Empire of Difference

Empire of Difference: The Ottomans in Comparative Perspective is a comparative study of imperial organization and longevity that assesses Ottoman successes and failures against those of other empires with similar characteristics. Karen Barkey examines the Ottoman Empire's social organization and mechanisms of rule at key moments of its history: emergence, imperial institutionalization, remodeling, and transition to nation-state. She reveals how the empire managed these moments to adapt and avert crises and examines what changes made it transform dramatically. The flexible techniques by which the Ottomans maintained their legitimacy, the cooperation of their diverse elites both at the center and in the provinces, as well as their control over economic and human resources were responsible for the longevity of this particular "negotiated empire." Barkey's analysis illuminates topics such as imperial governance, institutional continuity and change, imperial diversity and multiculturalism, multifarious forms of internal dissent, and the varying networks of state–society negotiations.

Karen Barkey is professor of sociology and history at Columbia University. She is the author of *Bandits and Bureaucrats: The Ottoman Route to State Centralization*, winner of the Social Science History Award in 1995, and coeditor with Mark von Hagen of *After Empire: Multiethnic Societies and Nation-Building: The Soviet Union, and the Russian, Habsburg, and Ottoman Empires.*

She has been awarded fellowships from the United States Institute of Peace, Social Science Research Council–MacArthur, and the National Humanities Center.

Empire of Difference

The Ottomans in Comparative Perspective

KAREN BARKEY
Columbia University

CAMBRIDGE
UNIVERSITY PRESS

CAMBRIDGE UNIVERSITY PRESS
Cambridge, New York, Melbourne, Madrid, Cape Town, Singapore, São Paulo, Delhi

Cambridge University Press
32 Avenue of the Americas, New York, NY 10013-2473, USA

www.cambridge.org
Information on this title: www.cambridge.org/9780521715331

First published 2008

Printed in the United States of America

A catalog record for this publication is available from the British Library.

Library of Congress Cataloging in Publication Data
Barkey, Karen
Empire of difference : the Ottomans in comparative perspective / Karen Barkey.
  p. cm.
Includes bibliographical references and index.
ISBN 978-0-521-88740-3 (hardback) – ISBN 978-0-521-71533-1 (pbk.)
1. Turkey – History – 18th century. 2. Turkey – History – Ottoman Empire,
1288–1918. I. Title.
DR531.B37 2008
956′.015–dc22   2007046782

ISBN   978-0-521-88740-3 hardback
ISBN   978-0-521-71533-1 paperback

FOR TONY MARX

Contents

Preface   *page* ix

Transliterations   xv

PART I AN IMPERIAL MODEL

1. Introduction   3
    Empire: An Analytic Framework   9
    The Longevity of Empires: Critical Concepts and Issues   15

2. Emergence: Brokerage across Networks   28
    A Frontier Society: Contradictions, Constraints, and Opportunities   36
    Osman: The Construction of a Network (1290–1326)   45
    The Internal Boundaries of the New State   58
    Conclusion   64
    Appendix to Chapter 2   65

3. Becoming an Empire: Imperial Institutions and Control   67
    From Conquest to Imperial Domains   72
        Establishing a Strong Center: Patrimonial Army and Peoples   74
    Establishing Provincial Rule and Managing Frontiers   83
        Establishing Control: A Segmented Society and a Flexible
           Economy   93
    Legitimating a Normative Order   98
    Conclusion: The Role of Islam   104

4. Maintaining Empire: An Expression of Tolerance   109
    Ottoman Tolerance: Marking the Boundaries   119
        The *Devshirme*   123
        Conversion   125
        The *Sürgün*   128
    A Capacious Administration of Difference   130
        Institutional Genesis   132
        Alternatives to Religious Community   143

The Absence of Intercommunal Violence   146
Conclusion   150

5. The Social Organization of Dissent   154
    Persecuting the Past: Heterodoxy under Fire   164
        Şeyh Bedreddîn   169
        The *Kızılbaş* (Redheads)   175
        Celalis   178
    Islamic Ultra Orthodoxy and Jewish Messianism: Dissent in the
        Seventeenth Century   181
    Conclusion   190

PART II   THE TRANSFORMATION OF THE EIGHTEENTH CENTURY

6. An Eventful Eighteenth Century: Empowering the Political   197
    A Short Historical Account of the Eighteenth Century   201
    State Power and Social Forces: Three Episodes of Learning
        the Politics of Opposition   205
        The Edirne Event: 1703   206
        The Patrona Halil Revolt: 1730   213
        The *Sened-i İttifak*: 1808   218
    Conclusion   225

7. A Networking Society: Commercialization, Tax Farming,
        and Social Relations   226
    Tax Farming and Commercialization   228
        The Extension of Ottoman Tax Farming   229
        The Brave New World of Trade   236
    Reworking Elite Networks: Institutions, Actors, and Activities   242
        Notables, State Positions, and Tax Farms   244
        Notables and Trade   252
    The Transitional Modernity of Notables   256
    Conclusion   262

8. On the Road out of Empire: Ottomans Struggle from Empire
        to Nation-State   264
    Toward State Centralization   266
    Decentralization, Decline, or Restoration under Federalism: The Role
        of Tax Farming   270
    Minorities at Risk: Toleration Unraveled and the Construction of
        "Bounded Identities"   277
    Religion and Legitimacy   289

Bibliography   297
Index   323

Preface

From the hill of Çamlıca on the Anatolian side of Istanbul, one has a majestic view of the multireligious, multiethnic character of the imperial city, the hub of many civilizations founded from 658 to 657 B.C., captured by Justinian and named the "New Rome" in 324 A.D., further named Constantinople in 330 A.D., and conquered by the Ottomans in 1453, to be designated Istanbul (from the Greek, *eis tin polin*: toward the city). In 1458, Istanbul became the capital of the Ottoman Empire.

From this hill of Çamlıca, I often watched my city and listened to two different lessons of history. One was related by my grandfather, an Ottoman subject and a soldier for the empire in World War I, and the other recounted by my father, a modern citizen of the Turkish Republic, born during World War I and coming of age at a time of national reconstruction.

The history that my grandfather told was one of imperial diversity, toleration, and a cultural bazaar. He worked very close to Yeni Cami and Mısır Carşısı (the Egyptian Market) and Rüstem Paşa Cami, finished in 1561 by the architect Mimar Sinan. His retelling of Ottoman life and culture mirrored the sites that he moved through – religious spaces of quietude and serenity; a multi-hued and vibrant display of eastern smells and tastes; perfumes, incense, drugs, and spices; and along squares filled with boisterous itinerant peddlers, street vendors, and mothers pulling their sons, with threatening images of boogey men lurking around the corner. He took his grandchildren to eat at the Ottoman restaurant Borsa, where he let us order specialties unlike our home cuisine, and filled our minds with the poetry of Bâkî, Fuzulî, Nedîm, and many other Divan poets of the empire. His was an Oriental version of the Orient.

The history that my father told was one of the need to move with history, to acknowledge the necessity for modernity, industry, and national consciousness. His was a tale of modernity locked into an Atatürkist version of history, serene in its notion of progress based on diligence and strength. Ottoman greatness for him was embedded in Byzantine continuity; in the early achievements of the Turks; and in what he saw to be the impeccable way in which the Roman,

Byzantine, and Ottoman worlds produced marvels of architecture, which he tirelessly narrated to every foreign tourist who visited during his long career as an engineer and businessman. His Orient was on the move, but somewhere entirely different than my grandfather's Orient: the hustle and bustle he saw and appreciated was that of industry and commerce, of trade and economic development, caught up in the relations between the West and a modern Turkey. His was an Occidental version of the Orient.

When I later became interested in the past of this extraordinary city and empire, I realized that neither one of the histories I so carefully listened to were complete, and, in their different understandings of the past and their vision of the future, they did not easily speak to each other. Instead, I have lived with the two pictures together. The manner in which I tried to rearticulate these histories remained unproductive until I understood that the way to bridge these two pasts was through a much more consciously analytic history of the empire. I have tried to understand empire by giving both visions their place, while forging my own representation and interpretation of what I saw as meaningful in my ancestors' past. For me, trained in sociology, such an enterprise would focus on the actual workings of empire, to uncover the manner in which empires became such powerful political formations, ruled differentiated groups, and maintained cohesion in times of upheaval. In such a moment of upheaval – a period of widespread banditry – I had earlier discovered an important key to empire: that empire was a "negotiated enterprise," and regardless of its strength an empire has to work with the peripheries in order to maintain a mix of compliance, tribute, and military cooperation, as well as to ensure political coherence and durability.

This theme is further developed in this book, in which my main interest is to understand the longevity of this particular political formation called empire. I carry out an analysis of the Ottoman Empire's social organization and mechanisms of rule at four carefully selected moments of its history: emergence, imperial institutionalization, imperial remodeling, and transition to nation-state. Unlike most comparative studies, my study also examines Ottoman imperial longevity from the Ottoman point of view and assesses Ottoman accomplishments and failures against those of other empires of similar characteristics. My goal is to understand the organization of empire through different moments and therefore contribute to comparative imperial studies. But I also want to better integrate Ottoman history into comparative imperial studies. In writing this book, I was interested in highlighting the mechanisms and machinery of empire, rather than the narratives of battles, wars, and treaties. I am also not setting out to chart a history of the multifarious relations between layers of text produced during the empire and their historical context. Rather, I am trying to understand how institutional and organizational structures enable or hinder the actions of the agents and networks of agents whom I consider crucial to my analysis. Developing an explanation for the longevity of empire, for me, means reconstructing a relatively faithful representation of a social process and identifying the typical actions, interests, and meanings of agents, and networks of agents, relating to each other through webs of association.

To this end, rather than going for new sources and archival material, I have made use of the abundant and carefully researched historical work and published data and have marshaled a theoretical framework and used a wide array of methodological tools to make this history analytically coherent and intelligible. In this process, I have also been highly selective; some institutions are highlighted, some regions underlined, and some processes stressed to the detriment of others.

This book took a long time to come to fruition. During this time, many individuals and institutions have been helpful. I first got a Social Science Research Center–McArthur fellowship to initiate this research, and spent a year at the National Center for Humanities reading and preparing what would become a segment of this book. After a long break from it, I returned to the project, and, despite a major reorganization of my thoughts, I was still able to use the research that these institutions made possible for me to carry out.

I am indebted to many scholars and friends in this endeavor. Two scholars have shaped my work in more ways than I can ever retell or thank them for. Daniel Chirot, with whom I have worked closely for more than 20 years now, directed me toward historical sociology, and toward comparative political analysis that insists on asking questions about large-scale outcomes that are substantively and normatively important and have an impact on the world in which we live. His intellectual mark is at the core of this book because his interest in what makes societies flourish or turn toward the abyss, his interest in ethnic conflict and genocide, and his interest in the far corners of the world has been with me since the day I met him. As is his style, his friendship and advice come with both encouragement and trenchant critique: these have helped me improve my questions and my analysis.

Harrison White has been the other similarly powerful figure since I arrived at Columbia University more than a decade ago. Harrison's analytic insight has transformed my work because he possesses such a fine capacity for sociological theorizing and combines it with deep and distinctive historical knowledge, in many ways different and at odds with the manner in which historians tell the story of societies. From his early reading of my previous book, *Bandits and Bureaucrats*, to the reformulation of my work on time and scheduling in the Ottoman Empire, he has pushed me toward more innovative and original directions. I have been influenced by his acute sense for finding what traditional narratives have missed and what analysts have overlooked. Dan and Harrison have read and commented on multiple drafts of my manuscript with interest, care, and much more than a sense of scholarly duty. I remain indebted and hope that I have taken advantage of their excellent insights and counsel.

Although I have not seen him in many years and miss his strong intellectual presence, Halil İnalcık, my mentor in Ottoman studies, remains with me all the time.

In my department, thanks also go to Peter Bearman and Charles Tilly, who carefully read and commented on the manuscript at a critical stage of revision. Two wonderful colleagues, George Gavrilis and Yonca Köksal, have been close friends, as well as patient and knowledgeable readers with expertise in the Ottoman and theoretical fields. Mark von Hagen and Ira Katznelson, with whom I have cotaught and coauthored work, have kept me on my toes, helping sharpen my arguments. Jean-Francois Bayart and Romain Bertrand, loyal colleagues and friends, have given me many occasions to present my work at Sciences-Po in Paris, providing me with analogies and counterexamples from Africa to Indonesia. Nader Sohrabi and Etem Erol, both superb scholars of the empire, have provided many forums at Columbia for me to present work and have engaged me on several occasions. I owe the specifics of my network analysis and the models to the marvelous work of my coauthor on another project, Frederic Godart, whose expertise and effectiveness remain unmatched. Rudi Batzell spent at least a summer reading and commenting on my work. His equally sharp attention to detail and ideas make him a special Columbia College student with a bright future ahead. Finally, Figen Taşkın researched most of the material on the networks of the early sultans; Işıl Çelimli helped with the figures and tables in the book; and Cenk Palaz, whose Ottoman historical and linguistic expertise I could not do without, worked day and night on the details of Ottoman and Turkish transliteration problems. At Columbia, I also have to thank a continuous wave of serious, thoughtful, and committed graduate and undergraduate students, whose relationships have been vital to me, among them Adoma Adjei-Brenyah, Zoe Duskin, Sara Duvisac, Aurora Fredrikson, Lena Friedrich, Bedross der Matossian, Neema Noori, Neha Nimmagudda, Onur Özgöde, Harel Shapira, Natacha Stevanovic, Arafaat Valiani, Kineret Yardena, Murat Yüksel, and Xiaodan Zhang. They have inspired me and have sustained my enthusiasm throughout my career. In Sociology, I also thank Dora Arenas, who has helped to facilitate my administrative burden as much as possible.

In Amherst I have benefited from the friendship and intellectual camaraderie of Sam Bowles and Libby Wood. Sam delved into the depth of Ottoman tax farming, providing me with comparative examples and clarifying the economics of such systems. Libby read segments of my manuscript and generously introduced me to the editors of Cambridge University Press, forging the decisive tie in this publication. Amrita Basu and Uday Mehta read, commented, and supported the sometimes relentless process of writing and doubting. Paola Zamperini kept me positive throughout. I cannot thank Daria Darienzo of Amherst College Library enough. Even before we arrived at Amherst, she wrote to me to give me a sense of the materials the library had in my field, and her continued support of my research was invaluable. Jayne Lovett has provided me with indispensable computer expertise and backup support for the past four years. Debby Goan, Denise Twum, and Jacqueline Makena helped with library research, editing, and manuscript work. Marion Delhaye also helped during the summer of 2006 with manuscript editing of French sources. Finally, for the past four years, Sabra Mont and Karl Long have selflessly helped take care of Joshua and Anna-Claire, making it possible for me to commute to Columbia University and write this book.

In the field of Ottoman studies, Reşat Kasaba, Çağlar Keyder, Şevket Pamuk, Fikret Adanır, Hasan Kayalı, Aron Rodrigue, Linda Darling, Virginia Aksan, and Halil Berktay stand out. Their continued interest in my work and their openness and inclusiveness have made it possible for me to continue my effort in darker moments. I particularly thank Reşat, who has followed this project from its inception, invited me to numerous conferences to present various parts, and whose suggestions have helped me think through history more carefully. In many ways, I owe to this group my continued participation in the field of Ottoman studies.

I thank Julie Perkins who edited the manuscript through the summer of 2007. I thank Eric Crahan, my editor at Cambridge University Press. Mary Paden on the production side has been very patient with me, and many thanks go to Ken Hassman, whose wonderful expertise at indexing I could not do without. Many friends had a hand in the making of the cover: George Gavrilis, Michael Chesworth, as well as my brother, Henri Barkey. It is an honor to have the work of Turkey's great modern photographer, Izzet Keribar, on the cover.

Finally, family and friends have been very influential as well. My mother and my brother have encouraged me, giving me love and support whenever and wherever needed. I am most grateful to my brother's sustained interrogation of my knowledge of dates of Ottoman wars and treaties throughout my childhood! My father passed away when I was still working on this manuscript, and, despite the time spent in the care and sadness of his long illness, what I miss most was his continued vitality, his headstrong and conscious effort to always be there to improve, and his luminous trust in me. My children miss him as well, but they have also missed their mother, whose attention to the Ottomans has sometimes overwhelmed them, angered them, and led them to enticing alternatives. Joshua, for a long time, asked me to write a *Lord of the Rings* version of the Ottoman Empire with him, as he thought a collaborative project would draw my attention. Anna-Claire's favorite phrase has been "is it done already?" as little kids on long road trips ask their parents "are we there yet?" So, my darlings, we are there.

My life companion, Tony Marx, to whom this book is dedicated, has lived with this book since we both got tenure at Columbia in 1997/98. He is the only man I know who is truly a feminist, an equal–opportunity husband, who has devoted his life as much to my career as to his own. I admire most his superb generosity of heart, his tremendous warmth, his devotion to his family, and his ability to remain good humored while juggling serious social and political problems of consequence.

Karen Barkey
Bargecchia

Transliterations

There are various ways of doing the transliteration of foreign words. In this book, I have used Turkish words as much as possible to remain consistent in usage. However, words such as "pasha," "vizier," or "devshirme," which have become quite well known in English, are used in their English spelling. Similarly, although I kept to the Turkish place-names of many regions and towns, I have maintained the English place-names for well-known cities such as Rome, Istanbul, Salonica, Aleppo, and Cairo. I use "Constantinople" to denote the Byzantine city and "Istanbul" the city after 1453.

The following is a key to the pronunciation of Turkish letters:

C: "j" as in Josh
Ç: "ch" as in chess
Ğ: very soft, not really pronounced
I: without a dot, pronounced like the "o" in atom
Ö: pronounced like the French sound "eu"
Ş: pronounced like "sh" in shawl
Ü: pronounced like the French sound "u"

The use of a circumflex indicates a lengthened vowel.

PART I

AN IMPERIAL MODEL

The first part of this book explores the imperial model, defining empire as a "negotiated" enterprise where the basic configuration of relationships between imperial authorities and peripheries is constructed piece meal in a different fashion for each periphery, creating a patchwork pattern of relations with structural holes between peripheries. In that construction we see the architecture of empire emerge: a hub-and-spoke structure of state-periphery relations, where the direct and indirect vertical relations of imperial integration coexist with horizontal relations of segmentation. After I define empire, I argue that to preserve this structure, its dominance and durability, an empire needs to maintain legitimacy, diversity, and various resources through a stable relationship with intermediary elites. No matter how strong an empire is, it has to work with peripheries, local elites and frontier groups to maintain compliance, resources, tribute and military cooperation and ensure political coherence and stability.

In different chapters, I analyze the social organization and mechanisms of rule of the Ottoman Empire. For this, I carefully select historical and organizational moments of Ottoman tenure from its inception as a "brokered" frontier state in the early fourteenth century through the seventeenth century after which a large-scale remodeling of imperial relations occurred. In several chapters then, I undertake analytic and where possible, explicitly comparative studies of the emergence, the imperial institutionalization, the organization of diversity and its outcome in the form of a constructed toleration and, the response to dissent in the first four centuries of Ottoman rule. In each chapter, I analyze intermediary processes such as the multiplicities of flexible arrangements, networked structures, institutional mixes, in the form of the layering of old and new institutions, bringing together actors, and their networks in the governance structures, the negotiated arrangements in different domains and structural and symbolic sites of agreement and contention. In each chapter, I demonstrate that the lesson of imperial flexibility and therefore longevity comes from this intermediary level of negotiations.

I

Introduction

When Mahmud II peacefully closed his eyes in his sister's Çamlıca Palace on 30 June 1839, he had successfully shepherded his empire, its institutions, and its diverse peoples toward the road that would ultimately lead "out of empire." A staunch believer in the westernization of Ottoman political thought, culture, and institutions, he had engineered a series of reforms that culminated in the famous Tanzimat reorganization, a program that would make the empire look more like a Western nation-state. Unfortunately, the reality on the ground was far from national. From the demography of the empire, the ethnic and religious mixes, and imperial ways – from the unwarranted violence of petty officials to the lenient and sometimes negligent deal making of the imperial ruling elites – to the half-hearted recognition of the importance of territory and frontiers, most indicators of social and political life were redolent of empire. What ensued was a race against time. Although without knowledge of what was to come – the watershed event of World War I – Ottomans engaged in a race to combine "saving the empire" with "becoming a modern nation." It is in this contradictory duality that the Ottomans lost their empire and the best of what they possessed: their diversity, ingenious flexibility, and resiliency.

At a time when we ask ourselves how to forge long-lasting political and economic cohesion in the midst of ethnic and national diversity on a multinational scale, the current fascination with the study of empire is understandable. It is driven by the recognition that empire is a valuable historical analogy for understanding and informing our current dilemma and possibilities. Many traditional empires were political formations, systems of rule that lasted a long time mostly due to their flexibility and capacity to adapt and innovate. Longevity, resilience, and flexibility remain key features of empire that have been undertheorized. To understand empire is to be able to follow analytically the slow but critical transformation of imperial states, their adaptation and robustness in the face of diversity, crisis, and change.

Heretofore, most studies of empire have been weighed down by a few paradigms that have not served it well. Historiographical tradition has focused on the rise and decline of empires, especially after Edward Gibbon's *The Decline and Fall of the Roman Empire*.[1] Narratives of rise and decline have had a deleterious effect on our understanding of empire. Telling history backward with the knowledge of the end has affected our understanding of the possibilities of empire, as we have searched for a unidirectional explanation from rise to decline. Similarly, the concern with rise and decline pushed historians to separate imperial history into set periods – rise, apogee, stagnation, and decline – casting molds into which chunks of history were neatly arranged. Even the most sophisticated political histories of empire – even of the comparative sort – have not been able to shed this straitjacket. The question of decline has so captured our imagination that we have spent much energy manipulating the onset and timing of decline. I suggest an alternative approach to the study of empire that stresses longevity and resilience.

The theoretical study of empire has also followed the pendulum swing of fashion in the field of comparative historical studies, moving from macrostructural studies to more cultural studies with different agendas. The main macrohistorical questions that we have abandoned for more formal, yet micro-level studies, or for cultural and linguistic studies, have diverted us from remaining relevant to the social transformations of the world today.[2] Scholars have asked important questions and have theorized on topics ranging from large-scale social and economic transformation, state formation, and the rise of capitalism, to civilizations, social control and discipline, the *longue durée* in the temporal dimensions of change, to population movements, and revolutions. These questions asked by a generation of scholars about how to understand the large-scale structures and processes that are continuously remolding our world have been put aside somewhat.

Cultural studies have gone too far in the direction of ignoring the basic structural determinants of social change, political institutions, and socioeconomic structures that are so important in light of the tremendous political and socioeconomic transformations of the global world today. From such perspectives, a central goal of understanding empire – its administrative and organizational ability to maintain power and establish control over vast and different populations for a long period of time – in brief, an important claim to decode imperial systems of rule, is lost.

What is more, for a long time the understanding of the "state" in the social sciences has been oriented from the European perspective. That is, the social sciences have conceptualized the state from the narrow experience of European

---

[1] Edward Gibbon, *The Decline and Fall of the Roman Empire* (London: Orion Publishing Group, 2005).

[2] From the old masters, such as Herbert Spencer, Karl Marx, and Max Weber, to the generation of European historical scholars, such as Norbert Elias, Marc Bloch, Fernand Braudel, E. P. Thompson, and Michel Foucault, to the Americans, such as Reinhard Bendix, Barrington Moore, Charles Tilly, Immanuel Wallerstein, and Theda Skocpol, macrohistorical studies has retreated to just a few good practitioners of the trade, such as Thomas Ertman, Rogers Brubaker, Kathleen Thelen, and Paul Pierson, among others.

states, limiting themselves to a set of particular state structures, in fictive opposition to the East. The classical theorists and shapers of the terms of sociology made their mark by careful, rich, and analytically informed historical analysis. This has been the core of our conceptual and theoretical thinking on the state. Moreover, even though recent attempts to bring back other, non-Western cases can be cited, they have rarely engaged with the theoretical perspectives of the West.[3] Furthermore, many such attempts result in postmodern critiques of the West, with no effort to rethink the ways in which diverse systems of rule may be articulated and studied under the same analytic umbrella. These developments, then, do not bode well for the study of empire. The irony, of course, remains the steady growth of the study of empire despite the larger historical and theoretical issues that plague it as an enterprise.[4]

In this book, I want to rethink the study of empire. First, instead of asking about rise and decline, I ask questions about the organization and longevity of empire, about the critical but slow processes of transformation that empires underwent as they inserted themselves into an international arena, constructed domestic institutions of rule, and adapted to change as they navigated the complexity of foreign and domestic tensions. Although empires ultimately gave way to other forms of political organization, the most important historical examples were marked by a special longevity and durability that is worth recognizing and engaging. I argue that our historical analysis has to take temporal processes more seriously and must analyze the manner in which institutions are shaped by historical processes and persist over time, or change in subtle, if not striking, ways. Therefore, I want to suggest, first, that we look at empire as a set of slow-moving, temporally based, entrenched, yet also changing political formations that need to be studied to understand how they change, adapt, and move on to maintain themselves, partly through reproduction and partly through innovation of their institutional structures.

Second, I want to refocus interest on the study of large-scale historical questions that help enlighten the historical and theoretical dilemmas we encounter today. More recently, James Mahoney and Dietrich Rueschemeyer made an important contribution to reinvigorating the study of comparative historical and political analysis.[5] With them, I believe in the sustained effort necessary to ask questions of relevance and world-scale interest. I still see the role of sociology as striving to understand the larger frame of how social systems and societies maintain themselves, and for that the work of Talcott Parsons,

---

3 Commendable exceptions are Eiko Ikegami, *The Taming of the Samurai: Honorific Individualism and the Making of Modern Japan* (Cambridge, MA: Harvard University Press, 1995); R. Bin Wong, *China Transformed: Historical Change and the Limits of European Experience* (Ithaca, NY and London: Cornell University Press, 1997); Miguel Centeno, *Blood and Debt: War and the Nation-State Latin America* (University Park: Pennsylvania State University Press, 2002).

4 A recent search shows that Amazon has approximately 207,000 books with the word "empire" in the title.

5 James Mahoney and Dietrich Rueschemeyer, *Comparative Historical Analysis in the Social Sciences* (Cambridge, UK: Cambridge University Press, 2003).

for modern society, and Eisenstadt, for historical empires, remains essential. Their attempts to address these questions were on a grand scale; sociology has increasingly shied away from them. In the United States, in particular, where professionalization has narrowed the scope of disciplines, among recent publications, Harrison White's *Identity and Control*[6] is the only large-scale attempt at understanding how our world functions.

Third, I want to add new verve to the study of empires as macrostructural formations. That is, I want to remain loyal to the main macrohistorical questions of state and social transformation that we have asked in the field, although by moving away from a practice that has often consisted of macrohistorical causes too easily tied to macrohistorical developments. In these explanations, large-scale changes, such as warfare, state centralization, state decentralization, or world systemic adjustments, are all assumed to cause other large-scale transformations, such as revolutions, capitalism, or imperial decline. Instead, I want to ask macrohistorical questions and resolve them from a meso-level of analysis. Often a macrohistorical occurrence, such as war or famine, causes a chain of events that engages the interface of society, that intermediary space where state actors and social actors meet and resolve their needs, interests, and ideals, deciding and shaping the outcome that we study. This is inline with Harrison White's insight that "social reality is in the middle range order."[7]

Overall, then, I argue that the answer to the question of the longevity of empire can be found in analyses of the organizations and networks connecting large segmented and constantly changing structures, and by focusing on the multivalent, networked, vertical, and horizontal linkages and the malleable compacts established between state and social actors. I show that such were the elements that enabled the Ottoman Empire to survive for a long time and over a large territory, my aim being to understand state transformations and enrich the corpus of social science thinking on this issue. This can be done not only by paying attention to state actors, but also to varieties of social and political actors who interact with the state, share power, and aspire to positions of power and privilege, as well as those who try to poke holes in the various hegemonies of imperial control, dissenters. The distinctive contribution of the work, however, lies in the attention paid to the middle level of interactions and relations, embedding it firmly into the movement between institutions and individuals.

I ask a large-scale historical question by focusing on the unfolding of one historical case over time. The larger question, however, is really comparative: what explains the long-term survival of political formations such as empires? In this case, how do we explain the long-term success of Ottoman imperial institutions? In comparative perspective, how does it compare to other empires with similar characteristics, not only its contemporaries and rivals, such as the

---

[6] Harrison White, *Identity and Control: A Structural Theory of Social Action* (Princeton, NJ: Princeton University Press, 1992).

[7] Harrison White, March 2006. *Identity and Control Revisited.* (Talk at the New School of Social Research.)

Habsburg and Russian Empires, but also its predecessors in the same region, the Romans and the Byzantines? In that sense, the tension in this book between a theory of empire and the uniqueness of the Ottoman Empire is constantly regenerated. I see this as a constant and healthy challenge to bring together places where imperial institutions and networks are comparable and transportable with examples where unique features claim our attention.

The Ottoman case is an excellent one to study. Notwithstanding the numerous misconceptions about it that remain to be clarified, the Ottomans were successful at maintaining imperial rule over a vast territory for many centuries. This success was based on their intrinsic flexibility and ability to adapt. Contrary to the image of wild barbarians who conquered territory and then degenerated into unyielding Asiatic forms of despotism, they showed tremendous adaptability. Furthermore, although they were often brutal warriors, warfare was only part of their success. What was unusual in the Ottoman Empire was an early ability to absorb diverse populations and create new institutions and a new elite, which was the hallmark of all successful empires. Rome and Byzantium also manipulated local elites and created a group of new men, constructed from the best among the different communities. Perhaps specific to the Ottomans was continued flexibility and adaptability. Ottomans persisted in their mode of absorption and adaptation for a long time, showing rigidity only in the nineteenth century, and more so among actors who pursued national solutions than among those who continued to look for imperial ones.

The Ottoman Empire linked three continents, Asia, Europe, and Africa, encompassing an array of cultures, languages, peoples, climates, and various social and political structures. Ottomans negotiated between the contradictory, yet also complementary, visions and organizational forms of urban and rural; nomad and settled; Islamic and non-Muslim; Sunnî Muslims, Shiites, and Sufi sects; scribes and poets; artisans and merchants; peasants and peddlers; and bandits and bureaucrats. They forged political institutions, combined military talent with territorial good fortune, and remained flexible and cognizant of the vastness of the imperial reach. In ways similar to the Romans, the Ottoman Empire was "a haven of relative peace, security and tolerance which the Ottomans offered not just to Muslims but also to Christian and Jewish subjects of their would-be universal empire."[8]

No wonder the early Ottomans saw, proclaimed, and titled themselves as the successors of Rome – they also crafted a uniquely hybrid civilization. Civilizations are hybrid when they contain elements of different traditions that are brought together by "institutional bricolage"[9]; force of circumstance; and exigencies of climate, environment, and territory. The Ottomans constructed

---

[8] Dominic Lieven, *Empire: The Russian Empire and Its Rivals* (New Haven, CT: Yale University Press, 2001), 13.

[9] "Bricolage" is a term used in the historical institutional literature that conveys a sense of how institutions and organizations are not built from scratch but through the "reworking of the institutional materials at hand." David Stark and Laszlo Bruszt, *Postsocialist Pathways: Transforming Politics and Property in East Central Europe* (New York: Cambridge University Press, 1998).

an uneasy, distinctly productive, and purposefully diverse, but nevertheless homogeneous and unifying, culture. That is, while accepting difference, they built their governance over similarities based on institutional structures and the shared understanding these generated. This achievement, however imperfect, lasted for many centuries. Its remnants are evident today when traveling in the Balkans or in the heartland of Anatolia: we see not only the market building, the *macellum*, imported from Roman times, but also its near Eastern rendering in the form and content of social relations of the bazaar.[10] We see the feat of Byzantine architecture in Hagia Sophia, as well as the Ottoman renewal and its insertion of the minaret as the symbol of the newest religion to conquer these lands. The Mediterranean Basin, although never fully conquered by the Ottomans, became the site of layers of civilization – Greek, Roman, and Ottoman – each of which contributed to the richness, texture, and local color of the canvas of the modern world. Consequently, especially early on, it did not easily fit any particular category exclusively; it was not just Ottoman, Turkish, or Islamic. It was all these combined with Roman and Byzantine, Balkan, and Turco-Mongol institutions and practices. It is as an important cultural and institutional medley that Ottomans gained their identity. Located at the center of where the West meets the East, the Ottomans gained their identity and forged a balance of coherence and diversity that remains a landmark in the modern world's search for precisely that balance.

There have been many social and political histories of the Ottoman Empire. Most of them have been arranged around the question of rise and fall of the empire, with increasingly detailed narrative histories some of which are placed in interpretive frameworks of imperial change. The most recent attempt, by Caroline Finkel is perhaps the most ambitious, detailed and encompassing work to date.[11] Finkel offers the history of the Ottoman Empire primarily in military and diplomatic terms, providing a detailed political history where the focus is on the central state's leading elites, the loyal statesmen who carried the business of the state, with a focus on what happened when. It does not, however, offer insights into the modalities of this empire, on how it was ruled, organized, how its populations understood and participated in the task of empire building or rejected the paradigm of the Ottomans.

My questions are different. How was this empire ruled? How was such diversity contained and managed? How did it maintain itself for centuries, outwitting the predictions and lamentations of many contemporaries and the readings of scholars? What was the logic of empire, the precarious balance of center and periphery, imperial and local institutions, and core structures and frontier plasticity that were all adapted to each other? How was the diversity of cultures, languages, and religions organized? How was dissent organized in empire, around which actors and issues, and for what purposes? Which

[10] Ramsay Macmullen, *Romanization in the Time of Augustus* (New Haven, CT: Yale University Press, 2000), ix.
[11] Caroline Finkel, *Osman's Dream* (New York: Basic Books, 2005).

groups in imperial society were capable of organizing, and what were their relations with state institutions? What were the forces that triggered state transformations at different periods of Ottoman history? In short, how did this complex political formation live and adapt? These are questions geared toward understanding the puzzle of empire.

These are the questions that cohere around the themes of longevity and flexibility as they apply to the empire. That is, there is an inherent flexibility built into the structure of empire that can be maintained for a long time. We can explore these features both in the definition of empire and in what makes and keeps empire a dominant political formation. In the following sections, I explore what I mean by empire, set the scope of my inquiry, and provide a framework to understand what keeps empires dominant. I then link these to the question of flexibility and present the concepts and tools that I deploy throughout the book to undergird this notion of flexibility.

Empire: An Analytic Framework

There have been so many definitions of empire that I am reluctant to add to the long list. Among the studies and definitions that have shaped our thinking most dramatically have been those by Michael Doyle and S. N. Eisenstadt, Charles Tilly, and, more recently, Alexander J. Motyl.[12] I provide my own definition, which is not very different, but is more thoroughly specified.[13]

An empire is a large composite and differentiated polity linked to a central power by a variety of direct and indirect relations, where the center exercises political control through hierarchical and quasi-monopolistic relations over groups ethnically different from itself. These relations are, however, regularly subject to negotiations over the degree of autonomy of intermediaries in return for military and fiscal compliance. The central state negotiates and maintains more or less distinct compacts between itself and the various segments of this polity. Last, but not least, one can say that most of the different segments of the polity remain largely unconnected among themselves. That is why an imperial system is best represented in terms of the hub-and-spoke network structure, where the rim is absent.

Empire, then, is about political authority relations (as well as many other transactions) between a central power and many diverse and differentiated entities. Such a characterization of empire underscores the importance of relations between the imperial state that is in a core central structural position and

---

[12] Michael W. Doyle, *Empires* (Ithaca, NY: Cornell University Press, 1986); S. N. Eisenstadt, *The Political Systems of Empires* (Glencoe, IL: Free Press, 1963); Charles Tilly, "How Empires End," in *After Empire: Multiethnic Societies and Nation-Building*, ed. Karen Barkey and Mark von Hagen (Boulder, CO: Westview Press, 1997); Alexander J. Motyl, *Imperial Ends: The Decay, Collapse, and Revival of Empires* (New York: Columbia University Press, 2001).

[13] Here I present a model of empire that is likely to fit many cases with variations across cases. The deviations from the patterns remain real, and although I present a model as the analytic base of my work, I also continually underscore the degree to which movement and flexibility existed.

the different segments that comprise the imperial domain, where power and control remain key to the state, yet the imperial state does not have complete monopoly of power in the territory under control. It shares control with a variety of intermediate organizations and with local elites, religious and local governing bodies, and numerous other privileged institutions. To rule over vast expanses of territory, as well as to ensure military and administrative cooperation, imperial states negotiate and willingly relinquish some degree of autonomy. No matter how strong an empire is, it has to work with peripheries, local elites, and frontier groups to maintain compliance, resources, tribute, and military cooperation, and to ensure political coherence and durability.

Imperial state–periphery relationships are not direct relationships between state and individual subjects; rather, intermediate bodies, networks, and elites mediate the relationships. Therefore, the authority relations flow from the central state to the local elites and from them to the local populations. Imperial power, then, has a crucially negotiated character, where different negotiations emerge from sets of relations in which state actors and elite groups are engaged. Once the multifarious settlements between state and different communities diminish and stabilize, and standardized relations apply to all segments of imperial society, we are not talking about empire anymore, and have moved toward an alternative political formation, perhaps on the way to the nation-state. That is why, first and foremost, we need to conceptualize empire in terms of one center with many differing political authority relationships between the center and the pieces of the imperial domain.

As such, empires conquered and ruled by maintaining a pattern structurally resembling hub-and-spoke network pattern, where each spoke was attached to the center but was less directly related to the others. The fact that imperial relations were vertically integrated, and that peripheral entities communicated mainly with the center and with one another only through the center, provided centers with added control over the various peripheral entities. Divide and rule, "brokerage," segmentation, and integration become the basic structural components of empire. Ronald Burt and many others define "brokerage" as a structural position or role in which an actor makes transactions and resource flows possible between two other social sites.[14] Particularly when the state has captured the brokerage functions between elites, it can use such structural advantage to separate, integrate, reward, and control groups. Such separation is not sealed tight in the sense that despite this general model, there are always obvious deviations to the pattern as well as tensions on the different parts of the system to rework these relations to the advantage of regional actors. However, that such segmentation and brokerage was important to imperial relations is demonstrated by how actively the Ottoman state, for example, fought the increasing connectivity and alliances between peripheral groups such as the nomads and the local notables in the eighteenth century.

---

[14] Ronald S. Burt, *Brokerage and Closure: An Introduction to Social Capital* (Oxford, UK: Oxford University Press, 2005).

One by-product of this is that in terms of state–periphery relations, because the different segments of the "imperial domain" functioned through intermediate organizations but without high levels of association and mobilization among them, an imperial whole was not highly and continuously mobilized. Mobilization was achieved under extraordinary circumstances, often at state initiative. What we might call "imperial society"[15] was very weak because it lacked the features whereby it could act coherently and unilaterally to safeguard its own social and political interests. This was certainly true of most land-based traditional empires, especially Rome, where public opinion or a common understanding of an imperial community was lacking.[16] Empires, then, are complex political formations that do not form one "national" community, but rather multiple networks of interaction, different communities with varying institutions and state–domain compacts. This is what empires strived for – they governed over diversity by creating the conditions whereby differentially incorporated communities remained separate in their development.[17] As long as communities continued as differentially incorporated parts of empire, imperial unity could not be achieved, even if a veneer of it was showcased at moments of high tension or war.

In part, that this pluralism did not add up to a whole was due to historical contingency and the eventful unfolding of imperial growth, that is, the fact that empires took over territories, peoples, and communities with different, established political and social systems and traditions piecemeal and at different times, incorporating by conquest, alliance, and marriage. The conquest of the Balkans or the Arab lands by Ottoman forces; the Habsburg expansion based on marriage alliances; or the Russian expansion into Ukraine, Poland, Belarus, the Baltic states, or the Muslim communities in Central Asia or the Caucasus provides a good example of such contingent, parceled, and successive incorporation. With each conquest and integration into empire, new entities negotiated different arrangements, levels of recognition, submission, or accommodation.

As they fought the imperial conquering armies, local groups not only further developed strong and cohesive communities, both in their rhetoric of war and heroism, but also in the organization necessary for resistance. The manner in which Serbian nationalists evoked the Battle of Kosovo (1389) in the 1990s only reminds us of the force of history, both its symbols and its myths.

---

[15] I use the term "society" for lack of a better way to describe the aggregation of networks that are artificially bounded by frontiers, territorial and other. In this appropriation of the term "society," I understand imperial societies to overlap only partly and unevenly with territory, population, frontiers, and boundaries, as well as with cultural identities. Rather, I see these networks as intersecting and overlapping. Yet, we also need to acknowledge the specific entities that individuals, state makers, scholars, and others were aware of and to which they referred.

[16] Gary B. Miles, "Roman and Modern Imperialism: A Reassessment," *Comparative Studies in Society and History* 32 (October 1990): 629–659.

[17] It is interesting to note that there are some examples of these arrangements in modern and very diverse countries such as India, where similar to empire, society is rather weak because relations between the center and the different regions mimic more empire than nation-state.

That the Battle of Kosovo was a major defeat that left deep scars among the Serbian population and served as part of a large bundle of facts, practices, and relations that unified Serbs throughout the centuries cannot be denied. Boundaries between communities were reinforced when empires attempted incorporation guided by a primordial sense of communities. Ethnic, racial, and religious categories promised to make administrative tasks easier, to generate legibility across the differentiated and diverse character of premodern societies. James Scott uses legibility to refer to the diverse practices that states engage in to make the tasks of administration, accounting, and control feasible.[18] In the Ottoman Empire, the construction of an administrative system, *millet*, around the ethnoreligious distinctions of the conquered peoples demonstrates this basic view of empire building. In the Habsburg Empire, the distinctions among *nationalität* were allowed to designate existing distinct communities of culture, history, and language, marking differences regarding groups that should be discriminated against and those who should not be. Such was the fate of the Protestants in Bohemia and Hungary, the Orthodox in Transylvania, and the Jews almost everywhere in Habsburg lands. Similarly, sharp contrasts among the Ukrainian, the Baltic, and the Muslim states existed in the minds of Russian elites who incorporated these regions. In many ways the Romans were similar; they had notions of the conquered peoples and territories often only as they conquered them and walked through them, but adapted their rule to the variations they perceived.[19] In these cases, territories that were incorporated as conquest not only were drawn in, settled, and accommodated into empire, but also remained separate because of the conquests that occurred as processes in time.

As much as empires were committed to the age-old adage "divide and rule," there were also many contingent reasons for segmented rule. Moreover, unlike nation-states, empires were or learned to be less committed to constructing an encompassing collective or to making political relations uniform. Moreover, empires did not have constitutions to regularize rights until they moved into a mixed political mode between empire and nation-state. It was the diversity of peoples, communities, and territories, as well as the diversity of rule, that made empires. This leads me to an overall characterization of empires at the height of their power as strong states, in relation to weak overall "societies" that may have incorporated strong local, ethnic, and religious subimperial communities. Such a characterization is consistent with the remnants of empire that are still around today, where authoritarian states rule over societies divided along religious, ethnic, and tribal dimensions. In what Gerard Prunier observes in the Sudan today, or what Daniel Chirot has called "mini-empires" we have seen

---

[18] James C. Scott, *Seeing Like a State* (New Haven, CT: Yale University Press, 1998).

[19] Susan P. Mattern, *Rome and the Enemy: Imperial Strategy in the Principate* (Berkeley: University of California Press, 1999). Mattern makes this argument by reminding us that the Romans did not really have maps or any ideas about the territories that lay ahead. They discovered them as they marched through territories.

the continuation of empire in modern, multiethnic, authoritarian contemporary states such as Iraq and Afghanistan.[20]

In summary, empires have been a widespread, durable, and flexible form of political organization. We can argue that empires remained so because of the segmented and weak nature of imperial domains and the capacity of states to make the necessary arrangements to integrate the peoples and the resources of the segmented regions. To maintain domination and longevity of the imperial form requires that empires ensure the articulation of three conditions:

1. Imperial states maintain authority over their population through the legitimation of a supranational ideology that often includes a religious claim to be protectors of Christendom or Islam, and an elaborate ideology of descent and lineage. Each imperial power has articulated and maintained such a supranational ideology. From the Romans down to the colonial empires of the past centuries, variations on the theme of *"mission civilisatrice"* have been quite common. The imperial supranational ideology is a symbolic expression of rule, the glue that offers spiritual cohesion to the elite upper classes of the empire, encouraging their participation. The elements of imperial culture are seen both in the ideas and the practice of empire.

2. Imperial states maintain rule over multireligious and multiethnic diversity through a variety of policies, from the "toleration" of diversity and its incorporation to forced conversion and assimilation. Religious, utilitarian, and strategic reasons drive imperial state elites to incorporate and order diversity. In a sense, to remain dominant, empires have to find a "solution" to diversity; more often than not, they choose an intermediate solution between conversion and toleration. They do so by instituting boundaries of different degrees of permeability, while organizing communities around and across such classificatory systems. But the boundary marking itself happens in the messy intermediate space in which state makers meet different groups and negotiate the terms of separation, difference, similarity, and cooperation.

3. Imperial states maintain control over a diversity of peripheral elites for political and economic reasons. Politically, states maintain control through "divide and conquer" strategies, keeping elites separate, distinct, and dependent on the central state. Such control also entails vertical integration into the state, but is accompanied by fragmentation at the horizontal level of social arrangements. Economically, the structure of elite arrangements also determines how a state will provide for its fiscal and military needs.[21]

---

[20] Gerard Prunier, *Darfur: The Ambiguous Genocide* (Ithaca, NY: Cornell University Press, 2005); Daniel Chirot, "Concluding Talk," Empire and Nation Conference, 5–7 Dec. 2003.

[21] Richard Lachmann expands on this idea in "Elite Self-Interest and Economic Decline in Early Modern Europe," *American Sociological Review* 68 (June 2003): 346–372.

Empires are dominant as long as they can maintain the combination of an ideological/cultural form of legitimation, along with appropriate mechanisms of rule over cultural diversity and modes of appropriation of political and economic resources. In this book, I pay particular attention to these three conditions. That is, I maintain that empires become and remain dominant polities as long as they can maintain the structure that ensures control over the decision-making processes of elites, can rule over diversity, and can claim a legitimate motivation for their existence. The balance among these factors keeps changing throughout imperial rule, especially as the relations between the center and elites change, often in relation to larger, international, geopolitical, and economic transformations that affect the imperial polity's capacity to rule and mobilize resources. These preconditions are loosely incorporated into the workings of empire, demanding that we evaluate what each statement means for a particular empire under study.

Not only are these the necessary components of imperial dominance and durability, but they also relate directly to their flexibility. That is, into each of these components of empire is built a possibility for flexibility; successful empires demonstrate over time that they can exploit these conditions to remain resilient in the face of change. Flexibility means not getting locked into enduring forms, being able to change according to circumstances, and maintaining a certain degree of elasticity of structure. In empires, the very nature of segmented rule – the making of separate bargains of rule based on the exigencies of empire and local existing institutions, practices, and relationships – is the hallmark of flexibility. The nature of the incorporation and brokerage that is necessitated by empire is also a source of its flexibility. Similarly, the ability to forge organizational structures and understandings that relate diverse ethnic, religious, and racial groups, and convince them to participate in the maintenance of interethnic/religious peace – that is, effective boundaries between groups and the continual adaptation of the boundary conditions – promotes flexibility. Finally, the construction and reconstruction of imperial legitimating ideologies to maintain relations with the elite and accommodate to the changing conditions of empire signal the suppleness of the imperial idea. Clearly, rigidity can also set in with each of these three conditions.

The definition and model of dominance for empires remain for me a Weberian ideal type that I present to be analytically rigorous; yet, as with ideal types, the reality is that the many historical cases are only approximations, and as we negotiate between theory and case, we will contribute to the knowledge of each. This definition and depiction of empire encompasses the traditional, contiguous, land-based empires, such as the Habsburg, Russian, and Ottoman and their illustrious ancestors, the Romans and the Byzantines. In Asia, the Persians, the Mughals, the Mongols, and the Chinese built successful empires. At the same time, this definition accommodates the colonial empires of Europe, where the central state and the peripheries were distinct. Although this definition applies to many cases, I restrict my comparative attention to the traditional, contiguous, land-based empires – the Ottomans' two neighbors, the Habsburgs and the Romanovs – and draw inspiration from the successes of the Romans and the Byzantines, the predecessors of the Ottomans in the same Eurasian land mass. The rationale for looking at Rome and Byzance is internal to the case because Ottomans claimed to be the heirs of these civilizations and continued in the practices they had developed.[22]

The Longevity of Empires: Critical Concepts and Issues

There is no doubt that one of the most intriguing features of empires has been their longevity. The Roman, Byzantine, Ottoman, Habsburg, and Russian Empires were political formations that endured for centuries. Such durability was remarkable, although also explainable. Rome as an empire lasted from 31 B.C. to A.D. 476. Byzance after the rise of the Eastern Empire continued from 527 to 1453. The Ottoman Empire formally existed from 1300 to 1918. The Habsburgs ruled nearly 400 years, and the Romanovs ruled from 1613 to 1917. These are impressively long stretches of time, especially compared to the longevity of the nation-state, the relatively new political formation that followed empire. The discussion of what keeps empires dominant and durable for a long period of time raises questions of grand strategy, state ability to control populations, and the structure of relations between the imperial state and the multiple domains that comprise the periphery.

The question of longevity and durability of empire used to be formulated in terms of actors' intentionality and strategizing, as contrasted to the *longue durée* transformation of social structures and of large-scale frames of relations. Among the most interesting, for example, is the debate that arose among the historians of the Roman Empire since Edward Luttwak argued, in his classic work, that it is through a grand military strategy that Roman frontiers were transformed from "undefined zones of dynamic expansion into static, scientific and highly visible lines of defense."[23] Although Luttwak attributed this transformation and stability of empire to the strategy of rulers, many Roman historians have actually argued against his interpretation. Notwithstanding the fact that we often lack the information to decide on the motives and intentions of actors, especially in the historical field, most scholars of the Roman world have instead argued either for a psychology of rule based on the basic needs for glory and grandeur, or a more crisis management approach to imperial thinking, arguing that ruling elites often patched over problems in an ad hoc fashion. The historian C. R. Whittaker, who studies the reports of imperial *consilia*, concludes that "while there was some, low-level, strategic thinking, it is difficult to detect any Grand Strategy, in the sense of an integrated effort towards a political end. There did exist the broad, ideological desire,

---

[22] On the comparison between the traditional empires and the colonial European empires, see E. J. Hobsbawm, "How Empires End," in *After Empire*, ed. Karen/Mark Barkey and von Hagen.

[23] Edward N. Luttwak, *The Grand Strategy of the Roman Empire* (Baltimore: Johns Hopkins University Press, 1976).

deeply entrenched in the Roman psyche, to extend imperial power forever, *sine fine.*[24]

The debate about strategy and intentionality in the Ottoman context is somewhat distorted because scholars are particularly sensitive to the idea of the state as initiator of change.[25] The traditional history of the Ottoman Empire has been told from the perspective of the state, its achievements, its rise and decline, and its own internal reevaluation and initiation of processes of modernization. State intentionality and strategy was therefore naturally built into arguments of Ottoman imperial tenure. Recent scholarship, however, has reacted to such focus on state actors and intentionality by drawing attention to nonstate forces and the manner in which opposition to the state can change the policy agenda. Reşat Kasaba, for example, convincingly argues that nonstate forces throughout the empire constrained and molded the power of political authorities in the nineteenth century. He claims that the organization of trade and commerce; the migratory and seasonal movement of people in the empire; and the variety of nationalist, religious, and sectarian movements shaped the imperial state's response, as well as restricted its ability to maneuver through crises.[26]

Less prevalent are the studies of empire that have intently asked questions about longevity and flexibility. Şevket Pamuk's recent work exemplifies the best of this scholarship with economic institutions in mind, and Gabor Agoston's work places long overdue emphasis on the variation and flexibility of Ottoman frontiers.[27] Both scholars underscore the degree to which the Ottomans were able to adapt to newly rising circumstances. Yet, what is not clearly said is that this was not just because they were flexible, but rather because the manner in which institutions and relations were forged left space for negotiation and adaptation. My own work on Ottoman centralization and bargaining raised similar issues, especially with regard to processes of negotiation with military groups, bandits, and mercenaries, although as with other works in the field, it focused on the state–social forces dichotomy.[28]

---

[24] C. R. Whittaker, *Rome and Its Frontiers: The Dynamics of Empire* (New York: Routledge, 2004), 37.

[25] There have been many critiques of the state-centered approach in Ottoman history. See Halil Berktay, "The Search for the Peasant in Western and Turkish History/Historiography," *Journal of Peasant Studies* 18 (April–July 1991): 109–184. More recently, Donald Quataert, "Ottoman History Writing at the Crossroads," in *Turkish Studies in the United States*, ed. Donald Quataert and Sabri Sayari (Bloomington: Indiana University Press, 2003), 15–30.

[26] Reşat Kasaba, "A Time and a Place for the Nonstate: Social Change in the Ottoman Empire during the Long Nineteenth Century," in *State Power and Social Forces: Domination and Transformation in the Third World*, ed. Joel S. Migdal, Atul Kohli, and Vivienne Shue (Cambridge, UK: Cambridge University Press, 1994), 207–230.

[27] Şevket Pamuk, "Institutional Change and the Longevity of the Ottoman Empire, 1500–1800," *Journal of Interdisciplinary History* 35 (2004): 225–247; Gabor Agoston, "A Flexible Empire; Authority and Its Limits on the Ottoman Frontiers," *International Journal of Turkish Studies* 9:1–2 (1993): 15–31.

[28] Karen Barkey, *Bandits and Bureaucrats: The Ottoman Route to State Centralization* (Ithaca, NY: Cornell University Press, 1994).

In this study, I take an analytic historical approach to understand state transformation. I link historical institutionalism with network analysis because the mechanisms of institutional continuity, flexibility, and change are embedded in the meso-level network structures that link macro-level events and phenomena to macro social and political outcomes. State transformation then is the resolution of organizational and boundary problems realized in the intermediate zone by state actors and social actors embedded in networks of negotiation. Each of the major transformations and challenges of empire was resolved in the intermediate space where relationships between actors took shape, within the ambit of organizations, boundaries, and other social formations that were molded and remolded to maintain empire.

I examine these resolutions within a relational, process-oriented historical analysis of the intermediate levels of interaction where relations between actors remain the dynamic constructions that shape the social world, and are continually remade, refined, and altered. Furthermore, these relations were the product of strategies of actors who were working to gain durable footing in their positions, mobilize people and resources, and establish themselves. Yet, they did so as they were embedded in networks of relations, as they forged the organizational arrangements that enhanced the practices and the interests of each side. The shape of these networks, whether cohesive or fragmented; the interdependencies they created; and the opportunities for action, reaction, maneuvers, and adjustments that they shaped remains crucial to understanding the strategic action that tends to emerge in such intermediary zones.

The various social forms that are produced out of the strategic negotiations between actors embedded in various networks do not operate in a vacuum of social meaning. On the contrary, throughout this analysis I try to extricate the various meanings that get attributed to the relational process I underscore, accepting with Max Weber and Clifford Geertz that *verstehen* completes our insight into the social world we study.[29] This analysis then allows me to move from the individual level to the intermediate level of networks of relations that more generally engage the institutional level where a set of practices and procedures provide and reproduce common understandings about how the world operates.

By far the more important arguments regarding the durability and longevity of empire have been structural. Yet, as I develop these concepts I hope to add more texture and depth to the structural dimension. The success of empire is based on the resolution of two challenging ideas: segmentation and integration. On the one hand, the structure of empires is based on the notion of segmentation. The basic definitional aspect of empire that has been used time and again, "divide and rule," flags the notion of separation and conquest, or separation and integration, into the power structure. More sophisticated is the hub-and-spoke metaphor, where the structure of relations between the center and the periphery both maintained the provision of goods and services to the

[29] Clifford Geertz, *The Interpretation of Cultures* (New York: Basic Books, 2000).

center as part of imperial state–society contracts, as well as made peripheral elites dependent on the center, communicating only with the center rather than with one another. The segmentation principle at the heart of empire remains the vertical integration of elites at the expense of horizontal linkages.[30] Such a structural arrangement provided power and influence to the state as the central actor that could behave as the broker among different sectors. In that sense, to the degree that communication, economic resources, migratory patterns, and political rewards were carried out between center and periphery, rather than among peripheral entities, empires remained in control of segmentation.

However, when we separate one slice of empire and concentrate on one particular state, intermediary, or locality relationship, we can see how the principle of segmentation can work against the center. That is, intermediaries between the state and the local population could also, in particular circumstances, become central and behave as brokers, providing the only linkage between state and locality. Under such circumstances, state actors might have built alternate routes or parallel structures to bypass potential blocking through these indirect relations. Empires could maintain themselves as long as the imperial center remained at the core of the exchange system; the elites enjoyed the privileged status they earned by being intermediaries between the state and the local populations, and were cognizant of the larger imperial picture, while still competing among themselves.

Segmentation and integration are the basic structural dimensions of empire; segmentation alone is not enough. I understand incorporation as integration with a further component: it might include a psychological and symbolic component that indicates that one has become part of the whole. To incorporate means to embody, and in that sense, it is more than just a structural feature. It is cultural and refers in a Weberian sense to the meaning orientations of social actors as well as the meanings that are attributed to actors and actions. As a result, the longevity and resilience of empires have also been explained in terms of a genius for incorporation. Unlike modern nation-states, empires have been political entities willing to maintain a kind of "open society." In Whittaker's terms, "empires have distinguished themselves from the nation-state by their recognition of people rather than territory and of borders rather than frontiers."[31]

The Roman, Byzantine, and Ottoman Empires present especially good examples of this feature. Scholars have demonstrated that longevity and maintenance were the result of the empires' ability to constantly renovate themselves and to incorporate the best available men. Ronald Syme, in his now classic work on Rome, argues that the governing class of both Republican and Imperial

---

[30] This was one of the major arguments I made in *Bandits and Bureaucrats*, a study of state centralization in the Ottoman Empire (*ibid.*); see also John Padgett, and Christopher Ansell, "Robust Action and the Rise of the Medici, 1400–1434," *American Journal of Sociology* 98 (1993): 1259–1319. It is also the main argument in Motyl, *Imperial Ends*.

[31] Whittaker, *Rome and Its Frontiers*, 3.

Rome demonstrated a remarkable ability to transform itself throughout the ages. Syme does not argue that this was the result of careful planning, but rather, he says, it was the product of pressure on the ground, the facts of conquest and expansion. As Rome dominated Italy in the time of the Republic, she brought into the fold the finest and most capable men from the conquered Italian communities, and later, when the republic gave way to the empire, the new imperial system did "not hold down or exclude the nations and cities that had come under Rome's dominion.... "[32] Another aspect of Roman imperial integration was the rulers' disregard for the racial and ethnic origins of the people they incorporated and made Romans. In the Roman understanding, Syme argues, "if a man was good enough to fight for Rome, he was good enough to be a citizen."[33] Romans were mixed from the outset, being from Latin, Sabine, and Etruscan origins, and in the tradition of empire, the realm displayed a myriad of languages, among them Oscan, Etruscan, Celtic, Illyrian, Venetic, and Ligurian, with Latin as the common language.

Roman political and administrative concepts that made for flexible and adaptive rule became the hallmark of the Byzantine Empire as well. In the combination of Roman political concepts with Greek culture and Christian faith, the Byzantine rulers demonstrated ingenuity at mixing the old and the new, forging alliances that would mark success. After the early establishment of Byzantium, in a meritocratic wave of appointments, a series of new men were selected by emperors to fill the administrative and military hierarchy of the state. The result of this understanding was that ruling cadres of the empire had many more Caucasians (Armenians, Georgians, and Lazs) in the elite of the empire than represented in the "native" populations. The former became emperors and empresses, trusted administrators and military men, running the empire.[34] They combined skill, knowledge, and an initial power base that made them essential to the empire. Byzantine rulers also understood well the value of incorporation in its multiple dimensions because they not only accepted barbarians into their polity, but also granted them lands and territories and spent resources educating their children both to manipulate and to include them.[35]

The same principles of integration and incorporation were present in the Ottoman domains, where institutional longevity was partly the result of ingenious openness, flexibility, and willingness to negotiate for *"raison d'empire,"* and where the continual ability to draw the best men, and to borrow and imitate successful institutional practices as well as technology, served them well. The

[32] Ronald Syme, *Colonial Elites: Rome, Spain and the Americas* (London: Oxford University Press, 1970), 3.

[33] *Ibid.*, 17.

[34] *The Oxford History of Byzantium*, ed. Cyril Mango (London: Oxford University Press, 2002); George Ostrogorsky, *History of the Byzantine State* (New Brunswick, NJ: Rutgers University Press, 1957).

[35] John V. A. Fine, Jr., *The Early Medieval Balkans: A Critical Survey from the Sixth to the Late Twelfth Century* (Ann Arbor: University of Michigan Press, 1999).

extension of this open and flexible vision of empire is displayed in many different venues, from the understanding of territoriality and frontier to the carrying on of negotiations with bandits and militias. Not only was this vision displayed in the realm of the state, however, but as we will see also in the domain of social dissent and opposition to political authority structures. From the moment of conquest, Ottomans demonstrated their openness to the forces of the "local" by spending much time learning, assessing, and adapting to indigenous practices. Although such careful assessment has been seen as both early bureaucratization and merely the greed of taxation, early success demonstrates that it was quite possible that Ottomans convinced the vanquished of their conquerors' larger interest in their well-being. Just as Rome deemed outsiders to be worthy of inclusion, the Ottomans did so as well, coexisting, comingling, and intermarrying with conquered populations, elites, and common people alike. Furthermore, just as Romans paid attention to preserve a class of provincials that did not feel alienated from the state, Ottomans maintained a set of provincial office holders who were both dependent on and rewarded by the state. Local leaders felt privileged in the local exercise of administration and control and understood such privilege, especially in the form of upward mobility, to come from the center.[36]

When we discuss the integration and incorporation of many different peoples into empire, the concepts of boundary and diversity emerge as essential to underscore the complexity of empire, as well as the conditions and exigencies under which boundaries were articulated and diversity was maintained. Incorporation is not possible without acknowledging difference. If empires are also worlds of social boundaries, how can we argue for fluidity? How can boundaries and openness coexist within the same society? Again, social networks provide a tool for understanding the functioning of these concepts. That is, fluidity is about crossing networks and establishing far-reaching ties, whereas boundaries are about interrupting networks and closing them in, making them more localized and cohesive. I take social boundaries to be the markers of social differences manifested in differing forms of social organization and association, and different access to resources and social opportunities. That is, groups that interact with one another across social boundaries not only have different patterns of organization, but also different understandings of association and community. Boundaries separate, make categories, and shape and channel social action. They also produce the conceptual distinctions that people overlay on the objective boundary; that is, they create the restrictions, symbols, practices, and ways of identifying and separating.[37]

---

[36] Miles, "Roman and Modern Imperialism," 640. See also Richard P. Saller, *Personal Patronage under the Early Empire* (Cambridge, UK: Cambridge University Press, 1982).

[37] Fredrik Barth, "Introduction," in *Ethnic Groups and Boundaries: The Social Organization of Culture Difference*, ed. F. Barth (London: Allen & Unwin Books, 1969), 9–38; Michele Lamont and Virag Molnar, "The Study of Boundaries in the Social Sciences," *Annual Review of Sociology* 28 (August 2002): 167–195; Aron Rodrigue, "Difference and Tolerance in the Ottoman Empire," *Stanford Humanities Review* 5.1 (1995): 81–90.

Part of the success and longevity of empires has been explained by their openness and their ability to accept different peoples into their polities, even though they also changed these people in the process. Does this mean that empires did not have objective social boundaries cutting across groups? Or does this mean that boundaries did not carry any social significance in social relations? I suggest neither.

Within empires, social boundaries existed around many different organizational criteria, and in many ways defined the interaction within and across categories. This is not what is really interesting about empire and social boundaries. Rather, empires viewed social boundaries as *mobile markers of difference*, understanding that diversity was a fact of empire and that not only marking it, but also employing it, was necessary. In that sense, it was not that boundaries "did not exist"; rather, state and social actors perceived their location and significance to be variable and somewhat open to manipulation. It was also clear that boundaries were not "blurred" because difference was meaningful to the members of society.[38] Therefore, if we want to understand how empire is organized, we need to understand how diversity in empire is organized and pay particular attention to shifting boundaries. This is because the patterns of change in boundaries – their formation and activation, their maintenance and reinforcement, and their suppression and obliteration – tell us a lot about how empires understood and organized diversity in different times. Understanding this variation gives us insight into the workings of imperial society.

Imperial states maintain rule over multireligious and multiethnic diversity through a variety of policies, from the "toleration" of diversity and its incorporation to forced conversion and assimilation. Religious, utilitarian, and strategic reasons drive imperial state elites to incorporate and order diversity. Yet, this is not to argue that empires had tolerance or intolerance as direct goals. Rather, their goal was to maintain power and to conquer or hold territories. Tolerance, assimilation, and intolerance were on the menu of strategies designed to squeeze resources out of minorities and to enforce allegiance to the imperial state.

There are at least four different strategies that empires have exhibited toward ethnic and religious communities: toleration, persecution, assimilation, and expulsion.[39] Empires have differed along this continuum; some have emphasized assimilation over toleration, whereas others have moved quickly toward the persecution of groups perceived as a threat to the empire. Imperial states have also displayed a combination of strategies, defining groups differentially and therefore applying different measures for dealing with diversity. They have also altered the trajectories, moving between tolerance and intolerance

---

[38] The syncretic traditions of the early Ottomans, the constant movement between Christianity and Islam, and the sharing of confessional spaces may be seen as a historical moment of "blurred" boundaries, although as I explore in Chapter 2, such mixing seems to have occurred within existing separate understanding of each religion as well.

[39] I thank David Laitin and Richard Lachmann for insights on this at the November 2003 Social Science History Association convention.

or vice versa for the same particular groups. This shows the degree to which social boundaries were manipulated and constructed to fit the strategies of empire. In this book, I focus on the emergence of policies dealing with diverse populations in the Ottoman Empire, the original encounters and the shaping of initial boundaries, and the understanding of difference. However, I also look at the manner in which such boundaries changed over time, under a variety of state and social forces, and show how dissent, trade and commerce, population movements, and foreign intrusion helped shape and reshape the boundaries between groups, in the process shifting the organization of empire.

Finally, we must clarify the concept of decline. It is clear from the foregoing that I concentrate on organizational and institutional longevity rather than on decline. The use of the term "decline" has been quite unfortunate in the Ottoman discourse because traditional scholarship has maintained that anything beyond the Classical Age (1300–1600) – a label that itself is the product of a decline thesis – was disintegration, decay, and the final collapse of the Ottoman polity.[40] In employing this term "decline" and in locating Ottoman decline in the sixteenth century, scholars have contributed to the pernicious comparison of Western rise and development as opposed to Islamic decline. If Ottoman society was in decline, then its social, political, and cultural production was deemed in the negative, a lesser and wanting polity that would end up imitating the West. Such a representation has had unfortunate consequences for the larger imagination of relations among cultures and civilizations. Use of this term, however, is of great significance in the study of social and political change because it has stifled the study of how states and societies transform themselves, adapt to new circumstances, and reformulate new state–society relations that work. Adaptation is not decline, so categorizing all adaptation as such dismisses it as failure rather than understanding it as flexibility and durability.

The decline thesis, happily, has become an endangered species. Because more and more studies are reconsidering the temporal and causal interpretations of the Ottoman decline, the focus is changing to state–society negotiations and recalibration,[41] institutional longevity,[42] military technology and diffusion,[43] and the reevaluation of relations between the state and local intermediaries

---

[40] Bernard Lewis, *The Emergence of Modern Turkey* (London: Oxford University Press, 1968); Halil İnalcık, *The Ottoman Empire: The Classical Age, 1300–1600* (New Rochelle, NY: Orpheus, 1973); Halil İnalcık and Donald Quataert, *An Economic and Social History of the Ottoman Empire, 1300–1914* (Cambridge, UK: Cambridge University Press, 1994); Cornell H. Fleischer, *Bureaucrat and Intellectual in the Ottoman Empire: The Historian Mustafa Ali, 1546–1600* (Princeton, NJ: Princeton University Press, 1986).

[41] Barkey, *Bandits and Bureaucrats.*

[42] Pamuk, "Institutional Change and the Longevity."

[43] Jonathan Grant, "Rethinking the Ottoman Decline: Military Technology Diffusion in the Ottoman Empire, Fifteenth to Eighteenth Centuries," *Journal of World History* 10 (January 1999): 179–201.

under the nineteenth-century reforms.[44] Rhoads Murphey has also skillfully advocated that if we stop seeing the Ottoman Empire as a compact totality, but rather as a conglomerate of pieces, we will be able to understand and analyze the location, impact, and implications of such episodes as the "agrarian crisis in Anatolia" or the "trade crisis in the Aegean."[45] These present alternative explanations that discuss state transformation rather than decline, and underscore the degree to which the Ottoman Empire remained a viable and distinct polity until the end of the nineteenth century.

Yet, it is also clear that we cannot dismiss decline so easily because its discourse was not simply an invention of modern scholarship and Orientalist thought. It was also the product of Ottoman society itself. That is, within the empire, once a self-described apogee was reached, subsequent transformations were perceived from the point of view of this initial height. That is, regardless of whether they were lacking, later moments were always compared to the former and deemed to be so. Such a discourse did several things to Ottoman society. It tempted the rise of religious zealotry that argued for Islamic purity and morality as a way to set the clock back. It also narrowed the options available to state actors because a discourse of decline permeated the mentality of state makers. After that moment of imperial height, the empire's thinkers would all be tormented by a single thought, as Coetzee once vividly remarked, "How not to end, how not to die, how to prolong its era."[46] Such fears were widespread in empire: Romans, Byzantines, Ottomans, and Russians certainly experienced this fear vividly. In fact, this is still an issue in modern societies, which have come more or less to mark the apogee of their power and hegemony and become obsessed with its maintenance. This tells us that we cannot just dismiss the decline thesis; we need to assess its effect on the imperial actors themselves.

It is within this perspective that I place my analytic and historical study of empire. This book is the product of a perspective that underscores durability, longevity, and continuity, where I try to locate the network and organizational underpinnings of such an imperial formation and its transformation. I attempt a systematic, process-oriented, and comparative study of Ottoman state transformation in which the emphasis is on process over time, contextualized comparisons to offer historically grounded explanations of important social outcomes such as imperial longevity and immutability, and state transformation in and out of "imperial formations." With a temporal dynamic in mind, I focus on the emergence of a political entity with imperial claims, its becoming an empire as well as its transformation and its transition to nonempire

---

44 Yonca Köksal, "Local Intermediaries and Ottoman State Centralization: A Comparison of the Tanzimat Reforms in the Provinces of Ankara and Edirne (1839–1878)," Ph.D. dissertation, Columbia University, 2002.

45 Rhoads Murphey, "Review Article: Mustafa Ali and the Politics of Cultural Despair," *International Journal of Middle East Studies* 21 (May 1989): 243–255.

46 J. M. Coetzee, *Waiting for the Barbarians* (New York: Penguin Books, 1982), 133.

on its way to multiple, modern nation-states with different characteristics. Again, a process-oriented outlook on empire requires me to study the strategic negotiations between actors embedded in networks of relations and institutionally structured fields in order to understand the unfolding of different social and political forms.

The processes I trace and put down on paper are the multiplicities of flexible arrangements, networked structures, institutional mixes, the layering of old and new, winners and losers in the governance structures, the negotiated arrangements in different domains, and structural and symbolic sites of agreement and contention. I argue that these intermediary processes in which socially embedded actors negotiate, appropriate, and innovate are critical for explaining the Ottoman experience. But more than that, they are also critical for showing why the terms of the Ottoman experience help us understand not just empire, but systems of rule and governance more generally.

The questions and issues that I have outlined cannot be pursued without a continuous effort at building complex and historicized notions of empire. Beyond a persistent attempt to balance historical specificity and case-based generality, I also remain methodologically eclectic because I believe that different historical questions can be answered best by a variety of tools and methodologies that respond to the questions at hand and to the available evidence. Such eclecticism also stems from my effort to continually pay attention to the articulation of social structures, cultural idioms, and human agency. Given different articulations of these three slices of social reality, I deploy various historical methodological tools such as network, event, and institutional-cultural, as well as comparative historical analyses to best highlight the articulation at hand. Overall, then, I claim to be working on three levels: a historical (empirical) level, an analytic level (stressing a class of new methods and ways of seeing and organizing data that should be useful for others working on other problems), and a substantive level (i.e., one with implications for our understanding of rule, empires, and the management of diversity and dissent).

The book is organized around two main parts. Part I focuses on the arrangements and understandings that made for flexibility and adaptation in empire, and Part II underscores how change occurred to undermine the negotiated and flexible arrangements of empire. In Part I, I concentrate on the networks and institutions that undergird the system from the fourteenth to the eighteenth centuries; in Part II, I study the ways in which such imperial arrangements transformed themselves, becoming different political formations that were perceived to be more adaptable to the new world order. Such transformations began in the eighteenth century and culminated in the late nineteenth century. The book is written in seven chapters that represent different moments and different aspects of imperial organization.

In Chapter 2, on the emergence of the state, I explain Ottoman emergence in terms of brokerage across different cultural and religious systems, within the context of a frontier society that allowed the extension of such linkages. The basic argument is that the Ottoman state grew out of post-Seljuk, post-Byzantine imperial formations, using many of the existing ideological and organizational tools, but with one added element – brokerage of networks used to build and unite – a tool that was lacking among other similar emerging political formations in the plateau of Bithynia. In this chapter, I reconstruct the ego networks of the first two sultans of the Ottoman Empire to demonstrate the manner in which they brokered across many diverse groups. I emphasize the innovative manner in which religion was used as a tool of brokerage, connecting networks rather than bringing closure and establishing boundaries.

In Chapter 3, I focus on the imperial threshold by asking how a state becomes an empire and establishes the institutions of empire. In this chapter, which is organized comparatively, the parallel transformations from statehood to empire (republic to empire in the Roman case) focus on the strategies and institution building by Mehmed II and Augustus. I argue that both empires emerged by focusing on successful elites, on institutional "bricolage," drawing on practices that worked, and discarding those that proved not adaptable. Empire building was a messy enterprise where existing and new elites needed to be incorporated and featured as part of empire, but where social and economic imperatives created political divisions that worked against consolidation. The chapter as such is also in constant dialogue with the three features of imperial domination: legitimacy, diversity, and the distribution of resources. In this chapter, I also discuss the peculiar role of Islam in the construction of Ottoman social and political life. Even though the Ottomans settled on a form of Sunnî Orthodoxy in the period of imperial institutionalization, they did so by allowing multiple visions of religious understanding to flourish in the empire. Over time, however, such forbearance of Islamic diversity was retracted in view of international and internal crises of governance. How religion was negotiated in empire, and how it was understood at various layers of imperial state and nonstate actors, is discussed here, yet also emerges in every chapter because it remains a crucial ingredient of the confrontation between various established forms of faith and the adaptation to changing conditions of life.

Chapter 4 is an in-depth study of the organization of diversity in empire as a tool for long-term stability and maintenance. How was diversity encountered? How was it institutionalized and accepted? Studies of multiculturalism today emphasize values, beliefs, and discourse in the language that people use to define their identity and to participate in modern society. Unlike such studies, there is less discourse and ideology in this organizational perspective on diversity. Diversity is embedded and maintained by organizational practices, in the relationship between the center and the composite parts of society, and in the outcomes of negotiations. That is, diversity contributes to the success of empire in its organizational features. In the process, I also develop a more complex and historicized notion of Ottoman toleration. I argue that Ottoman toleration emerged out of a top-down and bottom-up concern for boundaries and for peace between religious and ethnic communities. For as long as it lasted, until sometime in the eighteenth century, this toleration and diversity was the product of both state management and negotiations with social forces, especially with key interlocutors between state and society, both representatives of communities and agents of the state.

Chapter 5 looks at the organization of dissent in early empire, assessing the categories around which dissent was organized, the demands and the absorption, and the transformation of dissent. I do not survey the whole history of early dissent; rather, I attempt to understand dissent in imperial categories. The question of dissent becomes important, especially against the backdrop of toleration that Ottomans demonstrated toward non-Muslims. In contrast, the Ottoman state was not tolerant toward the Muslim heterodox orders, Sufi sects that were alternatives to the Sunnî orthodoxy of the Ottomans. In this chapter, I try to understand why the Ottoman state chose to tolerate non-Muslims, but to persecute its own Muslim heterodoxies. Not only is this chapter, then, very much about an important sectarian division that continues to plague the political landscape of the Middle East, but it also sheds new light on the old argument that the closer are the groups, the harder it is to read and accept differences and the sharper the struggle. I place this argument regarding the violence among brothers into an organizational perspective. We can explain the rise of sectarian dissent with an organizational argument about the inability of the state to create legibility, to order the different Muslim groups, and to administer them. Here, the proliferation of networks of dissent and the indeterminacy of the relations between state and dissenters pushed the state toward much more violent action.

I then move to Part II, which underscores the reorganization of empire. The eighteenth century was to become a transitional phase; state and social reorganization pushed toward new patterns of imperial formation, leading in the nineteenth century to a shift away from some of the key aspects of empire – negotiations, diversity, and legitimacy – toward less negotiation, more uniformity, and standardized rules and regulations, all of which culminated in the nineteenth century. Two parallel processes of change undergird the transition of the eighteenth century. First, political participation expanded in the Ottoman century, and second, the empire experienced a tremendous social-structural revolution as the result of economic expansion and tax farming. Both the political and the economic processes of transformations engendered a local indigenous modernity that provided the new counterweight to traditional state society arrangements. Chapter 6 deals with the slow reorganization of dissent throughout the eighteenth century into a coherent political movement whose effects became cumulative and that finally represented the empowerment of different components of imperial society. In this chapter, I study the events of three important moments in eighteenth-century Ottoman history, 1703, 1730, and 1808, showing how different groups enter the political arena from one event to the other and become empowered to gradually challenge the state. In this chapter, modernity is in the new forms of dissent.

Chapter 7 then presents the transformation of the relations of domination over the long eighteenth century. In this chapter, I show how the institutionalization of life-term tax farming, working in tandem with the development of extensive trade relations, transformed Ottoman society into a networking one in which horizontal ties and associations proliferated. I argue that in this new networking society, members of the local elites relied on one another as easily as they used to rely on the state; embedded in local networks, they gained the confidence and assertiveness to challenge the state. The spokes were joined, not just at the hub, but now also on the rim of the periphery. The combination of a new political economy and the emergence of innovative and connected actors in the local networks slowly shifted the balance between state and social forces. Finally, I trace the manner in which such reorganization in subtle ways promoted an indigenous modernity, one established before the Western reforms of the nineteenth century. I explore the consequences of such political, economic, and social transformations in the concluding chapter, which explores the forging of new patterns of social organization, *faute de mieux*, away from empire and toward the nation-state.

Thus, Chapter 8 is meant to tie together the three aspects of imperial domination, demonstrating that each one of them was transformed throughout the centuries via the formation of new institutions that moved Ottomans willy-nilly toward the forms of the nation-state. In this chapter, I demonstrate the impact of changing networks on the imperial state, deeply aggravated by the manner in which the system of tax farming that had served them so well became a strong liability in the nineteenth century. That is, not only were Ottoman imperial relations transformed through the dense horizontal networks of trade and cooperation across the empire, but these relations were also exceptionally widespread and decentralized, making it practically impossible for central state elites to rein them in. In comparison to the European tax farming systems that were controlled by centralized organizations, the Ottoman one was unmanageable.

However, I also show that one of the strongest features of Ottoman rule, the management of diversity, became the locus of imperial failure. That is, under conditions of economic transformation, the comparative differential success of ethnic and religious groups emerged as a threat rather than an impulse for improvement. Locally, as well as more centrally, competition between Muslim and non-Muslim merchants – relations fueled by ethnic entrepreneurs – led to the hardening of boundaries between groups and to the formation of separate identities where groups were in relations with each other but clearly forming distinct and bounded understandings of each other. A threatened state entered the fray of relations and committed atrocities. Had the Ottomans not been propelled toward a new world order, had they not used Islam and new Turkish identities as oppositional identities and as their new tool for legitimacy, they might have avoided the unraveling of violence. Yet, it is quite unlikely that they would have escaped the inescapable: the trajectory from empire to nation-state.

2

Emergence: Brokerage across Networks

> The Turkish raiders are called in their language *akandye* [sic. *akıncı*], which means "those who flow," and they are like torrential rains that fall from the clouds. From these storms come great floods until the streams leave their banks and overflow, and everything this water strikes, it takes, carries away, and moreover, destroys, so that in some places they cannot quickly make repairs. But such sudden downpours do not last long. Thus also the Turkish raiders, or "those who flow" like rainstorms, do not linger long, but whatever they strike they burn, plunder, kill, and destroy everything so that for many years the cock will not crow there.

This chilling description of Turkish cavalrymen descending on villages in northwestern Anatolia at the frontiers of the Byzantine Empire was reproduced many times by numerous fifteenth-century chroniclers of various origins; this particular one is from the pen of Konstantin Mihailovic, a Serb who served in the Janissary army.[1] These authors reflect a certain reality of the frontier zones, where boundaries between fractured and decaying empires and past kingdoms were eroding, where the further one got from centers of authority, the further removed from law and order, the lower the stakes, the greater the thrills, and the more the expectation of "chaos." Yet, in many ways it was from the disorder and uncertainty of the frontier that a world-class empire was born at the twilight of the thirteenth century. The construction of this formidable political apparatus of authority and control was not just the result of fire, plunder, rape, death, and destruction. It was also the result of brokerage among different religious, social, and economic groups that formed new social relations, combining diverse ideas and practices and forging new identities. This chapter explicates in analytic terms this process – the genesis of a new, lasting political form.

Perhaps at the moment of emergence the Ottomans had an initial spatial and temporal advantage, which they were able to turn into an organizational

---

[1] Quoted in Heath W. Lowry, *The Nature of the Early Ottoman State* (Albany: State University of New York Press, 2003), 47.

asset. Yet the members of the family who were to construct the Ottoman polity lived among many Turcoman populations and principalities, located in the geographic, social, and cultural space of the frontier, at the interstices between powerful empires, a space that was pregnant with possibility and that promoted organizational innovation. Not all of these Turcoman leaders were able to organize strong and stable organizational forms; many emerged, lasted for some years, and were conquered by others. The leaders who emerged as real state makers were located at the boundaries of various systems, and could communicate across groups, ideas, and cultural formations. As they brokered across cultures and social formations, they constructed a political form that combined centralism and regionalism, eclectic structures, and fixity and elasticity of boundaries, together with the incorporation and toleration of diversity, dissent, and, even when necessary, a certain defiance of the societal order. A historical network framework helps demonstrate that the Ottomans built a hub-and-spoke network structure of which they became the center, and that institutional innovation and political emergence resulted from building relations across otherwise separate and competing groups and communities.

Just as the Ottomans emerged from the frontiers as a dominant imperial power, so, too, did the Russian Empire, where brokerage across boundaries proved critical to establishing the supremacy of Moscow and to laying the foundations for imperial expansion and conquest. The rise of Muscovy from an undistinguished principality at the beginning of the fourteenth century to an expanding multiethnic and multiconfessional empire in the sixteenth century reflects the unique talent of Muscovite princes for brokering political deals across cultures and religions with their Tatar overlords in the Mongol Empire and the Golden Horde. Although the "symbiosis between Rus and the Tatars is only imperfectly reflected" in the primarily ecclesiastical sources,[2] like their empire building contemporaries in Anatolia, the Muscovite princes generally pursued a policy of pragmatic cooperation within a power structure that required frequent political and economic contacts across cultural and religious boundaries.

To understand the Ottoman emergence, we need to study the geography and the social and political structures of the frontier between two struggling empires, Byzantium and the Seljuks. It is within this frontier space that actors brokering among spatial, religious, and productive populations built resilient coalitions and mobilized various identities. Within the constraints of the frontier, within the institutional framework of two empires and of the multiple networks created across these institutional spaces, actors strategized and built an emergent political form. Because at that time and in that larger frontier space only one important empire emerged and persisted, the comparative question of why other principalities (*beylik*) constructed around similar ideas and frames did not succeed is also important. I conclude by stressing the early

---

[2] Andreas Kappeler, *The Russian Empire: A Multiethnic History*, transl. Alfred Clayton (New York: Pearson Education, 2001), 22.

characteristics and engagement between state actors and social actors, and the possibilities for change.

The ancestors of the Ottomans are said to have emerged in the second millennium B.C. from the space between the Siberian forests and the Mongolian plains on the Asian continent. Restless, they moved, fought the Chinese, and separated into multiple branches to emerge as the Oghuz peoples, and spread through Turkestan, the Caucasus, Iran, northern India, the Middle East, and Armenia. When they entered Anatolia after the battle of Manzikert (Malazgirt) in 1071, they crossed the threshold into a new Byzantine world and territory. The leader of the victorious nomads was Seljuk, who accepted Sunnî Islam and facilitated the settlement of Muslims in Anatolia. The early vigor of the Seljuk dynasty was unmatched in the region until Gengiz Khan, bent on destroying Turkic nomads in Central Asia and their settled brothers in the sultanate of Rum (the new name of the Seljuk Empire, 1077–1307), defeated their armies in Kösedağ in 1243. The sultanate shattered and split, with a few surviving families able to hold on to some territory. The latter formed small-scale emirates such as the Menteshe, Sarukhan, Karesi, and Aydın (*beyliks*), competing among themselves and with the emerging Ottomans for resources and booty. Among them was the rebellious and indomitable Osman (d. 1326), whose warrior habits attracted the attention of Byzantine and nomadic Muslim fighters; together they engaged in skirmishes and booty collection in northwest Anatolia. Osman initiated the scaffolding on which the foundations of the Ottoman state were erected. It was his son Orhan (1326–1362) who conquered Brussa (Bursa) in 1326, Nicea (Iznik) in 1336, and Lopadion (Ulubat) and Nicomedia (Izmit) in 1337. Orhan confronted the other nomadic survivors of the Seljuks as well; he annexed the lands of the Karesi emirate, and in 1354, he crossed into Europe by capturing Gallipoli (Gelibolu). In reality, he had been invited during the struggles between Byzantine dynasties, and once there, his men settled and stayed, establishing their leader's first bridgehead in Europe. Satisfied, Orhan declared himself emir and settled down in his capital of Bursa. His son Murad I (1362–1389) focused on the western and central Anatolian *beyliks*, taking Germiyan, Hamid, Teke, and Karaman between 1375 and 1380. In Europe, the earliest conquest was of Adrianople (Edirne) in 1362, the second capital of the Ottomans, but their first capital in Europe. After defeating the Serbs in Macedonia, Murad took Philippopolis (Plovdiv/Filibe), much of Bulgaria, Nis, and Thessaloniki (Salonica/Selanik); he died during the Battle of Kosovo Polje in 1389, fighting the Serbian armies.

His son, Beyazıd I, the Thunderbolt (1389–1402), saved the day by finishing off the battle, having Prince Lazar executed and moving back into Anatolia to penetrate deep into Turcoman *beylik* territory. The *beyliks* of Menteshe, Aydın, Saruhan, Germiyan, and Hamidili (1389–1390) ceased to exist, and Karaman surrendered; furthermore, major towns such as Sıvas, Kastamonu, Erzincan, and Sinop were taken, ensuring that the northern Anatolian ports on the Black Sea entered the new polity. When Beyazıd returned to advance into Europe, the news of the threat of the Turk had spread far and wide, and a crusade was on its way. Defeated by the Turks, the motley armies of French, English, German, and some Hungarian crusaders returned to their respective countries (1396). Expeditions into Europe continued until the Balkans south of the Danube were under Ottoman control. Similarly in Anatolia, Beyazıd did not rest until most of the east, west, and everything in between accepted his sovereignty, stopped only by Tamerlane (Timur) in 1402. In 1451, Mehmed II became the sultan of a renewed empire, but in 1453, he became "the Conqueror."[3]

The traditional narratives of Ottoman emergence have downplayed much of the relational and cultural dynamism of the region and have suggested single-minded accounts of the rise of the Ottomans, their ethnic and religious force, and their ability to overwhelm through Holy War.[4] Competing explanations emphasize religion, ethnicity, tribalism, demographic conditions, or a cultural symbiosis effect to explain the swift emergence of Turcomans from a small principality to a world-class empire. Although they emphasize the complexity of the moment and the relations emerging in the northwestern corner of Anatolia at the time, most scholars still present a smooth narrative in which the outcome – the emergence of the Ottoman state – is posited at the outset. The story is told through a narrow causality that minimizes the rise of the Ottomans to that of a religious *gazâ* (Holy War) ideology, a trope used successfully by the Ottomans much later in the fifteenth century to construct for themselves glorious and legitimate Islamic origins.[5] Linda Darling's study of the emergence period presents an alternative reading that emphasizes the historical practice of *gazâ* in the Muslim world for a long time before the rise of the Ottomans. She argues that it was probably one of the many and contending ways in which various groups presented and differentiated their interests and practices.[6]

---

[3] The early history of the Ottoman expansion can be read in detail in Claude Cahen, *Pre-Ottoman Turkey: A General Survey of the Material and Spiritual Culture and History, c. 1071–1330* (New York: Taplinger, 1968); Georges Castellan, *Histoire des Balkans XIVe–XXe siècles* (Paris: Fayard, 1999); Colin Imber, *The Ottoman Empire: 1300–1481* (Istanbul: Isis Press, 1990); Halil İnalcık, *The Ottoman Empire: The Classical Age 1300–1600* (London: Weidenfeld & Nicolson, 1973); Robert Mantran, *Histoire de l'empire Ottoman* (Paris: Fayard, 1989).

[4] Among those who have argued for a religious *gâzî* ideology, see Paul Wittek, *The Rise of the Ottoman Empire* (London: Royal Asiatic Society, 1938). Halil İnalcık still stresses ideology and organizational innovation. Halil İnalcık, "The Question of the Emergence of the Ottoman State," *International Journal of Turkish Studies* 4:4 (1980), 71–79; idem, "The Ottoman State: Economy and Society, 1300–1600," in *An Economic and Social History of the Ottoman Empire, 1300–1914*, ed. Halil İnalcık and Donald Quataert (Cambridge, UK: Cambridge University Press, 1994). Fuad Köprülü has advanced a thesis based on a Turkic ethnic identity. See M. Fuad Köprülü, *The Origins of the Ottoman Empire*, transl. and ed. Gary Leiser (Albany: State University of New York Press, 1992); finally, Rudi Lindner proposed an alternative explanation involving tribal and Central Asian traditions and religions that drove Turcoman nomads away from *gazâ* and early centralized power. Rudi P. Lindner, *Nomads and Ottomans in Medieval Anatolia* (Bloomington: Indiana University Press, 1983).

[5] Cemal Kafadar, *Between Two Worlds: The Construction of the Ottoman State* (Berkeley: University of California Press, 1995).

[6] Linda T. Darling, "Contested Territory: Ottoman Holy War in Comparative Context," *Studia Islamica* 91 (2000): 133–163.

More recently, Colin Imber argued that early Ottoman history is based on fifteenth-century writings on Ottoman origins and cannot be shown to be truthful; therefore, it is basically a "black hole" that we should not bother to use.[7] However, Halil İnalcık and Heath Lowry both show that there are "accounting"-type documents of the early state, land registers that corroborate the narratives that historians have used.[8] Furthermore, Lowry in a new book presents an analytically coherent argument based on meticulous study of the documentary and physical sources, giving the first account of the Ottoman rise to power within the constraints under which these men worked, the strategies they developed, and the outcome of their actions.[9] Lowry cogently argues that these early state makers were neither fanatic believers in Islam nor wishy-washy, tolerant, obliging men, but rather that their actions have to be understood within the context in which they found themselves. Under conditions of rapid expansion and lack of adequate manpower, the state that was constructed was necessarily a hybrid one in which Christians were as necessary and welcome as Muslims. Yet, Lowry's framework is missing a sociological accounting of how a few men make a revolutionary change in their immediate social relations and transform them into relations of power and influence. How was the state built? What were the initial steps in the development of the early form of the state?

I adopt a Weberian definition of the state in which it is an organization that successfully claims a monopoly on the legitimate use of physical force over a given territory, with the accent on "legitimate." Although most scholars start with this definition, the notion of legitimate control drops off relatively quickly, and the emphasis remains on the use of violence. Combining territorial control and legitimate control adds subjective forms as in "the mental structures and categories of perception and thought," which also agrees with Bourdieu's conceptualization of the state, where he talks of "*symbolic* violence over a definite territory and over the totality of the corresponding population."[10] I am, however, much more interested in understanding how this organization and its legitimacy is initially constructed by actors taking steps to convince different populations, soldiers, and elites to mobilize and join their efforts.

---

[7] Colin Imber, "The Ottoman Dynastic Myth," *Turcica* 19 (1987): 7–27; idem, "The Legend of Osman Gazi," in *The Ottoman Emirate*, ed. Elizabeth Zachariadou (Rethymnon: Crete University Press, 1993), 67–77; idem, "Canon and Apocrypha in Early Ottoman History," in *Studies in Ottoman History in Honor of Professor V. L. Menage*, ed. Colin Heywood and Colin Imber (Istanbul: Isis Press, 1994), 117–137. He instead reconstructs an explanation of early Ottoman times based more on *shari'a* and Islamic legal principles, which remains similarly contested. See his *Ebu's-su'ud: The Islamic Legal Tradition* (Edinburgh: Edinburgh University Press, 1997).

[8] Halil İnalcık, "How to Read Ashık Pasha-Zade's History," in *Studies in Ottoman History in Honour of Professor V. L. Menage*, 139–156.

[9] Lowry, *The Nature of the Early Ottoman State*. This chapter relies heavily on the arguments of this book.

[10] Pierre Bourdieu, Loic J. D. Wacquant, and Samar Farage, "Rethinking the State: Genesis and Structure of the Bureaucratic Field," *Sociological Theory* 12 (1994): 3.

Consequently, we have to conceptualize early state formation as moments when contenders for power have minimal organizational structures at hand, but have many social relations and ties that they need to manipulate in order to influence, control, and increase their social and cultural resources. In this way, we can begin to understand why and how they will generate social institutions, and why they will attract followers. These individuals start with existing relations, mostly horizontal ties that have to be converted into vertical ties of authority, thereby changing the content of the old networks of social relations. The question then becomes one of understanding how would-be leaders can transform existing horizontal ties into vertical relations of power while they continue to accumulate good will and supporters.

As studies of brokerage across structural holes show, networks provide the context for would-be leaders to expand their influence and power through brokerage. People who are located at the boundaries of systems, who can communicate across structural holes, and who can bring opinions, beliefs, and practices together are more likely to have good ideas and to promote change and innovation.[11] Although this consideration is not entirely new, its network conceptualization as brokerage across structural holes is very useful, both in studies of organizations and in historical settings.[12] Social actors who are located at the boundaries of systems at the interstices of different groups and who can learn from both, connect them, find analogies between them, and exploit the best practices and beliefs of each end up innovating. According to Ronald Burt, "good ideas emerged from the intersection of social worlds, but spread...in a way that would continue segregation between the worlds."[13]

When we attempt to map Osman's social networks, we can follow the manner in which he connected the worlds of Byzantium, the Seljuks, and the various principalities that emerged in the post-Seljuk era. Despite the paucity of data, we can trace the strategic family and political alliances that he constructed to bring together Christian and Muslim frontiersmen and women, religious figures, and important merchant and literate scholarly families, and employed the structures and cultures of both to build a new political entity. Here, then, our principal actor, Osman, was able to join previously unconnected elements and to build new networks from the recombination of existing networks. When connections can be made, over time patronage can be claimed, and companions can be turned into clients and vassals.

Yet, the emergence of any new organizational structure from among existing forms in society is usually the result of a recombination of existing socially

---

[11] Ronald S. Burt, "Structural Holes and Good Ideas," *American Journal of Sociology* 110 (2004): 349–399; idem, *Brokerage and Closure: An Introduction to Social Capital* (Oxford, UK, and New York: Oxford University Press, 2005).

[12] Such a concept in varying forms has been used in many management studies, but in the historical literature, the most successful application has been that of John F. Padgett and Christopher K. Ansell, "Robust Action and the Rise of the Medici, 1400–1434," *American Journal of Sociology* 98 (1993): 1259–1319.

[13] Burt, "Structural Holes and Good Ideas," 394.

structured channels of interaction with the practices and ideas available in that setting.[14] Brokerage across networks, recombination through alliances, and key moves from one network to another represent the social structural dynamics of this process. However, these structural transformations occurred in a frontier environment with several characteristics. On the one hand, the frontier was an inherently uncertain environment in which actors had to strategize to achieve "lasting footing,"[15] and where cross-cutting ties among religious, ethnic, and culturally distinct groups were possible and were understood as part of a repertoire of frontier negotiation. Osman and Orhan's brokerage across world religions was therefore acceptable as part of the larger cultural understanding that permeated frontier society. Yet, their brokerage was also in part strategic manipulation to achieve stability in their coalitions, resiliency in their network associations, and resources in their mobilizational capacity.

Each of Osman's rival principalities could have had access to the same arsenal of social and cultural ideas and innovations. Therefore, we also need to ask the comparative question why only one principality, that of the Ottomans, succeeded and others did not. One explanation lies in the differences between network structures that emphasize closure rather than brokerage, and that therefore lead to different patterns of trust and social capital.[16] Burt shows that networks that emphasize closure tend to reinforce existing ideas and prejudices; we can extend this argument to infer that they rarely lead to innovation. In this case, we have to look at what kind of structures existed in the other principalities that were, in the long run, all defeated by the Ottomans. Another explanation might lie in the difference that Mancur Olson discusses in his theory of state formation in which he argues that stationary bandits steal less than roving bandits because they have more incentive to allow the population to reproduce its assets. Therefore, those who decide to settle will be more likely to make the population safer and willing to generate wealth.[17] The Ottomans, as we will see, combined both brokerage across networks and good ideas, strategies that worked. To return, however, to the original quotation from Mihailovic, by stressing brokerage across networks, good ideas, innovations, and the transformation of ties, I do not want to underestimate the explanatory power of warfare, the push of a booty economy, and violence in conquest. The two working together, sometimes even taking turns, explains the rise of the Ottomans.

Similar questions can be raised about the emergence of Muscovy and the success of some rather than others, and the manner in which brokerage and war combined in other settings. During the fourteenth and fifteenth centuries,

[14] See John Padgett, "Organizational Genesis, Identity and Control: The Transformation of Banking in Renaissance Florence," *Journal of Economic Literature* 41 (2003): 211–257.

[15] Harrison C. White, Frédéric C. Godart, and Victor P. Corona, "Mobilizing Identities: Uncertainty and Control in Strategy," *Theory, Culture & Society* 24 (2007): 191–212.

[16] Ronald S. Burt, *Bandwidth and Echo: Trust, Information, and Gossip in Social Networks* (New York: Russell Sage Foundation, 2001), 30–74.

[17] Mancur Olson, *Power and Prosperity* (New York: Basic Books, 2000).

the Mongol Empire and its successor, the Golden Horde, played a decisive role in what would become the Russian Empire. Although the initial conquest by the Mongols was extremely destructive, they were mainly concerned with exacting tribute and maintaining stability. Thus, rather than interfering in the politics of the Russian principalities, the Mongols built on existing structures and forms of legitimacy by lending "support to two institutions that served as rallying points and sources of cohesion within the Russian community – the office of grand prince and the Eastern Orthodox Church."[18] In the early fourteenth century, Muscovy was undistinguished from the other principalities that competed for ascendancy within the Russian lands and for the title of grand prince. As in the Ottoman Empire, the Muscovites occupied a unique structural position that encouraged brokering and innovation to extend their power. Because Muscovite princes had lost their traditional claim to the title of grand prince, they were forced to make innovative alliances with their Islamic overlords, embracing "radical new methods to increase their power and defeat their rivals."[19] The Muscovite princes displayed remarkable "political dexterity" in their "ability to manipulate the rulers of the Golden Horde."[20] Through a combination of bribes, diplomatic skill, and social graces in a foreign court, the Muscovites "time and again . . . convinced the khans and their advisors to invest them with the title of grand prince and support them against the other princes of Russia."[21]

Successful brokerage across boundaries not only helps explain the emergence of Muscovy as the dominant Russian principality, such a pattern of emergence also established a repertoire of cultural and political practices of leniency and toleration that allowed the tsars to rule a vast and religiously, linguistically, and ethnically diverse empire. As the Mongol Empire and its successor, the Golden Horde, declined, the Muscovite principality successfully expanded by following the "rules laid down by the Mongols and the world of the steppes," including respect for traditional forms of legitimacy and "for foreign religions and cultures," as well as flexible and shifting alliances.[22] Although the Russians were flexible in that they did not demand sovereignty from subjugated territories, they maintained firmer control over conquered areas compared to the Ottomans, who successfully managed temporary and shifting borders. In Russia, the secession of peripheral territories would call forth a brutal reconquest by the center. Although the Ottomans were fully steeped in a politics of temporary alliances, Russian expansion often involved differing interpretations by central and peripheral actors, with the Russian center viewing alliances as pacts of "eternal submission" and peripheral brokers often construing alliances as only a "temporary subservience," which could be broken if better

---

[18] Robert Crummey, *The Formation of Muscovy 1304–1613* (New York: Longman, 1987), 31.
[19] Ibid., 36.
[20] Ibid.
[21] Ibid., 36, 38.
[22] Kappeler, *The Russian Empire*, 23.

circumstances arose.[23] Forced to innovate under the domination of the Mongols, adept bargaining and deal making by the medieval Muscovites produced a repertoire of tactics and policies that "constituted an important group of preconditions for the multi-ethnic empire that came into being around the middle of the sixteenth century."[24] In the cases of both the Ottoman and Russian emergence from minor principality to world-class empire, the context of frontiers as networks of uncertainty and innovation, as well as the conceptual framework of political brokerage across diverse cultural and religious networks, provides a powerful explanation for their emergence as major powers and their later ability to administer, rule, and exploit a diverse population.

A Frontier Society: Contradictions, Constraints, and Opportunities

The rise of the Ottoman state occurred at the frontier of empires, principalities, and small-scale landed powers. From the mid-thirteenth century onward, the political system of the Seljuk Empire shattered, and the imperial order of the Byzantine Empire, which had previously entered a precarious phase of decay (since the western Crusader attack and sacking of Constantinople in 1204), faltered, with increasing loss of control of its eastern lands.[25] Relations between these two imperial states and the struggle for control on both sides provided the opportunity for the construction of an intermediary frontier space that everybody seemed to have crossed. Ottoman leaders found themselves in the thick of this domain with the privileges, opportunities, and hazards that it provided.

Borders among states, frontier zones between empires, where both separation and connections are made with different groups, represent ecologies of constraint and opportunity. Between contending states and imperial powers, frontier spaces present those who live by or control the borders with varying sets of opportunities, inventive responses, prospects for brokerage, and alliances in war and peace. In this intermediary space shared and crossed by many networks of actors, there developed over time a common local knowledge, a shared understanding of the cross and no-cross zones, of imperial rules and regulations to uphold or ignore, and cultural idioms that facilitate everyday life in harsh environments. In this particular situation, the borders were vast territories where the Byzantine Empire ruled and where the Seljuks once ruled, which were now spaces where members of these different communities entered each other's space rather easily, treading on and claiming control over resources. There has been a lot of debate on what the Byzantine borderlands looked like at this time and whether the Turcoman warriors encountered ruins or riches as they raided deep into Christian territory. We can describe

[23] Ibid.
[24] Ibid., 18.
[25] Castellan, *Histoire des Balkans XIVe–XXe siècles.*

this border zone, its people, networks, institutions, and shared cultural idioms relatively well.

The Seljuks, whose fragmentation had already started in the mid-thirteenth century, left behind perhaps twenty or so small competing principalities, with some more powerful than others. They were all, however, pressed toward the west for fear of Mongol invasions. Especially after the Seljuk collapse, the reorganization of frontiers around successor states, with emirates rising out of the fetters of the empire, provided a different structure and stability to the frontiers. The Byzantine forces were more focused on Europe, and the Turcoman chieftains were able to expand westward toward the Aegean Sea. Among the most important of these emirates, the Menteshe and Germiyan became independent dynasties, to be followed by many others: Aydın, Sasan, Osman, and others who founded their own political entities. In part, opportunities were seized because some of these men had been settled in these frontier (*uc*) regions by the Seljuk sultans; they were either potential guards, or they were simply allocated land as tax farms.[26] These frontier guards/tax farmers were supplied with manpower because of the pressure from the Mongols forcing Turcoman movement toward the west. Settling, forming their dynasties, and taking the names of the local areas, they survived on raids into Byzantine territory and a thriving regional economy. By the mid-thirteenth century, not only were the Karamanids, the Hamids, and Menteshe principalities heavily engaged in raids, but they had also hired Greeks as their professional crew.[27] During the Seljuk Empire and after its disintegration, there was a continuous push toward the west, entailing the settlement of various frontier principalities at the edge and then slowly inside the Byzantine territories.

In their own remaining heartlands, the Byzantines were forced to confront the six new Frankish states, emergent regional formations after the 1204 Crusader takeover of Constantinople. Whereas the Byzantine Empire reconquered Constantinople in 1261, it was still overwhelmed by religious and schismatic struggles with the West and the Church of Rome. Yet, the Byzantine eastern periphery would not have been "lost" if it were not for the awkward consolidation after the mid-thirteenth century. After all, the eastern frontiers were richly endowed lands with powerful overlords ensconced in the countryside. However, Michael Palaiologos (1259–1261), who effected the reconquest of Constantinople and opened up an era of consolidation and renewal, reorganized state–society relations at the frontier, putting the Byzantine warriors on the defensive rather than incorporating them. Especially in the rich and fertile valley of Bithynia, taking away the lands of the soldiers and tying them

---

[26] Ismail Hakkı Uzunçarşılı, *Anadolu Beylikeri ve Akkoyunlu, Karakoyunlu Devletleri* (Ankara: Türk Tarih Kurumu Basımevi, 1988); Yaşar Yücel, *Anadolu Beylikeri Hakkında Araştırmalar: XIII–XV Yüzyıllarda Kuzey-Batı Anadolu Tarihi* (Ankara: Türk Tarih Kurumu Basımevı, 1988).

[27] Halil İnalcık, "The Rise of the Turcoman Maritime Principalities in Anatolia, Byzantium, and Crusades" *Byzantinische Forschungen* 9 (1985): 184.

to a salary after they had enjoyed a largely freer system of land in return for warfare pushed the warriors to the edge, creating a disaffected force ready to make allies across the border. Such action hindered the goal of keeping western Anatolia under Byzantine control, and Andronikos (1282–1328) was forced to contract with Catalans, in the process adding to the confusion and chaos of the region.[28] To add to the layers of confusion and discontent on the periphery, by the mid-fourteenth century the center of Byzantium was engaged in destructive civil wars. Geopolitical, imperial, and religious struggles ate at the Byzantine core, reducing its ability to rein in its periphery.

What did the Turcoman warriors find when they fought the Byzantine forces? First, nearly continuous warfare on land and sea for about two centuries had undoubtedly left clear signs of devastation. However, new research has shown that the devastation that the raiders of Turcoman origin found was also due partly to prior demographic crises and the Black Death, together with excessive demands on the soil. Accordingly, "by the fifteenth century, the population had fallen back to the twelfth-century level."[29] The consequences of this finding are that the wars with the Christians were not so devastating and soldiers found many deserted villages, and it is also possible that the easy Islamization and Turcoman naming of villages was due to this low density of Christians. In the towns, the situation was also mixed, with some having no stable settlement or commercial life, making them easier to incorporate, and others having more varied resources and settlement. Yet, the emerging consensus among Byzantinist scholars is that the situation was complex and varied, and that the weakening that was experienced between 1350 and 1450 was due to a long-term demographic decline as much as it was to conquest and a structural deficit already on the ground.[30]

The deep internal rumblings in the Orthodox corridor, caught between Western crusader enthusiasm and eclectic heterodox Islam, provided added opportunity for action. The exposed lands between central Anatolia and the easternmost boundaries of the Byzantine Empire became a frontier: a haven for all those swashbuckling, fortune hunting men, Christians, Muslims, orthodox, heterodox, eclectic preachers, and followers who roamed the countryside and the cities in search of a new life. This frontier was politically multilayered, historically always evolving and unpredictable, as well as pioneering and culturally heterogeneous. It had been so for at least a century before the Ottomans first appeared on the scene. Many of the social and cultural interactions had become institutionalized, with comfortable exchanges between governments, as would be expected with the repeated cycle of violence and cooperation

[28] *The Oxford History of Byzantium*, ed. Cyril Mango (Oxford, UK: Oxford University Press, 2002); Jacques Lefort, "Tableau de la Bithynie au XIIIe siècle," in *The Ottoman Emirate (1300–1389)*, ed. Elizabeth Zachariadou (Rethymnon: Crete University Press, 1993), 101–117.

[29] Klaus-Peter Matschke, "Research Problems Concerning the Transition to Tourkokratia: The Byzantinist Standpoint," in *The Ottomans and the Balkans: A Discussion of Historiography*, ed. Fikret Adanır and Suraiya Faroqhi (Leiden, The Netherlands: Brill, 2002), 79–113.

[30] Ibid., 92.

among frontier groups. My purpose in describing the unfolding of this frontier throughout the century is to demonstrate the degree to which exchange was allowed and expected, so that it therefore had become a sort of "habitus";[31] forms were mixed and fluid and much more complex and indefinite than previously presented. The Ottoman rise has to be reinterpreted in this light.

Prior to the fragmentation of the Seljuk polity, the frontiers between these two declining powers were carved as a practical space, claimed as *akra* by the Byzantines and as *uc* by the Seljuk state. This space, which often develops at the interstices of empires, was important not only in terms of its own social and cultural identity, to which I return, but also because both empires defined their relations to each other and their influence on each other through their penetration of these spaces into the territories of the other. Thus, for the Byzantines, the cultural hegemony they exercised in the Seljuk *uc* and beyond, evident in the churches, artifacts, Christian liturgical documents, and important Christian influence in the lands of the Seljuk Empire during the late thirteenth and early fourteenth centuries, was a sign of their continued success. In contrast, as Keith Hopwood argues, the reverse was also true: we need only mention the nature of Komnenian Turkophiles, the example of the emperor Manuel I (1143–1180), who had parts of his palace decorated in the Turkish style and who promoted Turkish or pro-Turkish councilors in his government.[32] In this frontier space, it became common for both sides to provide leadership for the other. Examples among the Byzantines are Manuel Komnenos, Manuel Mavrozomes – the high-ranking Byzantine officer appointed to the Seljuk regional administration – and Manuel Palaiologos, who alternated between Seljuk service and the throne of Nicea. These three were all interstitial men who belonged to both sets of elites. This was what the *akra/uc* was about, the continual presence of one in the house of the other.

Yet, lest we become complacent about this image of the frontier, we should be reminded that Manuel Palaiologos himself, who was close to the Seljuk sultan and escaped into his territory in 1256, was first robbed by the Turcoman nomads and then sent on to the court.[33] The terrain was rough; sedentary populations were in perpetual danger of invasion; and the *akınjıs* were ready for the next call to action, often operating in mixed Turkish-Christian groups of men participating in the action for the spoils, the division of booty and slaves. There is no estimating the damage that these swift and terrifying bands of Turcoman

---

[31] I use the term from Bourdieu. See Pierre Bourdieu, *Outline of a Theory of Practice* (Cambridge, UK: Cambridge University Press, 1977).

[32] Keith Hopwood, "The Byzantine–Turkish Frontier c1250–1300," *Acta Viennensia Ottomanica* (Vienna: Im Selbstverlag des Instituts für Orientalistik, 1999): 153–161; Keith Hopwood, "Low-Level Diplomacy between the Byzantines and Ottoman Turks: The Case of Bithynia," in *Byzantine Diplomacy*, ed. Jonathan Shephard and Simon Franklin (Aldershot, UK: Variorum, 1992), 151–155. See also Michel Balivet, *Romanie Byzantine et pays de Rum Turc: Histoire d'un espace d'imbrication Greco-Turque* (Istanbul: Les Éditions Isis, 1994); Osman Turan, "Les souverains Seldjoukides et leurs sujets non-Musulmans," *Studia Islamica* 1 (1953): 65–100.

[33] Hopwood, "The Byzantine–Turkish Frontier," 155.

warriors perpetrated. Between the violence of the pack and the strategic and accommodative movement of the elites back and forth, regional lower-level chieftains and Christian feudal castellans were in continual interaction in frontier territory. Turcoman chieftains taunted their Christian neighbors, and the Christian feudal castellans in return pestered Muslim nomads, often blocking their seasonal migration or their access to pasture lands.

Another important aspect of the relations at the frontier was trade and opportunities for resource mobilization. In trade, competition for booty, and wartime alliances, Turcoman chiefs from different principalities also became close to the Christians in the territories they raided. The trading zones in the frontier areas included Byzantine Christians, Latins from the Latin Kingdoms,[34] and members of the different post-Seljuk principalities. When the Byzantine Christians and the Muslims became closer and developed effective ties in trade and in frontier alliances, the Latins became apprehensive. They did not understand the relative closeness between these two religions, nor some of the circumstances under which they became closer, which included their loathing of their common enemy, the very Latins themselves.[35] Over time, these Turkish pirates in cooperation with Byzantine leaders would come to attack Latins who had occupied much territory, especially in the Aegean islands, the Morea, and Greece.[36]

More important, recent researchers show that Greek entrepreneurs benefited from the presence of the Ottomans even in the fourteenth century, early on when the frontier was still being redefined and warfare was going on. They argue that these traders sent their men both to trade with the West and move at the same time to trade within the confines of the eastern frontier. The Byzantine-Greek entrepreneurs chose to trade with the rising Ottomans out of necessity as well as a result of "personal decisions," and as Matschke explains, it was these men who made the transition to the Ottoman system after the conquest of Constantinople and who survived.[37]

More generally, international trade encouraged state building in early Ottoman times. As the Ottomans were expanding, they incorporated important trading ports, bringing cities on trade routes under their control. From the very beginning, the conquest of Bursa, the center of silk trade in Anatolia, and control over western Anatolian and northern Black sea zones of trade

---

[34] By Latins, I refer to the Latin Kingdoms that were formed after the first Crusade in 1099, became established in the region, and were part of the geopolitical and commercial competitions of the larger Mediterranean world. The first of the Latin Kingdoms was the Kingdom of Jerusalem (1099–1291), but there were many others in this immediate region. Their ties to Catholic Europe made the Byzantine elite both fear and loathe them.

[35] Alain Ducellier, "Byzantins et Turcs du XIIIe au XVIe siècle: du monde partage à l'empire reconstitué," in *Chrétiens et Musulmans à la Renaissance*, ed. Bartolomé Bennassar and Robert Sauzet (Paris: Honoré Champion Editeur, 1998), 11–49.

[36] İnalcık, "The Rise of the Turcoman Maritime Principalities in Anatolia," 184. This argument has been contested by some historians. See Matschke, "Transition to Tourkokratia," 104.

[37] Matschke, "Transition to Tourkokratia," 106.

encouraged the collection of customs duties and regular taxation and helped develop mercantile relations, especially with the Genoese and the Venetians. Recent studies have emphasized the degree to which Muslim merchants of the rising empire pursued their trade partnerships with the Genoese. Kate Fleet demonstrates the impact of trade on the formation of the Ottoman state.[38]

Regardless of whether Muslims and Christians felt the urge to mark their frontiers as boundaries and to delineate them, boundaries were *mobile markers of difference*, allowing both sides to make ample use of them, ordering a pattern of communication between groups because both sides used each other's markers liberally. For example, what became an important monument to Seyyit Battal Gazi (located at Nakoleia/Seyyit Gazi) was turned into a pilgrimage site for all who considered themselves of frontier heritage. Moreover, they told analogous narratives and even cohabitated, increasingly adopting each other's characteristics. Their myths and legends emphasized interfaith alliances and passions, often crossing geographical and cultural frontiers. For example, the Byzantine tale of Digenis Akrites was based on Arab-Byzantine wars, but Digenis himself was "the offspring of a cross-frontier love match," and Battal Gazi, the Turkish counterpart, was inadvertently killed by his Byzantine beloved.[39]

The culture that developed was certainly multiethnic, multireligious, nomadic, and sedentary, conflict-ridden and peaceful, all at the same time. On the ground, social relationships accrued through simple contact. Nomads and settled agriculturalists lived in precarious symbiosis on both sides of the frontier, where, among the peasantry and the nomads, the similarity of occupations and the resemblance between the Turkic *yürüks* and the Christian nomadic elements in the Balkans would facilitate not only exchange and cooperation, but also, when necessary, conquest.[40] Religious ceremonies linked to the local church, evoking fertility rites for land and animals, were shared by Christians and Muslims, indicating the closeness between the two traditions, as well as the willingness of local populations to mesh their rituals.[41] Besides, as the result of at least a century of frontier confrontations, Muslim and Christian forces had grown to know each other, and had developed a syncretic understanding with militaristic overtones. There is no denying that this was a disputed frontier where Greek *akritoi* confronted Muslim fighters, and they raided on each other and stole from each other. However, in the process, they also learned from each other, growing closer and each discovering the sociopolitical and economic exigencies of the other. As Pachymeres, a contemporary historian, tells the story of these frontier scuffles, "the damage was not so great, since 'our

[38] Kate Fleet, *European and Islamic Trade in the Early Ottoman State: The Merchants of Genoa and Turkey* (Cambridge, UK: Cambridge University Press, 1999).
[39] Hopwood, "The Byzantine–Turkish Frontier," 155–156.
[40] Fikret Adanır also makes this point for the period during which the Ottoman invasion of the Balkans accelerated. See Fikret Adanır, "The Ottoman Peasantries, c. 1360–c. 1860," in *The Peasantries of Europe from the Fourteenth to the Eighteenth Centuries*, ed. Tom Scott (London and New York: Longman, 1998), 277.
[41] Matschke, "Transition to Tourkokratia," 94–95.

own' did the same sort of thing. There was considerable local collaboration with the Turks."[42] The concept of comradeship (*nöker*) became widespread, enabling the leader to have an entourage of friends who cooperated under pressure. In conquered regions, Muslim leaders left their Christian allies in charge to ensure continued stability as much as defense and settlement. Such relations of equal partnership spread beyond the Turcoman warriors to appeal to the Christians, many of whom became the comrades of Muslim frontier chieftains. Heath Lowry calls them "a plundering confederacy."[43]

The conditions and culture of a hybrid frontier also promoted companionship, mutual assistance, and concerted action, especially in warfare, as well as festivity, gift giving, and building of reciprocity, often as ways of reducing uncertainty. Populations across the frontiers sometimes fought battles, at other times shared their provisions and exchanged gifts or traded at will, mostly taking advantage of being far from the center. No doubt there were strategic reasons for the Byzantine and Turcoman forces to cooperate and help each other. Yet, there were also much deeper cultural and civilizational reasons for these two cultures to grow closer together. On the tactical side, collaboration was also the result of different Turcoman forces fighting each other. In Asia Minor, the Mongol invasions and the ensuing struggle for predominance among the diverse Turkish groups had pitted Muslims against one another and therefore pushed some Turkish fighters closer to the Christian frontiers. In turn, Orthodox openness to the Turks was partly the result of the antagonism between Greek Orthodoxy and western Catholicism. The Byzantine elites had experienced the disintegration of their empire at the hands of the Latins, and many of them were dead set against any rapprochement with Catholic Europe. This schism would both bring peoples of different religions closer together, and later even provide the conquering Ottoman principality with room to maneuver and exploit divisions outside its realm.

The production of a hybrid frontier culture was not solely the work of disaffected elites and warriors. Rather, it had emerged from the slow synthesis of ideas and practices brought to this area by each group and integrated into the deep layers of society by the most itinerant and approachable groups in the region. Ensconced within the space between so many once powerful, but now waning empires, Greek elites, Turcoman chiefs and beys, their retinues and mercenaries, and peasants and nomads were all attracted to religious figures, heretical *babas* or just eccentric dervishes who preached cultural symbiosis and doctrinal syncretism, which pulled Greeks away from the ossified and rigid orthodox hierarchy and Muslims away from the fast developing and more rigid Sunnî milieu of the cities. Many wandering dervish figures, *baba*s and *abdal*s, were fed and housed by Christian and Muslim villagers alike. Therefore, just as groups of different religious traditions were meeting one another in war or in daily productive practice, broad-minded, tolerant, and

[42] Lindner, *Nomads and Ottomans in Medieval Anatolia*, 15.
[43] Lowry, *The Nature of the Early Ottoman State*.

experimentally minded men were easing their transitions, smoothing over their quest for heaven and earth, and constructing an environment promoting the free circulation of myths, rituals, symbols, beliefs, and gossip among different communities.

Seljuks had been known for their heterodox, heterogeneous, and mobile populations, many of them dervish colonies, preaching an Islamic–Christian synthesis. Sufi orders, which spread in Anatolia in multiple waves during the thirteenth century, extended mystical, heterodox Islam to different classes in society. Also, every city and town of Anatolia had *akhi* corporations, mystical associations organized around the various trades and crafts of the city.[44] These corporations and associations acted as repositories for many syncretic ideas that traveled into different frontier regions with the *abdal*s, *baba*s, dervishes, and *akhi*s on their journeys. The leaders of the Anatolian religious orders used to visit the frontier territories where they were always warmly welcomed and invited to stay. When they arrived, frontier people of all stripes flocked to experience the ceremonies and to share in the reflections and learning of the Sufi leaders. The result was in many ways another significant but promising contradiction in which an Islamic–Christian synthesis was spreading in the countryside, while the cities maintained the more learned urban Islamic culture, fueled by the migration of Muslim scholars into those cities conquered by Turcoman leaders. The other result that has been observed is the growing Turkification of the popular narratives of the region. Increasingly, the narratives that people invoked, the stories that they liked to tell, captured a rising dominant Turcoman version of history.

It is in this particular environment where political exigencies and alliances fashioned a social and cultural frontier of relations and cultural idioms, that we place Osman, his companions and followers, the future leaders of the Ottoman dynasty. Although Osman's rise and success is still debated, Greek writers and Muslim travelers put him in the fertile region of Bithynia in the first part of the fourteenth century. Bithynia, a protected space in the larger frontier, was located near the eastern lands of the Marmara Sea, delimited in the south by Mount Olympus (Uludağ), in the east by the Sangarios River Valley (Sakarya), in the north by the Gulf of Nicomedia (Izmit), and on the westernmost point of the small peninsula at Cyzicus.[45] According to the sources, this region had an immediate past as a fertile and prosperous area, where small towns and villages were densely populated with an extensive network of towns and fortifications, making them attractive both for raiding and eventually settling.[46] Documents also make it very clear that though the valleys were populated by Christians

[44] Ahmet Yaşar Ocak, "Les milieux soufis dans les territoires du Beylicat ottoman et le problème des Abdalan-Rum," in Zachariadou, ed., *The Ottoman Emirate*, 145–158.

[45] Lefort, "Tableau de la Bithynie"; Angeliki E. Laiou, "The Agrarian Economy: Thirteenth–Fifteenth Centuries," in *The Economic History of Byzantium: From the Seventh through the Fifteenth Century*, ed. Angeliki E. Laiou (Washington, DC: Dumbarton Oaks Research Library and Collection, 2002), 311–375.

[46] Lefort, "Tableau de la Bithynie."

and the mountains by Muslims, the village networks were mixed: in many villages, Christians and Muslims lived together. In this frontier zone, devastation resulted from the absence of state rule, harsh Byzantine taxation and the intensifying pace of Turcoman raids. Therefore, a given leadership in the frontier would have to know how to balance the need for pillaging and booty with the tremendous possibilities of growth. In a sense then, the next set of would-be state builders in this space would have to combine these incompatible elements of warfare, raids, and local development.[47]

We might surmise that Osman did relatively well for himself and his followers because, in less than one century, the political map of Asia Minor would be completely altered. From approximately 1314 to 1398 the forces of the Ottomans, still a small principality, had defeated most of their rival emirates. In fact, by 1400, it looked like none of these emirates had survived. Although some of them would get a short reprieve after the Ottomans were defeated by Tamerlane in 1402, they had pretty much been erased from the map after at least a century of existence.

First, it seems important to understand that in the context of the frontier, as described in this study, a form of state building – accumulation of power and legitimacy around a territory – was part of the context in which actors interacted. This recalls the manner in which Harrison White described the games in a playground, where identities emerge in the clusters of children that form repeatedly. State building in many ways is analogous to play in a playground; events occurred and groups combined and recombined along some dimension that they understood to be the main activity. Also, as in the playground where a certain game might become the understood shared activity, in thirteenth-century Bithynia it was warfare that became the collective activity by which everybody lived, regardless of their origins, descent, or religion. State building and consolidation of power was the result of a metaphor for interaction, the political action being played out in the frontier.[48]

The rise of Osman as a leader able to consolidate a state-like structure around him was made possible both by the nature of his horizontal relations and by his ability to broker across different previously unconnected groups. Osman straddled structural holes among many groups of potential followers, so that when he had consolidated his position, he had around him a network of interdependent groups connected to him. Osman, who initially had no large-scale constraints, managed to remain free and flexible rather than locked into some sort of action. Through his actions, he connected many different groups, behaving like their broker and resolving social problems arising in his environment. Furthermore, operating in a multivocal environment, his various declarations were interpreted coherently from multiple perspectives. It seems

---

[47] Olson, *Power and Prosperity*.

[48] Harrison White, *Identity and Control: A Structural Theory of Social Action* (Princeton, NJ: Princeton University Press, 1992).

that Osman carried out two crucial tasks of leadership successfully: with bro-kerage and redistribution of booty from successful warfare, he was able to demand allegiance and to transform horizontal relations into vertical relations of command and control.

At the same time, part of the puzzle of the Ottoman rise to power is that the principalities of the time were all quite similar. These emirates were orga-nized around one major activity, raids on Byzantine territory for booty. The emirs were described as *gazi/akınjı*, ambitious warriors who plundered at will. Although the emirates were spread across western Anatolia, they were ensconced mostly at the edge of Byzantine territory, benefiting from their proximity to rival lands. They also resembled one another in their simple organizational structure: a gathering around chiefs with simple rules for the distribution of booty, and which responded to demographic imperatives of their time and place. They also were identical in the more categorical markers of identity: they were comprised of Muslims by religious persuasion and eth-nically by what came to be known as Turkish. We then have to explain what made possible the rise of one group to the detriment of the others.

Except for Umur Bey, leader of the Aydın emirate, who seems to have partly succeeded at the same type of network connections, the other emirates were stuck in a much more conservative, hierarchical network, where rather than brokerage, some sort of closure was the rule.[49] In these other emirates, raiders were indirectly connected to the leader and aggrandized themselves through warfare and booty, distributed according to Islamic principles. There is much less indication here that the leaders had solid ties other than to their immediate lieutenants. The historical record allows us to infer some of these networks.

Osman: The Construction of a Network (1290–1326)

We can understand the rise of Osman (1290–1324) and his son Orhan (1326–1359) as the leaders of an incipient state in terms of their initial construction of a hub-and-spoke network structure of which they became the center, as well as the brokerage they initiated among otherwise separated groups and their effective multivocality maintained by the network structure they assembled through their actions. In ways that are reminiscent of the rise of the Medici in Renaissance Florence,[50] Osman and later Orhan found themselves at the center of a network structure that they might not have intended to create, but which they established as they became the brokers among groups. Communication among different kinds of actors occurs over bridge relations. Members of two

---

49 Here I use the distinction made by Ronald Burt between social capital that arises from hier-archical networks or from brokerage networks. He argues that those networks where there is closure (as in a hierarchical network) fare less well in the construction of social capital. See his two recent books on this issue: *Bandwidth and Echo* and *Brokerage and Closure*.

50 John Padgett and Chris Ansell, "Robust Action and the Rise of the Medici," *American Journal of Sociology* 98 (1993): 1259–1319.

disconnected groups can transcend these mostly through weak ties. However, when a third actor becomes the only way to connect two disconnected parties, he or she becomes a broker. Holes in a social structure represent opportunities to promote and take advantage of relations among contacts. Brokerage as the activity of people who belong to the intersection of multiple worlds and who connect them remains an important mechanism for state building. That is, those who engage in brokerage not only tie together different worlds, but also develop new and good ideas that they transfer to their own network. Brokers, according to Burt, are adaptive and can facilitate the "adaptive implementation" of ideas and policies.[51] This ability to maintain contact and control through multiple networks includes the notion that such actors respond in ways that appeal to each group separately. This is multivocality. Padgett and Ansell demonstrate the manner in which the Medici were positioned in a strategic structural place as a bridge between separate, competing, and unconnected groups. They were therefore able to connect different and unconnected groups through their actions and their adept multivocality, given that any single action on their part was interpreted coherently from multiple perspectives.

Most of the narratives of the rise of the Ottomans have turned to Osman, the leader of the dynasty, describing him as an illiterate man who was not a city dweller but the chieftain of a small pastoral and nomadic community at the edge of Byzantine territory in Bythnia, surrounded by other Turcoman emirates on its southern and eastern flanks. They also make clear that he came of age at a time when the absence of state power and activity was unmistakable. Accordingly, as central state power receded, local leaders were left to maintain their men and their activities through their own resources.[52] It is said that he acquired his territory from his father around 1284, and proceeded to build his empire from this small territorial nucleus. Such traditional narratives, as I mentioned previously, use the religious ideology of conquest as a trope to explain the motivation behind Osman's and other contemporary leaders' actions. Recent research provides a more sophisticated image of him in which, rather than being a simple nomad or peasant, he was from a more significant background, a man who already had his own slaves and eunuchs. This research also questions the religious or ethnic motivations that have been used to narrate the rise of the Ottomans. Rather, it provides simple interest-based, context-based explanations, arguing for geopolitical and demographic conditions that pushed leaders into action. The particular conditions on the frontier between empires on the wane and the demographic circumstances of the different groups undoubtedly play an important role in the context of state building.

However, the real difference in Osman's and Orhan's abilities to shape an alternative and durable state structure seems to be related more to their skillful brokerage across vast networks of people, by which they garnered

[51] Burt, *Brokerage and Closure*.
[52] Darling, "Contested Territory," 156–157.

substantial strength from the connections they enabled. They emerged in a frontier environment of high uncertainty where many different networks – religious and ethnic, economic and status based – flourished, cooperated, and also entered intense conflict. The absence of state authority at this time made local power holders more willing and able to inflict violence, bypass rules and regulations, and behave like warlords. Even though they were embedded in these networks of constraint and opportunity, early Ottoman leaders were able and willing to build resilient coalitions across networks, and strategize to build emergent identities that would last for centuries. To understand this process, I use an added analytic lens, that is, a network approach that studies Osman's and Orhan's ego networks and their connections.

According to some European sources, it seems likely that Osman and his family were one among three important founding warrior families: Osmanoğulları, Mihaloğulları, and Evrenosoğulları. The Ottoman state was cofounded by these three families, one of Islamic descent and the other two converted Christians. According to Spandugnino's *On the Origins of the Ottoman Emperors*, during the reign of Michael Palaiologos (1261–1282), four lords of the Turks in the vicinity of Byzance (Michauli, Turachan, Evrenes, and Ottomano) knew of the opportunities in the frontier region, but were also aware of the constraints, their fragmentation, and their potential weakness against a more powerful enemy:

They saw that the power of the Christians was too great for them to resist it singly, and they soon decided to look not to their own self-interest but to their common good; and they did something generous and memorable.... One day they assembled together to elect one lord from among them. Each of these present had his own say but all were agreed that none could match Ottomano [Osman] in authority, courage and strength of character. They found it hard to decide, for by common consent they would rather have had a brother than a sovereign lord. But they elected Ottomano as such; and he became the first emperor of the Turks.[53]

If this is the correct story, why did they choose Osman? I think not only because he was strong physically and mentally, but mostly because he could connect them most effectively to many other groups. First, Osman had demonstrated the ability to foster relations with Christians, warriors, friends, castellans, and entire villages. We learn from the sources that Osman spent his early years building friendships, going to war, and trading with members of disparate groups. He befriended both local Christian and Muslim lords and *gâzîs* in hunting expeditions, campaigning, or in simple day-to-day transactions of trade, protection, and mutual relief. Many stories of local interactions present him helping local castellans in their struggles against other local Byzantine lords, easing the negotiation process between sedentary and mobile populations,

---

[53] Quoted in Lowry, *The Nature of the Early Ottoman State*, 55. I have used Lowry's research and conclusions – with which I am in complete agreement – although without going into the details of how he reached his conclusions.

supporting trade and market activity, and providing justice even when this meant backing Christian peasants against Muslims, in short constructing a social network of local allies and a solid reputation for justice and cooperation. For example, when the castellan of Bilecik asked him for help against his rival at Koru-Hisar, he obliged by sending Tundar, whom he appointed as his deputy. The latter defeated the castellan of Koru-Hisar but also stayed on and kept Koru-Hisar as his patrimony. Neither Osman nor his allies went after Tundar to take over Koru-Hisar, and in light of his noninterventionist response, Osman and Tundar probably both knew that they could rely on each other in the future. The castellan of Bilecik, in contrast, was easily able to ask Osman for help because in a previous transaction Osman had successfully negotiated safe passage with the castellan for his people and had paid him back with pastoral gifts such as "fresh butter, cheese and meat."[54] In these stories, we see not only negotiation, but also ties of friendship and trust, as well as the transformation of a horizontal relationship into a vertical one, when Osman assigned Tundar as his deputy.

A network analysis of the relationships that Osman entered into demonstrates the manner in which a variety of structural gaps were bridged through social relations. Figure 1[55] shows that Osman had close friends with whom he went to war, described in the sources as comrades (*nöker*); many fighters (*akınjı-uc beyis*) who fought with him; Greeks whom he fought but who then joined his forces and converted; relations with religious leaders of various persuasions; and family and marriage ties. Through such relations, Osman connected many previously unconnected or warring factions, bringing them closer to one another through their relations to him. He also extended his reach into many different settlements, enterprises, and communities that might not have been aware of him previously. That is, he extended his reach to various religious groups, Orthodox Sunnî and heterodox Sufi groups, *akhi* organizations of trade, and religious men of learning. Although the data were not sufficient to demonstrate that these ties connected him to others who were part of a large network of alternative communities, they are still significant. We know, for example, that the *akhi* organizations reached through Şeyh Edebali, Akhi Hüseyin, and Akhi Şemseddin were important groupings that had to lend their support to Osman for him to succeed. We can now analyze Osman's patterns of relations through local narratives and bring more life to the visual representation of Osman's network. (See Figure 1.)

Osman's entourage was built on close friendships, with both Muslim and Christian men who shared the same lifestyle, and with local Christian

---

54 Hopwood, "Low-Level Diplomacy between Byzantines and Ottoman Turks," in *Byzantine Diplomacy*, Shepard and Franklin, eds., 151–152; Lowry, *The Nature of the Early Ottoman State*, 68; Kafadar, *Between Two Worlds*, 126.

55 I constructed the two network models for Osman and Orhan with historical information I gathered on the ego networks of these two leaders. See the appendix at the end of this chapter.

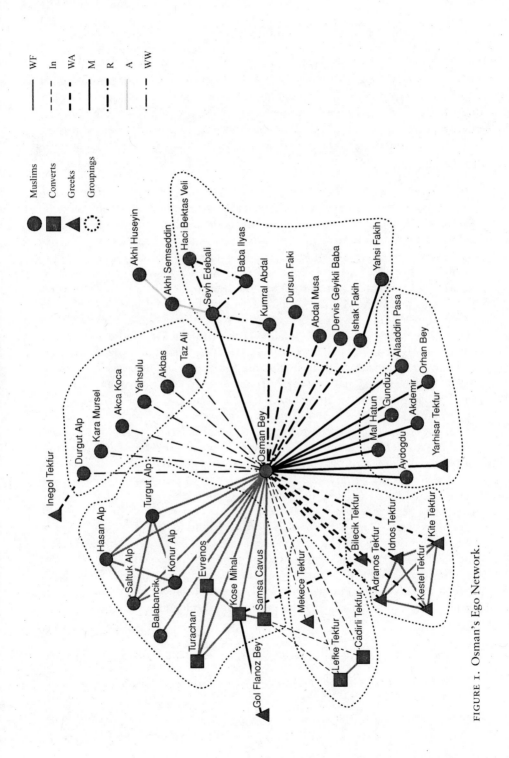

FIGURE 1. Osman's Ego Network.

Muslims ●
Converts ■
Greeks ▲
Groupings ⭕

WF |
In |
WA |
M |
R |
A |
WW |

Akhi Huseyin
Akhi Semseddin
Haci Bektas Veli
Seyh Edebali
Baba Ilyas
Kumral Abdal
Dursun Faki
Abdal Musa
Dervis Geyikli Baba
Ishak Fakih
Yahsi Fakih

Taz Ali
Akbas
Yahsulu
Akca Koca
Kara Mursel
Durgut Alp
Inegol Tektur

Osman Bey

Mal Hatun
Gunduz
Alaaddin Pasa
Akdemir
Orhan Bey
Aydogdu
Yarhisar Tektur

Hasan Alp
Turgut Alp
Saltuk Alp
Konur Alp
Balabancik
Evrenos
Kose Mihal
Samsa Cavus
Turachan
Gol Flanoz Bey
Lefke Tektur
Cadirli Tektur
Mekece Tektur
Bilecik Tektur
Idnos Tektur
Adranos Tektur
Kite Tektur
Kestel Tektur

49

chieftains joining him as his comrades (*nökers*), such as Mihal from Har-mankaya; Evrenos, a converted Christian of Aragonese or Catalan origin[56]; or the numerous Christian friends he acquired through his associate Samsa Çavuş.[57] That both Köse Mihal and Evrenos Bey saw themselves as near equals of Osman, and that they were the only two converted companions of Osman to have been addressed with the title "malik," usually reserved for the sultans, indicates the degree to which these two men were above the others in their closeness to Osman, and their relative equality. This is why they are mentioned in the European sources as close friends and allies of Osman, who could have become leaders themselves.

For warfare, Osman relied on voluntary Turcoman horsemen and border raiders (*akıncı*) who usually gathered around small and semi-autonomous com-manders of frontier districts, but who now came to join Osman in his raids.[58] Although his troops were primarily Turcoman, there is no doubt that as Chris-tian elites joined Osman, more and more Christians joined the Turcomans in their raids. Köse Mihal and his son Gazi Ali, as well as Evrenos, became hereditary commanders of the *akıncı*s, the light forces that usually preceded the Ottoman armies in battle. Of more serious consequence was the other side of the coin: Byzantium's loss of its best men to the Turkish fighters when so many Christian warriors were joining Turkish raiders. In Figure 1, we have the examples of the castellans (*tekfur*s) of Lefke, Çadırlı, and Mekece, who were incorporated after defeat. By the mid-fourteenth century, this loss of men would become so endemic that the Patriarch of Istanbul wrote to the Christians of Nicea urging them not to renounce their faith and become Muslims.[59]

Osman treated all his men well and gave them what they wanted most: access to booty. He was able to control access to pasture, hunting grounds, warfare and booty, and freedom to move. After war, they followed the Islamic tradition of the equal division of the spoils after the chief had taken one-fifth. Although these men operated jointly when they raided, part of the secret of their success was their equally cherished independence in how they exited. That is, these frontier raiders came and went as they pleased. They had to be recruited each time. A century or more later when Beyazıd II sent an order to recruit *akıncı* raiders for his campaign, he used the same basic mobilizational rules, bringing the men together, promising rewards, refraining from discrimination based on religion, and opening his armies to Muslim and Christian warriors.[60] If this was still the case in the fifteenth century after the establishment of more permanent armies, it certainly must have been the operating rule in earlier times.

---

[56] It is possible that he might have been a Spaniard in service of the Karamans and joined the Ottomans later.

[57] Lindner, *Nomads and Ottomans in Medieval Anatolia*, 24.

[58] Rhoads Murphey, "Yeni Çeri," EI2 322–331; J. A. B. Palmer, *The Origins of the Janissaries* (Manchester, UK: Manchester University Press, 1953).

[59] Lowry, *The Nature of the Early Ottoman State*, 67.

[60] Ibid., 50–53.

Chronic warfare can result in serious devastation of territory, leading the local inhabitants to move away and leave the lands unattended. Osman seems to be the first among the emirs of the region to show concern for the devastation implied by Turcoman raids. Osman refused to destroy many of the lands that he overtook, ensuring that the population returned and remained comfortable in their original locations. A policy of accommodation (*istimalet*)[61] was developed, as the example of the town of Yar-hisar shows: "All the villagers came back and settled in their places. Their state was better than it had been in the time of the unbelievers. When the word spread of the comfort enjoyed by these unbelievers, people began to come from other places as well."[62] Numerous other reports confirm that peasants came back, that they were often better off than when the land was under Byzantine control, that they enjoyed lighter taxation, and that even the leadership understood that their people did not really miss them. Yet, such actions created tension within Osman's family, especially between those who argued for continuous predatory raids with no discrimination among the Christians (like most of the other Turcoman principalities), and members of his camp, who were much more careful about building alliances and convincing productive populations to stay on the land. Osman combined strategy with brokerage in the sense that his bridging between groups mobilized allies and built coalitions that would bring long-term benefit.

Osman had therefore been able to make important alliances with local Christian leaders, enjoying their loyalty and trustworthiness, and building close ties through a policy of accommodation and respect. Everywhere he went, he left Christian soldiers to defend conquered areas, made military alliances, and provided local soldiers with more status than their previous leadership had. *Istimalet* was then a strategy for the stabilization of power. His two companions, Köse Mihal and Evrenos Bey, were both able to contribute to such activity. They were equally successful in convincing local populations to stay, to continue their productive activities, and to demonstrate to other local Christian rulers the benefits of belonging, as, for example, Köse Mihal had done with his fellow Christian lords of Harman Kaya.[63] Yet, neither Köse Mihal nor Evrenos were able to connect to the local Turkish populations with different origins. Osman's friendship with Köse Mihal and Evrenos Bey brought him widespread Christian networks.

Marriage connected Osman, located him at the center of the old and established families of the region, and helped him manage access to the key social classes in Anatolian society, the fighters (Gaziyan-i Rum), the religious orders (Abdalan-i Rum), and the craftsmen and traders (Akhiyan-i Rum). By marrying the daughter of one of the most central religious Sufi sheiks of the period, Osman became a broker between different Sufi groups and Akhi organizations,

---

[61] Halil İnalcık, "The Status of the Greek Orthodox Patriarch under the Ottomans," *Turcica* 21–23 (1991): 407–436.

[62] Ibid., 69.

[63] Lindner, *Nomads and Ottomans in Medieval Anatolia*, 5.

as well as important regional notable families with economic and symbolic capital. Şeyh Edebali, who belonged to the Abdalan-i Rum milieu (the collective name for the religious orders in Anatolia that were tied to the Baba'is, who revolted during the Seljuk tenure), and the Akhi brotherhoods became the key link between these two and Osman. Furthermore, Şeyh Edebali is said to have been close friends with Hacı Bektaş, the founder of the famous Bektaşi dervish community, active colonizers of the frontiers. With Edebali's connection and prestige among these different dervish and *akhi* groups, Osman could count on support, peacefulness, and compliance from these groups, which had had a tendency to oppose state authority.[64] Edebali was also key to linking what were going to become three important families in early Ottoman rule – that of Osman, Çandarlı Halil, and Taceddin-i Kürdi – bringing together military and learned scholarly families.[65]

As Figure 1 clearly shows, Osman added precious new networks to the emerging power structure in Bithnya.[66] Although we have little information on what Osman, Köse Mihal, and Evrenos might have thought and discussed, we can infer from the available histories that while originally Evrenos and Mihal were linked to the Christian warriors and their retinues, Osman's capacity for brokerage was greater. He brokered through more varied populations, Christian and Muslim, orthodox and heterodox associations, and trade and *akhi* brotherhoods, and especially because he married into one of the key religious families in Anatolia, he was able to connect much further than his two key allies. On the warfare front, the openness and allure of both Christians and Muslims doubled the potential population from which Osman could draw. Success and rewards in terms of wealth in cash and land and freedom of movement provided just enough incentive for the Turcoman and Christian *akınjıs* to come back. On another front, consolidation of rule occurred with the dramatic spread of social and religious networks. In the towns, connections were formed under *akhi* brotherhood organizations, bringing together those involved in the production and distribution of goods.[67] New markets, old and new traders, merchants, and artisans were brought together through a web of brotherhood rules and relations meant not only to harmonize, but also to regulate. At the frontiers, religious leaders, dervish zealots who broke ground at the edges of the world, tied the center to the periphery, not only through their close associations with the rising Turkish leaders, but also through their untiring movement back and forth between urban and rural, settled and nomadic, ecstatic in their worship and tolerant in their interfaith linkages.

[64] Ocak, "Les milieux soufis," in ed. Zachariadou, *The Ottoman Emirate*, 154.
[65] Kafadar, *Between Two Worlds*, 127–129.
[66] See Aşıkpaşazade, *Tevarih-i Al-I Osman*, ed. Ali Bey (Istanbul: Matbaa-yi Âmire, 1913); Atsız Nihal, *Aşıkpaşaoğlu Tarihi* (Istanbul: Milli Eğitim Bakanlığı, 1970); Sencer Divitçioğlu, *Osmanlı Beyliğinin Kuruluşu* (Istanbul: Eren Yayıncılık, 1996).
[67] G. G. Arnakis argues that the Akhis were the most important organizations that maintained the social fabric of Anatolian society during the most vulnerable period of frontier struggles. See his "Futuwwa Traditions in the Ottoman Empire: Akhis, Bektaşi Dervishes, and Craftsmen," *Journal of Near Eastern Studies* 7 (October 1953): 232.

By the time Osman died in 1326, Ottomans were poised to capture Brussa (Bursa), the first truly central Byzantine city and were fast on their way to the conquest of many more. Osman had established control through broker-age across structural holes where he brought connected layers of Byzantine, Turkic, peasant, nomad, orthodox and heterodox Islamic men of learning, and popular dervishes who appealed to Greeks and Muslims alike. Therefore, Ottomans under Osman's leadership emerged out of frontier warfare, but as the inclusive, resilient, and syncretic force of the region. His son Orhan did not deviate from this path. We see the same patterns of networking as with his father, but with more interfaith mixing. Orhan married the daughter of John VII Kantakouzenos, sealing an alliance with the ruling Byzantine families. Through his brother (who had joined the ranks of the dervish orders), he con-nected with the Bektaş i order, and it is said that he took his brother's advice and put the embryonic Janissary army under the protection of the Bektaşis.[68] Ottomans needed skilled administrators; they had been skilled warriors and had enlisted talented Greek fighters. Orhan's tenure was also one of the defin-ing realms of administration. The religious men he embraced put pen to paper, and recorded the wealth and resources of this incipient state. Religious foun-dations in Ottoman Yenişehir and Bursa are exemplars of the initial adminis-trative effort of an incipient state. Orhan also enlisted many Greek advisors to help administer the lands they had administered under Byzantine rule. When we look at some of the ties that emerge in the documents related to Orhan, we see that he bestowed property on a manumitted eunuch named Şerefeddin Mukbil; that the command of the siege of Bursa was shared by a slave named Balabancık; that the surrender of Bursa was negotiated between Köse Mihal and a Byzantine adviser to the ruler, Saros, who then promptly joined the Ottoman side; that the *subaşı* of Bursa was Koskos; and that the *subaşı* of Biga was Mavrozoumis.[69] (See Figure 2.)

Although the historical material does not lend itself to a full-scale analysis of the networks of these individuals, the networks we could construct and the narratives of their transactions with different groups during raids and at other times remain powerful examples of the manner in which they brokered through different communities. That they were able to do so was first and foremost due to a long tradition of interfacing at the boundaries of different systems of rule. Furthermore, we have seen that not only in the frontier zones, but also in larger expanses in the ruling houses of the avowed enemy, intermixing occured, bring-ing varying, and even opposing, cultural idioms together, and bringing religious believers together despite the recriminations of their orthodox leadership. What I have described was a frontier where boundaries were acknowledged but con-tinually evaded. Differences remained, yet they were evoked strategically, and no one ever argued seriously that they could be eliminated. Osman, Mihal,

---

[68] Irène Mélikoff, "Un ordre de derviches colonisateurs: les Bektachis. Leur rôle social et leurs rapports avec les premiers sultans Ottomans." *Mémorial Ömer Lûtfi Barkan* (Paris: Librairie d'Amérique et d'Orient Adrien Maisonneuve, 1980), 153.

[69] Lowry, *The Nature of the Early Ottoman State*, 45–55.

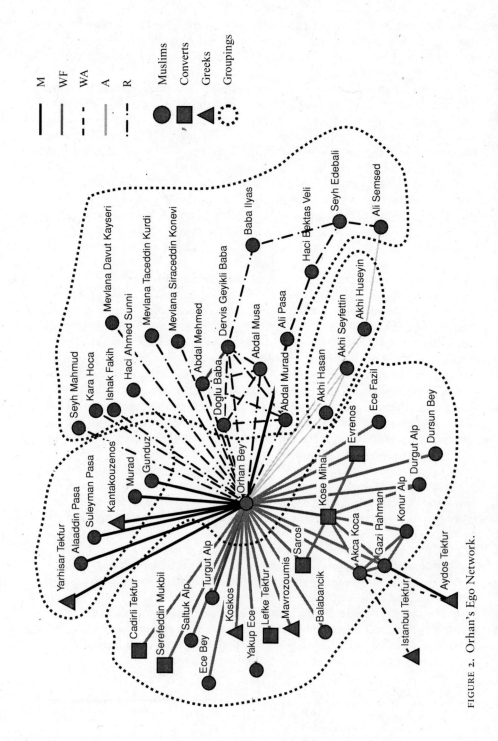

FIGURE 2. Orhan's Ego Network.

Legend:
M
WF
WA
A
R

Muslims
Converts
Greeks
Groupings

Yarhisar Tektur
Alaaddin Pasa
Suleyman Pasa
Kantakouzenos
Murad
Gunduz
Seyh Mahmud
Kara Hoca
Ishak Fakih
Haci Ahmed Sunni
Mevlana Davut Kayseri
Mevlana Taceddin Kurdi
Mevlana Siraceddin Konevi
Abdal Mehmed
Doglu Baba
Dervis Geyikli Baba
Baba Ilyas
Abdal Musa
Ali Pasa
Abdal Murad
Haci Bektas Veli
Seyh Edebali
Ali Semsed
Akhi Seyfettin
Akhi Huseyin
Akhi Hasan
Orhan Bey
Kose Mihal
Evrenos
Ece Fazil
Durgut Alp
Dursun Bey
Konur Alp
Gazi Rahman
Akca Koca
Saros
Balabancik
Istanbul Tektur
Aydos Tektur
Mavrozoumis
Lefke Tektur
Yakup Ece
Koskos
Ece Bey
Saltuk Alp
Turgut Alp
Serefeddin Mukbil
Cadirli Tektur

54

and Evrenos in many ways succeeded at crossing boundaries, bringing different communities together, and enlisting them in a common project in a way that would continue the segregation of these worlds and different societies. The foundation of Ottoman power then was the result of brokerage across boundaries, especially religious ones. The irony of this construction should not be missed because it is clear that as the West consolidated Latin Christendom, opposing and oppressing Orthodox Christianity at every turn, Muslims and Greek Orthodox Christians were laying the foundations of a hybrid state.

Finally, the question remains why the other rival principalities were unable to endure and were incorporated into the larger Ottoman project. The answer seems to lie in the absence of continued brokerage among extended networks and also in the more hierarchical system of rule that we detect among many of the other frontier principalities. I use the case of Umur Pasha from Aydın, which was, according to many sources, closest to independent statehood.

During the hundred years that followed the Mongol invasion of Anatolia, the frontier between Byzantium and the Seljuk Empire was organized around at least twenty emirates. Insofar as these emirates were organized around powerful chieftains, and their retinues engaged in local warfare and local diplomacy and organized themselves around a booty economy, they were more or less similar to the early Ottomans; therefore, they could have been serious contenders for the consolidation of the Anatolian plateau. Yet, they were all erased from the map, the result of warfare and an inherent inability to extend into larger networks of brokerage. Especially in western Anatolia, the maritime principalities of Menteshe, Aydın, Saruhkan, and Karesi were also engaged in similar activities, with the added advantage of combining land and sea warfare. Among them Umur Bey was perhaps the most distinguished, his navy in full throttle, his seamen responding to his call for naval warfare and booty from all over Anatolia, especially between 1330 and 1337.[70] In fact, Halil İnalcık, the dean of Ottoman history, considered Umur Bey to have been the foremost rival to Osman and Orhan in the construction of an alternative imperial state.

Osman and Umur were competitors until the Hospitalers took Smyrna (Izmir) in the 1340s and the principality of Aydın fell apart. Although both Osman and Umur's principalities were positioned to take advantage of raids into Christian territory, Osman was geographically better placed and bordered Byzantium, attracting many more Turcoman warriors in search of booty and also drawing disaffected Christians into his lands and armies. It is likely that the relative excess of warriors gave Osman the ability to organize them loosely, allowing them freer movement to come and go as they pleased. This is confirmed by the fact that warriors were recruited for specific battles. If, however, Umur had fewer warriors and they were located in a less receptive area, we can surmise that he organized his army more hierarchically and tried to hold onto it more permanently. Such differences would have led to more egalitarian methods of rule among the followers of Osman and less so for Umur.

---

[70] İnalcık, "The Rise of the Turcoman Maritime Principalities in Anatolia," 179–217.

The initial establishment of power relations for Umur and Osman thus demonstrates quite different logics. From the beginning, the reign of Umur Pasha announced itself as more hierarchical, more divided along its perception of Muslim-Christian boundaries, and certainly more destructive of the communities that were attacked. Umur came to power when his father divided his territories among five sons, giving the best area, Izmir, to his son Umur, who assembled his men to take charge of his domain. What we learn first are the various positions he distributed as rewards to his lieutenants and that he was surprised to see that so many Christians inhabited the lands he had just been offered.[71] Immediately thereafter, he engaged in fierce raids into the Christian communities, where it is said that he battled for 2 years before he was able to defeat the enemy, that is, the Christian inhabitants of Izmir.[72] Umur Pasha continued his devastating raids and built a small navy; he joined the seafaring pirates of the Aegean.

Ahmet Yaşar Ocak, the foremost scholar of Sufi movements in medieval Anatolia, differentiates between those groups who followed Osman's campaigns and those who joined the other emirates. He argues that the more established and traditional Sufi orders (e.g., Mevlevis, Halvetis, Rifais) connected better with the other principalities, where they performed their rites and rituals and remained away from battle, protected by the emir. Those who joined the Ottomans through Şeyh Edebali were descendants of the more rebellious leaders, were military minded, followed their beys into battle, and colonized new regions. Thus, we can see that even the şeyhs who followed the Ottomans joined previously weakly connected groups and networks.[73]

That Osman and Orhan were able to broker relations with Christians and incorporate many more castellans, warriors, and administrators into their expanding realm meant that they were also able to use their knowledge and skills for taxation and the management issues that come with incipient government. From the sources on Umur Bey, we have no information regarding the incorporation of Christian administrators; there are indications that many of these emirates fell apart because they were internally incapable of administration once they could not expand further.[74] These differences were only enhanced during the participation of Turkish forces in the civil war in Byzantium.

When in 1341 civil war erupted in Byzantium between John VI Kantakouzenos and John V Palaiologos, both parties appealed to Turkish principalities

---

[71] Irène Mélikoff-Sayar, *Le destan d'Umur Pacha (Düsturname-I Enveri): Texte, traduction et notes* (Paris: Presses Universitaires de France, 1954).

[72] The differences between Osman and Umur might be an artifact of the available documentation, that is, that the major document on Umur is a *destan*, an epic poem, naturally inclined to glorify the warrior of Islam. Yet I still think that the fact that so many documents on Osman mention his refusal to pillage and devastate Christian villages is indicative of their differences.

[73] Ocak, "Les milieux soufis," 154.

[74] John V. A. Fine, Jr., *The Late Medieval Balkans: A Critical Survey from the Late Twelfth Century to the Ottoman Conquest* (Ann Arbor: University of Michigan Press, 1987); George Ostrogorsky, *History of the Byzantine State* (New Brunswick, NJ: Rutgers University Press, 1957).

for help against each other. Three principalities got involved: Umur Bey of Aydın, Orhan Bey of Ottomans, and Süleyman Bey of Karesi. The manner in which each used his access betrays his world view and his interests. Kantakouzenos enlisted Orhan and the neighboring Umur Bey Aydın to join him in his fight against fellow Christians in Thrace and Macedonia.[75] At the same time, Süleyman Bey of Karesi was also enlisted by an ally of Kantakouzenos. The Turks helped this latter defeat his enemy rival, Palaiologos. When the news came that Batatzes and his ally Süleyman Bey had switched sides and were now working for Palaiologos, their interference annoyed the Ottoman forces, who had different plans for the area. Not only were Turkish forces now competing for booty and slaves, the erratic behavior of the Bey of Karesi encouraged Orhan to conquer Karesi on the mainland and get rid of these rival forces. Consequently, the legendary sailors of Süleyman Bey joined Orhan (1345).

With Karesi eliminated, the forces of Orhan and Umur were more in step with each other and worked together to raid the region and seize much booty. For the forces of both Orhan and Umur, victory meant that they could stay there in the Balkans, opening the road to more conquest in Europe. The leaders used such advantage differently. Whereas Orhan's forces (first under his son Süleyman's command and then under his son Murad's command) went on to settle in Europe, lay siege to Adrionople (Edirne), and establish a permanent foothold there, Umur Bey was pleased that his Christian allies in ports watched his ships while he and his troops engaged in extended forays for booty. In fact, according to İnalcık, Umur Bey, "content with finding employment and booty for his ghazis, did not seek territorial gains."[76] By the time he lost Smyrna (Izmir) to the crusading forces, his reputation as a powerful chieftain was tarnished. His heir to Aydın chose a quiet path of peace with the Christians and abandoned warfare and booty-seeking altogether. Meanwhile, Kantakouzenos gave his daughter to Orhan in marriage, and the two men were sighted spending much time in festivities, hunting, and banquets on the outskirts of Constantinople.[77] The leaders of the Ottomans had preferred to use these opportunities as a way to build networks and a bridgehead into Europe, while Umur Bey had just resumed his old habits of raiding.

It should be clear that not all chieftains or beys had grand schemes of imperial conquest. Most were content to remain free and to roam the countryside in search of booty, maintaining minimal organization and gathering fighters in the cause of accumulating booty rather than land. As many contemporary

---

[75] The unfolding of the struggle for domination in Byzantine politics and the role of the Turcoman principalities is complex and has been told by distinguished historians. Although the details are interesting, they do not bear on the argument I am making. I therefore skip to the conclusion of hostilities and the final settlement. For full narratives, see Elizabeth Zachariadou, "The Emirate of Karesi and That of the Ottomans: Two Rival States," in *The Ottoman Emirate (1300–1389)* (Rethymnon: Crete Press, 1993), 225–236; İnalcık, "The Rise of the Turcoman Maritime Principalities in Anatolia," 179–217.

[76] Ibid., 195.

[77] Elizabeth A. Zachariadou, "Histoire et legendes des premiers Ottomans," *Turcica* 27 (1995): 52–53.

Byzantine authors have maintained, these Turcoman chiefs would come, pillage, take slaves, and then retreat, showing no interest in the permanent occupation of territory. They remained open to all kinds of itinerant men, drifters, and mercenaries who were willing to fight under their banner and share in their booty. Therefore, the half-century of raiding did not quickly produce a gathering of the lands. These groups did not deviate from their established trajectories of raids and booty. The external stresses imposed on them did not cause much further social differentiation or integration of different types. They were defeated, for example, by the Catalan Company of mercenaries hired by Byzantium in 1304–1305, and some of the seabound principalities had trouble raiding because of the Knight of St. John. However, again, for the Turcoman principalities, these were temporary setbacks; no urgency was recorded in their activities, and not much change occurred over their tenure. Also, when their Anatolian land base had been saturated, they had turned to the sea, developing as seafaring pirates. This lasted until 1344, when the Knights Hospitaller came from Palestine, settled in Rhodes, and allied with the Europeans and the Byzantines to defeat Umur Bey, who had just returned from helping his ally, Kantakouzenos. The Knights took Smyrna and defeated Umur Bey. From this moment on, Umur's ability to engage in further sea raids and his access to European frontiers was blocked.

In contrast, only the Ottomans were able to open new frontiers with the conquest of the Gallipoli Peninsula in 1354 by Orhan's son Süleyman Pasha. Thus, Orhan, by extending his stay in Europe, marrying a Byzantine princess, building further networks, and providing his troops with the opportunity to learn the topography of the Gallipoli Peninsula, had provided his descendants with both access to booty from warfare in Byzantine Europe and the right to tax those who returned. In fact, Murad instituted a tax of one-fifth of the booty for the ruler's household there.[78] This was quite important because many of the slaves for the household of the ruler came from this one-fifth.[79] In a sense, had Umur Bey done what Orhan had done – establish a foothold on the European side of the peninsula when they were both there – he might have succeeded in establishing a state.

The Internal Boundaries of the New State

That the construction of an early Ottoman state took place as an enterprise of brokerage and coalition building across different groups and within a fluid and uncertain frontier environment hardly meant that identities did not emerge and that differentiation would not occur over time. As boundaries and

---

[78] Metin I. Kunt, "State and Sultan up to the Age of Süleyman: Frontier Principality to World Empire," in *Süleyman the Magnificent and His Age: The Ottoman Empire in the Early Modern World*, ed. Metin I. Kunt and Christine Woodhead (London and New York: Longman, 1995), 12.

[79] Ibid., 15.

identities were constructed, they transformed the freely flowing associations into more solid markers of identity, although with enough pragmatism and flexibility built into the system that resilience and mobility were concurrently maintained.

We first reconsider the stereotypical rendering of the period. Cemal Kafadar, in his book on the origins of the Ottoman Empire, struggles against these embedded histories and stresses cultural syncretism, ideological and regional opposition, and alliances that provided for new patterns of state building,[80] although he also understands that a milder form of the *gazâ* thesis (Turcomans as warriors of Islam) must have been part of the discourse of the time. Such a discourse is a prime example of the multivocality of the Turkish raiders and Ottoman conquerors, the rationale for which is provided by Kafadar in the following statement: "Obviously, then, the people of the marches did not see a contradiction between striving to expand their faith and engaging in concilia-tory (not necessarily insincere) gestures toward members of the other faith. One insight gained from the hagiographies of dervishes like Sari Saltuk is that an atmosphere of 'tolerance' and symbiosis ... does not preclude a desire to gain converts."[81] Linda Darling offers an even stronger *gazâ* thesis, arguing that *gazâ* was used and interpreted in a myriad of ways by different groups with varying interests. In her words, "As an ideology, *gazâ* was flexible enough to be represented as an Orthodox Islamic activity to/by the '*ulema*,' an unorthodox activity to/by antinomian Sufis, an economic activity to/by tribesmen, and a political activity to/by aspiring rulers. As such, it might have been the most powerful and inclusive unifying device available to conquerors on the frontier, more so than tribalism, origin, religion, language or culture."[82] These were not contradictions, but ambiguities and multivocality of rule in early Ottoman Bithynia, where tolerance and conversion, accommodation (*istimalet*) and war-fare, and friendship and vassalage worked together and were interpreted con-sistently from multiple directions.

The focus on the essentialist identities of the "Turks" and their religious ethos completely misses the point. It was not that the rising Ottomans did not understand the differences between religions and cultures, it was rather that once they became brokers and brought together diverse populations, they understood better than anyone else that the acquisition of power and respect, the construction of a new order, necessitated working with differences, accept-ing them, and crossing over boundaries. Moreover, they needed to be inclusive because they did not have the forces to afford a strategy based purely on

---

[80] Kafadar, *Between Two Worlds*. See also Ömer Lûtfi Barkan, "Osmanlı Imparatorluğunda bir Iskan ve Kolonizasyon Metodu Olarak Sürgünler," *Iktisat Fakültesi Mecmuası* 11 (1949–1950): 539–540, and Rudi Paul Lindner, "Stimulus and Justification in Early Ottoman History," *The Greek Orthodox Theological Review* 27 (1982): 207–224. See also Gyula Kaldy-Nagy, "The Holy War (jihad) in the First Centuries of the Ottoman Empire," *Harvard Ukrainian Studies* 3–4 (1979–1980): 467–473.

[81] Kafadar, *Between Two Worlds*, 72.

[82] Darling, "Contested Territory," 157.

adversarial tactics.[83] At this juncture, religion at the frontier was not institutionalized. The Turcoman tribes and the new leaders of the frontier raids had not developed a strong institutional Islamic identity. Moreover, on neither side did frontier life lend itself to strong orthodoxy; religious leaders were less permanent and more transient like the populations they tried to influence. Churches and mosques, institutions of religious learning, were in the larger towns or urban centers, less so at the frontier. Words, actions, and ideologies were expressed similarly to all, but interpreted differently across networks.

Over time, the boundaries between conqueror and conquered, Christians and Muslims (but also Jews), and nomadic and settled populations would emerge. Initially, however, şeyhs and dervish leaders who colonized the frontier territories did not use Islamic precepts to separate, but rather to bring people together toward common goals. Accordingly, Islamization as it transpired was the result of a heterodox understanding of Islam, an active dervish-based proselytism, and the prevalence of Islamo-Christian sanctuaries. Balivet perceptively shows how the two faiths increasingly came to use the same sacred space, the same locales that had been consecrated to the memory of ambiguous religious figures, bringing the faithful closer together.[84] Christian monasteries became *tekke*s, yet they kept many of their religious symbols, including the cross, that were adopted by Muslims. Hasluck's work is convincing with regard to an early religious symbiosis, as exemplified in the cases of saints worshipped by both Christians and Muslims.[85]

To the degree that boundary production was starting, it was not hegemonic; rather, it was multi-locational in style, with the conquering *gâzî* leader, the newly appointed regional *bey*, the dervish and the imam, the priests, and the Greek Orthodox theologians all involved in defining boundaries. That a newly appointed pasha would break the ground for a new town, and build a mosque and a *medrese* (religious school) as centers of worship and learning was as likely as an elder dervish opening up a *tekke* (monastery) to gather the faithful around him. Many followed the teachings of the dervish leader Bektaşi whose *tekke* in the thirteenth century became a refuge not only for those from Christian and Sunnî backgrounds, but also from the heretical orders on both sides: Nestorians, Bogomils, and Shii believers. They followed the rites of the *tekke*, and lived in communities of unity and peace. Greek followers of the wandering dervishes were numerous, for example, the residents of still-Byzantine Bursa who sent food to Abdal Murad throughout his time in the region.[86]

---

[83] Lowry makes the point that the Turkish *akınjıs* did not have a demographic advantage and therefore were forced by circumstances to look for allies across the boundaries. See *The Nature of the Early Ottoman State*, 139.

[84] Michel Balivet, "Aux origines de l'islamisation des Balkans ottomans," in *Les Balkans à l'époque ottomane, La revue du monde musulman et de la Méditerranée* 66 (1992/4): 11–20.

[85] F. W. Hasluck, *Christianity and Islam under the Sultans* (Oxford, UK: Clarendon Press, 1929), vol. I, 9–31. See also Elizabeth A. Zachariadou, "Co-Existence and Religion," *Archivum Ottomanicum* 15 (1997): 119–129.

[86] Michel Balivet, "Culture ouverte et échanges inter-réligieux dans les villes ottomanes du XIVe siècle," in *The Ottoman Emirate*, ed. Zachariadou, 3.

The movement across religions sometimes even emboldened Greek Orthodox theologians to preach in conquered Ottoman territory and to engage Muslims in theological debates.

The courts of the sultan were also eclectic, combining Christian theologians, Jewish philosophers and theologians, dervish leaders, and many others giving and getting advice. At the same time, the tolerant and liberal discourse of the Ottoman leaders toward other groups and religions was the result of multivocal signaling. That is, the manner in which the religious discourse was formulated was correct, but was also partly a mechanism of survival in a multiethnic, multireligious society. When Ottoman leaders accepted Christian faith, they were behaving according to the precepts of Islam that accepted Christianity and Judaism as the other religions of the book that were fully pleasing to the Muslim population. Yet, they were also agreeable to and welcomed the Christians themselves, who perceived their discourse as open minded. Gregory Palamas, archbishop of Salonica, who was captured by the Turks and spent time with them in the sultan's court, relates many court gatherings in which the Turks questioned him and other Christian theologians regarding their faith, especially on their unwillingness to accept Mohammed as a prophet, given that Turks readily recognized Christ![87] Palamas also described many interactions in the streets in which the relative merits of Islam and Christianity were compared, discussed, and accepted as alternative and compatible ways of approaching faith,[88] so much so that Palamas assumed that the Turks and Byzantines were going to reach an inter-confessional concordat. Some scholars believe that many Jews, mainly Christians converted to Judaism, were also present at these religious discussions, brought in especially for their religious acumen.[89]

Crossing religious networks also had familial implications. Marriage alliances reinforced the overall perception that the Ottomans were possible acceptable local players. Ottoman leaders married Christian princesses freely, sealing their alliances with local dynasties. Orhan had first married the daughter of a Christian lord, and in 1346, he married Theodora, the daughter of Jean Cantacuzenes. Murad I, who was the son of Theodora, married Helena, the Byzantine princess, daughter of Jean V, and Beyazıd I married a Serbian woman. Their marriages to elite Christians notwithstanding, the early sultans remained simple, unassuming men known to join the people, live simply, and enjoy local traditions and festivities.

There is, however, a danger in reading history from one lens only. That such symbiosis had set in did not preclude different demands and contingencies also altering relations between ethnic and religious populations. In the first two centuries of Ottoman rule, no forceful state policy had yet settled in to regulate relations between groups. Boundaries were uncertain, relations

---

[87] G. G. Arnakis, "Gregory Palamas among the Turks and Documents of His Captivity as Historical Sources," *Speculum* 26 (1951): 108.

[88] Balivet, "Culture ouverte," 1–6.

[89] J. Meyendorff, "Grecs, Turcs et Juifs en Asie Mineure au XIVe siècle," *Byzantinische Forshungen* 1 (1966): 211–217.

were fluid, and the emerging rulers fully enjoyed maneuvering in this kind of plastic and adaptable environment. Moreover, as the analysis in the following chapters shows, boundaries were established based on a series of Islamic and cultural principles, as well as the organizational needs to maintain such diversity. So, despite the fully open tolerance of this "dervish time," new loci of Muslim/non-Muslim boundaries were also emerging and settling among populations.[90] Again, despite the forceful optimism of Gregory Palamas, who predicted the eventual conversion of Muslims to Christianity as Turks conquered Christendom, relations between the two groups would become more clearly differentiated over time.[91]

The boundaries that were established, however, never functioned as rigid and impermeable markers of difference. They were conceived as mobile markers of difference and were to remain so until the nineteenth century, when boundaries were reorganized to separate and differentiate, and were infused with content that led to "bounded identities." Until then, however, despite moments of high insecurity for Christian or Jewish populations or specific ethnic and religious enclaves, the pendulum always swung back to the original concepts of mobility, movement across boundaries, and the sense of elasticity in the networks of inter-religious arrangements.

It is impossible to close this discussion of emergence without acknowledging that there is a traditional Christian historiography of the period that emphasizes the devastation, havoc, and ruin that the Turks brought with them.[92] This history makes the case that Ottomans treated well only those who surrendered; they destroyed and enslaved those who resisted. They cite Islamic law, and present the cases in which the Ottomans transformed churches and monasteries into centers of Islamic learning, *medreses*, or official centers for the magistrate and the *subaşı*, the local peacekeeper.[93] They refer to the land distribution after conquest: the need to harness and redistribute new land resources, especially since the land regime was based on the *tımar*, which was understood to be reward for prowess in service. They argue that the population suffered under agents who surveyed the land and acquainted themselves with all the sources of revenue, assessing taxes, deliberating on collection, and establishing themselves as the new sovereigns. Such proceedings left many distraught at the loss of their land or the disappearance of their overlords.

There is no doubt that many of the cities conquered in Byzantium were sacked. The tradition was to allow warriors to plunder a conquered locality for 3 days. The story goes that Mehmed the Conqueror cut short the looting of Constantinople, ending it after 1 day because he was impatient to claim

[90] H. T. Norris, *Islam in the Balkans: Religion and Society between Europe and the Arab World* (London: C. Hurst & Co., 1993), 52.

[91] Aristeides Papadakis, "Gennadius II and Mehmed the Conqueror," *Byzantion* 42 (1972): 93.

[92] Apostolos E. Vacalopoulos, *Origins of the Greek Nation: The Byzantine Period, 1204–1461*, transl. Ian Moles (New Brunswick, NJ: Rutgers University Press, 1970).

[93] Ibid., 80.

his city and also worried about the damage. These initial acts of brutality left many families without homes and resources, often forcing them to emigrate. Ottomans quickly repopulated these areas, especially as dervishes led their followers and established *tekke*s in these new outposts. Added to the brutality was the capture of slaves and their sale in slave markets. Everyone participated in these markets: Turkish warriors bringing Christian slaves, and Christian warriors bringing Christian and Muslim slaves. Turks were sellers and buyers of slaves, engaging in markets in their regions as well as in Aegean markets farther away. Slaves certainly were highly valued as a commodity in the medieval trade economy, engaging Europeans, especially the Genoese, in trading with the Turks.[94]

It also makes sense that as Ottomans established themselves, gained supporters, and increased their hold over territories, they became more confident in their own local networks, their own localities and identities, and their ability to dominate. Therefore, religious boundaries emerged slowly, presenting the need for the assertion of one's religious identity. By the reign of Murad II (1421–1444) interfaith constructions would be replaced by encroachments onto Christian religious sites. Murad II transformed the church of Acheiropoietos into a mosque after he conquered Salonica, an act that would soon be emulated by many of the high-ranking Ottoman officials as they settled in their posts.[95] As a result, not only were quite a significant number of churches made into mosques, but also many villages were transformed into *vakıf* (pious foundation) villages destined to redirect their revenues for the maintenance of newly converted religious shrines. Dimitriades, who has carefully located these transformations from the fifteenth to the seventeenth centuries for the region of Chalkidiki and the city of Salonica, reports that many villages where both Christians and Muslims lived were transformed over time. Such acts by the ruling elite destroyed traditional Christian locales of worship and ensured the emergence of dichotomous views of rule, clearly separating the ruling Muslim elite from subordinate Christian peoples.

By the sixteenth century, the comfortable multi-confessional space maintained by a remarkable absence of structured orthodoxy was no longer possible, with a dominant Sunnî Islamic state using its relational and cultural domination to erect important boundaries. Historical circumstances especially contributed to this transformation. Starting in the sixteenth century as the Ottoman-Safavid crises were developing, rulers increasingly defined themselves in more orthodox ways, in terms of Sunnî Islam (especially as it meant opposition to Safavid Shi'ism).[96] For example, as a result of such Islamization,

---

[94] Fleet, *European and Islamic Trade in the Early Ottoman State*, chapter 4.

[95] Vasilis Dimitriades, "Ottoman Chalkidiki: An Area in Transition," in *Continuity and Change in Late Byzantine and Early Ottoman Society*, ed. Anthony Bryer and Heath Lowry (Washington, DC: Dumbarton Oaks Research Library and Collection, 1986), 39–50.

[96] Nathalie Clayer, "Des agents du pouvoir Ottoman dans les Balkans: les Halvetis," *Les Balkans à l'époque Ottomane* (2004): 21–29.

we observe that Selim II (1566–1574) confiscated numerous churches in the Balkans and had them sold, allowing the church the possibility of buying them back.[97] This was a way to make money for the treasury, yet it was only possible because the Sunnî Islamic identity of the rulers was becoming stronger. The result was the construction of "the other" in religious terms and a gradual move away from a comfortable multi-religiosity. The state also now became the sole locus of boundary mediation, setting down the rules for living in the empire. We return to the topics of the construction of boundaries between Muslims and non-Muslims, rulers and ruled, and the sultan and his flock. Suffice it to say that a new phase in interfaith relations would emerge, one where boundaries and identities were certainly identified, where markers of difference were discussed and relied on, and where therefore a tolerant order needed more intentional construction.

Conclusion

Throughout history, large empires have been built, and over time these large state systems have fallen apart, often into many different pieces, principalities, small states, mini-empires, and other forms of political structures. Again, throughout history some have been able to reconstitute empire from these pieces; sometimes the core – in ways similar to what modern post-Soviet Russia is trying to do – and sometimes a tiny segment of the periphery reemerged. This is the cycle of change in Ibn Khaldûn's famous tension between center and periphery.

So perhaps that the Ottoman Empire rose out of the ramshackle pieces of the Seljuk Empire is not news. It is part of the cycle of history. Yet, this analysis of the rise of the Ottomans provides many lessons in history. First, the Ottomans became powerful by building an inclusive polity and society, rather than an exclusive one, as its closest neighbors attempted but failed to do. That is, the Russian Empire, even though it emerged on similar principles of brokerage and alliances across groups, carried on a policy of conversion of non-Christians, whom they incorporated from the initial gathering of lands around Muscovy to the conquest of Khazan, when it became a truly multiethnic empire well into the eighteenth century. Similarly, in Habsburg lands divided during the Protestant Reformation, the policy of the Catholic Church and the imperial state went hand in hand with a policy of counter-Reformation.

Not only did the founders of the Ottoman state choose to bridge across social and cultural systems, bringing together religious networks and innovating to construct a hybrid state, they also moved further to base their emerging empire on a remarkable new elite that combined the best warriors and administrators: they included the best Christian and Muslim fighters, the ablest Christian and Muslim administrators, and religious men of many different persuasions: Greek

[97] Aleksandar Fotic, "The Official Explanations for the Confiscation and Sale of Monasteries (Churches) and Their Estates at the Time of Selim II," *Turcica* 26 (1994): 33–54.

Orthodox, Jewish, Sunnî, and Sufi Islam. They coopted their enemies; instead of pursuing a policy of de-Byzantification, they recognized the value of their rivals, accepting Byzantine and Balkan aristocracies into their new administration. They valued innovation and change as much as they valued and needed institutional continuity. The next chapter explores the institutionalization of such an imperial construction.

Finally, that this corridor between east and west, the frontier zone between a Christian empire and a Muslim empire, gave birth to such a powerful symbiosis of sorts is important. It is also important to understand that much of this Islamo-Christian synthesis was built not just because there was hybridity in the air. Rather, it was built because of the exigencies on the ground, because people realized that they required allies, and because they understood that the construction of a new society, a better edifice, would have to incorporate rather than exclude. This lesson has long since been forgotten.

Appendix to Chapter 2

I constructed two networks – one for Osman and one for his son Orhan – using historical information gathered from the best-known histories of the period. These networks are represented by Figures 1 and 2. Especially informative were Aşıkpaşazade, *Tevarih-i Al-I Osman*, edited by Ali Bey (Istanbul: Matbaa-yi Âmire, 1914); Atsız Nihal, *Aşıkpaşaoğlu Tarihi* (Istanbul: Milli Eğitim Bakanlığı, 1970); and Sencer Divitçioğlu, *Osmanlı Beyliğinin Kuruluşu* (Istanbul: Eren Yayıncılık, 1996).

The two networks are "egocentric" in the sense that they are centered on the two sultans, Osman and Orhan. I gathered the most significant relationships for each sultan, based on the aforementioned historical accounts. I collected information on as many relations as possible, with the knowledge that these are not complete networks, and I included relations among acquaintances of the sultan when they were available.

I coded the individuals – the nodes – according to their religion, Muslim (circles), Greek (triangles), and Convert (squares), and coded the different relations that individuals had with each other. When there was more than one type of relation, I reported the one that seemed strongest, given the narrative in the history.

The relations are as follows: M for family or kinship ties; R for religious ties; WF for ties based on durable war friendships; WA (war against) for ties that occurred through conflict and paved the way for an allegiance; WW (war with) for ties among individuals who fought together, but with a lower intensity than in a WF relationship; In for incorporation (allegiance after a war was lost); and A for ties with members of *akhi* religious trade corporations. In Figures 1 and 2, ties are coded. I also drew groupings to indicate the important clusters across which these sultans brokered in their quest to maintain a central position and to increase their power. Such groupings also help demonstrate the increasing consolidation that occurred even in one generation from the networks of father to son, where the grouping of friends of war grew to incorporate multiple previous smaller groups. Similarly, the religious grouping grew to include previously differentiated groups that became increasingly integrated into the networks of the sultan.

I used Ucinet and Netdraw to construct the networks of the two sultans and to draw the graphs.[98]

---

[98] I thank Frederic C. Godart at Columbia University for his expertise in constructing these models. We used Borgatti, S. P., Everett, M. G., and Freeman, L. C. (2002). *Ucinet for Windows: Software for Social Network Analysis.* Cambridge, MA: Analytic Technologies. The version 4.14 of Netdraw is distributed along with UCINET.

3

Becoming an Empire: Imperial Institutions and Control

A young man of 26 [actually he was between 19 and 21], well complexioned, large in body rather than middling in height, noble in arms, of an aspect inspiring fear rather than reverence, sparing of laughter, a pursuer of knowledge, gifted with princely liberality, stubborn in purpose, bold in all things, as avid of fame as Alexander of Macedon. Everyday he has Roman and other histories read to him ... chronicles of the popes, the emperors, the kings of France, the Lombards; he speaks three languages, Turkish, Greek, and Slavonic. Diligently he seeks information on the position of Italy ... the seat of the Pope, of the Emperor, and how many kingdoms there are in Europe, of which he has a map showing the states and the provinces. Nothing gives him greater satisfaction and pleasure than to study the state of the world and the science of war. A shrewd explorer of affairs, he burns with desire to rule.[1]

Giacomo de' Languschi (Langusto), a Venetian visitor who met Mehmed II (1451–1481) right after the conquest of Constantinople, described the conqueror as a bold man, an avid learner, and an heir to the Romans and the Byzantines, whose personal inner strength and might was matched by his open-minded vision and his curiosity about other peoples and cultures.

The 1453 conquest of Constantinople was a key event in the construction of the Ottoman Empire. Although the early trajectory of the state was toward an imperial formation, the chaos after the battle of Ankara against Tamerlane had temporarily halted expansion and consolidation, which was forthwith restarted after 1453. The empire that was built after 1453 became a robust, flexible, and adaptive political entity where a patrimonial center, a strong army, and a dependent and assimilated state elite interconnected with many diverse and multilingual populations ensconced in their ecological and territorial niches. The Ottoman imperial order was to be found in the three components of empire – legitimacy, control over elites and resources, and the maintenance of

---

[1] Description of Mehmed II, cited in Bernard Lewis, *Istanbul and the Civilization of the Ottoman Empire* (Norman: University of Oklahoma Press, 1963), 26–27.

diversity – each forged through the relations between state forces and social forces, center and periphery, state and regional elites, and central officials and local populations.

This chapter seeks to explore this Ottoman imperial construction. I inquire how Ottomans were able to construct the political institutions of empire, to set the rules and practices of governance, to ensure the assimilation and participation of new and old elites and the military, and to forge varying relations and compacts with the conquered regions because each region belonged to and participated in the empire in a different way. Once central power was consolidated around the emperor, perhaps the greatest remaining challenge to centralizing the empire was incorporating the diversity of frontiers, populations, religions, world views, and the centrifugal tendencies of many regions. How to spread a supranational umbrella that provided some sense of commonality but that also accommodated a diversity of peoples and places became important to making empire. The challenge previously experienced and finessed by the Romans, and also to some extent by Byzantium, would now be embraced in turn by the Ottomans.

In Chapter 1, I argued that empires are dominant as long as they can maintain the combination of legitimacy and appropriate mechanisms of rule over cultural diversity and modes of appropriation of political and economic resources. In this chapter, I focus on the incorporation of elites and resources and on the expression of legitimate conceptions of rule. I am interested in demonstrating how central imperial state institutions were forged, how the institutionalization and vertical integration of a diverse group of elites were affected, and how multiple state-locality arrangements of rule were articulated and maintained as the product of negotiated alliances between the state and social actors. Because empires are negotiated enterprises, the concept of bargaining between the state and social groups helps demonstrate that state interests and realities on the ground shaped the different compacts of rule.[2] Furthermore, the multiple roles of intermediary officials shows that the categorical divisions that we assume to exist between "state" and "society" are never really that rigid, but often blurred. The particular permeability of state and society in the interwoven networks that cross these so-called categories suggests a way to rethink state power and put it into the context of the regional and local.

How was a legitimating language formulated to solidify these bonds and to convince groups of the legitimacy of the sultan and his imperial project? Legitimacy was based on the notion of a normative order that produced concrete and reproducible relations between the ruler and his subjects. This order was constructed and understood as such. The internal and external relations of empire presented opportunities for the language of legitimacy, for an assessment of how far or how close real relations were to the ideals of the normative order. In the following sections, I develop two parts of a three-part discussion

---

[2] This argument was developed in my earlier work. See Karen Barkey, _Bandits and Bureaucrats: The Ottoman Route to State Centralization_ (Ithaca, NY: Cornell University Press, 1994).

of empire making: first, relations of rule (imperial governance and institution building), and second, legitimacy. The next chapter deals with the third part, diversity.

Behind the need to understand how this empire was built lies the question that we asked in the first chapter; that is, what were the reasons for the longevity and successful adaptation of the empire to diverse threats and challenges? What were the chosen strategies and institutions that brought about flexibility and the ability to integrate overlapping social formations and to adapt to new circumstances over time? What were the origins of the institutional practices, and how did this polity combine its ruling and economic institutions, frontiers, and overall state–society structures with an apparent flexibility that lasted a long time?

Here, the predecessors of the Ottomans give us some clues and comparative leverage to solidify our arguments. On the one hand, Ottoman sultans styled themselves after the Roman and Byzantine examples, and learned and adapted many of their practices. The Ottomans were very conscious, as Europeans were, of the value of using and learning from the Romans and the Byzantines, who had ruled these territories before them successfully for a long time. To such an imperial heritage, the Ottomans added Turkic traditions and Islamic practices. On the other hand, many decisions and strategies resulted from how empires organize: how the intermediary network and organizational solutions are arranged at the interface where state and social actors meet and resolve their differences. That is, state and social forces showed considerable adaptability in the intermediate arrangements that were forged and reshaped in order to maintain continuity and stability. We therefore have to understand both what mechanisms of rule were learned or were locked in from the past, and what other forms were adaptations of state–society relations that were produced in similar ways in many different contexts.

We see such similarities both in the fact that these three empires were equally long lasting, strategically interesting, and administratively both mixed and flexible, and, moreover, that there was learning across cases. That is, Byzantines certainly duplicated aspects of the western part of the Roman Empire, and Ottomans knew and adopted many of their practices. After the Turkic peoples entered Anatolia with the Battle of Manzikert (1071), they learned Roman and Byzantine forms and practices; these lessons were reinforced especially by the Byzantine advisors at the court of the Seljuk sultans, as well as when the Byzantines used powerful Turkic leaders in their own internal struggles, incorporating them into Byzantine army and political forums. The exchange of such personalities across borders, the large numbers of slaves who were brought into the sultan's court, as well as the marriage alliances contracted across the two cultures, all contributed to a great deal of learning across the two sets of political formations.[3]

---

[3] Speros Vryonis, Jr., "The Byzantine Legacy and Ottoman Forms," *Dumbarton Oaks Papers* 23 (1969–1970): 251–308.

Ottoman imperial institutions were built in a manner most similar to those of the Roman Empire, which also succeeded by its openness, flexibility, and ability to incorporate the most able, training them and making them organizationally coherent. Although the Ottoman system lacked the concept of citizenship – a key to the organizational and ideological success of the Romans – in a sense the equivalent to Roman citizenship was the military institution of the empire (*askeri*). Roman citizenship and Ottoman *askeri* status were not the same. Although Roman citizenship varied according to different historical periods, it was a privileged status given to certain individuals with respect to laws, property, and governance. Ottoman *askeri* status that included the *devshirme*, a mechanism through which non-Muslims were incorporated into Ottoman life and trained and included in military and political participation, and other forms of incorporation such as that of Christian cavalrymen and nobility, was also a privileged status given to certain individuals. Both were structurally similar and performed a comparable task for the imperial institutions: assimilation. They each identified the most qualified men and gave them opportunities for success. Citizenship in Rome and the army in both empires were institutions of assimilation. Like their august predecessor, the Ottomans did not produce a distinct class or group of officials and administrators that had reason to be disgruntled or alienated if not empowered. This was due largely to the practice of incorporation of elites that provided incentives for belonging, along with the building of legitimacy and the distribution of resources. Both empires also left the bureaucracy light. Only later, as bureaucratic offices enlarged and as administration became engorged with people expecting positions, did the empires begin to falter.

The other asset of this empire was its institutional flexibility and diversity. Again, not unlike the Romans, the Ottomans understood well the limits of their rule, in terms of both the geographical reach of their control and their limited manpower, and fashioned an empire that was based on organizational diversity. That is, they were accepting of multiple systems of rule, multiple negotiated frontiers, laws and courts, forms of revenue management, and religious diversity. Rather than attempt to impose new or uniform forms of rule, they built on and took advantage of systems already in place. The Ottomans were institutionally omnivorous. This pragmatic flexibility made for the accommodation of many layers of administration from the core to the periphery to the faraway frontiers of the empire.

Finally, I show how this pragmatic flexibility, this acceptance of the incorporated peripheries with their cultural and systemic peculiarities, changed the empire itself. The Ottoman Empire during the sixteenth century moved from being an open and multivocal empire with a candidly Islamo-Christian orientation (in which multiple groups of Islamic, orthodox Sunnî, heterodox Sufi, Christians, and Jews coexisted and had participatory voice) to one in which Islamic religiosity, especially of the Sunnî orthodox stripe, gained ground. This occurred with Beyazıd II (1481–1512) and then with Selim I's (1512–1520) conquest to the east in the Islamic world; the empire found itself in a different demographic, institutional, and cultural framework that changed its main constitutive identity, causing it to mold itself more clearly as an Islamic empire.

This chapter combines the study of the leaders' strategies to consolidate their rule with an institutional perspective to help understand the ways in which political decisions were mediated and made sense of in an institutional framework. In this regard, I bring together human preferences with questions of institutional persistence or change.[4] Such a perspective allows me to study the particular inclinations of the rulers who were key actors in empire building. Their decisions were not made in a vacuum, however, and were part and parcel of a pre-existing institutional environment and new rules and procedures that accompanied conquest. That is, the power struggles between the conqueror and the old Turkish aristocracy, the institutional facility with which the Byzantine and Turkish political forms blended, and the concrete manpower and resource needs of a new administration shaped the state and its long-term structure.

In contrast, there were also moments when becoming imperial was not a result of institutional openness and flexibility, such as when, during the initial phase of centralization, Mehmed II pushed against some of the earlier flexibility in order to consolidate his power, centralize his apparatus of rule, and establish effective control over imperial domains, revenues, and resources. We therefore need to be able to identify the manner in which the particular exigencies and preferences of the key actors affected this institutional flexibility and the choices this implied. Similarly, for Selim I, the inherent openess toward heterodoxy became a moot point when the empire was threatened from the east.

Finally, the institutional framework is helpful in explaining the larger identity and legitimacy of the empire. That is, the transformation from the more syncretic and eclectic vision of Ottoman identity toward an evidently Muslim identity was the result of both institutional reproduction and innovation, the latter in the form of "institutional layering," which involves attaching new elements onto an otherwise settled institutional frame.[5] In reproduction, "initial outcomes were [also] strongly self-reinforcing,"[6] and in openness, the layering of different institutional forms – Roman, Byzantine, Turkic, and Islamic – occurred with continuous compromise between old and new. It was this institutional flexibility that had originally consented to the inclusion of Byzantine forms that then allowed the insertion of Islamic modes of organization and legitimacy that remade Ottoman political concepts.

The construction of this political and cultural arrangement into an imperial formation occurred during the tenure of four sultans, Mehmed II (1451–1481),

---

[4] Kathleen Thelen, "How Institutions Evolve: Insights from Comparative Historical Analysis," in *Comparative Historical Analysis in the Social Sciences*, ed. James Mahoney and Dietrich Rueschemeyer (Cambridge, UK: Cambridge University Press, 2003), 208–240.

[5] Kathleen Thelen, *How Institutions Evolve: The Political Economy of Skills in Germany, Britain, the United States, and Japan* (Cambridge, UK: Cambridge University Press, 2004), 35.

[6] Paul Pierson, *Politics in Time: History, Institutions, and Social Analysis* (Princeton, NJ: Princeton University Press, 2004), 3.

Beyazıd II (1481–1512), Selim I (1512–1520), and Süleyman the Magnificent (1520–1566). This period in Ottoman history was, in many ways, remarkable for the ability of state actors not only to build and frame the governmental structures of the Ottoman state, but also to control power relations as far as the North African littoral and Yemen. I emphasize the balance among central authority, institutional rigidity, and flexibility during the reign of Mehmed II as the vertical integration of elites was carried out. I compare Mehmed's incorporation of new Byzantine elites to Augustus's appeasement of the Italian elites after the Republican Civil Wars. I discuss the layering of Byzantine and new Ottoman organizations and practices, demonstrating that the new rulers built in flexibility and a certain degree of plasticity in the state by allowing this bricolage of institutions to happen, rather than destroying everything associated with the "enemy." I also discuss the connected forms of legitimacy during Mehmed's tenure that merged dynastic, imperial, and military symbols of legitimacy. Moving from the center to the provinces, I demonstrate how the knowledge that Ottomans had of the peoples they conquered helped them shape the foundations of rule in the periphery. As in many other empires – here, significantly, those of the Romans and the Russians – the perspective of the center helped shape the state–society compact that emerged. The Ottomans also tried to learn a great deal about the provinces, with the aim of establishing efficient and responsive systems of rule.

With Selim I, I emphasize the development of a new form of religious Sunnî zealotry that was both exploited and harnessed by the state. In this context, I take into consideration the extension of religious institutions, their ability to link elite and popular circles through the *kadı* court, and the implications of such linkages. Finally, I return to state and provincial institutions to analyze the levels of institutionalization, innovation, and diversity in the incorporation and control of elites. Sultan Süleyman embodied – as he himself declared – the concept of perfect justice and the formulation of a precarious balance between religious (*Sharia*) and secular dynastic (*kanun*) law. It is in this context that I bring in the legal institutional structure of the empire, through the formalization it acquired in Süleyman's last years. If innovation and diversity of institutional structures were the reflection of the early Süleymanic era, codification and formalization became the hallmark of the end of his reign. I therefore follow the institutional unfolding by studying the historically contingent and culturally enabling context in which struggles for domination and legitimation occurred. Through each of these reigns, I also follow the formalization of rule and its representation in the more excessive and elaborate forms of ceremonials, and the progressive physical separation between ruler and ruled that resemble earlier forms of imperialization, especially among the Romans.

From Conquest to Imperial Domains

On the twenty-ninth of May [1453], the last day of the siege, our Lord God decided, to the sorrow of the Greeks, that He was willing for the city to fall on this day into the hands of Mahomat Bey the Turk son of Murat, after the fashion and in the manner described below; and also our eternal God was willing to make this decision in order to fulfill all the ancient prophecies, particularly the first prophecy made by Saint Constantine, who is on horseback on a column by the Church of Saint Sophia of this city, prophesying with his hand and saying, "From this direction will come the one who will undo me," pointing to Anatolia, that is Turkey. Another prophecy which he made was that when there should be an Emperor called Constantine son of Helen, under his rule Constantinople would be lost, and there was another prophecy that when the moon should give a sign in the sky, within a few days the Turks would have Constantinople.[7]

Whether the Turks knew of these prophecies or not, they had coveted the imperial city for a long time. When Mehmed II succeeded to the throne in 1451, he was ready for this next challenge. He knew well the dissent in the Christian ranks; the rivalries that had torn the city; and the divisions among the Greeks, the Genoese, and the Venetians. However, he also knew well that Constantinople would *make* the Ottomans. Not only would the Turks be safer by holding the city, but they would also truly become a force to be reckoned with. He would be one step closer to claiming the succession to the throne of the Caesars, maybe even closer to the conquest of Rome, symbolized as "*kızıl elma*," the "golden apple," held by the Roman emperors.[8]

Mehmed carefully devised a plan to reinforce the Ottoman navy, build fortresses on both sides of the Bosphorus, and prevent the city from getting outside help, cutting off the Black Sea, the Mediterranean, and the land routes. Attacks on the walls of the city exhausted the population, who repeatedly spent their energies repairing them. The actual siege lasted 54 days, and on 29 May, the Janissaries made a final attack on the walls of the city, breaking through and triumphantly entering the city as the conquerors of a new world.[9] Although the fall of Constantinople brought humiliation to the Western world, from the perspective of the Turks it also brought the start of a transition from conquest to rule, even as further conquest was pursued.

The capture of Constantinople also signaled the initial reformulation of Ottoman thinking, first in grand imperial terms, and second in seeing themselves as the legitimate heirs to a series of great empires. Not only did this dramatic event indicate shifting eras in world history, but it also shifted the definitions that Ottomans had of themselves, as they enthusiastically installed the sultan on the throne of the Romans. With the securing of Constantinople, the Ottomans were now able to construct a much stronger and deeper legitimating ideology that evolved from a narrower charismatic (focused on the

---

[7] Nicolo Barbaro, *Diary of the Siege of Constantinople 1453* (New York: Exposition Press, 1969), 61.

[8] Halil İnalcık, "State, Sovereignty and Law during the Reign of Süleyman," in *Süleyman the Second and His Time*, ed. Halil İnalcık and Cemal Kafadar (Istanbul: SIS Press, 1993), 68.

[9] Numerous books discuss the conquest of Constantinople; among them are Barbaro, *Diary of the Siege of Constantinople*; Sir Steven Runciman, *The Fall of Constantinople 1453* (Cambridge, UK: Cambridge University Press, 1990); and Franz Babinger, *Mehmed the Conqueror and His Time* (Princeton, NJ: Princeton University Press, 1978).

person of Osman) and also syncretic (based on the open and inclusive cultural understandings of the period) legitimation to a much broader set of legitimating claims. The Ottomans were now *imperial*; that is, they began to imagine and construct an Islamic-Ottoman polyglot empire that claimed its roots as much in Byzantium as in the steppes of Central Asia. With the conquest of Constantinople, they lay claim to the Roman imperial title, although Mehmed II did not really use it. It was Süleyman the Magnificent who would finally wrest the title away from Charles V and begin using it in public. The synthesis that was constructed drew equally on Islamic, Central Asian, and eastern Roman heritages, offering an ideology of imperial stability and hegemony symbolized in the success of the conqueror.

Establishing a Strong Center: Patrimonial Army and Peoples

The year 1453 signaled the end of the Byzantines and the imperialization of the Ottomans. The immediate aim of the sultan was to fashion his own absolute rule and power. Consequently, his actions were organized to eliminate dissent and reward loyalty, and to construct stable yet compliant vertical relations of subordination.

The fifteenth-century Ottoman centralization policies mirror those of Augustus, who had imperialized Rome, skillfully making the transition from republic to empire by supporting and drawing in the previously disgruntled Italian and provincial landed gentry, reforming the administration, recentralizing the army to eliminate the potential for any coup d'état, and initiating the procedures for pulling the frontier provinces into his administration. What Michael Doyle calls the "Augustan threshold" was the moment at which the republic was reconfigured as a much more centralized and powerful imperial authority.[10] The genius of Augustus was to transform Roman imperial rule dramatically through his ability to effect change and to make a whole category of elites feel incorporated and grateful to the emperor. From the Civil Wars to the Battle at Actium where Octavian (Augustus) defeated Mark Anthony and Cleopatra in 31 B.C., the Roman Republic had been divided, and its Roman elites were alienated and at war with one another. Augustus brought them together not only by defeating the harshest contenders, but also by preserving traditional republican offices and forms of government while including many members of the Italian elites in the government. From the Roman imperial center to the provincial administrative class, the transformation entailed the integration of local native elites in ways that prevented feelings of exclusion.[11] Such a process was comparable in the eastern Roman Empire, when Byzantion was made into a new imperial capital, Constantinople, and emperors brought into their

[10] Michael W. Doyle, *Empires* (Ithaca, NY: Cornell University Press, 1986), 92–97.
[11] Ronald Syme, *The Roman Revolution* (London: Oxford University Press, 1960); Gary B. Miles, "Roman and Modern Imperialism: A Reassessment," *Comparative Studies in Society and History* 32:4 (October 1990): 640.

new city an entirely new set of worthy individuals that they organized into a new senatorial aristocracy that became, at least at the beginning, institutionally dependent on the center.

Augustus also reshaped the military, balancing central and peripheral forces, both reducing the size of the Roman legions to 28 (from 60) and strengthening them by creating the first western standing army, the 15,000 soldier legionaries. Pushing his twenty-eight legions to border provinces, he consolidated power from outside toward the center, taking for himself control of the outer provinces and leaving to senators the internal provinces. Among the most troublesome during the late Republican era had been the proliferation of personal armies that Augustus eliminated along with the riffraff in his own ranks. In the end, the army was pushed away to the frontiers of the territories, being used to protect and expand when necessary, but with the intent that provincial armies should not intervene in central politics. The imperial army was rewarded, paid, and kept in strict control; they performed swiftly. Thus, the manipulation of frontiers, provinces, the military, and the Roman elite came together in the space of a few years and provided Augustus with central dictatorial power.

After the collapse of 1402 and the reordering of the Ottoman factions under Murad II and the young Mehmed II, the year 1453 represented an opportunity similar to the entry of Augustus into republican politics. Mehmed needed to shape a strong, central, imperial state based in Istanbul, and to tame the centripetal forces seeking easy semi-feudal compromises with the sultan. Otherwise, he would have lost the battle to become emperor, an opportunity that he saw as God given after the taking of Constantinople. Like Augustus, Mehmed eliminated elites potentially hostile to change, and rewarded groups with the fewest prospects and the most to gain from promotion and integration, therefore ensuring their loyalty. Both emperors during their reigns successfully constructed an autonomous state and bureaucratic apparatus, ensuring that the interests of the empire would come first, before those of individual groups, aristocratic elites, or the military.

Although most scholars concentrate on the centralization activities of the conqueror that were related to the repopulation of Istanbul, the issues of economic centralization, and, finally, legal and administrative consolidation,[12] such measures would not have been possible before the simple reestablishment of central control, especially after the rivalries and splintering that followed 1402. Mehmed's restructuring effort – starting from the center and expanding toward the frontiers – created layers of winners and losers. A group of frontiersmen, dervish leaders, and landed Turcoman families, some of whom had been at the forefront of frontier expansion, became the steady losers as imperial

---

[12] Rhoads Murphey, "External Expansion and Internal Growth of the Ottoman Empire under Mehmed II: A Brief Discussion of Some Contradictory Aspects of the Conqueror's Legacy," in *The Great Ottoman-Turkish Civilization*, ed. Kemal Çiçek (Ankara: Balkan Ciltevi, 2000), vol. I, 155–162.

statehood advanced. A new breed of men, pulled in from foreign aristocracies and from simple Balkan peasantries, emerged as the winners in the new imperial formation. To entice the new members of the elite, incentives would have to be provided. To subdue the losing forces of the new empire, the military would be needed. The question, however, remains as to why the Ottoman sultan would display such preferences toward men of enemy ranks, rather than toward his own companions and followers who perceived themselves as the rightful beneficiaries of the conquests.

The strategy was to eliminate those entrenched in their lands and the power resources that had the potential to create rivalries to the Ottoman household, and to build the loyalty of and reward an already trained and savvy group of men who had nothing to expect or demand from the new imperial state. Besides, the sultan needed these men to rule newly conquered lands and decisively to remake devastated cities; vanquished foreign populations were more likely to respond to their own former leaders. In this endeavor, he behaved much like Augustus, merging his reform of the military, the construction of a new loyal elite, and the remaking of the provinces.

For his military reform, he started with the traditional division of Ottoman society into two groups, the ruling class – the *askeri* (literally, the military), the army, the civil servants, and the *ulema* (doctors of Muslim theology) – versus the *reaya*, the flock or subjects. The *askeri* were exempt from taxation, and the military filled the ranks of the standing infantry (the Janissary army), the *sipahi* (provincial cavalry), and other central and auxiliary troops. One could become part of this privileged elite by birth into a high-ranking *askeri* household, or through the *kul* (slave–servant) system, that is, by becoming one of the sultan's loyal servants who were drawn from slaves acquired during war or through the *devshirme* institution.

The *devshirme*, a levy of Balkan Christian young boys, had emerged as an institution during the reign of Murad as part of the natural transition from a small emergent state based mostly on horizontal kinship and friendship relations, to a hierarchical and vertically integrated structure. When such kin and brokerage relations could not maintain loyalty any longer, leaders needed a central patrimonial army completely devoted to the sultan. The early practice of transforming captured slaves into the personal armies of Seljuk or Ottoman sultans or Turcoman tribal leaders gave way to a more institutionalized procedure of levying Christian boys from the conquered territories. Young Christian boys were taken from their families, converted to Islam, sent to live with Turkish families for up to 8 years, and taught Turkish, thus undergoing serious cultural assimilation, with the most promising among them educated for palace service. The finest among them went on to become state leaders. The vast majority were trained and incorporated into the Janissary corps. This army corps, a cross between a standing and a patrimonial army, the faithful slaves of the sultan, came to symbolize the power of the sultan and his household.

When Mehmed II ascended to the throne, he had inherited a Janissary corps of modest size – but demonstrably a powerful and fearless force at the walls of Constantinople – a land tenure system based on military cavalry in the provinces, and an entrenched Turkic "aristocracy" that was resourceful, powerful, and oppositional. In his dealings with these families, Mehmed II brought together three main goals: to tame these landed Turkic aristocratic families that were deeply rooted in the Anatolian countryside, to make the land state land (*miri*) according to Islamic law, and to distribute it to reward service and loyalty through the granting of rights to taxation of the land. He achieved this through the expropriation of Anatolian families whose long-standing inherited lands and pious foundations (*vakıf*) were seized and converted into *timars*, prebendal benefices on state-owned land. The *timar* holders were members of the Ottoman cavalry, positioned in the provinces, and entrusted with the task of taxing the peasantry and maintaining an army. Raising the numbers of the *timar* holders also increased the number of provincial warriors available to the state.

Military consolidation then was effected in a practice of isolating competitors, where Janissaries were recruited from among young men/soldiers with no ties to the Anatolian Turkic families, and was further consolidated as a sort of counterweight to the provincial forces, which were developed to counter central military regiments.[13] The two armies differed in military style and weaponry, in the mode of their livelihood, and in their particular functions within the Ottoman system. The advantage of the provincial cavalry was that it shifted the imperial burden onto other groups. Partly because the *timar* holdings were not part of the money economy and because they shifted the burden of tax collection and military readiness to the provinces, thereby keeping the central bureaucracy light, the *timar* was an important administrative, fiscal, and military institution to maintain and was, at least in the central provinces of the empire, the backbone of the provincial army. Mehmed II, then, had succeeded in the separation and differential integration of various military groups. He planned the expansion of the Janissary army from about 5,000 to perhaps 10,000 soldiers, and his successor Beyazıd II added another 13,000 to the mix.[14] During this time, the central army was reinforced and the frontier Turcomans settled on land away from military action.

These numbers represented the gains that the Christians made at the expense of the traditional Turkic groups. The Christian element was particularly powerful when whole groups of palace officials or Janissary soldiers originated from a particular region and maintained close ties to their communities. It is

[13] We should note that this practice of isolating competitors was also very much the case in the early sultans' marriage alliances. Not only did marrying Christian women consolidate their ties to the regions they wanted to conquer, but also by not marrying Muslim or Turkic women, they isolated the Anatolian families who were competing with them. After many of the Anatolian principalities were incorporated, marriage alliances with Muslim women gained prominence. See Leslie P. Pierce, *The Imperial Harem: Women and Sovereignty in the Ottoman Empire* (New York: Oxford University Press, 1993).

[14] Rhoads Murphey, "Yeni Çeri," *Encyclopedia of Islam*, 2d ed. (Leiden, The Netherlands: E. J. Brill, 1965), EI2.

said, for example, that Mehmed II filled the palace with Trapezuntine (from the empire and region of Trebizonde) slaves and that they formed a powerful bloc connected to their families, not only bestowing help and privileges on them, but also trying to interfere in the workings of the Orthodox Church. Legislation was passed to prevent similar occurrences in the future.[15]

Again, a similar pattern can be observed in the history of Russian centralization and expansion. In the emergence and construction of the Russian Empire, the Muscovite Grand Prince Ivan III (1462–1505) used strategies and structures similar to Mehmed II. The origins of the Russian Empire lie in the mid-fifteenth century. Similar to the conquest of Constantinople in the ideological and structural transformations it triggered, one of the critical aspects of Russian imperial emergence was the subjugation and final annexation of Novgorod during the reign of Ivan III. It placed the Muscovite state in a new and enduring military strategic position and led to rearrangements in property relations with "momentous consequences."[16] No longer threatened from three sides, Russia's expansion was defined by a southeastern frontier with the Kazan, Nogai, and Crimean Tatars, and a western frontier facing Sweden, Poland, and Lithuania.[17] The annexation of Novgorod province around 1480 set in motion modes of conquest and patterns of imperial rule that would define the emerging Russian Empire. Particularly important was the establishment of the *pomest'e* system of cavalry service lands. After gaining control of Novgorod, thousands of elite landholders were deported to the imperial center, opening up millions of acres of land, which was distributed to the newly recruited military servitors of the central state.[18] Ivan III, having successfully centralized the state, became "the father of the *pomest'e* system," a practice of provincial landholding and cavalry military mobilization remarkably similar to the Ottoman *tımar* system.[19] In both the Russian and Ottoman Empires, conquest and imperial centralization were facilitated through military organization based on state-controlled land systems of military servitors.

The other piece of central consolidation was the elimination of individuals who threatened the state from the center. An immediate overhaul in the corridors of power was initiated with the dismissal and then the execution of Çandarlı Halil Pasha and his sons. This old scion of a Turkish family was brazen in his betrayal, especially by showing restraint during the siege of Constantinople and by accepting bribes from the Greeks. Yet, much more significant than his immediate betrayal was the fact that this family behaved as a potential alternative network of state power. As an established Turkic aristocratic family, it had a long tradition of closeness to the Ottoman ruling family, and a

[15] Vryonis, "Byzantine Legacy," 272.
[16] Robert O. Crummey, *The Formation of Muscovy* (New York: Longman, 1987), 90.
[17] Richard Hellie, *Enserfment and Military Change in Muscovy* (Chicago: The University of Chicago Press, 1971), 21.
[18] Ibid., 90; idem, *Enserfment*, 27.
[19] Ibid.

monopoly over the most important state offices, the grand vezirate and the kadıasker positions.[20] For more than 60 years, the Çandarlı family had developed a small-scale capital city in Iznik, had close relations to the *ulema* and the military, and controlled significant wealth, creating the potential for centrifugal tendencies.[21] Similarly, other members of old aristocratic Turkish families, some members of the *ulema*, and some of the more rebellious frontier families were either eliminated or subjugated to the imperial will. The immediate goal was the eradication of the potential refeudalization of the conquered territories.

Clear financial incentives also applied to land appropriation. The revision and appropriation of all private property (*mülk*) and pious foundation (*vakıf*) lands under the control of the Anatolian landholding families, religious groups, and hundreds of pious foundations established to provide for dervish lodges (*zaviye, vakıfs*) would increase the revenues of the state. Tursun Beğ, in his history of Mehmed II, counts as many as 20,000 villages and different land tenure arrangements (*mezra'as* and *çiftliks*) that were confiscated by the state and redistributed to the military as their fiefs.[22] Because it was Mehmed's group of Byzantine tax farmers who attended to these fiscal matters, many landed families were infuriated by these "infidels," whom they believed had taken over all the important positions while Turks were being dislocated.[23] Since this was done, however, at the expense of the old traditional Anatolian aristocratic families, they resisted fiercely, forcing Beyazıd II to reverse his father's policy by expanding only the Janissary army and returning fief land to the members of the propertied families.[24] However, "infidels" were targeted as well. On the Byzantine side, those with potential to revive the empire were also quickly eliminated; the small empire of Trabzon (1461), the Palaeologs of the Morea, and some Genoese with connection to the ruling houses were removed from their positions of power.

Also similar to Mehmed II's attack on entrenched landed interests in order to consolidate imperial power, Ivan IV's (1533–1584) experiment with the *Oprichnina* expanded the state service land system initiated by Ivan III at the expense of the hereditary nobility in Russia. The interests of the military servitors and the state coincided in opposition to the Boyars, monasteries, and other private landholders. Both the state and its servitors desired to reduce private, hereditary ownership and increase the domain of the *pomest'e* landholding

---

[20] Cemal Kafadar, "Yeniçeri- Esnaf Relations: Solidarity and Conflict," M.A. thesis, Institute of Islamic Studies, McGill University, Montreal, Quebec, Canada, 1981, 50.

[21] Ibid.

[22] Tursun Beğ, *The History of Mehmed the Conqueror*, transl. Halil İnalcık and Rhoads Murphey (Minneapolis and Chicago: Bibliotheca Islamica, 1978); Halil İnalcık, "How to Read Ashık Pasha-Zade's History," in *Studies in Ottoman History in Honour of Professor V. L. Menage*, ed. Colin Heywood and Colin Imber (Istanbul: ISIS Press, 1994), 146.

[23] İnalcık argues that because Ashık Pasha-Zade himself suffered from these fiscal changes, his views on the conqueror were tainted. İnalcık, "How to Read Ashık," 145.

[24] Murphey, "External Expansion and Internal Growth," 161; İnalcık, "How to Read Ashık," 145–147.

system.[25] Although Ivan IV's experiment with the *Oprichnina* was disastrous in most respects, many Boyar estates were expropriated in favor of the *pomest'e* system with the result that "service land holding became the predominant form of tenure," and it appeared in the 1580s as if hereditary landownership might expire altogether.[26]

Mehmed chose his closest allies and administrators from among both Muslim and Christian elites, building a small but robust network of advisors tied not only to one another, but also to the important dynasties of each community. The grand vezirate, secured as the first official position right below the sultan and as the sole representative of the government, was filled with the sultan's trusted advisors, his two closest companions in war, Ishak Pasha and Zaganos Pasha, and later followed by Mahmud Pasha, a converted Christian noble who became a powerful and consequential grand vizier. Even more significant than this immediate reorganization of power at the very top were the next layers where administrative continuity became the hallmark of Mehmed's policy. Already in the fourteenth century the emerging Ottoman state had largely been administered by a complex medley of Christian and Ottoman administrators, and this pattern was then extended to the higher levels of government. After 1453, the Ottoman palace was packed with "Byzantine and Balkan aristocrats turned Vezirs."[27]

The Sultan chose to retain and empower a hybrid group of top elites who represented both the power structures of the past and the emerging ideologies of the present. These Byzanto-Balkan elites also made some choices because many of them crossed over first by converting to Islam, and then by taking government positions. Those who were clearly not interested in living under Ottoman rule had long disappeared into Latin Christendom. Even among the heirs to the Byzantine Empire, two out of three of the nephews of the dead emperor Constantine, Mesih Pasha and Murad Pasha, both converts to Islam, rose to the pinnacle of Ottoman power, taking on important military and administrative positions. Mahmud Pasha was another member of the Byzanto-Serbian nobility who rose to the position of grand vizier, a man whose tenure was described by the Ottoman chronicler Tursun Beğ: "Mahmud Pasha was now at the height of his glory. It was as though the Sultan had renounced the sultanate and bestowed it on Mahmud."[28] Mahmud Pasha's brother was the "grand voivode" of Serbia, and their mother had been endowed with a monastery in Istanbul.[29]

In a manner that might seem out of character for a conquering power, the Ottomans chose to incorporate the defeated elites at the highest echelons of

---

[25] Hellie, *Enserfment*, 40.

[26] Ibid., 41.

[27] Heath Lowry, *The Nature of the Early Ottoman State* (Albany: State University of New York Press, 2003), 118.

[28] Quoted in Tursun Beğ, *The History of Mehmed the Conqueror*, 124.

[29] Julian Raby, "A Sultan of Paradox: Mehmed the Conqueror as Patron of the Arts," *Oxford Art Journal* 5 (1982): 3–8.

government. As a result, out of the fifteen grand viziers who occupied their positions between 1453 and 1515, eight were of Byzantine or Balkan nobility, four rose to the ranks from the *devshirme* system, and only three were of Muslim Turkish origin.[30] The result of such a policy of empowering men who would have remained outside the new reorganized power structure was the creation of a tight group of sultan's servants who were employed at every level of the Ottoman administration. Mehmed II made these men his tax collectors, tax farmers, grand viziers, and other viziers, promoting them to political positions. He also enlisted the help of many other Greeks, some as his secretaries and some erudite writers who produced a series of Greek manuscripts for the sultan, mostly it seems to teach the next generation of courtiers, translators, and scribes the Greek language; in short, he was laying down the foundations of his own Greek chancellory staff. Many of these men had been prominent in Constantinople because they had close ties with the Byzantine imperial family.[31]

Although we can look at this as one of Mehmed II's most consequential moves (matched by his organization of non-Muslim communities, as chapter 4 shows) in his imperialization strategy, this policy was not entirely novel. It certainly was continuous with the practices of his ancestors who had chosen to roam the frontier lands shoulder to shoulder with local Greek warriors. The early Ottoman rulers had also relied on skilled Byzantine administrators to govern their expanding realm. What had been forged out of necessity during the early period of incorporation was now restated and applied as a positive philosophy of rule that did not repress talent or exclude the peoples who came under Ottoman rule. Such a policy forcefully signaled that the Ottomans would rely on a significant stream of foreign talent into the higher ranks of administration and into the army through the *kul-devshirme* system. Thus, the Ottomans became among their contemporaries the only empire to espouse most clearly this aspect of Roman and also Byzantine administrative traditions.[32]

Comparing the Roman consolidation during the Principate and the Ottoman consolidation during the time of Mehmed II, we find that both leaders, Augustus and Mehmed II, used existing institutions and practices and reinforced them to strengthen their personal power (directly associated with the state). They both developed a strong understanding of service to the state that provided the reasoning behind reward and assimilation. Both took the military as an important central institution and reinforced it to serve their interests. For Augustus, this meant restricting the Senate's access to the military, and developing checks and balances among inner and outer provinces. It also meant that even more than

[30] Lowry, *The Nature of the Early Ottoman State*, 120–123.
[31] Julian Raby, "Mehmed the Conqueror's Greek Scriptorium," *Dumbarton Oaks Papers* 37 (1983): 15–34; Nicolas Vatin, "L'Emploi du Grec comme Langue Diplomatique par les Ottomans (Fin du XVe – Debut du XVIe Siecle), in *Istanbul et les Langues Orientales*, ed. Frederic Hitzel (Paris: Harmattan, 1997), 41–47.
[32] Although more guarded, the Byzantines also followed this rule since their Armenian and Georgian peoples rose to become powerful in the ruling administration and even became the rulers.

before, the elite of the conquered peoples were allowed into the inner sanctum of Roman politics and administration, and were provided with the overwhelming sense that they were ruled by consent rather than force.[33] Although at first Roman citizenship was a way to distinguish people who lived in Rome from those who came from other lands, it was later extended to allies whom the Romans deemed to be sympathetic and positive, and finally, it reached its apex in AD 212 when Caracalla issued an edict in which citizenship was given to all free people in the empire.

Ottomans also focused on the military and the central apparatus of rule, with a developed conception of who could be included in the favors of the state. Both polities conceptualized entry, the Roman around the granting of citizenship and participation and the Ottoman around the assimilation into the army and upward mobility. In both cases, the motivation of empire was to stimulate the growth of armies and to ensure the loyalty of larger and larger segments of the population. Such practices of imperial rule determined success and longevity because they continually drew from a new and diverse pool of successful men who provided novel means of control and renewed energy to the empire.

The inclusion of so many Christian noblemen in the Ottoman government was undoubtedly institutionally a clever policy to espouse. At the symbolic level, this was a remarkable ideological/geopolitical move for the Ottomans to legitimize their entry into the European world scene, not just by conquest, cruelty, or captivity, but rather through the incorporation and acceptance of the senior leadership of the conquered peoples. They would conquer deep into Europe, and they would rule with Christians. This way the Ottomans forcefully signaled that they were the natural heirs to Byzantine civilization. There could be no better proof than allowing Byzantine elites to ensure institutional continuity: the rising Ottomans were linked with their Byzantine contemporaries. In many more gestures of goodwill, the sultan used conciliatory and appeasing language to convince different communities with external ties in Europe that they would honor their long-held privileges.[34] As Rhoads Murphey reminds us, European commentators nonetheless held a low opinion of Mehmed.[35]

Sultans claimed to unite plural cultures and to spread their civilization. They "styled themselves as *Kaysar* (Ceasar), *Basileus* (King – the primary title used by the Byzantine Emperors), *Padisah-i Konstantiniye* (Emperors of

---

[33] P. A. Brunt, "The Romanization of the Local Ruling Classes in the Roman Empire," in *Assimilation et Résistance à la Culture Gréco-Romaine dans le Monde Ancien*, ed. D. M. Pippidi (Paris: Société d'Edition "Les Belles Lettres," 1976), 161–173.

[34] In a letter addressed to the Genoese community, Mehmed II declared: "Let them observe their own laws and customs and preserve them now and in the future; and we will keep them as earnestly and hold them as dear as those which are current in our dominions." Rhoads Murphey uses the English translation found in J. R. Melville Jones, *The Siege of Constantinople 1453: Seven Contemporary Accounts* (Amsterdam: Hakkert, 1972), 156.

[35] Murphey, "External Expansion and Internal Growth of the Ottoman Empire under Mehmed II."

Constantinople), and as *Padisah-I Rum* (Emperors of the Romans), all titles that clearly underline a belief in their role as inheritors of universal power."[36] In 1466, Mehmed II was so hailed: "Nobody doubts that you are the emperor of the Romans. A ruler who controls the center of the empire is the emperor of that empire, and Istanbul is the center of the Roman Empire."[37] In a book published in 1505 by Theodore Spandounes, the author argued that Mehmed II had claimed that he was descended from the Komnenian lineage of Byzantine ruling families, a prestigious and noble Greek heritage.[38] On a visit to Troy in 1462, Mehmed II inquired about the tombs of Achilles, Ajax, and the others, telling his entourage that he, Mehmed II, was avenging the Trojans and the East against the West.[39]

Establishing Provincial Rule and Managing Frontiers

Establishing provincial rule for an empire involves negotiating the relationships between the center and those who become subjugated to the center. Because empires grow gradually by gaining territory piecemeal and by defining relationships at the period of conquest, and because they remain reliant on the concept of vertical rather than horizontal integration of relations, the process of marking provincial rule and maintaining it tells us a lot about the nature and type of imperialization. The variation in provincial rule defines the structure of empire because empires involve not uniformity but diversity of rule. Center–provincial relations therefore are varied, and even within provinces, the inner and outer provinces, the frontier regions, and core regions remain different. Although it is impossible to provide a full analysis of the Ottoman provincial or frontier system, we can assemble our thoughts around a few organizational principles and their effects. Although Ottoman expansion could seem disorganized, it was in fact governed by principles of expansion, conquest, and negotiation across boundaries of governance, culture, and religion that underpinned the empire's remarkable expansionary success and durability.

Similarly, the Roman and Russian Empires displayed important variation along their expansion, incorporation, and administration of territories that they saw as different. The Roman Empire displayed different forms of incorporation with different types of provinces (*provinciae*) – areas that were directly administered by the government – and regions of Allied Kings, a status assigned to those who were conquered and who administered, as friends of the emperor,

---

[36] Lowry, *The Nature of the Early Ottoman State*, 119.

[37] Cited in Halil İnalcık, "An Overview of Ottoman History," in *The Great Ottoman-Turkish Civilization*, vol. I, 41.

[38] Hakan Karateke, "Legitimizing the Ottoman Sultanate: A Framework for Historical Analysis," in *Legitimizing the Order: The Ottoman Rhetoric of State Power*, ed. Hakan T. Karateke and Maurus Reinkowski (Leiden, The Netherlands, and Boston: Brill, 2005), 1352.

[39] Julian Raby, "East & West in Mehmed the Conqueror's Library," *Bulletin du Bibliophile* 3 (1987): 296–318; Stefanos Yerasimos, "Türkler Romalıların Mirasçısı mıdır?" *Toplumsal Tarih* 116 (2003): 68–73.

free cities where treaties maintained the power and prestige of the old forms of legal and military institutions. A last category included those communities with no special status.[40]

In the Russian Empire, variations in the incorporation policies of empires can be discerned by looking at the imperial state responding to the conditions on the ground. Incorporation into the Russian Empire was attempted in three different ways, each a combination of the local social structures that the conquerors found and the manner in which they understood and interpreted these realities on the ground. The Russians gave most favored lord status to Ukrainian elites that they incorporated, colonial status to the elites in Kazakhstan and to other Muslim elites, and adopted an integralist perspective in the Baltic states. That is, they perceived that the Ukrainian elites would become part of the imperial elites and therefore provided them with opportunities to do so, while they colonized the Kazakh elites only to the extent that they would become mediators between the Russian center and their own communities. Russians perceived the Muslim communities to be tribal and did not expect their elites to be more than mere intermediaries, so they empowered them as such. Finally, Russians negotiated a third alternative with the established and developed Baltic states, which were to be ruled only indirectly through their German aristocratic elites. Although the Ukrainians were to adapt to the core culture to become part of the imperial elite, in the Baltic case, the Russians who found themselves in the region had to adapt to the peripheral culture. It is in these established forms of incorporation that we see the nature of imperial rule, where the initial definition of a province and its later administrative articulation resulted from scrutiny of conditions on the ground.[41]

The Ottoman Empire exhibits remarkable variation and complexity across frontiers and provinces. The patterns of the Ottoman processes of incorporation do not entirely reproduce those of the Russian Empire, yet the Ottomans made some similar decisions based on their reading of local conditions and power relations. First, they valued provinces for their potential contribution to empire, whether financial, territorial, or cultural/symbolic. Some areas were of clear economic value, such as the province of Egypt, whereas others were of clear military and strategic value, such as the Hungarian province that maintained an important frontier and could be subject to irredentist claims because a large part of its historic kingdom was under Habsburg rule. Furthermore, the border with the Habsburg Empire remained contested and was the site of military campaigns and political negotiation. There were also regions that had more symbolic value than real military or fiscal importance. These were important to maintain and subdue, but this was done with relatively peaceful means.

[40] Andrew Lintott, *Imperium Romanum: Politics and Administration* (London and New York: Routledge, 1993).

[41] David D. Laitin, *Identity in Formation: The Russian-Speaking Populations in the Near Abroad* (Ithaca, NY and London: Cornell University Press, 1998).

Second, Ottoman power and practice had the effect of altering local social structures. The Ottomans created new economic opportunities, brought an influx of new populations, and often brought in new roads and urban facilities that changed the manner in which locals lived. Ottomans took over native systems of rule, entered into negotiated state–regional compacts, and learned to rely on local knowledge, making distinctions between areas that could be incorporated and assimilated, such as the Balkans where elites were granted favored status, and other regions that might just be kept in a form of mild integration as long as resources were allowed to flow to the center. Overall, Ottomans showed tremendous flexibility and ease, accepting local institutions, languages, and organization.

Third, the Ottomans employed different timing and styles of incorporation, using tools of accommodation. They integrated privileged foreign elites before assimilating them completely. Especially in the core provinces, the timing of accommodation and assimilation was different. In the distant border provinces, they imposed less, left arrangements supple and variable, and adapted to local conditions lest they be confronted by strong rivalries. The Ottoman-Safavid border region was one such area that affected the forms of internal provincial arrangements. By far, the most variation in center–provincial arrangements was found in the East, where frontiers were permeable and regions went in and out of Ottoman rule, and where political and ideological contestation remained significant.

Fourth, modern province and frontier studies emphasize the notions of identity, discourse, and ideology. The relationship between frontiers and modern notions of sovereignty and identity in modern nation-states is quite robust. In contrast, overall imperial provincial rule had less to do with religious differences because empires by definition accepted diversity along various dimensions, especially, religion. Religious ideology, however, could become consequential when rivalries between empires were represented in ideological and religious or confessional terms. In the Ottoman Empire, religious ideology came into play when it was imposed from the outside, especially in the struggle between Sunnî and Shia visions of Islam, during war with the Safavids.

Finally, scholarship on empire has traditionally looked at the effects of imperial power on subject populations, analyzing the manner in which imperial states, armies, and elites fashioned the peoples and the institutions they encountered. Rarely has the locality been taken into consideration in terms of its influence on the political culture of the state itself. Particularly in the Ottoman Empire, which emerged with such a local articulation, we have to evaluate the impact of incorporation on imperial thinking and institutional development. The most momentous example of this was the Islamization of the Ottoman Empire. The Ottomans who first conquered the Christian populations of the Balkans had balanced a hybrid empire and had worn their religion rather lightly. The effort at that time to convert the masses was minimal, and conversion was a means to create loyal military and administrative elites. The Ottomans also understood, as I argued in Chapter 2, that they were not numerous enough to overwhelm the enemy and that they would have to rely on the locals for administration.[42] Local Christian populations, in contrast, saw the advantages of joining the conqueror, either for political or economic reasons, often simply to avoid the *cizye*, the tax on non-Muslims. The extension of the empire toward the East and the conquest of the Arab provinces crystallized and solidified an imperial Islamic identity, one that strengthened the hand of Islamic institutions in the empire.

The most reputable studies of the Ottoman Empire simplify for the lay reader, dividing the empire between the core provinces (*tımarlı*) and the outer provinces (*salyaneli*), which separated direct rule from indirect rule.[43] The core provinces were ruled directly through the *tımar* system, the main land tenure institution. The outer provinces, either farther away or not fully conquered, became the *salyaneli* provinces, left to different arrangements of indirect rule where local administration otherwise remained relatively untouched. The first form represented a secure relationship with the region of assimilation – here, the Balkans, similar in ways to Russian Ukraine – where indigenous populations and elites were perceived as similar and open to assimilation. The second form in regions that were far away from the center and outside the reach of the empire was administered as military and economic outposts. Changes occurred that moved provinces from one form of rule to another, based not only on the local state arrangements, but also on where the region was located. That is, as the empire expanded, frontiers became closer territories, bringing about expected changes in rule. For example, the province (*sanjak*) of Adana had been a hereditary patrimony since early Anatolian dynasties had ruled in the area, but it became a regular Ottoman province as the Ottomans were able to extend their frontiers eastward.[44] By the time the province reached the eighteenth century, as discussed in Tamdoğan-Abel's study, Adana had become a regular core Ottoman province.[45]

Salyaneli provinces were organized around tax farming as the main revenue collection method. The governor general of the region who was involved in tax farming was to draw his salary from the collected amount and send the rest to the central treasury. For example, in the distant Arab provinces – Egypt,

---

[42] This point has been made most forcefully by Heath W. Lowry, both in *The Nature of the Early Ottoman State* and *Fifteenth Century Ottoman Realities: Christian Peasant Life on the Aegean Island of Limnos* (Istanbul: Eren, 2002).

[43] I do not elaborate on the numbers and the basic administrative structures of these provinces because they have been presented in many works. See, for example, Halil İnalcık, *The Ottoman Empire: The Classical Age 1300–1600* (London: Weidenfeld and Nicolson, 1973); I. Metin Kunt, *The Sultan's Servants: The Transformation of the Ottoman Provincial Government 1550–1650* (New York: Columbia University Press, 1983); Colin Imber, *The Ottoman Empire 1300–1650* (New York: Palgrave Macmillan, 2002).

[44] Gabor Agoston, "A Flexible Empire: Authority and Its Limits on the Ottoman Frontiers," *International Journal of Turkish Studies* 9:1–2 (1993): 15–31.

[45] Işık Tamdoğan-Abel, "Les Modalities de L'Urbanité dans une Ville Ottomane," Ph.D. thesis, Ecole des Hautes Etudes en Sciences Sociales, Paris, 1998.

Yemen, Abyssinia, Lahsa, Southern (Basra) and Northern (Baghdad) Iraq, northern Libya, Tunis, and northern Algeria – which had been assigned governors and governors general, revenue collection was locally farmed out to tax farmers, thereby providing salaries for the officials, revenue to maintain a local army, and a surplus to send to the central treasury.[46] The similarly more distant provinces of the Balkans, which were never fully conquered and assimilated – Moldavia, Wallachia, Transylvania, and Dubrovnik – were tribute-paying principalities to which the Ottomans granted self-government in return for an annual tribute to the empire's treasury. In these distant lands, the Ottomans were flexible; they allowed the princes to rule as they pleased, although in return they demanded revenues and some political-military loyalty expressed by "be friend of our friends and enemy of our enemies."[47]

In the Balkans and Anatolia, where we see the core values of the Ottoman system at work, the Ottomans systematized an administrative system based on careful balancing of central versus local interests. Overall, the cooptation of elites followed a two-tiered process that first incorporated local elites and nobilities as vassals of the empire, and only later assimilated them as genuine Ottoman provincial officials. Vassalage was a form of indirect rule that was followed by the second step, direct rule, when Ottoman land tenure arrangements could be fully implemented. The more entrenched the nobility in the area, the more difficult it was for them to accept Ottoman rule. Perhaps the differences between the Balkans and the Anatolian Peninsula were ironic because Anatolian Turkish families were much less willing to accept Ottoman rule than were Christian elites in the Balkans.[48] In the Balkans, direct control was possible practically by the reign of Beyazıd I (1389–1402), whereas the local Anatolian dynasties were not subdued until the reign of Mehmed II (1451–1481) and even his grandson Selim I (1512–1520). For a long time, these dynasties resisted participating in the imperial campaigns, doing so only when they expanded westward and the government seemed to be restoring land and maintaining ties with the old Anatolian beys.

In general, vassalage, initiated with the first Balkan conquests, allowed local landowners to remain on their land, to maintain their religion and become Ottoman vassals, and to see themselves as privileged Christians. The benefit of vassalage was that it left the local leadership in place, but as vassals who had to participate in the Ottoman campaigns and fight alongside the sultans. This early process fit with the policy of accommodation (*istimalet*), a strategy of encouraging local populations and nobilities to accept the new rule through

---

[46] İnalcık, *The Ottoman Empire*, 107; Agoston, "A Flexible Empire," 17.

[47] Viorel Panaite, "The Voivodes of the Danubian Principalities: As Haraçgüzarlar of the Ottoman Sultans," in *Ottoman Borderlands: Issues, Personalities, and Political Changes*, ed. Kemal Karpat with Robert W. Zens (Madison: University of Wisconsin Press, 2003), 58–78.

[48] Irene Beldiceanu-Steinherr, "Loi sur la Transmission du *Timar* (1536)," *Turcica* 2 (1979): 89–90.

incentives and concessions before they became fully incorporated.[49] In a second round, the *tımar* system was established, opening the way for the Islamization of Christian Balkan landed elites. In some regions, Islamization was completed rather quickly, such as in the Bulgarian lands where the process was complete by the end of the fifteenth.[50] In other regions of the Balkans, Christian *tımar* holders remained part of the Ottoman army as Christian soldiers in the early sixteenth century.[51] In addition, the Ottomans retained the Byzantine *pronoia* land system that was very similar to the *tımar* land administration. Given that the Seljuk articulation of the practice (*ıkta*) derived from their knowledge of forms of land tenure, it made even more sense to adopt the *pronoia* wholesale. This way not only did they not disturb existing arrangements that worked, but they also remained faithful to their own practices. Consequently, it seems that Ottomans simply incorporated Serbian and Greek *pronoia* holders as Christian cavalrymen, calling them *tımar* holders.[52] These vassals were then given a status similar to Russian most favored lord, ensuring further assimilation into the imperial system. This soon-to-be Islamicized nobility was now part of the provincial military and administrative structure of the empire, having gained a status equivalent to that of the conquering elite.

Even more Christians gained relatively privileged positions, including the *"voynuks"* or *"martolosi,"* a variety of auxiliaries and guards who were exempted from taxation. These were the lesser Balkan nobility, the Christian *voynuks* of Bosnia, Serbia, Macedonia, Albania, Thessaly, and Bulgaria, who became men of Ottoman military status with commensurate status in the Ottoman army, the ability to stay on their lands (albeit with different requirements), and the possibility of advancement in the Ottoman administration (if they chose to convert to Islam). Special status and privileged positions in the administrative hierarchy were meant as incentives to join imperial ranks.[53] The

---

[49] Halil İnalcık, "Ottoman Methods of Conquest," *Studia Islamica* 2 (1954): 103–129; "The Status of the Greek Orthodox Patriarch under the Ottomans," *Turcica* 21–23 (1991): 407–437. Such tactics were widespread among empires, especially as David Laitin discusses for the Russian and Soviet Empires in "The National Uprisings in the Soviet Union," *World Politics* 44 (October 1991): 139–177.

[50] Dennis P. Hupchick gives the example for the conquered Bulgarian lands in his "Orthodoxy and Bulgarian Ethnic Awareness under Ottoman Rule, 1396–1762," *Nationalities Papers* 21:2 (1993): 77.

[51] Halil İnalcık, "Stefan Duşandan Osmanlı Imparatorluğuna: XV. Asırda Rumeli'de Hiristyan Sipahiler ve Menşeleri," *Fuad Köprülü Armağanı/Melanges Fuad Köprülü* (Istanbul: Ankara Üniversitesi Dil ve Tarih-Coğrafya Fakültesi Yayınları, 1953), 207–248.

[52] Vryonis, "Byzantine Legacy," 273–274.

[53] It seems that Beyazıd I (1389–1402) was the only sultan among the early rulers to provide an alternative style of conquest through his swift, fierce, and decisive campaigns. Under him, vassals and other remnants of pre-Ottoman military groups were quickly transformed into members of the Ottoman provincial army paid in land (prebend or in Turkish *tımar*). He had therefore pushed further the reconstruction of incorporated territory into an Ottoman domain. Yet, the defeat at Ankara would wreak havoc with these domains. İnalcık, "Ottoman Methods of Conquest," 103–127. See also Fikret Adanır, "The Ottoman Peasantries, c. 1360–c. 1860,"

economic taxation and legal institutions that were left intact just made the task easier. Christian secretaries in the service of the sultan in the provinces were to further ease the communication problems, bringing together a people, inscribing their practices, and using their language in an administrative arrangement that was foreign, yet open to others. It is not surprising, therefore, that the tax system of Ottoman Anatolia and the Balkans was complex and mixed, and that scholars found elements of Islamic, Mongol, Byzantine, Armenian, and Slavic tax systems in the records.[54] What the Ottomans clearly demonstrate then is an ability to incorporate and introduce Christians and other conquered populations into the growing Ottoman polity and society, here making the *askeri* status one of the key mechanisms of integration and assimilation, comparable to citizenship in Rome.

Although it is impossible to survey the extensive variation of forms, comparisons of different regions demonstrate the logic of empire at the frontier provinces. I look first at the example of two *timar* provinces. Overall, in the southern Balkans and the Aegean Islands of the Greek archipelago, the imperial government often relied on the Byzantine and local Christians to perform administrative tasks. On the island of Limnos, the Ottomans not only left a very small military contingent, but they also depended on the local Christian auxiliary units – a few of the converted Janissary men – to protect and administer the island. That Limnos was conquered after a bitter struggle with the Venetians (1463–1479) seemed not to worry the Ottomans, who left a contingent of only twenty military men on the island in 1490. By 1519, there were fifty-three *timar* holders making a Janissary garrison.[55] Ottomans continued the Byzantine *pronoia*, assigning state agricultural revenues to cavalrymen who would tax peasants to maintain small military posts, and the typical practices of land sales, protection of the islands, the role of the peasantry in local defense, and other key local institutions.[56] Making concessions that were visibly contrary to the typical Ottoman landholding rules, they allowed landholders to transfer their lands to their sons because heredity was already established as a practice on the island. The Ottomans must have believed that they enjoyed the support of the Christian inhabitants of the islands because they so easily

---

in *The Peasantries of Europe from the Fourteenth to the Eighteenth Centuries*, ed. Tom Scott (London and New York: Longman, 1998), 278; and Georges Castellan, *Histoire des Balkans, XIVe–XXe Siècle* (Paris: Fayard, 1991).

[54] Halil İnalcık, "Osmanlılarda Raiyyet Rüsumu," *Belleten* 23:92 (1959): 575–610; Ömer Lutfi Barkan, *XV ve XVI Asırlarda Osmanlı Imparatorluğunda Zirai Ekonominin Hukuki ve Mali Esasları, I, Kanunlar* (Istanbul: Burhaneddin Matbaası 1945); Vryonis, "Byzantine Legacy," 276.

[55] Lowry, *Fifteenth Century Ottoman Realities*, 23.

[56] See also Speros Vryonis, "Local Institutions in the Greek Islands and Elements of Byzantine Continuity during Ottoman Rule," *Godishnik na Sofiski a Universitet Sv. Kliment Okhridski* 83:3 (1989): 1–60; Anthony Bryer and Heath Lowry, eds., *Continuity and Change in Late Byzantine and Early Ottoman Society* (Birmingham, UK: University of Birmingham, 1986).

left only twenty men in 1490. Also, these low numbers could partly be the result of a "severe manpower shortage," which Lowry believes helped make the Ottomans more accommodating.[57]

In contrast, the defense of the frontiers with Hungary was much more costly in men and resources. The nature of the tripartite division of Hungary, its strong polity, and the permanent role of the Habsburgs made this province and the frontier regions virtual strongholds. Hungary's dealings with the Ottomans started with Süleyman I (1520–1566) in 1521, when the key defense systems in southern Hungary and Belgrade were occupied, and by 1526, the Hungarian feudal army was defeated at the Battle of Mohacs. Not long after, in 1541, Süleyman occupied Buda, the capital of Hungary, and incorporated central Hungary into Ottoman territory. If we look at the activities that transpired around the Hungarian frontiers and hinterland, we see that the Ottomans were uneasy with regard to this region. Their incorporation of Hungary required much investment in manpower and resources, although little in terms of settled communities and their social and cultural institutions.[58] That is, here Ottomans did not seek to alter local social and cultural institutions, but clearly spent much time and resources in altering the defense structure of the land. In the 1520s, the total number of Ottoman soldiers who were in Balkan fortresses was 27,000, in Hungary alone 18,000, and this number was to increase over time. If we add the number of *tımar* holders in this region, then the total number of soldiers numbered 30,000.[59] Recent research also shows that there was a steady stream of volunteers in this region, adding as much as 20% to the already existing numbers.[60] Furthermore, Ottomans moved from the outer frontiers toward the inner provinces to build an elaborate fortress system that would hold military forces large enough to fight the enemy, protect the local population, and expand when necessary. This was the result of much greater insecurity within this territory and the need to man numerous fortifications between the Ottomans and the Hungarians, as well as in the Habsburg Empire.[61]

It is within this complex system of military institutions that *tımar* holdings, local arrangements, and compromises fit next to one another, creating direct and indirect rule in the same territory. Special land arrangements in which the Hungarian nobility and the Ottoman governors shared the administration, jurisdiction, and taxation duties implied that peasants paid both their

[57] Ibid., 27. See also Lowry, *The Nature of the Early Ottoman State*.
[58] For the dearth of cultural institutions in the Ottoman part of Hungary, see Gabor Agoston, "Muslim Cultural Enclaves in Hungary under Ottoman Rule," *Acta Orientalia Academiae Scientiarum Hung* 45:2–3 (1991): 181–204.
[59] Geza David and Pal Fodor, "Introduction," in *Ottomans, Hungarians, and Habsburgs in Central Europe: The Military Confines in the Era of Ottoman Conquest*, ed. Geza David and Pal Fodor (Leiden, The Netherlands: Brill, 2000), xi–xxvii.
[60] Pal Fodor, "Making a Living on the Frontiers: Volunteers in the Sixteenth Century Army," in *Ottomans, Hungarians, and Habsburgs in Central Europe*, 229–265.
[61] Klara Hegyi, "The Ottoman Network of Fortresses in Hungary," in *Ottomans, Hungarians, and Habsburgs in Central Europe*, 163–193.

Hungarian and Turkish overlords. As Gabor Agoston relates, this seemed natural to contemporaries holding these positions, who corresponded quite oddly about this form of possession: "Your village, Nagyegros, is in my possession in Turkey, I mean, it is in your possession in Hungary."[62] Hungary required more in terms of resources, manpower, and investment, whereas the island of Limnos practically ruled itself for the empire.

Not only much farther away from the political center of the empire, the eastern frontier was much less tidy or well demarcated. Selim I was credited with having altered the geographical scale of the empire and driven the Ottomans eastward. Two forces in the East hindered Ottoman security and expansion: Shah Ismail of Iran and the Mamluks of Egypt. The defeat of Ismail in 1514 initiated the conquest of eastern Anatolia and its incorporation into the larger empire. Two years later, with the defeat of the Mamluks in 1516, came the major conquests in the Arab world – Syria, Jerusalem, and Egypt – opening the way to further expansion. In this region, the military and ideological battle with the Safavid Empire made the Ottomans pay even more attention to local arrangements, power structures, and elites because they were wary about cross-frontier fertilization, attempts by the shahs to infiltrate Ottoman territory, and the impact of population movement across porous frontiers. At the heart of the military and ideological frontiers of the empire, what kind of bargain would bring the most security was crucial. The geopolitics of a region, the relative threat to the empire, the religious and ethnic composition of the area, and the strength of its local elites affected the negotiations between the government and the local groups.

Two different regions of present-day Iraq were incorporated in ways that suggest different state-local administrative elite negotiations. It was much harder for the Ottomans to control the province of Basra where the population and elites were mobile and commercially successful, However, Mosul, an important military outpost for the Ottomans that was crucial to the geopolitics of the region, turned out to be more easily controlled through the cooptation of a reliable, settled, and influential local elite.[63] That Mosul and Basra were at the frontier with the Safavids and that Hungary was contested between the Habsburg and the Ottoman Empires, as well as having its own independent territory, made the Ottomans set policies but continually recalibrate them to fit these politically unstable regions.

The more Ottomans engaged in war on multiple fronts, and the more significant their territorial gains, the greater the need for accommodation and flexible provincial and frontier arrangements. This was especially true of the Süleymanic era, when the Ottomans were also assuming their new role as the leaders of the Islamic world. The conquest of Iraq was settled with great

[62] Agoston, "A Flexible Empire," 24.
[63] Dina Rizk Khoury, "Administrative Practice between Religious Law ('Sharia) and State Law (Kanun) on the Eastern Frontiers of the Ottoman Empire," *Journal of Early Modern History* 5:4 (2001): 328.

care, and when they conquered Baghdad, the Ottomans were fully committed to the best accommodation possible to demonstrate the benefits of association with the Ottoman Empire. So, while the Safavid governors had collected heavy taxes, the Ottomans abolished these taxes, providing the population with important financial and subsistence relief.[64] In the Hijaz, the Ottomans not only maintained the area, but also spent resources on the provisioning of the Holy cities, Mecca and Medina. Here, issues regarding the Islamic legitimation of the empire led to the design of an entirely more constrained policy of incorporation.[65]

In the intermediate zones of the Ottoman-Safavid struggle, the Ottoman government granted eight Kurdish tribal leaders the position of governor (*sanjak beyi*) and awarded their domains as family properties (*ocaklık* or *yurtluk*), arrangements premised on the fact that lands and tribes would be passed on to the descendants of the leaders. Five more tribes were rethought as administrative categories of *hükümet* lands exempt from taxes but subject to state control. In return for special privileges such as heritable land and status, the Ottomans stipulated that the Kurdish tribal leaders join the army when appointed by their governor-general.[66] The *hükümet sanjaks* of the empire were the most autonomous of the possible arrangements that the Ottomans contracted in eastern Anatolia. Another province of tremendous political import, Diyarbakır, had became a buffer zone between the Safavids and the Kızılbaş rebels of Anatolia, and therefore was worth many concessions by a state eager to stop frontier interference. Here there was no trace of *timar* arrangements or even standard bookkeeping with an eye to revenue management. Instead, there was intense negotiating, trading of incentives, and threats of military intervention. In the eastern provinces during the seventeenth century, the trend was toward the transformation of regular Ottoman provinces (*sanjaks*) into *hükümet sanjaks*, where much more autonomy was allowed.[67] The net effect of frontier contestation and distance away from the center was the carving of significantly looser arrangements whereby local chieftains felt the weight of Ottoman control only lightly, and felt independent and empowered to maintain the rivalry between states.

Lest we assume that such a spirit of negotiation was always possible, we should consider the conquest of Crete at the end of the seventeenth century. Crete, another Greek island, long under Venetian rule, confronted a different

[64] Rhoads Murphey, "Süleyman's Eastern Policy," in *Süleyman the Second and His Time*, 228–248.

[65] Suraiya Faroqhi, "Trade Controls, Provisioning Policies, and Donations: The Egypt–Hijaz Connection during the Second Half of the Sixteenth Century," in *Süleyman the Second and His Time*, 131–143.

[66] İnalcık, "An Overview of Ottoman History," in *The Great Ottoman-Turkish Civilization*, 61–63. The best piece on this topic is Agoston, "A Flexible Empire"; see also Mehmet Öz, "Ottoman Provincial Administration in Eastern and Southeastern Anatolia: The Case of Bitlis in the Sixteenth Century," in *Ottoman Borderlands*, 143–155.

[67] Agoston, "A Flexible Empire," 20–22.

set of challenges that the early conquerors had not imposed. The public administration of Crete did not resemble that of Limnos nearly two centuries earlier. The more relaxed the Ottomans were about their rule and their dependence on Byzantine institutions in Limnos, the more anxious they seemed to be in Crete. They established much stricter rule, despite the demise of the *timar* system and despite the seeming havoc of Ottoman administration. They also made Crete into a new province and established a series of officials to administer the island.[68] Oddly, Ottoman officials and administrators in Crete relied on the Sharia. The typical Ottoman land regulations, which had usually been part of secular law (*kanun*), were now undermined and replaced by a perspective that insisted "that the land and tax regime on the island be established in accordance with the seriat or Islamic law."[69] Between the conquests of the Balkans and of this Aegean island, the Ottomans had expanded eastward, with Selim I adding Egypt, Syria, Mecca, and Medina – the Holy places of Islam – to the Ottoman Empire. Had Islam now become the main conquering and legitimating force of the empire?

Establishing Control: A Segmented Society and a Flexible Economy

The overall Ottoman model of rule was based primarily on the vertical integration of elites and corporate groups into the political system with flexibility evident in the state's willingness to allow for different styles of incorporation. Along dimensions of revenue management and geopolitical strategy, especially relating to distance from the center and threats to the empire, the central authorities and local power holders came to important agreements that were all predicated on some form of vertical integration. This was true for the social control and administration of the empire and for resource collection and economic management of commerce, provisioning and trading activity. Working from the center toward periphery, and periphery toward center, the imperial elites made different arrangements with the locals, reflecting their mutual strengths and interests.[70]

Although most scholars acknowledge the vertical integration of elites into the state as a significant aspect of Ottoman state power, they do not take the next step to underscore the degree to which these vertically integrated elites also remained separate. For one thing, elites were incorporated and assimilated from different regions and at different times, with some variation. However, other state policies, such as rotation, in their unintended consequences reinforced integration toward the state, keeping elites separated from one another like the spokes of a wheel. The result was state control that was exerted through ties from the periphery to the center, with elites responsive to the center rather than to one another. Strong vertical relations from locality to center developed,

---

[68] Most of my information on Crete comes from Molly Greene, *A Shared World: Christians and Muslims in the Early Modern Mediterranean* (Princeton, NJ: Princeton University Press, 2000).

[69] Ibid., 26.

[70] Agoston, "A Flexible Empire," 15–31.

but left local groups and communities relatively weak and unconnected. The accompanying political culture that emphasized strong ties to the center encouraged a diffuse social disorganization and consequently hindered the development of autonomous corporate entities throughout the empire.[71]

At the local level, control over resources and institutional flexibility worked together. At the micro level of daily practice, the surveyors of the state flagged differences and local particularities, and helped the state adjust, negotiate, and separate according to indigenous practice. Ottomans started very early surveying and registering the conquered populations. They insisted that the essentials – the land structure, the produce, and the required revenues – be carefully inscribed by officials and maintained as land records (*tahrir*) for the next set of officials to acknowledge, abide by, and amend. İnalcık, who calls these registers "the doomsday books" of the Ottoman Empire, emphasizes the degree to which they were meant both to determine all available sources of public revenue and to be basic reference books in the government offices of the empire.[72] The *tahrirs* were the records of the resources and manpower that existed in the provinces as they became incorporated. In this task the *tahrir* officials, the traveling bureaucrats, have been described as inconsequential, as the slight footmen of a powerful central administrative machinery. On the contrary, these men actually forced the local onto the center. In the formidable detail they related to the center, these men seemed to say, "Unless you understand the particularities of these regions, towns, and communities, it would be unfair to tax them in routine fashion," confirming by their work the facts and figures on the land and the previous surveys. Significant changes in the provincial tax districts were carried out after a three-way negotiation process that entailed reaching a consensus among survey officials, the local population, and the central government.[73]

For a large part of its existence, the Ottoman Empire was a large agrarian empire where the interests of the state determined economic and agrarian policy. As it grew, the Ottoman economic system was based on the principle of control of basic factors of production, that is, land, labor, and capital. From the direct ownership of land to the control of physical capital and labor enterprises, as well as the restrictions on labor mobility, it would be easy to classify the Ottoman system as a strict command economy with a centralized state at the helm. Yet, overall, the Ottoman state fiscal machine demonstrated a relative degree of flexibility over a long period of time. That is, it was able both to maintain control over the vital resources of the empire, varying and adapting

---

[71] For a detailed version of this argument, see my *Bandits and Bureaucrats* and idem, "In Different Times: Scheduling and Social Control in the Ottoman Empire, 1550–1650," *Comparative Studies in Society and History* 38:3 (1996): 460–483. For the argument on the lack of corporate bodies in the Ottoman Empire, see Şerif Mardin, "Power, Civil Society, and Culture in the Ottoman Empire," *Comparative Studies in Society and History* 11 (1969): 258–281.

[72] Halil İnalcık, "State, Sovereignty and Law During the Reign of Süleyman," in *Süleyman the Second and His Time,* 83.

[73] Rhoads Murphey, "Ottoman Census Methods in the Mid-Sixteenth Century: Three Case Histories," *Studia Islamica* 71 (1990): 115–126.

its needs and consequent exploitation of these resources, and to alter the forms of fiscal arrangements over time.

The expansion of the Ottoman principality was based on a grant of land (*timar*) in return for service, thereby establishing an agrarian system at the very base of the empire. At the very core of the agrarian system was the family farm unit, a basic productive, fiscal, and administrative form of land exploitation based on the Byzantine model, where a peasant family lived and paid taxes to the state. The landed cavalrymen who were to collect taxes from the peasants administered a given region and maintained themselves and their armies. A simple yet also sophisticated administrative superstructure was constructed above the small agrarian units, which maintained order and stability. Lest these military/administrators become entrenched in a local region, ally with the peasantry, and disrupt local production or rebel against the state, they were rotated every 3 years and sent to other provinces. With rotation, they were often transferred to new regions where they would have to reintegrate themselves and acquire new peasants and clients. On top of such transition problems, often the villages to which they were assigned were not contiguous, making both tax collection and organization difficult.[74] Despite hardships and lack of autonomy, the prebendal cavalry must have been pulled in by the dominant logic of acquisition of land as a state reward. As such, from the lowest level of the *timar* to the highest levels of the governors, provincial men moved, breaking their local ties, learning about new areas and new practices, but remaining loyal to the Ottoman sultan.

In the cities, local production was based on the guild system. The awkward monetarization of the rural economy was certainly overshadowed by the fluidity of monetary exchanges in urban milieus. Institutions and practices such as guilds, money lending, long-distance and international trade, and state collection of *mukataa* revenues were all based on a more extensive money economy.[75] Yet, we should not overemphasize the monetary fluidity of the state. We know that the Ottoman state could not pay decent wages to craftsmen and workers engaged in state projects; they used a blend of administrative coercion, slave labor, and low wages to get local populations to join in state projects. In lieu of wages, the state often offered exemption from certain taxes, access to raw materials at lower prices, and sometimes guaranteed outlets for goods produced.[76]

---

74 Much of this information on the hardships of the local provincial officials comes from my *Bandits and Bureaucrats*. The assignment of noncontiguous villages could easily have been the result of the manner in which land parcels were recorded in the central state office; it might not have been a state-planned policy to separate peasants from officials and disrupt their relationships.

75 Şevket Pamuk, "Money in the Ottoman Empire," in *An Economic and Social History of the Ottoman Empire, 1300–1914*, ed. Halil İnalcık and Donald Quataert (Cambridge, UK: Cambridge University Press, 1994), 947–953.

76 Suraiya Faroqhi, "Labor Recruitment and Control in the Ottoman Empire (Sixteenth and Seventeenth Centuries), in *Manufacturing in the Ottoman Empire and Turkey, 1500–1950*, ed. Donald Quataert (Albany: State University of New York Press, 1994), 13–57.

Mehmet Genç has argued that three main principles – fiscalism, provisionism, and traditionalism – guided Ottoman economic reasoning.[77] These have been interpreted as being formal, rigid, and interventionist. All three of these principles, but especially fiscalism and provisionism, meant that the state engaged in a high degree of economic policing. Yet, as demonstrated by the basic laxity in Ottoman control of the monetary system after the fifteenth century, Ottoman state makers also had a keen understanding of the limited extent of their economic and political reach. Fiscalism, the main guiding policy of a centralized bureaucratic empire, ensured that all levels of the bureaucracy strove for the maximization of treasury income, viewing all economic activity as a source of tax income.[78] Provisionism, the second principle, was based on the principle that the Ottoman capital city especially, as well as other cities and markets, were to be maintained cheaply and reliably with a steady supply of goods and services. Finally, traditionalism was an attempt to maintain the status quo, not to shake up the system too much, and to rely on past experience to define the future.[79]

The Ottoman economic mind was part fixed by such fiscal understandings, part adaptable given the scale and diversity of imperial financial arrangements. A carefully monitored taxation system specified the amount, the potential augmentation and the form of collection according to each category of individual and group. From early on, the most important taxes were the poll tax (*cizye*) – the Islamic tax on non-Muslims – an onerous tax that varied from region to region and tended to increase with the accession to the throne of new sultans and the revenues from *mukataas*, mostly tax farms. The *mukataas* included various revenues from mints to mines, to customs dues, to market dues. The fiscalism of the empire was moderated by its inability to maintain a coherent and cohesive monetary system throughout the vast lands under imperial control. Many conquered regions maintained their coinage, and many foreign coins made the rounds of Ottoman markets.[80] Şevket Pamuk argues that despite the Islamic prohibition on interest, the development of credit institutions in the empire was remarkable. Many studies of court records actually demonstrate the networks of credit, lenders, and borrowers around the many towns of the empire.[81] Pamuk also contradicts the research of many traditional historians who have argued that the state regularly imposed artificial price ceilings

---

[77] Mehmet Genç, "19. Yüzyılda Osmanlı Iktisadi dünya Görüşünün klasik prensiplerindeki değişmeler," *Divan* 1:6 (1991): 1–8.

[78] Mehmet Genç, "Ottoman Industry in the Eighteenth Century: General Framework, Characteristics, and Main Trends," in *Manufacturing in the Ottoman Empire and Turkey*, 60.

[79] Ibid.

[80] Pamuk, "Money in the Ottoman Empire."

[81] Şevket Pamuk, "Institutional Change and the Longevity of the Ottoman Empire 1500–1800," *Journal of Interdisciplinary History* 35 (Autumn 2004): 225–247; idem, "Osmanlı Ekonomisinde Devlet Müdahaleciliğine Yeniden Bakış," *Toplum ve Bilim* 83 (Winter 1999/2000): 133–145; Ronald Jennings, "Loans and Credit in the Early 17th Century Ottoman Judicial Records: The Sharia Court of Anatolian Kayseri," *Journal of the Economic and Social History of the Orient* 16 (1973): 168–216; Karen Barkey and Ronan van Rossem, "Networks

(*narh*) in the markets. Through studies of Istanbul courts, he demonstrates that such price ceilings and controls were established only in periods of extraordinary economic instability. Although the state intervened much more frequently in the economic processes and guilds of Istanbul, it neither had the capacity nor the interest to intervene in all the towns of the empire. Such examples provide us again with a sense that despite such formal assessment of imperial needs, the Ottomans were pragmatists and only cautiously interventionist in economic matters. In these matters, the Ottomans were on a par with the Byzantine state, which was neither interested in commerce and economic institutions, nor had the capacity to seriously manipulate them.[82]

Despite a certain inherent lack of interest, the establishment of Ottoman rule, connected many zones of commerce, redrawing trading zones that became pockets of international influence. Foreign and local merchants, state officials, and appointed provisioners followed the lucrative path of resources, developing local economic zones and linking them to international trade routes. Some of these zones remained from pre-Ottoman times and represented important trade routes; others were developed based on Ottoman needs and new territorial connections made through conquest. For example, Bursa continued to be one of the most famous silk entrepots between the East and the West. The Balkans became the breadbasket of the empire, and expanded trade in other foodstuffs and raw materials, with Dubrovnik serving as a key port between the Balkans and the Western world. Not only did the Black Sea continue as the link between eastern Europe and the Ottomans, but together with the Aegean Sea it settled into a closely knit zone of commerce where various groups met to buy and sell foodstuffs, raw materials, and slaves.[83]

Provisioning, whether through internal trade routes or sometimes through international channels, directed economic expansion as it brought necessary and valued goods into the empire. Regions were developed to respond to Ottoman provisioning needs, such as the plains of Thrace, the Danubian Basin, Bulgaria, the steppe from Dobruja to the Don River, the plain of Thessaly, western Anatolia, and Egypt, areas focused on feeding Istanbul.[84] Especially after the sixteenth century, both trading and provisioning created lengthy and well-traveled transportation networks and market hubs in the empire. Such provisioning needs led to the settlement of populations in certain areas, such as the Turcoman and Tatar *yürüks* who were forcibly settled in the Dobruja steppe to grow grain for Istanbul.

of Contention: Villages and Regional Structure in the Seventeenth Century Ottoman Empire," *American Journal of Sociology* 102: 5 (March 1997): 1345–1382.

[82] John Haldon, in his paper titled "Empires and Exploitation: The Case of Byzantium," presented at the Social Science History Institute, Stanford University, 2001, compares Byzantium to the Italian city-states with which the empire was trading to demonstrate the degree to which Byzantine merchants were neither helped nor appreciated.

[83] For a much more complete image of the trading zones of the empire, see İnalcık's contribution in *An Economic and Social History*, 179–380.

[84] Ibid., 180.

To jump-start commercial linkages and to provision the palace and the elite, the Ottomans gave trading privileges – capitulations – or friendship pledges to those nations they favored and used such concessions as a form of international alliance making. The capitulations provided those members of European nations holding pledges the ability to travel and trade unhindered within the Ottoman realm as long as they paid the required customs duties. In return, Ottoman traders were to be treated similarly in foreign ports. It was mostly non-Muslim merchants who relied on the capitulations in order to have Ottoman protection abroad, and who established merchant colonies abroad in places such as Venice, Ancona, and Lwow. Ottoman officials tracked the foreigners and regulated their behavior, especially through customs zones. These became especially important as centers where considerable state resources were collected and where trading networks coalesced. The Ottomans might have inherited both the idea and the actual customs zones from the Roman and Byzantine Empires. Customs zones were both centralized and decentralized at the same time. The Ottomans maintained customs zones as central economic-fiscal units under the tax farming system. However, because the tax farm could be delegated and broken up into smaller units, many local ports had their own customs houses. This led to a composite of customs zones, complete with their separate regulations and rates. Ships were to arrive at designated districts, and caravans had to travel supervised roads and pass through specified custom houses. Foreign and indigenous merchants became accustomed to operating within these zones of control and restriction, finding ways of bypassing regulations, bribing officials, and even sometimes developing alternative provisioning routes. At the same time, these trading zones became important webs of interaction, with customs becoming hubs where foreign merchants encountered state officials and local intermediaries.

Legitimating a Normative Order

In all empires, rulers have had to justify their governments and to clarify their actions to maintain their legitimacy. Legitimacy means that rulers uphold an effective and ordered government where subjects feel secure. For Weber, domination is legitimate when the subjects recognize, obey, and consider domination to be acceptable, or at least tolerable and not worth challenging.[85] Legitimacy is not maintained just by the actions of the ruler, but also by the willingness of those who are subordinate to believe in the legitimacy of the ruler's claims. The legitimate ruler claims the right to be in power, and the population accepts this claim.

In the context of this study, the question of longevity is closely related to that of legitimacy. We have to assume that the Ottoman Empire, as well as the other long-lasting empires, were legitimate enough that they were not violently

---

[85] Max Weber, *Economy and Society*, ed. Guenther Roth and Claus Wittich (Berkeley: University of California Press, 1978).

challenged and overthrown. To return to my original argument regarding imperial domination, empires that dominated large territories for a long time were able to organize their empires to draw resources from them, to successfully manage multiethnic and religious populations, and to develop a supranational and relational form of legitimacy over their populations. The legitimation of empire is dynamic, constantly renewing itself and adapting to the challenges of domination. It includes many internal relational aspects (justice, security, welfare, and order), as well as a broader discourse that ties these internal components to supranational understandings of the role of the ruler and his government.

Many imperial states maintained authority over their populations through the legitimation of a supranational ideology that included a religious claim to be protectors of a world religion: Islam or Christianity, for example, which they connected to an elaborate ideology of descent and lineage. The supranational imperial ideology was a symbolic expression of rule, the glue that offered the spiritual cohesion of the elite upper classes of the empire, encouraging their participation. When empires confronted each other in the international arena, they developed such ideologies partly in relation to each other, as was the case with the Ottoman and the Habsburg Empires. The Habsburg monarchy was based on the expansion of one dynasty through alliances and skillful marriages over time, and on its special position as the holders of the crown of the Holy Roman Empire, the protectors of Roman Catholic Christianity, and the guardians of a central European culture, if not more generally of Europe, especially against the Turks. The Habsburg dynasty's sense of itself and its legitimacy was derived especially from being a European empire opposed to and threatened by the East. Similarly, the Russian Empire saw one of its main legitimating tasks to be the protection of the Orthodox Christian Church, but in relation to the Ottoman Empire, this ideology grew to incorporate safeguarding the Orthodox populations living under Islam. Imperial military victories, international acclaim, and fear and respect from other political entities are all ingredients of this form of legitimacy.

The Ottoman Empire also developed a supranational ideology based on the Ottoman dynasty representing the realm of Islam against the infidels. Yet, although the dynastic element was always there, the Islamic segment of the supranational idiom was not always clearly articulated or used. The dynasty descended from the first legitimate ruler, Osman, and the principle of rule by the members of the House of Osman was the simplest and deepest source of legitimacy for the Ottomans. Ottomans played around with elaborate lineages, but settled on a rather forceful but also simple genealogy that tied them back to the tribe of Oghuz Khan, the legendary Turkic leader in Central Asia.

The Ottomans built a strong dynastic legitimation that accepted and promoted only the descendants of Osman as the legitimate heirs to the throne. Rulers were dethroned later in history after fierce discussion about the legality of such action and its validation through a *fetva* (written answer to legal question) of the Şeyhülislâm. When they were deposed, moreover, sultans had to be replaced by members of the House of Osman. No other dynasty had any claim to the throne of the Ottomans. It is important to ponder the consequences of such attention to the principle of maintaining the primacy of one household. First, it did not hinder the development of alternative important households; they flourished, as we will see, after the mid-seventeenth century. Yet, these other households competed among themselves, not for the throne, but rather for the favors of the imperial household. Second, that the focus was on the rulers rather than on the "empire" made the Ottoman different from Rome or Byzantium, but also different from the more modern European imperia. Rome, then, as well as the European Atlantic empires, existed much more as an *empire*, where rule was subordinate to empire. The Russian example was intermediate in the sense that "belief in and hope for a harmonious Muscovite political family" was at the root of a strong unifying myth for all members of the empire until the transformation that Peter the Great achieved an impersonal and remote bureaucracy as a mediator between the ruler and his subjects.[86] At the end, the Ottomans and the Habsburgs were more ready to change the political form and the institutions of empire, but were both quite loyal to their ruling houses.

Most empires had a distinctive central concept that provided members of society with an important sense of belonging, giving meaning to the subjects' aspirations that cut against remaining remote from the essence of imperial domination. In the Roman Empire, such meaning was based on a combination of liberty, patriotism, and ambition, distinct ways in which the Roman center managed its imperialist goals while remaining stable for a long time.[87] In the Ottoman Empire, legitimacy was based on the notion of a normative order that produced concrete and reproducible relations between the ruler and his subjects. This normative order was imagined and maintained by the Ottomans in the concept of a well-ordered society (*nizam-i âlem*) in which the relations between the ruler and his people remained reciprocal. The concept of justice (*adâlet*) was an internal pillar of state–society relational forms of legitimation. Such legitimation was understood in terms of a larger theory of the state adapted by the Ottoman thinker Kınalızâde, the Circle of Equity, a basic compact between state and society that emphasized not only state supremacy, but also justice as state protection. Accordingly,

> There can be no royal authority without the military
> There can be no military without wealth
> The subjects produce the wealth
> Justice preserves the subjects' loyalty to the sovereign
> Justice requires harmony in the world

[86] Valerie A. Kivelson, *Autocracy in the Provinces: The Muscovite Gentry and Political Culture in the Seventeenth Century* (Palo Alto, CA: Stanford University Press, 1996), 14–15.
[87] Doyle, *Empires*, 85.

The world is a garden, its walls are the state
The Holy Law orders the state
There is no support for the Holy Law except through royal authority[88]

This compact, among the oldest Islamic and central Asian-Turkic teachings, was the foundational component of rule whereby the state was defined, judged, and legitimated by how well it dispensed justice to the people. The expectation of justice was deeply embedded in everyday practice, with the people eager to ensure and preserve the distribution of justice by the state. In practice, every petition that came to the center asking those in charge to guarantee the welfare of the petitioners and every response that state officials diligently wrote back enabled the provision of justice. In symbolic terms, the compact was also renewed every Friday at the mosques throughout the empire, with rulers who were not named and prayed for during the Friday sermon considered not legitimate.[89] The sultan provided justice, and his approval rating was assessed in the mosques of the empire. That justice was centered on the sultan again underscores the importance of the house of rule to the legitimacy of empire. Even though there were significant changes in the ideological discourse and in propaganda as well as in the behavior of sultans, strong and universal legitimacy based on justice endured throughout the centuries. Sultan Süleyman was the most ardent upholder of the concept of justice, and in the sixteenth century under his patronage, this relational form of legitimacy was firmly institutionalized. Moreover, because the notion of justice is also associated with toleration, in the Ottoman case, it is clearly the case that moments of a strong understanding of justice were also periods of robust toleration.[90] In contrast, for a long period of Muscovite rule, the relations of power and fundamentals of rule were based "on mercy, personal intercession, and divine instruction," making Russian rule seem more dependent on privileged and personalized rule than its contemporaries.[91]

The sultans who consolidated the empire also defined in many ways three different periods of legitimacy, in which the particular events of their reigns, as well as their particular inclinations, fashioned an explicit content to the normative order. The reconstruction of Constantinople into an Ottoman city, the organization of religious and social welfare institutions, and finally the construction of the palace – a space both dignified for a conqueror and a ceremonial space for imperial sovereignty – were achieved and performed within the political context of power struggles, as well as within the larger cultural

---

[88] Quoted in Cornell H. Fleischer, *Bureaucrat and Intellectual in the Ottoman Empire: The Historian Mustafa âli (1541–1600)* (Princeton, NJ: Princeton University Press, 1986).

[89] İnalcık, "State, Sovereignty and Law During the Reign of Süleyman," in *Süleyman the Second and His Time*, 66.

[90] Ingrid Crepell, *Toleration and Identity: Foundations in Early Modern Thought* (New York: Routledge, 2003).

[91] Kivelson, *Autocracy in the Provinces*, 277.

umbrella defined by the early Ottomans. It is in this time period that the contradictions of some of these actions speak to the diversity of the empire and
the perceptive multivocal signaling that was carried out by Mehmed II. The
triumph of Islam was clear in the pronouncement of Abu Ayyub al-Ansari, the
patron saint of an Ottoman Islamic city, and in the conversion of churches and
other Christian edifices into mosques and religious schools (*medreses*), Hagia
Sophia being the most famous example. In an act of war, but also an act of
religion, Constantinople saw the enslavement and removal from the city of
more than 30,000 of its Christian inhabitants.[92] The Sufi Şeyh, Aq-Şemseddin,
accompanied Mehmed II later for the first prayers at Hagia Sophia, and was
also charged with finding and marking the tomb of the prophet's companion.
Such actions facilitated becoming an empire that claimed universal legitimacy.
The empire, which had roots in the central Asian steppes, was now declared
heir to the Roman and Byzantine Empires, destined to combat and unite these
previously distinct worlds, those of Latin Christianity, eastern Orthodox Christianity, and its own faith, Islam.

If the initial encounter of the Turcoman principalities were with Christianity
and its Byzantine representation, the second major forceful "encounter" of the
Ottomans was with Islam in the Arab provinces. Centuries of cross-frontier
articulation and the final conquest of Constantinople had brought about a
degree of both institutional stability and change. This is because institutional
layering not only brought about the renegotiation of some aspects of Byzantine
and Turkic practices, but also entailed some degree of stability since on both
sides layering also maintained important elements of local rule. By the mid-
sixteenth century, the conquests of Arabia, the Ottoman–Safavid conflict, and
the increasing centralization of the state brought about a remarkable strengthening of the Islamic institutions of the empire, placing at center stage the Islamic
identity of the empire. The buttressing of Islamic institutions did not eliminate
other more multireligious and cultural forms of state–society arrangements,
but they did acquire a relatively more stringent Islamic rationalization.

The Ottoman Empire became more forcefully Islamic in its identity and
world view after the conquests in the East and the resulting changing demographic makeup of the empire. As long as the majority of the conquered peoples
were Christians, the empire bowed to the West, and therefore it did not make
sense to have stringent policies of Islamization. Islam had been the religion
of the rulers since the inception of the Ottoman principality; as such, both in
the ideals of holy war (*gaza*) and in the various institutions of rule, Islam did
have an impact on the organization of Ottoman society. After the conquest of
Constantinople, Mehmed II had converted eight churches into religious schools
(*medreses*) for famous scholars, while later the construction of the Fatih complex – a mosque and eight *medreses* – signaled not only the religious inclination
of the conqueror, but also his new integration of religious institutions into the

---

[92] Halil İnalcık, "Istanbul: An Islamic City," *Journal of Islamic Studies* 1 (1990): 7; and İnalcık,
"Istanbul," *EI²*, 4 (1973): 224–248.

grip of the state. Religious scholars were tied in as salaried officials of the state who worked in the highly sophisticated *medrese* network of the city, among them the sultan's mosque complex, which gathered the best religious minds of the realm.[93] Mehmed II nurtured relations with many Sufi dervish leaders, among them the Haydaris to whom he assigned the Aya-Marina monastery as a dervish lodge. Mehmed expropriated and angered equally the Christians from the city and the dervish and fief holders from Anatolia and Rumelia, but he also relied on an eclectic mix of Sunnî, Sufi, and Orthodox Christian advisors. Therefore, we can surmise that Mehmed never intended Islam to be the only hegemonic legitimating force in the empire.[94]

It is Selim I who is credited with having altered the population balance of the empire, making Sunnî Muslims the majority through his conquests in eastern Anatolia and the Arab territories, and through his harsh policies toward the Kızılbaş (redhead) Shiite groups of Anatolia, who backed the Safavids against the Ottomans.[95] He was also less tolerant of the Sufi leadership. The increasing centralization of the state had led to the radicalization of the Sufi element who therefore became eager to support the enemy of the Ottomans. Selim I dealt a harsh blow to these groups, signaling the further centralization and strengthening of the state.[96] The turning point in Ottoman self-identification came with Selim's great victories against the traditional axis of the Islamic world and culture. With such military expeditions, classical Islamic civilization, which had arisen in Arabia, finally reached the Ottomans. Selim was adorned with the title of Muslim Caliph (although he did not use this title) and was sent the keys to the Holy Cities by the Sherif of Mecca in 1517. From then on, confronted in the East with the rising forces of Shah Ismail and his infiltration of Ottoman Anatolia with Shiite forces, sultans would increasingly define themselves in the Sunnî Orthodox tradition.

The addition of important Arab territory and sites of Islamic culture rene-gotiated Ottoman identity. The old reliance on the Byzantine elites diminished, partly as the natural result of their previous assimilation into the empire and their Islamization, and also because a new pool of ideological and admin-istrative manpower would now join the center at Istanbul. The "new men"

---

[93] Franz Babinger, *Mehmed the Conqueror and His Time* (Princeton, NJ: Princeton University Press, 1978).

[94] İnalcık, "Istanbul: An Islamic City," 4.

[95] Rudi Matthee, "The Safavid–Ottoman Frontier: Iraq-I Arab as Seen by the Safavids," in *Ottoman Borderlands: Issues, Personalities, and Political Changes*, ed. Kemal Karpat with Robert W. Zens (Madison: University of Wisconsin Press, 2003), 157–173.

[96] Irene Beldiceanu-Steinherr, "Le Regne de Selim Ier: Tournant dans la Vie Politique et Religieuse de l'empire Ottoman," *Turcica* 6 (1975): 34–68; Markus Dressler, "Inventing Orthodoxy: Competing Claims for Authority and Legitimacy in the Ottoman–Safavid Conflict," in *Legit-imizing the Order: The Ottoman Rhetoric of State Power*, ed. Hakan T. Karateke and Maurus Reinkowski (Leiden, The Netherlands, and Boston: Brill, 2005), 151–173; Yusuf Kucukdag, "Precautions of the Ottoman State against Shah Ismail's Attempt to Convert Anadolu (Anato-lia) to Shia," in *The Great Ottoman–Turkish Civilization*, ed. Kemal Çiçek (Ankara: Balkan Ciltevi, 2000), 181–193.

were not Byzantine elites anymore; they were Islamic religious scholars who filled the ranks of the *ulema* and who crowded the *medreses* and slowly but surely transformed Ottoman imperial understandings of rule. As a result of his Muslim conquests, Selim I had imported numerous Muslim learned men into the Ottoman bureaucracy, and had endowed and developed many religious schools and complexes in Istanbul, by which he managed to make the empire much more Muslim in its identity. Selim I inaugurated a period of greater religious orthodoxy, a form of Sunnî zealotry that was, however, in the tradition of Mehmed II, strongly harnessed by the state. Süleyman strengthened his predecessors' legitimacy by inscribing it into law and making a move toward organized, legalistic, and scriptural Islam.

Conclusion: The Role of Islam

The question of Islam remains germane to discussions of legitimacy, partly because many empires used religion as a way to legitimize imperial rule, and also because Islam has been made into one of the most important components of the Ottoman Empire. The Arab predecessors of the Ottomans, the Umayyad and Abassid Empires claim Islam as their major ideological, legitimating force, and the Ottomans' contemporaries, first the Byzantines and then the Habsburg and Russian Empires, claimed an ideological component through religion that represented their empire to the world. There is no doubt that Islam was important in the "identity" of empire, but more as a self-consciously constructed and strategically displayed one, rather than an overriding distinctiveness that made the Ottomans clearly different than others. The outward international dimension undoubtedly had an impact on the internal dynamics of how state, society, and religious institutions related to one another, although the internal material and the relations that were forged as states imperialized defined the role of religion.[97]

It is fair to say that Ottoman Islam's role in the empire was constrained by the structural position in which Islam was embedded. We can claim Islam as part of the identity of the empire, especially after the conquests of Selim I, but we have to be careful about this claim because Islam was not ideationally or

---

[97] Much has been written on the question of religion in the Ottoman Empire, but the work of two Turkish scholars, Şerif Mardin and Ahmet Yaşar Ocak, stands out. As Ocak tells us, there are four different realms in which Islam presents itself: the state; the *medreses* and *ulema* (religious education); the Sufi, heterodox segment; and popular folk Islam. Although this differentiation is certainly representative, it is really the relations among the four sectors that will give us an understanding of Islam in the empire and its role. Şerif Mardin, "Power, Civil Society, and Culture in the Ottoman Empire"; idem, "Religion and Secularism in Turkey," in *Atatürk: Founder of a Modern State*, ed. Ali Kazancıgil and Ergun Özbudun (Hamden, CT: Archon Books, 1981), 192–195; and idem, "The Just and the Unjust," *Daedalus, Journal of the American Academy of Arts and Sciences*, 120: 3 (Summer 1991), 113–129. For Ahmet Yaşar Ocak, see "Islam in the Ottoman Empire: A Sociological Framework for a New Interpretation," in *Süleyman the Second and His Time*.

institutionally dominant in the empire; we cannot use Islam to explain both the identity and all the basic structures of the Ottoman Empire.[98] Especially if as in the Weberian tradition, we see religion to be complex, varied, and assembled from a combination of institutional and ideational structures. Religion in the empire was a world view, a set of ideas, institutions, and practices that actors believed, interpreted, and lived their lives according to.

The reasons why Islam was not institutionally dominant are complex, yet can be analytically summarized. First, Islam was tamed mostly because the empire's construction and relations with it were carefully balanced from early on, with the Greek-Byzantine element as the counterpoint. Second, the particular construction of the Ottoman state was such that it maintained and nurtured an important separation between religion as an institution and religion as a system of meanings and relations that connected a community of faith. Religion as an institution would help administer the empire. Religion as a system of beliefs would provide the tools for everyday practice. The two were not entirely separate; they were connected in the person of the judge.

The state also facilitated a pattern of negotiating between alternative legal and institutional frames, between dualities that allowed the state both to segment and integrate religion along multiple dimensions, making religious institutions compliant to its interests. The sultan maintained control over sultanic (*kanun*) and religious (Sharia) law, and maintained both heterodox and orthodox leaders at the palace, often playing them against one another. There is no doubt that the Ottoman state benefited from tensions between Sunnî and Sufi and Sunnî and Shi'ia practices, from the division of secular and religious law, and especially, from the embodiment of such tensions in the person of the magistrate, the religious official versed in both religious and secular law.

That is, Islam could be publicly welcomed as the great universal religion that would bind the empire together and provide legitimacy to the imperial house of rule. Yet, it could also be brought in and its institutionalization marked by existing conditions and shaped by the rulers to adapt to their superiority. In what Mardin has called the "empiricism of Ottoman secular officialdom," Ottoman rulers embarked on a bid to build a religious elite and an educational system that would be controlled by the state.[99] Thus, although Islam was understood as the religion of the state, it was subordinated to the *raison d'état*. Religion functioned as an institution of the state, and its practitioners emerged only as state officials. There was therefore an intricate relationship between Islam and the state in which the state provided for the flourishing of Islam as an institutional practice, with the *medreses*, the *ulema*, and the positions

---

[98] Here, I wholeheartedly agree with Halil Berktay, who argues that the Western tradition and its followers have erroneously identified the Islamic tradition as the main component through which they think they can explain the empire. See his "Studying 'Relations' or Studying Common Problems in Comparative Perspective," in *Chrétiens et Musulmans à la Renaissance: Actes du 37e Colloque International du CESR*, ed. Bartolomé Benassar and Robert Sauzet (Paris: Honoré Champion Editeur, 1998), 313–315.

[99] Mardin, "Religion and Secularism in Turkey."

they held. In return, "Ottoman Islam bestowed sacredness on the concept of sovereignty and, at the same time, performed an active function by providing a means of governing."[100]

The role of Islam as an institutional structure, as an ordinary branch of the state bureaucracy, or as an ideational system with its pervasive cultural frame of action changed according to the exigencies of rule and the relations between the state and religious institutions. Although Mehmed II, Beyazıd II, and Selim I had harnessed Islam as they accommodated to the natural balance of the imperial population and their needs, Sultan Süleyman applied himself to the institutions of Islam because he wanted to expand the physical and intellectual capacity of and grow the numbers of students in the medreses. First, creating a sophisticated group of learned scholars to represent Sunnî Islam, particularly of the Hanafi school, helped set the Ottomans apart. But second, as the empire expanded, more administrative power and therefore also more magistrates (*kadıs*) would be needed, who would also be much better educated and finer representatives of the state in the empire. Under Süleyman, they reached every corner of the imperial lands. Given that their livelihoods and their careers were dependent on state rewards, these men were fully integrated into the state and acted on behalf of its maintenance both as a religious Islamic state and as a secular bureaucratic state. At the top of the religious hierarchy, the Şeyhülislâm was the source of spiritual advice and companionship to the sultan and the author of religious opinions on matters of state and empire. The sultan appointed the leader of the religious community of Ottoman Islam, but the grand vizier appointed all other members of the religious hierarchy. In such a move, we see the dependence once again on the state for positions and rewards. Religion had been subjugated to the state. However, the state had also acquired the most well-organized bureaucratic machinery in the Islamic world. Therefore, part of Islam in the Ottoman world was an organizational, administrative Islam.

The manner in which Islam became administrative under Ottoman rule animated another important set of relations between the state and the people. The local magistrate became the intermediary between state and folk, between high culture and folk culture, and between literate society and illiterate understandings of religion. The role of the *kadıs* was manifold; they were the administrators of the empire, and they were also entrusted with the maintenance of basic moral and cultural unity through the application of religious law (Sharia) and Sultanic law (*kanun*), both as judges and as *medrese* teachers. They were bred and educated in the religious *medreses*, and then spent time in retraining, especially in secular and regional law; they went out into the provinces and cities of the empire as men of the empire; and they adjudicated according to the Sharia and sultanic law, but were much more than representatives of Islam in the empire. They were the main intermediaries between the state and the

---

[100] Ocak, "Islam in the Ottoman Empire," 188.

people. They tied the state to the people; they were the source of unity between center and periphery. As such, they could not just be religious men; they had to be religious men of the center. In this sense, the mixture they represented would have seemed odd to a medieval Catholic man. For the common folk, the Ottoman administrator represented both Islam and the state.

In the routines of daily court practice, the *kadıs* reproduced the demands of the Sharia: that they watch over the lives of those who were of Islamic faith. They both watched for transgressions against Islamic precepts and helped define the parameters of Islamic practice. That is, they performed Islamic practice, and even though they ruled in religious and customary local terms, they still represented the institution of Islam and connected people to the religion and its forms of thinking. The way in which they carried out their practice – listening to cases, judging in Sharia terms, and abiding by religious regulations – richly conveyed a sense of Islamic identity to the people. When common folk came to court asking for justice between adversaries, and the *kadı* ruled as the representative of the sultan, all members of the community were reenacting an old traditional Islamic concept of the just ruler. Beyond the performance side of this relationship, the fact that the religious official and the religious court offered resolution, clarification, support, and relief to the inhabitants of a region focused the people on religion and its day-to-day signs and symbols. The court was among the most important source of linkage between the state and religion because it functioned parallel to the mosque and the Sufi lodges, and worked to satisfy the spiritual needs of the people while administering them.

Clifford Geertz sees religious patterns as "frames of perception, symbolic screens through which experience is interpreted; and they are guides for action, blueprints for conduct."[101] To the degree that Islam was "the bedrock of the Ottoman social system," it was shared by Ottomans of high and low status, and many different art forms were used to bridge this relation with Islam.[102] In these ways, religion functioned to repeatedly confirm through everyday life the shared legitimacy of a system of beliefs for the people and for the state.

As such, Islam then helped define relations to the outside world, but more importantly, it both facilitated the administration of the empire and the crucial integration of the people into the state. Religion was the mechanism of integration, and the magistrate was the tool with whom the state implemented this important connectivity. Therefore, it was perhaps not just the conquest to the East and the Sunnî–Shia rivalry that helped the Ottomans define themselves in Sunnî religious terms, but it was more the administrative and organizational aspects – the crucial state–society connectivity constructed by the networks of

---

[101] Clifford Geertz, *Islam Observed: Religious Development in Morocco and Indonesia* (Chicago: University of Chicago Press, 1968), 98.
[102] Mardin, "The Just and the Unjust," 119–120. See also Walter Andrews, *Poetry's Voice, Society's Song* (Seattle: University of Washington Press, 1985).

the magistrate – that helped hold the empire together and vertically integrated. Such a conclusion gives us an insight into at least one aspect of the construction of religious imperial legitimacy. Force of circumstance made the empire lean more toward Islam, but administrative needs helped solidify its role. To assess this argument further, we need to turn to the issue of religion and diversity in empire.

4

Maintaining Empire: An Expression of Tolerance

[L]et us suppose two churches – the one of Arminians, the other of Calvinists – residing in the city of Constantinople. Will anyone say that either of these churches has right to deprive the members of the other of their estates and liberty (as we see practiced elsewhere), because of their differing from it in some doctrines and ceremonies, whilst the Turks in the meanwhile silently stand by and laugh to see what inhuman cruelty Christians thus rage against Christians?[1]

Let us get out of our grooves and study the rest of the globe. The Sultan governs in peace twenty million people of different religions; two hundred thousand Greeks live in security in Constantinople; the muphti himself nominates and presents to the emperor the Greek patriarch, and they also admit a Latin patriarch. The Sultan nominates Latin bishops for some of the Greek islands, using the following formula: "I command him to go and reside as bishop in the island of Chios, according to their ancient usage and their vain ceremonies." The empire is full of Jacobites, Nestorians, and Monothelites; it contains Copts, Christians of St. John, Jews and Hindoos. The annals of Turkey do not record any revolt instigated by any of these religions.[2]

John Locke wrote the "A Letter Concerning Toleration" in the seventeenth century; Voltaire wrote *Toleration* a century later. Both remain key texts that transcend the times and places of their composition. They both refer to the Ottoman form of government and the Turk as tolerant, and their observations are in sharp contrast to the harsh realities of medieval and Reformation Europe.

The contemporary literature on religious and ethnic diversity in the Ottoman Empire has adopted the term "toleration" to refer to the relatively persecution-free centuries of early Ottoman rule. This toleration in the empire has been

[1] John Locke, "A Letter Concerning Toleration" (with an introduction by Patrick Romanell) (Indianapolis: Bobbs-Merrill Educational, 1955).

[2] Voltaire, *Toleration and Other Essays*, translated with an introduction by Joseph McCabe (New York and London: Knickerbocker Press, 1912), 23.

contrasted to the "persecuting society" of the medieval West.[3] As the West banished its Jews, enclosed them in small and filthy ghettos, burned their heretics, unleashed its inquisitors among its own people, and tore apart the fabric of society in religious wars, the realms of the Ottomans were mostly peaceful, accepted diversity, and pursued policies of accommodation (*istimalet*). Especially for the Jews of Islamic countries, historical analyses maintain that they suffered much less persecution than did their brethren in medieval and Reformation Europe.[4] Most scholars provide an explanation that lies with Islam as a body of religious thought and practice that classifies non-Muslims, Jews, and Christians as protected people. According to Islam, they argue, as long as these groups recognized their second-class status, they were protected. This emphasis on religious and cultural reasons for toleration leads us away from the political, economic and mainly administrative functions of toleration in a multiethnic, multireligious empire.

This chapter develops the organizational basis for toleration. I argue that toleration as it developed was a way to qualify and maintain the diversity of the empire, to organize the different communities, to establish peace and order, and to ensure the loyalty of these communities, and had little to do with ideals or with a culture of toleration. Toleration is neither equality nor a modern form of "multiculturalism" in the imperial setting. Rather, it is a means of rule, of extending, consolidating, and enforcing state power. Toleration is therefore one among many policies of incorporation such as persecution, assimilation, conversion, or expulsion. I define toleration as more or less the absence of persecution of a people but not their acceptance into society as full and welcomed members or communities. Toleration refers to the relations among different religious (and ethnic) communities and secular authorities, and is the outcome of networked, negotiated, and pragmatic forms of rule.

Whereas toleration emerged to provide a sense of imperial order and an organizational advantage to the state, it also grew to mean something specific in the context of the Ottoman Empire; it referred to a cultural understanding that, as a rule, non-Muslims would not be persecuted. No doubt, as *dhimmis*, according to Islam, they were second-class citizens with certain prospects and some disabilities who endured a healthy dose of daily prejudice. They would be tolerated as long as they did not disturb or go against the Islamic order. If they did transgress, their recognition could easily turn into suppression and persecution. Moreover, the Ottoman understanding – similar to the Roman conception – was that difference was tolerated because it had something to contribute. That is, difference added to the empire; it did not detract from it, and therefore, it was commended. Toleration had a systemic quality; maintaining

[3] R. I. Moore, *The Formation of a Persecuting Society* (Malden, MA: Blackwell, 1990).

[4] Mark R. Cohen, *Under Crescent and Cross: The Jews in the Middle Ages* (Princeton, NJ: Princeton University Press, 1994); and "Persecution, Response, and Collective Memory: The Jews of Islam in the Classical Period," in *The Jews of Medieval Islam*, ed. Daniel Frank (Leiden, The Netherlands: E. J. Brill, 1995), 145–164.

peace and order was good for imperial life, and diversity contributed to imperial welfare.

Empires have shown much variation in how to treat and incorporate different ethnic and religious groups. Among the predecessors of the Ottoman Empire, Rome can be distinguished with regard to its ability to permit the existence of many diverse peoples, religious groups, and cults, embracing a religious pluralism that was the result of the polytheistic character of the Roman religion. It is only with the rise of Christianity and its threat to Roman paganism that the empire incited the persecution of Christians.[5] In contrast, the eastern Roman Empire, Byzantium, was not only torn by religious strife, but overall it used toleration sparsely and only when needed. The Byzantines assimilated and empowered the elites of various groups that they had conquered, but were not very willing to tolerate much religious variation, and tried as hard as possible to convert Jews and Muslims.[6] In the Byzantine Empire, the closer relationship between religion and the state, the particular religious struggles around Orthodox Christianity, and the greater cultural imperialism of the Byzantines led to much greater pressure on different religious groups.

The contemporaries of the Ottomans, the Habsburgs and the Russians, also faced similar questions of toleration and persecution as they extended their frontiers. In the Habsburg case, in which toleration was the exception rather than the rule until the eighteenth century, persecution was the result of the particular moment at which the consolidation of the Habsburg Empire occurred, bringing it fully into the religious controversies of the Reformation. The Habsburgs emerged from the Holy Roman Empire with strong Catholic institutions and values that not only were fully fused with the political order, but that also enhanced their view of themselves as the guardians of Christendom. The Habsburgs consolidated through a policy of "confessional absolutism," which had three essential features: centralization, princely predominance of the estates, and the advancement of Catholicism.[7] The result of this consolidation was persecution, forced conversion, and assimilation. The Habsburg Empire became more tolerant as it assimilated the lessons of diversity and began to value the economic gains that diverse commercial populations brought to the empire in the eighteenth century under the rule of Maria Theresa and her son, Joseph II.

The Ottoman and Russian policies toward diversity are comparable in many respects, especially with regard to state pragmatism, flexibility, and toleration,

[5] Perez Zagorin, *How the Idea of Religious Toleration Came to the West* (Princeton, NJ, and Oxford, UK: Princeton University Press, 2003), 4–5.

[6] George Ostrogorsky, *History of the Byzantine State* (New Brunswick, NJ: Rutgers University Press, 1957); Cyril Mango, *The Oxford History of Byzantium* (Oxford, UK: Oxford University Press, 2002).

[7] Charles Ingrao, *The Habsburg Monarchy 1618–1815* (Cambridge, UK: Cambridge University Press, 1994); Robert Bireley, S. J., "Confessional Absolutism in the Habsburg Lands in the Seventeenth Century," in *State and Society in Early Modern Austria*, ed. Charles W. Ingrao (West Lafayette, IN: Purdue University Press, 1994), 36–53.

although in Russia the history of state–religious group relations is more criti-
cally interspersed with episodes of conversion, assimilation, and standardization, and therefore, persecution. In both empires, as some groups were granted
protection and privileges, others were persecuted. The Russians wavered in
their policies toward the "foreign" or "uncivilized" peoples they encountered,
mostly under the influence of the Orthodox Church. For example, the expansion into the Khanate of Khazan in 1551–1552 started with the influence of an
Orthodox clerical elite that made for disastrous conquest and violent assimilation, which led to a period of relative peace to be interrupted by Peter I,
who renewed the antagonism against these groups as he tried to construct a
uniform imperial polity.[8] In the early eighteenth century under the auspices
of the Agency for Convert Affairs (1740–1764), the state oversaw the most
organized, sustained, and violent attack on the religious beliefs of the people of
Khazan. In Russia, especially during the sixteenth and seventeenth centuries,
a mix of state exigencies and the changing relationship between the Orthodox
Christian Church and the state lay at the basis of policies of toleration and
of persecution. In Russia, however, where strong missionary activity occurred
in which the government itself was closely involved, religious conversion was
quite different than under Ottoman rule. By the reign of Catherine the Great
(1762–1796), Ottoman and Russian rule of religious communities appeared
to be similar in the sense that the recognition and forbearance of Ottoman
religious communities could be compared to the Russian notion of "tolerated
faiths."[9] By then, given the position and the significance of the Muslim community, religion became an essential tool of imperial rule, and Muslim religious
leaders were integrated into the state, forging new institutions of Islamic authority modeled on the Orthodox Church and the Islamic religious structure in the
Ottoman Empire. What Catherine the Great accomplished in the eighteenth
century, Mehmed II had carried out after the conquest of Constantinople.

Religious, utilitarian, and strategic reasons drove imperial state elites to
incorporate and order diversity. Empires did not have tolerance or persecution
as direct goals. Rather, their goal was to maintain power and to conquer or hold
territories. Tolerance, assimilation, and intolerance were strategies designed to
order imperial society and to increase legibility to squeeze resources out of
diverse communities and to enforce allegiance to the state. "Legibility" in this
context indicates a central task of imperial states to map the conquered terrain,

[8] Andreas Kappeler, *The Russian Empire: A Multiethnic History,* transl. Alfred Clayton (New
  York: Pearson Education, 2001); Michael Khordarkovsky, "'Not by Word Alone': Missionary
  Policies and Religious Conversion in Early Modern Russia," *Comparative Studies in Society and
  History* 38:2 (April 1996): 267–293; Marc Raeff, *Understanding Imperial Russia,* transl. Arthur
  Goldhammer (original title: *Comprendre l'ancien régime russe* [Paris: Editions du Seuil, 1982])
  (New York: Columbia University Press, 1984); Robert Crews, "Empire and the Confessional
  State: Islam and Religious Politics in Nineteenth-Century Russia," *American Historical Review*
  108:1 (February 2003): 50–83.
[9] Robert D. Crews, *For Prophet and Tsar: Islam and Empire in Russia and Central Asia*
  (Cambridge, MA: Harvard University Press, 2006), 355.

the people, and the resources.[10] Along with cadastral surveys, population registers, and land recalibration comes manipulation of religious and ethnic understandings, settlement attempts, and so on. Empires exhibited four different strategies toward ethnic and religious communities: toleration, persecution, assimilation, and expulsion, which emerged largely out of imperial understandings of difference and imperial willingness to use violence.

The Ottoman Empire fared better than did its predecessors or contemporaries on this score until the beginning of the eighteenth century, largely as a result of its understanding of difference and its resourcefulness in organizing an intermediate set of corporate networks that maintained order and legibility. That is, it maintained relative peace with its various communities and also ensured that interethnic strife would not occur.

Policies of toleration or persecution in the Ottoman Empire cannot be understood as a single unidirectional narrative from toleration to persecution. Rather, periods of high insecurity and even state persecution that did occur – especially during the seventeenth century – can be understood as localized and historically particular cases that demand our analytic attention. Ottoman sultans, for example, were strongly pressured by a group of zealot Sunnî preachers (*Kadızadelis*) who tried to cleanse the realm of Jews, Christians, and especially Sufi orders such that these groups experienced high levels of insecurity. Religious and ethnic violence also happened much earlier under Selim I (1512–1520), when the most vicious state action was reserved for the Kızılbaş and Safavid supporters, who were perceived as a political threat to the survival of the Ottoman state and its rising Sunnî identity. Throughout Ottoman history, deportations and conversions took place during periods of political and economic insecurity, especially during and after war when the state elite felt most vulnerable. Ottoman settlement policy encouraged the movement of Muslims and Christians to settle border regions, forced population movements to respond to labor scarcity, or moved groups to frontiers to punish rebels among them. Although deliberate state policy was possible, it was far from uniform, organized, or premeditated.

Violence was also inflicted by individual Ottoman officials who took advantage of their positions of power to harass, exploit, and inflict serious damage on communities.[11] The following illustration makes the point. It seems that when the future Şeyhülislâm Hocazade Mesut became the judge of Bursa in 1642, he discovered that previous judges had allowed Christians to build a new church. Hocazade Mesut ordered the church to be closed because it was built despite the Shari injunction against the building of new temples and churches. When

[10] James C. Scott, *Seeing Like a State: How Certain Schemes to Improve the Human Condition Have Failed* (New Haven, CT: Yale University Press, 1998).

[11] The Armenian author Eremya Çelebi Kömürciyan in his manuscript on Istanbul in the seventeenth century provides vivid examples of such individuals who took it on themselves to terrorize non-Muslims. See his *Istanbul Tarihi: XVII. Asırda Istanbul* (Istanbul: Eren Yayıncılık ve Kitapçılık Ltd. Şti., 1988), 50–53.

the Grand Vizier heard about this, he dismissed the judge. In response, Muslim mobs in Bursa vandalized the city, although their leaders were promptly arrested and punished.[12] Although the actions of the local official and the larger populace displayed religious prejudice, the Grand Vizier in the name of the state made every effort to err on the side of the non-Muslims. Rabbi David Ibn Abi Zimra, who lived earlier, did not feel the same about state protection: "In this Diaspora, we cannot live among them except through bribes and [monetary] losses, for what shall a lamb do among the wolves, for naught will they tear out his wool."[13] The existence of numerous justice rescripts (*adâletnâme*) dispatched from the center ordering local judges to monitor such demonstrations of prejudice is itself evidence of the fact that serious breaches of tolerance occurred at the local and individual levels.

Toleration emerged as the negotiated outcome of intergroup relations and was maintained in the first three centuries of Ottoman rule, both from the top down by the state and from the bottom up by communities where each shared an interest in the maintenance of intercommunal peace and order. The state institutionalized existing religious boundaries, and adapted its rule based on an understanding of Islamic domination over diverse non-Muslim communities, molded to its own interests in governance and legibility. Local community leadership entered negotiated agreements with Ottoman rulers based on their desire to maintain their religious autonomy and community existence free from interference. The result was multiple, bounded, yet also overlapping corporate networks of religious and ethnic communities integrated into the state, where a degree of separation was desired by both sides.

Nevertheless, important transformations of state–community boundaries and relations occurred in the eighteenth century, paving the way for interethnic violence. Violence, especially in the form of large-scale state-sponsored massacres, did not occur until it was clear that the empire was not sustainable and that all constituent parts were experiencing lowered "expectations of many future interactions,"[14] making it possible for ethnic and religious violence to escalate. Such lowered expectations facilitated ethnic and religious massacres, which were administered and organized from the center and carried out at the eastern periphery of the empire. The Armenian population of the empire was

---

[12] Madeline C. Zilfi, *The Politics of Piety: The Ottoman Ulema in the Postclassical Age* (Minneapolis: Bibliotheca Islamica, 1988).

[13] Leah Bornstein-Makovetsky, "Jewish Lay Leadership and Ottoman Authorities during the Sixteenth and Seventeenth Centuries," in *Ottoman and Turkish Jewry: Community and Leadership*, ed. Aron Rodrigue (Bloomington: Indiana University Press, 1992), 87–121.

[14] Fearon and Laitin use this phrase when they explain the problems of opportunism, in James D. Fearon and David D. Laitin, "Explaining Interethnic Cooperation," *American Political Science Review* 90:4 (December 1996): 715–735. The "expectation of many future interactions" is what maintains cooperation and trust in small groups, trade associations, and so forth. However, this temporal consideration is similarly valid for states, especially as they become convinced that secession will occur or that they risk losing territory, which may cause them to abandon appropriate behavior.

by far the most victimized by the genocidal unraveling of ethnic and religious corporatism. Chapter 8 provides analytic insight into the grievous mistakes that led to this tragic turn of events.

It is important to provide a historical narrative of the moment of institutional integration at which relations between the state and the communities were formalized. In the historical process whereby particular circumstances and explicit organizational and cultural frameworks came together, an institutional recalibration of sorts occurred as a result of the mixing and layering of old and new institutional operations. Given different community arrangements, the three main groups – Orthodox Christians, Jews, and Armenians – were incorporated and administered differently. The main similarity was the establishment in each case of intermediaries who managed relations for the state. These were either religious or secular community leaders, who displayed a keen interest in maintaining authority over their communities because they had everything to gain from their position and its privileges. For an extended period of time, the interests of the state and those of the community leaders coincided. Three analytic themes undergird the different historical narratives: (1) the identification of boundary markers in Ottoman society; (2) the institutionalization of an ad hoc system of state–religious community relations; and (3) the role and control of the intermediary authorities. However, first I examine what has been said on this topic.

The historiography of Ottoman religious and ethnic relations has fluctuated widely, from representations of the "terrible Turk" toward much more benign depictions of hybridity, toleration, and intercultural understanding. The first image brings to mind a rigid multiplicity that was separated and defined, with little positive interaction. In the second, the hybridity of a class of travelers, scholars and mystics, and merchants has been stretched to include all, extrapolating from the rather unusual experience of a few. More balanced is the view presented by Aron Rodrigue in which Ottoman Islam did not lead to an essentialized version of intergroup relations, but rather to a framework where religion, language, and structure provided the milieu in which groups interacted,[15] although the danger here is that such a view underestimates the degree to which Islam was pervasive in Ottoman society and provided the litmus test for political inclusion.[16] Islam provided a clear political identity; a state-sponsored version of Islam was institutionalized by members of the religious elite (*ulema*) and was diffused from the top down into the far reaches of Ottoman society.

From another viewpoint, the notion of a "millet" system, an organization for diversity established from the initial moments of the conquest of Constantinople, has been sharply criticized. According to Benjamin Braude, there

---

[15] Aron Rodrigue, "Difference and Tolerance in the Ottoman Empire," *Stanford Humanities Review* 5:1 (1995): 81–90.
[16] Bruce Masters, *Christians and Jews in the Ottoman Arab World: The Roots of Sectarianism* (Cambridge, UK: Cambridge University Press, 2001).

was no institutionalized system until the nineteenth century.[17] By making ten-
dentious the early contacts between the sultans and religious communities, by
calling such accounts "foundation myths" that have no basis in reality, and by
arguing that Ottomans did not use the word "millet" to refer to their communities in documents, Braude misleadingly argues that all arrangements between
the state and the newly conquered groups were ad hoc.[18] As we will see, not
only is there strong historical evidence that is at odds with such a characterization, but this argument also makes little sense when we think of how states
work to increase legibility in the societies they encounter, and thus classify and
organize them.[19] Many scholars of ethnicity have argued that states through
their actions and policies can create, define, and manipulate ethnicity. If the
state organizes political access and participation along ethnic lines, then these
lines will be reinforced.[20] More important for the study of empires, whether
the state organizes around existing ethnic and religious boundaries (social and
territorial), or whether they create new administrative boundaries, they run the
risk of creating, maintaining, and reinforcing ethnicity and religious identification. Therefore, an imperial state in search of order and legibility is liable
to shape further religious and ethnic boundaries and organize them around its
own cultural understandings.

  To explain the first few centuries of relatively peaceful interreligious and
interethnic living, when neighborly relations and a kind of sociability came
about from both the presence and absence of contact, we need to pay attention
to transactions across groups and to how Ottomans lived. On the one hand,
relations organized around family, neighborhood, village, and religion and its
institutions sustained a certain kind of sociability that was community based.
Members of the same religion and community encountered one another on
family visits, holidays, and occasions in their own neighborhoods (*mahalle*).
To the degree that urban neighborhoods were separate and closed up at night,
people gathered around the familiar, the language, and the identity of the
brother. Separation, however, was mostly induced by the location of each
group's religious institution. Similarly, village life was organized around rural
needs and institutions, with local relations based on communities of people of
similar ethnic, religious, and linguistic background.

  When people of diverse persuasions lived close to one another in mixed
spaces, members of different communities finding themselves in contact were

---

[17] Benjamin Braude, "Foundation Myths of the Millet System," in *Christians and Jews in the
Ottoman Empire*, ed. Benjamin Braude and Bernard Lewis, 2 vols. (New York and London:
Holmes & Meier, 1982), 69–88.

[18] Unfortunately, such an argument in effect stymied the field of research, and many have espoused
it without much corroboration. See Daniel Goffman, "Ottoman Millets in the Early Seventeenth Century," *New Perspectives on Turkey* 11 (Fall 1997): 135–158; Michael Ursinus in his
"Millet" entry in the *Encyclopedia of Islam* (2d ed., 1993) starts to move away from such a
restrictive argument.

[19] Scott, *Seeing Like a State*.

[20] Joane Nagel, "The Political Construction of Ethnicity," in *Competitive Ethnic Relations*, ed.
Susan Olzak and Joane Nagel (Orlando, FL: Academic Press, 1986), 93–112.

often not comfortable with one another. Sometimes, the dwellings of Jews were just a little too close to the local mosque, or Greeks could catch a glimpse of the courtyard of a Muslim house, so friction was possible. However, when the men of these neighborhoods opened up their doors during the day, they entered a plural society, where they bought and sold in the marketplace and bargained fiercely to get the best merchandise; where salesmen lured their customers in Turkish, Greek, or Armenian; where Jews and Christians strove to use Muslim dress to hide their natural disabilities; and where contact created conflict, cooperation, and transgressing of social boundaries.

That there was little escalation into intercommunal violence is interesting not because there was no potential for it, but rather because state and community leaders did their utmost to contain and quash quarrels that might have escalated. For example, relations between Greeks and Jews were always tense. Greeks manipulated their Ottoman connections against the Jews, commercial rivalries exacerbated intercommunal relations, blood libels emerged in the late sixteenth century, and sometimes looting and attacks on Jews got out of hand.[21] The Ottoman state, like the Russian, throughout its history tried to use a policy of containment rather than letting religious rivalries get out of control.

Recent analyses of ethnic conflict suggest that the more communities engage in interethnic relations, especially of a formal and organized kind, the better the chances for peace among groups.[22] Ashutosh Varshney explains that such communities are strongest in resisting attempts by politicians who want to manipulate ethnic rivalries. Paul Brass contends that riot systems are formed by networks of specialists who play diverse roles in instigating, maintaining, and disseminating communal rivalries and ethnic hatreds.[23] Therefore, ethnic conflict is more likely to occur when communities are closed in on themselves, separated from others, and engaged only in intraethnic relations, and when political entrepreneurs are allowed to manipulate and use ethnic differences to their advantage. To the degree that interethnic relations are maintained by brokers, we can also argue along with Ronald Burt that a combination of conditions under which closure and brokerage occur together can enhance social capital.[24] Here, religious and ethnic communities can have dense internal relations, but if they also engage in relations that are brokered by community leaders, merchants, or religious and secular interlocutors with interest

[21] Gilles Veinstein, "Une communauté Ottomane: Les Juifs d'Avlonya (Valona) dans la deuxième moitié du XVI siècle," *État et société dans l'empire Ottoman, XVIe–XVIIIe siècles: la terre, la guerre, les communautés* (Aldershot, UK: Variorum, 1994), 781–828; Mark Mazower, *Salonica, City of Ghosts: Christians, Muslims, and Jews 1430–1950* (New York: Alfred A. Knopf, 2005), 49.

[22] Ashutosh Varshney, "Ethnic Conflict and Civil Society," *World Politics* 53 (April 2001): 362–398; *Ethnic Conflict and Civic Life: Hindus and Muslims in India* (New Haven, CT: Yale University Press, 2002).

[23] Paul Brass, *The Production of Hindu–Muslim Violence in Contemporary India* (Seattle: University of Washington Press, 2003).

[24] Ronald S. Burt, *Brokerage and Closure: An Introduction to Social Capital* (Oxford, UK: Oxford University Press, 2005).

in maintaining community, conflict does not necessarily arise. James Fearon and David Laitin focus on the strategies of group actors that ensure peace and prevent violence from spiraling. Key to averting a spiral of violence, in which one side punishes the other collectively, is self-policing, and in their view, group-to-group interactions largely unmediated by public authority.[25] More radically, Ken Jowitt employs the concept of "barricaded social entities" for groups whose "primary imperative is 'absolute' separation from what are seen as contaminating others," where such identities can lead to violence.[26]

In the Ottoman Empire, because religious identity determined a person's legal and political status, boundaries and belonging were essential; ethnic and religious peace could be maintained by both respecting boundaries and allowing movement across them. Therefore, a mix of relations within and across communities, brokered by boundary managers, community leaders, and state officials, was key to peace. Contrary to Fearon and Laitin, serious attempts to control spiraling conflict occurred along with robust state action. The role of public authorities in shaping the boundaries between, and the outcome of, ethnic and religious interactions needs clarification; the concept of boundaries has to be problematized more carefully. Fredrik Barth pointed out the importance of boundaries in the creation and reproduction of ethnicity when he argued that boundaries shape and canalize social life and shape social relations among groups. What occurs at the boundary has a tremendous effect on the self-definition and identification of a group as well as on its relations with others.[27] I adopt a Barthian perspective with regard to the importance of boundaries in the creation and the reproduction of ethnicity. Social boundaries existed between religious communities, in which people knew where they belonged, were clear about their religious identity, and entered into relationships fully cognizant of who the other was, and what was expected of him or her.

Similarly, a certain fluidity of relations was the result of the existence of boundaries. That is, boundaries not only separated, but also pointed out sites of weakness that were susceptible to manipulation. Where religion and key institutional policies clearly demarcated boundaries between Muslims and non-Muslims, other institutions, such as markets and especially everyday practices, made possible the flow from one category to the other (as we will see, this was unidirectional toward becoming Muslim). As if to attest to the importance of boundaries, when boundaries were blurred, people spent much time and energy trying to define them, making sure that categories were settled. Explaining interethnic and interreligious peace requires that we look at how people were

---

[25] Fearon and Laitin, "Explaining Interethnic Cooperation."

[26] Ken Jowitt, "Ethnicity: Nice, Nasty, and Nihilistic," in *Ethnopolitical Warfare: Causes, Consequences, and Possible Solutions*, ed. Daniel Chirot and Martin E. P. Seligman (Washington, DC: American Psychological Association, 2001), 28.

[27] Fredrik Barth, *Ethnic Groups and Boundaries: The Social Organization of Cultural Difference* (Boston: Little Brown and Co., 1969), 14; Charles Tilly, *Durable Inequality* (Berkeley: University of California Press, 1998).

defined and categorized, and in turn how they defined themselves in the context of their relations.

Charles Tilly helps explicate further the role of boundaries by specifying the conditions under which social transactions across boundaries vary. Both the degree of "localized common knowledge that participants in a transaction deploy" and the extent of "scripting for such a transaction that is already available jointly to the participants" are important for understanding the circumstances under which groups tend to engage in transactions across boundaries. Local knowledge includes tacit understandings, such as those about spatial go and no-go areas, and memories of earlier conversations and interactions. Scripts are models – both normative and practical – for how interaction is supposed to occur, often secured by both formal and informal rules and institutions backed by sanctions.[28] These scripts, such as Islam had for the Ottoman Empire, can specify boundaries between groups and conditions of interaction at the boundary between public authorities and groups. Yet, the separation or accommodation between groups would often result from an exchange between religious and/or public authorities and various groups, grounded in a set of local understandings and traditions. Especially when boundaries are essential to everyday discourse and relations, the fact that people are separated by a boundary becomes more important and is the focus of their behavior. As a result, when boundaries are evident, actors try to undermine them, to exploit their weaknesses; conversely, where boundaries are ambiguous, actors try to affirm them, often calling attention to their social relevance.

Political and religious authorities mark boundaries, but they are also manipulated, maintained, and recast by boundary managers, that is, brokers and interlocutors between different communities, among themselves, and with the state. Such intermediaries might be appointed by the state or by the community – sometimes both – and are different from the riot specialists of Brass's India. These boundary managers are the connective tissue between communities and the state and ensure that relations remain smooth. In the Ottoman Empire, these were the religious and secular authorities of each community who represented the state and the community.

Ottoman Tolerance: Marking the Boundaries

From very early on, a relatively strong and confident state expanding into a stable empire constructed a social order whose legibility overall tended toward toleration, not only because the state was interested in maintaining diversity and managing the resources of this diversity, but also because the communities themselves and the leadership were concerned with this issue.

The result of imperial recognition of the tremendous religious and ethnic diversity the Ottomans confronted as part of becoming imperial-led sultans, as Rodrigue maintains, to make no attempt to transform this "difference" into

---

[28] Charles Tilly, *Durable Inequality* (Berkeley: University of California Press, 1998), 53.

"sameness."[29] Difference was perceived as the norm, a condition that need not be altered, but managed. Between 1520 and 1530, the populations of seventeen principal cities in Anatolia and the Balkans in terms of households were 29,728 Muslim, 12,937 Christian, and 4,930 Jewish.[30] Because Christians and Jews, in the urban setting at least, made up more than 30% of the population, consideration first had to be given to how to run an Islamic state with non-Muslim populations ensconced in their particular religious and ecological niches. As the foundational legal and cultural system of the state, Islam provided the guidelines under which Muslim and non-Muslim communities would be incorporated into the Ottoman society and state. Islamic law and practice dictated a relationship between a Muslim state and non-Muslim "Peoples of the Book," that is, Jews and Christians. According to this pact, non-Muslims (*dhimma*) would be protected, could practice their own religion, preserve their own places of worship, and, to a large extent, run their own affairs provided they recognized the superiority of Islam. As such, Islam was pervasive and the primary marker of inclusion in the political community.[31] Its impact can be summed up in three words that described Muslim and non-Muslim communities: *separate*, *unequal*, and *protected*.

The immediate public markers of a boundary between Muslims, Jews, and Christians were codes of conduct: rules and regulations concerning dress, housing, and transportation. Jews and Christians were forbidden to build houses taller than Muslim ones, to ride horses, or to build new houses of worship. They had to make way for Muslims and engage in continuous acts of deference. For example, Minna Rozen cites two *fermâns* (sultanic decrees) in the mid-sixteenth century in which the argument is made that the distinction between Muslims and non-Muslims is blurred when non-Muslims do not abide by the clothing codes.[32] Periodically, then, sultans issued edicts describing what non-Muslims could and could not wear and the punishment necessary to maintain the hierarchical ordering of religious society. The edict of Sultan Murad IV in 1631 makes these boundary distinctions clear:

According to the religious requisites based on sharia and *kanun*, infidels are not to mount a horse, wear a sable fur, fur caps, European silk velvet, and satin. Infidel women are not to go about in the Muslim style and manner of dress and wear "Paris" overcoats. Thus

---

[29] I borrow the term "difference" from an inspirational piece by Rodrigue, "Difference and Tolerance."

[30] Because these are taken from taxation records, nontaxable populations are not included. Taken from Ömer Lütfi Barkan, "Essai sur les données statistiques des registres de recensement dans l'empire Ottoman au XVe et XVIe siècles," *Journal of the Economic and Social History of the Orient* 1 (1957): 35.

[31] Benjamin Braude and Bernard Lewis, "Introduction," in *Christians and Jews in the Ottoman Empire: The Functioning of a Plural Society* (New York and London: Holmes & Meier, 1982), 1–34; C. E. Bosworth, "The Concept of Dhimma in Early Islam," in *Christians and Jews in the Ottoman Empire*, 37–51; Masters, *Christians and Jews*, 17–40.

[32] Minna Rozen, *A History of the Jewish Community in Istanbul: The Formative Years, 1453–1566* (Leiden, The Netherlands, and Boston: E. J. Brill, 2002), 21.

they are to be treated with contempt, made submissive, and humbled in their clothes, and styles of dress. For some time, however, these rules have been neglected. It has been communicated to my felicitous threshold and made known that with the permission of the magistrates, infidels and Jews go about in the marketplace on horseback and wear sable fur and sumptuous garments. When infidels encounter Muslims in the marketplace they do not get off the pavement, and they and their women have become the possessors of more pomp and circumstance than the people of Islam. Since it is imparted to my exalted ears, and communicated and made known to my felicitous threshold that they are not being treated with contempt, or made submissive and humble, act accordingly and henceforth do not allow such things to take place. This time it is my command that such acts be hindered by means of the appointed agent, the model of his peers and equals, one of those on my current imperial campaign, Mustafa, may his value increase! I order that when it arrives, act upon my order proclaimed in this matter. Insult and humiliate infidels in garment, clothing, and manner of dress according to Muslim law and imperial statute. Henceforth, do not allow them to mount a horse, wear sable fur, sable fur caps, satin, and silk velvet. Do not allow their women to wear mohair caps wrapped in cloth and "Paris" cloth. Do not allow infidels and Jews to go about in Muslim manner and garment. Hinder and remove these kinds. Do not lose a minute in executing the order that I have proclaimed in this matter.[33]

This Islamic framework represented the formal discourse of relations that established boundaries between communities and provided the expectations for the behavior of each group. However, in reality, this discourse was constantly reassessed, and as was the case with the Jewish community, many of the rules were broken, new synagogues built, and white turbans (special to Muslims) worn, at least in foreign lands. Despite frequent references – such as the edict of Murad IV – to physical markers of difference such as clothing, colors, height of residences, and ownership of slaves, the Ottomans, it seems, were unable or unwilling to enforce such regulations. Often by citing ancient practice and previously allowed local custom, various Ottoman communities interpreted and gave meaning to this Islamic framework as their repertoires of lived and shared experiences helped them develop common strategies of action. This was possible because Islam had erected such boundaries. There would have been no negotiation, no bargaining about rules and regulations of ethnoreligious coexistence, had there been no formal boundaries established by the Ottoman authorities. Those who argue that there were never clear-cut boundaries between communities and the state and among communities underestimate *the degree to which such perception of fluidity was due to bargaining around rules.* An exemption provided to the Jews by Mehmed III illustrates this point. An imperial order (*fermân*) dated September 17, 1593, exempted Jews from butchering-related taxes. This exemption was negotiated by Jews who

---

[33] Ahmet Refik, *Onbirinci Asr-ı Hicri'de Istanbul Hayatı (1592–1688)* (Istanbul: Enderun Kitabevi, 1998), 52, document #98. I take the translated text from Marc Baer, "Honored by the Glory of Islam: The Ottoman State, Non-Muslims, and Conversion to Islam in Late Seventeenth-Century Istanbul and Rumelia," 2 vols., Ph.D. dissertation, University of Chicago, Chicago, 2001, vol. I, 153–154.

pointed out that butchering was carried out on the Sabbath and that they could not engage in it, so they should not have to pay taxes on an economic activity in which they could not take part. In return, however, they pledged a significant sum of cash for the exploitation of mines.[34] Beyond codes of conduct and dress, the existence of multiple systems of justice (Christian Orthodox, Armenian, and Jewish rabbinical), local community centers of worship, and multiple languages demonstrated diversity and provided temporal, spatial, and cultural allowances for individuals and communities both to experience the "other" and also to be separate. Another entire study could be devoted to language, law, and centers of worship to explain how they were used interchangeably and also slowly separated over time.

Three large-scale relational and administrative policies marked and regulated the boundaries between Muslims and non-Muslims, state and non-state between the fifteenth and the seventeenth centuries. These policies have been frequently misunderstood, misused, and taken at face value, and deeper layers of institutional meaning in them with regard to Ottoman thinking have not been explored. On the one hand, there is a tendency to understand such policies as "us" versus "them" distinctions that are drawn by communities at different stages of their existence under Ottoman rule.[35] In some ways by sharply marking a boundary, moreover, they made people cognizant of their religious identity. On the other hand, they were not simply ways of dividing that allowed no movement, as was clear in most European premodern polities.[36] These policies represented a polity that drew boundaries, but nurtured movement across them. As such, I have called them "mobile markers of difference."

Each policy was carried out with a strong Ottoman belief in the value of Ottoman heterogeneity that enhanced a culture and a people. The Ottomans extolled the virtues of these practices, while also drawing strong lines between communities. The policies in many ways became the markers of such difference. The first two, the levy of Christian children (*devshirme*) and conversion, actually belong to the same family of policies. Yet, I separate them since the *devshirme* was a fully institutionalized state policy that entailed the conversion of a specific segment of the population with a precise rationale. Conversion more generally, however, was not institutionalized; it increased at moments of imperial uncertainty or during war and conquest. It was a provisional strategy rather than a policy. In contrast, the same would not be said of the Russian effort at conversion, which was more clearly associated with the Orthodox Church, its close relationship to the Russian state, and the latter's underlying plan aiming toward uniformity and Russification. In the Ottoman Empire, conversion evidently also involved voluntary communal or individual conversion

[34] Avram Galante, *Histoire des Juifs de Turquie*, 9 vols. (Istanbul: Isis Press, 1940), vol. 1, 122.
[35] Rozen, for example, makes this explicit by using the *responsa* literature of rabbis, who wrote responses to their congregationists on various issues. Rozen, *A History of the Jewish Community in Istanbul*, 40–41.
[36] Anthony W. Marx, *Faith in Nation* (New York: Oxford University Press, 2003).

for better economic and social status, less taxation, and the privilege of belonging to the victorious class. Again by moments the state made such acts of belonging either relatively simple or even forced, demonstrating particular political and religious fervor. The third policy, forced migration (*sürgün*), established a boundary by its actual modus operandi and by the hardship and opportunity imposed on communities differentially. Moreover, all three policies were differentially applied; they were likely to be applied to non-Muslim populations, but not to all non-Muslims.

The Devshirme

The Balkan population must have experienced the religious Muslim–Christian divide sharply with the incorporation of the *devshirme* style of recruitment into the slave-*kul* system of Ottoman rule. The earliest contemporary reference (1395) to the practice of levying Christian boys was a deep expression of grief by Isidore Glabas, the metropolitan of Thessalonica (Selanik), on the effect on the Balkan population of the seizure of Christian children by the decree of the amir: "What would a man not suffer were he to see a child, whom he had begotten and raised . . . carried off by the hands of the foreigners, suddenly and by force, and forced to change over to alien customs and to become a vessel of barbaric garb, speech, impiety, and other contaminations, all in a moment?"[37] Conquests, wars, and devastation occurred many times in the lifetime of a peasant, and billeting was a well-known evil, although it was not particularly Ottoman. However, when Turkish warriors remained and established a sometimes open, sometimes forced channel to belonging to the ruling class, they introduced a novel level of cognition of difference and distress. Aware of the hardships this levy must have imposed, Ottomans never took an only son or two sons from one family. They supplied this institution carefully both to minimize damage to the families and to the agricultural system that required able-bodied youths. The levy was carried out on an ad hoc basis when a genuine need was faced, thus the unrelated dates of recruitment – 1543, 1546, 1553, 1557, 1559, and 1565 – for the sixteenth century.[38] Nevertheless, this practice was in many ways more forceful a marker than taxation, which, according to Islamic regulations, was higher for non-Muslims.[39]

Children who were removed from their families clustered into groups of 100 to 150 boys, were brought to Istanbul (notwithstanding the attempted bribery by parents and agents, abuse on the road, and sale of children) where they were converted, inspected, and distributed to dignitaries, with the rest hired out to Turkish peasants in Anatolia who would break them in and assimilate

---

[37] Speros Vryonis, Jr., "Isidore Glabas and the Turkish Devshirme," *Speculum* 31 (July 1956): 433–443; *Encyclopedia of Islam*, "Devshirme," 210.

[38] Cemal Kafadar, "Yeniçeri-Esnaf Relations: Solidarity and Conflict," M.A. thesis, Institute of Islamic Studies, McGill University, Montreal, Quebec, Canada, 1981, 25.

[39] Taxation had been very heavy during the late Byzantine period; the early Ottoman state was known for its relatively light taxes.

them into Muslim culture and ways of life. Then they would receive specific training for the Janissary army or administrative posts in the bureaucracy and state. It is through these channels of both assimilation and upward mobility that Christian children were directed, many toward the life of Janissaries.

The debate about whether the Christian population of the Balkans was forced or willingly joined the *devshirme* levy to enhance their opportunities has not been resolved. It will probably remain unsettled. Evidence indicates that parents tried to both pay off officers to keep their children home or bribe them to smuggle their children into the *devshirme*. Nonetheless, that the Ottoman elite recruited from among various religious and ethnic groups, or that non-Muslims opted for government service through conversion, are important markers for emerging boundaries. The differential application of this system of recruitment sharpened boundaries, creating many inequalities in the overall application and perception of the institution. For example, it did not apply to all non-Muslims, leaving Jews and most Armenians aside. However, western Anatolia was added on later, leading to much local discontent that was duly registered, but rarely resolved. Peter Sugar, in his now classic work on southeastern Europe, comes to the moderate conclusion that during a period of approximately 200 years, about 200,000 Christians were converted and included in the *devshirme*. He also reminds us that despite the formal end of this practice with Ahmed II (1691–1695), it was probably phased out earlier with Murad IV (1623–1640).[40] As the *devshirme* took root in Ottoman society, those who became Muslim often kept their language and maybe even their allegiance, some returning to their region of birth as governors, others commanding in their native tongues, and many trying to help family members back in their homeland.

Even more dramatic was the inevitable irony of the Serbian brothers separated by the *devshirme*, one becoming Grand *Vizier* (Mehmed Sokullu) and the other becoming the head of the Serbian Orthodox Church (Makarius), with his brother's help. One brother, a converted Muslim, headed the Ottoman state; the other brother, a devout Christian, led the Serbian Church. The two brothers corresponded in Serbian.[41] Many such examples – perhaps not as dramatic – were reproduced, making the boundaries between ruler and ruled, Muslim and non-Muslim quite unequivocal to the elites and the populace. At the height of the *devshirme*, between the mid-fifteenth and mid-seventeenth centuries, only five grand viziers out of forty-seven were of Turkish origin; the others were of Albanian, Greek, or Slavic origin and had risen from the *devshirme*.

---

[40] Peter Sugar, *Southeastern Europe under Ottoman Rule, 1354–1804* (Seattle: University of Washington Press, 1977), 56; V. L. Ménage, "The Islamization of Anatolia," in *Conversion to Islam*, ed. Nehemia Levtzion (New York: Holmes & Meier, 1979), 65–66.

[41] Sugar, *Southeastern Europe under Ottoman Rule*, 58. Ties of this nature across boundaries no doubt contributed to the control that the Ottoman center garnered from center–periphery relations. The Serbian brothers are a micro-level example of control that was effected through easy surveillance across state/nonstate boundaries.

Diversity was firmly a part of the Ottoman political culture. The Ottoman administration might have perceived the *devshirme* in actual military and administrative terms, citing the previous practice of capturing slaves during *gazâ*, yet there is little doubt that the larger implications of the process with regard to political culture were part of the discourse of the early Ottoman Empire.[42] *Devshirme* was discussed not only in terms of religion and conversion to Islam, but also in terms of ethnicity. In the writings of the famous sixteenth-century Ottoman bureaucrat and intellectual Mustafa Ali, we get a sense of this discourse. Mustafa Ali discussed the ethnic heterogeneity of the empire and the contribution of the *devshirme* to it as a distinct characteristic of the empire, separating it from the previous Islamic states. Describing Mustafa Ali's remarks, Cornell Fleischer brings the thinking of the time back to life:

By virtue of its geographical location and origins as a Muslim *gâzî* state, the Ottoman Empire acquired unique human resources. Mingling of constituent ethnic groups potentially allowed for optimal combinations of physical, moral, and intellectual characteristics within that heterogeneous population; physical strength and beauty came from the non-Muslims, intellectual prowess and piety from representatives of the heartlands of Islamic civilization.[43]

Ali also acknowledged the darker side of this tremendous heterogeneity by lamenting the potential for conflict that emanates from "difference."[44]

Conversion

Conversion was an ambiguous practice that marked separation and difference, especially by its unidirectional nature under Islam. It allowed Jews and Christians to become Muslims, but strictly forbade Muslims from converting under the threat of apostasy; punishment was even harsher when converted Muslims tried to go back to their original faith. Conversion could be of different types, individual or collective, and voluntary or forced. In the absence of a clear-cut, uniform, and continuous state policy on conversion, multiple religious, economic, social, and political motives explain why individuals, groups, or whole communities either chose to convert or were pushed to do so.

Early on, Sufis played a major role in the colonization of territory and in the conversion of Christians to a mild heterodox Islam in the early moments of territorial incorporation, especially in the Balkans. Economic motivations and the desire to enhance one's social status led Jews and Christians to convert, especially as a way to avoid the heavier taxation that they would have had to

---

[42] An Orientalist discussion of the *devshirme* system attributes the greatness of the empire to the prowess and strength of the converted Christian element. It is partly in the writings of travelers to the empire as well as in those of scholars who analyzed the success of the empire, the most prominent being H. A. Gibbons, in *The Foundation of the Ottoman Empire: A History of the Osmanlis up to the Death of Bayezid I, 1300–1403* (London: Frank Cass & Co., 1968).

[43] Cornell H. Fleischer, *Bureaucrat and Intellectual in the Ottoman Empire: The Historian Mustafa Ali (1541–1600)* (Princeton, NJ: Princeton University Press, 1986), 256.

[44] Ibid., 255–258.

endure otherwise. According to Islamic law, the *dhimmi* population paid all the regular taxes imposed on the Muslims, plus an additional tax, the *cizye*. This tax varied according to region and period, but all told, it could be an onerous obligation, especially in the later centuries of Ottoman rule. Conversions to avoid this tax were conflict-laden because the *cizye* was collected on communities, and the conversion of some necessarily increased the tax burden on others in the community. Whole communities converted precisely to avoid this issue. Sultans also varied in their religious zeal, defining periods of relative religious freedom versus times of greater pressure to convert, for example, Sultan Beyazıd II (1481–1512), who put pressure on Jews to convert, or Selim I (1512–1520), who was interested in converting Bulgarians.[45] A wave of religious zealotry and purification during the reign of Mehmed IV (1648–1687) led to the conversion of Jews in the capital.[46]

Debates about conversion persist mostly among Balkan scholars because both the total number and the method of conversion are crucial to some of the continuing contentions regarding territory in the postimperial nation-states. Was conversion state forced or voluntary, and do we have accurate accounts of the populations involved? There have been various efforts made to answer these questions but no clear resolution. This is not the place to resolve such divergent opinions based on questionable sources. For our purposes, conversion is central as a boundary marker in that conversion makes boundaries salient, especially when it is carried out in public ceremonies as it was during the seventeenth century. Conversion was also momentous because unlike in the *devshirme* system, the Ottomans did not have a clear policy of conversion, yet every religious group and many ethnic communities were affected by gains and losses due to conversion. Locally, conversion also constructed ties across communities, rather than breaking ties as other boundary practices did, thereby maintaining difference in very visible ways. Therefore, there is some value to understanding how conversion proceeded throughout the empire, yet the social and relational aspects are clearly more significant to our argument.

Some scholars have argued that Anatolia went from being predominantly Christian in the mid-eleventh century to claiming a large majority of Muslims in the early fifteenth century.[47] Heath Lowry tackles this question for Trabzon, a northern Anatolian city on the Black Sea, the seat of the Pontus Kingdom, where Islamization occurred to a significant degree. He finds the process to be quite intricate, with layers of movement, forced settlement, and conversion, and complicated population changes in the area. However, in ways that confirm the

[45] Mark Epstein, *The Ottoman Jewish Communities and their Role in the Fifteenth and Sixteenth Centuries* (Freiburg, Germany: Klaus Schwarz Verlag, 1980), 30–31.

[46] Baer, "Honored by the Glory of Islam."

[47] Ménage, "The Islamization of Anatolia," 52–53. Barkan's figures for Anatolian towns also show a majority of Muslim households. See Barkan, "Essai sur les données statistiques," 20; Speros Vryonis, Jr., *The Decline of Medieval Hellenism in Asia Minor and the Process of Islamization from the Eleventh through the Fifteenth Century* (Berkeley: University of California Press, 1971); Osman Turan, "L'Islamisation dans la Turquie du Moyen Âge," *Studia Islamica* 10 (1959): 137–152.

insights of a tolerant beginning, Lowry finds conversion not to be significant early on, but only much later in the late sixteenth century as the benefits of becoming Muslim became clearer in an increasingly Sunnî-oriented empire.[48]

For southeastern Europe and especially Bulgaria, Dennis Hupchick argues that Muslim immigration and forced conversion was a significant policy of the Ottoman authorities in the region.[49] Bulgaria experienced a steady flow of Muslim immigration so that the major Bulgarian urban centers – Sofia, Plovdiv, Nikopol, Varna, Turnovo, Vidin, and Ruse – had become important centers of a mixed Muslim and Orthodox culture.[50] Although the earlier conversions were often voluntary, after the seventeenth century, conversions become political and coerced, such as the conversion drive of the populations in the Rodope and Pirin mountains from 1666 to 1670, which engendered a new demographic population category of converts named Pomaks.[51] Anton Minkov's work on southeastern Europe reveals that Islamization occurred starting in the 1530s, peaked in the mid-seventeenth century, and tapered off after the 1730s. He also finds that conversion was the result not of economic need as much as it was a way for elites and their followers to enhance their status and ensure social advancement. He also attributes much of the initial zeal to the receptivity of popular Islam conveyed by the Bektaşî and Mevlevî orders that were close to both Muslims and Christians. Others such as Zhelyzakova forcefully argue that the Ottomans did not have an official policy of converting the ordinary subjects of the empire.[52] Conversions could follow conquests, especially in regions where religion was multilayered, varied, and ambiguous, and where conversion could simplify relations of domination as well as previous social and cultural structures.

In Bosnia, the Christian population had converted to Islam in large numbers after the conquest in 1463. The particular situation of Bosnia can be attested to by the Bosnians' somewhat unorthodox request that their sons not be exempted from the *devshirme*, now that they had converted to Islam![53] Bosnia produced some of the most interesting high-ranking converts, who succeeded in their official positions in the capital, and also contributed substantially to their home communities by finding positions for their relatives back home, endowing

---

[48] Heath Lowry, *Trabzon Şehrinin İslamlaşma ve Türkleşmesi, 1461–1583* [1981] (Istanbul: Bosphorus University Press, 1998).

[49] Dennis P. Hupchick, *The Bulgarians in the Seventeenth Century: Slavic Orthodox Society and Culture under Ottoman Rule* (Jefferson, NC: McFarland and Co., 1993).

[50] Dennis P. Hupchick, "Orthodoxy and Bulgarian Ethnic Awareness under Ottoman Rule, 1396–1762," *Nationalities Papers* 21:2 (Fall 1993): 77.

[51] Ibid., 78.

[52] Anton Minkov, *Conversion to Islam in the Balkans: Kisve Bahasi Petitions and Ottoman Social Life, 1670–1730* (Leiden, The Netherlands: Brill, 2004); Antonina Zhelyzakova, "Islamization in the Balkans as a Historiographical Problem: The Southeast-European Perspective," in *The Ottomans and the Balkans: A Discussion of Historiography*, ed. Fikret Adanır and Suraiya Faroqhi (Leiden, The Netherlands: Brill, 2002), 223–266; Süphan Kırmızıaltın, "Conversion in Ottoman Balkans: A Historiographical Survey," *History Compass* 5 (2007): 646–657.

[53] Vryonis, "Devshirme," *Encyclopedia of Islam*, 211. See also Ahmet Refik Altınay, *Sokollu* (Istanbul: Tarih Vakfı Yurt Yayınları, 2001), 4.

many charitable establishments, and opening businesses in towns.[54] Although in some way conversion represented the reaffirmation of difference, it also was part of the mechanism that maintained connections between groups and kept the networks of intergroup relations well oiled. In many ways, when conversion was not forced, it was made very easy. In fact, there is evidence that even just wearing Muslim clothing and saying that one wanted to become a Muslim was enough to make it so. Forced conversion would be the stronger marker of difference, whereas the easy availability of individual conversion promoted the awareness of access and the possibility of upward mobility. Converts were also the main linkages between communities, bringing people together and maintaining open channels of communication.[55]

Perhaps the difference with the Habsburgs and the Russians was the much less consistent policy of conversion that marked difference in a more subtle and mobile way, both marking difference and accommodating its existence.

The Sürgün

Another practice of dubious origin, deportations (*sürgün*), brought different groups together into the same region. Like most agrarian empires, the Ottomans were interested in securing their borders, feeding their troops at the frontiers, and promoting settled agriculture that could be easily taxed; therefore, they promoted the migration of peasants and nomads to open and cultivate new land and to secure new borders. From the very beginning, the Ottomans felt the need to bring in populations of Muslim peasants and nomads to the Balkans, while Christian military men were sent to Anatolia "so that they cannot give us trouble in the future."[56] Some of these measures were attempts at repopulating; some were ways to deport troublesome groups such as the Turkish nomads organized under a military format (*yürük*). For example, the rebellious Cepni Turcomans from the Black Sea region of Canik were deported to Albania, and Tatars from the Tokat-Amasya region were forcibly settled in the Maritsa Valley in the fourteenth and fifteenth centuries.[57]

Beyond the strictly administrative advantage they imparted, deportations were practiced for cultural integration and ideological purposes. Mehmed II made extensive use of deportations from Serbia, Albania, Morea, and Caffa to repopulate Istanbul.[58] He also made sure that a significant number of non-Muslim merchants were settled in Istanbul to revive trade in the city. To convince Greeks, Jews, and Armenians to repopulate this once prosperous city,

---

[54] Alexander Lopasic, "Islamization of the Balkans with Special Reference to Bosnia," *Journal of Islamic Studies* 5 (1994): 163–186.

[55] For the town of Bursa in the Ottoman Empire, Osman Çetin has demonstrated the degree to which converts continue to be part of their old and new communities and bring the two together. See Osman Çetin, *Sicillere Göre Bursa'da İhtida Hareketleri ve Sosyal Sonuçları (1472–1909)* (Ankara: Türk Tarih Kurumu Basımevi, 1994).

[56] Cited from a letter of Süleyman Pasha, the son of sultan Orhan in İnalcık, "Ottoman Methods of Conquest," 123.

[57] İnalcık, "The Ottoman State: Economy and Society," 32.

[58] Ibid., 124.

Mehmed II brought the Greek Orthodox patriarchate to Istanbul, invited the Armenian patriarch, and started conversations with various Jewish religious leaders. Such gestures were facilitated by a cultural recognition of the strength created by ethnic heterogeneity and openness to refugees from different lands. Especially in the fifteenth century, when Jews migrated to the empire from Spain, Portugal, and Italy, they were decorously received and widely tolerated. A century later, when Istanbul's population grew to about 400,000, its central political and economic might was partly the result of this earlier inclusion. Another example of historical consequence was the conquest of the Peloponnese from Venice in 1714, which triggered serious efforts from Ottomans to repopulate this region devastated by warfare. They improved local conditions by bringing in Greeks who maintained control over important commercial networks.

The attempt to rebuild Constantinople brought communal and economic problems. Jews from Salonica; Armenians and Muslims from Anatolia; and Greeks from the Morea, Izmir, and Trabzon were deported to the city and provided with incentives to start rebuilding it and their communities.[59] Although the long-term effect of such migrations could be advantageous to the migrants, in the short term they were devastating. Many established and wealthy merchants resisted, and the state insisted on sending many follow-up orders to depart and resettle. Lowry finds from records of fifteenth- and sixteenth-century Trabzon that *sürgün* populations returned to Trabzon as soon as they were able. Hacker, for example, describes the hardships of Jewish families forced to leave their communities, their livelihoods, and their traditional lives for uncertain conditions. *Sürgün* created many familial, social, and economic dislocations.[60]

Beyond simple hardship, forced migration contributed to the formation of boundaries and their maintenance as markers of difference. As described in the Jewish manuscripts of the period, when communities had to adapt and move to Istanbul (or to other cities as would occur later), they often tampered with their own traditional and communal law and practice. They adapted by bending their own rules to those of the Ottoman state. Often, they acquired a novel legal status, and were even differentiated within their own religious and ethnic communities.[61] Similar to the case of converts, those who were relocated through forced migration always retained the label of a "*sürgün* population."

---

[59] Uriel Heyd, "The Jewish Communities in Istanbul in the Seventeenth Century," *Oriens* 6 (December 1953): 299–314. In this article, Heyd shows district by district where the Jews of Istanbul came from, including the many *sürgün* communities that had settled after implementation of Mehmed II's policy.

[60] Joseph R. Hacker, "Ottoman Policy toward the Jews and Jewish Attitudes toward the Ottomans during the Fifteenth Century," in *Christians and Jews in the Ottoman Empire*, ed. Braude and Lewis, 117–126. See also Hacker, "The Sürgün System and Jewish Society in the Ottoman Empire during the Fifteen to the Seventeenth Centuries," in Rodrigue, ed., *Ottoman and Turkish Jewry*, 1–65. Minna Rozen describes similar reluctance in *A History of the Jewish Community in Istanbul*.

[61] Heyd, "The Jewish Communities in Istanbul"; Hacker, "The Sürgün System," 28–29 and 36–37.

To the existing distinctions were added *sürgün*-based differentiation between communities that emigrated of their own will and communities forced to move, leading to more fractionalization than community building. Such distinctions were used to regulate marriage between communities in ways that paralleled status and economic differences.[62] Furthermore, given that the existing synagogues were not sufficient for the newcomers, these new Jews practiced their religion in rooms and small buildings, and were sometimes allowed to build new houses of worship, despite the Shari.[63] It was at such moments of upheaval that intense recognition of difference arose during moments of population displacement, when representatives of the communities were forced to negotiate with authorities, and boundaries were erected not only within communities, but also between groups from different origins, each maintaining their communal and religious organizations and forms of worship. Difference was then experienced in everyday practice, dress, and encounters between groups of different religious persuasions. Yet, it was also made salient by state practice that highlighted the different categories and made movement from one category to the other part of society's nearly natural expectation.

A Capacious Administration of Difference

The core of an Ottoman version of indirect rule vis-à-vis different religious communities was what scholars have called the *"millet"* system. The *millet* system, a loose administrative set of central-local arrangements, was a script for multireligious rule, although it was neither fully codified nor comparable across communities.[64] It started with the regularization of state–Orthodox Christian relations and became a normative and practical instrument of rule. The Ottomans had several goals: to ensure the loyalty of a growing Christian community with important economic skills, to increase legibility and order, and to enable the administration to run smoothly and taxes to flow to the center while also reinforcing the wedge between the Orthodox and Catholic worlds of Europe.[65] In addition to the Muslims, three non-Muslim *millets* – Greek Orthodox, Armenian, and Jewish – were organized around their dominant religious institutions, with the understanding that religious institutions would define and delimit collective life.

---

[62] Rozen, *A History of the Jewish Community in Istanbul*, 327.

[63] Epstein, *The Ottoman Jewish Communities*, 28.

[64] I agree that this was not a fully centralized and coordinated administrative blueprint applied evenhandedly to every religious community. Yet, we cannot dismiss the governing process, the establishment of a form of organization, and some strategizing behind the incorporation of difference. For the classic treatment of the *millet*, see H. A. R. Gibb and Harold Bowen, *Islamic Society and the West: A Study of the Impact of Western Civilization on Moslem Culture in the Near East*, 2 vols. (London: Oxford University Press, 1957).

[65] Charles A. Frazee, *Catholics and Sultans: The Church and the Ottoman Empire 1453–1923* (London: Cambridge University Press); Goffman, "Ottoman Millets in the Early Seventeenth Century."

The aftermath of the conquest of Constantinople was the most plausible moment for the emergence of new and somewhat still opaque organizational forms that grew into three large-scale identity vessels that organized diversity in the empire. As such, these were separate from one another, contained within their institutional forms, and internally administered by boundary managers who acted as intermediaries between the state and the religious community. The Orthodox *millet* was recognized in 1454, the Armenian in 1461; the Jewish *millet* remained without a declared definite status for a while, although it was unofficially recognized around the same time as the other two. In 1477, there were 3,151 Greek Orthodox; 3,095 Armenian, Latin, and Gypsy combined; and 1,647 Jewish households in Istanbul. The number of Muslim households had reached 8,951.[66]

Sultans, and Mehmed II in particular, forged the early arrangements that were then periodically renewed by diverse communities. These arrangements did not even entail much innovation because they folded into their practice the existing authority structures of each community, and thereby provided them with significant legal autonomy and authority. Attention was paid to maintain the internal religious and cultural composition of communities. Where there was strong community organization and/or strong ecclesiastical hierarchy, the central state adopted these institutions as the representative structures of the community. In this sense, joining with existing institutional structures both maintained the old and added some new features of Ottoman rule. In this we see what Kathleen Thelen describes as layering, a mechanism of institutional change. Institutional layering "involves the grafting of new elements onto an otherwise stable institutional framework."[67] She argues that such layering can actually change the course of an institution's development. For the Greeks, the conqueror recognized the Greek Orthodox patriarchate in Constantinople as the most powerful force among the Christian population. The Orthodox Church would dominate ethnically and linguistically diverse populations that followed more or less a uniform Orthodox practice. For the Jewish population, a different mechanism of institutional change was applied, that of conversion. For Thelen, conversion is "the adoption of new goals or the incorporation of new groups into the coalitions on which institutions are founded."[68] Jews – smaller in number, urban, and inconsequential to international politics, and with no overarching rabbinical authority, but rather an assembly of religious and lay leaders – were first forced into the pattern of the Orthodox Church, in fact converting the existing goals and structure of the community in the process.

[66] Halil İnalcık, "The Policy of Mehmed II toward the Greek Population of Istanbul and the Byzantine Buildings of the City," *Dumbarton Oaks Papers* 23 & 24 (1969–1970): 247; İnalcık, "Foundations of Ottoman-Jewish Cooperation," in *Jews, Turks, Ottomans: A Shared History, Fifteenth through the Twentieth Century*, ed. Avigdor Levy (Syracuse, NY: Syracuse University Press, 2002), 5.

[67] Kathleen Thelen, *How Institutions Evolve: The Political Economy of Skills in Germany, Britain, the United States, and Japan* (Cambridge, UK: Cambridge University Press, 2004), 35.

[68] Ibid., 36.

When this attempt failed, the administration went back to recognizing Jews as a series of communities with their own leaders and layered new elements onto this form of organization. The Armenians were in an intermediate position with a regionally complex configuration of communities and few patriarchs claiming jurisdiction over them. Consequently, the integration of the Ottoman Armenian community might have taken longer and have been more contested. The Armenian Church dominated many smaller and less significant religious groupings that did not fit other categories, but that had their own religious practice. In each encounter, relations between state and religious communities, as well as the particular network of leaders and their interests, helped negotiate and recalibrate the institutional framework to best suit the interests of governance.

Managing diversity remained the *sine qua non* of imperial persistence, requiring mechanisms that were flexible enough to endure. Institutional reproduction, continuity, and change were based on three principles. The first principle, the acceptance and internalization of existing organizational forms and their adaptation to an Ottoman model of indirect rule through intermediaries, calls for the analysis of the genesis of the relations between communities and the state. The second principle, the creation of competing alternative organizational forms that acted as checks and balances to the accumulation of power in intermediate groups, necessitates the study of the structure of multiple competing brokers. Finally, the third principle, the management and diffusion of religious and ethnic tensions by intermediaries with a vested interest in the reproduction of institutional arrangements, makes us look at how the religious or lay leadership that acted as the intermediaries between public authorities and the communities administered their realm, collected the taxes, and helped maintain inter- and intraethnic peace and security. For brokers who became boundary managers, we need to understand how and why they were keen on keeping violations of existing rule to a minimum.

Institutional Genesis[69]

The conquest of Constantinople came at a critical juncture when conquerors and conquered elites encountered each other, and when old institutions were

---

[69] Benjamin Braude has called the initial contact and its representation "foundation myths," a term that he elaborates to show that there was little systemic relationship established between Ottoman leaders and the communities; he described contemporary accounts as myths. Elizabeth Zachariadou, in contrast, deals with this issue by saying that there were some exaggerations in contemporary accounts mainly because their authors were eager to argue that the Orthodox Church was so great that even the infidels were forced to deal with it. Presentation at "In Honor of Professor İnalcık: Methods and Sources in Ottoman Studies," April 29–May 2, 2004, Harvard University, Cambridge, MA. Halil İnalcık in his two seminal articles demystifies the initial relations between Ottomans and Greek Orthodox subjects of the state. These are "The Status of the Greek Orthodox Patriarch under the Ottomans," *Turcica* (1991) 231–249; 407–437 and "The Policy of Mehmed II toward the Greek Population of Istanbul and the Byzantine Buildings of the City," *Dumbarton Oaks Papers* 23 & 24 (1969–1970): 231–249. As this section shows, I argue in opposition to the "foundation myth" argument to emphasize institution building instead.

recalibrated rather than changed, with layers of previous and new practices being joined together by Ottomans and Greeks. Even though the Greek Orthodox patriarchs were to become the main interlocutors with the Ottoman state, conquerors and conquered elites initially agreed on secular rule by established notables led by Loukas Notaras. Mehmed II first summoned and delegated authority to the Grand Duke Notaras, a distinguished and lay member of Byzantine officialdom, only to move on to the religious leaders relatively quickly.[70] Why did Notaras not work? Apart from local political intrigues, Islamic understandings trumped political desires. It was also the case that for the past few centuries of Byzantine rule, the Church had taken over the execution of judicial authority from the state.[71] Geopolitical strategy must have led Mehmed II, who was keenly aware of the troubles between the western and eastern Churches, to reinforce eastern claims and make an eventual alliance against the Turks more difficult.

Besides, the Orthodox Church had become the predominant institution in the Greek lands. The conquests of the Balkans by early Ottomans had come with the protection and acceptance of the Greek Orthodox Church.[72] Everywhere they went, Ottomans had incorporated metropolitans into the empire and had allowed them to maintain their rich lands as *timars*.[73] Moreover, Ottoman rulers had developed an important tradition of communicating with Greek metropolitans in conquered regions, urging them to make contact with other metropolitans in regions soon to be added to Ottoman territory.[74] Thus, even as the conquest of Constantinople was being planned, Ottomans were cozying up to the religious leadership in the city, using allies and well-known religious figures to establish their credentials.

The moment of institutional genesis built as much continuity with the past as innovation for the future. Historians of the time agree that whether orally or in writing, Mehmed II sanctioned the election of Gennadios as the Patriarch of the Greek Orthodox Church, probably providing him with a diploma, called *berat*, that gave the patriarch jurisdiction over the Christian Orthodox population of the empire. This would not have been against tradition because both Seljuk leaders and Ottoman rulers were known to provide *berats* to subjugated populations.[75] Pantazopoulos underlines the fact that Mehmed II sanctioned the patriarch's judicial authority by saying: "Be the Patriarch in happiness and

---

[70] For a discussion of the emergence of a formal relationship between the Ottoman state and the Greek Orthodox Church, see Theodore H. Papadopoullos, *Studies and Documents Relating to the History of the Greek Church and People under Turkish Domination* (Brussels: Bibliotheca Graeca Aevi Posterioris, 1952), and N. J. Pantazopoulos, *Church and Law in the Balkan Peninsula during the Ottoman Rule*, no. 92 (Thessaloniki: Institute for Balkan Studies, 1967). See also the article by Ralph S. Hattox, "Mehmed the Conqueror, the Patriarch of Jerusalem, and Mamluk Authority," *Studia Islamica* 90 (2000): 105–123.

[71] Pantazopoulos, *Church and Law*, 43.

[72] See İnalcık, "The Status of the Greek Orthodox Patriarch," and "The Policy of Mehmed II toward the Greek Population of Istanbul."

[73] İnalcık, "The Status of the Greek Orthodox Patriarch," 409.

[74] Ibid., 410.

[75] Ibid., 415, and İnalcık, "The Policy of Mehmed II," 237.

have our friendship on anything you wish and enjoy all your privileges, *as all the Patriarchs before you also had.*"[76] Here we see not only the importance of the Church prior to conquest, but also the interest in building continuity between Byzantine and Ottoman practices. With this move, Mehmed II extended three centuries of a form of ecclesiastical rule that was at once very traditional and quite novel.[77] It was traditional because in this historical era when religion was predominant, the Orthodox Church continued to be of great significance. It was novel because it extended into a new civil realm. The jurisdiction that the Patriarch now acquired extended to all religious and civil matters of the Orthodox peoples of the realm, and was significantly different from his previous authority under the Byzantine Empire. The combined secular and religious authority made sense to the Ottomans, who themselves combined religious law (*Shari*) and secular law (*kanun*) in the person of the sultan. Furthermore, this partnership was more than administrative; there was a symbolic resemblance in the claims both the Ottomans and the Orthodox Church made. Braude and Lewis express this claim elegantly: "Constantinople's claim to authority over all Orthodox Christians in the Empire, consistent with its ecumenical pretensions to universal authority, dovetailed with the Ottomans' own claims to universal empire, heir to the traditions of Byzantium and Rome."[78]

In addition, for the Orthodox Church and the Orthodox population, this endorsement signaled not only a new form of administration, but also an extended one, where Orthodox Christians of the empire, from the Balkans to the edges of the Middle East, despite their diverse ethnic, tribal, and regional backgrounds, clearly became subjected to one formal religious authority. All Orthodox Christian taxpaying subjects of the empire were bound to the cause of the Church, and evidently, the Church had become the counterpart of the Ottoman state in boundary maintenance. Moreover, the patriarchs as the single ethnarchs of the Christian Orthodox community certainly acquired much power over their subjects, yet they were reminded of their limited power as they encountered different forms of state abuse. For example, because patriarchs had to buy *berats* of appointment, every time a new patriarch came into office, the state made some money. Patriarchs were also executed at the whim of the sultan or of his mobs.[79] As the payments for office increased, especially in the eighteenth century, patriarchs borrowed from rich merchants, important political families, or even foreign states eager to have a say in Ottoman politics.

---

[76] Ibid. (my emphasis). See also Steven Runciman, *The Great Church in Captivity: A Study of Constantinople from the Eve of the Turkish Conquest to the Greek War of Independence* (Cambridge, UK: Cambridge University Press, 1968), 169.

[77] Both Dimitri Cantemir in *History of the Growth and Decay of the Ottoman Empire* (p. 104 Note) (London, 1734) and Hammer-Purgstall in *Histoire de l'empire Ottoman* (vol. III, 2–5) provide details about what this jurisdiction entailed.

[78] Braude and Lewis, eds., *Christians and Jews in the Ottoman Empire*, 13.

[79] See B. J. Kidd, *The Churches of Eastern Christendom* (London: The Faith Press, 1927), 304; Sir Charles Eliot, *Turkey in Europe* (London: Frank Cass & Co. Ltd., 1965), 248; and Pantazopoulos, *Church and Law*, 25.

In this way, these high-ranking men got caught between their obligation to the Ottoman state and their financial patrons.

The *berat*, a document providing the patriarch with authority over the Christian Orthodox community, also authorized the patriarch and the metropolitans to collect taxes from the community, for the church and for the state. The same document entitled patriarchs and metropolitans to deal with lower-level clergy on community issues, administrative and educational activities, and monasteries. It also provided the Church with its own courts to administer justice in civil matters such as marriage, but not on penal issues, which were left to the Muslim courts.[80] İnalcık cites the text of a *berat*, clarifying the nature of the compact between the state and the religious representatives of the Greek Orthodox *millet*:

The order of the imperial diploma (*nishan*), may God keep it in force until the final day, is this:...My order is that from now on he be the Metropolitan there, and, as God ordered: "Leave him in what they profess," he perform their rites as they have been performed, and that he exercise authority as a Metropolitan over the priests, monks (*kalyoros*), and other orthodox Christians of that district and place as his predecessors did, and that he enter into possession of the churches, vineyards, orchards and plots of land which were in the possession of his predecessors, as that he be exempt from the *djizya*, and all extraordinary impositions such as the *ulak* and the *djere-hor* as his predecessors were, and that the priests, monks and Orthodox Christians of that place acknowledge him as their Metropolitan and bring to him all the litigations under the jurisdiction of the metropolitanate.

The relationship between the state and the Orthodox Church was formulated partly at the time of Mehmed II when the territorial, administrative, and symbolic aspects of an agreement were specified, after which the state did not claim to meddle in the relationship between the Church and the Christian population. More often than not, it was the patriarchs and the metropolitans who appealed to the Ottoman court for help in running their own affairs. The Church had extensive administrative authority to oversee church lands, and to control the educational and legal institutions of the Orthodox community. Ecumenical courts handled matters dealing with the daily lives of the Christian communities, their births, deaths, marriages, and other civil issues. With this compact, which encompassed Greeks as well as other Christian Orthodox peoples, especially the Slavic population of the Balkans, the Ottoman state had found and empowered an intermediary institution to govern those who were across the boundary.

The financial aspect of the Ottoman–patriarchate relationship is another good example of the institutional arrangements that were made by layering different practices, the Greek Orthodox religious entity and the Ottoman fiscal unit being harmonized in the interests of legibility. That this intermediary organization resembled many other Ottoman institutions supports the point

---

[80] The text of a *berat* clarifies this arrangement: See İnalcık, "The Status of the Greek Orthodox Patriarch," 418–419.

that Ottomans assimilated the Greek Orthodox Church into a pattern with which they were familiar; they were keen to formulate stable relations that would ensure the administration of peoples and the assimilation of revenues. The patriarchate was tied into the Ottoman system as a financial institution. Since 1474, the position of the patriarch had been tied to a monetary gift, the *pishkes*, which established parallels with other Ottoman financial institutions. Ottomans then thought of the patriarch as a state official, in ways parallel to the *kethüdâ* of the craft guild. *Kethüdâs*, patriarchs, and metropolitans were all elected officials, and the state showed similar concern regarding the elections of each official. As the tax collectors of the Christian population, metropolitans were compared to tax farmers collecting on state lands (*mîrî*).[81]

Once the office of the patriarchate was tied to revenues, it was fully constituted as an Ottoman fiscal unit (the *mukataa*), as is made clear in the request Patriarch Jeremie 1st makes in 1544: "I took on the engagement to give yearly to the Imperial Treasury as a *mukataa* the sum of four thousand pieces of gold on the condition of being the Patriarch of Istanbul-the-well-protected and of the dependent domains and the regions and the countries of Moldavia and Wallachia. Accordingly, I was given an imperial *berat*."[82] To administer such revenues, the Ottomans organized a special office at the department of imperial finances "for the collection of the revenues connected with appointment of the religious heads of the Christian communities in the empire," led by a head secretary (*hoca*) under the finance minister and designated as under the direct control of the grand vizier's office.[83] That is, not only did the Ottomans create a special office, but this office was significant enough to be placed under the jurisdiction of the grand vizier. The records in the register were collected regarding the Orthodox patriarchate of Istanbul, the patriarchates of Jerusalem, Alexandria, Antioch, Ohrid, and Pec, as well as the Armenian patriarchate of Istanbul.

The Greek Orthodox patriarchate developed to become the institution of indirect rule par excellence. Had the patriarch become a mere administrator with his own financial interest at heart, or was his loyalty to his people? Was his role as a religious and cultural leader still intact?[84] Konortas makes the "mere administrator" argument quite forcefully, arguing that the patriarchate was transformed into a fiscal shell with no real content that hindered the other functions of the office. The tremendous amount of religious authority delegated to this Orthodox center over others led to the development of an inherently hierarchical and unequal form of administration that tolerated other Orthodox

---

[81] İnalcık, "The Status of the Greek Orthodox Patriarch," 420–423.

[82] Quoted in Paraskevas Konortas, "Considérations Ottomanes au sujet du statut du patriarcat orthodoxe de Constantinople 15e–16e siècles: quelques hypothèses," *Congrés International des Études du Sud-est Européen* 6 (1989): 221.

[83] İnalcık, "Ottoman Archival Materials on *Millets*," in Braude and Lewis, eds., *Christians and Jews*, 437–449. Most of the following information on the sources comes from the work of İnalcık.

[84] Konortas, "Considérations Ottomanes au sujet du statut du patriarcat."

patriarchs but did not allow the fragmentation of religious sovereignty.[85] The older sees of Jerusalem, Antioch, and Alexandria delegated authority to Istanbul. Chief among those autochthonous churches that suffered directly from the establishment of the Greek Orthodox Church were the Serbian and Bulgarian churches. Therefore, the Orthodox Church came to be seen as an instrument of the Ottoman state and, in return, the Ottoman rulers made use of the Church as an instrument of administration. In the words of Papadopoullos, "the history of the Greeks and of the other Christian subjects during the period that followed the fall of Constantinople up to the nineteenth century cannot be separated from the history of the Eastern Church."[86]

There was no equivalent to the dominant Eastern Church for the other non-Muslim groups of the empire. Much of the administrative practice established with the Greek Orthodox Church could not be replicated with relation to these other populations. Neither the Jewish nor the Armenian communities initially fit this mold. They did not have a well-defined ecclesiastical hierarchy ready to take over jurisdiction from the Ottoman state. Although Ottomans forced some patterns, they also had to come to terms with such institutional variation, especially with the Jews.

The history of the Jewish communities in Europe and in areas under Byzantine control greatly affected the encounter between Ottomans and Jews. First, throughout Europe, Jewish communities had scattered with neither the tradition nor the administrative reality of a centrally defined rabbinical authority, making centralized rule similar to that of the Orthodox Church impossible. Although they were dispersed into multiple smaller communities, they retained strong communal ties and organizations, mostly stemming from their precarious Diaspora existence. They were also used to being the only significant minority in the Christian countries in which they lived. They were not only a visible minority, given their differences from Christian society, but they were also visible in that in Europe they mostly existed by reason of state, dependent on the latest interest or wish of the kings. They were thus accustomed to building strong ties to existing public authorities, but as individual communities, rather than as national communities. By the time they encountered Ottoman rulers, first in the Balkans and then in Constantinople, Jews had suffered under great uncertainty in Christian lands. Similarly, they were to suffer discrimination in the Habsburg and Russian lands. Habsburg policy resembled that of other Catholic western countries, while the Russian policy was much more complex, changing, and, especially later, based on internal attempts to divide and conquer, what Nathans calls a policy of "selective integration."[87]

---

[85] Papadopoullos, in *Studies and Documents Relating to the History of the Greek Church*, makes a similar argument in which he regrets the loss of democratic rule by the Church. See 11–12.

[86] Ibid., 26.

[87] Benjamin Nathans, *Beyond the Pale: The Jewish Encounter with Late Imperial Russia* (Berkeley: University of California Press, 2002).

The Ottoman–Jewish contact promised to bring substantial change to Jewish uncertainty. Initially, the Ottomans encountered Jewish communities when they conquered the Balkans, and there is evidence that Jewish scholars and rabbis were part of the multireligious encounters and discussions at the sultan's table. As small communities were incorporated, more often than not, Jews cooperated with the Ottomans, clearly showing their preference for a new system of rule. The Jews settled in the lands of the Ottomans in three different periods. At first, small Romaniot and Karaite communities came under Ottoman rule in Anatolia and the Balkans. Second, immigrants from northern Europe followed. The third and major immigration into the Ottoman lands, however, especially to the newly conquered city of Constantinople, started in the Iberian Peninsula with the persecution of Jews during the Inquisition. The initial significant encounter between Jews and Mehmed II, however, took place with the *sürgün* population, a series of different Jewish communities relocated to Constantinople from towns in the Balkans and Anatolia. They had been resettled in the Venetian districts to reproduce the former occupants' talent at commerce. In 1477, there were 1,647 Jewish households in Istanbul.[88] Sephardic Jews were settled not only in Istanbul, but also in Salonica, Valona (Avlonya), Patras, Edirne, Bursa, and other towns, many of whose Jewish trading families had been removed by Mehmed II.[89]

The modern accounts of the initial establishment of a relationship between Mehmed II and the Jews are contentious because scholars have been at odds about the structure of the Jewish community. The best narrative has to reconstruct the encounter to represent the Ottoman and Jewish needs and strategies of the moment within the field of available options. From this perspective, Mehmed II, a pragmatist, appreciated the multiple implications of Jewish settlement in his empire; that is, on the one hand, Jewish commercial and professional acumen was valuable, yet many communities without an overarching organizational framework created practical problems of administration.[90] With this problem in mind, Mehmed II appointed Moshe Capsali as the leading rabbi and honored him as the leader of the Jewish community, in many ways attempting to reproduce the Orthodox pattern. He did so without the approval or the opposition of the Jewish community. Jews were not used to having a leading rabbi, but they were probably keenly aware that opposition to the sultan at such an important moment of contact would only hurt them. That such a position did not continue beyond 1526 shows that the Jewish tradition of multiple communities with multiple leaders would reassert itself, forcing the Ottoman administration to reconsider adopting Jewish institutions rather than changing them. Braude has defined the parameters of the Ottoman–Jewish administrative existence quite succinctly: "in the absence of regular formal representation

---

[88] İnalcık, "Foundations of Ottoman–Jewish Cooperation," 5.
[89] Ibid., 7.
[90] Avigdor Levy, *The Sephardim in the Ottoman Empire* (Princeton, NJ: Darwin Press, 1992), 45; Levy, ed., *Jews, Turks, Ottomans*.

to the authorities, the Jewish communities of the empire employed a system of special envoys and court favorites to plead their causes – a custom prevalent among Iberian Jews before the expulsion."[91] Yet, the absence of such formal hierarchical leadership was more than compensated for by the organizational detail and significance of Jewish communities.

Diaspora Jews had always organized to keep their internal affairs coherent, protected, and autonomous. Accordingly, Jews were initially organized into multiple small congregations (*kahal* in Hebrew and *cemaat* in Turkish), voluntary associations of families and individuals who knew each other from their original towns of immigration and who assembled around a synagogue. These congregations operated as religious and secular units of administration in which elected lay and religious leaders handled issues of religion, education, taxation, and communication. In larger towns, such smaller units were often organized into larger, town-wide organizations (*kehillah*).[92] Especially as the Ottoman communities flourished in their urban settings, these larger units became the administrative units that dealt with the state, operating as fiscal and legal units, and were also the markers to Jews of an institutional Jewish presence. Moreover, in urban centers where multiple congregations of different backgrounds were forced into a *kehilla*, alternative arrangements loosely named "councils" emerged, especially as a way for leadership to meet and discuss social and political issues.

That the Ottoman authorities adapted to this multilayered, complex, and fiercely protective system without undermining its autonomy is a testament to the flexibility and expediency of their rule. Unlike any other group, Jews early on had penetrated the imperial palace as high government functionaries, doctors, and advisors, and made it possible for rulers and communities to understand that there existed an open channel of communication, ready to be deployed.[93] Ottomans therefore negotiated with each community separately, adopting the community leadership structures whereby those lay leaders chosen by the community were responsible both for the management of internal affairs and for negotiation with state representatives. Yet, they also maintained an encompassing administrative perspective in that they stipulated a set amount of taxation from the Jewish communities and were indifferent to the manner in which it was divided up among communities; they expected payments to be made promptly. Internally, community leaders divided up the sum into communal responsibilities and collected from each community. The imperial authorities were not interested in the community details of taxation, and community leaders were keen on maintaining such tasks as a matter of internal concern.

---

[91] Braude, "Foundation Myths," 80–81.

[92] Levy, *The Sephardim in the Ottoman Empire*, 48–49.

[93] Aryeh Shmuelevitz, *The Jews of the Ottoman Empire in the Late Fifteenth and the Sixteenth Centuries: Administrative, Economic, Legal, and Social Relations as Reflected in the Responsa* (Leiden, The Netherlands: E. J. Brill, 1984), 24.

That the Jewish community and its leadership never became centralized made the issue of leadership much more complex for both sides. The boundary managers of the Jewish community then were necessarily less hierarchical as well as more numerous and varied. Even if the leading rabbi, Moshe Capsali, had acted as the tax collector initially, the geographic and demographic growth of the Jewish communities would have made this task impossible for one man without a formal religious hierarchy below him. Therefore, again, by necessity and by custom, Ottoman–Jewish relations developed to be managed by a series of religious and lay leaders, acting on behalf of specific communities. Each community had its own rabbinic and judicial authorities, although ultimately brokerage was maintained by the true intermediaries of each community. These were prominent Jews at the court and state-appointed special functionaries – Jewish *kethüdâs* – responsible for keeping the records of the community, whether they were taxation, business, or tax farming records. With the development of a successful repertoire of relations, the lay leader appointed from below and the Jewish representative appointed from above came to be the same person. As they mediated community affairs and taxation with local government officials, contacted prominent Jews at the center to raise their concerns with the sultan, or managed intercommunity relations in their particular settings, both religious and secular leaders became boundary managers for the empire.

The institutionalization of such relations for the most important centers of Jewish life, such as Istanbul, Salonica, Safed, and Jerusalem, meant that they could easily be reproduced, for example, when new cities such as Izmir emerged. Istanbul, however, being close to the seat of power, naturally retained primacy, which is evidenced by the increasing number of appeals by leaders of local communities for help in bringing a community's case to the Porte.[94] The networks that connected Jews across communities often went through the capital, making Istanbul a de facto center. We can thus see that the Jews of Istanbul, as a result of their locational and financial advantages, acquired intermediary positions. The upshot of being both without a hierarchical religious order and of having multiple communities within a *millet*-style organizational format was that Jewish communities remained autonomous, connected among themselves, and responsible for their own tax burden.

The Ottomans recognized the Armenian community right around the same time as they did the Greek Orthodox one, without fully realizing its ecclesiastical and regional complications. Because it emerged after the fourteenth century to be the only remaining center of Armenian identity, the Armenian Church might have evinced a structure similar to that of the Greek Orthodox Church. Yet, this would initially be difficult because there were various such centers that claimed ecclesiastical authority over a specified territory. Furthermore, early on the centers of Armenian religious authority lay outside the Ottoman frontiers. The stronghold of Armenian identity lay with the head of the Armenian Church,

---

[94] For more concrete details of Ottoman–Jewish relations, see Bornstein-Makovetsky, "Jewish Lay Leadership and Ottoman Authorities."

the Catholicos, in Erivan (Echmiadsin), outside Ottoman territory. Ottomans established two centers within their territory, appointing a patriarch for each, in Constantinople and in Jerusalem. Later, other patriarchates were incorporated, and the empire was divided among numerous religious sees with varying jurisdictions. Recent work on the Armenian community stresses the complexity of the territorial divisions, the various jurisdictions, and the fact that there were large chunks of territory that remained outside the existing system. Where they had jurisdiction, the Armenian patriarchs were responsible for tax collection and administration, and outside their jurisdiction, simple local prelates performed these duties.

The moment of Ottoman–Armenian acquaintance was a moment of creation of legibility, partly the result of Mehmed II's campaign to the East, where he conquered most of the northern coast of Asia Minor to the borders of Armenia. It is said that he returned from his Trabzon expedition in 1461 and then addressed the issue of Armenians in his city.[95] The immediate community of Armenians was also a *sürgün* population of artisans and traders from Sıvas, Tokat, and Kayseri, who had recently been joined by a group from Bursa, Ankara, and other Anatolian towns. It is said that Mehmed II looked around to fit the Armenians and other splinter groups into a category other than the Greek Orthodox, and remembered that his acquaintance in Bursa, Bishop Horaghim (Joachim/Hovakim), was the highest Armenian religious authority in the realm; he therefore invited him to come and head the Armenian community.[96] The patriarchate in Istanbul represented a growing population of Istanbul Armenians, but not the remaining population of Anatolia. In addition, making internal patriarchate affairs more complex, other Christian groups that did not easily fit into the Orthodox category, such as the Monophysites of Syria and Egypt, the Bogomils of Bosnia, and the Copts, were added into the Armenian Gregorian Church.

Established in his headquarters, the Byzantine Church of Sulu Manastır, the Armenian patriarch was made to parallel the Greek Orthodox model; he was an Ottoman administrative official who farmed out the office of the patriarch from the Ottoman state in the same way the Greek Orthodox patriarch did. In 1587, for example, a *berat* was provided to the Armenian Patriarch Serkis, who had bought the right to the *mukataa* of the Armenian patriarchate for 126.920 *aspres* or 1,056 gold coins.[97] As the patriarch of the Armenian community of Istanbul, he was to enjoy jurisdiction over the community's spiritual administration, its public instruction, and its charitable and religious institutions. Similar to the situation in the Greek Orthodox and Jewish communities, the Armenian patriarch had his ecclesiastical courts in which members of the community presented their cases, except those involving "public security and

[95] Franz Babinger, *Mehmed the Conqueror and His Time* (Princeton, NJ: Princeton University Press, 1978), 197.

[96] Sugar, *Southeastern Europe under Ottoman Rule*, 49; Georges Castellan, *Histoire des Balkans, XIVe–XXe siècle* (Paris: Fayard, 1991), 120.

[97] Konortas, "Considérations Ottomanes au sujet du statut du patriarcat," 221.

crime." According to some sources, much authority was exercised over the members of the community who transgressed religious law or neglected to pay their taxes; they were tried by the patriarch and then accordingly punished by his *vekil* (vicar), a high-ranking cleric working closely with the administration.[98]

With the large-scale movement of Armenians to Istanbul, the patriarch accumulated power and influence until, in the late seventeenth century, he was able to centralize jurisdiction and take control of the other existing patriarchates. Therefore, on the one hand, Armenians developed a tendency toward the Orthodox pattern of hierarchical control. Yet, on the other hand, by the mid-sixteenth century, similar to the situation in Jewish communities, Armenian lay leaders (Armenian *Çelebis*, later also called the "Amira" class) had taken on some of the broker functions between the Istanbul community and the Anatolian settlements. The relationship between the Ottoman state and the Armenian communities then resembled both that of the Greek Orthodox and that of the Jews. Ottomans wanted to provide religious authorities with the sanction to administer their people. However, because many such religious centers existed with no centralized authority, the Ottomans found themselves negotiating complex issues of religious and territorial jurisdiction with the leadership. Moreover, those Armenian patriarchs farthest from Constantinople would have to rely on intermediaries at the capital, which therefore inadvertently promoted the rise of a new class of secular Armenians. In the case of the Jews, the secular leadership was homegrown, part of the community structure. In the Armenian case, a secular leadership seems to have emerged as a result of church fragmentation and needs. The Armenian community organization and its religious structures dictated an intermediate position between the overly centralized and hierarchical Greek Orthodox Church and the decentralized and more popular Jewish communal organization.

At each encounter, transactions between the state and community leaders set a modus vivendi with an Ottoman script that was the by-product of a syncretic interpretation of the Turkic past and of Islam mixed in with the requirements of ruling a vast, heterogeneous empire. Each community in turn had its own set of institutions and understandings of relations with the conquering forces. The strongest script, the Greek Orthodox religious one, had been dominant during Byzantine rule, and had therefore facilitated a religious perspective on defining and delimiting collective life. Others had different scripts that were produced by different historical experiences. Nevertheless, by the end of the fifteenth century, the Ottoman state had replicated its pattern of vertical integration through indirect rule; it had created dependent and compliant elites who had been incorporated into the state and who were given favored status over other potential religious and ethnic elites. Yet, their position was also balanced by a series of other local community structures and public officials.

[98] Vartan Artinian, *The Armenian Constitutional System in the Ottoman Empire 1839–1863: A Study of its Historical Development* (Istanbul: V. Artinian, 1988).

Alternatives to Religious Community

The advantage of indirect rule with a stratum of incorporated elites is that the ruling elite does not have to engage with the details of everyday rule in multiple and varied settings. Yet, the danger of fully empowering intermediaries is that they will become connected to those they rule, stop complying with the state, and organize dissent. It is only natural to ask then why these men who acted as intermediaries between the state and their own communities did not find a way to become empowered by their position and decide to use it for collective action against the state? After all, they ruled over their own peoples for an alien state.

The Ottoman state had empowered these religious elites (also secular elites in the Jewish case) with positions that had all the trappings of officialdom: tax exemption, freedom to travel, and rule over communities. Nevertheless, the state also promoted administrative conditions that both destabilized intermediaries and promoted alternatives to them. These intermediaries were strictly controlled by the state, and often were unappreciated by their religious disciples and communities. That they were recognized as Ottoman officials, that they bought their offices at very high prices and had to collect through onerous exactions to reimburse themselves hurt their legitimacy vis-à-vis their religious communities.

The integration of communities along religious lines existed alongside a variety of other territorial and political forms of integration. I have already discussed the integration of frontiers, the conquered elites, and the absorption of the landed estates. Added to the religious and military elites, alternative and parallel local elites and institutions of rule engendered multiple tracks of indirect integration. Given the nature of piecemeal conquests and the need to pull in territory quickly after incorporation, the Ottoman leaders left communes intact with their local self-government. Although at the very top they had empowered the Christian Orthodox Church as an umbrella organization, at the district level, existing local structures, communal organizations, village centers, and indigenous leadership remained. Especially in the Balkans, where conquest happened early and quickly, the Church was one of the most important institutions of indirect rule, but not the only one. In addition to the local bishops and metropolitans, local chiefs and notables at the rural level and neighborhood chiefs (*mahalle başı*) and guild leaders (*kethüdâ*) in the urban centers organized the community and maintained its diverse internal workings. In Serres, local memoirs tell the story of the rivalry that existed between the metropolitan and the local notables, as well as the continual interference of the local clerics and low-level Christian religious administrators in the affairs of the church and the community. They conclude that even though the metropolitan might have had a position of authority in the local Ottoman hierarchy, it was always tempered by the local notables, the priests, and the laity.[99]

---

[99] Paolo Odorico, ed., *Conseils et mémoires de Synadinos, prêtre de Serrés en Macédoine (XVIIe siècle)* (Paris: Editions de l'Association "Pierre Belon," 1996).

By allowing a complex and intricate set of networks of alternative community and neighborhood leaders and organizations, the Ottomans enhanced a
division of labor that made it impossible for any one patriarch or metropolitan
to dominate the entire community. The potential power of the church was
diminished by the Ottoman acceptance of local secular leadership acting to
balance ecclesiastical concerns. Diverse administrative tasks such as tax collection, provisioning, and regulation were carried out by local intermediaries,
from the *knez*, the *voyvoda*, the *çorbacı*, the *primkuran* to the *kocabaşı* and the
archons, who staffed a "secular" administrative hierarchy of linkages to the
regional Ottoman officials and their superiors at the center. These local leaders
were exempt from taxation and reported directly to the government representative in the area, generally the *subaşı*.[100] Thus, the lower-level members of the
Ottoman secular administrative hierarchy were helped in their duties by their
secular counterparts in the local communities. In Muslim communities, Muslim notables (*ayan*) performed exactly the same tasks for the local provincial
leaders. We see then that parallel structures were employed in the governance
of rural communities, be they Muslim or Christian.[101]

In many conquered areas, typical forms of community self-government had
evolved in previous centuries and functioned to maintain communities as well
as distinct ethnicity and religion. These communal forms, the Serbian joint
family organization (*zadruga*) and self-governing community (*knezina*), the
Balkan pastoral community (*katun*), and the Greek free communities (*eleutherochoria*), were accepted, and the community was implicitly inaugurated as
the administrative unit that populated the larger geographical units. Wayne
Vucinich argues that "for a long time, it was to the advantage to both the
ruling Turks and the subject peoples to perpetuate organizations of this kind,
even though their existence promoted social exclusiveness, minimum social
interaction, and the perpetuation of old social norms."[102] Recent research has
shown that these communities were more than just vessels of taxation and subordination to the Ottoman authorities; rather, they organized and took part in
decision making, distributing the tax burden, and imposing it on households
after having negotiated with the central authorities.[103]

Similarly, the organization of urban social and cultural spaces, as well as the
distribution of religious institutions throughout these spaces, reproduced parallel structures of the governing administration. That is, on the one hand, the

---

[100] Kemal H. Karpat, *An Inquiry into the Social Foundations of Nationalism in the Ottoman State:
From Social Estates to Classes, from Millets to Nations* (Princeton, NJ: Center of International
Studies, Princeton University, 1973), 35.
[101] There are really no data on the numbers of these men who laid the basis for local administration,
apart from the fact that they were in every district and urban location of considerable size.
[102] Wayne S. Vucinich, "The Nature of Balkan Society under Ottoman Rule," *Slavic Review*
21 (1962): 608. See also N. Pantazopoulos, "Community Laws and Customs of Western
Macedonia under Ottoman Rule," *Balkan Studies* 2:1 (1961): 1–22.
[103] Eleni Gara, "In Search of Communities in Seventeenth Century Ottoman Sources: The Case
of Kara Ferye District," *Turcica* 30 (1998): 135–162.

smallest urban unit was the neighborhood (*mahalle*) of the religious communities gathered around their religious center, whether it was a mosque, synagogue,
or church.[104] Despite this tendency to gather around religious institutions, religious groups were not separated from one another. In principle, Jews and
Christians were not allowed to live by a mosque, but this was often not fully
enforced.[105] On the other hand, the guild system functioned as the occupa-
tional category under which urban space was organized. Guilds were primarily
a Muslim institution, but over time Jewish and Christian artisans and merchants joined them. Jews and Christians could develop their own section of a
certain guild and choose a Jewish or Christian functionary (*kethüdâ*) to lead
them. In such cases, the *kethüdâs* of different religions communicated among
themselves, agreeing and disagreeing on policy.[106]

Second, the uneasy and awkward establishment of one church over many
different ethnic groups helped break the power of the patriarch. Each *millet*
umbrella had its own internal complexity of competing leaders and institutions,
making it impossible to capture in its entirety. The Greek Orthodox Church
was the institution for the Orthodox community, although in the other two
cases, leadership was more fragmented, especially among the Jews. The Greek
Orthodox Church had been empowered by the Ottoman state to maintain the
Orthodox community as a religious community, with a shared religious identity, and not to concern itself with the ways in which it had lumped together
many diverse ethnic groups.[107] The church had the potential to be a national
institution, yet its uneasy management of diverse groups hindered such an
inclusive goal. Clearly, religion and ethnicity were not fully compatible with
nationhood. At the top of the church hierarchy, the patriarchs sitting in Constantinople guarded a boundary based on universal religious claims. As one
descended the hierarchy and entered the communities of the faithful, the local
prelates guarded more than just religious difference; in their daily interaction,

---

[104] Ahmet Refik, *Onuncu Asr-ı Hicri'de Istanbul Hayatı* (Istanbul: Enderun Kitabevi, 1988); idem,
Onikinci Asr-ı Hicri'de Istanbul Hayatı (Istanbul: Enderun Kitabevi, 1988).

[105] Stéphane Yerasimos, "La Communauté juive d'Istanbul à la fin du XVIe siècle," *Turcica* 27
(1995): 101–130 indicates a real entanglement of Jewish and Muslim properties in Istanbul; see
also Veinstein, "Une Communauté Ottomane"; Ronald C. Jennings, *Christians and Muslims
in Ottoman Cyprus and the Mediterranean World, 1571–1640* (New York and London: New
York University Press, 1993), 136; Molly Greene, *A Shared World: Christians and Muslims in
the Early Modern Mediterranean* (Princeton, NJ: Princeton University Press, 2000); Masters
thesis, *Christian and Jews*.

[106] Yücel Özkaya, *XVIII. Yüzyılda Osmanlı Kurumları ve Osmanlı Toplum Yaşantısı* (Ankara:
Kültür ve Turizm Bakanlığı, 1985); Eremya Çelebi Kömürciyan, *Istanbul Tarihi: XVII. Asırda
Istanbul* (Istanbul: Eren Yayıncılık ve Kitapçılık Ltd. Şti., 1988); T. Tankut Soykan, *Osmanlı
İmparatorluğu'nda Gayrimüslimler: Klasik Dönem Osmanlı Hukukunda Gayrimüslimlerin
hukuki statüsü* (Istanbul: Ütopya Kitabevi, 1999).

[107] The Orthodox Church had jurisdiction over many different ethnic groups, such as Greeks,
Albanians, Bulgarians, Serbians, Moldavians and Wallachians, Ruthenians, Croats, Syrians,
Caramanians, Arabs, and Melkites. See Karpat, *An Inquiry into the Social Foundation of
Nationalism in the Ottoman State*.

they maintained ethnicity and language because the local prelate or the local bishop belonged not only to the larger Orthodox community, but also to the local Greek, Serbian, Albanian, or other Slavic ethnic and linguistic community. The local church and village communities therefore took over as the strongholds of ethnic and cultural identity and linguistic continuity as they functioned as the centers of education, promoting local language and religion regardless of who was at the top. Hupchick, for example, demonstrates the degree to which an Orthodox Bulgarian Church was instrumental in maintaining a Bulgarian identity, separate and opposed to the larger Greek Orthodox confessional *millet* identity.[108] Such local institutions existed as early as the sixteenth century and sometimes even earlier, as was the case of the Bulgarians.[109] It is in this way that despite the Ottoman state's relative inattention to ethnicity, it was in fact maintained deep in the thick of Balkan communities despite the limited resources of the local peoples. Karpat elegantly summarizes the maintenance of religion and ethnicity: "the millet system therefore produced, simultaneously, religious universality and local parochialism."[110]

The different layers of religious, fiscal, and administrative forms of organization show us that the Ottomans not only shaped and organized religious identities, but also left in place many communal forms that served local and regional functions, maintaining linguistic and ethnic enclaves that they did not care to possess as long as intermediaries, boundary managers, and tax officials carried on the functions of indirect rule.

The Absence of Intercommunal Violence

Most notable is the absence during the centuries under consideration of large-scale violence within and among religiously and ethnically differentiated communities. Although many attest to the potential for conflict between groups, to the intense animosity between Christians and Jews, and to the varying dominance of groups in demographic, economic, and trading terms, the centuries of Pax Ottomanica were relatively calm and free of ethnic or religious strife. Furthermore, when local incidents occurred, they were not allowed to spiral out of control. Court records show that Muslims and non-Muslims and non-Muslims among themselves came to court expecting the *kadı* to resolve their conflicts, especially in matters of trade, sales, and payment. Non-Muslims attended Muslim court, expecting both impartiality and a record of their transaction. It is also significant that in the thousands of cases in which members of different communities engaged in fights across boundaries, their actions did not get out of hand.[111]

---

[108] Hupchick, *The Bulgarians in the Seventeenth Century.*
[109] Hupchick, "Orthodoxy and Bulgarian Ethnic Awareness," 79.
[110] Kemal H. Karpat, "Millets and Nationality: The Roots of the Incongruity of Nation and State in the Post-Ottoman Era," in *Christians and Jews*, ed. Braude and Lewis, 147.
[111] Jennings, *Christians and Muslims in Ottoman Cyprus.* Jennings studied 2,800 cases in judicial court records from 1580 to 1637. He found that 15% of the cases involved just non-Muslims; 34% of the cases involved at least one non-Muslim (pp. 163–168). See also Greene, *A Shared World.*

The desire and attempt on the part of the state to maintain boundaries and order between Muslims and non-Muslims, as well as among non-Muslims, cannot be the only explanation for this relative stability of relations. It is not only that states make and maintain boundaries, but that religious and ethnic communities often acquiesce in this process, strenuously holding on to their distinctiveness. For intercommunity peace to exist, the communities themselves or, at the minimum, their leaders must have a direct interest in the maintenance of peace. Fearon and Laitin, who discuss interethnic peace, call such attempts "institutionalized in-group policing," where leaders successfully police their own members within the community and in transactions across communities. They use the Ottoman example along with Paul Dumont's description of interethnic relations, which, although based on the nineteenth century, could have been similar in earlier centuries: "the slightest spark sufficed to ignite a fuse. Whenever a young Christian disappeared at the approach of Passover, Jews were immediately accused of having kidnapped him to obtain blood necessary for the manufacture of unleavened bread. Threats and violence followed close behind the suspicions and generally things ended with a boycott of Jewish shops and peddlers."[112]

So that such incidents did not to blow up into large-scale ethnic conflict, the intermediaries, whether religious or secular leaders, were empowered by the state to monitor their internal affairs in return for continued benefits and autonomy. Community leaders who maintained peace and paid their dues on time would be rewarded with continued appointment and increased opportunity for wealth. Community leaders who were embroiled in violence and could not maintain calm in communities and across communities, or who were unable to garner enough authority to collect taxes, lost their livelihoods and, more often, their heads.

Much of the relationship between communities occurred in the market, in the production and consumption transactions that members of the different communities engaged in daily. Jews, Christians, and Muslims not only bought and sold from one another, but they also formed business associations, dissolved them, and committed fraud and crimes that required the arbitration of courts. However, even further than that, especially when they got along, as was exemplified by relations in the town of Avlonya, Muslims testified for Jews, Jews testified for Christians or served as the guarantors for Christians in Muslim courts, and the *kadı* used Jews and Christians to add to his list of court witnesses.[113] In the city of Lefkosia on the island of Cyprus, Muslims and Christians engaged in intercommunal land and property transfers quite frequently at the *kadı* court. As Jennings demonstrates, the more they bought and sold property from each other, the more they intermixed in their urban living

---

[112] Quoted in Fearon and Laitin, "Explaining Interethnic Cooperation," 728. See also Paul Dumont, "Jewish Communities in Turkey during the last Decades of the 19th Century," in *Christians and Jews in the Ottoman Empire*, 222–223.

[113] Gilles Veinstein gives many good examples of such tight intercommunal relations. See Gilles Veinstein, "Une Communauté Ottomane," 790.

space.[114] Similarly, Bruce Masters reports a relatively harmless picture of inter-communal relations in Arab cities of the seventeenth century, where Muslims and non-Muslims lived together and worked freely in many guilds together, although over the centuries of Ottoman rule spatial clustering around religious dimensions did occur.[115] Community members also struggled and engaged in many conflicts that often originated from differences in their treatment by public authorities, or from the real or perceived differences in economic and financial superiority. Veinstein explains that in Avlonya some conflict arose from the fact that Jews were financially more successful; therefore, competitive animosity was directed against them. He provides examples of the petty and not so petty crimes that were committed against the Jewish population of this town.

Given that in most of the unresolved cases litigants ended up in court, the separate, autonomous, yet somehow interactive legal institutions of the empire – whether Jewish, Muslim, or Christian – became centers of intercommunal conflict resolution. Therefore, much of the information on how conflict was diffused comes from court cases. However, even before looking at the cases, we need to look at the actors involved in conflict resolution. Contact between court systems bred knowledge. In each of the three *dhimmi* communities, the legal executives (whether rabbis, judges, or ecumenical court officials) were forced to study and be fully conversant with Ottoman law in order to make sure that the members of their communities did not commit offenses serious enough to harm relations between the communities and the authorities.[116]

Community leaders at many different levels were interested in boundary management. Among them, religious leaders were most naturally inclined to maintain boundaries. Such leaders were always interested in maintaining a community of the faithful for both financial and religious reasons. The literature attests to the fact that the most important struggles between patriarchs, rabbis, and their constituencies were related to keeping the basic religious functions of the community within its boundaries. That is, rabbis in numerous *responsas* demanded that Jews be married in Jewish court and not in the *kadı* court; ecclesiastical courts struggled to maintain marriages that had been dissolved at the *kadı* court. In both cases, members of the community had crossed the boundaries of their community to seek a better deal at the dominant court. The rabbis threatened their people, whereas the patriarchs excommunicated their people and prohibited their burial after death.[117]

Religious leaders restricted the movement of their members toward the dominant legal institutions of the country for many reasons. Both rabbis and

[114] Jennings, *Christians and Muslims in Ottoman Cyprus*; see also Greene, *A Shared World*.
[115] Masters, *Christians and Jews*, 33.
[116] Shmuelevitz reports that that the fifteenth- and sixteenth-century rabbis whose *responsas* he read demonstrate that they were fully conversant with secular and Islamic law (*The Jews of the Ottoman Empire*, 38–40).
[117] The best sources on this for the Jewish community are Shmuelevitz, *The Jews of the Ottoman Empire* and for the Greek Orthodox community, Pantazopoulos, *Church and Law in the Balkan Peninsula*.

patriarchs believed in the superiority of their indigenous laws. Rabbis wanted members to respect Jewish law; more important, they maintained restrictions in order to avoid decisions that contravened Jewish law. Rabbis voiced their fear of assimilation and conversion because they believed that the more Islamic courts became the final recourse of Jews, the more likely were the Jews to become assimilated. Often, rabbis made concessions just in an effort to keep their communities from disintegration.[118] In the Balkans, official Orthodox Christian ecclesiastical law struggled to maintain its predominance over popular law, but more important, over Islamic law. Metropolitan and Episcopal courts in the provinces and the patriarchal court in Istanbul worked hard to apply patriarchal law because they not only believed in its sanctity, but also, especially in matters internal to the community, such as in cases of family law and inheritance, abhorred interference from the conquerors' laws. In the case of marriages, for example, a temporary type of marriage between Christian women and Muslim men and between Christians was frequently approved by the *kadı* court, but was seen as endangering the soul of Christian communities. Ecclesiastical courts imposed harsh penalties to keep these marriages from occurring.[119]

In the case of Jewish courts, Shmuelevitz reports that rabbis often restricted the access of Jewish litigants to the Islamic courts because they wanted to maintain the good reputation of the Jewish community, being concerned that intracommunity struggles showed the uglier side of the community. In cases where they found infractions by Jews, rabbis were torn between reporting or not reporting them to the authorities because they feared not only for the community, but also for the individuals involved. Significant also was the fear of false accusations, especially when struggles between Jews led to false denunciations in the *kadı* court, sometimes leading to communities rather than individuals being threatened. When a Jew harmed his own community in such a way, he was severely punished. Christian leaders must have been similarly concerned because under the domination of a foreign power, the mentality of keeping internal conflicts within the community becomes a mode of survival. Furthermore, given the harsh conditions of prison, religious leaders always sought to protect their people from the prisons of the conqueror.

Although intracommunity relations and conflicts were easier to control, avoiding their escalation into unmistakable public cases or intercommunal struggles, especially between Christians and Jews, was much harder to achieve once the escalation had begun. Despite the fact that Jews mostly preferred to live in Muslim neighborhoods and avoided Christian – especially Greek – locales for fear of abuse, relations between Jews and Christians were difficult to restrict in the major cities of Salonica, Istanbul, and others. In such cases, relations had to be as stylized and controlled as possible. That is, when a Christian and a Jew

[118] Shmuelevitz, *The Jews of the Ottoman Empire*, 68–69.
[119] John C. Alexander, "Law of the Conqueror (The Ottoman State) and Law of the Conquered (The Orthodox Church): The Case of Marriage and Divorce," *International Congress of Historical Sciences* 16 (1985): 369–371.

entered a relationship, especially in business, they were eager for the Islamic court to register it because this ensured that their transaction would be honored. Relations between these two non-Muslim communities were sometimes so tense that litigants were afraid to use their own courts and instead used the Muslim courts, where they sought impartial treatment.[120] Blood libels were an instance of conflictual relations between the two communities, when Jews were accused of using Christian blood to make their Passover bread. Given the gravity of such accusations and their potential for violent conflict, Mehmed II had issued a *ferman* asking the *kadıs* of the realm to refer such cases to the Divan, the Imperial court. Despite the reissuing of this *ferman*, local *kadıs* preferred to keep such matters within their realm, perhaps also maintaining in their own view some sort of intercommunal policing function. The important point is that more often than not the leaders concerned carefully monitored such cases to avoid the spiraling of confrontation. Such behavior on the part of the rabbis and lay leaders of the Jewish community is especially evident in the rabbinical *responsa* literature of the Jewish community.[121]

These communities and their leaders were also keen to preserve boundaries. The manner in which this occurred was through in-group policing by which the leadership exercised great care and authority to maintain community boundaries, to keep contention from developing beyond boundaries, and especially to keep cross-community struggles under control.

Conclusion

The historical examination of the Ottoman establishment and maintenance of relations with the multiethnic and multireligious communities throughout the first three centuries of rule demonstrates that toleration was the preferred solution to imperial rule over diversity. It was in the nature of Ottoman rule to find an intermediate organizational solution with which it could exploit the manpower, skills, and resources of various populations by enlisting local elements into the imperial way of life. This practice then was applied to a diverse population, to religious and ethnic groups, which were maintained in their traditional social and cultural positions and brought in to participate in empire.

Whether the organization of religious communities was called *millet* or something else, we have unequivocal evidence that the early Ottoman rulers established a relational format of state-religious community interaction. Given the Islamic notions of boundary between Muslims and non-Muslim communities, and the Turkic tribal understandings of incorporation, the Ottoman state developed a policy toward these groups that was flexible and that adapted itself to local conditions and needs. In this arrangement, it allowed

[120] Ibid., 46.
[121] Esther Benbassa and Aron Rodrigue, *Sephardi Jewry: A History of the Judeo-Spanish Community, 14th–20th Centuries* (Berkeley: University of California Press, 2000), 18.

for existing communities to persist and to determine key intermediaries between communities and the state. Therefore, from the micro levels of established community practices, such as the Serbian *zadruga* (family organization) to the more meso structures of the *katin* (pastoral community), the *knezina* and *eleutherochoria* (respectively, free and self-governing Serbian and Greek communities), to the macro communal and religious organization of the church, the Ottomans accepted what was there and designated a few agents as the key interlocutors across boundaries.

Ottomans paid much more attention to administrative boundaries of rule than to physical or symbolic markers of difference. Despite frequent references to physical markers of difference such as clothing, colors, height of residences, and ownership of slaves, they were unable or unwilling to fully enforce such regulations. From time to time they did fine individuals or communities through their representatives, but this was an economic device rather than one of policing religious boundaries. Only during periods of state zealotry did obvious physical markers become critical to maintaining boundaries. Mostly, the state allowed a multicultural society where it was possible to acquire multiple languages, to interact with multiple others, to be cosmopolitan, and to adopt the practices and the knowledge of others. This was allowed as long as everyone was controlled, paid their taxes, and was accountable to the state through a "unit."

The administrative structure of the Greek Orthodox Church with its typical hierarchical arrangement headed by an ecclesiastical leader as the main representative of the whole community of Orthodox Christians was the preferred model for the state. For the conquered populations, it was different. Had religion and ethnicity been congruent in this classification, the Balkans might have emerged as rebellious forces long before nationalism came on the scene. The Jewish model of multiple autonomous communities with their distinct leadership led to the proliferation of intermediaries, a situation that was administratively remedied by forcing Istanbul Jewry into a dominant role. Over time, through different channels of rule, both Jewish and Armenian communities would be forced into the simpler and more straightforward pattern of Greek Orthodox organization. The Ottoman state interfered most vigorously in the administration of the Armenian community, having recognized a strategic need as well as an administrative difficulty with the existing forms of multiple and fragmented religious sovereignty. This again reminds us of the degree to which organization and rule were constantly rethought and better models tried.

Much of the discussion of community and religious diversity has been blurred by the apparent inability to reconcile Ottoman Islam with notions of community. Among Ottoman historians, both claims have been made: that Ottoman Islam nurtured the "community" or that it rejected the "community" as a legal entity. Robert Mantran in his discussion of guilds in the Ottoman Empire maintains that Islam is a community-based society. Economic and religious forms of organization, he says, make the isolation of the individual practically impossible.[122] However, others have forcefully argued that the concept of corporation did not exist in Ottoman Islam and that the law favored the individual.[123] Joseph Schacht, in his classic book *An Introduction to Islamic Law*, argues that "the concept of corporation does not exist in Islamic law (neither does that of a jurisdic person)."[124] Still others make the argument that it is only with the developments of the eighteenth century that corporations were understood as real formations in the empire. The community unit was the main organizational unit of the Ottoman Empire. Religious communities, local administrative community units, and guilds as economic communities represent the means through which Ottomans administered and controlled society.

The concept of boundaries as elaborated by Barth is brought to bear in explaining the dilemmas that arise from the notions of community and individual. Communities were understood and separated by boundaries, and many mechanisms maintained boundaries for the state. Examples from studies of Jewish–Ottoman relations demonstrate the degree to which local officials and central state officials understood Jews to form a community, yet searched for a few representatives to mediate relations. Many cases show how the local officials, *sanjak beyis*, *kadıs*, and other power holders referred to the "Jewish community," extorted money from the "community," and accommodated them or threatened them as a group. Most often, the Ottoman magistrate who recognized the need to deal with a collectivity handled the situation by appointing a representative body that would negotiate personally with it.[125]

Boundaries were produced and maintained by each side. Despite the greater prospect for the Ottoman state to make, break, and maintain boundaries, communities of faith were also interested in remaining separate. That is, whether it was the Greek Orthodox Church, the different Armenian patriarchs, or the various scattered Jewish communities of the empire, they all recognized their precarious condition, yet insisted on their separateness. From the sixteenth century on, records of communities show the degree to which they responded to the Ottoman government in collective terms, as communities with an understanding of their existence as a people apart whose existence and liability within the system was open to negotiation. We have to conclude that difference and separation was a value pursued by the state and the communities themselves.

---

[122] Robert Mantran, *Histoire de l'empire Ottoman* (Paris: Fayard, 1989).

[123] Eleni Gara argues that in Islamic law the corporation does not exist ("In Search of Communities in Seventeenth Century Ottoman Sources"). Timur Kuran argues similarly that the individual actor is recognized, but not the collectivity. See Timur Kuran, "Islam and Underdevelopment: An Old Puzzle Revisited," *Journal of Institutional and Theoretical Economics* 153 (March 1997): 41–71.

[124] Joseph Schacht, *An Introduction to Islamic Law* (Oxford, UK: Oxford University Press, 1964), 155.

[125] Amnon Cohen, "Communal Legal Entities in a Muslim Setting, Theory and Practice: The Jewish Community in Sixteenth-Century Jerusalem," *Islamic Law and Society* 3:1 (1996): 75–89.

Finally, we return to the comparison of the Ottomans with their contemporaries. There is no doubt that there was a difference between Islam and Christianity with regard to how subject communities experienced diversity in Islamic and Christian empires. Islam no doubt moderated the impact of empire on diversity. Islam had a script for how to deal with Jews and Christians, whereas Christianity, especially in the age of the Crusades and its aftermath, conducted itself as an exclusive religion with an organized body ideally unified with public authorities. The history of the Habsburg and Russian Empires, especially early on, demonstrates this unity in which the polity and the religious authorities worked in tandem to administer empire, whereas Islam was subordinated to the will of the polity, but also provided an inclusive script for the administration of religious groups. It is interesting that both the Russians and the Habsburgs moved toward a more pragmatic model of religious incorporation, with the Russians developing the idea of "tolerated faiths" and the Austrian politicians especially discussing the *millet* system as an option.

5

The Social Organization of Dissent

Rumelia, Serrai,
And an old expression:
>HIS IMPERIAL PRESENCE.

At the center,
Straight as a sword stuck in the ground,
>The old man.

Facing him, the Sultan.
They looked at each other.
...
The rain hisses.
Swinging from a bare branch,
getting wet in the rain
late on a starless night,
>the naked body of my sheik ... [1]

In this poem by Nazım Hikmet, Şeyh Bedreddîn, the fifteenth-century Ottoman mystic and rebel, faces Sultan Mehmed I before he is finally hanged for leading a rebellion against the sultan. The image of empire and dissent is forcefully represented throughout the epic narratives and poems that relate the story of the şeyh, one of the most influential mystical figures of Ottoman times. In this particular poem, the meeting of the two men, the rebel and the sultan, reveals the poignancy of the situation. The deep sense of ambivalence that Hikmet wants to convey comes from the knowledge that these two men had been allies and have become mortal enemies. Hikmet got it right: the essential ingredient of this narrative is the contest between şeyh and sultan, rebel and state. Among the many reasons for Şeyh Bedreddîn's continuing influence was his impressive learning and his drawing together of Muslims, Christians, and Jews under a syncretic and enlightened vision of religion. Şeyh Bedreddîn is also fascinating

---

[1] Excerpts from "The Epic of Sheik Bedreddin," by Nazım Hikmet. See *Poems of Nazım Hikmet* (New York: Persea Books, 2002).

because he belongs in the transitional space between acceptance and dissent, between authority and subjection, and between popular and elite culture, and temporally to the historical shift from syncretism to Sunnî hegemony. Moreover, the stories of Bedreddîn and those of other instances of dissent reveal a lot about the relationship among dissent, imperial longevity, and the organization of difference and boundaries in the empire. A corollary is that the inquiry into empire and dissent reveals the workings of Sunnî–Shiite sectarian divisions, especially as Sunnî orthodoxy once again assumed an imperial posture and the Shiite religious approach became defined as the opposition.

Imperial domination is never complete; it is negotiated. Therefore, the space for acceptance and dissent is both available and contested. Throughout the centuries, empires as a form of domination inspired, furthered, and shaped dissent. If empire held together through the social organization of difference and control, dissent thrived in the recesses of empire that remained outside the purview of the rulers. Domination that is not complete creates opportunities in its fissures and cracks. Scholars have studied the relationship between empire and resistance with the overall goal of understanding empire as a form of rule and resistance as a form of multivalent opposition. For the most part, they have also assumed that mounting opposition to imperial rule brings about the demise of empire. If dissent is in fact what leads to this demise, then we have to look at how empires successfully withstood opposition for centuries, incorporated dissent into their ranks, and eliminated their adversaries without crumbling.

The analysis of the relationship between empire and dissent contributes to our understanding of imperial longevity. How does dissent originate, what sort of transformations does it undergo, and under what circumstances does it become perilous to imperial forms of rule? How have empires survived dissent? What were the mechanisms of survival for empires and for dissenters? How did they confront each other, and under what circumstances did empires become violent and repressive of dissent?

The Ottoman Empire is a rich case to study because deep contradictions and ambiguities existed in the relationship between the empire and those who dissented. Especially through the sixteenth and seventeenth centuries, the Ottomans encountered widespread heterodox and "heretical" Muslim religious and sectarian dissent, which they fought vigorously, persecuting the extremists and assimilating the moderates. Persecution resulted from an inability to include, incorporate, and make relations and groups legible for the central authorities. The more diffuse and less organized the dissenters were, the more subversive they were deemed to be. In the seventeenth century, the central government found itself pulled by various forms of dissent, each claiming a different origin and purpose and with their actions organized differently. The popular heterodox forces pulled for more syncretism and less imperial domination, whereas the Kadızadeli religious reformists pushed for radical Puritanism so as to disengage Islam from its syncretic and impure applications, and Jews followed a messianic movement that responded to the malaise and pull and push of the period. The way in which the Ottomans responded to each episode of confrontation and continued to endure reveals much about the process of empire.

The question of dissent has been asked about all empires in one way or another. Who opposed imperial domination, and how did the center respond? Rome did not allow dissent to escalate into full-scale revolt. The Roman example has been explained by the strategy of incorporation, the implicit equality of all subjects in front of the emperor, the incorporation and privileging of local elites, and the patronage system that linked such local elites to the local people in tight and assimilated networks of reciprocity. In this way, elites were responsible and positively inclined toward the imperial state because they were given most favored lord status; the locals, however, were also dependent and loyal as they were beholden to the elites.[2] However, because Rome was a slave-based society, slave rebellion could have been a genuine problem. Many have argued that the extreme brutality with which the Romans punished their errant slaves acted as a deterrent, convincing the slaves that rebellion could end in a total bloodbath. Jews who rebelled between 66 and 70 A.D. in Judea were severely punished for their infractions. Moreover, the patronage system, friendship demands, and possibility of upward mobility and freedom from slavery facilitated the control of slaves. Yet, the Roman and Byzantine Empires encountered different forms of dissent. Dissent in the Byzantine case was much more religious; it took shape in the iconoclast conflict and in the state struggle against heretical forms, such as Bogomilism. In each case, imperial governments cajoled and fought, absorbed rebellious tendencies, and tried to eliminate dissent before it spread.

In the Habsburg and Russian Empires, as well as in the Ottoman, dissent manifested itself in religious terms more than in other dimensions, although religion was often a cover for socioeconomic issues. In the Russian Empire, the state's response to the organization of dissent was similar in many ways to the policies of the Ottoman Empire. Although Jewish and Muslim communities experienced a complex and evolving combination of persecution, cooptation, cooperation, and violence in their relations with Russian imperial authorities, the forms of dissent that the Russian state found most threatening were the Old Believers and the Uniates. These were non-Orthodox Christian sects that, like the heterodox orders of the Ottoman Empire, either resisted cooperation and cooptation and remained subversively diffused – for example, the remarkably persistent faith of the Old Believers – or else occupied a threatening intermediary space with loyalties outside the empire – such as the Uniates who swore allegiance to the Pope in Rome. These non-Orthodox Christians experienced more consistent and sustained pressure to convert and assimilate than did other non-Orthodox communities with which the Russian state brokered agreements and whose elites they coopted. For instance, the Lutherans of the Baltic German states and Finland were easily assimilated into the imperial

[2] Gary B. Miles, "Roman and Modern Imperialism: A Reassessment," *Comparative Studies in Society and History* 32 (October 1990): 629–659.

structure. The well-defined hierarchies and regional concentration of Lutherans allowed arrangements to be established in which imperial authorities felt firmly in control.

In this pairing of empire and dissent, I broadly understand dissent as the effect of a set of relations that brings empire to the people. That is, it is in the political, social, and cultural organization of imperial relations that people experience empire. Moreover, in response, they accept, rethink, reshape, or reject these relations, allowing some to become practices and others to disappear. Yet, by defining dissent in this way, I do not confine it to imperial boundaries. Dissent may be confined to the boundaries of empire, but more often than not, it transgresses boundaries and settles in interimperial spaces, exploiting interstate rivalries. Russia had to deal with such interstate positioning with regard to the Uniate Church. Formed in the Union of Brest in 1596 in an attempt by the Polish-Lithuanian Commonwealth to consolidate the Orthodox of the East with the Catholics, the Uniate Church occupied a threatening interstitial and indeterminate locus that challenged Russian authorities as they expanded into the Ukraine and Poland. As Tsar Paul I (1796-1801) complained in reference to the Uniate Church, "I don't like it. It is neither one thing nor the other, neither fish nor fowl," reflecting the problems of legibility and boundary management that this organizational form prompted.[3] From the Union of Brest until the partition of Poland in the late eighteenth century, the Uniate Church was an instrument "for extending political and cultural hegemony" by both sides in the imperial rivalry between the Poles and the Russians.[4] In the seventeenth century, Russia and the Polish-Lithuanian Commonwealth were partitioned along the Dnepr River, with Russia in control of the left bank and Kiev. In the eighteenth century, the Uniate Church in right-bank Ukraine under Polish supervision developed closer ties with the Catholic Church, shifting the boundaries and making the division between Orthodox and Uniate confessions more differentiated.[5] A complex blurring of ethnicity and confession occurred along the border, as Orthodox faith was intertwined with Russian identity, and Catholic and Uniate faith represented Polish influence. Orthodox bishops engaged in aggressive campaigns to convert Uniates in the right-bank Ukraine and to organize parishes, effectively shifting the ecclesiastical border and blurring the political border.[6]

In many ambiguous ways, empires experience in some transitional populations the simultaneous potential for both legitimation and opposition. That is, dissent can sometimes help further legitimate the imperial order; opposition that wants to be incorporated into empire can bring legitimacy to empire.

---

[3] Theodore R. Weeks, "Between Rome and Tsargrad: The Uniate Church in Imperial Russia" in *Of Religion and Empire: Missions, Conversion, and Tolerance in Tsarist Russia* (Ithaca, NY: Cornell University Press, 2001), 73.

[4] Ibid., 71.

[5] Barbara Skinner, "Borderlands of Faith: Reconsidering the Origins of the Ukrainian Tragedy," *Slavic Review* 64 (Spring 2005), 97–98.

[6] Ibid., 101.

Within the larger system of competing states, empires encountered fluid movement back and forth from resistance to incorporation, especially at the frontiers. Populations that inhabited the spaces between empires often successfully negotiated moves from one rival empire to another. In such moves, they helped legitimate one empire over the other in the domestic and international arenas. Therefore, dissent played a role both at the core and at the frontiers.

Before turning to the analysis of the empire–dissent pairing in the Ottoman context, we need to make a few conceptual clarifications. First, "dissent" is more appropriate than "opposition" or "resistance" as a term of study because it connotes ambiguity better and can be used to denote forms of organization that might be embedded in the workings of the state, yet still promote dissent. Although opposition and resistance are clearly much sharper forms of disagreement, dissent fits better with the negotiated aspect of imperial rule, where it might mean acceptance of the bargaining process in some ways, while still being subversive through the mechanisms of indirect rule. Dissent thus differs from opposition and resistance in representing different forms of social organization and different analytic and historical literatures. Although "opposition" implies a practice fully outside and opposed to the state, "resistance" is a term of postcolonial studies that has signaled a move away from the traditional historiography of colonialism; its use has become too fluid and diffused in ways that make it impossible to actually study. In the Foucauldian sense, if power and resistance are everywhere, then they are really nowhere. I would rather use "dissent" and concentrate on the networks, types, and textures of imperial rule in various domains and the array of responses that such rule elicits.

Second, much of the dissent that percolates in an empire, and the politics associated with it, does not become full-fledged opposition. Rather, it is absorbed into the politics of rule; it might look fully accommodating, while transforming imperial relations in small, subtle, but significant ways. Empires have encountered dissent from the moment they emerged, especially in the form of armed resistance to conquest and colonization. Yet, opposition changed as conditions of rule transformed the relations between the rulers and the ruled. The form of dissent can be as simple as rogue elements wanting to become part of the system or religious reform movements with conformist agendas pushing the state further than it is willing to go. The question then becomes how is dissent organized, and what provokes different styles of dissent?

Third, because coercive power is certainly at the center of dissent, what can we say about the nature and strength of the state that affects the rise as well as the strength of the opposition? States engender opposition to their rule when they are strong or when they are weak or weakened.[7] When states are

---

[7] Pierre Birnbaum was among the first to theorize this relationship among strong states, weak states, and collective action; *States and Collective Action: The European Experience* (Cambridge, UK: Cambridge University Press, 1988). Similarly, the work of Michael Mann, especially the distinctions between infrastructural and coercive states, is also important to this thinking. See *The Sources of Social Power: A History of Power from the Beginning to A.D. 1760* (Cambridge, UK: Cambridge University Press, 1986).

strong, they elicit movements in opposition to their rule, but when they decline, they provide opportunities for oppositional groups to organize. Imperial states on the rise are often forces with which to be reckoned; they are strong and ruthless warriors bent on the consolidation of territory. At such moments, militant, armed resistance to invaders can mix with other social and cultural forms of resistance, sometimes even with religious, mystical movements whose constituencies react to the tremors that displace their comfortable accommodation. During the height of imperial rule, movements range from accommodationist to treacherous, often in cooperation with foreign powers. When states become unable to organize the collection of resources or to maintain their organized diversity, they provide opportunities for groups to assemble around ideas of opposition and to explore opportunities for better rule.

"Dissent" is also better suited than either "opposition" or "resistance" to a corollary argument: that is, when imperial rule is ambiguous, fluid, and flexible, dissent is more incorporative than oppositional. When imperial rule gains clarity, is visible, and becomes more rigid and less adaptive, dissent in turn becomes more oppositional. This is well shown by movements of early dissent in the Ottoman Empire when rule was not fully clarified, when accommodation was predominant, and especially when religious and mystical leaders found it beneficial to organize dissent, mostly as a way of forcing rulers to adjust to the demands of local populations. Similarly in the Russian Empire, until an increasingly self-conscious Orthodox Muscovy reinforced its missionary spirit, non-Christians in the early empire both accommodated and dissented to negotiate the limits of rule with the new conquerors.[8] In contrast, the frighteningly unequivocal Catholic zeal for converting of the early Habsburg rulers triggered straightforward Protestant opposition.

Finally, I also make a counterintuitive argument that when dissent is fluid, vastly networked through individuals, and not regionally circumscribed in closed homogeneous groups, it is more threatening to powers seeking hegemony. When individuals and groups connect various fluid social networks that cut across communities, locate themselves in interstitial spaces, and are the means by which members pass on information, communication, and resources, dissent can become dangerous to state control. The opposite is also correct. That is, in many ways the Romans could deal with the three Jewish uprisings of Judea – the Great Revolt (66–73 A.D.), the Kitos War (115–117 A.D.), and Bar Kokhba's revolt (132–135 A.D) – and inflicted great casualties on the Jews located and concentrated in one area. However, Ottomans had a much harder time dealing with the mystical dervish orders spread through rural and urban spaces; the Byzantines similarly were continually fighting sectarian groups widely spread and networked through the Balkans. In Russia, Old Belief as a recognized form of dissent emerged in reaction to the liturgical reforms of the Patriarch Nikon in the mid-seventeenth century, in ways similar to the

---

[8] Michael Khodarkovsky, "'Not by Word Alone': Missionary Policies and Religious Conversion in Early Modern Russia," *Comparative Studies in Society and History* 38:2 (April 1996): 267–293.

scriptural turn within official Islam in the Ottoman Empire.[9] Old Belief was particularly troubling to the Russian authorities because its adherents completely rejected involvement with a state that they perceived as corrupt; they also jealously guarded their religious autonomy at a time of increasing centralization and consolidation of ecclesiastical control. Responding to the intrusion of the Church into the popular traditions of the "hinterlands," Old Belief was a movement of dissent with "mass appeal" that attracted "independent-minded individuals and social outcasts who acted for their own reasons."[10] Peasants and charismatic holy men organized clandestine communities of religious dissent and, without exception, the state responded with intense persecution and massive violence, leading some dissenters to organize raids and violent attacks against the established Church and Russian authorities.[11] Similar to the radical dervish orders of the Ottoman Empire, Russian Old Believers posed an organizational threat to the logic of imperial control in managing diverse populations.

In the Ottoman Empire, religion, especially the Muslim mystical orders (*tarîkat*), was at the center of dissent. In previous chapters, I illustrated and discussed the ways in which the Ottoman Empire assured that its rule tended toward stability through negotiated settlements between the state and diverse social groups, creating intermediary organizational solutions with varied outcomes. I argued that Ottoman inclusion of Christian and Jewish lay and religious leadership and the organization of intermediary arrangements simultaneously preserved social boundaries and interreligious peace. The resulting toleration afforded non-Muslims centuries of persecution-free existence. In contrast, the Ottoman state was not so tolerant of its Muslim populations and victimized all kinds of heterodox Islamic movements that came to be known under the umbrella of Sufism. Why did the Ottoman state persecute adherents of heterodox Islam – especially because we know they were the staunch allies and fighters of the first sultans and were culturally close to the ruling members of the state – while they tolerated and protected the various groups of non-Muslims who were more different and separate than the Ottoman Muslims? This is even more perplexing because the Ottoman state emerged at the cusp of networks that bridged heterodox with orthodox Sunnî Islam and with various forms of Christianity, and the foot soldiers, colonizers, and early ideologues supporting the state were the Sufi şeyhs and dervishes of these groups.[12]

[9] Georg Bernhard Michels, *At War with the Church: Religious Dissent in Seventeenth-Century Russia* (Palo Alto, CA: Stanford University Press, 1999), 96.

[10] Ibid., 218–220.

[11] Ibid., 6, 46, 78–79, 206, 221.

[12] Much of this was discussed in Chapter 2. See especially Ömer Lütfi Barkan, "Osmanlı İmparatorluğunda bir İskan ve Kolonizasyon Metodu olarak Vakıflar ve Temlikler I: İstila Devirlerinin Kolonizatör Türk Dervişleri ve Zâviyeler," *Vakıflar Dergisi* 2 (1942): 281–365; Ahmet Yaşar Ocak, "Les milieux soufis dans les territoires du Beylicat Ottoman et le problème des 'Abdalan-I Rum,'" in *The Ottoman Emirate (1300–1389)*, ed. Elizabeth Zachariadou (Retymnon: Crete University Press, 1993), 145–158; Irène Mélikoff, "Un Ordre de derviches colonisateurs: les Bektachis," *Mémorial Ömer Lütfi Barkan* (Paris: Librairie d'Amérique et d'Orient Adrien Maisonneuve, 1980), 149–157.

Dervish orders spread throughout the Ottoman territories, representing schools of thought and practice of various origins. The Sufis in early Anatolia were of pre-Seljuk origin, although they were originally from Central Asia and were mostly immigrants from regions of what are today Iraq, Iran, and Syria. They were welcomed in the Seljuk state and established convents in the heartlands of Anatolia, in the cities of Kayseri, Konya, Tokat, Sıvas, and Amasya, and in many rural regions. In the post-Seljuk period, some ended up in the territories that emerged as the emirate of the Ottomans, and they vigorously followed Ottoman leaders. It was during this period that they helped cross-fertilize ideas and practices, fought in the wars, and colonized much new territory as they brought their convents to the frontiers of the emirate. The dervish convents that spread with the Ottomans became sites for religious mysticism and popular movements with more socioeconomic bases. In the cities, they interwove with the practice of Sunnî Islam, providing for more theosophical variations. At the frontiers, the Mevlevîs, Nakşbendîs, and Bektaşîs remained anchored in the popular imagination as the architects of the rise of the Ottomans.

Over time, these dervish orders claimed a space between institutionalization and acceptance of the Ottoman center and dissent.[13] The Bektaşîs, for example, became institutionalized as the Janissary corps embraced them as their official order. In 1416, the Şeyh Bedreddîn rebellion, to which I return, ignited many fires in parts of the Balkans and Anatolia, with many followers continuing the rebellion and their activities into the sixteenth century. However, more extreme were the Hurûfîs, Melâmîs, Melâmetîs, and others who defined themselves against the Ottoman state and fought its centralizing efforts. In their dealings with these groups, the Ottomans were ruthless, and as the flaying of poet Nesimi, an outspoken Hurûfî, in 1408 was to foreshadow, greater violence against the Hurûfîs followed in 1444 and later in the slaughter of Filibe in Bulgaria. In the frontier struggles between the Ottomans and the Safavids, when groups sustained by the Safavids threatened the Ottomans, they struck back.

During the time of Selim I, especially between 1511 and 1514, draconian measures were taken, and thousands of Shiites were now defined as heretics; those with Safavid leanings and support were massacred. During the sixteenth century, attacks against the Bayramîs-Melâmîs were reinforced after the reorganization of this particular order under a young enthusiastic Şeyh, Ismail Masuki.[14] He was decapitated in 1529. Other segments of the same movement were organized in Bosnia and Herzegovina under the leadership of Hamza Bali; he was also executed with many of his followers in 1561. Although these are the most conspicuous instances of persecution, they are by no means exhaustive. Persecution also meant continued control, secret policing of the

[13] See Halil İnalcık, *The Ottoman Empire: The Classical Age, 1300–1600* (New Rochelle, NY: Aristide Caratzas, 1989).

[14] The order was first formed in the early fifteenth century under the leadership of Hacı Bayram, a mystic who caught the attention of Murâd II.

orders – especially when defined as Shi'ia – testimonies and trials, and executions of people deemed dangerous, although without much evidence or procedure. Such are the moments when the relationship between dissent and empire led to violence and when Ottomans demonstrated a persecuting mentality. How do we explain the relationship between empire and dissent, the variety of forms of dissent, and the episodic outbreaks of persecution?

Nizâm-ı Alem, the Ottoman conception of order, was the basis of the rationale for state action; that is, those who disturbed the order of the realm were not tolerated. Furthermore, it was not really the ideas as much as the activities of these groups that public authorities found unacceptable. To the degree that dervish leaders connected different sites of contention, enabled movements to spread, and enlisted dispossessed landholders and peasants, disgruntled artisans, and all those who might have lost ground vis-à-vis a centralizing state, they represented a threat to the existing order of Ottoman society.[15]

To understand the particular nature of the relationship between empire and dissent we need to marshal once again the concepts of difference, boundary, and the creation of legibility through the organization of difference. What facilitated the incorporation of the non-Muslim communities and their administration was the straightforward Islamic set of guidelines for Muslim–non-Muslim relations; the clear-cut boundaries that such principles advocated; the deep organizational structure of the communities prior to their incorporation; and the eagerness with which community leaders maintained the boundaries, pursuing the state ideal of difference and separation and a perception of the Byzantine urbane culture as closer to the high culture to which the new rulers aspired. Islam provided a blueprint, the Ottomans had an organizational need, and community leaders were positioned to become mediators and peacekeepers. Communities had their own organizational structures, a dominant church hierarchy, or, as in the case of Jews, strong community organizations with leaders who were coopted as intermediaries between state and community.

When we analyze the relationship between the myriad of mystical groups and the state, we observe a different set of contingencies. Simply put, the multifarious heterodoxies under the Sufi umbrella did not fit any organizational pattern; they were comprised of overlapping, constantly changing, and recombinant networks of religious groups. Whereas their ideology and doctrines were familiar to the sultans and were even espoused by many of them, the continued fluidity of movement, the covert activities, and alternative assemblies and ceremonies became a threat because they remained outside the purview and organization of the state. The emergence and close partnership of the Ottomans with the Sufi dervish orders, the fuzzy and ambiguous boundaries between orthodox and heterodox Islam during early colonization, and the constant repositioning of Sufi groups along a continuum of incorporation and dissent, together with their

---

[15] Ahmet Yaşar Ocak, "Les Melamis-Bayrami (Hamzavi) et l'administration Ottomane aux XVIe–XVIIe siècles," in *Melamis-Bayramis: études sur trois mouvements mystiques musulmans* (Istanbul: Éditions Issis, 1998), 99–114.

vast amorphous multiplicity and the lack of a strong organizational principle by which they could be ordered, made these popular religious movements more difficult to dominate than were non-Muslim communities. Therefore, the particular cultural and organizational features of the groups that defined Ottoman heterodoxy rendered their relationship to the established authorities not only less formal and more supple, but also more ominous. Thus, it is important to understand general state policy, as well as the manner in which state authorities read the different contextual and local variations on the ground. The variation in state policies is not simply the outcome of state interests, but more of state interests as grounded in and in relation to the local networks, structures, and cultural meanings.

To return to the slow but steady evolution of an official and increasingly formalized Sunnî orthodoxy at the very core of Ottoman legitimacy, the fight against the unruly orders of Sufis and the overly puritanical Kadızadelis represented the struggle for religious domination. Beyond simple organizational principles, the whole construction of Ottoman state legitimacy was shifting toward one that combined the sultan's dynasty and the Sunnî orthodoxy. State centralization coincided with the conquest of the Arab lands and overlapped with a "scripturalist interlude"[16] in Ottoman state making. To construct such authority, the state would have to have increasing monopoly and legitimation based on religion; however, dissent among the multifarious Sufi orders impeded such development. Centralization and universal legitimation produced scripturalism: a turn toward the Koran, the Shari'a, and many discussions and interpretations of religious authority. Such religious consolidation was certainly the product of the late fifteenth century, and had flourished in the sixteenth under Selim I and Süleyman I. The effects of such scripturalism changed the early classical understanding of Ottoman Islam, which was open, syncretic, and tolerance based. Scripturalism appealed for harsher and better-defined boundaries, whereas Sufi dissent called for syncretism and porous boundaries.

When we trace the historical and organizational aspects of this relationship, we can demonstrate a simple idea: *that the Ottomans were more likely to persecute those who did not easily fit their organizational mode: those who defied boundaries and those for whom a blueprint did not exist.* For the Ottomans, these happened to be their closest allies in the past, their brothers in arms, from whom they tried to dissociate while retaining important symbolic and religious ties. In the process of subduing the Sufi orders, the Ottomans were able both to demarcate the realm of their legitimacy and to selectively incorporate in order to reach out and symbolize their openness. The same can be said of the Russians, for whom the Old Believers and the Uniates were both close and yet still the objects of persecution.

In the rest of this chapter, I analyze several examples of the relationship between empire and dissent. One example, that of Şeyh Bedreddîn, represented

---

[16] Clifford Geertz, *Islam Observed: Religious Development in Morocco and Indonesia* (Chicago: University of Chicago Press, 1968), 56.

everything Ottomans had been when they emerged, yet wanted to distance themselves from as they became imperial. *Celalis*, the bandit militias, in contrast, were organized as military units whose "rebellions" were absorbed into the state in ways that demonstrate that Ottomans knew how to deal with pre-modern forms of organized crime. Kadızadelis, an ultra-orthodox conservative movement that challenged the hard-earned toleration of the system, emerged to challenge the state for not being tough enough on "difference." Finally, the messianic movement of the Jew Sabbatai Sevi, who led the Jews of the empire into disarray, became one further link in the chain reaction between empire and dissent. This movement both underscored difference and was effortlessly absorbed into the Ottoman fold. That the Ottomans were able to resist and reestablish their bounded accommodation has to be seen as the result of strength and stability of rule.

None of these religious forms of dissent were entirely accepted or eliminated. The Ottomans learned to maintain a flexible Sunnî orthodoxy bolstered by the individual power and the symbolic demonstration effect of particular mystical religious figures, who advised rulers, maintained a presence in the imperial palace, and adjudicated among different views. Sultans also, as we will see, learned that the Sunnî–Shi'ia struggle was even less likely to be resolved because it had been effectively superimposed onto a political competition between states and thrived at the frontier.

Persecuting the Past: Heterodoxy under Fire

Although the early history of Ottoman conquest and incorporation under-scores the work of colonizing dervishes and the alliances between emerging state actors and religious actors, it is hard to imagine that armed opposition, contestation, and dissent was not part of the building of a great imperial state. Already in fourteenth-century Anatolia, many heterodox sects under the larger umbrella of Sufism had brought their central Asian traditions and were spread-ing, attracting tribal and peasant groups, and providing them with the contrast between the more established cultural and spiritual influence of Sunnî Islam and the heterodox beliefs and superstitious traditions of a popular religion. These groups were numerous, differentiated, and ranged from mild forms of mystical thought to religious radicalism to politically active Shi'ia Muslims stirred up by the Ottoman–Safavid conflict.

To understand the manner in which the state came to perceive these groups as a threat and to decide to persecute their leaders and members, we need to understand their social organization, their evolving position in Ottoman social and cultural structures, and their relationship to an increasingly more formal and authoritarian state. We also have to understand the manner in which the Ottoman state was changing during this time period, transforming into an empire claiming universal legitimacy, with a cultural and literary educated center and a sultan increasingly identified with this separation, who formalized his distance from his subjects.

Nevertheless, the key aspect of Ottoman rule – its openness to negotiation with social groups – cleared the way for agreement and compromise, even if this was temporary. Thus, the Ottomans incorporated many important and lesser known Sufi orders into their realm. In response, groups tended to move back and forth from more to less legitimate activities, occupying the pivot of this empire–dissent duality, acting simultaneously as the missionaries of Islam and as an enduring subversive force. The result was complex relations with the state because movements were not always clearly subversive. For example, a blurred case of dissent and compliance was embodied most significantly in the Bektaşî and Halvetî orders, both strategically important orders because they had strong bases in the Balkans.

The authorities watched, controlled, and preferred to incorporate such mystical orders into the normative order of the state, trying to approximate the known models of religious patronage, not in the form of Sunnî *ulema*, but at least by settling their convents on the lands of pious foundations, affording them a comfortable living. The Bektaşîs were known for the manner in which they settled on recently conquered but deserted lands, opening convents (*zâviyes*) and offering opportunities for disciples, who followed with profitable agricultural and educational activities that led toward the intentional growth of a village and the spread of Islam and early Turkic culture in the region.[17] The Bektaşîs were also connected to other parts of Ottoman society, most important, to the Janissaries, a connection that made them an urban order. At the Bektaşî end, the state patronized, protected, and used the mystical insight of the şeyhs, elevating them to positions of importance in the palace and society.[18] Kalenderîs, originally itinerant dervishes, were another example of a mystical fraternity organized around incorporation and dissent, who participated early on in the anti-Ottoman movements of Anatolia and who later organized a revolt in 1527, along with the Bektaşîs, with between 20,000 to 30,000 partisans. Another Kalenderî rebel assassinated the Grand Vizier, Sokullu Mehmed Pasha, in 1579, although by the seventeenth century the Kalenderîs had all but merged into the Bektaşî order that by now was more respectable.[19] This easy

---

[17] Ömer Lütfi Barkan, "Osmanlı İmparatorluğunda bir İskan ve Kolonizasyon Metodu olarak Vakıflar ve Temlikler I: İstila Devirlerinin Kolonizatör Türk Dervişleri ve Zâviyeler," *Vakıflar Dergisi* 2: 279–386; Mélikoff, "Un ordre de derviches colonisateurs"; Irène Mélikoff, "Les Origines centre-asiatiques du soufisme anatolien," 7–18; Suraiya Faroqhi, "The Tekke of Haci Bektash: Social Position and Economic Activities," *International Journal of Middle Eastern Studies* 7 (1976): 183–208; Suraiya Faroqhi, "Agricultural Activities in a Bektashi Center: The Tekke of Kizil Deli 1750–1830," *Sudost-Forschungen* 35 (1976): 69–96; Suraiya Faroqhi, "Agricultural Crisis and the Art of Flute-Playing: The Worldly Affairs of the Mevlevi Dervishes," *Turcica* 20 (1988): 43–69.

[18] John Kingsley Birge, *The Bektashi Order of Dervishes* (London: Luzac & Co., 1965).

[19] Ahmet Yaşar Ocak, "Quelques remarques sur le rôle des derviches Kalenderîs dans les mouvements populaires et les activités anarchiques aux XVe et XVIe siècles dans l'empire Ottoman," *Osmanlı Araştırmaları* 3 (1982): 69–80; Ocak, "Kutb ve İsyan: Osmanlı Mehdici (Mesiyanik) Hareketlerinin İdeolojik Arkaplanı Üzerine Bazı Düşünceler," *Toplum ve Bilim* 83 (1999/2000): 48–56.

movement is again a testament to the flexibility of empire and its allowance for passage from one degree of legality to another.

The history of other orders, such as the Bayramîs, is more complicated as they separated into two movements, one that accepted Sunnî Islam and the protection of the state, and the other, the Melâmîs, that became a secret sect opposed to the government, with ties to different urban guilds and that showed heretical leanings,[20] having proclaimed a more audacious interpretation of the doctrine of the Unity of Being (Vahdet-i Vücud).[21] A deep opposition to established religion and the manner in which the separation of man from God is effected in Sunnî Islam was at the base of the Melâmî dissent from the Ottoman state and established religion.

The Melâmîs represented a vast network of leaders and followers strewn over different parts of the empire. Different in their potential for social organization and mobilization from the mystical orders with state backing such as the Bektaşîs-Kalenderîs, they were more threatening to the state. Much less open to negotiation with the Ottomans, they cast a wide net because under the leadership of Ismail Masuki, they were able to move from being a simple rural order to a sophisticated urban movement that assembled many intellectuals, poets, *ulema*, state bureaucrats, and rich merchants in Istanbul. They were organized around many different leaders who operated in various locations, with Hamza Bali in Bosnia-Herzegovina, Şeyh Ali Rumi (known as Idris Muhtefi), who was a well-regarded merchant and Mclâmî leader in Istanbul, or Sütçü Beşir Ağa, who had entered the Palace Imperial Guard (Bostancı Ocağı), influencing the members of the unit. Sütçü Beşir retired and became a milkman and a şeyh before he was decapitated at the age of 90, together with forty of his followers. After he died, a letter was found in which he advised his followers to conform to the Shar'ia, to speak moderately, and to be both prudent and disingenuous, for the state authorities would certainly get them.[22]

The complexity, range, and lack of formal organization of these secret religious societies, which were unwavering in their mobilization of larger networks of adherents and in their forceful dissent from the state, made the authorities apprehensive.[23] According to sixteenth-century letters and documents, Melâmîs were supposed to follow Sunnî rites; learn the Koran, Hadîth, and

[20] İnalcık, *The Ottoman Empire*, 192.

[21] Ahmet Yaşar Ocak, "Idéologie officielle et réaction populaire: un aperçu général sur les mouvements et les courants socio-religieux à l'époque de Soliman le Magnifique," in *Soliman le Magnifique et son temps: actes du colloque de Paris, Galeries nationales du Grand Palais, 7–10 mars 1990*, ed. Gilles Veinstein (Paris: Ecole du Louvre, 1992), 185–194.

[22] Ahmet Yaşar Ocak, "Les Melamis-Bayrami (Hamzavi) et l'administration ottomane aux XVIe–XVIIe siècles," in *Melamis-Bayramis: études sur trois mouvements mystiques musulmans* (Istanbul: Éditions Issis, 1998), 99–114.

[23] Although there have been excellent studies of these different movements, there are no reliable statistics, and even the numbers of participants in rebellions have been vastly exaggerated. See Abdülbâki Gölpınarlı, *Melâmîlik ve Melâmîler* (Istanbul: Devlet Matbaası, 1931); Ahmet Yaşar Ocak, *Osmanlı Toplumunda Zındıklar ve Mülhidler (15.-17. yüzyıllar)* (Istanbul: Tarih Vakfı Yurt Yayınları, 1998).

Islamic sciences (*fikh*); differentiate themselves from the "uneducated Sufis"; and never subject themselves to the court system of the empire. Moreover, Melâmîs were not supposed to open up dervish lodges or to settle as leaders of the order where they would become more easily accessible to the state.[24] They were to shun all forms of collective settlement, giving the state no organizational structure in which to encounter them. They remained secret societies, spread by leaders and word of mouth. The known individuals for each Melâmî group were the leader (*kutb*) and someone close who looked after him (*kalbe bakıcı* or *rehber*). These leaders attached themselves to other Sufi organizations and lodges so government-subsidized Bektaşîs, Kalenderîs, and Halvetîs had among their members many who were actually Melâmîs and who were ready to mobilize when their leader's call came. Also according to their regulations, these orders, especially the Melâmîs, were not supposed to be on the government payroll, and their şeyhs were to make a living independently from the state. As a result, we find among them many who had very respectable positions, earning their living, who became intricately embedded in the networks of their vocations.

These orders attracted many disgruntled artisans, low-level traders, and itinerant merchants in urban centers (e.g., Ismail Masuki and Şeyh Ali Rumi, mentioned previously); in the rural areas, they mingled with the landless peasants or the dispossessed landholders, each group with a particular grievance against Ottoman authorities. Nomads and semi-nomads opposed the state's policies of sedentarization, and many Turcoman families had lost their lands starting with the centralization policies of Mehmed II (1451–1481). The relative ease with which the leaders of these dissenting orders participated and mobilized in the trade and artisan groups is explained by a historically close relationship between dervish orders and *ahî* organizations, where shared activities such as vocational training led over time to significant similarity of social and cultural understandings of social welfare, solidarity, and peaceful coexistence. The dervish orders and the *ahî* organizations had been natural allies in the establishment of the Ottoman state and would similarly be joined in opposing a hardening Sunni orthodox state. In central Anatolia, a prime region of such discontent, nomads, peasants, and cavalrymen joined the leaders of the Bayramî-Melâmî order, Bünyamin-i Ayaşi, in the region around Ankara in 1521–1522, Pir Ali Aksarayi around Niğde-Aksaray in 1527–1528, and Hüsameddin Ankaravi in 1568 in Ankara.[25] That the Bayramîs, the Halvetîs, and Melâmîs were spreading across Ottoman lands, mushrooming into additional movements, and attracting adherents from both rural and urban populations was of grave concern, even before the Safavid threat became

[24] Ocak, *Osmanli Toplumunda Zındıklar ve Mülhidler*, 254–255.
[25] Ahmet Yaşar Ocak, "XVI. Yüzyıl Osmanlı Anadolu'sunda Mesiyanik Hareketlerin Bir Tahlil Denemesi," *V. Milletlerarası Türkiye Sosyal ve İktisat Tarihi Kongresi: Tebliğler* (*International Congress on the Social and Economic History of Turkey 5th*) (Istanbul: Türkiyat Araştırma ve Uygulama Merkezi, 1989), 817–825.

real.[26] Furthermore, they outlived the Safavid threat and continued into the nineteenth century because their existence was based on their practices of dissimulation (*takiyye*) and informal, underground organization.

The continued production of local branches of mystical orders and secret Melâmî societies linked lawful Sufi orders with unorthodox and hidden movements, intertwining them at their base, spreading dissent further. Between the two extremes existed a vast network of individual dervish figures (Haydarîs, Babaîs, Hamzavîs, and Abdals), who were mostly in ideological and cultural conflict with the centralizing Ottoman state and who were especially dangerous to the state because they traveled, spreading ideas and sedition and taking advantage of the fluidity of premodern society as well as of different centers of heterodox worship. These şeyhs were as diverse as the peasant and nomadic social and cultural world onto which they grafted; they combined and recombined into different units, gave rise to many submovements, and because they were itinerant, they carried the thoughts and the ties of one order to the other.

The identification of the Ottoman state with an increasingly distinct Sunnî identity sharpened the contrast between state-sanctioned institutions and the rather free-floating, diverse, and diffuse networks of dervish orders and peoples. Certainly, the beliefs and practices of the various groups were divergent from Sunnî ones, among the most important being the beliefs in reincarnation and the manifestation of God in human form. Groups differed slightly in their beliefs beyond the doctrine of reincarnation, such as on questions about what was permitted or prohibited, or on the concepts of heaven and hell as relative rather than absolute. Given the mix of beliefs and practices, as well as the variety of social arrangements that propagated them, the Ottoman state had no straightforward and clear set of guidelines for how to organize the expanse of such Sufi movements in society. Besides the provisions within Sunnî Islam against such divergence and heresy, the boundary between orthodoxy and heterodoxy was blurred, not by the doctrines as much as by the fluidity of movement. Learned Islamic scholars studied both the different Sunnî schools of Koranic interpretation and Sufi thought and practice. Despite or perhaps because of such blurred boundaries and constant interlacing, state officials and the *ulema* within them recognized these orders as alternatives to central institutional religion, and settled, domesticated, and monitored those who were willing and persecuted the reluctant.

Particularly urgent for these groups was the trajectory of the Ottoman state itself, which had complicated relations between the authorities and the dervishes. In the move from popular to high culture, from frontiers and marshlands dominated by Turcoman raiders and dervish mystics to the rarefied atmosphere of the urban Sunnî culture, they had alienated many of their loyal foot soldiers. Despite long incubation in the networks of popular mystical orders and manipulation by many influential members of these orders, the territorial and organizational changes that the imperial state engendered shifted its focus

---

[26] Ocak, "Idéologie officielle et réaction populaire," 186.

to be more urban and settled. Under the protection of the state, trade and towns flourished and its successive capitals – Bursa, Edirne, and then Istanbul – became centers where the concentration of power and capital became the alternative to territorial consolidation and further expansion. In a sense then, as it grew and became more settled and urban, the state did not need to rely as much on dervish orders for colonization. Instead, in Bursa and Edirne, the sultans established dervish lodges as part of a network of welfare institutions created to take care of the poor, regardless of religion and social status. The more successful the Ottomans were, the better they shaped their central order of beliefs and symbols, increasing the value accorded to learned and refined thought. With literacy came a scriptural tendency, an attempt to codify both Islamic law and secular law.[27]

Despite the larger move away from popular mysticism, the sultans continued to patronize Sufi dervish mystics and to deploy them as elements in the balance of forces between increasingly institutionalized orthodox Sunnî Islam and progressively more subversive heretical Shi'ia Islam. The sultans chose to emphasize Sunnî Islam, but nurtured both Sunnî and judicious Sufi leadership, often consulting Sufi leaders about the people. Şeyh Bedreddîn, the mystical rebel we consider next, could have been an essential link in the Ottoman patronage arrangement, although he chose rebellion instead. He remains an excellent case study of the movements we have considered because he was educated in traditional Sunnî teachings, but met and learned from the Hurûfîs, Melâmîs, and other mystics, synthesizing their influence into a thoroughly personal perspective.

Şeyh Bedreddîn

Şeyh Bedreddîn (1358/1359–1416), the fifteenth-century Ottoman mystic, was among the first rebels trapped in the dualities of a transitional age: orthodoxy and scripturalism versus heterodoxy; popular versus high culture. He embodied these apparent contradictions: the teachings of different forms of mysticism and Sunnî Islam, the entwining of religion and politics, and the continual cross-fertilization of popular and high culture. He linked these two parts of Ottoman existence: in his being, he demonstrated the artificiality of this boundary because he continually crossed it in his readings and his life.[28] In many ways, Şeyh Bedreddîn was a more organized and rebellious, as well as better traveled and more learned, Menocchio, the sixteenth-century protagonist of Carlo Ginzburg's book, *The Cheese and the Worms: The Cosmos of a*

---

[27] Jack Goody, *The Logic of Writing and the Organization of Society* (Cambridge, UK: Cambridge University Press, 1986).

[28] Much has been written about Şeyh Bedreddîn. Among the most important works that have directly informed this chapter are Michel Balivet, *Islam mystique et révolution armée dans les Balkans ottomans: vie du Cheikh Bedreddin le "Hallaj des Turcs" (1358/59–1416)* (Istanbul: Les Éditions Isis, 1995); Ocak, *Osmanlı Toplumunda Zındıklar ve Mülhidler*; İnalcık, *The Ottoman Empire*; Abdülbâki Gölpınarlı, *Simavna Kadısıoğlu Şeyh Bedreddin* (Istanbul: Varlık Yayınevi, 1966).

Sixteenth-Century Miller; that is, in his essence he traversed culturally charged fields through his different schooling and his varied travels and contacts, which he then brought together in his own synthesis.[29] In contradistinction to Menocchio, who was killed for his *ideas* by the Catholic Inquisition, Bedreddîn met his death for his *actions*, which linked a whole universe of mystical and heretical Islam with the oppressed and demoralized element of postimperial centralization. It is in the response to his dissent that we locate another step toward consolidating Sunnî identity.

With the şeyh, we travel back in time to when the Anatolian hinterland had been home to many alternative, heterodox movements and "mentalités," some pre-Islamic and others fundamentally Islamic. Both Ibn Arabi (1165–1240) and Mevlânâ Celâleddin Rumi (1207–1273) were instrumental in making Anatolia an important site in the spread of their mystical traditions and syncretic beliefs. Under the Seljuks, Anatolia had become open to many cross currents, a space for easy religious syncretism, a tolerant place where Islamic and Christian understanding flourished together, sharing some beliefs, traditions, and often rituals. When dissent took a religious form in early times, it was a reaction to the emergence of a new power that would unquestionably shake up the comfortable fusion, cultural symbiosis, and syncretism that made medieval Anatolia and part of the Balkans havens of forbearance.

The revolt of Şeyh Bedreddîn in 1416 and that of his followers in 1421 and 1422 represents the clash between two world views that would continually mesh and separate from each other and vary over time. The oral, popular, and localized culture of the empire was increasingly squeezed into the interstices of an imperial hegemony represented by the growing supremacy of orthodoxy and by the urban high culture of the state. These two cannot be equated or sternly separated; on the contrary, they interlaced often and seeped into each other by means of ideas, actions, and people. Therefore, there are many sides to the Şeyh Bedreddîn story. His dissent connected the popular and higher levels of culture, helping him fashion his own world view that was opposed to what he saw as an increasingly hegemonic and monolithic power. His particular synthesis was the result of his travels, learning, and connections. His was a vision that helped reconnect the oral culture of the peasant-nomadic background with its erstwhile and somewhat buried beliefs in utopianism, toleration, egalitarianism, and material needs. His ideals were both the result of and pushed against the emerging Ottoman state, reasserting its domination in an increasingly hostile environment. Rival Turkish principalities and crumbling states, such as those of the Byzantine Empire, the Serbian, and the Bulgarian kingdoms were each vying for control over territory and resources, mostly emboldened after the defeat of the Ottomans by Tamerlane (1402).

Bedreddîn's story demonstrates the possibilities of movement, of connectivity, of switching identities at a moment where identities were not fixed, when

---

[29] Carlo Ginzburg, *The Cheese and the Worms: The Cosmos of a Sixteenth-Century Miller* [1976] (London: Routledge and Kegan Paul, 1980).

travel and movement between regions seemed extraordinary. It also shows that a state on the way to consolidation wanted order and legibility. It did not want free-floating individuals connecting groups and talking to potential and existing enemies. Bedreddîn represents a moment when the Ottomans were maneuvering out of unrestrained mystical diversity and syncretism to a more controlled order of state-policed orthodoxy. Şeyh Bedreddîn also demonstrates for us the degree to which one individual could link multiple sites and forms of religious belief with the political interests and activities of many regional leaders, creating a network spanning from the Balkans to Egypt to Azarbaijan in the Safavid heartlands. That his travels and intellectual, religious, and political development occurred during perhaps the most difficult period of Ottoman consolidation – before and after the battle at Ankara (1402), after which Ottomans were left scrambling for their territory and troops – indicates that when state power is weakened, those who have the connections and the ability to mobilize can benefit.

Şeyh Bedreddîn was himself the product of mixed traditions and a multireligious family: he was born in Samavna (a town close to Edirne) in 1358/1359 to a Christian mother and Muslim *gâzî* father who was among the first conquerors of Rumelia; his grandfather was of Seljuk lineage. His mother was an important Christian woman, the daughter of the viceroy of Samavna, who had chosen to convert with 100 of her closest relatives before she got married in the old church that had been transformed into the residence of the conqueror of the region. Bedreddîn was trained in Islamic sciences in Edirne, but left for Bursa in 1380, where the Islamic establishment flourished and where opportunities for serious legal training were possible. From Bursa, he went on to Konya in 1381 (where he might have encountered some Hurûfî dervishes) and continued on to Cairo in 1383, another university town where Islamic training flourished and whence many famous scholars of the period would emerge. From Egypt, he went to Mecca and Medina and returned to Cairo in 1384, where he was introduced and became the disciple of Hüseyin Ahlati, who invited him to a *sema* ceremony.[30] It is said that following the ceremony, Bedreddîn put on the bristle coat of the dervish, distributed his goods, and threw his books into the Nile, signaling a different kind of education. This move from serious Islamic studies to mystical knowledge was then further developed in Azarbaijan, where in Tabriz he mingled in Safavid convents. We also know that it was at this time (1403) that Tamerlane returned from his victorious battles and met Şeyh Bedreddîn in Tabriz, offering him a post at his court.[31] However, Bedreddîn returned to Cairo to be chosen as the successor to Hüseyin Ahlati, his mentor, who had passed away.

Bogged down in controversy, he chose to leave Egypt for Aleppo in 1405, where his contacts became increasingly wide ranging. He connected with

[30] The sema ceremony or ritual began with the inspiration of Mevlânâ Celâleddin Rumi (1207–1273) and is meant to represent the spiritual journey of the individual in Sufi beliefs.

[31] Balivet, *Islam mystique et révolution armée.*

Turcoman tribes and Hurûfî dervishes, and met the poet Nesimi. It is said that he also met the imam, who later proclaimed a fetvâ against the poet, leading to his flaying in public. In fact, his sojourn here among the Hurûfîs was significant in his heterodox formation.[32] Returning to Rumelia via Karaman and Germiyan, he met with the leading emirs who were trying to reconstitute their principalities because the Ottoman defeat had opened a window of opportunity in these lands. Here and in the western Anatolian hinterlands, he found among the emirs fierce opponents of the Ottomans, for example, Izmiroğlu Cüneyd. It is in this region that he met Torlak and Börüklüce, future rebellious chiefs who would emulate Bedreddîn. These men were converts to Islam and gathered people at the fringes of their religions, whether they were Jewish, Christian, or Muslim. A trip to the Genoese-controlled island of Chios across the Aegean Sea contributed to Bedreddîn's Christian contacts; he is said to have gathered many adherents there, even among the clergy. From another source, we learn that Crete, Chios, and Sisam were all in contact with one another, connected by dervish routes across the islands. Again, Bedreddîn traveled from one to the other and connected them even further.

It might be impossible to imagine that he traveled so easily as local emirs, sultans, and members of ruling households allowed him across their territories freely without any need for assurance or pledge of return. Often, his travels were punctuated by encounters with important political figures eager to preserve some of his rich syncretic contemplation as part of their ruling power. Given the nature of his thought and the special spirit of the times, Şeyh Bedreddîn located himself at the entwining of religion and politics, in a world where religion and politics enthusiastically embraced each other.

That Bedreddîn was just at the place where religion and politics met is made clear in many ways. The patterns of power, the winners and losers in the struggles in western Anatolia and the Balkans, often determined his particular position. After the defeat of 1402 by Tamerlane, the multiple reconfigurations of power in Anatolia, especially within the principalities, affected Bedreddîn's political and religious influence. When Musa Çelebi (1411–1413) – one of the sons of Beyazıd I, contenders to the Ottoman throne – had defeated his rivals and ruled in Edirne, he made Bedreddîn his principal army judge (*kadıasker*) between 1411 and 1413. By giving Bedreddîn a stable, official state position for 3 years, Musa allowed him the opportunity to develop ties in and out of government and local politics, making alliances with the Turks of the Danube, Deliorman, the Dobrudja region, nurturing relations with disgruntled landholders, and cultivating important contacts with the prince of Wallachia, Mircea. In that sense – although it was not going to last – he had become an official of this temporary local "Ottoman" government. The tables turned in 1413, when Mehmed I took over and, aiming to establish a more permanent Ottoman regime, had Bedreddîn's patron Musa Çelebi killed. Musa's men were removed from political and religious office in disgrace. The Şeyh himself was exiled to

---

[32] Ocak, *Zındıklar ve Mülhidler*, 184–185.

Iznik with his family; this brush with power, in and out of officialdom, helped crystallize some of his uncertainty and vague reactions to the rising Ottoman hegemony. Yet, Bedreddîn did not choose to revolt immediately. It was only after his close disciples had rebelled in western Anatolia and only after he had traveled and gathered possible allies through a strong propaganda campaign that Şeyh Bedreddîn chose armed insurrection.

In his travels, the şeyh encountered various Balkan and Anatolian groups who had become disenchanted with Ottoman rule. Who were they? What were the circumstances of their discontent and how did they become mobilized? In his rebellion, we find gathered Turcoman nomads, *gâzîs*, *sipâhîs*, Christian peasants, and others, mostly those with local grievances, the importance of which is not to be underestimated given the post-1402 chaos in Anatolia. Bedreddîn knew the disgruntled well because when he was a government official, he had provided them with the land that they lost once again under Mehmed I. Bedreddîn had different elements in his multilayered identity that appealed to different groups; his mixed *gâzî* and Seljuk credentials, his Christian background through his mother, and his frontier mentality became the symbols of his mobilization. He preached his syncretic understanding of religion, opposed the reorganization of the Ottomans, and gathered rebels around him. His rebellion was not successful in that Mehmed's agents heavily infiltrated the movement; finally, Bedreddîn was betrayed by his own men. Sadly, he was converting people to his creed as fast as the Ottoman armies were executing them as rebels. The numbers of state executions was high: from 6,000 to 8,000 were executed among the three rebels – Şeyh Bedreddîn, Börüklüce Mustafa, and Torlak Kemal – and their followers. Such numbers are significant in that they indicate that by then, the sultan's men were unwilling to tolerate dissent and to let it percolate and dissipate, as they had previously done.

To the Ottomans, Bedreddîn was more than just one more heterodox dervish who could be integrated into the state and settled into a convent. He represented the ideals of the Islamo-Christian synthesis that they had so usefully deployed at their emergence, but his actions and the combination of these ideals in a rebellious context, mixed in with elements of urban and rural discontent, demonstrated that such ideals might become dangerous to the Ottoman order. That is, more than the ideas themselves, it was the *actions* of Bedreddîn, his *networks*, and his *potential for upheaval* that engaged state response. Bedreddîn and those who followed his rebellion were successful in the rural areas of the western Anatolian littoral, especially where the greater mixes of religions, creeds, and heterodox beliefs existed and matched well with Bedreddîn's ideological system. The more marginal the population, the better suited they were to following the Şeyh.

Yet, neither Bedreddîn nor his followers could have sustained long-term opposition to the Ottomans, especially without interference from outside forces. That Bedreddîn attempted outside contacts was also a marker of peril for the state. Mircea, Prince of Wallachia, helped Bedreddîn in his revolt, and Byzantine forces and renegades assisted Düzme and Cüneyd, two of his disciples who continued the rebellion after him. Such outside forces were vying for control inside the expanding borders of Mehmed's realm, hoping to detract from the reunification of Ottoman forces. Both for Bedreddîn and his supporters and foreign neighbors, fomenting dissent became an option after Ottoman reunification was a reality in the region, and rebellion was a form of opposition to state making. In this sense, the movement became political; in response, the growing Ottoman government fought them and formulated an ideological blueprint for rebels such as these, bringing their religious rather than political features to the limelight, calling them heretical, faithless, disloyal atheists and other damaging epithets, and in the process shaping the state's opposition as well. An Ottoman political culture was thus being forged in state–Bedreddîn relations, a political culture that accepted dissent that demanded incorporation, but refused political interference from internal or external forces.

Bedreddîn perceived that the Ottoman system was consolidating toward a more urban and Sunnî Islamic culture, to the detriment of other prior elements that had been part of the early Ottoman mix. He was the most significant syncretic force when a popular Islamo-Christian syncretism was starting to clash with an urban high Islamic Sunnî system.[33] The kind of life that he led, as well as the type of learning and cultural blend that he represented, were becoming marginalized in favor of a more rigid and legible social order. He fought to reassert the past and to be included in a system that remained open. His was a popular world of heterodoxy that questioned authority against the austerity of a type of Durkheimian understanding of religion that promoted consent to the existing social order. Şeyh Bedreddîn might have represented the key moment of transition between the unbounded order of multiple forms of worship to the austere world of institutionalized religion. He rebelled to force the state to turn back toward its early syncretism, and it was a tribute to him and his beliefs that Ottomans realized the power of his ideas; Mevlana Haydar-ı Herevi, who conducted Bedreddîn's trial, asked the sultan for private time with the Şeyh in order to benefit from his wisdom before he was put to death! Therein lay the duality of a state that both punished and learned from dissent.

The dervish orders with their various şeyhs and disciples represented a local force with which centralizing Ottomans had to contend. They had been among the brokers of the state-building enterprise. On the one hand, the dervish orders grounded the Ottomans in local realities and forced them to capitulate to existing configurations of religions, ethnic and kin groups, local traditions, and deep-rooted superstitions, what James Scott calls *metis*.[34] For those who chose to remain connected to the state, both their missionary activity and their subversion were worth incorporating. On the other hand, those who defied the social order became transient and connected many sites of dissent and simple

---

[33] Lowry, *The Nature of the Early Ottoman State*, 138.

[34] Scott, *Seeing Like a State*, 6. Here Scott uses and defines *metis*, "which descends from classical Greek and denotes the knowledge that can come only from practical experience."

socioeconomic discontent. In this case, religion at the hands of dervish leaders worked as a source of both consent and dissent. Through missionary activity, dervish leaders contributed to the spread of state power by working through the colonization process; their religious activity in its syncretic and multivalent form became a key source of consent to imperial rule. This was possible as long as new rulers were open to and willing to accommodate multivalent, heterodox, and mystical forms of worship that brought together different religious groups, thereby enhancing their control over territory. The dervish orders were the colonizing intermediary, but their job as translators of power relations was facilitated by the fact that the leaders and the people were not that far apart in their religious and mystical understandings.

The Kızılbaş *(Redheads)*

The *kızılbaş* (redhead) movement in the Ottoman heartland was perceived as much more dangerous to the state since in Anatolia it represented groups of Turcomans of Shiite persuasion and strong partisans of the Safavid rulers; in the eastern provinces, especially in Iraq, it epitomized the Ottomans' inability to fully reconcile their rule. The term *kızılbaş* appeared at the time of the father of Shah Ismail, Şeyh Haydar, who called those populations who followed the Safavids *kızılbaş* because they were wearing red headgear. These populations were local heterodox rebel Muslim Turcomans who were disgruntled at Ottoman rule and initially followed the Safavid order for socioeconomic reasons. Local conditions of rural dispossession, landlessness, and periodic crop failures presented severe challenges to the rural population of the empire. They were the nomads, villagers, and poorer members of rural society who switched to Shi'ia orders, drawn to a Turcoman version of Shi'ia Islam[35]; they were further agitated, provoked, and subsidized by the Shah of Iran who sent spies into Ottoman territory to feed, clothe, convert, and politicize these poorer nomadic populations. As Irène Mélikoff argues, "*kızılbaş* is a Turcoman phenomenon,"[36] although a Turcoman phenomenon with dire consequences. The rebellion of the *kızılbaş*, their adherence to Shi'ia rites and traditions, as well as their support of the Safavid Shah were the apparent reasons for persecution. The Turcoman-*cum*-Shi'ia populations of the Ottoman Empire were more dangerous than the many different groups and assemblies of roving dervishes because they had an enemy state backing them. Their potential organizational and oppositional power was less negotiable, although the solution for dealing with them was also clearer to Ottoman state elites: persecution.

---

[35] The initial differences between the Sunnî and Shia also arose from the political process for choosing the caliph of the Muslim community, Ebu Bekir, against Ali Ibn Abi Talib, the cousin and son-in-law of the prophet Muhammad. Over time, as the divisions between the different groups consolidated, the Shia also began to compile their own books of *hadîths* and provide their own Quranic interpretation of Islam. As a result, the Shia differ from the Sunnî on many issues of interpretation, as well as on issues of leadership and practice.

[36] Irène Mélikoff, "Le Problème kizilbas," *Turcica* 6 (1975): 49–67.

The persecution of the Shi'ia became routinized in the fifteenth and sixteenth centuries, when it was intensified with the rebellion of Shah Kulu in 1511, who was defeated in 1512–1513. Sources report many local acts of harassment, of hounding of Shiites as individuals or groups, especially in central and eastern Anatolia. Among those harassed for their views were Şeyh Celâl and the better-known religious *kızılbaş* chief and poet, Pir Sultan Abdal,[37] who celebrated their connection to the Shah in his verses in which the Shah was immortalized through the imagery of the crane, also the manifestation of Ali:

> The voice of his Majesty the Shah
> Is found in a bird called "turna" (the crane)
> His Stick is found at the bottom of the Nile
> And his robe is on a dervish.[38]

The rivalry between Sunnî and Shi'ia Islam increasingly became a self-fulfilling prophecy in the sense that the geopolitical rivalries and the Shi'ia-Sunnî struggles came to be superimposed. With the Battle of Çaldıran in 1514, Selim I first subdued the local *kızılbaş* element to continue with a holy war against the Shah, who he argued was corrupting Islam. With the acquisition of Iraq, the Shi'ia problem was accentuated. The Iraqi lands between Basra and Mosul and the province of Şehrizol were not fully consolidated under Ottoman rule, and given the presence of religious differences, the hold of the Ottomans was more tenuous. Basra, Baghdad, and Şehrizol had been under Safavid rule before passing into the Ottoman Empire and were therefore strongholds of Shi'ia Islam, which was well established among the elite, the notables, and the landholders of Syria and the province of Iraq. In Iraq, Shiites were particularly active since they organized in Najaf and Karbala, the cities where the shrines of Ali, Huseyn, and Abbas, the key figures of Shi'ia Islam, were located.

The struggle between the Shiite elite of Iraq and the Ottomans shows that imperial authority had not yet been established in this region and that the officials of the state were scrambling to find solutions to the low-level religious and militant insurgency fomented by the local leadership. In fact, imperial edicts show that the government perceived Iraq to be a province of dissent and made concerted efforts to control the region by limiting the number of fiefs distributed to local notables, testing for indications of heresy, and, when necessary, banning the Ashura ceremonies[39] that had become the site of religious and political

---

[37] Irène Mélikoff, "L'Islam hétérodoxe en Anatolie: mon-conformisme – syncrétisme – gnose," *Turcica* 14 (1982): 142–154.

[38] Translated from ibid., 151.

[39] Ashura ceremonies take place on the tenth day of the month of Muharrem. Shia Muslims have been taking part in this religious ceremony commemorating the death of the Imam Hussein at the battle of Karbala in 680 A.D. The event is the most significant moment in Shiism because it marked the divide in Islam between Shias and the majority Sunnîs. Ashura is the culmination of 10 days of mourning during the Islamic month of Muharrem. In some Shi'ia regions today, men flagellate themselves in rituals to demonstrate that they share the suffering of the imam. Clerics hold their heads and weep as they listen to stories of their Shia leader Hussein.

tensions. The Ottomans also exiled known religious fomenters from Iraq to the Balkans, where they expected them to settle down and give up their political activities. Yet, documents show that they kept coming back to continue the struggle against the Ottomans in Iraq.[40] The result was that the persecution of Shiites stemmed from multiple policies at both state and local levels. Locally, *kadıs* ordered the breakup of Ashura processions: the participants were arrested and beaten, and their flags broken; individuals accused of Shiism were burned alive; or executions were ordered with no trial, where often all the *kadıs* had to do was wait for witnesses to come forth voluntarily.[41] It is also noteworthy that the standards of evidence for who was a *kızılbaş* heretic were also seriously lacking. Often, as Imber discovered in a record, accusations were vague: "they have held mixed gatherings of men, women and girls, ever since Shah Ismail became Shah in Persia, and they have clearly displayed the marks of heresy."[42]

The consolidation of Sunnî and Shi'ia identities and their subsequent transformation into "bounded identities" was the result of regional geopolitical developments. The rivalry between the two imperial states exacerbated the religious differences between the two peoples, making the Ottomans more Sunnî and the Persians more Shi'ia. By the time of Süleyman the Magnificent, the Ottomans had become the rising Sunnî Islamic empire of the region and had institutionalized Sunnî Islam as the state religion. By the mid-sixteenth century, especially under the watch of Şeyhülislâm Ebu's-su'ud Efendi, Sunnî traditions had become dominant, and with Süleyman, the regularization and evening out of religious and secular law produced the empire's legal order. The rivalry with the Safavid Empire strongly contributed to this development since the enmity between the Ottomans and the Safavids was maintained not only at the level of territories and politics, but also at the cultural and ideological level where they fought for the allegiance of Muslims. This was not a matter of the state attempting to create order and legibility, but rather attempts to use the notion of heresy as a trope for simultaneously persecuting the enemy within, the *kızılbaş*, and the external enemy, the Safavid. Markus Dressler argues that this was a process for legitimating the rivalry of the two states on both sides of the border. That is, he argues, Ottomans and Safavids were "acting in the same discursive field, drawing on similar symbols and arguments."[43] Once caught up in this rhetoric, when religious orders became secret orders and showed Safavid leanings – especially some of the Melâmîs and Hurûfîs – the government justified

---

[40] C. H. Imber, "The Persecution of the Ottoman Shi'ites According to the Muhimme Defterleri, 1565–1585," *Der Islam* 56:2 (1979): 247.

[41] Personal communication from Professor Michael Winter about the persecution in Damascus, from the chronicles of Shams al-Din Muhammad Ibn Tulun. See also Imber, "The Persecution of the Ottoman Shi'ites."

[42] Imber, "The Persecution of the Ottoman Shi'ites," 248.

[43] Markus Dressler, "Inventing Orthodoxy: Competing Claims for Authority and Legitimacy in the Ottoman-Safavid Conflict," in *Legitimizing the Order: The Ottoman Rhetoric of State Power*, ed. Hakan T. Karateke and Maurus Reinkowski (Leiden, The Netherlands and Boston: Brill, 2005), 164.

persecution for their beliefs and political alliances. Political relations then trumped religious conflict, which was constructed and emphasized to fit the political needs of each state.

The kızılbaş situation had elements of state–society dissent with little negotiation. That the Ottomans as a rising imperial power responded so harshly to the kızılbaş threat in their territory indicates how seriously they took threats from rival powers, especially from their Safavid neighbor to the east. They also understood that the lack of integration in important provinces such as Iraq could have significant consequences for imperial prestige and growth. Once again, in a world view with such strongly entwined understandings of religion and politics, the kızılbaş were a perfect case of religion and politics reinforcing each other, with dire consequences. As networks of Turcoman peasants and tribesmen got caught in the web of geopolitical rivalries, they added a religious-ideological layer to their socioeconomic discontent, expressing themselves through the Sunnî-Shi'ia divisions, which provided Ottoman authorities both opportunity and cause for further consolidation of the political and religious identity of the empire. In this way, the kızılbaş from within their own political perspective contributed to the further consolidation of a Sunnî Islamic identity.

Celalis

Another relatively complex phenomenon of the sixteenth century was the rise of banditry, which developed into a form of mercenary or quasi-military organization with leadership. The Ottoman government's dealings with this form of banditry – which plagued the empire between approximately 1550 and 1650 – demonstrate an altogether different understanding of the implications of dissent. In fact, that state authorities were open to incorporating these bandits was almost entirely due to their ability to understand and put to use their organizational structures. They thus handled bandits with a different set of policies, which included both deal making and brutal destruction; they also clearly perceived them as cooptable and less threatening than the kızılbaş.

The development of Ottoman banditry, a phenomenon of the sixteenth century located especially in the southeastern frontiers of the empire, resulted from many state policies of territorial consolidation and demilitarization after war. When peasants, vagrant students, and others were drawn into the army and given clothing, shelter, arms, and a salary, they became soldiers. However, demilitarized after war and deprived of their shelter and salary, soldiers turned into mercenaries, gathering around band chiefs who refocused their energies on looting and banditry. As these former soldiers-cum-mercenaries grew in number and sophistication, they organized their forces around pools of men ready for hire by the state or by powerful grandees out to challenge local control. Such actions militarized the countryside, and as mercenaries waiting to be hired, these loose networks of soldiers not only competed among themselves, but also inflicted much damage on local populations, inspiring terror and complaints.

Responding to demands from local populations under siege, the state engaged the bandits at different times, and often struck bargains with bandit chiefs, reconverting mercenaries into soldiers and making their leaders officials of the state. Given that no common ideology or political goal beyond participation in Ottoman institutions ever emerged, the *celalis* remained powerless to effect major change or to constitute a clear threat to Ottoman politics and territory. Furthermore, banditry did not threaten the state as such because it quickly became incorporated into the state through bargains. State–bandit relations can be viewed as an alternative method of centralization through bargaining and incorporation, a method that the Russians used with their Cossack bands at the edges of their territory. Bandits, formerly mercenary soldiers, were not interested in rebellion but concentrated on trying to gain state resources, more as rogue clients than as primitive rebels.[44]

Unlike the Shiite threat from the Iraqi provinces where deal making was not really considered, *celalis* were eminently cooptable. They were recognized military units, demanded positions in the Ottoman state, and organizationally were a known quantity. This is easily demonstrated by the letters of intent bandit leaders wrote the sultans, offering their mercenaries for military use during campaigns in return for positions in the local state hierarchy and patronage networks. In one famous letter, Canboladoğlu Ali Pasha, a *celali* chieftain, promised the sultan more than 16,000 soldiers in return for fourteen high-level administrative positions for himself and his lieutenants.[45] The rhetoric of deal making between state makers and bandits was quite revealing: bandits felt free to write the sultan to ask for state positions; they believed that they could ask to be made part of the state's ruling hierarchy. Given examples of bandit leaders who had been incorporated into the state, received with pomp and ceremony by sultans, and even one famous outlaw who was buried next to the Grand Vizier – a man who spent his career fighting bandits – the message was clear: you can be one of us! You are part of us – we can negotiate with you. This was one way that the Ottomans dealt with the rambunctious populations of their frontiers across Anatolia. In such ways, dissent born out of Ottoman state policies was later incorporated into the state administrative structure, becoming part of regular consensual politics.

The history of Russian incorporation of the Don Cossacks fits this framework of warfare, bargaining, and integration, as Cossacks developed into a frontier people buffering Muscovy from the Tartars and encroaching on the Polish, Ottoman, and Muscovite borders. They had developed around 1550 as a depot of vagrant peasants, pirates, bandits, and mercenaries whose fame princes, kings, and emperors knew. They were engaged to fight wars for King Stephen Bathory (1524 and 1572) and for Muscovy, when they aided Ivan the

---

44 For a more elaborate exposition of this argument, see Karen Barkey, *Bandits and Bureaucrats: The Ottoman Route to State Centralization, 1550–1650* (Ithaca, NY: Cornell University Press, 1994).
45 Ibid., 190.

Terrible in his capture of Kazan. Before the Russians, the Polish government had developed a tradition of deal making with the Cossacks. Especially in the heyday of their strength in the sixteenth century, Cossacks presented the Polish government with armies in return for political concessions. In a manner quite similar to the Ottoman center, the Polish government sought to recover the privileges they had handed out after the war.[46]

Despite this precedent of bargaining and deal making at the frontiers of another kingdom, the relationship between Russians and Cossacks was not always predictable early on; the Russian state used Cossacks either as trading partners or as mercenaries for hire. Cossacks, for their part, also actively fought the Romanovs. When Cossack ranks were swelled with peasant runaways who were escaping Russian centralization efforts and increasing regulations on serfs, Cossacks actively involved themselves in the fight against the Russian establishment. In a series of rebellions – where a mix of rebellion and banditry was the norm – Don Cossacks resisted the incursion of the Russian forces. From the time of Peter the Great through the reign of Nicholas I, each rebellion was followed by imperial success because the Cossacks were mostly not very well organized in military terms, and each time they were further incorporated into the Russian lands. In a careful policy that benefited both sides, the Russian imperial policy of "subordination and perpetuation" assured that the Don Cossack leadership would be incorporated into the empire, while the imperial forces made sure that they maintained their military usefulness.[47]

As both the Ottoman and Russian cases demonstrate, consent and dissent were entwined in a precise way in the case of banditry. Although Ottomans understood well the ways in which such organized demands for political space and influence should be handled, they also understood the necessity for an imperial state to keep peace and order and to protect its subjects from plunder and rape. The accommodation of banditry and its invitation into regular politics came with a price. That is, while the state accepted these mercenaries into its fold, it also developed a rather sophisticated narrative of banditry and rebellion against the state. During the time when elaborate efforts were made to incorporate banditry into society, and the state provided symbols of acceptance into the state (e.g., ceremonies, burials), it also actively developed a narrative of opposition to the state.[48] Rebels who were thus wooed into the system were labeled *celalis* after a rebel leader in the early sixteenth century named Şeyh

[46] William H. McNeill, *Europe's Steppe Frontier, 1500–1800* (Chicago: The University of Chicago Press, 1964), 116; Philip Longworth, *The Cossacks* (New York: Holt, Rinehart and Winston, 1969).

[47] Bruce W. Menning, "The Emergence of a Military-Administrative Elite in the Don Cossack Land, 1708–1836," in *Russian Officialdom: The Bureaucratization of Russian Society from the Seventeenth to the Twentieth Century*, ed. Walter McKenzie Pintner and Don Karl Rowney (Chapel Hill: University of North Carolina Press, 1980), 131–135.

[48] In Barkey, *Bandits and Bureaucrats*, I document this in relation to *softas*, religious students, and low-level village militarization. I show how committees were formed: rebel leaders were invited to Istanbul, were provided with benefits and deals, and were convinced to participate in Ottoman society.

Celâl.[49] Given the severe brutality inflicted on Şeyh Celâl and his followers, the incident was in the collective memory of the people as one of great state violence; the state label of *celali* warned of the great danger that could befall those who opposed the state.

Şeyh Celâl, like the *kızılbaş*, dared to challenge the ideological frontiers of Ottoman state culture: by playing the Shiite card and getting Safavid help, he challenged not only territorial, but also ideological conceptions of the state; he would not survive. *Celalis*, the mercenaries of the seventeenth century, would not threaten this ideological concept of the state. Yet, the Ottoman state played both cards: it convinced bandits of the benefits of incorporating and becoming loyal servants of the state, while also rejecting the bandits as outcasts to be crushed through violent wars. It fought internal wars against the bandits and rewarded them at the same time. The very survival of the bandit rebels whom the Ottoman state engaged a century later was predicated on their not being true rebels; they were clients who had never developed an ideology of opposition. As such, they were never fully annihilated. In this sense, for them dissent was about becoming marginalized, which they did not want; rather, they were eager for positions in the Ottoman ruling order.

In the movements of Şeyh Bedreddîn and other dervish orders and in the struggles and incorporation of the *celalis* into the Ottoman political order, the Ottoman state confronted the dissent of the marginalized, those who perceived their relative weakening position vis-à-vis the state and who struggled to gain legitimacy, purpose, and possible incorporation. They expressed dissent, but dissent within the established framework of the state and its institutions. The dissent was strategic in the sense that its agents, the leaders of the rebellions, were aware of the social and cultural framework of the state and formulated their dissent from it, but used it to get benefits within the system, rather than trying to destroy it. They were handled partly through violent retribution, enough to maintain the coercive apparatus of the state, as well as through infrastructural mechanisms of appropriation. In this way, the movements of some of the dervish leaders and various *celali* leaders were similar. Theirs was dissent, not opposition. Ottomans expended not only energy on ideological justification, but also much time and resources on the persecution, exile, and annihilation of such religious and political heretics as a way of dealing with the allies of the Safavids, the *kızılbaş*, and the Shiite men of learning.

Islamic Ultra Orthodoxy and Jewish Messianism: Dissent in the Seventeenth Century

They [the preachers] must not spread extremist notions and so provoke the people and slow dissension among the community of Muhammad. This is not a subject either for

---

[49] Şeyh Celâl had been a true rebel, who capitalized on the discontent among Turcoman nomads and the Shiite infiltration from the Safavid lands, and declared a rebellion against the Ottoman state. The Ottomans violently crushed this rebellion, showing their territorial and ideological strength, and proceeded to call all rebels, bandits, and opponents of the state *celalis*.

excessive subtlety or for excessive crudity. It is better not to forbid any custom that takes the shape of worshipping God, for that would give rise to zeal and persistence.... It is among the duties of the Sultan of the Muslims to subdue and discipline ranting fanatics of this sort, whoever they may be, for in the past manifold corruption has come about from such militant bigotry.[50]

By the time Katib Çelebi, Ottoman scholar and literary figure, warned of the dangers of extremism, the movements of popular dissent observed at the height of imperial consolidation had given way to the strenuous reaffirmation of a certain type of traditional orthodoxy. The rise of such new and different protests in the urban, intellectual, and official religious quarters of the empire was a reaction to the discourse regarding the position of the empire. The matter was no longer whether a rising empire was perceived as perturbing the effortless compromise and collaboration between complex historical forces and networks of popular mystics and heterodox orders. It seemed just the reverse. Rather, Ottomans were now observed from the very core of society by the traditional *ulema* and preachers who blamed them for having incorporated too much of the periphery and its ideas, traditions, and cultural mores that diluted the ambitions and objectives of this grand empire. Greater international difficulties and internal repercussions were a clear sign for conservative elements to question whether imperial greatness would continue.[51]

The seventeenth century, a century of long-lasting wars on two fronts, with both Europe and the Safavids having exhausted the Ottomans, presented economic and social hardships for both urban and rural populations. The wars with Iran lasted from 1603 to 1639, whereas the Ottomans were engaged on the Polish, Ukrainian, and Russian borders from 1600 to 1681 and then at war with the Habsburgs from 1683 to 1699. At the same time, the Cretan crisis from 1654 to 1669, when Candia was captured, put tremendous stress on the government and the people of the empire. This meant that there was hardly any year in which the empire was free of war mobilization and expenses. During this century of continued warfare and internal destabilization of men and resources, two quite different movements of dissent appeared on the Ottoman scene.

The first, the Kadızadeli movement – rather conservative, exclusively Islamic, and in retrospect, short lived – gathered many devotees and fanatics in the urban spaces of the empire, especially in the main core cities. Their platform,

---

[50] Katib Chelebi, *The Balance of Truth*, transl. G. L. Lewis (London: George Allen and Unwin Ltd., 1957), 133–134.

[51] Such a discussion had already started in the Süleymanic era, when adaptations and signs of imperial flexibility were seen as examples of decline. A vigorous literature developed for talking about decline and the necessary response to loss of imperial greatness. See Bernard Lewis, "Ottoman Observers of Ottoman Decline," *Islamic Studies* 1 (1962): 71–87. The two major texts he analyzes are important discussions of perceived decline: Koçi Bey, *Risale*, ed. Zuhuri Danışman (Istanbul: Milli Eğitim Basımevi, 1972), and Aziz Efendi, *Kanun-name-i Sultani li Aziz Efendi, Aziz Efendi's Book of Sultanic Laws and Regulations: An Agenda for Reform by a Seventeenth-Century Statesman*, ed. and transl. Rhoads Murphey, Sources of Oriental Languages and Literature series no. 9. (Cambridge, MA: Harvard University Press, 1985).

one of conservative return to traditions and to pure Sunnî Islam, advocated the exclusion and destruction of heterodox orders and preached the submission of non-Muslim communities. Given the influence of Kadızadeli preachers, the relations between the Muslim majority and the Jewish communities started to deteriorate, affecting relations between Christians and Jews, as well as leading to an outburst of messianic activity in the Jewish community. The second, a Jewish messianic movement – fascinatingly, the most important one in Jewish history – arose within the empire during the middle of the Kadızadeli crisis, in the city of Izmir. The rise of the Jewish messiah, Sabbatai Sevi, undoubtedly resulted from the conjuncture of many European events (e.g., the massacres of Jews in Poland) and Ottoman social and political conditions at the same time. It is important to remember, however, that it became inflamed during the Kadızadeli ascendancy; therefore, there was an expected confrontation between the two sets of contentious actors, pressing the state to mediate among orthodox and heterodox Islam and now, messianic Judaism. It is fair to argue that the same social and political conditions gave rise to the conservative orthodox movement and to the Jewish messianic movement, so that not only did they coincide in space and time, but they were also born out of the same social malaise. As the ultra orthodox influenced the state to become more rigid, Jewish messianism promised a better life, one less affected by the travails of the new conservatism of the Ottoman state. In that sense Jewish messianism and Sufi heterodoxy resembled each other and became cognate movements, drawing the distance between conservative Islam and latitudinarian alternatives further apart.

Medieval Catholic Europe's persecution was slow and steady in its development. Throughout the eleventh and twelfth centuries, in particular, persecution became habitual: "deliberate and socially sanctioned violence began to be directed, *through established governmental, judicial, and social institutions*, against groups of people defined by general characteristics such as race, religion, or way of life; and membership of such groups in itself came to be regarded as justifying those attacks."[52] Violence against others on the basis of religion and ethnicity did not become the rule in the seventeenth-century Ottoman Empire, although subtle and deliberate changes appeared in the discourse and actions of state and religious actors and their social allies. As the high stress of warfare and competition on multiple fronts solidified, the empire embarked on the discourse of imperial greatness and decline and what to do to avoid decline. Marc Baer also argues that it is during this period that a new discourse developed on the part of the Ottoman government, especially under the influence of conservative Kadızadeli preachers, which started defining external and internal enemies: foreign powers as external enemies and the internal Christians and Jews as domestic enemies.[53] Although the empire ruled

---

[52] R. I. Moore, *The Formation of a Persecuting Society* (Malden, MA: Blackwell, 1990), 5.
[53] Marc David Baer, "Honored by the Glory of Islam: The Ottoman State, Non-Muslims, and Conversion to Islam in Late Seventeenth Century Istanbul and Rumelia," Ph.D. dissertation, University of Chicago, Chicago, June 2001.

by marking boundaries, separating and incorporating difference, these boundaries had not been static; they had absorbed and cushioned much movement
along with conversions, individual and communal relocations, and confrontation and dissent. The state had succeeded at being flexible by working with
movable boundaries that marked separation, but also allowed crossover. In
the seventeenth century, the ultra orthodox movement would question such
movement across boundaries, and would try to push the state toward a more
bounded and more rigid view of interreligious relations. In the confrontation
that ensued, each group tended toward the most extreme position, leading to
serious but temporary violence.

The consequence of this was the transformation of the language of war
and defeat, the violence of the conquests of central European citadels, and
the takeover of Kamanica (1672) and Yanik (1666) citadels, after which the
Ottomans aggressively put thousands of warriors to the sword.[54] Within the
empire between 1660 and 1680, a series of dramatic assaults on the person,
property, and culture of Sufis and non-Muslims disrupted the tolerance and forbearance of Ottoman authorities, shaking the trust of the empire's non-Muslim
communities. Although short lived, such demonstrations of zealotry across
boundaries imprinted imperial relations. The great conflagration in Istanbul
in the summer of 1660 was followed by a decree banning Jews from living in
much of Istanbul and ordering them to sell their property and give their trusts
to Muslims. In 1661, laws regarding the dress of Jews and Christians were
redeployed; Jewish and Christian property was confiscated, and some churches
and synagogues were destroyed. In 1662, seven churches were razed. Between
1663 and 1671, Jewish palace physicians were converted, and many public conversions were performed (1666–1687). During these years, Sufis were actively
persecuted, some executed, and their ceremonies banned, culminating in the
destruction of the shrine of Kanber Baba in 1667. Other assaults on Jews and
Christians included the razing of taverns, the prohibition of the wine and spirits
trade in Istanbul – a direct attack on their livelihood – and finally, the public
stoning of a Muslim adulteress whose Jewish convert partner was beheaded in
1680.[55]

By far the worst conflict occurred between the conservative Kadızadeli
preachers and Sufi şeyhs of the Halvetî order. By the seventeenth century,
the Halvetî order of dervishes had become devoted to the ruling circles, working close to the sultan as his advisors and holding positions in the mosques
as imams. The conservative Kadızadeli movement developed in opposition to
the domination of the Halvetî order. An initial auspicious encounter between
Murad IV (1623–1640) and Kadızade Mehmed Efendi established a relationship between this first preacher and the young sultan, who was searching for
ways to centralize the empire further, protect the frontiers, and reestablish

[54] Ibid., 117–119.
[55] Most of these events are culled from Baer's dissertation, in his chronology of events and from
his excellent analysis of the events themselves in the text.

peace and order. He found religious fundamentalism to be a strand that could be cultivated to help establish this order.[56] He therefore unleashed a novel force that lasted until nearly the end of the seventeenth century and damaged established notions of interfaith relations. It was during the initial struggles between the Halvetîs and Kadızadelis that the Jewish rabbi Sabbatai Sevi declared himself the messiah and promised a better life to Jewish Ottomans and to Jewish communities that he visited in Europe. The Halvetîs and Kadızadelis confronted each other for the better part of the century, but it turns out that both had the ear of Murad IV. Part of a pragmatist manipulative strategy that had served them well in the past, Ottomans displayed integration with segmentation, incorporation with pomp and ceremony, and participation sometimes with no serious responsibility.

The cultural conservatism of the Kadızadeli movement expressed itself in terms of opposition to innovation (*bida*) and adamant aggression against the established Sufi movements, especially the Halvetîs.[57] From about 1633 to 1694, three important preachers (*vaizan*) captivated the Istanbul faithful by squaring off in public with important Sufi counterparts. Each side employed extremist rhetoric, excited the crowds, and rallied their followers to violence that they happily carried out inside and outside the religious compounds of the city. Yet, it was the Kadızadelis who surprisingly continued to insist on their adherents' loyalty, their own self-purification, and the targeting of others for the same purpose. The Kadızadeli movement was one of extremism and vigilantism that, if kept under control by strong rulers who invoked Çelebi's advice for balance, might remain just a nuisance, but under weaker rulers had devastating potential.

Dissent in this war-torn period of Ottoman history played itself out as the public contestation between different world views: radical purist and heterodox, permissive movements vying for the attention of an increasingly solid Sunnî orthodox center. Zilfi argues that the movement for reform and renewal was both positioned against the Sufis and the more established *ulema* of the empire, those learned religious leaders who embodied the institutionalization of Ottoman Islam. Kadızadeli preachers with access to the crowds of the major cities of the empire believed that they were neither respected nor remunerated sufficiently for their efforts. Yet, Ottoman state makers were reluctant to

[56] Ahmet Yaşar Ocak, "XVII. Yüzyılda Osmanlı İmparatorluğu'nda Dinde Tasviye (Puritanizm) Teşebbüslerine bir Bakış: 'Kadızadeliler Hareketi,'" *Türk Kültürü Araştırmaları* 17–22 (1979–1983): 215.
[57] The best work on the Kadızadeli movement has been done by Madeline C. Zilfi, *The Politics of Piety: The Ottoman Ulema in the Postclassical Age, 1600–1800*, Studies in Middle Eastern History, no. 8 (Minneapolis: Bibliotheca Islamica, 1988); "The Kadızadelis: Discordant Revivalism in Seventeenth-Century Istanbul," *Journal of Near Eastern Studies* 45 (October 1986): 251–269; Semiramis Çavuşoğlu, "The Kadızadeli Movement: An Attempt of Seriat Minded Reform in the Ottoman Empire," Ph.D. dissertation, Princeton University, Princeton, NJ, 1990: Ocak, "XVII. Yüzyılda Osmanlı İmparatorluğu'nda Dinde Tasviye (Puritanizm)"; Ismail Hakkı Uzunçarşılı, *Osmanlı Tarihi, III* (Ankara: Türk Tarih Kurumu Basımevi, 1983).

commit themselves on the choice that was presented to them. They had maintained Islamic mysticism and traditional Sunnî religious orthodoxy, and even though Sultan Murad IV might have inadvertently added to this mix of religious perspectives by drawing the Kadızadelis closer to him, he skillfully played groups off against one another. Thus, Sufi Sivasi Efendi participated in conversations with the trusted members of the sultan's entourage, while Murad condoned some of the actions of the Kadızadeli crowds. That the *ulema* allowed Sufi şeyhs into state deliberations was the product of a relatively easy relationship between the *ulema* and the şeyhs of the period because many şeyhs were educated in Sunnî religious schools, and many *ulema* had mystical tendencies. At least 22% of the şeyhs operating in dervish orders (*tarîkats*) in the seventeenth century had been educated in *medreses* and *tekkes*.

When Kadızadeli Mehmed Efendi was nominated to the post of preacher at the Ayasofya mosque in 1631, he and Sivasi Efendi started to square off in public. Mehmed Efendi pleased his crowds by attacking Sufi religious tenets, and by preaching religious fundamentalism and a return to a traditional orthodoxy with harsh simplicity, straightforward boundaries, and certainty. Sivasi Efendi pleased his own crowds by disparaging the conservatism of Mehmed Efendi, making the case for a tolerant, unbiased, and syncretic world in which the complexity and uncertainty of our being and our thought was only a reminder of our fragility. Moreover, each provided his own analysis of particular subjects.[58] A brief respite was provided by Köprülü Mehmed Pasha (1656–1661), a forceful opponent of preacher zealotry, as well as a strong advocate of calm and order in the capital, who moved relatively quickly to eradicate potentially explosive conservative dissent. However, his son-in-law, Köprülü Fazıl Ahmed Pasha (1661–1676) reversed his actions, giving rise to the most hateful of the Kadızadelis, Üstüvani Mehmed Efendi (referred to as Vani Efendi), whose period of influence during the reign of Mehmed IV (1648–1687) lasted a long time and caused much damage to relations among the multiple social groups in the Ottoman capital.

Vani's reign in the mosques of Istanbul lasted from 1659 to 1694; during this time, relations soured among the different ethnic and religious communities of Istanbul. The increased radicalization of the Kadızadeli had found a public supporter in Köprülü Fazıl Ahmed Pasha, the grand vizier of the period, who allowed the zealotry to flourish, especially when the empire was engaged in difficult international struggles, such as the siege of Candia. External hardships were compounded by the renewed project of Islamization that was touted as a solution to enhance the somewhat battered legitimacy of the Ottoman state. The 1660 fire in Istanbul provided a suitable moment for the project of Islamization. Already in the earlier part of the century, Safiye Sultan, the mother of Sultan Mehmed III (1595–1603), had attempted to build the Yeni Camii complex by appropriating the houses and properties belonging to the Jews in this particular district of Istanbul. Not fully successful, the project was restarted

---

[58] Ocak, "XVII. Yüzyılda Osmanlı İmparatorluğu'nda Dinde Tasviye (Puritanizm)," 217.

after the conflagration of 1660, during which many Jewish homes were burnt.[59] Not only was the new mosque erected, but also the fire and the displacement afterward provided the opportunity for the Islamization of the space and the subsequent rise in interethnic strife. The Christians complained that the Jews were moving into their neighborhood, and the Muslims similarly complained that Jews and Christians were settling beyond permissible areas, close to the mosque or public space. After the fire, Jews and Christians lost their properties, moved to other locations in the city, and watched the transformation of their land and houses of worship into Islamic spaces. Such action was supported by imperial decrees and encouraged by the *fetvâs* of the religious authorities.[60] Between the reconquest of Bozcaada (1658) and capture of Candia (1669) and the impounding of non-Muslim land in the capital city, we can see that a larger process of "reconquest of infidel space" was taking place.[61]

Although the rise of the Kadızadeli movement was grounded in the perception of changing Ottoman territorial superiority, the rise of the Jewish messiah, Sabbatai Sevi, was the result of manifold factors coming together at this particular juncture when the news of European massacres of Jews, the local effort at Islamization, and the outbreak of intercommunal tensions were further exacerbated by the first warnings of future European influence with respect to the Christian populations of the empire. There has been a rich literature on the causes of Jewish messianism and Sabbatai Sevi. Most of these sources focus on the effect of the expulsion from Spain, on the spread of Jewish communities in the Ottoman Empire, the Balkans, the Near East, and on their relations with the European communities. They emphasize the different internal conditions of the Jewish communities, their tendencies toward messianic thought, the European context, and discrimination and persecution in Europe, without paying much attention to the changes undergone by Ottoman Jews at that time.[62]

During the seventeenth century, the position of Jews in the Ottoman Empire started to decline. With increasing economic relations between the Ottomans and the Europeans, both internal rivalries and European Christian influence made for unsavory relations between Jews and other groups, and furthered interethnic tensions, so much so that Christians and Muslims allied to oppose Jews. Furthermore, the Kadızadeli preachers had adopted an openly anti–non-Muslim attitude and were preaching the elements of prejudice and fanaticism to larger crowds. It is within this context of increased animosity, competitive dealing, and Ottoman geopolitical travails that the Messiah announced himself. Marc Baer makes a cogent argument linking the decline in Jewish social and

---

[59] Lucienne Thys-Şenocak, "The Yeni Valide Mosque Complex at Eminönü," *Muqarnas: An Annual of the Visual Culture of the Islamic World* 15 (1998): 58–70.

[60] Baer, "Honored by the Glory of Islam," 130–135.

[61] Ibid., 40.

[62] Jacob Barnai, "The Spread of the Sabbatean Movement in the Seventeenth and Eighteenth Centuries," in *Communications in the Jewish Diaspora: The Pre-Modern World*, ed. Sophia Menashe (Leiden, The Netherlands: E. J. Brill: 1996), 313–337; Gershom Scholem, *Sabbatai Sevi and the Sabbatean Movement in His Lifetime* (Jerusalem: 1957).

economic position, as well as the Ottoman malaise to the rise and acceptance within the community of the self-declared messiah Sabbatai Sevi. Among other issues, he argues that even the sultans who had promoted many Jews to sensitive palace positions stopped appointing doctors, translators, and diplomats from among Jews and turned to the Orthodox community.[63]

As did Şeyh Bedreddîn, Sabbatai Sevi had spent time traveling through the empire, visiting potential ally communities, building contacts, and gathering followers before he rose into the limelight and declared himself the savior of the Jewish people. He traveled from Izmir to Salonica and other Greek cities, Petras, and then to Rhodes, Tripoli, Cairo, and Jerusalem. In Jerusalem and Cairo, he developed ties to many communities; in Gaza in May/June 1665, the community sent word that "the messiah of Jacob's God" had arrived.[64] From there, Sabbatai Sevi traveled to Safed, Damascus, and Aleppo, coming back to Izmir before landing in Istanbul where he gathered a large following.

Although there is no doubt that the empire had been a fertile ground for Muslim and Jewish mysticism and that Sabbatai had tapped into these mystical teachings and the Kabbala through his travels, in many ways like a Jewish Şeyh Bedreddîn, Sabbatai Sevi's initial success can be explained by the fact that Jews had recently suffered at the hands of the Ottoman state, especially the grand vizier, the Valide sultan, and the preacher to the sultan, Kadızadeli Vani Efendi.[65] They had become the more apparent victims of the project of reinforcing Ottoman legitimacy through the Islamization of one of the most non-Muslim commercial districts of Istanbul, then focused primarily on Jews, Jewish houses, and resources. The construction of the Yeni Camii Mosque complex right on the land where Jews lived and where the fire had razed their property was a clear demonstration by the state of power and authority, a symbolic display of Islamic hegemony and imposition of interreligious boundaries. To the palace preacher, Kurd Mustafa, "The aforementioned mosque showed itself and became manifest just as the Muhammadan religion appeared out of the darkness of infidelity."[66] Such a change in attitude was painfully apparent to Jews who had fled persecution in Europe. Sabbatai's success is also explained by his ability to use the vast network of diaspora Jewish communities that were so tightly knit together through different channels of communication and an already developed press.

Sabbatai Sevi was a messianic religious figure, but he had also successfully spread his word through many communities across a wide geographical area throughout the empire, the Balkans, Egypt, Anatolia, and the Holy Land, gaining many followers among community leaders and their people, thereby

---

[63] Baer, "Honored by the Glory of Islam"; and "The Great Fire of 1660 and the Islamization of Christian and Jewish Space in Istanbul," *International Journal of Middle Eastern Studies* 36 (2004): 159–181; and "17. Yüzyılda Yahudilerin Osmanlı İmparatorluğu'ndaki Nüfuz ve Mevkilerini Yitirmeleri," *Toplum ve Bilim* 83 (Kış 1999/2000): 202–222.
[64] Barnai, "The Spread of the Sabbatean Movement," 326.
[65] Ibid., 160.
[66] Ibid., 172.

gathering a potentially powerful opposition movement. These organizational factors would certainly have alerted government officials to the potential danger of Sabbatai's movement. However, for the Kadızadeli element, Sabbatai brought together mysticism, messianism, influence from Sufi traditions, and Judaism, thereby combining in his dissent many elements that ultra orthodox circles vehemently abhorred and decried. Such were the reasons for his arrest.

Given no choice but conversion or execution, the messiah converted, pulling his followers into Islam. According to a palace Jew, the converted physician of the sultan, Sabbatai Sevi had "turned the world on its head,"[67] and his conversion was a relief. After his conversion to Islam and his earnest work to convert his fellow Jews, Sevi, now Aziz Mehmed, became the companion of Vani Efendi, the most passionate of the conservative preachers. Together, they convinced many Jews to follow them into the Islamic fold. Not only were Jews converted, this occurred with great pomp and ceremony in which the public ritual of conversion – the cloaking of Jews in new Muslim clothing and the white turban, which symbolized Islam – fulfilled two important functions.[68] At this juncture when the doctrines of Islam were forcefully disputed, what better show than the public conversion of Jews to the true faith? Furthermore, public conversion ceremonies – the marking of movement across the boundary with conscious, deliberate, and physical markers of difference – were the best way to reinforce flagging boundaries.

In the end, the sultan reasserted mainstream accommodationist principles and, especially after the banishment of the central actors in this religious drama (the grand vizier, the preacher, and the Valide sultan), it looked as if the state had successfully ridden a terrible wave of potential disaster. The preachers had organized, used the pulpit to appeal to popular religious fanaticism, and manipulated the crowd to construct a more Sharia-based culture of Islam, which underplayed the legitimacy of popular Sufi learning and questioned the easy interface between traditional *ulema* and Sufi şeyhs. They had used their expanding authority and voice to spread their venom to interreligious relations in Ottoman cities where an overall conservative Muslim mood was already in place and where they ensured that the population of mosque-goers noticeably increased. It is said that a crowd larger than 60,000 attended the main mosque after the siege of Vienna. Jews and Christians were bound to feel the pressure of religion, the pull away from toleration and from the basic values of Ottoman Islam.

Whether the Grand Vizier Fazıl Ahmed Pasha would have continued his agenda of Islamization and conservative reform from within is not known. One interpretation of the Kadızadeli and Sabbatai Sevi episodes of seventeenth-century Ottoman history is that the Ottoman state rode the crisis by manipulating it, promoting the extremists while appointing their favorite Halvetî şeyhs

---

[67] Zilfi, *The Politics of Piety*, 155.
[68] Baer describes in detail the public ceremonies that displayed the conversion of Jews in chapter 6, "The Conversion of Sabbatai Sevi," of "Honored by the Glory of Islam," 286–316.

as preachers in the most important mosques. On another score, promoting Islamization was not only a by-product of the Kadızadeli position, but also perhaps the first true political response of the state taking a chance to reinforce its legitimacy at a time of international difficulty. Jews became pawns in the struggle between orthodoxy and its opponents, although they also became victims of a temporary lapse in Ottoman organization of boundaries and difference. The Kadızadeli episode therefore threatened to change Ottoman rule from toleration to large-scale conversion and assimilation.

Conclusion

In these various movements of dissent that interacted and interlaced with the Ottoman state, we recognize the rising significance of religion, although not just religion as such, but religion in its various forms of organization and institutionalization. If we take the *celalis* out of the equation (which some authors have associated with the *kızılbaş*, but I do not), the other movements of dissent in the first four centuries of Ottoman rule could be seen as repeated struggles for the religious leadership of the empire: scripturalism and Sunnî orthodoxy versus heterodox movements spread all over the Ottoman provinces fighting a trend of spiritual consolidation. The conflict, however, as I have explored, emerged and consolidated itself into a religious one as a result of systematic issues of the organization of rule. That the Ottoman state managed the control of well-organized non-Muslim communities, but fought more amorphous and unorganized networks of Muslim heterodoxy, indicates the degree to which the differences in response were originally based on organizational issues. The competition between the Ottomans and the Persians was only going to exacerbate this religious difference.

Groups pulled at the state from several directions. On the one hand, a variety of Sufi movements – from institutionalized, state-reliant dervish orders to secret societies with strongly antinomian practices – wanted to maintain an open, syncretic society and appealed to the disgruntled landless or nomadic Turcomans and urban artisans and traders, providing the antidote to the increasing scripturalism and Sunnî orthodox practices of the center. The more the Ottomans institutionalized Islam into a Sunnî orthodox framework, the greater the proliferation of this heterodox counterweight. The core provinces, especially the Balkans and Anatolia, were strewn with these orders, participating in the construction of everyday religiosity. Whereas the magistrate, as the state official, negotiated between the individual or the community and the state, the dervish leaders and the members of the convent provided an alternative space for religiosity. These spaces were not always contradictory or at odds with one another; they composed a mosaic of alternative practices and affiliations that bound people to some form of Islam. The state became the enemy of alternative forms of religiosity mostly when they were diffuse, not grounded in a traditional framework of land tenure and production, and moved from village to village and province to province to proselytize. It was not the ideas of

Şeyh Bedreddîn but his movement and his actions that concerned state authorities and prompted conflict with them. Bedreddîn refused to fit the pattern of Ottoman balance and order.

On the other hand, an externally stimulated but largely internal upheaval within Islam threatened the state's classical Sunnî order from the ultra orthodox right. The preachers of the Kadızadeli era were oppositional Muslims in the sense that they worked to push Islam further down the road of scripturalism and orthodoxy, to cleanse it of the infidels within and beyond. They were forceful advocates of a purist Islam, but to the detriment of the precarious balance that the Ottomans had established between the competing demands of empire. If the Sufis pulled for more flexibility, complexity, and amalgamation of tradition and practice, the Kadızadelis pulled for more rigidity and harshness of rule. The Ottoman state for a while embodied both forces within itself, responding and assessing the impact of each, and integrating these groups for its own purposes. In the seventeenth century, the objective was unclear, shrouded in doubt about the strength of empire; therefore, the solution became Islamization and rigidity.

Dissent was a response to empire. Yet, in its encounter with dissent, the imperial state understood the opportunities for shaping empire further. Dissent here was more about the confrontation with one religion, Islam, but in many different manifestations and political forms. Taming Islam and settling on a classical style proved to be much more challenging than dealing with the diversity of the empire. This was a struggle for identity, a struggle that was carried on in different spiritual climates with different forces that challenged the state. Yet, the reorganization of the relationship between religion and politics favored the state. This outcome would be transformed with the eighteenth-century reorganization of dissent.

PART II

THE TRANSFORMATION OF
THE EIGHTEENTH CENTURY

I n Part I of this book, I explored the organization of empire. I asked about imperial longevity, and focused on the structural features of empire that contribute to its flexible and pragmatic persistence. Empires are negotiated enterprises in which the basic pattern of relationships between imperial authorities and peripheries is different for each periphery, creating a patchwork pattern of relations with structural holes between peripheries. I argued that to maintain this structure and remain dominant and flexible, an empire needed to maintain legitimacy, diversity, and the flow of resources and manpower through a stable relationship with the intermediary elites. To present my argument, in Part I, I followed a temporal narrative of empire in which I analyzed the emergence, development, and maintenance of the Ottoman Empire in the context of other imperial cases.

The Ottoman Empire was formed within the existing ideological and organizational world of the frontier in the post-Seljuk and late-Byzantine era using loose and fluid integration as components of a deliberate strategy in which brokerage across networks of region and religion succeeded in giving rise to a new polity. Brokerage was key to the establishment of the incipient state, whereas its development into an empire was constructed as a hub-and-spoke structure, maintaining vertical integration and horizontal segmentation at the same time. The institutionalization into empire can be compared to that of the Roman world, especially as Augustus transformed the republic into an empire. Similarly, Mehmed II transformed a regional state into an empire, once again by relying on the extension of government institutions to include the most administratively savvy and militarily skillful of both worlds, the Ottoman and the Byzantine, thereby creating a hybrid world in which institutional layering became the preferred method of imperial construction.

Settling into empire, state control was ensured through the vertical integration of elites and the continual segmentation of horizontal networks. The potential for the development of strong social networks ready to coalesce against the state was continually minimized. Longevity and success were the results of flexible state–society arrangements, pragmatic decision making, and the provision of varying career alternatives and choices for the uppermost elites of the empire. The roots of Ottoman diversity and integration can be found in an early expression of tolerance that functioned by establishing and maintaining boundaries between religious and ethnic groups and allowing for some movement across boundaries. Interethnic peace and order were predicated on Ottomans' ability to provide segmented minority elites with the incentives to maintain boundaries.

Such openness and toleration was also possible given the particular role of Sunnî orthodox Islam in the Ottoman state–society configuration. Religion functioned to legitimate empire, yet it also remained subservient to a strong and pragmatic state in which it functioned as an institution of rule and a mode of everyday life. The trajectory of state–religious relations was never unidirectional, uniform, or predictable. Whereas orthodox Islam had played a minor role in early Ottoman times, it was reinforced by conquests in Islamic lands and the influx of religious teachers and schools built by religiously inclined sultans. Sunnî orthodoxy was reinforced in the seventeenth century, when it became somewhat restrictive in doctrine, but consolidated its institutional control.

Dissent in the Ottoman Empire involved a recurrent struggle for the religious leadership of the empire that emerged from organizational challenges and happened to coincide well with economic and political marginalization. In the midst of a Sunnî spiritual consolidation and unable to impose order on these multifarious communities and brotherhoods, the Ottoman state made dissent visibly possible and in turn persecuted its perpetrators. The struggle was never resolved because the dissenters' ideas were less of a dilemma than were their potential rebellions. A religious division between a state-defined orthodoxy and a localized, latidunarian, heterodox piety always coexisted with Ottoman rule, moving from cooperation to dissent to collaborationist behavior in border regions.

In each chapter, I follow the historical unfolding of an organizational logic, one that privileged networks and institutions as the stepping stones to a stable, pragmatic, and open system that, ironically, believed ideologically in the illusion of an existing order that had to remain undisturbed. Although, in fact, the structure of the empire was quite loose, its ideology of order was quite strict, which explained how the state allowed both movement and diversity, but lashed out harshly when it perceived this "order" to be threatened. Both the organizational openness and the strength of imperial protection can be compared to the Roman and Byzantine worlds, perhaps even more than to its contemporaries, the Habsburg and the Russian Empires.

Part II of this book traces the manner in which the organizational modus vivendi that had been accomplished operated in the eighteenth century to produce alternative forms of organization and adaptation. *Adaptation was a sign of flexibility and pragmatism, not a sign of decline.* As the circumstances of international warfare, politics, and the economy had changed, the protected order of

Pax Ottomanica came under threat. The systemic changes that were undertaken by the crown reflected its need for greater resources to fight increasingly powerful and successful Europeans, as well as its ability to adapt rapidly to overhaul established taxation systems. Taxation was altered to provide greater resources for the center; the economy was restored, and new actors were empowered to control the periphery.

The seeds of transition from empire to a different political formation were sown in the eighteenth century. The central and local structures of the empire began to take a different shape, connecting nodes and further decreasing peripheral segmentation. This time period saw deep structural changes whereby social actors of different origins, locations, and interests connected through political and economic networks of association, and explored the means by which they could become empowered vis-à-vis the state, perceiving alternatives not fully within the imperial vision. Two central processes provided the basis for alternative horizontal linkages to develop in Ottoman society: tax farming and international trade. Both provoked the development of long chains of association and dependence, embedding actors in dense networks of relations. Two central chapters explore political and economic empowerment, setting the stage for a more direct struggle between state actors and social actors for control over the destiny of Ottoman modernity and refashioning.

Reform and modernity were also discussed with varying results in the eighteenth-century transformation. Reform took on alternative meanings and provided different platforms for action, depending on who appropriated the reform discourse. As Chapter 6 shows, it could be defined and appropriated by quite conservative groups such as the Janissaries and the *ulema*, with some effect, if their grievances were perceived as legitimate. However, these groups switched to antireformist platforms rather easily.

Like reform, modernity also had multiple meanings throughout this time period. Modernity is a difficult concept to discuss because it is fraught with Western definitions and cross-cultural biases. In the Ottoman context, modernity has mostly been used to characterize a reformist and modern center pitted against conservative and traditional regional actors. However, there were many more alternative locations of modernity in the empire. I take modernity to be characterized by multiple paths that maintained and adapted religious and imperial traditions at the same time as actors searched for new resolutions to their contemporary dilemmas. In this sense, modernity is not just one central state path toward increased standardization, rationalization, and uniformity of relations and processes; rather, it is inline with Eisenstadt's definition of actors' engagement with gradually larger sectors of their respective societies.[1]

In the Ottoman context, starting with the eighteenth century, modernity was being imagined and acted on in a variety of ways, in multiple locations. Each chapter follows the location of modernity in another set of institutions and actors. In Chapter 6, we see that modernity concerns the constitution of

---

[1] S. N. Eisenstadt, "Multiple Modernities," *Daedalus* 129 (2000): 2.

a political arena with a variety of central, and later regional, actors asserting their ability to act politically in unison. In Chapter 7, the slow and steady empowerment of regional notables as economic and political actors through tax farming and international trade brings about a different modernity, both of local involvement and of investment for further growth, but also again a structural possibility for concerted action through the associative capacity of new horizontal networks. In Chapter 8, with the assertion of an alternative state-based centralizing modernity, but one that was also under the dictates of the West, a liberal notion of reform and citizenship came to be held and acted on, transitioning from empire to nation-state.

Chapters 6 and 7 first trace the political process of empowerment in the eighteenth century, then the economic and networking structure of change; Chapter 8 discusses the contest of the nineteenth century.

6

An Eventful Eighteenth Century: Empowering the Political

> The government which has been depicted as so despotic, so arbitrary, seems never to have been such since the reigns of Mahomaet II, Soliman I or Selim II, who made all bend to their will.... You see in 1703 that the padishah Mustafa II is legally deposed by the militia and by the citizens of Constantinople. Nor is one of his children chosen to succeed him, but his brother Achmed III. This emperor is in turn condemned in 1730 by the janissaries and the people.... So much for these monarchs who are so absolute! One imagines that a man may legally be the arbitrary master of a larger part of the world, because he may with impunity commit a few crimes in his household, or even the murder of a few slaves, but he cannot persecute his nation, and is often the oppressed rather than the oppressor.[1]

If Ottoman historical eras were to compete for lack of scholarly interest and attention, there is no doubt that the eighteenth century would win. Wedged between classical greatness and renewed centralized vigor, the eighteenth century has been both neglected and misunderstood. From the perspective of classical glory, how could the empire sink so low? From the lens of nineteenth-century centralized reform, where did they get the strength to start again? Undoubtedly, the larger historiographical issue of the eighteenth century in the West as well has been the transitional nature of this century between premodern and modern political formations.

From contemporary observers to European travelers to historians of the empire, those who have been tempted to describe this "dark century" did so with a vengeance. To the Ottomans living in the empire, nothing was the same any longer: the traditional system of rule had been abandoned, and the division between classes was forsaken for a porous and dangerous movement filling the ranks of the military with undeserving and untrained men. The sultans did not

---

[1] François-Marie Voltaire, *Oeuvres complètes de Voltaire: Essai sur les moeurs et l'esprit des nations* (Paris: Gallimard, 1858), vol. 3, bis, 271. Translation taken from Selim Deringil, *The Well-Protected Domains: Ideology and the Legitimation of Power in the Ottoman Empire, 1876–1909* (London and New York: I. B. Tauris, 1999), 4.

take rule as seriously and engaged in the pleasures of the palace. To Europeans traveling through on diplomatic missions or for pleasure, the exotic Orient had now turned into a despotic Orient. The Europeans were the products of the Reformation and the burgeoning Enlightenment, and they viewed Ottoman traditions with increasing suspicion. When these differences were seen against the increasing military might of the West, Europeans described the East and the West in terms of "barbarian" versus "civilized." Historians fell prey to these images, which reproduced much of the malaise of their contemporaries, without questioning their validity.

If the empire in the sixteenth and seventeenth centuries was suspected of being in decline, in the eighteenth century it was indisputably so. For historians of the empire, its inability to expand, its defeat in war, and the slow diminution of its territories did not portend success. Especially because scholars of the Ottoman Empire had glorified its frontier expansionist and warfare economy, they identified the end of expansion and the cutbacks of the Ottomans as indicators of decline. The expansion of the early centuries could not continue; the Ottoman Empire had reached its technological and geopolitical limits. Maintaining its far-flung territories would prove difficult, especially as Europeans were developing new military technology and the Russians were flourishing into an equally strong and ambitious empire. Pressure from most of the Christian–Muslim borderlands in the west and Shiite–Sunnî frontiers in the East continued unabated throughout the seventeenth and eighteenth centuries. While wars with the Habsburg Empire and the Persians dominated in the seventeenth century, wars with Russia engaged the Ottomans and overburdened its socioeconomic and military apparatus in the eighteenth century. These wars have defined the Ottoman centuries.

The domestic transformations experienced by both state and social forces in Ottoman society were understudied and misunderstood.[2] Internally, the classical social organization of the empire was described as rigidly separated between the ruling institution, and when scholars found movement between institutional fields, they interpreted this as decline. Yet, Norman Itzkowitz had provided excellent examples of individuals whose trajectory he described as from "efendi to pasha clearly showing that the discussion of the eighteenth century should be about the adaptation of institutions and the ability for individuals to move from one central institution to the other, providing flexibility to the system.[3] It is now much more common to be a revisionist historian of the empire and to declare war on the decline paradigm. The pendulum has now swung in the direction of demonstrating imperial health through state–provincial relations.

---

[2] Ottomans were mostly understood from the viewpoint of Albert K. Lybyer, *The Government of the Ottoman Empire in the Time of Suleiman the Magnificent* (Cambridge, MA: Harvard Historical Studies, 1913) and H. A. R. Gibb and H. Bowen, *Islamic Society and the West: A Study of the Impact of Western Civilization on Moslem Culture in the Near East*, 2 vols. (London: Oxford University Press, 1957).

[3] Norman Itzkowitz, "Eighteenth Century Ottoman Realities," *Studia Islamica* 16 (1962): 73–94.

As a rethinking of the Ottoman social order has unfolded, many studies have focused on reconstructing the provincial perspective in the empire, focusing on state–provincial relations in many different regions to understand the dynamics of eighteenth-century rule. In these studies, we see the emergence of a novel picture, in that many of them show how involved the state was with control of the provinces. The central state was active in controlling its governors, the local notables, and the various Janissary corps in the provinces. In one important study, Karl Barbir analyzes another trajectory – from "pasha to efendi," from a military administrative to a civilian administrative position – and demonstrates how the state coopted and integrated these notables who lived in eighteenth-century Damascus and who were often of military origin.[4] Many other studies have brought eighteenth-century state involvement in the provinces to extraordinary light, demonstrating the degree to which the Ottoman administrative structure functioned, adapted, and conveyed the necessary control to the provinces that they deemed important to maintain in a well-integrated fashion.[5] The shift toward studying provincial arrangements, however, led to the neglect of the central unfolding of events that demonstrates the immediate state–society reorganization at the center.

I use this chapter to present a perspective on the domestic political transformation of the Ottoman center in order to underscore the degree to which, during the eighteenth century, movements of opposition to the state (or to particular segments of the state) were developing to connect, unite, and develop common platforms of action; social forces were starting to frame a new state–society compact. To accomplish this goal, I provide two histories of the eighteenth century: one short traditional one, focused on wars and international developments, and the other – a more analytic one – an eventful history of the eighteenth century focusing on three main internal junctures during this period – 1703, 1730, and 1808 – each at the pinnacle of internal developments. I aim to assess the meaning of the succession of these events and to understand the depth of the structural changes they engendered.

Focusing on particular events, in the genre of an eventful sociology, as advocated by William Sewell, Jr., helps us understand the path dependency of historical processes, their contingency as well as the rearticulation of structures that results from events. Events, as Sewell defines them, are a subclass of happenings that transform structures. That is, many different things happen all

---

[4] Karl K. Barbir, *Ottoman Rule in Damascus, 1708–1758* (Princeton, NJ: Princeton University Press, 1980); idem, "From Pasha to Efendi: The Assimilation of Ottomans into Damascene Society 1516–1783," *International Journal of Turkish Studies* 1 (1980): 67–82.

[5] Michael Robert Hickok, *Ottoman Military Administration in Eighteenth-Century Bosnia: The Ottoman Empire and Its Heritage* (Leiden, The Netherlands, and New York: E. J. Brill, 1997); Dina Khoury, *State and Provincial Society in the Ottoman Empire, Mosul, 1540–1834* (Cambridge, UK: Cambridge University Press, 1998); Ariel Salzmann, *Tocqueville in the Ottoman Empire: Rival Paths to the Modern State* (Leiden, The Netherlands: E. J. Brill, 2004); Beshara Doumani, *Rediscovering Palestine: Merchants and Peasants in Jabal Nablus, 1700–1900* (Berkeley: University of California Press, 1995).

the time, but only some of them have a transformative effect.[6] In choosing to look at the these three events, I intend to show the manner in which they were connected through the goals of the actors, the process of learning opposition, and the incremental changes that occurred as a result. From this perspective, I look at events as discrete social happenings that are concatenations of networks that coalesce in time and space to transform the social-structural elements and cultural understandings of the period. For each event, I not only provide the historical unfolding of activities and actions, but also focus on the actors, their ties, and coalitions to understand how they came to see, organize, and effect their opposition. In this sense, the focus is on events, but as moments when resources, information, and associations flowed through distinct webs of social transactions. Once again, actors embedded in their networks of association are clearly seen as mediating within institutions, changing somewhat, but also maintaining significant continuity in the institution of the state and the meaning attached to its legitimate rule.

Although the events I discuss constituted three remarkable moments in the history of the empire, they were relatively neglected because they were not "revolutions." Yet, they were fundamental as they engendered transformations in the associative ability of different social groups and classes in Ottoman society, and signaled a transformation in the political culture of the empire. They represented a trend of empowerment that spread to the military classes, the *ulema*, the artisans, and the masses in coalition with a variety of groups. The result was a forceful broadening of the base of political power in the empire, in which each event appealed to and called for broader political participation. Such a process definitely marked the reorganization of dissent into opposition politics, a process of politicization that ratcheted up significantly the stakes in politics, spread to the provinces, ignited rebellions, and transformed the nature of factions and alliances in faraway regions of the empire. At face value, however, each event ended up merely with the deposition of a sultan and the execution of his close advisers. Amazingly, the state remained intact through these ruptures, indicating its continuing resilience.

By the end of 1808, Ottoman politics had been transformed in several ways. Dissent had moved from mostly religious, amorphous, pervasive, and extensively and loosely networked movements into more organized and coordinated forms of political alliances in which nonstate actors moved toward participation in state politics. The institution of the *ulema* had been strengthened through its participation in the multiple opposition movements. Politics had changed in its location, moving from center to periphery, and, finally, movements of self-determination became active toward the end of the century.

Among the three events of the eighteenth century and the continuing transformation of the *ulema* demands and of education, both the institution of Sunnî orthodoxy and the members of the corps of religious learning increasingly consolidated in the eighteenth century. *Ulema* families became better organized and

---

[6] William H. Sewell, Jr., *Logics of History: Social Theory and Social Transformation* (Chicago and London: University of Chicago Press, 2005), 100.

centralized at the very height of the religious hierarchy, as fathers increasingly transferred their positions to their sons, and sultans confirmed the special status of the *ulema* during this period. The *ulema* also participated actively in the opposition movements of 1703 and 1730; from their positions on both sides of the debate, they managed to gain prominence and assert the importance of their location in politics. If anything, the Kadızadeli episode had helped consolidate a more orthodox Sunnî reading. Now, in the eighteenth century, the conservative reading of religious texts was further consolidated by the increasing strength of Sunnî orthodoxy itself, reinforced by the politics of its constituents. Therein lies part of the continuity in the trajectory of the gradual reinforcement of a Muslim Sunnî identity in the empire.

The new politics of empire in the eighteenth century began at the center, in the imperial city of Istanbul, in the regional capital of Edirne, and in the Balkans, with troops moving to control the capital. Regardless of whether they entered politics with the belief that they could participate in state politics, the political actors of the eighteenth century created a space for the next generation. In the post-1808 era, the state had to confront political actors from the center and the periphery whose actions moved from the local to the national. The realm of politics widened with the rebellions in the Balkans and the demands for autonomy and national self-determination, beginning with the Serbs (1803 and 1805) and continuing with the Greeks (1812) and the Romanians (1821). Although some of the Balkan rebellions were the early precursors of the larger politics of separation from empire, many other provinces remained quiescent until much later.

Although they have not been compared previously, the rebellious interludes of the eighteenth-century Ottoman Empire have similarities to the revolutions of 1848 in Europe. The economic, political, and nationalist causes that led to the movements in France, Germany, Italy, and especially the Habsburg Empire have been accorded much weight in the political learning that occurred, despite the reestablishment of absolutism at the end. European sources describe 1848 as the beginning of nationalism, liberalism, and socialism. Beyond the ideologies that fueled the revolts, serious economic crises and the immediate misery of the people also triggered these movements. In the case of Europe, the ideas and the means of revolt spread across the continent, and regional variations in the involvement of different social groups was based more on the political exigencies and the particular power structures of the place. In the Ottoman Empire, the economic and political exigencies of continued warfare, increased taxation, and poverty reached the empire earlier, resulting in manifold rumblings of state–society readjustments. Set in a different imperial context, 1703 and 1730 were the 1848 of the Ottoman Empire.

A Short Historical Account of the Eighteenth Century

As an empire surrounded by at least three rival imperial political formations with their own varied capacities and objectives, the Ottoman Empire rarely saw periods of extended peace. At most, when possible, the Ottoman government tried to minimize warfare on multiple fronts. Warfare triggered many internal imperial developments, from the organization of society along military lines, to the growth and maturity of taxation systems, to politically costly internal transformations such as dissent and formal opposition to war and government. This was no different in the eighteenth century. In fact, many consequential wars framed the century, and in the narratives of historians, they plagued the empire, facilitating its downfall. Here, there is a clear causality established between warfare and decline. Let me follow this particular story line.

Although there had been a lull in warfare at the beginning of the century, wars had been relentless since the seventeenth century; they had fatigued the Ottoman system and depleted its treasury. They forced Ottoman state makers to consider new ways of enhancing their revenue, and in the eighteenth century, wars also brought Ottoman leaders to consider reform, at least of some military techniques. In the first half of the seventeenth century, Ottomans were seriously engaged in war against the Safavids, with campaigns in 1634 in Erivan and Tabriz and in Baghdad until the formulation of a peace treaty in 1638. Starting in the mid-seventeenth century, strong grand viziers such as Köprülü Mehmed or Fazıl Ahmed had been able to organize armies and fight wars on many fronts, maintaining naval warfare with Venice and fighting over rule in Transylvania with the Habsburgs. Fazıl Ahmed Pasha orchestrated the conquest of Crete from Venice in 1669. As the Ottomans expanded to the west of the Black Sea with the Polish wars from 1672 to 1677, they had demonstrated their continued military competence. War with Russia over the control of the Cossacks was hastily terminated when the new grand vizier Kara Mustafa turned his attention to Hungary and the Habsburgs, with a new attempt to conquer Vienna in 1683. Vienna remained Austrian, and the Ottomans were defeated by a concerted European effort mobilized against the Turks.

The adversaries of the empire had forced the Ottomans to spend decades fighting on many fronts at the same time. Ottoman armies confronted the Habsburgs in various regions, such as Bosnia and Serbia. They engaged Venice on three fronts in Albania, Dalmatia, and the Morea. They fought the Russians in the Crimea and in the principalities of Wallachia and Moldavia. Finally, they also fought the Poles. Ottoman populations suffered from such a widespread waging of war; they were drafted, taxed inordinate sums, encountered famine and food shortages, and finally fought the plague. From the loss of territory, especially in Hungary and Transylvania, they endured the influx of cavalry-men, *tımar* holders who had lost their domains. Furthermore, although the early sultans had to implement repopulation through forced migration, by the eighteenth century, authorities were trying diverse strategies to keep demobilized soldiers, peasants, and vagrant populations from overwhelming urban centers, especially Istanbul, a city that lived through at least sixty plague epidemics during this century.

The population felt the increasing tax burden in the transformation of traditional dues in kind to cash revenues, the restructuring of the tax burden, and the higher sums demanded. For example, after 1683, two taxes associated with war that had been collected in cash and in kind in alternating years were now demanded in cash every year from the rural population. In 1691, the government had insisted that the poll tax on Christians and Jews be collected from every taxable individual and not from communities as a whole. Both measures were taken to augment the flow of cash into the treasury, which spent almost two-thirds of its budget on the military.[7] The defeat at Vienna, the dislocation suffered by the Ottoman population, and the seeming neglectful attitude by Mehmed IV (1648–1687) to his peoples' suffering led a council of leaders of the state to depose the sultan.

The Habsburg offensive continued, and the Ottomans lost Belgrade (1688), Nis, Vidin, Skopje, and Prizren (1689). As was often true of this century, the tables turned quickly when the Habsburgs engaged in war with France, which provided the Ottomans with the opportunity to take back most of its lost territory. In 1697, however, the Ottomans lost yet another war against the Habsburgs, met their enemies at Karlowitz, and surrendered significant territory. Although recent research shows that had it not been for the diplomacy of the Ottoman officials, the empire might have lost more territory, the impact of Karlowitz was not pretty.[8] To the Habsburgs, the Ottomans gave part of Hungary and Transylvania, to Venice the Morea and Dalmatia, to Poland Podolya and the Southern Ukraine, and to Russia Azov and the lands north of the Dniester River. In 1700, the Turks formally signed the Treaty of Karlowitz, undoubtedly a blow to Ottoman foreign standing and international relations. Three years later, Mustafa II (1695–1703) was deposed, and his faithful but dishonest Şeyhülislâm, Feyzullah Efendi, was executed.

At first, wars against Russia were mildly successful; against the Venetians, from whom they took the Morea, Ottomans registered important successes. However, the treaty of Passarowitz (1718) reminded them of the strength of the Habsburgs who had won Serbian territory and more of Wallachia, only for it to be reclaimed by the Turks at the next round. After Passarowitz, a relatively peaceful period provided an opportunity for internal changes. An onerous tax that had been assessed only rarely – on the basis of urgent need called *imdadiye* – was collected yearly after 1718. The Grand Vizier Damad Ibrahim Pasha was instrumental in the consolidation of the Tulip Era, a time of relative peace, cross-cultural germination, leisure, and certainly much conspicuous consumption. However, the start of the wars with Iran in 1723 and the renewed threats from the eastern front in 1727 exacerbated already existing tensions, hurt the sultan and his grand vizier, and put a stop to their rule. The

[7] Suraiya Faroqhi, "Crisis and Change, 1590–1699," in *An Economic and Social History of the Ottoman Empire, 1300–1914*, ed. Halil İnalcık and Donald Quataert (Cambridge, UK: Cambridge University Press, 1994), 538–541.

[8] Rifa'at Abou-el-Haj, "The Formal Closure of the Ottoman Frontier in Europe: 1699–1703," *Journal of the American Oriental Society* 89:3 (1969): 467–475; "Ottoman Diplomacy at Karlowitz," *Journal of the American Oriental Society* 87:4 (1967): 498–512.

Patrona Halil rebellion of 1730 led to the abdication of Ahmed III (1703–1730) and the execution of Damad Ibrahim Pasha.

The new sultan, Mahmud I (1730–1754), was quickly thrown into renewed warfare with the Austrians, Russians, and Persians. The peace of Belgrade (1739) was quite favorable to the Ottomans, who gained territory and time, affording them a respite from war to rethink the traditional system of military training and warfare. Despite Mahmud's efforts, reactionary forces limited the extent of military reform, and redirected some of it into city administration and infrastructure. The empire paid dearly for the lack of serious military reform in the second half of the century, when three wars with Russia (1774, 1792, and 1812) contributed to the direct loss of territory and to the strengthening of the independence movements in the Balkans. The Treaty of Küçük Kaynarca in 1774 established Russia in the northern and eastern section of the Black Sea, and with the annexation of the Crimea in 1783, it consolidated its control of the Black Sea region. Russia could navigate in the Black Sea, cross the Straits, and gain access to the Aegean and the Mediterranean. It was also able to assert its right of protection over the Orthodox population of Istanbul, thereby inaugurating a process of internal manipulation and intimidation. The wars with Russia and Austria continued unabated. Unfortunately, it was during these wars (especially with Russia from 1787–1792) that Selim III (1789–1807) became the sultan and attempted the most courageous reforms, which catapulted him into the tragedy of 1808 when he lost his life, to be replaced by another reformer, Mahmud II (1808–1839).

Reports similar to the brief one presented previously on Ottoman fortunes in the seventeenth and eighteenth centuries were usually followed by extended discussions of the weakness of the state. New generations of sultans intoxicated by the pleasures of harem life impressed historians with their inability to make decisions while the nefarious influence of the sultanate of women – the wives and mothers who connived and intrigued to keep their sons and husbands in power – continued. Furthermore, in the provinces, taking advantage of this central weakness, newly emerging notables keen on gaining independent power and separating the empire into multiple regions rose to claim regional sovereignty. Accordingly, the demise at the top was proclaimed as the cause of the Ottoman malaise that started with military defeats and ended with internal revolts. In such an account, the role of the state is accorded exclusive importance, while social forces remain invisible until they explode into revolts. Although there is no doubt that war and state policies were critical in determining Ottoman fortunes, the focus on these macro-level occurrences – to the detriment of the intermediary layers of networks of actors who engaged in eventful politics to raise their opposition and demand better rule – has to be seriously questioned. It is in these intermediate political networks of opposition, organized and reorganized to address a variety of issues of public concern, that we detect the beginnings of renewed state–society relations, as well as adjustments by the state and other institutional agents.

State Power and Social Forces: Three Episodes of Learning the Politics of Opposition

We can start an alternative version of Ottoman eighteenth-century history with an entirely different set of dates, marking internal developments rather than major battles, victories, defeats, and peace treaties.[9] Such a history starts with 1703, the rebellion known as the Edirne Event, that led to the deposition of Sultan Mustafa II. It continues with the 1730 Patrona Halil revolt that shook Istanbul and ended in the removal of Sultan Ahmed III. Repercussions of this rebellion continued into the middle of the century. The history then follows the narrative to the rise of the dynasties of provincial notables in Rumelia and Anatolia, the most important of whom arrived in Istanbul to participate in central politics and, in 1808, to sign the famous deed of agreement, the Sened-i İttifak with Sultan Mahmud II.

The movement from 1703 to 1730 to 1808 tells the story of a substantial transformation in state–society relations that led to a more organized and asso-ciative social sphere. Not yet a part of burgeoning civil–society associations, the provincial notables who were part of this sphere were a motley group of social actors, state actors at first, but also increasingly members of different classes who rose up to challenge the state or some segment of it, replacing the leader-ship and slowly altering the nature of state–society relations in the empire. The social and political empowerment of these actors depended on their construc-tion of a more integrated and associative network society. In 1703, the empire encountered opponents who came together in various cross-class and intraelite horizontal alliances, composites that invoked many different interests; by 1808, social actors had perfected the skill of negotiating with the state as an interest group. They demonstrated the confidence that comes from acting as a coalition of strong actors. The result was not to dismantle the state; the coalition aimed rather to reform the state and impose the rule of new sultans and new officials who would reinstitute the older and romanticized political rule of the past. Especially in 1808, the notables who followed Bayraktar Ali Pasha claimed to have come from Rumeli and the Balkans to strengthen the center. As a result, 1808 became an important precursor to yet another reordering of state–society relations in the nineteenth century; it was not, as many historians have claimed, a symptom of state decentralization and weakness. However, the 1808 deed of agreement was also not a mini Magna Carta, as some scholars have claimed. It was not a break toward constitutional development. As we will see, it was a negotiated pact, although different from previous ones because negotiations were carried out between the Ottoman state and a coalition of organized and

---

[9] In this alternative history, I remain focused on the center, even though I am aware of and appreciate the breadth and depth of repercussions in the various provinces. Focusing on them here would draw attention away from the central stage of eventful politics oriented toward the state, where events as they unfolded increased the various groups' sense of empowerment. I focus on the provinces in Chapter 7.

associated actors, here the notables of Rumelia and Anatolia. The important imperial analogy – the hub-and-spoke network structure that had been dominant until then – demonstrated significant horizontal linkages, bringing regions and actors together.

Were these new political actors modern? If we define modernity in Weberian terms to mean the unraveling of the accepted order together with increased rationality, the modernity of these actors was questionable. The narrative of events highlights the slow questioning of the accepted Ottoman order and demonstrates that rebels reverted to traditional Ottoman understandings in each situation. However, if by modernity we mean the constitution of a political arena increasingly defined by a struggle over the definition of the political, eighteenth-century developments certainly qualify as such.[10] The movements of this century politicized the demands of the different groups of society, defining their interests while still seeking redress within their given system of justice. Traditional forms of legitimation were not abolished, yet a new sphere of the political, carved and shaped by networks of contention, initiated the process by which different social groups made alliances to bring about change in the politics of the empire. Although their tools of dissent were modern, their demands were not.

These events were not without historical precedent. Ottoman history contained important examples of uprisings against the state and the sultan, and both the deposition and assassination of sultans. The moment of imperial transformation occurred in 1622 when the Janissary and Sipahi armies dethroned Osman II, a young reformer sultan with ambitions to create alternative military organizations, and brutally slaughtered him. Although they seemed to have had some support from the *ulema*, their act of fitful revenge was more an internal patrimonial action than a state–society confrontation. Despite the fact that according to the Islamic legacy of the empire, as well as the understanding of justice that provided the rationale for unjust rulers to be removed, the vicious assassination of Osman II somewhat diminished the symbolic legitimacy attached to the person of the sultan, the head of the patrimonial household. This act initiated a path of opposition to the sultan and possible consequences of such opposition that had not occurred previously. After this particular event – at least until the end of the eighteenth century – seven out of fourteen sultans were deposed. Coup politics of this style became a viable alternative. What was different about this new century were the different coalitions and interclass and intergroup alliances that fueled the politics of opposition.

The Edirne Event: 1703

Contemporary histories of the 1703 rebellion argue that it stemmed primarily from discontent with the close association between Sultan Mustafa II (1664–1703) and his şeyhülislam, Feyzullah Efendi. They claim that Mustafa brought his childhood teacher and adviser to the palace, provided him not only with

[10] S. N. Eisenstadt, "Multiple Modernities," *Deadalus* 129 (Winter 2000): 6.

the highest rank in religious affairs, but also surrendered political affairs to him – for the first time in Ottoman history submitting the grand vizier to the power of the şeyhülislam.[11] Once installed in a position of privilege, Feyzullah exploited the tax farming advantages to increase his fortunes and to spread wealth and available positions to members of his family. Histories also focus on the relocation from Istanbul to Edirne where Mustafa and Feyzullah had settled, depriving the Istanbul populace of much of its economic activity and livelihood. Therefore, the initial urge to rebel can be attributed to a reaction to favoritism and corruption, and to poverty. Sources further claim a military element to this rebellion because it was the 600 armorers (*cebeci*) who started the rebellion by demanding that the central state pay their salaries before sending them to western Georgia. Yet, what was interesting about this rebellion was not so much the entirely predictable scenario of privilege and corruption, but the slow concatenation of networks of actors and groups that coalesced to oppose the sultan and his adviser. Also interesting is the manner in which the rebellion moved from one stage to the next, appealing to different constituencies, while also showing the value of wanting to act within the bounds of the law.

As Rifa'at Abou-el-Haj elegantly shows, this was a rebellion undertaken by a conglomerate of actors: networks of merchants and religious students, soldiers, and Janissaries provoked by the heads of pasha and vizier households.[12] The rebellion that started with the planting of the regimental banners at the traditional parade grounds in Istanbul was soon joined by the merchants, disgruntled *ulema* leaders, and finally by the Janissary army sent to confront the rebels, but who were unwilling to fight their fellow soldiers with whom they shared many grievances. The historical narratives agree on the participation of these military, religious, and mercantile elements that were brought together by the opportunistic moment started by the *cebecis*. Yet, they mostly fail to identify the leaders of the rebels. Abou-el-Haj argues that the leadership originated from among the clients of the strong vizier and pasha households (*kapı*) that had taken hold of the expanding polity of the empire.

The growth of households (*kapı*) in the late seventeenth century had transformed an increasingly differentiated and complex state structure by providing an alternative to the regular channels of palace and political appointments. Especially in Istanbul, Rumelia, and Anatolia, vizier and pasha households became strong patronage networks of men, members of an extended family, friends, and clients who were offered training and education for government positions in return for loyalty and service. Members of the households could

---

[11] Silahdar Mehmet Ağa, *Nusretname*, transl. İsmet Parmaksızoğlu, 2 vols. (Istanbul: Milli Eğitim Yayınları, 1962–1969); Rifa'at Abou-el-Haj, "The Narcissism of Mustafa II," *Studia Islamica* 40 (1974): 115–131.

[12] Rifa'at Ali Abou-el-Haj, *The 1703 Rebellion and the Structure of Ottoman Politics* (Istanbul: Nederlands Historisch-Archaeologisch Instituut, 1984). This is by far the best analysis of the events of 1703. Most of my summary of the events of 1703 relies on this text.

become part of a pasha's retinue for war or follow him in the palace administration. The pasha households in effect reproduced the model of the household
of the sultan, where the most effective and developed patronage system was
prevalent.[13]

The households represented an alternative form of organization, especially
useful for high-ranking elites. As Carter Findley rightly points out, the household must have developed early on from a need for protection. That is, state
officials who wielded power but who were at the same time dependent on the
whims of sultans built up a household of clients and protégés who could provide them with protection and information. Also, the household was a subtle
adaptation to the transformation of the regular sources of state personnel, especially the end of the *devshirme* system of recruitment. With fewer *devshirme*
soldiers, household soldiers became a valuable commodity close to the palace.
Households where young men were trained and then placed in positions of
employment became feeders into the Ottoman administrative and military hierarchies. The religious establishment, the *ilmiyye*, which produced many more
graduates than there were available positions in the empire, also naturally
found a place in strong *ulema* patronage households.[14] In a different manner,
but with similar consequences, the Ottoman bureaucracy evolved a family-
and patronage-dominated career structure as well.[15] High-level administrative
and military elites, as well as high-ranking *ulema*, therefore developed large
networks of patronage, with the sultan having his own very large household
comprised of all officials of the Ottoman administration. These households,
which originated with a series of strong grand viziers – all initially members of
the same Köprülü family – provided an alternative route of recruitment into
politics, different from the palace and the military that had been until then
controlled solely by the sultan's household. During the reign of the Köprülü
dynasty, multiple households developed, which made for much competition
among factions within the state, forcing the sultan to moderate between factions and tamper with his absolute authority.[16] For example, between 1683

---

[13] Carter V. Findley, "Patrimonial Household Organization and Factional Activity in the Ottoman
Ruling Class," in *Turkiye'nin Sosyal ve Ekonomik Tarihi (1071–1920)*, ed. Halil İnalcık, Osman
Okyar, and Ünal Nalbantoğlu (Ankara: Meteksan, 1980), 227–235; Suraiya Faroqhi, "Civil-
ian Society and Political Power in the Ottoman Empire: A Report on Research in Collective
Biography (1480–1830)," *International Journal of Middle Eastern Studies* 17 (1985): 109–117;
Michael Meeker, *A Nation of Empire: The Ottoman Legacy of Turkish Modernity* (Berkeley:
University of California Press, 2002).

[14] Faroqhi, "Civilian Society and Power," 112.

[15] Joel Shinder, "Career Line Formation in the Ottoman Bureaucracy, 1648–1750: A New Perspective," *Journal of the Economic and Social History of the Orient* 16:2–3 (1973): 217–237.
See also Madeline Zilfi, *The Politics of Piety: The Ottoman Ulema in the Postclassical Age
(1600–1800)* (Minneapolis: Bibliotheca Islamica, 1988). While Shinder concentrates more on
the chancery, Zilfi makes a similar argument for the *ilmiyye*, the religious establishment.

[16] Rifaat Ali Abou-El-Haj, "The Ottoman Vezir and Pasa Households 1683–1703: A Preliminary
Report," *Journal of the American Oriental Society* 94:4 (1972), 438–447.

and 1703, *kapı* appointments to high positions were as high as 40%, with 26.3% appointed to the palace and 21.3% to the military.[17]

Two conclusions are to be drawn from this process of the reproduction of power within the state. First, in what Salzmann calls "corporate patrimonialism,"[18] these *kapı* households and *ulema* aristocracies expanded into quasi-permanent aristocracies (especially among the *ulema*) and households, becoming engaged in the concentration and reproduction of their power through privilege and patronage. In this sense, the state structure had already been altered with a different concentration of power at the top, not based solely on a few of the sultan's slaves who were raised, educated, and formed at the center of the palace, but on a much larger patronage structure that inflated the ranks of the state. Second, these political networks at the core of the state disrupted the fundamental vertical integration of state officials into the ruling apparatus. These patronage networks combined both horizontal and vertical ties of association, where loyalty to the patron became as important as to the members of the household, a basis for association and cooperation later in politics, as is demonstrated in the 1703 rebellion. For example, when a servant (*kul*) of the sultan died, the members of this servant's household could petition to be transferred into the sultan's household and become vertically integrated into higher-level positions. However, at the same time, the members of the same household were often attached to one another by kin, friendship, and ties of support and therefore also acted on the basis of on such notions. The transformation that resulted from this particular evolution of households in the Ottoman polity created tensions between supporters and detractors of each interest group. Households were evolving, competing and attracting adherents; yet, they were also still contested, and sultans themselves were not always in support of the corporatization of power.

One such contest between households and their detractors led to the crisis of 1703. When Mustafa II had ascended to the throne, he declared his intention to be a strong activist sultan, making decisions on his own, and later with the help of Feyzullah Efendi, his chosen associate and religious leader. He intended to keep members of the households away from central positions, even though they had successfully run the state since the mid-1650s. This resulted in the dismissal and execution of incumbent grand vizier Sürmeli Ali Pasha, member of a *kapı* household, and the reversal of a household-based pattern of appointments. Nevertheless, after the military defeat at Zenta in 1697, Mustafa had to rely on the household; he appointed a Köprülü man[19] to the grand vizierate. Amcazade Hüseyin maintained peace and order, brought about

---

[17] Abou-el-Haj, *The 1703 Rebellion*, 49.

[18] Salzmann, *Tocqueville in the Ottoman Empire*, 102.

[19] The Köprülü dynasty was an important family of powerful grand viziers and viziers who ruled the empire from the mid-seventeenth to the mid-eighteenth century. There were six Köprülü grand viziers in this period.

important fiscal reforms, and tightened the military organization by lowering the numbers of paid Janissaries, although in the long run he was prevented from making a lasting impact: when he retired, Feyzullah nullified his reforms. The rebellion of 1703 coalesced at a moment when such tensions between a simple patrimonial model (preferred by Mustafa II and his şeyhülislam Feyzullah) and a more corporate one (favored by the members of *kapı* households) were becoming more evident.

On the morning of 17 July 1703, 600 Istanbul-based armorers (*cebecis*) defied orders to march toward western Georgia, but instead headed toward the central military parade grounds, where they planted their regimental banners on the ground, enacting a ritualized action in an open sign of revolt. Within the next 3 days, they gathered around them members of the *ulema*, the military, and the merchant classes of Istanbul.[20] To rally the *ulema* and the Janissaries around this rebellion, undoubtedly would have conferred legitimacy on the rebels, so they promptly sent a mission to convince the *kadı* of Istanbul to come and join them. Two days later, the Janissaries who had been assembled to suppress the armorers joined them in a show of support, preferring to ally with rather than fight their fellow soldiers.

By 20 July, the four elements of the rebellion coalesced as the *ulema*, and other religious figures such as şeyhs joined the armed rebel forces. Some *ulema* were invited to join and others came of their own will. *Ulema* in the eighteenth century were gaining power, consolidating their social and religious bases, and reinforcing their own corporate-institutional structure. Yet, as an elite, they had also been unhappy with the policies and the corruption of the şeyhülislam.[21] Accounts of the early days demonstrate the degree to which this rebellion was initiated and pursued carefully as the rebels struggled to maintain their cause, but also to tread a fine line between opposition to the sultan and the state. The *ulema* declared the Friday prayers to be inappropriate because the rebels had revolted against the sultan, and therefore should not offer him their loyalty at the prayers.[22] However, the rebels were not immediately ready to withdraw their allegiance to the sultan and debated whether they should do so.[23] At this particular juncture, by following the letter of the law, the rebels sealed their alliance with the *ulema*, gaining further legitimacy for their actions.

Once an initial coalition was assembled, rebel leaders asked that members of the sultan's entourage be replaced with new men. The rebels' prospective appointees turned out to be mostly members of the Köprülü households, men effectively related to the extended family of the Köprülüs as well as clients of the family. According to Abou-el-Haj, this marked the official entry of the

---

[20] Abou-el-Haj, *The 1703 Rebellion*. The events of the rebellion are described in this book in a detailed fashion. I highlight the relevant moments of key transformation.

[21] See Silahdar Ağa, *Nusretname*.

[22] Friday prayers were the weekly moment of public prayer, and they were given in the name of the sultan to affirm his position as sovereign and leader of the Islamic community.

[23] Abou-el-Haj, *The 1703 Rebellion*, 24.

household faction into the rebel movement: "the rebellion itself was occasioned by the failure to peacefully resolve the conflict over the question of membership in the government."[24] Therefore, it was not purely a movement against the state; it was also an intrastate struggle for governance. Rather, this was a moment of alliance among various networks of corporate interests in the empire, with one segment of the state. Disgruntled members of the extended polity were actually reaching out to the local social actors and using their grievances to reorganize the internal authority structure of the state. As the state apparatus itself had become more differentiated and organized along separate and competing network factions, the possibility for struggles to spill out and exploit responsive social forces had become greater.

In the next few days, the rebels proceeded to prepare a document of their demands. The petition that ensued had two conditions: that the Şeyhülislam Feyzullah Efendi and his entourage be dismissed, and that the sultan and the Ottoman court return to Istanbul. Not only were the demands and the rebellious actions of the opposition striking in their moderation, but also the deliberative process described by contemporaries attests to the care that they took to remain within the bounds of the law. Even when the more extreme elements took over and imposed their will, the result was mild; the most aggressive lines in the document were "Let the padishah know that upon the receipt of our letter, Feyzullah Efendi should be taken and dispatched in chains to Istanbul."[25] Again, that the final draft was read to the representatives of all the rebel groups, signed, and sealed before it was sent on to Edirne by trustworthy men indicates the degree to which the process was cautious and guarded, with the various factions trying to maintain a precarious balance between unbridled contention and a semblance of law and order. This was further signaled by the precautions that the rebels took to minimize violence and to avoid harming the residents of the city in a bloody confrontation. The movement unfolded into a series of negotiations between Edirne and Istanbul, respectively the seat of power and that of rebellion.

Confronted with the corruption of his closest associate, the man who happened to be the representative of the Muslim community, Feyzullah Efendi, the sultan dismissed him. Thus, it looked like Mustafa II was responding to the crisis, though in reality the tensions between Edirne and Istanbul were continuing and the sultan was preparing for action. In Istanbul, a vigorous rebel coalition remained within the bounds of legitimacy, but set out to prepare a second set of *fetvâs* issued by the *ulema* to justify the removal of the sultan from office. What had become the next logical step of a rebellion against the sultan coincided with official religious justification, giving the rebellion a sense of moderation and legality. In a series of *fetvâs*, the causes for the removal of the sultan were carefully spelled out. These *fetvâs* challenged the rule of the sultan, providing sufficient cause for his removal. The last *fetvâ* is especially

---

[24] Ibid., 88.
[25] Ibid., 33.

interesting because it points to a significant turning point in a larger under-standing of empire, especially its territoriality. The rebels blamed the sultan for negotiating with the enemies in the West and by accepting their terms, closing the frontiers that were imperative to the self-definition of the Ottoman imperial ideology. When frontiers solidified into borders, the natural zeal for expansion through raids had to be stopped. The rebels saw this constraint as treason to the Ottoman *raison d'être*.[26] The defeat at the hands of the enemy and the deep humiliation of the Treaty of Karlowitz (1699) were compounded by the dashing of hopes for the resumption of raiding activities. Rebels thus gave voice to a larger popular view that Karlowitz was a loss, not a relative success.

The crisis of 1703 was resolved in a final dramatic confrontation. Although Mustafa violated many of the principles of Ottoman state–society relations in gathering as large an army as possible around himself, handing out benefices for life, and promising income and heritability to those who did not deserve it, he nevertheless did not manage to amass a large army. Moreover, even before his men confronted the rebels at Hafsa, the two sides had contacted each other and had made a deal. At the prearranged hour, after a loud explosion, both sides joined hands![27] The niceties ended there as vandalism and unlawful behavior gained acceptance. Yet, when the rebels got ready to execute Feyzullah Efendi, the dismissed şeyhülislam, they went through an implicit subterfuge to change his *ulema* status, turning him into a simple military man in order to take his life. Clearly, they were still in search of validity and legitimacy and were concerned that neither the members of the polity nor the populace lose sight of the limits of behavior that were within the bounds of the law of the realm. If rebels could so easily execute grand *müftis*, what was left that was sacred in the Ottoman Empire for successors to claim?

The impeccable analysis offered by Abou-el-Haj demonstrates that despite their serious intent and their final success at replacing the sultan, the rebels remained loyal to the ideals of the Ottoman state, the rule of law, and the power of the *Sharia*. They wanted a change in the seat of government, but at no time did they argue for regime change or the abolition of the sultanate. Their actions demonstrated that they were content to work within the old regime framework, but with some changes. First, in the attempt to negotiate with both state members and social groups we find that they extended the bounds of negotiation. Mustafa II conceded advantages and forms of dispen-sation to landholders and military groups that the state had never provided previously; "in his final bid to keep the throne this ruler was willing to barter his constitutional and executive prerogatives."[28] Furthermore, a few months

---

[26] Again, Abou-el-Haj has made the most interesting contribution in a series of articles and in *The 1703 Rebellion,* in particular. See Abou-el-Haj, *The 1703 Rebellion,* 70–72; see also idem, "The Formal Closure of the Ottoman Frontier in Europe: 1699–1703," *Journal of the American Oriental Society* 89:3 (1969): 467–475; and idem, "Ottoman Diplomacy at Karlowitz," *Journal of the American Oriental Society,* 87:4 (1967): 498–512.

[27] Abou-el-Haj, *The 1703 Rebellion,* 78.

[28] Ibid., 91.

down the line, his successor Ahmed III would do the same, finding that consolidation and centralization could not be carried out in the same manner. Thus, to secure the loyalty of the various military groups, he compensated them generously and gave up Edirne as an alternate seat of government. The actions of these two sultans led toward a clear-cut deterioration in their powers and ability to negotiate.

Another result was an interesting amalgam of forces different from the traditional alliances. An alliance between conservative *ulema* and disobedient and reactionary Janissaries as champions of the old order had already started to emerge in the late seventeenth century, and was to become the main aggravation of reformist leaders in the next two centuries. Yet, in this case, the *ulema* and the Janissaries were willing to work for the cause of a more progressive outcome. So, although ostensibly the revolt was about soldiers' pay, it developed into an interesting struggle against the more conservative elements that had captured the state. Numerous times in Ottoman history, soldiers had risen up to force the sultans to remunerate them. More distinctive was this slow-but-sure association among otherwise separated groups in society who were able to bring their opposition together, form alliances, and think about one another's demands and capabilities because they all shared basic grievances against the state. In these alliances, both vertical patron–client relations and horizontal ties of loyalty and involvement worked to provide support for the rebels. This was really the first serious episode of opposition in which multiple networks of groups coalesced and carried out unremitting contention. The last time a sultan had been deposed – Mehmed IV in 1687 – it was entirely at the hands of a palace coup led by the Köprülü faction. No other groups had been involved.

The Patrona Halil Revolt: 1730

In 1703, the masses had not yet been involved in the struggle. On the contrary, the crowds were scared away by the boisterous *cebecis* and the defiant and refractory Janissary element, while disgruntled merchants who had joined in and approved were also cautious. By the time the revolt of Patrona Halil occurred in 1730, however, there was no hesitation among the crowds, artisans, petty bourgeoisie, small-scale merchants allied with religious students, *ulema* leaders, and Janissary men to stop the regime that robbed them of their daily living.

Ahmed III was put on the throne after 1703, and soon after he appointed Nevşehirli Damad Ibrahim Pasha to the grand vizierate, a man known for his peaceful and reforming tendencies. When they could, between wars and raising taxes, Ottoman leaders of this period engaged in a small-scale cultural revolution that encouraged the Istanbul elite to engage in a lifestyle that promoted the beauty and pleasures of life and nature, consumption of foreign goods, and acquisition of material possessions. Labeled the Tulip Period for its impassioned devotion to tulip gardens and the fierce competition among grandees for the most magnificent tulips, this era caught men of the state neglecting state affairs to indulge in the pleasures of tending their gardens or relaxing on the waterways and in the gardens of the Golden Horn and the new Palace, the Sadabad (the abode of happiness). The Tulip Era inaugurated the first significant opening to the West, a process by which the flow of goods, people, and dialogue brought Ottomans to rethink their traditional attitude of exalted superiority and to begin to appreciate some of the developments in Western lands. The Ottoman ambassadors and observers of the West had brought back with them a flavor of Occidental living. Its appeal was not lost on men like Sultan Ahmed III and his grand vizier, refined and educated people who appreciated this cultural and technological intervention and intended to develop it fully.[29] Yet, the more visible outcome of this short-lived Western fugue was elite luxury and extravagance. The Ottoman elite in the main cities built gardens and small palaces (*konak*), and invested time and money in lavish festivities and displays of power and wealth, perhaps compensating for a comparative international decline in their power and prestige.

Ariel Salzmann elegantly describes how this consumer culture managed to envelop the elite of the empire, men and women who separately delighted in their freedom of movement, their leisure, and their expensive habits, in close proximity to the urban populace packed into the shadows of filthy, narrow streets. The more the elite engaged in festivities, festivals, and processions, making space by taking it from the poor, the more charged the atmosphere of the city became.[30] It was not new that the elite engaged in merrymaking and pleasure seeking; it was that they did so increasingly in public view.[31] The crowds of Istanbul watched the cavalcades, carnivals, picnics, and frolicking, all deemed to be too ostentatious for the poor and too amoral for the religious. The Sadabad was the Versailles of Istanbul.

Ottoman society was not a strongly demarcated class society. Groups associated around their neighborhoods, their religion and ethnicity, and their occupations, with criss-crossing ties that produced alternative foci of relations and allegiance. The depiction of contemporary observers presents Istanbul in the late 1720s as a city of contrasts and stark inequalities, where vagrancy and poverty were rampant and disparities in fortune were flagrant. Leisure activities and associated construction projects provided jobs for the poor and the artisans, but not nearly enough employment, especially because migration into the city was soaring. Wars and dislocation had brought large numbers of Anatolian peasants, Balkan vagrants, Albanian militia, and many artisans from smaller

---

[29] There are contradictory reports on both the openness to the West and the conditions in the Ottoman capital at the time. See, for example, Lavender Cassels, *The Struggle for the Ottoman Empire 1717–1740* (London: John Murray, 1966).

[30] Ariel Salzmann, "The Age of Tulips: Confluence and Conflict in Early Modern Consumer Culture (1550–1730)," in *Consumption Studies and the History of the Ottoman Empire 1550–1922*, ed. Donald Quataert (Albany: State University of New York Press, 2000), 95–96.

[31] Madeline C. Zilfi, "Women and Society in the Tulip Era, 1718–1730," in *Women, the Family and Divorce Laws in Islamic History*, ed. Amira el Azhary Sonbol (Syracuse, NY: Syracuse University Press, 1996), 290–303.

towns, overwhelming the city and swelling the ranks of the unemployed; these migrants forced themselves on the guilds, or worse yet, managed to compete with the guilds outside their formal structure. It is said that there were around 12,000 Albanian immigrants in Istanbul during the 1730s.[32] Immigrants overwhelmed city resources and welfare services, spreading into different neighborhoods and bringing people into a larger web of discontent. After the rebellion of 1730, there would be a concerted effort to chase them away from Istanbul.[33]

The war brought burdens other than restless and jobless immigrants into the city, especially as the artisans and shopkeepers were already reeling under the pressures of war taxation. With the opening of the war front with Iran, extraordinary campaign taxes were reimposed, and a large share of the burden fell on the peasants and the artisan population, the latter also having to pay the special tax (*ordu akçesi*) during mobilization for war. Much of this happened as the continued devaluation of the currency shook the local economy, providing little maneuvering room for these impoverished groups. Artisans in the cities experienced significant declines in their production since the Ottoman state officials were unable to supply the raw materials necessary for manufacture. Moreover, the increasing integration of the empire into the world economy and the importance of Europeans in the trading activities with the West had thrown the traditional guild structure into disarray. As Engin Akarlı has shown, the artisans of the empire had never before worked for larger international markets; they had produced for the state with a provisioning mentality and were therefore not quick to adapt to the transformation brought on by this new commercialism.[34] The foreign agents operating in the main cities also favored the Christian and Jewish artisans and masters because many could speak at least one European language. As a result, Muslim and non-Muslim artisans who had shared the same space and administrative structure of the guild for many centuries started to experience tension, especially as the Muslim artisans believed that their non-Muslim counterparts were enjoying better opportunities.[35] Consequently, the tensions in the bazaar were rising. By August 1726, signs of these tensions were already apparent when crowds rallied together and assaulted the imperial palace in the Beşiktaş district of Istanbul.[36]

Patrona Halil – a soldier of Albanian origin turned petty trader/artisan – and many of his friends were part of the disgruntled crowd who periodically came

---

[32] Münir Aktepe, *Patrona İsyanı (1730)* (Istanbul: Istanbul Üniversitesi Edebiyat Fakültesi Yayınları, 1958), 70, 170.

[33] Ahmet Refik, *Onikinci Asr-ı Hicri'de Istanbul Hayatı (1689–1785)* (Istanbul: Enderun Kitabevi, 1988).

[34] Engin Akarlı, "Gedik: Implements, Masterships, Shop Usufruct and Monopoly among Istanbul Artisans, 1750–1850," *Wissenschaftskolleg Jahrbuch* (1985–1986): 223–232.

[35] Onur Yıldırım, "Ottoman Guilds as a Setting for Ethno-Religious Conflict: The Case of the Silk-Thread Spinners' Guild in Istanbul," *IRSH* 47 (2002): 407–419. See also *Crafts and Craftsmen of the Middle East: Fashioning the Individual in the Muslim Mediterranean*, ed. Suraiya Faroqhi and Randi Deguilhem (London and New York: I. B. Tauris, 2005).

[36] Aktepe, *Patrona Isyanı*, 68.

together in the streets of the bazaar inciting brawls and making boisterous demands on the state. On 28 September 1730, about twenty-five of Patrona Halil's friends entered the bazaar and started marching, crowds following them as they rallied their comrades and stormed the city streets, burning their way through the abodes of pleasure. Whereas they started with disgruntled and demobilized soldiers, artisans, and shopkeepers of various religious persuasions, they were soon able to gather the support of higher elite society, especially some members of the *ulema* who were more than happy to endorse the rebellion and legitimize the movement by proclaiming the appropriate *fetvâs*. Acting swiftly, and still somewhat according to the collective understandings of the times, Patrona and his associates nominated a new *kadı* for Istanbul on the second day of the rebellion, and by the third day, they had moved on to the Janissary corps, choosing a new leader. The reports of the early days indicate that the size of the rebellious crowds quickly soared, taking the Istanbul merrymakers by surprise.[37]

The rebels demanded the execution of the grand vizier, their immediate target and the agent of their misery. They did not, however, ask for the sultan to be dethroned or killed, again demonstrating some constraint. Rebels also obtained the support of the *ulema*, who joined them because they opposed the new ways of the court, the Western outlook of the secular leadership, and the moral depravity of Sadabad luxury. Once again, the coalition against the state brought together not altogether strange bedfellows: the Janissaries and the *ulema* were becoming used to allying against the leaders of the state, while the Janissaries and artisans had become enmeshed as the Janissaries increasingly joined the ranks of artisans. The rebellion did not last long; Damad Ibrahim Pasha was quickly executed, and by the beginning of October, Ahmed III was deposed and replaced by Mahmud I (1730–1754).

Mahmud 's accession was conditioned on multiple political moves, such as repealing most of the onerous taxes from which people suffered, paying the Janissaries a hefty coronation award, appointing new members to the government, and giving the order to tear down the palace his predecessor had so lovingly constructed.[38] In the intermediate moment between deposition and consolidation of the new regime, the rebels were able to make many demands and place thousands of demobilized vagrants and immigrants into military positions, drawing salaries.[39] The government did strike back, however, in turn eliminating Patrona Halil and his comrades, restoring order to the city, and reestablishing the authority of the state. Istanbul remained insecure despite

---

[37] Most of this information comes from Abdi, *Abdi Tarihi: 1730 Patrona İhtilâli Hakkında bir Eser*, ed. Faik Reşit Unat (Ankara: Türk Tarih Kurumu, 1943); and Aktepe, *Patrona İsyanı*.

[38] Robert W. Olson, "The Esnaf and the Patrona Halil Rebellion of 1730: A Realignment in Ottoman Politics?" *Journal of the Economic and Social History of the Orient* 17:3 (1974): 329–344; Salzmann, "The Age of Tulips," 96–97.

[39] Abdi says that tens of thousands entered the Janissary corps, although others believe that this is exaggerated. See Aktepe, *Patrona İsyanı*, 159.

the defeat of the rebels and the support of the artisans and shopkeepers for the new government. The crowded bazaars were prone to brawls; each quarrel had the potential to quickly transform into a revolt of the populace. In fact, the 10 years following 1730 recorded many such events, where different articulations of alliances and powerful actors challenged the policies of the state.

Regardless of the similar outcomes – the dethronement of a sultan and the execution of a close advisor (a şeyhülislam and a grand vizier) – 1703 and 1730 were quite different from each other. The Patrona Halil rebellion coalesced into an important class movement, the revolt of the masses against a spendthrift state, far too many war taxes, and economic dislocation. The rebels tried to reconstitute the "moral economy" of Istanbul,[40] and in the process they aspired to a better administration, to a state that cared about the people rather than the enjoyment of endless varieties of tulips. Significant elite input into this movement came from the *ulema*, who associated with the rebels not for economic reasons, but for their own political and religious motives, swaying the Muslim masses against a Westernizing state. They preached in the mosques the evils of Western ways, deploring the alliances between the West and the Sultan, and also increasingly condemning the non-Muslim population of the city. Their sermons, their perceived fear of Western ways, and the discourse they espoused certainly helped put fear into the heads of good Muslims and eroded relations between the Muslim and non-Muslim elements in the city, bringing in ethnic frictions, especially as competitive tensions already existed within the guilds and trades. The events of 1730 brought about a series of cascading events with their own moments of rupture.

By the summer of 1740, another movement began to gather steam against Sultan Mahmud I, who had replaced Ahmed III. This time, the movement of revolt was initiated in the *sipahi* bazaar, where the immigrant Albanians pillaged, burned, and forced shopkeepers to close their shops. Reports by the British ambassador to the empire, Everard Fawkener, indicate that the cleavage between Muslim and non-Muslims in the bazaar was gaining ground. While the rebels ransacked and called Muslims to rebel, Janissary forces were called in to suppress the movement. It was after this episode that the government fully realized the degree to which the increased number of vagrants, jobless immigrants, and discontented elements among the masses had become dangerous. Thus, a concerted movement to rid the city of such elements began. State response ranged from killing thousands and dumping them into the Black Sea to forced exile to the plains of Anatolia, trips that all started on boats taking men far away from the threatened city.[41] After social control was reestablished, Istanbul remained peaceful for a while.

---

[40] The term "moral economy" is well known, but in this context Salzmann uses it first. See "The Age of Tulips," 96.

[41] Robert Olson, "Jews, Janissaries, Esnaf and the Revolt of 1740 in Istanbul: Social Upheaval and Political Realignment in the Ottoman Empire," *Journal of the Economic and Social History of the Orient* 20:2 (1977): 185–207.

The Sened-i İttifak: 1808

More than half a century passed between the revolts of the 1730s and 1740s to the coup d'état of 1807–1808 against Selim III – a reformist sultan – which was the third event that shook the relative calm of Istanbul. The coup against the sultan brought the best men of the provinces to the imperial center, the first such case of direct intervention from the provinces. The renowned notable Alemdar (or Bayraktar) Mustafa Pasha arrived in Istanbul with his provincial army to restore Selim III to his throne, and became instrumental instead in the establishment of Mahmud II. I return to these tumultuous events in the capital after briefly reviewing the antecedents that brought the periphery to the center.

In the post-Tulip period, two crucial developments came to maturation. First, the fiscal system of the late seventeenth century – initiated to collect money for the treasury – altered traditional sources of income into life-term tax farming, opening the way for the purchase of numerous sources of revenue by private individuals alone or in association with others. Life-term tax farming empowered a wealthy set of Istanbul elites and bureaucrats who bought these tax farms in the provinces, but farmed them out to provincial notables (*ayan*), who became their astute local entrepreneurs. Locally, these notables managed to take over both the lands and the administrative functions of the traditional elite, also currying favor with the state to assume important revenue-collecting positions. From the modest local notables who acquired positions and served the state loyally to the wealthy and powerful notables who threatened the local rule of the state, the provinces were strewn with these new landholders and tax collectors.[42] They developed their own households, patronage systems, local political culture, and local armies, which they headed to help the sultan at war when they felt so inclined.

Second, with the impact of a new world of trade engaging especially the western shores of the empire, these local notables and administrators became emboldened turning their tax farming into commercial enterprises, poised to profit. Internal fiscal reform and external commercial opportunities altered the social and administrative landscape of the provinces. The traditional forces of administration and taxation, the provincial landholding system and its managers, and the *tımar* holders were disappearing. The traditional functions of the state in the provinces were now taken over by these increasingly powerful local notables, who were organized as extended regional networks of family, kinship, and patronage ties, ensconced in the changing structure of land tenure and commercial expansion. The 1808 Agreement (Sened-i İttifak) was the fin-de-siècle episode of the most powerful among these men arriving in Istanbul to sign a political document of state–notable truce and cooperation, following their comrade from Rumelia, Bayraktar Mustafa Pasha.

At the center, Selim III (1789–1807) had come to power at a moment when the peripheries of the empire, both the near periphery of the Balkans and the

---

[42] Chapter 7 is devoted to an analysis of these state–society processes.

farther Arab provinces, were feeling the tension between the administration of the state and that of the local notables. Rumblings of regional rebellions for autonomy emerged. In the Balkans, the notables were competing for territory and influence, often bringing the state into their local struggles. Local rule by the agents of the center was increasingly varied: weakening in certain areas while steady and strong in others. For example, in the Serbian provinces, the Janissaries ran amok, but in the Bosnian provinces, law and order prevailed due to good central–local administration.[43] Yet, within this widespread variation of rule, movements for autonomy such as that of the Serbs and the Greeks emerged. In other regions, the near separation of Egypt, Syria, and Iraq became of vital importance. It is in this atmosphere that Selim III commenced a series of reforms, the most important of which was organized around the military. Selim III worked on the reorganization of a new military in comparative secrecy with the knowledge of a few reformer administrators; this indicated that they were worried about the potential reaction of the conservative Janissary forces and the *ulema*. For both groups, such reforms represented threats to the traditional order. Furthermore, that Selim was able to replenish his new army with soldiers and resources from among the provincial armies also demonstrates that there were among the powerful notables those who supported the new young sultan in his endeavor to reform the more traditional and reactionary forces at the center.[44]

A delicate and precarious balance between opponents and supporters of Selim's regime ensued as enemies of reform multiplied in the provinces and in Istanbul. The Ottomans had forever promoted power struggles on the periphery under the belief that local and regional struggles for control between different powerful notables was healthy and would deflect opposition to the state. At the same time, they also used armies of notables for the protection of the provinces and as another reserve of military recruits during war. The unintended consequence of such policies was that when a notable accumulated local power and military might and decided to turn against the state, he could cause significant damage to the empire. Complicating Selim's reform initiatives further was the Russian movement into the Danubian principalities in 1806, the culmination of Russian interference in the affairs of the Christian population of the Balkans, where they fomented discontent and also created alliances with the Muslim magnates of the periphery, especially in Egypt and northern Anatolia.

In the capital, the supporters and the enemies of reform battled among themselves until a coup led by the Janissaries supported by the *ulema* gave the upper hand to the enemies of reform. The coup was achieved on 25 May

---

[43] See Hickok, *Ottoman Military Administration in Eighteenth-Century Bosnia.*
[44] Ismail Hakkı Uzunçarşılı, *Meşhur Rumeli Ayanlarından Tirsinikli Ismail, Yılık Oğlu Süleyman Ağalar ve Alemdar Mustafa Paşa* (Istanbul: Maarif Matbaası, 1942); Stanford J. Shaw, *Between Old and New: The Ottoman Empire under Sultan Selim III, 1789–1807* (Cambridge, MA: Harvard University Press, 1971); idem, *Mustapha Pacha Bairaktar* (Bucharest: Association Internationale d'Études du Sud-Est Européen, 1975).

1807, when the reformer Raif Mahmud Pasha went to the headquarters of the old *yamak* troops to pay their salaries and to urge them to join the new army created by Selim III and his men. Instead, the soldiers savagely killed the pasha. The conservative forces fighting against change were at the forefront of the coup; the Janissaries were afraid that the new army, the Nizam-ı Cedid, was going to put them out of business; the *ulema*, meanwhile, steadfastly believed in the evils of European influence in reform. By 28 May, various contingents of the Istanbul military forces were having "a spirited debate over the legality of their actions," before all agreeing to join the rebellion at the Janissary barracks.[45] Many reformers were executed, the reforms abolished, and, finally, only after the tensions and the hazards of keeping Selim III as sultan mounted, he was dethroned to make way for Mustafa IV on 29 May 1807.

This rebellion and treachery of the Janissaries launched a coordinated response from the provinces, an alliance of the *ayan* of Rumelia and Anatolia marching in unison under the leadership of Bayraktar Mustafa Pasha, the most powerful notable of Ottoman Europe. The political divisions in Istanbul, the coup against Selim III, the ruin in the Balkans, and the increasing threat of the Russians came together to propel responsible notables into action. In the chaos of the palace and the confrontation between the new sultan and the leader of the provinces, Selim III was assassinated, thus depriving the counter-coup forces of their most important asset. The provincial leaders reacted quickly to install instead Mahmud II (1808–1839) to the throne, removing Mustafa for his younger cousin. Bayraktar Mustafa Pasha became the grand vizier of the new sultan and proceeded once again to gather reformers around him. From July to November 1808, Bayraktar remained the dominant force in the empire. Soon after becoming grand vizier, he appealed to his provincial comrades to come to the capital for a special session (*meşveret-i amme*) to discuss the affairs of the state. That he invited his former colleagues to this assembly is interesting in itself because it demonstrates the realization by a man of the provinces of the need to coopt the provinces into a project of the center. From this extraordinary meeting emerged the document entitled "Sened-i İttifak," a political agreement between state and provincial magnates.

The Sened-i İttifak (literally, a deed of alliance or a concord) was the first of its kind in political deal making in the Ottoman Empire. The Sened was the political culmination of the provincial march on Istanbul, *yet was negotiated within the context of strong state and societal actors*. Those historians who have emphasized the power of the *ayan* to the detriment of the state have a tendency to see the end point of this century – the takeover by Bayraktar Mustafa Pasha and the 1808 Sened-i İttifak – as catastrophic for state affairs. They see these events as heralding a serious loss of state power, and especially for those historians interested in nationalism, this historical moment signals a green light for local/regional movements of self-determination. Others argue

---

[45] Shaw, *Between Old and New*, 380.

for the relative insignificance of the event.[46] The Sened-i İttifak represented a pact signed between the state and the *ayan* with respect to their mutual responsibilities. In fact, careful study of the documents related to the pact provides us with an alternative explanation of centralization, espoused especially by one Turkish scholar, I. H. Uzunçarşılı, who claims that the Grand Vizier Bayraktar Mustafa Pasha strove to centralize the empire. I agree that reassembling these important nodes of local power under state supervision would certainly be a goal of centralization.

Centralization was necessary to reassert control over European provinces. Prior to the reign of Selim III, especially the European parts of the empire had plunged into anarchy. In the 1790s, the infamous notable Pasvanoğlu rebelled against the Ottoman state and its military reforms; many *ayan* operated rebellious armies and with the increasing presence of bandits, Macedonia and Thrace had fallen into complete disarray.[47] Centralization was also necessary to pull in as many local power holders as possible, reaffirming their role as agents of the state. Among them, those who opposed the reforms of the state perceived the efforts at centralization and the creation of alternative armies as a direct threat to their well–established provincial rights and privileges. Certainly the relationship between the state and the *ayan* of Vidin, Pasvanoğlu, suggests that the animosity was the result of the state's attempt to forge alternative sources of regional power in the provinces. Others however, in Rumelia and many in Anatolia had forged alliances with the state and remained loyal. Among those in Rumelia, Tirsiniklioğlu promoted Selim III's reforms, and Bayraktar Mustafa Pasha – despite some early hesitation, especially during the Russian

---

[46] Norman Itzkowitz, for example, delineates the eighteenth century with two events; the 1703 Edirne rebellion and the 1808 Sened-i İttifak. He interprets the latter as one more deadly nail in the Ottoman state's coffin, whereby a weak state made an agreement with strong feudal interests. Furthermore, in his view, this agreement is the first time old Islamic traditions of government and society were forever altered. See Norman Itzkowitz, "Men and Ideas in the Eighteenth Century Ottoman Empire," in *Studies in Eighteenth-Century Islamic History*, ed. Thomas Naff and Roger Owen (Carbondale: Southern Illinois University Press, 1977), 15–26. Furthermore, whereas both Halil İnalcık and Kemal Karpat wrote early on about the Sened-i İttifak in much more balanced terms, they have been ignored. See Halil İnalcık, "Sened-i İttifak ve Gülhane Hatt-ı Hümayunu," *Belleten* 28 (October 1964): 603–690; Kemal Karpat, "The Land Regime, Social Structure and Modernization in the Ottoman Empire," in *Beginnings of Modernization in the Middle East*, ed. William R. Polk and Richard L. Chambers (Chicago: The University of Chicago Press, 1968), 69–90; idem, "The Transformation of the Ottoman State, 1789-1908," *International Journal of Middle Eastern Studies* 3 (1972): 243–281. Şerif Mardin barely points to the 1808 pact, *en passant* in a footnote, declaring it to be "a burst of self-assertiveness on the part of the Ayans." See Şerif Mardin, "Power, Civil Society, and Culture in the Ottoman Empire," *Comparative Studies in Society and History* 11 (1969): 278–279, n. 2. For another overview of the historical events leading up to the pact and a description of the discussions around the pact, see Uzunçarşılı, *Meşhur Rumeli Ayanlarından Tirsinikli Ismail*.

[47] For a good overview of the chaos in the Balkans, see Deena Sadat, "Urban Notables in the Ottoman Empire: The *Ayan*." Ph.D. dissertation, Rutgers University, New Brunswick, NJ, 1969, and "*Ayan* Aga: The Transformation of the Bektashi Corps in the Eighteenth Century," *The Muslim World* 63 (July 1973): 206–219.

campaigns – had come around to supporting the sultan. In Anatolia, among the most significant supporters of the reforms were the *ayan* with the most power and wealth, Karaosmanoğlu and Çapanoğlu.[48] Therefore, by the end of Selim III's reign, despite the varying allegiances in the Balkans and Anatolia, there were still key notables who had tied their fortunes to those of the sultan. And for those men, there was no substitute.

These regional men were key to reestablishing order at the center. Their intervention at the center of imperial politics did not result in a takeover by the *ayan*; on the contrary, it was an act of loyalty to the state whereby they tried to reinforce the order they perceived to be legitimate. When Selim III was dethroned, Bayraktar and his friends/fellow *ayan* "Les Amis de Roustchouk," as Miller calls them, went to Istanbul in 1807–1808 to redress the situation, reinstate Selim III, and help him revitalize his reforms. They were organizing, in effect, a counter–coup in support of the Sultan, but against those who wanted a change in government. When the sultan was executed at the hands of the conservative alliance, Bayraktar put the young Mahmud II on the throne and took over the affairs of the state as the new grand vizier. His intention was to unite the provincial elements with the reformists in Istanbul, and thereby strengthen the reign of Mahmud II. The Sened-i İttifak was the pact that resulted when Bayraktar Mustafa Pasha, the new grand vizier, convened all of the large *ayan* of Rumelia and Anatolia. Not many came, but those who did were among the most powerful *ayan* of Rumelia and Anatolia, the brokers who held state positions and wielded great local power. Despite their known allegiance to the Ottoman state, these *ayan* showed up with their private armies, ready for all eventualities.[49] The result of many days of deliberations was a pledge of loyalty to the Ottoman state and an agreement to remain on the course of reform, and therefore to back the reformists within the government. In return, the *ayan* got a promise of autonomy only in the sense that they were now fully recognized as regional powers, respected in their positions, and provided with a sense of freedom of action.

The original speech by Bayraktar Mustafa Pasha both provided an explanation for interference from the periphery and put the actions of the *ayan* into context. Bayraktar justified the rebellious attitudes of the *ayan* during the reign of Selim III and presented their presence at the court as an act of generosity toward the state and Islam. The warriors of Islam, he argued, had become

[48] Shaw tells us that Karaosmanoğlu supported Selim III and his Nizam-ı Cedid army not only by supplying money and men to the corps in Istanbul, but also by accepting officers to train his men in the new forms of warfare. Similarly, Çapanoğlu engaged in Nizam-ı Cedid formation and support. Stanford J. Shaw, *Between Old and New: The Ottoman Empire under Sultan Selim III, 1789–1807* (Cambridge, MA: Harvard University Press, 1971), 215.

[49] Uzunçarşılı counts seven *ayan* at the events: the *ayan* from Bilecik, Kalyoncu Mustafa; the *ayan* from Manisa, Karaosmanoğlu Ömer Ağa; Çapanoğlu Süleyman Bey; the *ayan* of Şile, Ahmed Ağa; the *voyvoda* of Bolu, Hacı Ahmedoğlu Seyid İbrahim Ağa; the *ayan* of Serres, Ismail Bey; and the *ayan* of Çirmen, Mustafa Bey. See Uzunçarşılı, *Meşhur Rumeli Ayanlarından Tirsinikli Ismail*, 138. These men were supporters of state policy.

weakened and had to unite in order to glorify the faith and the empire. The general tone was that these actions were for the "good of the state," rather than in the interests of the *ayan*.[50] However, the language and the spirit of the speech were regional; Bayraktar addressed the *ayan* in their language and style and appealed to their popular understanding. Consequently, he successfully brought into the fold of the state those who clearly stood at the interface of state and society, and sent them back out again to preach order and incorporation.

The text of the agreement certainly confirms the sense that the strength of the state was preserved and that the *ayan* were given what they had already wrested for themselves. The 1808 agreement has often superficially been compared to the Magna Carta; however, this is erroneous. Unlike the Magna Carta of 1215, in which the king was assailed by numerous grievances by the nobles, the Ottoman document shows no such contentious spirit. It is also incorrect to assume that the Sened-i İttifak was the direct result of the struggles between state and notables. Conflict between these state and societal actors existed, yet those notables who came to Istanbul were in agreement with the state; that is, they were not its real opponents.[51] It is also worth looking at the beginning of these documents, especially the Ottoman one that starts with an appreciation of the institution of the state, and the English document that asserts the freedom and liberty of the church and all free men. That the Ottoman document started by underlining the special place of the sultan and the state, the importance of the protection of the state, and the need for submission to the authority of the sultan and the grand vizier was indicative of the centralization agenda. The benefits for the central state were apparent: the reinforcement of the new armies; the phasing out of the Janissaries by decreasing their salaries even further, thereby giving them practically no choice but to join the new military units and retrain; and financial repackaging of some taxes for further military use. The center had furthermore succeeded to appeal to the periphery, forcing it to retrain itself.

For the notables, the pact did not represent much change in their practices. The *ayan* who participated in this meeting were already the most important ones, and had in many different ways ensured that their sons and – even more consequential – their larger kinship network enjoyed the privileges of their dominant positions after they had passed away. In practice, they had already established a kind of "feudality."[52] They had informally established rights

---

[50] Uzunçarşılı provides the complete text of this speech. See Uzunçarşılı, *Meşhur Rumeli Ayanlarından Tirsinikli Ismail*, 141–142. For a French translation, see A. F. Miller, who presents segments of the speech given by Bayraktar at the opening session of the conference of *ayan*. See Miller, *Mustapha Pacha Bairaktar*, 312–313.

[51] See Footnote 48.

[52] See, for example, the various discussions of the Karaosmanoğlu family of western Anatolia. They did not directly relinquish their posts to their sons, but they ensured the prominence of their family in key administrative posts. The brothers and sons of Mustafa Ağa, for example, maintained posts in the region and struggled to keep these titles against other *ayan*.

and privileges over weaker and smaller *ayan*. These prerogatives were often enacted through the alliance of a few strong *ayan* pooling their resources to subordinate others.[53] As I show in Chapter 7, the notables who had come to Istanbul to throw their support to the grand vizier and the young sultan were well established. They had little to fear. They had woven strong horizontal networks of association and vertical lines of patronage that both protected them from above among the grandees of the state and created exploitative networks of production. Nothing in the agreement gave these men new powers. All the Sened-i İttifak did was encode this power in more public ways.

Yet, this agreement between state and notables was quite significant in other ways. It unmistakably represented a shift from a pattern of deal making between the state and the individual notable family to deal making between *the state and a group of elites*, who seemingly acted in concert. The main advantage to the *ayan* was not the concessions the state made, but rather their recognition of the efficacy of concerted action. For the first time, the *ayan* understood that they could act in unison and were empowered by the show of force that they had inadvertently demonstrated. By calling them to Istanbul, the grand vizier had opened the door for collective bargaining, a circumstance without much precedent in Ottoman history. As the notables came to the collective realization of the power of the message sent by thousands of men gathered at the doors of Istanbul, awaiting orders from their masters, the *ayan*, Mahmud II also understood the significance of such joint action of resistance to the state. Then and there must have come his resolve that the state could very well act to retrieve these privileges by waging war on the *ayan*. He showed much reluctance to sign the Sened document. Soon after, Sultan Mahmud II would reassert his and the state's power by waging war first against the most visible and the most powerful of the *ayan*, Ali Pasha of Janina (Tepedelenli).

Given such an analysis of the events that led up to the reign of Mahmud II and the pact with the *ayan*, it is difficult to interpret this history as one of decentralization. The Sened-i İttifak was a prelude to the much stronger efforts of consolidation of the nineteenth century. It represented an important attempt to convince those regional brokers most likely to be convinced, and to establish a covenant enabling reforms to be carried out with relative peace and quiet. For the state then, the Sened-i İttifak may not have been a complete political victory, but certainly it was a political act of consolidation. For the *ayan*, the Sened-i İttifak also was not a political victory, but an event that demonstrated their potential relational power. The peripheral elites had come to the center, empowered by horizontal ties, but saw their interest anew in bolstering central power over which they now had much sway.

---

[53] It is said that Tirsiniklioğlu Ismail Ağa of Rusçuk had allied with Osman Pasha Pasvanoğlu of Vidin in a regional coalition to ensure themselves the role of appointing *ayan* to positions in their regions, thereby constructing their own patronage networks.

Conclusion

From 1703 to 1730 to 1808, the unfolding of the eighteenth century tells an important story of political empowerment, of societal forces at different moments in different alliances forging an opposition to the state that saw its goal as reform. Reform, however, was defined in multiple ways through the course of this history. It came to mean a return to the old Süleymanic age as well as just its opposite, an acknowledgment of the need to espouse Western knowledge and practices. The meaning of reform very much depended on the forces trying to control state politics. When it was the Janissaries and *ulema* at the helm of opposition, reform was a return to the social and political order of the classical age as defined by the actors themselves. It conceived of bounded institutions, separation of realms and groups in society, and the reinstitution of imperial notions of conquest and territoriality. At the hands of such conservative religious forces, an increasingly narrow Sunnî orthodoxy would be protected and perfected by the increasingly centralized institution of the *ilmiyye*. In contrast, reform at the hands of Selim III, Mahmud II, and the powerful interlocutors of the state in regional politics meant continued flexibility at adapting and absorbing new developments, perhaps beyond a continued understanding of institutional continuity between the Ottomans and the West. In these contrasting views of reform, we have to conclude that an important segment of the provincial elites of 1808 acted in concert to stop the reactionaries at the center, and, as such, they made possible another round of more important reforms that were to be carried out by Mahmud II, the Tanzimat. Notables then proved to be the more flexible element of the empire at this moment, struggling against those who resisted change and adaptation. Chapter 7 further clarifies the reasons behind the pragmatism of this new class of actors. In the eighteenth century, these actors had acquired the capability for important economic and social growth and development, and it seemed to be in their interest to maintain the order that provided them with such privilege.

7

A Networking Society:
Commercialization, Tax Farming,
and Social Relations

> In this Empire of everlasting glory, which opens its portals to all Mankind . . . this empire is unwalled, its gates are open day and night, and anyone may freely enter and exit. . . . All who desire to purchase or trade are welcome.[1]

In the Ottoman Empire in the eighteenth century, two macrohistorical developments, commercialization and tax farming, opened the door to a series of new transactions that led to major social-structural changes. These changes included increased horizontal integration of the periphery with networks of new actors tied to one another, as well as to brokers vertically integrated into the state. Provincial notables emerged strongly out of these twin processes of macroeconomic change, and by the end of the eighteenth century, they had become significant political actors. Their political acumen was the result of their hard-earned financial success and the slow and sustained spread of their regional governance regimes. Throughout the eighteenth century, notables showed ingenuity at transforming social structures, forming networks of interaction, and connecting to other social groups – especially to central elites, merchants, and peasants – in order to protect their interests and their newly formed lifestyles.

The notables were the key agents of Ottoman social transformation because they developed social and economic linkages across their territories, perhaps inadvertently reorganizing the basic skeleton of imperial control that had been based on segmentation and vertical integration. They actively participated in politics, either for or against the state. Although many, especially in the Balkans, fomented dissent against Ottoman rule and dreamed of their own regional polities (Ali Pasha of Janina and Pasvanoğlu are classic examples), others, as Chapter 6 describes, marched to Istanbul to save empire and sultan. They also

---

[1] Quoted in Minna Rozen, "Contest and Rivalry in Mediterranean Maritime Commerce in the First Half of the Eighteenth Century: The Jews of Salonica and the European Presence," *Revue des Etudes Juives* 147:3–4 (1988): 311.

discovered, in their local social structures and in their relations with European others, some emerging principles of modernity and adapted to its ways.

The commercialization of the economic environment of the empire, together with the widespread growth of tax farming as a significant form of revenue collection and state–society contracting, made the eighteenth century the key transitional period between the traditional mode of "rule of empire" and the prerequisites of "modern state rule." Yet, during this century, both types of political formation coexisted, imperial and incipient national. Regional trade and tax farming encouraged local enterprises to flourish with opportunities for privatization, and when wealthy enclaves of modernity were formed, local notables with available cash were not averse to investing in the welfare and infrastructure of their communities. Simultaneously, state political appointments, rewards, and patronage of the traditional state–society form remained useful and recurred institutionally.

This political, social, and cultural vitality disappeared in the narrative of decline. The growth of notables was the telltale sign of decentralization, and scholars have called this century "the age of *ayan*." Ceding on paper much power and authority to these new men, most scholars characterized the central state as losing power vis-à-vis the provinces, thereby engaging in the inevitable decentralization that all empires must one day face.[2] When important regional actors rose to claim local positions and partially (fiscally and/or administratively) autonomous offices, this could only mean decentralization. Because centralization and decentralization were seen as a zero-sum game, the rise of regional power in the periphery implied devolution for the state. These scholars felt no need to look further at the manner in which these developments occurred, the intermediary processes of negotiation and distribution of rights and privileges, and the intense dependencies created on both sides.

In this chapter, I discuss commercialization and tax farming and show that the notables did have the ingenuity to fashion their multiple roles, especially their tax farming resources for a sort of local protodevelopment. From this, I infer an ability to invest in local developments, infrastructure, and the distribution of their wealth beyond their own families. Through their investments in trade, local agriculture, roads, employment, and urban growth, these notables

---

[2] Bruce McGowan, "The Age of the Ayans, 1699–1812," in *An Economic and Social History of the Ottoman Empire, 1300–1914*, ed. Halil İnalcık and Donald Quataert (London: Cambridge University Press, 1994), 639–758; Bernard Lewis, *The Emergence of Modern Turkey* (Oxford, UK: Oxford University Press, 1961). See also Halil İnalcık, "Centralization and Decentralization in Ottoman Administration," in *Studies in Eighteenth-Century Islamic History*, ed. Thomas Naff and Roger Owen (Carbondale: Southern Illinois University Press, 1977), 27–52; Albert Hourani, "Ottoman Reform and the Politics of Notables," in *Beginnings of Modernization in the Middle East: The Nineteenth Century*, ed. William R. Polk and Richard L. Chambers (Chicago: The University of Chicago Press, 1968), 41–68; Norman Itzkowitz, "Men and Ideas in the Eighteenth Century Ottoman Empire," in *Studies in Eighteenth-Century Islamic History*, ed. Thomas Naff and Roger Owen, 15–26; Halil İnalcık, "Sened-i İttifak ve Gülhane Hatt-ı Hümayunu," *Belleten* 28 (1964): 603–690; Deena R. Sadat, "Urban Notables in the Ottoman Empire: The Ayan," Ph.D. dissertation, Rutgers University, New Brunswick, NJ, 1969.

were initiating the first steps of a modernization process in their own regions. However, as I continue to argue in Chapter 8, there is nothing modern about tax farming, and we should not forget the lessons of tax farming in Rome or in *ancien régime* France. For now what I would like to show, however, is that given eighteenth-century realities, tax farming was a significant adaptive response that in itself demonstrated once again the pragmatism of this empire.

Tax Farming and Commercialization

Commercialization and tax farming were the two key processes underlying the transformation of the Ottoman Empire as it slowly and awkwardly moved from being an empire to being an aggregate of emerging diverse political entities. These new processes imposed significant relational changes on Ottoman society. They led to a network revolution, transforming relations between state and social actors and among different social groups. It is therefore important to look at this transformation not only through statistics – quantities of grain exported or taxes collected – but also by imposing a relational lens that tracks, marks, and provides meaning for the changes in the transactions among people. By engaging in such analysis, we can follow how imperial relations changed, how the main structural characteristics of state and society as defined by empire could or could not be maintained, as well as how these changes were understood. What we observe then is that macrohistorical changes transformed the network relations among actors, tempered by traditional state–society institutions, and slowly altered the meaning generated by these institutions. Thus, socially embedded actors transformed and reproduced structures, institutions, and the cultural categories with which they lived.

From the mid-seventeenth through the eighteenth centuries, the Ottoman Empire became increasingly engaged in the European processes of economic and commercial development. This period has been studied as the moment of the incorporation of the Ottoman Empire into the European world economy, when the peripheralization of the Ottoman economy steered it toward a dependent position, and in the long run toward economic backwardness. Although this view has persisted for some time now, new research has countered such assertions by responding that the Ottoman economy in the eighteenth century was on a par with the European one and had not yet developed dependent patterns. I am less interested in this particular controversy because I focus on the changes that occurred in the transactions among actors, groups of actors, and the state as the empire became more integrated into a larger commercial network. Integration facilitated new social and economic ties between actors, but also fostered instabilities, fears, and boundary issues that shook some of the traditional securities of imperial rule.

Similarly, analysis of tax farming in the Ottoman Empire has been severely restricted because it has been debated solely in terms of centralization and decentralization. Again, rather than focus on centralization/decentralization as the source of state strength or decline, I suggest that we understand the transactional shifts that occurred in the aftermath of the spread of tax farming to nearly all traditional lands of the empire. We need to understand these two large-scale processes in the relational adaptation that followed because this tells us a lot more about the ways in which the raw materials of this imperial structure were being remolded into a different political formation.

The Extension of Ottoman Tax Farming

Tax farming (revenue farming) means the subcontracting by the state to private interests the right to collect taxes. In return for an initial significant sum of money, and often extra annual payments, the state leases the right or grants a license to collect taxes in a region. Tax farming existed in antiquity; it was widely practiced in Egypt and the Greco-Roman world, as well as in classical Middle Eastern societies and in other Muslim empires.[3] Whether tax farming was a response to the low level of bureaucratization of some societies or to state need for reliable and recurrent sources of revenue as well as a certain degree of risk aversion, many states throughout history relied on tax farmers to collect taxes, especially indirect taxes such as sales, customs, or excise taxes because they were mobile, harder to assess, and more risky to reliably collect.

Max Weber, who was concerned with understanding the bases of various historical land regimes, especially the differences between feudalism and prebendalism, as well as the comparative advantages and disadvantages of Western and non-Western modes of development, wrote about tax farming in sometimes contradictory fashion. On the one hand, he viewed it as a genuinely effective instrument of state rationalization because it allowed rulers to know how much revenue to expect on a yearly basis. On the other hand, he argued that tax farming was the result of inefficiency and the "moral unreliability in the official personnel."[4] Weber also argued that in the long run tax farmers were rapacious and exploited their tax base because their interests were different from the state's. An extension of this idea was also inscribed in his comparative work in which he claimed that those countries with prebendal land systems and tax farming practices were unable to develop capitalism in the manner that western Europe did.[5] In fact, versions of this argument have become classic for explaining different rates of development in different parts of the world.

[3] J. P. Levy, *The Economic Life of the Ancient World* (Chicago: University of Chicago Press, 1967); Ernst Badian, *Publicans and Sinners: Private Enterprise in the Service of the Roman Republic* (Ithaca, NY: Cornell University Press, 1972); Ramsay Macmullen, *Corruption and Decline of Rome* (New Haven, CT: Yale University Press, 1988); Margaret Levy, *Of Rule and Revenue* (Berkeley: University of California Press, 1988); John F. Richards, *The New Cambridge History of India I-5 The Mughal Empire* (Cambridge, UK: Cambridge University Press, 1993); Irfan Habib, *The Agrarian System of Mughal India (1556–1707)* (London: Asia, 1963).

[4] Max Weber, *General Economic History* (Glencoe, IL: Free Press, 1961; reprinted 1993), 58–59.

[5] Max Weber, *Economy and Society*, ed. Guenther Roth and Claus Wittich (Berkeley: University of California Press, 1978); idem, *The Religion of India: The Sociology of Hinduism and Buddhism*, transl. H. H. Gerth and D. Martindale (Glencoe, IL: Free Press, 1958).

Tax farming involved much more than risk aversion and rational calculation of rulers and agents. It reformulated state–society relations, and jump-started the creation of intermediary networks of state–society articulation in which the state was able to gain some central power in return for relinquishing other forms of control. Tax farming was a discretionary and neutral institution inserted into the midst of state and social forces, and its role and development were necessarily dependent on how the relationship was structured and how it developed on the ground. Consequently, the comparative study of this institution is also quite complex. For example, as in the Ottoman Empire, both England and France relied extensively on tax farming in early modern times. Yet, when it became clearly in the interest of the rulers to do away with tax farming, the English and the French states were much more successful at switching to a public system of tax administration. The Ottoman Empire struggled longer for a reliable standardized form of tax administration. Needing clarification, therefore, is not whether tax farming was used as a system, but rather the complexities of its application and the switch to modern forms of tax administration by public rather than private officials. Although I describe the insertion of tax farming into the institutional framework of the empire and the positions and networks of the actors, I leave the task of clarifying the awkward position of tax farming in the transition from empire to more national forms of administration to Chapter 8.

We can confidently say that tax farming was among the most important institutions of the eighteenth-century Ottoman lands. Halil İnalcık, in fact, describes tax farming as "the backbone of the administrative structure of the state."[6] By means of its novel eighteenth-century implementation of life-term tax farming contracts, the Ottoman state had bargained both to extend its financial resources and to bolster its relationships with central and regional elites. Yet, the initial reorganization of Ottoman finances and the rethinking of tax farming tenures were the result of the long seventeenth-century wars and the resulting fiscal deficits of the state.

On the international front, the Ottoman Empire encountered serious difficulties in warfare starting in the mid-seventeenth century. The European theater of war engaged its attention until the end of the century. Ottomans fought for Crete starting in 1645; responded to the revolt in Transylvania; and encountered the Habsburg armies starting in 1663, the Polish armies in 1672, and the Russians between 1678 and 1681. In fact, for most of the time from 1683 to 1699, the Ottoman Empire was continually at war, extending its armies and resources beyond its capacity. The budgets of the late seventeenth century were never balanced because, on the one hand, state expenditure steadily increased to keep up with the war efforts, and, on the other hand, the fiscal crisis was compounded by increasing difficulties in tax collection. The old systems were in decay, and the intermediate mechanisms established as temporary fixes were

---

[6] Halil İnalcık, "Military and Fiscal Transformation in the Ottoman Empire, 1600–1700," *Studies in Ottoman Social and Economic History* (London: Variorum Reprints, 1985), 327.

leading to the relentless exploitation of the peasantry, but without much return to the state.[7] The financial burden was clearly steep. The state budget of 1660–1661 showed a deficit of 12,333,543 *akçes*,[8] and by 1692–1693, this figure had catapulted to 262,217,191 *akçes*.[9] Concomitant with external pressures on the state, internal strain heightened as vizier households expanded and demanded increased sources of revenue.[10] Warfare, fiscal strain, and developments within the state itself crystallized in a significant fiscal overhaul of taxation and reorganization of the economy.

After careful planning during the reigns of three sultans, Ottoman financiers promulgated tax reforms that corresponded well with the fiscalism of the empire, that is, with the strong tendency to maximize revenues to the treasury.[11] Fiscal reform was carefully applied to different regions, tested for effect and expanded only after some success, and monitored for popular disaffection, especially in non-Muslim areas of the empire. Fiscal transformation involved the reform of the poll tax on non-Muslims (*cizye*) (1691); another reform, a form of privatization, entailed the grant of life leases on tax farms (1695).[12]

Tax farming (*iltizam*) had functioned in parallel to the *tımar* system throughout early Ottoman rule. The state had moved into the realm of tax farming as it became more risk averse, encountered difficulties in tax collection, and needed cash income.[13] The practice involved a short-term contract available to state officials, who hired tax farmers as their revenue collectors, and to wealthy non-Muslim individuals, who often acted as the intermediaries between the people and the elites. Even in its early manifestation, tax farming brought many groups in Ottoman society together and provided incentives for them to cooperate.[14] When it engendered conflicts among partners, the state intervened to disentangle the types of association and the amounts involved. Given the decentralized

---

[7] Yavuz Cezar, *Osmanlı Maliyesinde Bunalım ve Değişim Dönemi* (Istanbul: Alan Yayıncılık, 1986), 32.

[8] One Venetian ducat was worth 190 *akçes* in 1659 and between 300 and 400 *akçes* in 1691. (The 300–400 range shows the variation in market rates throughout the empire.)

[9] Mehmet Genç, "Osmanlı Maliyesinde *Malikane* Sistemi," in *İktisat Tarihi Semineri*, ed. Osman Okyar and Ünal Nalbantoğlu (Ankara: Hacettepe Üniversitesi Yayınları, 1975), 236.

[10] Yücel Özkaya, *XVIII. Yüzyılda Osmanlı Kurumları ve Osmanlı Toplum Yaşantısı* (Ankara: Kültür ve Turizm Bakanlığı, 1985), 92–44.

[11] Mehmet Genç, "Ottoman Industry in the Eighteenth Century: General Framework, Characteristics, and Main Trends," in *Manufacturing in the Ottoman Empire and Turkey, 1500–1950*, ed. Donald Quataert (Albany: State University of New York Press, 1994), 59–86. See also his *Osmanlı İmparatorluğu'nda Devlet ve Ekonomi* (Istanbul: Ötüken, 2000).

[12] Ariel Salzmann, "Measures of Empire: Tax Farmers and the Ottoman Ancien Regime, 1695–1807," Ph.D. dissertation, Columbia University, New York, 1995, 134.

[13] Murat Çızakça, *A Comparative Evolution of Business Partnerships: The Islamic World and Europe with Specific Reference to the Ottoman Archives* (Leiden, The Netherlands, and New York: E. J. Brill, 1996); see also Mehmet Genç, *Osmanlı İmparatorluğu'nda Devlet ve Ekonomi* (Istanbul: Ötüken, 2000).

[14] Linda Darling, *Revenue-Raising and Legitimacy: Tax Collection and Finance Administration in the Ottoman Empire 1560–1660* (Leiden, The Netherlands, and New York: E. J. Brill, 1996), 136.

nature of the practice, the Ottoman state regulated and assigned many different officials to supervise the workings of the system. Despite this, short-term contracts generated much abuse of the peasantry because tax farmers tended to maximize their benefits to the detriment of long-term investment. Yet, tax farming was useful and entrenched enough that it lasted in this form for at least a century, from 1550 to 1650. The new advance, life-term tax farming (*malikane*), was devised as a way to inject a large amount of cash quickly into the Ottoman treasury, as well as to redress some of the improper and harmful practices the rural populations endured. The life-term version was a corrective to the old style, perhaps the most lucrative and least risky alternative for the state.

The *malikane*, a life-term revenue tax farm, sold by the state in return for a down payment of ready cash, enabled the contract holder to collect taxes on state revenues at certain fixed rates for the duration of his life.[15] The *malikane* was sold at Istanbul auctions (soon after at provincial auctions as well) where the amount to be paid was determined by competitive bidding. The payments were composed of the down payment (*muaccele*) and the annual rent for which the tax farm holder was responsible. The sale was executed at the finance department and recorded in a public finance register; then the *malikane* holder was given a deed (*berat*) spelling out his duties and responsibilities. Accordingly, he could manage his tax farm as he wanted, developing or selling it to others.[16] More often than not, many individuals came together as partners to buy a larger tax farm, committing themselves to sharing payment and profit. Life-term tax farming gave rise then to many different-size enterprises, with varied structures and partnerships.[17]

The *malikane* became one of the most important instruments for financing the state in the eighteenth century, demonstrating that Ottomans were flexible and creative pragmatists when it came to institutional adaptation. Life-term tax farming was revolutionary for the Ottoman fiscal system and its understanding of property, especially in comparison to the traditional landholding and tax collection systems instituted by the founding fathers of the empire. Although in reality a mix of forms of landholding existed, the empire had been built on

---

[15] Mehmed Genç, "Osmanlı Maliyesinde *Malikane* Sistemi," in *İktisat Tarihi Semineri*, ed. Osman Okyar and Ünal Nalbantoğlu (Ankara: Hacettepe Üniversitesi Yayınları, 1975), 231–296; and idem, "A Study on the Feasibility of Using Eighteenth-Century Ottoman Financial Records as an Indicator of Economic Activity," in *The Ottoman Empire and the World-Economy*, ed. Huri İslamoğlu-İnan (Cambridge, UK: Cambridge University Press, 1987), 345–373. Ariel Salzmann, "An Ancien Regime Revisited: 'Privatization' and Political Economy in the Eighteenth-Century Ottoman Empire," *Politics and Society* 21 (1993): 393–423.

[16] Mehmet Genç, "A Comparative Study of the Life Term Tax Farming Data and the Volume of Commercial and Industrial Activities in the Ottoman Empire during the Second Half of the 18th Century," in *La Révolution industrielle dans le sud-est Européen-XIX siècle* 9 (Sofia: Institut d'Etudes Balkaniques, Musée National Polytechnique, 1976): 247.

[17] Although the form, variety, and quantities of these different partnerships are important for understanding the operation of the system, even the best economic historians of the empire, Genç, Çızakça, and Pamuk, remain silent on the question.

the concept of state ownership of land. Not only did this new process allow for the privatization of land and enterprises and made enterprises alienable, but it also initiated a process of appointment that relied on the market. That is, by allowing for the highest bidder, it brought about market competition and facilitated market relations. Private enterprise was further enhanced by the operation of a market of buyers rather than by state-directed appointments.[18] That is, in this odd way, market relations evolved from tax farming rather than from commercialization. Competition also forced the formation of partnerships and the development of joint operations in the development of tax farming.

The agents of this privatization, *malikane* owners, were first the members of the military class of the empire; such membership was then extended to bureaucrats, *ulema*, and members of royal family, as well as to the provincial notables (*ayan*).[19] Because the *malikane* was devised to quickly tap private wealth, the contracts were extended to a privileged group of high-level Istanbul officers and patrons, which also suited the new structure of the state with independent and competitive pasha and vizier households. There were also institutional reasons – such as the central position of the state, the creditors, and the auctions – for the fact that Istanbul-based *malikane* contracts were dominant for a good part of the eighteenth century.

The contracts provided significant incentives. They offered sources of continued revenue for the military elites, especially because, as holders of fixed income, these men had seen their revenues plummet. Moreover, that 30% of the *has* (domains with revenue more than 1,000,000 *akçe*) holders returned and then bought back their own *has* as *malikane* demonstrates that they were eager to continue receiving revenues beyond their assigned period of office.[20] The acceptance of these contracts by the military elites further legitimated the state at a moment of fiscal crisis because they thereby signaled their continuing support of the state and their willingness to extend credit to this central institution. Consequently, in the first 2 years of the privatization program of the state, we see that 61% of the tax farms were sold to members of the military, who altogether deposited 71% of the total down payment (*muaccele*) received by the state. The civilian nonstate individuals, in contrast, bought up 39% of the tax farms but with a down payment of 29%, significantly less than the military contribution.[21]

Life-term tax farming reorganized Ottoman relations. As the eighteenth century unfolded, the capital and the provinces became increasingly more networked, interweaving fiscal relations both within themselves and across center–regional lines. The *malikane* system was lubricated with Greek, Armenian, or Jewish bankers and accountants as moneylenders involved in financing the

[18] Genç, "A Comparative Study of the Life Term Tax Farming Data."
[19] For an excellent analysis of the distribution of these groups, see Erol Özvar, *Osmanlı Maliyesinde Malikane Uygulaması* (Istanbul: Kitabevi Yayınları, 2003), part II.
[20] Ibid., 49.
[21] Ibid., 60.

buyers and the state. Substantial tax farms gave rise to partnerships between buyers, with 30% of the tax farms bought in partnerships in the first 2 years from 1695 to 1697.[22] Murat Çizakça argues that by 1774 there was a marked increase in the shareholders of tax farms, with as many as twenty to thirty individuals investing in one tax farm. These individuals were investing small shares in many tax farms to diversify their portfolios and reduce their risk. Sometimes such sharing gave rise to rotation (*münavebe*) arrangements for the management of a single tax farm. By the end of the eighteenth century, there were between 1,000 and 2,000 Istanbul-based individuals who owned one tax farm or shares in multiple tax farms.[23]

The Istanbul tax farmers engaged as agents, sub tax farmers, and local tax collectors – between 5,000 and 10,000 individuals based in the provinces – constituted an entirely new web of state–provincial relations.[24] The result was a gradual centrifugal expansion of contracts. Especially when central elites showed little interest in leases in the far eastern provinces of Anatolia (e.g., Damascus, Aleppo, Diyarbakır, Mardin, Adana), provincial notables in these regions were awarded contracts instead.[25] Even more widespread was the practice of farming out one's life-term tax farm to intermediary tax farmers (*mültezim*), in effect reproducing at the regional level some of the traditional patterns. Wealthy and distinguished pashas, viziers, and rich women who bought the tax farms in Istanbul would contract with Anatolian and Balkan notables to maintain their tax farms, collect their income, and send it on to the city. Although the state initially instituted tax farming to secure knowledge about taxable assets and to bring in higher and steadier revenues, tax farmers knowledgeable about local conditions excelled as native entrepreneurs, and participated fully in expanding it to many more realms in addition to traditional land and village tithes and taxes.

What were the advantages of this tax system for the Ottoman state? That it persisted through ups and downs until the Tanzimat reforms of the mid-nineteenth century, with new leases being added every year, is not necessarily evidence of its success. Instead, it was also relatively hard to eliminate. Yet, the contracts brought in a substantial amount of cash initially, especially because the down payment was calculated at the rate of between two and eight times the amounts of annual rent. The life-term contract was certainly minimally risky and ensured steady income. However, it was far from perfect and needed continual adjustment. For example, the state could not benefit from a *malikane* that developed more than expected and yielded higher revenues. Moreover, the initial calculations of the duration that a *malikane* owner would own the *malikane* were not accurate, and the actual durations were longer than

---

[22] Ibid., 84–85.
[23] Salzmann, "An Ancien Regime Revisited," 21.
[24] Ibid. Although the range here is fairly large, these are the only numbers available in the literature regarding these individuals, both central and peripheral.
[25] Özkaya, XVIII. Yüzyılda Osmanlı Kurumları, 95.

expected, preventing the reselling of the tax farm. Therefore, financial officers compensated for these inaccuracies in 1715, when they repossessed all the *malikane*s, announcing 2 years later that they would sell the tax farms to the previous owners for half the price of their initial down payment, but with an increase in the yearly tax amounts. As the yearly tax had been kept constant, this subterfuge increased the profit to the state. The finance department further expanded the fiscal network of *malikane*s, as Salzmann argues, creating "an evolving fiscal network encompassing not only many village tithes and tribal taxes, but marketplace, guild, and administrative offices, imperial domains, excise duties, and custom revenues across the empire."[26] The chief financial officers of the Ottoman state innovated by continually carving out increasing varieties of revenues that could be turned into tax farms and putting them on the market, thereby adding new leases to the pool every year. Although there are no accurate numbers for how many leases were sold during this period, estimates vary between 150 and 300 leases a year. Over time, *malikane* owners found themselves with added burdens to increase the cash flow to the treasury, such as taxes for sultans' swearings-in and payments for the maintenance of soldiers.[27]

The budgets show the monetary returns of this fiscal policy. In 1692–1693, the treasury was 262,217,191 *akçe*s in the red; in 1698–1699, only 63,560,888 *akçe*s in the red; and by 1701–1702, the treasury showed a surplus of 111,866,873 *akçe*s![28] Salzmann shows that from its inception, over a span of 8 years, a total of 897,705 k. advance payments were invested in these *malikane* contracts. Of this amount, the Ottoman Middle East (Syria, Kurdistan, Eastern Anatolia, and Iraq) accounted for 361,835 k. of the contracts, the Balkans 322, 278 k., and western and central Anatolia totaled 213,592 k.[29] McGowan calculates that the annual collection from the down payments (not the annual rents) accounted for 10% of budget revenue.[30]

From the available data (Graph 1), the amount collected by the state from down payments during the tenure of the system clearly underlines the reasons for its survival and expansion, showing a steady increase in state revenues until the mid-nineteenth century and then a sharp decline. Similarly, Table 1 demonstrates the tremendous expansion of the system from its inception to the start of experimentation with other financial solutions (1774).

Looking at the contracts and the enduring relations among the state, its officials, and the various levels of the regional notables, we see that tax farming fashioned new property relations that the state in turn tried to shape and alter to its own benefit. First, the choice of the military as the privileged and chosen

---

[26] Salzmann, "Ancien Regime," 402.

[27] Genç, "Osmanlı Maliyesinde," 246.

[28] Ibid., 236.

[29] "k" is an abbreviation for *kuruş*, which Mehmed Genç also uses in his work; in this period, it was approximately equivalent to 120 *akçe*s. See his "Comparative Study of the Life Term Tax Farming Data," 249.

[30] McGowan, "The Age of the Ayans, 1699–1812."

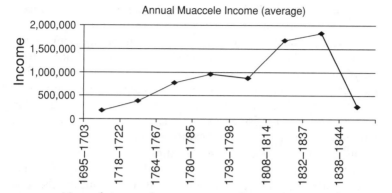

GRAPH 1. *Muaccele* income between 1695 and 1844. *Source:* Mehmet Genç, *Osmanlı İmparatorluğu'nda Devlet ve Ekonomi* (Istanbul: Ötüken, 2000) p. 115.

group for the life-term tax farms indicates the state's intention to solidify its relationship to this class. In return, that the *askeri* did not envisage great returns but were prepared to buy these farms indicated its willingness to help prevent state bankruptcy. Similarly, by extending these practices to members of the local notables, the Ottoman administration intended to restructure the relations between itself and the notables, making them if not government officials, at least loyal members of an extended state apparatus. Despite the fact that the central elites retained a lion's share of the contracts, such extension of rights to the provincial notables was the result of the state's recognition of the rising importance of this group. Both central and provincial groups were allowed to appropriate surpluses in return for their help in financing the state as well as their continued support of it. As such, this policy represented continuity, with seventeenth-century state officials often attempting to extend the net of government officials as far as it could stretch.[31] By renewing ties between the state and the provinces with the extension of these privileges to the local notables of the various provinces, the Ottoman center augmented its financial as well as its political control of this group. Yet, the unintended by-product of such an extension of distributive privileges was that it allowed provincials to develop their own new world.

The Brave New World of Trade
The perception of unrestricted trade with which we started the chapter might have been overstated; yet, the fact remains that during the eighteenth century, the Ottoman Empire became much more permeable to all kinds of trade with many European nations, and empire-wide trade routes and commodity markets flourished, bringing more and more people into contact with one another.

[31] This information fits well with the broader argument I made for seventeenth-century state practices. See Mehmet Genç, "Osmanlı Maliyesinde Malikane"; Yücel Özkaya, *Osmanlı İmparatorluğu'nda Ayanlık* (Ankara: Ankara Üniversitesi Dil ve Tarih-Coğrafya Fakültesi, 1977), 25, and Barkey, *Bandits and Bureaucrats*.

TABLE 1. Mukataa (tax unit) *income (years 1697–1698 and 1774 compared)*

	1697–1698	1774	% change
Number of *mukataa*	220	680	209
Income	199,838,944 *akçe*	375,171,600 *akçe*	88
Tax items sold as *malikane*	115	514	347
Malikane income	10,752,920	161,619,480	1400
% of *malikane* compared to all tax items	5.3	43	

Source: Mehmet Genç, *Osmanlı İmparatorluğu'nda Devlet ve Ekonomi* (Istanbul: Ötüken, 2000) pp. 116–117.

The result was a vast increase in the raw numbers of economic transactions and an unprecedented mixing of peoples from different religious and ethnic backgrounds and walks of life. As the networks brought imperial subjects of the sultan, foreign traders, and state officials together, an initial mix of relations led to fluid and open networks and increased communication. However, over time, this mix also brought about reorganization according to towns of origin as well as ethnic and religious networks.

In the fifteenth and sixteenth centuries, the Ottoman economy functioned with a traditional fiscal and provisionist outlook that ordered internal markets and imposed central economic interests on the immediate external world. Thus, the economic relations of some European countries with the Ottomans were intricate, with Ottomans behaving as the most powerful empire in the region, providing "capitulations" – permission to trade – which friendly foreign nations would acquire. The Europeans, in constrast, valued these capitulations as their trading licenses and watched one another compete for further dispensation. For the Ottomans, the preferred outcome was moderate commerce, driven by special needs and special regulations.[32] The domestic organization of trade and markets followed this provisionist and traditionalist mode, resulting in the growth of two distinct groups, one of merchants that grew to expand the boundaries of trade with Europe, and a second, traders and provisioners who bought grain, sheep, and other essentials from local producers at prices set by the state and brought them to Istanbul. Whereas the first group developed a freer, looser relationship to the state and prospered through its commercial acumen and network ties, the other group advanced through the regulation of its trade by the state, which made this trade both more controlled and more protected.[33]

[32] Probably the best summary of the Ottoman economic world is Halil İnalcık, "The Ottoman State: Economy and Society, 1300–1600," in *An Economic and Social History of the Ottoman Empire, 1300–1914*, ed. Halil İnalcık and Donald Quataert (Cambridge, UK: Cambridge University Press, 1994), 9–380.

[33] For the provisioning of the empire, see Lütfi Güçer, *Osmanlı İmparatorluğunda Hububat Meselesi ve Hububattan Alınan Vergiler* (Istanbul: Sermet Matbaası, 1964) and Lütfi Güçer,

Instituted early by the Ottoman government, provisioning had become stable by the mid-sixteenth century when traders, associations of traders, or official government buyers were specializing in purchasing goods for the capital and moving along established tracks between town and country. Most of these provisioning routes developed on the Black Sea coast of Bulgaria, the Romanian principalities, Thrace, Macedonia, Thessaly, Morea, and parts of Asia Minor, provisioning supplied cattle, sheep, grains, butter, honey, tallow, wax, and timber, many of the bare essentials for the capital to survive.[34] Local agents were drawn from among the wealthier local notables (*ayan*), the tax collectors (*mütesellim*), or other officials of the state. They were provided with cash to make all the necessary arrangements from purchase to transport and were bound to return any extra monies at the end of their efforts. For their work, they were given 1 measure (*kile*) of grain for each 10 collected, quite a generous payment.[35]

During the eighteenth century, commercial networks spread between Ottoman and European port cities.[36] Trade between European countries and the Ottoman Empire was concentrated mainly in the eastern Mediterranean, where the main Ottoman ports with access to the hinterland flourished. In

"XVIII. Yüzyıl Ortalarında Istanbul'un İaşesi için Lüzumlu Hububatın Temini Meselesi," *İktisat Fakültesi Mecmuası* 11 (1949–1950): 397–416; Marie M. Alexandra-Dersca, "Contributions a l'étude de l'apprivoisionnement en blé de Constantinople au XVIIIe siècle," *Studia et Acta Orietalia* 1 (1958): 13–37. See also the important piece by Tevfik Güran on the eighteenth-century transformation, "The State Role in the Grain Supply of Istanbul: The Grain Administration, 1793–1839," *International Journal of Turkish Studies* 3 (1985): 27–41; N. G. Svoronos, *Le Commerce de Salonique au XVIIIe siècle* (Paris: Presses Universitaires de France, 1956), 45–52; Bistra Cvetkova, "Les Celep et leur rôle dans la vie économique des Balkans à l'époque Ottomane (XVe–XVIIIes)," in *Studies in the Economic History of the Middle East*, ed. M. A. Cook (London: Oxford University Press, 1970), 176–177; and Anthony W. Greenwood, "Istanbul's Meat Provisioning: A Study of the Celepkesan System," Ph.D. dissertation, University of Chicago, Chicago, 1988.

[34] Traian Stoianovich, "The Conquering Balkan Orthodox Merchant," *Journal of Economic History* 20:2 (1960): 241.

[35] Güran, "Grain Supply of Istanbul," 33. He gives the example of Mahmud, the Salonica agent whose payment was 5,108 *kiles* of wheat, which he sold in the free market for a substantial amount.

[36] Reşat Kasaba, *The Ottoman Empire and the World Economy: The Nineteenth Century* (Albany: State University of New York Press, 1988), and "Incorporation of the Ottoman Empire, 1750–1820," *Review* 10 (1987): 805–847; Şevket Pamuk, *The Ottoman Empire and European Capitalism, 1820–1913* (Cambridge, UK: Cambridge University Press, 1987); Daniel Panzac, "International and Domestic Maritime Trade in the Ottoman Empire during the 18th Century," *International Journal of Middle Eastern Studies* 24 (1992): 189–206; idem, "Activité et diversité d'un grand paort Ottoman: Smyrne dans la première moitié du XVIIIe siècle," and "Affreteurs Ottomans et capitaines Français à Alexandrie: la caravane maritime en Mediterranée au milieu du XVIIIe siècle," *Revue de l'occident Musulman et de la Mediterranée* 34 (1982): 23–38; Elena Frangakis-Syrett, "Trade between the Ottoman Empire and Western Europe: The Case of Izmir in the Eighteenth Century," *New Perspectives on Turkey* (Spring 1988): 1–18; Necmi Ülker, "The Emergence of Izmir as a Mediterranean Commercial Center for the French and English Interests, 1698–1740," *International Journal of Turkish Studies* (Summer 1987): 1–37.

the Balkans, cities grew and craft industries and manufacturing developed, providing merchants with goods to trade, at first especially textiles from the Greek, Turkish, and Jewish textile manufacturers of Salonica, Bursa, Edirne (Adrianople), and Istanbul. Thessaly and Macedonia exported 40% of their grain and more than half their cotton and tobacco production in the late eighteenth century.[37] Macedonia and western Anatolia became the major entrepôts of grain trade, followed by trade in other commodities such as cotton, livestock, tobacco, and maize with Salonica and Izmir, the main cities benefiting from such production and demand. It is estimated that in the eighteenth century, cotton production tripled in these regions.[38] Other products came from other regions, with the Balkans becoming an important hub for livestock, where Serbian pig and cattle exports became legendary.[39] In the case of Izmir, the growth of the city both privileged some regions, such as Bursa (for silk) and Ankara (for mohair yarn), and hurt the growth of other regions, such as Chios and Kuşadası.[40] Izmir, in particular, attracted trade with France, surpassing all the other towns and port cities of the empire.[41] By 1765, Salonica and Kavala had become the principal ports of trade after Izmir, representing close to half of the trading activity of the latter.[42] Among non-Muslim communities, Jews focused their activity on wool and grains from the region of Salonica, and the Greek merchants of the Aegean came to prevail as the vital merchant community of the region.[43] To the east, Aleppo became a center of manufacturing and trade that rivaled surrounding towns and developed as an important intermediary in the transit of European goods from London, Marseille, Amsterdam, Livorno, and Venice, through the ports of Alexandretta and Latakia.[44]

[37] Stoianovich, "The Conquering Balkan Orthodox Merchant," 260; Svoronos, *Le Commerce de Salonique*, 364–366.

[38] Stoianovich, "The Conquering Balkan Orthodox Merchant," 260; Kasaba, *The Ottoman Empire*, 18–19.

[39] Stoianovich, "The Conquering Balkan Orthodox Merchant," 283.

[40] Elena Frangakis-Syrett, *The Commerce of Smyrna in the Eighteenth Century (1700–1820)* (Athens: Centre for Asia Minor Studies, 1992), 28–31.

[41] Frangakis-Syrett asserts that "Istanbul, Iskenderun, Sidon, Cyprus, Tripoli in Syria, Alexandria, Salonica, the islands in the Aegean Archipelago, the Peloponnese, Crete, and the Barbary Coast (Algiers, Tunis, and Tripoli in Libya) also traded with France, but for fifteen years between 1700 and 1749 Smyrna exported more goods in value to France than any other port in the empire." See ibid., 121.

[42] Ibid.

[43] For eighteenth-century Salonica, Svoronos provides the following population figures: the total population was between 60,000 and 70,000; among them were 25,000–30,000 Jews and 16,000–20,000 Greeks. See *Le Commerce de Salonique*, 7–11. The population of Izmir in the early eighteenth century was 100,000, with 1,800 Jews and 10,000 Greeks; by the end of the century, the Jewish community had risen to 5,000 and the Greeks to 25,000. See Elena Frangakis-Syrett, "The Raya Communities of Smyrna in the 18th Century (1690–1820): Demography and Economic Activities," *Actes du colloque international d'histoire: la ville néohellenique. Héritages Ottoman à état Grec* (Athens, 1985), vol. I, 28–29.

[44] Abraham Marcus, *The Middle East on the Eve of Modernity: Aleppo in the Eighteenth Century* (New York: Columbia University Press, 1989), 144–146.

Wars, especially the Seven Years' War, the War of American Independence, and the French Revolution, displaced French commerce in the eastern Mediterranean, providing Greeks and Orthodox Albanians the opportunity to trade. Stoianovich tells us that Greek merchants who brought grain to Marseille during the French Revolution became "millionaires."[45] The wars with Austria at the beginning of the eighteenth century (1716–1718) gave Austria new territories, whereas the wars in the middle of the century (1737–1739) forced her to give back some of these lands. With these territorial changes came various attempts at resettlement, colonization, and, especially in Hungary, a substantial effort to revitalize the commercial economy. Serbs were invited; Greeks, Macedo-Vlachs, Jews, and Armenians followed, gaining access to new commercial opportunities and exploiting them to their benefit. The result was an extraordinary intermingling of ethnic groups and talent in those regions of the two empires that connected through trade. When the Dutch and the British directed their attention to other areas of the world, the French expanded their trade with the Ottomans, representing by the 1720s more than 60% of this international trade.[46] The French were also, according to Eldem, most numerous and most widespread in the empire, as "French commercial activity was usually conducted by a more extended group of traders in practically every commercial center of the Levant, even including certain trading centres in the hinterland such as Bursa, Ankara and Aleppo."[47] In addition to strong political and cultural ties between the French and the Ottomans, the technical and military enhancement that French experts brought to the empire also reinforced relations, leading to dense networks of trade and cooperation.

Commercialization of relations with western Europe not only intensified relations among social, political, and economic actors, but it also reorganized populations and ethnic and religious groupings, their interests, and their needs. Some of this reordering occurred with regard to important trade goods. The European demand for cotton cloth established ties among cotton-growing regions, centers for weaving, and ports of export. For example, Edirne, Shkoder, and Salonica became linked among themselves as well as to the smaller Balkan towns of Tirnovo and Elassona. Izmir became linked to Ankara, Bursa, Tokat, and Antakya, but sometimes with cities as far away as Aleppo and Baghdad. In the absence of strong market structures, fairs became centers of trade frequented by large numbers of people intermingling and speaking a variety of languages. The Balkans especially were the hub of Ottoman fairs, with Austria and Hungary as eager customers of the Christian Orthodox merchants, who became the main intermediaries of the region. One fair in eastern Thrace, Uzuncaova, is said to have attracted 50,000 people.[48] Balkan merchants

---

[45] Stoianovich, "The Conquering Balkan Orthodox Merchant," 275.

[46] Edhem Eldem, "French Trade and Commercial Policy in the Levant in the Eighteenth Century," in *The Ottoman Capitulations: Text and Context*, ed. Maurits H. van den Boogert and Kate Fleet, *Oriente Moderno* 22:3 (2003): 27–43.

[47] Ibid., 28–29.

[48] McGowan, "The Age of the Ayans, 1699–1812," 701.

initially mixed quite easily, especially because most merchants operating in the Balkans spoke Greek and were called "Greek."[49] Yet, over time an ethnic division of labor also spread everywhere in the western part of the empire.[50] With the intensity of international trade came uncertainty, which many groups handled by forming associations centered around their trade or their religion and ethnicity. In fact, it is in the eighteenth century that the empire experienced the beginnings of a richer associational life, which was the result of fragile or no banking relations and of the need for security and protection.

As the volume of trade increased, more and more individuals acquired a variety of intermediate locations, official positions, and roles. By their nature, these intermediate locations not only connected different sites and were productive and enriching, but also focused the attention of all parties on them. Many individuals settled in intermediate locations such as key European ports, acting as trusted facilitators for their communities. Frangakis-Syrett notes that during trade between Marseille and Izmir, ships increasingly stopped in Livorno, Ancona, and Trieste, loading more goods and involving more merchants. The Italian ports such as Livorno and Ancona were important regions of settlement for liaison populations, especially Jews. Greeks traded with and then settled in Leipzig, Lwow, Vienna, Trieste, and many other Austro-Hungarian towns. These towns then became the intermediate zones where east and west met and where Ottoman Christian and Jewish merchants established family members in European cities, creating business kinship networks that spanned long distances and were built on strong loyalty ties.[51] The non-Muslim communities of the empire were located mainly in Istanbul, Salonica, Izmir, Aleppo, and other important trading cities, and as traders they strengthened the commercial and cultural ties between these cities and Livorno, Ancona, Trieste, Leipzig, Vienna, and Lwow.

The Ottoman state was not absent in the development of these new commercial relationships. It acted as the protectionist force of the market, restricting the access of foreign traders, but also more often than not interfering in the normal workings of market relations, demanding gifts, bribes, and making policy difficulties that were imitated and enhanced at the local level by

---

49 Stoianovich titles a section of his article "The Conquering Balkan Orthodox Merchant," "To Be a Peddler Is To Be 'Greek.'" See the revised edition of this classic article in *Between East and West: The Balkan and Mediterranean Worlds* (New York: Caratzas, 1992), 50.

50 Macedo-Thessalian and Epirote Greeks and Vlachs exported wool and cotton to Austria and Germany; Greeks, Macedo-Vlachs, Serbians, Jews, and Armenians controlled the commerce of Wallachia and Moldavia, Hungary, Vojvodina, Croatia-Slavonia, and parts of Transylvania and Moravia. The commerce of Buda, Pest, Eger, Szentendre, Keresztes, Arad, Debrecen, and Temesvar was under Greek and Serbian control. In general, Greeks, Vlachs, Albanians, Macedonian forwarding agents, agents from Thessaly and Epirus, Serbian pig merchants from the Sumadija, Armenians from Bulgaria, and agents from Bosnia spread across the border towns of the empire, setting up business and connecting with trading centers in Leipzig, Vienna, Amsterdam, Lyons, Livorno, and Naples. See George W. Hoffman, "Thessaloniki: The Impact of a Changing Hinterland," *East European Quarterly* 22:1 (1968): 1–27.

51 Ibid., 701. See also David S. Landes, *Bankers and Pashas: International Finances and Economic Imperialism in Eqypt* (Cambridge, MA: Harvard University Press, 1979).

government officials.[52] Although this demonstrated continued state engagement in local trade, it also created difficulties for all concerned, from the French traders to their consuls and the ambassador to local guilds and networks of Muslim or non-Muslim merchants. Although Ottoman state intervention and attitudes did not change over the eighteenth century, its relative power and advantage vis-à-vis the Europeans did change. The best example of this is that the balance of trade after 1740 was clearly more favorable toward the French. After this date, the European discourse of superiority and security began to spread, overlying the more neutral networks of association and commerce.[53] Ottoman Muslim and non-Muslim merchants, landholders, peasants, and *ayan*s now encountered not only the vagaries of the international market and the difficulties of a provisionist state, but also the increasingly negative, imposing, and demeaning language and discourse of the Europeans. As a result, the open, fluid, and far-reaching networks of commercial activity could not endure, and they reorganized along communal, protectionist lines.

Reworking Elite Networks: Institutions, Actors, and Activities

The institution was life-term tax farming; the key actors were the notables, whose activities ranged from cultivation, tax farming, and tax collection, to moneylending and local and international trade. In these activities, they engaged the state, the peasantry, and a rising group of Ottoman Muslim and non-Muslim traders and commercial agents, as well as European merchants. These actors also constructed regional governance regimes[54] that were to shape eighteenth-century state–society organization and force state actors to recentralize in the nineteenth century in an effort to reign in such powerful alternative centers of rule. In the rest of this chapter, I analyze the processes by which elite networks were configured into regional governance regimes.

I use the term "regional governance regimes" to indicate networks of large patriarchal families who established themselves around one or two leaders; developed their resources and influence through multiple state and nonstate activities and positions; extended their networks to incorporate clients, whether lesser notables or peasants; and both in their local rule and in their understanding of their legitimacy mimicked the ruling household of the sultan. There were many of these, though they were not all the same, varying especially with regard to relations with the central state.[55] Many lasted for at least a century

---

[52] Eldem, "French Trade and Commercial Policy," 38.

[53] See, for example, the reports of Felix Beaujour, *Tableau du commerce de la Grèce*, 2 vols. (Paris: Renouard, 1800), which exhibits a striking arrogance and sense of superiority vis-à-vis the Turk.

[54] The two works that have most forcefully argued for regional regimes are Dina Rizk Khoury, *State and Provincial Society in the Ottoman Empire, Mosul, 1540–1834* (Cambridge, UK: Cambridge University Press, 1997), and Salzmann, *Tocqueville in the Ottoman Empire.*

[55] That is, among them, the Anatolian regimes of Karaosmanoğlu, Çapanoğlu, Caniklioğlu, Tuzcuoğlu, Hazinedaroğlu, and the Balkan regimes of Tirsiniklioğlu, as well as around Alemdar Mustafa Pasha, maintained overall positive relations with the state, while such dynasties as

until the centralized regime of Mahmud II (1808–1839) tried to eliminate them. Some of these families, although stripped of their political power, have continued to survive as local notable families of high prestige in modern-day Turkey.[56]

The creation of these governance regimes was not the result of grand strategy by notables who wanted to seize power from the center. Rather, these actors seem to have taken advantage of available local positions, openings in the social structure that emerged out of a series of larger social and political developments. Given the opportunities that were presented by tax farming and international trading, they developed multiple interests, and as they pursued these interests, they engaged with others, forming extended networks of cooperation and conflict. So, on the one hand, their interests led to expansion in the size, scope, and range of networks, but on the other hand, in order to increase their wealth and influence they had to prevent others from such expansion. The result was that extended networks of regional governance grew as far as they could go, in the process subordinating smaller networks and locking out others who were regarded as threatening.

The men who established these networks originally accumulated positions, taking advantage of their place in local society. They then used the diversity of their positions and occupations and their involvement in many different activities to develop multiple interests, pursuing power, wealth, and influence in Ottoman society. They did this, however, within the norms and expectations of Ottoman society at that particular historical time, often replicating the structure of the ruling Ottoman household and its understanding of justice. The result was an equivalent sense of empowerment among the provincial new guard, both in terms of *ayan* independence and autonomy but also in the production of alternative, locally based regional networks of rule and incipient modernity. In this network, extension and reorganization differences in actors' positions and interests led to a variety of regional network regimes in which patterns of state–regional relations signaled different routes toward imperial accommodation. Among these, a Balkan, a western Anatolian, and a central Anatolian mode can be clearly discerned.

The study of these new networks relies on a few simple analytic propositions. In this chapter, I use the network idea more as a metaphor than as a qualified methodological tool though the shape and transformation of networks in historical time tells us a lot about changing relations between actors, groups and institutions. Lacking adequate data to formally substantiate these claims, I use the example of a few families to demonstrate how they developed their networks. Actors are always embedded in social relations, but the shape of their embeddedness is relevant. Eighteenth-century Ottoman provinces reveal a significant change in the orientation of elite actors and the prominence of their ties. Moreover, viewing these groups as overlapping networks of elites

---

Pasvanoğlu and Ali Pasha of Janina proclaimed themselves *ayan*, established their rule through illegitimate means, and remained mostly hostile to the state.

[56] Michael Meeker, *A Nation of Empire* (Berkeley: University of California Press, 2002).

provides us with much more leverage than does lumping them into a class and assuming common core interests.[57] I follow these individuals/families in their own trajectories as members of fluid networks of association rather than as rigid categories of actors unflinching in their interests, and I avoid attributing to them strong group identity or stable interests. The fluidity and multiplicity of their occupations, their diverse origins, and their varying relationships with the state make it impossible to group them as a class. Some tax farmers were officials of the state; some were provincial men drawn into a relationship with the state; others were military men of Janissary or *timar* origin; and still some others were intermediaries, contractors, and subcontractors with fleeting interests in the system. The sociological interest of these individuals is in their overlapping memberships in various groups, the affinity that emerges from this overlap, and the self-reliance that results from being embedded in these multiple networks. Consequently, I also do not separate and set state and society in opposition to each other; the relationship between state power and social power is not a zero-sum game, as in this case where a strong state coexisted with strong social actors.

Notables, State Positions, and Tax Farms

The provincial notables were a well-established local elite, with families of high social status derived from religious and scholarly backgrounds, although the importance of these features were to give way to wealth and local connections.[58] Notables and their families became powerful by investing in land and real estate in the cities, accumulating wealth, and building local social and political networks.[59] Originally, their power was based purely on local recognition

[57] This last point is especially important to Ottoman historians. Although there is an overabundance of material on these elites, they have been discussed in terms of categorical and bounded entities with one fundamental identity. Most Ottoman scholars would concur with Bruce McGowan's description of the eighteenth century: "two rising groups stand in dramatic profile: the tax-gatherers and the local committees (ayans) – at first as separate groups with distinct functions, but, with the passage of time, as a single merged class with roots both in the country and Istanbul." See McGowan, "The Age of the Ayans, 1699–1812," 661. Similarly, as is clear in the discussion of merchants, Stoianovich, the foremost historian of the Balkan merchants, treats this quite disparate and interconnected group as a class. Only Çağlar Keyder agrees with my argument that these groups did not represent classes. See Keyder, "Introduction: Large-Scale Commercial Agriculture in the Ottoman Empire?" in *Landholding and Commercial Agriculture in the Middle East*, ed. Çağlar Keyder and Faruk Tabak (Albany: State University of New York Press, 1991), 1–16.

[58] Although some would like to maintain the significance of religious and somewhat "noble" social origins, the fact is that these families had diverse roots, from rural peasant to religious to merchant and to military. For the best exposition of the various views on the diverse ways of becoming a notable, see Nurhan Fatma Katırcıoğlu, "The Ottoman Ayan, 1550–1812: A Struggle for Legitimacy," M.A. thesis, University of Wisconsin–Madison, 1984, 49–55.

[59] Meriwether shows the importance to the notables of urban real estate investments. She argues that it gave them stability and durability, protecting them from the vagaries of the market. Similarly, Nagata shows that the notables he studied were interested in both rural and urban real estate, and his analysis of the registers shows wide-ranging investment activity. See Margaret Lee

rather than on affiliation with the state.[60] Albert Hourani describes their political influence as stemming from a combination of their social power derived from local wealth and status and their "access" to power (as distinguished from holding official positions).[61]

Moreover, they rose to prominence by taking advantage of the growing structural holes in Ottoman society, that is, the increasing inability of the members of provincial elite society – from governors to the lower levels of the *timar* holders – to administer, collect taxes, and fight wars. When other members of regional society dropped out, the provincial notables were indirectly drawn into helping the local magistrates (*kadis*) and providing administrative services for the state, facilitating the transition from traditional tax collection to the innovative reorganization based on the *malikane*. However, unlike their predecessors, the notables were well ensconced in their towns and regions; it was only natural that such developments would increase their interest in creating around themselves networks of officials, peasants, and artisans dependent on *ayan* benevolence and wealth. The great Ottoman notables used their permanent location and their original local power and influence as springboards for developing extensive networks in almost every activity, including tax farming of state revenues, tax collection, recruiting of troops for the military, provisioning of city and army, moneylending (for both political and commercial purposes), and management of landholdings of various sizes for moderate commercial purposes. Given their local knowledge, they acted as honest brokers, bringing the state and the peasants to an acceptable compromise in the transitional stages of short-term tax farming (*iltizam*), collective taxation procedures (*maktu*), and drawing up the registers of apportioning (*tavzi defteri*).[62]

In 1695, when tax farms officially became available for lifelong acquisition, settled families bid for the taxation privileges of lands and revenue sources in which they had already been involved. Khoury, for example, describes the process in Mosul by which a few key local families immediately became involved. The most prominent family, the Umari family, which claimed descent from the second caliph of Islam and had strong ties to the Ottoman bureaucracy

Meriwether, "The Notable Families of Aleppo, 1770–1830: Networks and Social Structure," Ph.D. Dissertation, University of Pennsylvania, Philadelphia, 1981; Yuzo Nagata, *Materials on the Bosnian Notables* (Tokyo: Bunkyo Printing, 1985).

[60] H. A. R. Gibb and Harold Bowen, *Islamic Society and the West*, especially vol. 1, pts. 1 and 2 (London: Oxford University Press, 1957); İnalcık, "Centralization and Decentralization." Although Gibb and Bowen and İnalcık assume this intermediate position for the *ayan*, both Meriwether and Katırcıoğlu warn about the precarious nature of this relationship prior to the late seventeenth century. Meriwether, "The Notable Families of Aleppo"; Katırcıoğlu, "The Ottoman Ayan."

[61] Albert Hourani, "Ottoman Reform and the Politics of Notables," in *Beginnings of Modernization in the Middle East*, ed. William Polk and Richard Chambers (Chicago: The University of Chicago Press, 1968), 46.

[62] İnalcık, "Military and Fiscal Transformation," 327–337; Bruce McGowan, *Ottoman Europe: Taxation, Trade, and the Struggle for Land, 1600–1800* (Cambridge, UK: Cambridge University Press, 1981); Katırcıoğlu, "The Ottoman Ayan," chapter III.

and the Şeyhülislam, held the lion's share of the largest *malikane*s. The other main family, the Jalilis, were newcomers by comparison and were allocated smaller tax farms, although the strategic importance of some of these led to significant fortunes.[63] Meriwether also shows how local notables from Aleppo first became tax farmers with great estates, before obtaining official tax collecting positions. The opposite was equally possible: notables could begin as the deputy governors or provincial tax collectors (*mütesselim* or *muhassıl*) of a region, thereby gaining access to extended land revenues, and then overlay this access to lands with tax farming rights. Another example common in central Anatolia indicates the manner by which local notables stepped in to provide military and provisioning assistance during wartime, gathering military and tax official titles as they demonstrated their loyalty to the state. The fortunes of two Anatolian families, the Caniklioğlus and the Çapanoğlus, rose and fell according to their wartime performance because they had been called on to fill military leadership positions usually filled by members of the military hierarchy. The Caniklioğlus – successful in their services to the state – ended up consolidating a governance regime around a large territory as they acquired life-term tax farms in the areas of Canik, Amasya, and Karahisar-Sarki. Generally, the *ayan* understood well that whatever the route to and the requirements of a particular office, those who combined the esteemed communal title of local notable (*ayan*) with the state-conferred privileged office of tax collector (*muhassıl*) and the monetary benefits of tax farming (*malikane*) were poised to gain enormous power and influence and to become important local-imperial brokers.[64]

The genealogy of these families has been studied, but with little attention to the way in which they built network relations. Here the details of the construction of the Karaosmanoğlu dynasty, a key western Anatolian family with extended network ties, is instructive. The dynasty emerged by offering sultans their services during war or in local struggles requiring conflict resolution, acquiring titles such as deputy tax administrator of Saruhan and tax collector of Aydın, two western Anatolian provinces.[65] In Saruhan, they developed

[63] Khoury, *State and Provincial Society in the Ottoman Empire*, 89–95; Margaret L. Meriwether, "Urban Notables and Rural Resources in Aleppo, 1770–1830," *International Journal of Turkish Studies* 4 (1987): 55–73.

[64] Among them are the best-known names of the eighteenth century: Karaosmanoğlu, Çapanoğlu, Canikli, Kalaycıoğlu, Emirağazadeler, Zennecizadeler, Müderriszadeler, Nakkaşzadeler, Caffarzadeler, Mühürdarzadeler, Kalyoncu Ali from Anatolia, and the more rebellious *ayan* (warlord *ayan*) of the Balkan Peninsula: Osman Pasvanoğlu of Vidin, Ismail Bey of Serres, Ali Pasha of Janina, and Mehmet Buşatli of Shkoder. See İnalcık, "Centralization and Decentralization," 33. Işık Tamdoğan-Abel, in her study of the eighteenth-century Adana, demonstrates the degree to which numerous local notables successfully combined these three positions. See her brilliant study, "Les Modalités de l'urbanité dans une ville Ottomane," Thèse de Doctorat, Ecole des Hautes Etudes en Sciences Sociales, Paris, 1998.

[65] Reşat Kasaba, "Migrant Labor in Western Anatolia, 1750–1850," in *Landholding and Commercial Agriculture in the Middle East*, ed. Çağlar Keyder and Faruk Tabak (Albany: State University of New York Press, 1991).

a strong network of relations with every level of society and made their fortunes as government tax collectors and tax farmers of the wealthy central state grandees and estate owners. Another large part of their income was generated by commerce and by the taxes they imposed on commercial goods produced under their jurisdiction and sold to the West.[66] Perhaps the key to the early development of an important local dynasty in Saruhan was the lack of an established governor for this region in the eighteenth century; instead, the region functioned as a stipend (*arpalık*) for viziers and beys of distinction. In the absence of governors, a deputy tax collector could find his own space and opportunity for holding power. Also, as these Istanbul beys acquired Saruhan as their stipend, rather than move to the region, they farmed out its revenue to local entrepreneurs. The patriarch of the dynasty, Mehmed Çavuş (d. 1644), started out as the local representative of these Istanbul-based beys, acquired their trust, and became well known in political circles so that the central state set out to assign positions to members of this family. From among four sons, only one, Kara Osman (d. 1706), was to distinguish himself, diversifying his portfolio of state titles, acquiring tax farms, establishing quasi-private estates, and launching the name of the dynasty that was to continue at least until the end of the nineteenth century.

As the family was on the rise, the early network contacts seem to have been made through common state missions or campaigns; often the central authorities ordered neighboring *ayan* to go to the front together, sometimes sending them on joint missions against a rebellious governor or other notable, putting structurally equivalent individuals into contact with each other. Kara Osman and two other *ayan* were assigned to seize the crops of those who did not participate in the Vienna campaign. Both Hacı Mustafa (d. 1755) and his brother Hacı Ibrahim (sons of Kara Osman) made important contacts when they were commanders at the eastern front. Between 1724 and 1730, Hacı Mustafa refused to go to war, but was then forced to join the war on the eastern front with six other notables who had been similarly ordered. Likewise,

---

[66] To develop my argument regarding networks of association and patronage, I have used a variety of secondary and primary sources: Yuzo Nagata, *Tarihte Ayanlar: Karaosmanoğulları Üzerine bir İnceleme* (Ankara: Türk Tarih Kurumu Basımevi, 1997); idem, *Some Documents on the Big Farms (Çiftliks) of the Notables in Western Anatolia* (Tokyo: Institute for the Study of Languages and Cultures of Asia and Africa, 1976); idem, *Studies on the Social and Economic History of the Ottoman Empire* (Izmir: Akademi Kitabevi, 1995); Halil İnalcık, "The Emergence of Big Farms, Çiftliks: State, Landlords, and Tenants," in *Landholding and Commercial Agriculture in the Middle East*, ed. Keyder and Tabak, 17–24; Frangakis-Syrett, *The Commerce of Smyrna*; Çağatay Uluçay, "Karaosmanoğullarına Ait Bazı Vesikalar," *Tarih Vesikaları* II: 193–207, 300–308, 434–440; III: 117–126. Most of these books and articles provide not only analysis, but also much of the primary archival documentation on the dynasty. I have used this primary documentation extensively and have added it to the French consular reports on Izmir mentioned in note 57. See Ministère des Affaires Etrangères, Archives Diplomatiques, Mémoires et Documents, Turquie, vols. 8, 9, 13, 15, and Archives Nationales de France, Affaires Etrangères, Série Sous-Série Bi, Correspondance Consulaire, vols. 1051, 1052, 1053.

in 1743, Hacı Ibrahim was made commander in the Persian War, along with four other notables from the same region. In both cases, the Karaosmanoğlus went on campaigns with these men, and returned to the same region, because they were all notables from the same locality.[67] Some of these men figure in later records, especially in moneylending transactions, showing the ties that were formed during campaigns. The difference from past practice is important to note because before notables joined and replaced the provincial military-administrative officials (*tımar* holders, governors, and governors-general) as commanders in war, only peasants of the same region would go to war and return together. The multiple commanders, from the lowest *tımar* holders to the governors, would return to different areas, depending on their rotation schedule.

Whereas Hacı Ibrahim, who went to the Persian War, disappeared from the records, evidence shows that his brothers, Hacı Mustafa (d.1755) and Abdullah (d. 1779), became wealthy men who administered many large estates. Abdullah remained a tax farmer and owner of estates, whereas Hacı Mustafa became an important broker. He accumulated titles in the following order: commander, deputy tax administrator, and then tax farmer, having been offered tax farms by the state (Saruhan sanjak mukataası); the governor of Anatolia, Yeğen Ali Pasha; and a state official, İvaz Paşazade Halil Pasha, in the fertile Manisa plain (Koru-i Cebel-i Manisa). He also accumulated old or deserted villages, took over estates from other families, and gathered lands earmarked as grazing lands or pious foundation (*vakıf*) lands to create new estates under his jurisdiction.[68] As a tax farmer, he was able to provide himself with the title deeds to many lands, consolidating a large region of cultivation in the Manisa plain between his home village of Yayaköy and his central town of business, Manisa. This is not to say that there were no members of the dynasty who opposed the state and were therefore not allowed to flourish, or whose fortunes were confiscated by the fiscal authorities.

There was, however, another less legitimate route to "*ayan*hood" and a regional governance regime. Located more in the Balkans, for example, the infamous Osman Ağa Pasvanoğlu had espoused a different route to *ayan*hood, gathering his troops of irregular soldiers and bandits and claiming the region from Vidin to the banks of the Yantare River. Both he and his father forcibly extorted titles from the Ottoman state, establishing themselves on land as tax farmers, with Osman Ağa imposing himself by force on the administrative council of Vidin in order to acquire the title of *ayan*. At the height of his power, Pasvanoğlu had established a contentious governance regime by force,

---

[67] The towns that these *ayan* were from range from Edremit, the northernmost point, to Kırkağaç, Palamut, Gördes, and, finally, Turgut and Menteşe in the south. Yayaköy was the village of origin for this family, and Manisa and Izmir were their towns of temporary residence.

[68] It is important to recall that although land legally was state property (*mîrî*), in practice the manner in which it was used and passed on or sold brought it close to being private property (*mülk*).

but still controlled the lands and peoples in the strategic basin from Vidin to Lom to Nikopol, Plevne, and Tirnovo down to Tatarpazarcığı, Sofia, and Niş in the south. This was a significant part of the Balkan Peninsula.[69]

The central and eastern Anatolian dynasties of notables, which were intermediate between Balkan warlords and officially recognized dynasties such as Karaosmanoğulları, rose to positions of prominence after the treaties of Karlowitz in 1699 and Passarowitz in 1718, and especially during and after the war of 1768–1774, when local administrative and military duties were vastly expanded and notables began to participate, becoming central in all such arrangements. As such they were assigned to deputy-governor (*voyvoda*) and deputy tax collector (*mütesellim*) positions, establishing patronage that resembled the old style of relations between state actors and their immediate regional officials. The founder of one dynasty, Çapanoğlu Ahmet, for example, was quite willing to engage the Ottoman state and its provincial elites and to participate in their project of provisioning and expansion. He established a zone of security, free from banditry and extortion in the region he ruled, providing the state with a military force to fight unruly *ayan*, and with sheep to feed Istanbul during meat shortages. Between 1728 and 1765, he was rewarded with eight official positions bestowed by the governor or the state.[70] The best-known member of the family, Süleyman Çapanoğlu, assisted Sultan Selim III (1789–1807) in developing the Nizam-ı Cedid army in the southeastern region of Anatolia.[71] The resulting relationship between the two men grew to be special, with letters showing that Süleyman was by far the most trusted *ayan* in all of Anatolia. Süleyman earned this trust early on when he decided to forgo any riches that belonged to the family after the death of his brother Mustafa and, furthermore, forced his nephew and others in the family to turn over the estate to the state. Therefore, Süleyman's claim to an *ayan*ship came at the

---

[69] I have used a variety of sources to reconstruct the story of Pasvanoğlu. The most important among these are Ahmed Cevdet Paşa, *Tarih-i Cevdet*, 2d ed., 12 vols. (Istanbul: Matbaa-yı Osmaniye, 1884–1885); G. Iakichitch, "Notes sur Pasvanoğlu, 1758–1807, par l'adjudant commandant Meriage," *La Revue Slave* 1:1 (May 1906): 261–279; 1:2 (June 1906): 419–429; 2:1 (July–August 1906): 139–144; 2:2 (November–December 1906): 435–448; 3:1 (January–February 1907): 138–144; 3:2 (March–April 1907): 278–288. This report is also from the Archives du Ministère des Affaires Etrangères, Quai d'Orsay; Sadat, "Urban Notables in the Ottoman Empire: The Ayan."

[70] Among the eight titles that we know of, five were as military agent of the governor to collect his revenues in the proscribed area (*voyvoda*), one as lieutenant-governor (*mütesselim*), one as life-term tax farm owner (*malikaneci*), and one district was given to him as appanage (*arpalık*). See Özcan Mert, *XVIII. ve XIX Yüzyıllarda Çapanoğulları* (Ankara: Kültür Bakanlığı Araştırma ve İnceleme Yayınları, 1980), 28.

[71] The rivalry between Çapanoğlu Süleyman and the members of the Canikoğlu family is represented in the sources as one deriving from different positions regarding the new army. Süleyman's support was dismissed by Tayyar Mahmud Pasa, the chieftain of the Caniklis who openly opposed and worked against Selim III's reforms. Yet, there was much territorial rivalry between the two families as well. See J. H. Mordtmann and Bernard Lewis, "Derebey," *EI²* (1965), 207.

expense of his own family and of other regional power holders whose fortunes were confiscated. Such actions broke local ties and consolidated one important relation: to the sultan of the empire.

All these families used moneylending as a central activity to connect elites horizontally and notables and peasants vertically. *Ayan* lent money to other *ayan*, to deputy-provincial governors, townsmen, and villagers, either to help them pay their taxes or to set up and maintain small businesses. Müridoğlu, another local lesser *ayan*, used much of his cash to lend and to invest in small-scale business. Much of his wealth came from grain and oil production and tax farming.[72] Müridoğlu loaned money to the Karaosmanoğlu family and to the tax collectors of Karesi, among others. The inheritance registers of Karaosmanoğlu Hacı Hüseyin Pasha show a large number of transactions with other *ayan*, state officials, entire villages, towns, women, and Christians. For just the 3 years from 1813 to 1816, the registers show that Hacı Hüseyin had loaned money to nineteen officials with state titles, to ten men clearly identified as *ayan*, to twenty-four men most likely *ayan* but not clearly indicated as such, to one council of notables, to the workers of two of his estates, to various townsmen, to Christian peasants, and to at least two women. In all, we find sixty-five different references to individual transactions in which this *ayan* loaned money.[73] It is clear that these men loaned both for the economic gains to be had from such transactions (especially given that the interest rate was quite high, from 20% to 24%) as well as for the social value generated by the tie created by the transaction. It seems that the Karaosmanoğlu family often did not expect repayment from numerous debtors for their unpaid debts. This was probably more likely to be the case with peasants, artisans, and village communities than with state officials or other *ayan*. This was certainly an important mechanism in patron–client relations during the Roman Empire, when aristocratic Romans bound their clients to them in a patron–client relationship by lending money. It was not necessarily the expectation of financial return, but rather the creation or strengthening of unequal social bonds that lay behind the act of lending.

Other families such as the Tuzcuoğlus and the Hazinedaroğlus of the eastern Black Sea region emerged later and continued through the early nineteenth century. The Tuzcuoğlus also started as a patriarchal household, with Memiş (Mehmed Ağa) – their father notable, the *ayan* of Rize and Hopa – involved in agriculture and commerce. He later acquired many state titles, indicating his positive and useful relationship with the state. Tuzcuoğlu reached into larger

---

[72] Suraiya Faroqhi, "Wealth and Power in the Land of Olives: Economic and Political Activities of Muridzade Haci Mehmed Agha, Notable of Edremit," in *Landholding and Commercial Agriculture in the Middle East*, 77–95.

[73] Nagata, *Tarihte Ayanlar*, 248–251. It is important to note that the inheritance registers show only those transactions that were not completed. Presumably, there were more financial dealings in which this man engaged, but they were not recorded because they did not leave any debts on either side.

domains and often prepaid taxes for his peasants, and was involved with a neighboring notable family, the Hazinedaroğlus. Although these notable chiefs often loaned money to each other, they were also locked into an irrevocable competition over land and positions, engaged in a furious conflict that ended in the demise of Memiş Tuzcuoğlu, revered *ayan* of the region.[74]

Networks of contention defined the outer limits of these regional governance systems. That is, Karaosmanoğlus could grow through the incorporation of their diverse relations, constructing their networks and harnessing them to spread their authority and control. Yet, they also encountered limits to their expansion where contending families impeded their movement. The outer limits of the governance regime was either artificially produced by state action or through powerful *ayan* bumping into each other in their competition for state titles and resources. Most often, the divide-and-rule strategies of the state lay behind local conflicts. For example, decisions to sell tax farming rights were often carried out strategically to enhance the power of some family against another, sometimes to redirect the efforts of a troublesome notable family, and undoubtedly always with a keen interest in the potential value of the land and resources being auctioned out.[75] The central authorities knew that they had to keep any one notable family from becoming too powerful in a region, lest they break away. Central authorities also knew that by extending state titles and tax farms to notables, they had extended part of their own authority to them, hence, the use of notables in many matters of peace and order. For example, many of these notable strongmen, including Çapar-zade Süleyman of Ankara, Vanlı Çırağı Ismail, the *mütesellim* of Ankara, and Tiryakizade Mustafa, the *ayan* of Sorba, were summoned in 1797 to fight Pasvanoğlu, the infamous warlord-*ayan* of the Vidin region.

Governance regimes also arose from contention among famous pairs of men who started out together in campaigns, or in moneylending and trade. Their competition over land and resources, however, was bound to emerge given the proximity of territories and interests. Therefore, rivalries between major *ayan* dynasties in Anatolia – the Çapanoğlu dynasty from central Anatolia and the Canikli family of northern Anatolia, the Karaosmanoğlus and the Araboğlus, the Tuzcuoğlus and the Hazinedaroğlus – were celebrated products of state and local competition and manipulation. Unquestionably, powerful *ayan* built networks of patronage among the lower *ayan*; they both offered protection and expected loyalty. The powerful *ayan* were also able to provide the members of their extended kinship and friendship networks with *ayan* and

---

[74] Güçlü Tülüveli, "De-Mystification of the Contemporary Historiographical Paradigms: Ottoman Provincial Notables in Historical Perspective," M.A. thesis, Boğaziçi University, Istanbul, 1993.

[75] Khoury shows how the state's anxiety about the rebellious forces in Mosul's hinterland led state elites to sell the land in the area to the Jalili family, whom they believed would be able to counteract local insurgent power. See *State and Provincial Society*, 91.

tax farmer positions. By offering positions to lesser notables, powerful *ayan* were both reproducing the state's redistributive ethic and ensuring that they would be locked into positions while they themselves continued to expand their networks.[76] When conflict arose, much of the contention between *ayan* concerned regional power and staking out networks of patronage and spaces of influence.[77]

Notables and Trade

Dissimilar from networks of contention that marked the boundaries of the regime, networks of generosity deepened the vertical ties of patronage and the horizontal ties of association within the governance regime. These depended, however, on the relative wealth of the various actors involved. The issue of wealth rests on understanding the economic role of the *ayan*; were they involved in Western trade, did they "own" large-scale plantation style estates (*çiftlik*), and did they really alter the agrarian structure of the Ottoman landscape?[78] It made a difference whether the *ayan* were simply glorified tax farmers/tax collectors or self-interested economic actors willing to invest in the production of wealth. Although there are varying opinions in the scholarly literature,[79] the answer seems to be that where there were opportunities for the simultaneous exploitation of tax farming and trade, these pursuits were combined in the person of the *ayan*. The regions that combined Western trade intervention, commercialized agriculture, and changing relations of production were also places where the *ayan* could and did become central nodes among the Ottoman state, international and local merchants, peasants, and producers.[80]

---

[76] See John F. Padgett and Christopher K. Ansell, "Robust Action and the Rise of the Medici, 1400–1434," *American Journal of Sociology* 98 (1993): 1263–1264.

[77] See Özkaya, Osmanlı İmparatorluğunda Ayanlık, 244–247.

[78] See especially Gilles Veinstein, "'Ayan' de la region d'Izmir et le Commerce du Levant (Deuxieme Moitie du XVIIIe Siecle)," *Etudes Balkaniques* 12 (1976): 71–83, and all the articles in Keyder and Tabak, eds., *Landholding and Commercial Agriculture in the Middle East*, especially the introduction by Keyder.

[79] Some argue that the traditional land tenure system in the Balkans was transformed into large plantations based on commercial agriculture. Traian Stoianovich, "Land Tenure and Related Sectors of the Balkan Economy," *Journal of Economic History* 13 (1953): 398–411; Christo Gandev, "L'apparition des rapports capitalistes dans l'économie rurale de la Bulgarie du nord-ouest au cours du XVIIIe siècle," *Etudes Historiques* 1 (1960): 207–220; Fernand Braudel, *The Mediterranean and the Mediterranean World in the Age of Philip II*, 2 vols. (New York: Harper & Row, 1972); Sadat, "Urban Notables in the Ottoman Empire: The Ayan," and her "Rumeli Ayanlari: The Eighteenth Century," *Journal of Modern History* 44 (1972): 346–363; Keyder, "Introduction."

[80] Stoianovitch and others argue that European commercial needs and intervention in Balkan trade led to the relatively quick response of the mostly Muslim landholder/*ayan* to dispossess the mainly Christian peasantry, enclose the lands and pastures, and to hire wage laborers on plantation-like large farms (*çiftlik*). Accordingly, for them this "marks the transition from a social and economic structure founded upon a system of moderate land rent and few labor services to one of excessive land rent and exaggerated service." See his "Land Tenure," 401–402.

The Karaosmanoğlus responded to commercialization.[81] Ataullah and his brothers' estates were involved in both subsistence agriculture, with wheat, barley, vetch, and chickpea cultivation, and in cash marketing, with the excess wheat and barley being sold, bringing in considerable income.[82] Karaosman-zade Hüseyin Pasha (d. 1816) had eight *çiftliks* under his control, with a total value of nearly a quarter of a million *kuruş*, a substantial amount for the eighteenth century. His richest and most productive *çiftlik* was Karaağaçlı, where cash crops such as cotton were cultivated.[83] Although they were all located within the Saruhan Basin, they were not consolidated into European-style plantations. Rather, they remained dispersed, and furthermore, within each *çiftlik*, the traditional peasant family farm unit (*çifthane*) system continued to exist, with the lands divided among the peasants.[84] The manner in which this *ayan* benefited from these estates varied according to type of lands under cultivation and production issues. According to İnalcık, the estates of Hüseyin Pasha included three types of land: "those with fields in which the produce belonged entirely to the landlord, those combining fields of the former with fields rented to the *reaya*, and those *çiftliks* which were simply leased to tenants."[85]

Karaosmanoğlus were involved in production, cultivation, and labor decisions. Where they lacked agricultural workers, they brought in labor from outside; in need of an agricultural labor force for cotton cultivation, one member of the family settled 3,000 Greek peasant migrants from the region of Morea and the Aegean Islands on lands under his tax farming control.[86] The names of these Greek workers appear in the inheritance registers of their employers

---

[81] Although this point, as reported previously, is controversial, the data leave little doubt about its accuracy.

[82] Nagata provides the following information for five *çiftliks* (Papaslı, Mihaili, Cedid, Burunören, and Durasalli) owned by Ataullah and his brothers. Although the amounts provided are not overwhelming, the distinction between "for subsistence" and "for sale" is made, consistent with the understanding that they were aware of production for market but had not fully developed the necessary technology. In fact, Nagata speculates about the expected yields for the area, using these speculations to argue that the yields were not very lucrative. In this particular example, the wheat for subsistence was 2,000 Istanbul *kile* (51,300 kg), and the wheat for sale was 2,427.5 Istanbul *kile* (62,265 kg), bringing in 3,637.5 *kuruş* income. For 1 year and for three cash crops (wheat, barley, and vetch), these five *çiftliks* brought in an income of nearly 5,000 *kuruş*.

[83] This ayan's *çiftliks* have been subjected to careful analysis. Both Nagata and İnalcık have documented the extensive lands that he controlled. Karaağaçlı alone, for example, produced 12,000 *kuruş* worth of cotton, to be compared with the wheat production on five of his *çiftliks*, which amounted to 10,440 *kuruş*.

[84] Halil İnalcık, "Köy, Köylü ve İmparatorluk," *V. Milletlerarası Türkiye Sosyal ve İktisat Tarihi Kongresi, Tebliğler* (Ankara: Türk Tarih Kurumu Basımevi, 1990); "Osmanlılarda Raiyyet Rüsumu," *Belleten* 23 (1959): 575–610.

[85] İnalcık, "The Emergence of Big Farms, Çiftliks," 27. This division of labor becomes clear in the inheritance register of Hacı Hüseyin Ağa, published by Nagata. See Nagata, *Tarihte Ayanlar*, 232–244. These pages show the exploitation of these *çiftliks* as land that the *ayan* almost owned.

[86] Kasaba, "Migrant Labor," 116, and Yuzo Nagata, *Tarihte Ayanlar*, 112. Nagata lists other groups of migrants as well, from eastern Anatolia and the Black Sea region, the Balkans, the Crimea, and the Caucasus.

because they almost always rented rooms from the housing units and hostels that the Karaosmanoğlus endowed as pious endowments (*vakıf*). Similarly, many notables of the southern region of Adana developed many enterprises, especially as cotton became important in trade and they were thus able to turn lands into *çiftlik* estates.[87]

When tax farming was lucrative, but the location was not open to international trade, the *ayan* centered his efforts more on taxation activities.[88] The Çapanoğlus, interestingly, did not develop commercial enterprises or engage in large-scale farming. Mustafa Çapanoğlu is said to have disliked horse breeding and engaged in cattle herding; at his death, he had 80 camels, 80 mules, and about 1,000 head of sheep and goats. The produce from lands under his supervision were distributed to the poor peasants rather than marketed.[89] That the Çapanoğlus were not driven by commercial zeal makes sense for the early expansion of the dynasty, which was geographically located in the Anatolian Basin, circumscribed by the towns of Çorum, Tokat, Yeniil, Kayseri, and Niğde – an area without access to waterways and rather arid in comparison to the coasts. However, by the time Süleyman Bey had taken over in 1782, the region under their control had expanded south to Adana and Tarsus, rich cotton-growing areas of the Mediterranean littoral. That they did not seem to get involved in commercial activity in the face of growing opportunities is indicative of their complacent attitude toward their already existing sources of income. Rather, these *ayan* tax collectors maintained the land and the peasant-based household structure intact, content to collect the taxes prescribed by the state. Intermittently, they skimmed off the top and collected a little extra.

Halil İnalcık shows that in many of the areas cited, the *çiftlik* was developed in essentially different ways, but mostly as the *natural extension* of the increasingly more common practice of life-term tax farming, especially when the likelihood of commerce was high. The lack of state control of the *malikane* tax farms, the lifelong acquisition of these tax farms, and sometimes their extension to the heirs of the tax farmers themselves paved the way for such de facto property rights. İnalcık proposes that simply the stability inherent in rent from life-term tax farming was a motive for *çiftlik* extension.[90]

[87] Tamdoğan-Abel, "Les Modalités de l'urbanité," 88–90.
[88] Many Ottoman historians argue that privatized large properties were marginal in Ottoman lands, and even if they existed, they were not really commercialized. Veinstein, "'Ayan' de la region d'Izmir"; Bruce McGowan, *Economic Life in Ottoman Europe: Taxation, Trade, and the Struggle for Land, 1600–1800* (Cambridge, UK: Cambridge University Press, 1981). Gandev, who argues for the importance of *çiftliks*, also tells us that generally in the Macedonian, Bulgarian, and some Greek lands, *çiftliks* varied from 30 to 500 hectares, with many more concentrated at the bottom of the scale; "L'apparition des rapports capitalistes," 208. Many others have also used these figures when discussing *çiftliks*; see, for example, Kasaba, *The Ottoman Empire and the World Economy*, 24–25.
[89] Uzunçarşılı, "Çapan Oğulları," *Belleten* 38 (1974): 215–261, here 224.
[90] İnalcık, "The Emergence of Big Farms, Çiftliks: State, Landlords and Tenants," in *Landholding and Commercial Agriculture in the Middle East*, 25.

Finally, a careful regional perspective helps link these points together. First, in the regions where commercialization was prominent, there is strong evidence that all concerned – peasants, landholders (traditional or *ayan*), and merchants – responded to the attractions of increased production and commercialization. Areas where Western interests had not penetrated were freer of agricultural changes. It is easy, then, to see agrarian transformations in the Balkans (especially Thessaly, Epirus, parts of Macedonia, Thrace, Maritsa Valley, northwestern Bulgaria, and some coastal plains of Albania) and in western Anatolia (coastal and immediate hinterland).[91] Careful research places the *ayan* as the key regional figures who held tax farms in these areas.[92] According to Frangakis-Syrett, *ayan* were formally and informally involved, setting prices, negotiating with local and foreign merchants and consuls, engaging in competitive bidding among themselves, and ensuring that the production of valued raw materials continued.[93] If they were not involved in actual production for commercial benefit, they made their fortunes as administrative and fiscal authorities taxing commerce.[94] These cases clearly demonstrate that in regions of commercial development and stability of production, the *ayan* were state agents (as tax collectors), tax farmers, landholders, estate owners, merchants, commercial intermediaries, and moneylenders all at once.[95]

---

[91] Stoianovich asserts that by the 1720s Macedonia produced and made cotton available for export and that cotton went to Germany and Austria, first by the overland route from Macedonia to Belgrade and then by way of the Danube to Budapest and Vienna. By the late eighteenth century, half the exports of Macedonia and Thessaly went to Austria, Hungary, and Germany. By the end of the century, 70% of the imports of cotton into France originated in the Ottoman lands. See John R. Lampe and Marvin R. Jackson, *Balkan Economic History, 1550–1950: From Imperial Borderlands to Developing Nations* (Bloomington: Indiana University Press, 1982), 41; Kasaba, *The Ottoman Empire and the World Economy*, 19. The Macedonian region, Seres, known for cotton production, had 300 villages divided among powerful *ağas*, with each man counting between thirty and forty villages in his domain. Among these, for example, was *ayan* Ismail Bey of Seres, who was well acquainted with the merchants of the region. See Stoianovich, "Land Tenure," 403.

[92] In her dissertation, Salzmann places the region in the Balkans with the greatest concentration of *malikane-mukataa* as the following: "in eastern Rumeli in the region comprising the district or sanjak of Sofia, from Nikbolu on the Danube south to Gelibolu, Kavala, Serres, and westward to Kostendil." See "Measures of Empire," 177. Sadat places the *ayan* in the same region as Salzmann, but extends their scope beyond eastern Rumeli to the Danube Basin, to the Vardar, Maritsa, and Struma valleys, thereby covering the most fertile parts of the Balkans. See Sadat, "Urban Notables," 61. From the work of Yuzo Nagata and Halil İnalcık, we know that Bosnia was certainly an area where notables were involved in *çiftliks*, although of smaller size and of a different style than in western Anatolia, where larger estates dominated. See Yuzo Nagata, *Materials on the Bosnian Notables* (Tokyo: Institute for the Study of Languages and Cultures of Asia and Africa, 1979), and idem, *Some Documents on the Big Farms (Çiftliks) of the Notables in Western Anatolia* (Tokyo: Institute for the Study of Languages and Cultures in Asia and Africa, 1976); İnalcık, "The Emergence of Big Farms, Çiftliks."

[93] Frangakis-Syrett, "The Commerce of Smyrna."

[94] Veinstein, "'Ayan' de la region d'Izmir," 71–83.

[95] This information is corroborated many times by French consular reports ranging from Salonica to Izmir to many other port cities. They say that overwhelmingly Jews, Armenians, and Greeks

These commercialized regions also had important colonies of local and foreign merchants. Notables linked merchants to state officials and to landholders simply by virtue of their own trading activities and official positions, as well as through their broader interest in commerce and stability. Because notables belonged to merchant and state networks simultaneously, they brokered relations between them. Furthermore, the most powerful Balkan and western Anatolian notables protected foreign merchants, whom they saw as their main trading allies. Ismail Bey of Serres, Ali Pasha of Janina, and Mehmet Bey of Scutari were known to foreign merchants and consuls as reliable Ottoman notables who deployed their forces to maintain protected trade routes and ensure secure markets. Ismail Bey of Seres was also known to engage in contraband trade in wheat with foreign merchants. Karaosmanoğlu went even further in his sense of obligation toward the European merchant community: when he heard that the French had invaded Egypt, fearing reprisals against the French in the empire, he went to Izmir to convince the merchants there to withdraw with him to the safety of Manisa.[96]

It would not be an exaggeration to say that these regional notables constructed an alternative Ottoman social structure, one that was highly interconnected, yet also organized around powerful alternative nodes of authority, regional dynasties built around influential notables who reproduced central households, extending the business of government to the provinces in a novel manner. Although far from complete, these examples give an idea of the rise of important notable families in the Ottoman countryside, where the leadership, typically fathers and sons, shared in acquiring available local positions and tax farms, and expanded their networks through assistance and cooperation, moneylending, trade, and joint missions against state or other officials. As they negotiated their multiple positions, they constructed dyads and triads of various types of actors, in one transaction bringing state officials and merchants together, while another deal involved peasants and merchants, both foreign and local. The modernity of these actors lies partly in the multiple ways in which they made and remade relations.

The Transitional Modernity of Notables

Advocates of modernization theory have argued that the bourgeoisie has been at the forefront of modernity. In the Balkans, the merchants, especially in Serbia

were involved in industry and commerce. Comparatively, Muslims were less involved in direct commerce, but more in the production of essential materials for commerce. Reports point out that Muslims lived mostly off the revenue of their lands, the interest accrued from loans (interest in this period varied between 20% and 24%), and income from their tax farms. Each activity, in turn, often but not necessarily involved market decisions. I have gleaned this material from the different Consular reports in both Ministère des Affaires Etrangères, Archives Diplomatiques, Mémoires et Documents, Turquie, vols. 8, 9, 13, 15, and Archives Nationales de France, Affaires Etrangères, Série Sous-Série Bi, Correspondence Consulaire, vols. 1051, 1052, 1053.

[96] Sadat, "Urban Notables," 67–68. See also Archives Nationales, AE BIII, 20 December 1076.

and Greece, were the central actors who brought modernity and transmitted the ideas of the Enlightenment and development to the Ottoman provinces. As a result, it had always been assumed that it was really only the Balkan Peninsula that became modernized early and that other regions followed and imitated. At the same time, because the reforms of the nineteenth century were initiated by central government agents, the view of modernity in Ottoman history has been centered around the state. It was, furthermore, not only the state, but also the state in partnership with the West that produced the Tanzimat reforms of the nineteenth century. There is historical truth in both views, although they have operated to the detriment of a third perspective – a regional one – which is now being reinforced.

A careful regional view temporally located in the eighteenth century demonstrates that the notables of the empire were involved in economic growth and in the beginnings of modernity. It is possible, then, to account for a variety of different trajectories within the empire toward transition out of empire. S. N. Eisenstadt argued in his defense of multiple modernities that different forms and processes (not all inline with Western ones) and different sets of actors can promote different paths toward a modern outcome.[97] Even if in the long run they were not successful, the notables represented an alternative form of modernity in the empire, a modernity that they fashioned out of combined commercialization and tax farming opportunities and then extended to other realms of provincial life.

The apparent reorganization of the Ottoman provinces as the result of life-term tax farming and the rise of international commerce brought the Ottoman Empire into a new state–society arrangement that it had not experienced before. Early state–society relations had been based on the incorporation of strong vertical relations that promoted the state as the central node coordinating across numerous separate and often competitive provincial elites; a bird's-eye view of the empire at the end of the eighteenth century showed significant changes. First, the state itself had become more corporate in its organization, with vizier and grandee households competing for power and positions. Second, "society" had also become both more intensely interconnected and refashioned around multiple new nodes of competing local governance regimes. These regimes acted as small states, not only espousing some imperial forms but also advancing some creative adaptations that signaled an alternative transition to modernity.

The eighteenth-century reorganization demonstrated mixed modalities. On the one hand, the structure of domination was still imperial in the continuing strength of the center and in the vertical relations of authority that persisted. The financial data reveal that the state managed to cover its expenses and maintain its financial strength and centralization throughout the eighteenth century. The analysis of state–notable relations also demonstrates continued strength because life-term tax farming represented the extension of state services to the

[97] S. N. Eisenstadt, "Multiple Modernities," *Daedalus* 129 (2000): 1–14.

provinces and was a strategy of extension to the periphery. As such, tax farming, the privatization of public resources, and the strategy of venality of office
were used by the Ottoman state to pursue regional control and economic centralization. This continued extension of ties to the periphery and the insistence
on strong vertical integration was an Ottoman variation on an older practice.
That is, both by continuing to control and to engage in imperial state–society
relations on the periphery, the Ottoman state carried on like an empire. Also,
in its continued ability to protect the peasantry and to interfere in relations
in the provinces, the state demonstrated continued authority. Furthermore,
because not all the traditional prebendal actors had disappeared, and because
the provinces required adjudication between their old and new members, the
state continued to maintain local functions. However, in contrast, in the connections that were forged at the local and horizontal levels and in the struggles
against those who were vying for autonomy and alternatives to state control,
the state engaged in a transitional route to a different political form. Therefore,
the Ottoman Empire was slipping into a nonimperial structure in the expansion
in the number, density, and directionality of the networks in the empire.

The Ottoman state was pushed toward modernity because it had opened
the doors to a new understanding of private property and had cleared the way
for the opportunities associated with private enterprise and the development of
infrastructure and communications for the spread of private enterprise. For the
notables, their potential modernity emerged with the notion of private enterprise, the ability to invest in their future, and the confidence that arose from
being embedded in dense networks of association, but also by their increasingly autonomous agency that questioned the legitimacy of the old order. The
notables switched between roles and occupations, invested in their family enterprises, and consolidated their hold on large stretches of territory. Moreover,
these regional entrepreneurs fashioned themselves differently from the norm of
Ottoman provincial actors and from the centrally based group of rentier capitalists who were at the origins of the tax farming business. Because the rentier
capitalists were content to leave the development of their tax farms to regional
tax farmers, notables cultivated their enterprises and challenged the state on
the notion of private property, gradually turning their lands and sources of
revenue into private estates.[98]

Undoubtedly, notables understood the importance of this groundbreaking
policy of privatization of revenues, both in its impact on their entrepreneurial
abilities and its potential transformative impact on state control. The ambiguity between state portrayal and tax farmer representation of the *malikane*

---

[98] Mehmet Genç provides examples of this process of erosion that affected both the state and
the rentier class over time; see *Osmanlı İmparatorluğu'nda Devlet ve Ekonomi*, 111–117, and
Footnotes 30 and 31 in this chapter. He gives examples of investment in enterprises and argues
that the rentier class of Istanbul rarely developed enterprises, leaving the possibilities wide
open for the regional notables. See also the discussion of the struggles around a "discourse" of
privatization in Salzmann, "Measures of Empire," 151–156.

not only kept actors aware of both their new privileges and their actual limitations, but also affirmed the position of the state as the distributor of these incompletely privatized estates. The language adopted vis-à-vis the *malikane* system remained somewhat blurred, affording both the state and the tax farmers room to bargain. The classification of those who contracted *malikane*s as *sahib* (owner) or *mutasarrıf* (possessor), and in fact, even the use of *malikane*, the Persian–Arabic compound that can be translated as "as if to the owner," provided the tax farmer with a sense that he nearly owned the property.[99]

At various times during the eighteenth century, public discussion of the parceling and inheritance provisions of the *malikane* indicated the degree to which privatization was pregnant with meaning and consequence, and therefore contested by both sides. For the state, it was meant to increase the incentives for careful, long-term investment and care of property. For the notables, these enterprises meant labor and planning, and investment over time, and therefore a well-developed sense of property. However, when they went to court to maintain that this was in fact their property, they were rebuffed.[100] Throughout the eighteenth century, notions of private property were contested, keeping all involved alert and mindful of the limits of their actions. Yet, the state held the ultimate tool, that of confiscation (*müsadere*), which when exercised returned all lands, property, and personal effects to the state. The struggle over the parameters and definitions of private property would have never occurred in the earlier centuries; now it indicated both a challenge to the imperial state and the formulation of an innovative alternative to state control of resources. In various provinces of the empire, forms of privatization proceeded to impose new forms of land ownership and compromises with local landholders and elites. Cuno's analysis of eighteenth-century Egypt clearly demonstrates that one important aspect of an indigenous protomodernity was the way in which landholding rights were consolidated locally through life-term tax farming, inheritance, mortgaging, pawning, and outright selling of land. Once the institutional process was initiated, legal fictions were developed to ensure its continued stability.[101] In addition to Khoury and Salzmann, Doumani makes similar arguments for a local modernity; they each argue for a particular combination of networks of trade, taxation, and relations at the local level among merchants, elites, and peasants formulating novel ways of developing the immediate context.[102]

Two important developments are the structural precursors of this protomodernity. İnalcık's conclusion about the importance of the stability of life-term tax farming has to be considered most seriously. Life-term tax farming

---

[99] Salzmann does a good job of presenting the ambiguity of the terminology and the practice. See "Measures of Empire," 151–156.

[100] Ibid.

[101] Kenneth M. Cuno, "The Origins of Private Property of Land in Egypt: A Reappraisal," *International Journal of Middle Eastern Studies* 12:3 (1980): 247.

[102] Beshara Doumani, *Rediscovering Palestine: Merchants and Peasants in Jabal Nablus, 1700–1900* (Berkeley: University of California Press, 1995).

brought those who were involved in it a stability of tenure never really experienced before in the Ottoman lands. Despite the fact that the state remained strong and always willing to challenge the ownership of the tax farm, this form of tenure has to be seen as a prelude to the development of complete ownership rights in the empire. This revolutionized the individual's understanding of his venture, his willingness to invest in and develop it, and his moorings in the area of his enterprise. In this way, the *ayan* were most probably early entrepreneurs. Second, the conclusion by Rifa'at Abou-el-Haj regarding the development of households in the seventeenth century also has to be taken seriously. In his understanding, first within the state and then in the system at large, the notion of households that mirrored the state multiplied. The *ayan* families can be seen as a form of household, an extended family with servants and retinues. The social form of household and the economic form of the tax farm enterprise coalesced into a unit that could be at the root of the modernization of the empire. Economic enterprises developed around households, and competition – between households and with the state – resulted in the intensification of agriculture and commercialization. These notables were not all illegitimate holders of local state power (as when the state called them *mütegallibe*).[103] Many contemporary travelers commented on the prosperity and generosity of the notables they encountered, and later many would disapprove of the destruction of this regional network by the central state of Mahmud II.[104]

Local notables brought an organic, homegrown modernity to their regions through the development of private enterprises and interethnic relations, and through investment in their communities, their labor forces, and their dependent lesser notable families. Their modernity was reflected first in how seriously they developed their economic and agricultural ventures and in their ability to switch roles and positions; to combine multiple visions of themselves with their relations beyond the local communities; and to imagine communities, networks, and futures that were larger and distant from them. Those who combined tax farming, official taxation, and commerce were especially able to tap into three different forms of thinking and three different types of roles that brought them beyond the more narrow and fixed positions experienced by traditional actors in Ottoman society. They also invested in the infrastructure of their region, in the belief that better roads and better river, sea, and land

---

[103] I used both types as examples: Karaosmanoğlu as the mostly legitimate power and prestige holder whose redistributive ethic remained exemplary; and others, such as Pasvanoğlu, who extracted their positions and control from the state through illegitimate means, and developed exploitative relations with the peasantry, opposing the state at every opportunity. Çapanoğlus from central Anatolia were a more mixed case of a notable dynasty in which some very strong state–notable relations were replaced by weaker or contentious ones over time.

[104] Just a few examples are Adolphus Slade, *Records of Travels in Turkey, Greece, &c., and of a Cruise in the Black Sea, with the Capitan Pasha, in the Years 1829, 1830, and 1831*, 2 vols. (London: Saunders and Otley, 1833); Georges Perrot, *Souvenir d'un Voyage en Asie Mineure* (Paris: M. Levy, 1867); Charles Macfarlane, *Constantinople in 1828*, 2 vols. (London: Saunders and Otley, 1829), vol. II, 110.

communications increased their access to centers of capital and commerce, and provided further opportunities for development.

To take a familiar example, the Karaosmanoğlus were at the forefront of such incipient modernity. Although everywhere in the empire men of wealth established pious endowments (*vakıf*) in order to avoid confiscation of their wealth by the state, this western Anatolian dynasty endowed mosques and *medrese*s (in the traditional fashion), as well as bridges, roads, hostels, rental housing units, and shops. For example, the Greek peasants who emigrated from the Morea were housed in the hostels built by the Karaosmanoğlus, and after they started working, they paid rent to this family. Yuzo Nagata shows that the family constructed fourteen mosques, fifteen *medrese*s, two schools, two libraries, five bridges, thirteen roads, forty-one fountains, and fifteen canals for drawing water to the fountains. Furthermore, the profits from 816 buildings were used to endow pious foundations and were used to provide for the maintenance of these religious and public facilities.[105] Necdet Sakaoğlu provides an in-depth study of another notable who rose to become a vizier, yet who was best known for being the "father" of the region under his control, having established multiple pious foundations; public services; and public buildings, roads, and bridges. Sakaoğlu reports that Köse Pasha was well known for having built up and supported a region long forgotten by the Ottoman state.[106] Tuzcuoğlu, a notable in northern Anatolia, was also known as a father figure in the region. When the state decided to pursue him and empower a neighboring *ayan*, the populace hid him; protected him; and were unwilling to lose him, his services, and his benevolent tax collection because he often prepaid taxes for his peasants. Moving from Divriği, the eastern Anatolian lands of Köse Pasha, to the central Anatolian plateau, we find that in contrast, the Çapanoğlu family in central Anatolia preserved their wealth in precious goods, gold, silver, and furs rather than using it to endow religious or public projects. The Çapanoğlus, whom we have identified as a more intermediary governance regime combining strong state patronage with tax farming and limited commerce, developed pious foundations merely to protect their wealth or to keep shops in the market.[107]

These notables strike us then as the better architects of the modern social fabric of Ottoman society. Especially in western Anatolia and its immediate surroundings, but also scattered around the rest of the empire, notables promoted the wealth and development of their regions with a novel social consciousness that they derived from their close associations and numerous patronage

[105] Yuzo Nagata, "The Role of Ayans in Regional Development during the Pre-Tanzimat Period in Turkey: A Case Study of the Karaosmanoğlu Family," in *Studies on the Social and Economic History of the Ottoman Empire* (Izmir, Turkey: Akademi Kitabevi, 1995), 119–133.

[106] Necdet Sakaoğlu, *Anadolu Derebeyi Ocaklarından Köse Paşa Hanedanı* (Ankara: Yurt Yayınları, 1984).

[107] Osman Bayatlı, *Bergama'da Yakın Tarih Olayları, XVIII–XIX. Yüzyıl* (Izmir: Teknik Kitap ve Mecmua Basımevi, 1957); Ahmet Halaçoğlu, *Teke (Antalya) Mütesellim i Hacı Mehmed Ağa ve Faaliyetleri* (Isparta, Turkey: Fakülte Kitabevi, 2002).

ties. Men such as Araboğlu and Karaosmanoğlu are prominent in the archival records, as well as in the narratives of the people for reasons more than their wealth and their political acumen. They were acclaimed in the stories people told from generation to generation because they involved themselves in the affairs of the community, they made themselves known to everyone, and as patrons they both protected and punished in what seemed to be just ways. They built roads and bridges, and they brought water to the towns, and in all these activities they used the language of the people, engaging them to become members of the community. Osman Bayatlı collected many stories told by the elder citizens of Bergama, who have heard from their parents and grandparents the tales of Araboğlu and Karaosmanoğlu rule. One such story is about bringing water from the Geyikli River to Bergama. The narrative emphasizes both the importance of water and the consequences of its availability, and the manner in which Araboğlu enticed commoner and privileged alike to work at digging and constructing waterways, never shying away himself from actual involvement in labor.[108] While the men built, the women demonstrated a different kind of social involvement, entering the social and private lives of others, providing examples of dress and fashion and lifestyle. The French consul reported often on important social occasions, from the "jeered" parties to the wedding parties that the Karaosmanoğlu dynasty held.[109] It is therefore possible to think of these notable families as modern architects of Turkey, certainly more involved in local community building than the state ever was in this time period.

Conclusion

In the provinces in this century, then – through the development of networks of tax farming and trade – power, control, wealth, and social status became much more widespread in the empire, a development strongly analogous to the political empowerment described in Chapter 6. The notables, the architects of this new social and cultural structure, made and remade relations among diverse groups and contructed their own dynastic governance regimes by manipulating the interstices of the land and tax structure of the empire. They were able to do so not only because of their personal strength and acumen, but also mostly by exploiting the gaps in the provision of state services. Yet, they did not do this haphazardly, but in an organized, ordered, and semi-imperial way because that was their model. They reproduced at the regional level the relations of the center. They also added a novel form of governance; however, a new sensibility toward rule that stemmed from becoming a less segmented, more tightly integrated – both vertically and horizontally – and smaller unit.

---

[108] The stories that peasants from western Anatolia told early researchers at the turn of the century have been widely ignored. Yet, they are invaluable as sources for deeper understanding of how members of the society actually viewed these notables and recounted their interactions with them. A book that values such narratives is Bayatlı, *Bergama'da Yakın Tarih Olayları XVIII.–XIX. Yüzyıl*; see page 23 for details.

[109] Archives Nationales, Affaires Etrangères, BI 1053, letter written on 27 November 1752.

The eighteenth century produced transformations that altered the architecture of empire. Two major outcomes have been addressed in recent chapters: the empowerment of multiple and diverse social forces in society, and the politicization of demands in a series of nested households. In a paradoxical fashion, and unlike the other major example of tax farming, this quite old-fashioned scheme of indirect taxation that essentially lacked a system of accountability became a source for local movements of protomodernity. Although the immediate effects of such investment, development, and political mobilization were positive, in the long run, tax farming on such a widespread and extended scale became a liability. In Chapter 8, I explore why such changes brought about a road out of empire, rather than a readaptation of it. By the end of the eighteenth century, the empire was no longer fully imperial in its formal structure.

8

On the Road Out of Empire: Ottomans Struggle from Empire to Nation-State

The key transformations that pushed the empire toward a remodeling of state–society relations coincided, taking effect from the end of the seventeenth century through the beginning of the nineteenth century. Two connected processes pushed the state toward a recalibration of state–society relations: one mainly economic, the increasing commerce with western Europe and the overhaul of the tax system starting in the late seventeenth century; and the other political, the increasing empowerment of different social groups in the nonstate arena. The social transformation discussed in prior chapters had indigenous roots that adapted to social and economic conditions. Even if these indigenous forces did not pose a serious threat to the state, changes in them affected Ottoman central elites deeply, signaling an inevitable challenge to the premise of empire: state control through segmentation and vertical integration. That such internal reorganization was occurring during a period of intense warfare when the Ottomans were in a rather grim international position with respect to foreign affairs intensified the risks for the empire and made the role of the state even more critical.

Given such internal transformations and international exigencies, the Ottomans chose to embark on a period of remodeling and centralization that would result in the construction of a modern state. Yet, the new forms of centralization – conceived as responses to international threats, to Balkan demands for autonomy and independence, as well as to internal transformations of regional- and provincial-level administration – were without a doubt dissimilar to past imperial forms of centralization. The centralization measures were responses to the new patterns of associative social organization (emerging from commerce and taxation), the Balkan demands for autonomy and independence from imperial domains, as well as serious international threats. Consequently, the empire that in the past had centralized by vertical integration and coordination of multiple deals with various contenders for regional power would now have to emulate what was seen at the time as successful centralization, especially the new European models of standardized reform and consolidation of power at the center. Ottomans, therefore, in their new understanding of reform and centralization, embarked in the direction of nonempire, suspending negotiated forms of rule and the diversity of bargaining between state and society. They instituted standardized forms that signified a different idiom of rule with changing legitimacy and a new understanding of diversity that would accelerate the path to nationhood.

I do not intend to explicate here the full breadth of the nineteenth-century reorganization and construction of the foundations of the modern Turkish state. By instead returning to the three principles that keep empires dominant – legitimacy, control and integration of elites, and diversity – I want to address the unresolved issues of decentralization and decline, the changing role of Islam and its confounded legacy in the transition from empire to nation, and finally the construction of a new identity based not on diversity, but rather on nationality. Each was affected by a top-down, forced centralization, imposed from the end of the eighteenth century on, signaling a return to the state, but in a new form. Over time, most of the imperial forms withered away, taking empire as a political formation with them. In the nineteenth century, empire faded away in the face of a plurality of forms, some imperial, some national, and some more hybrid, leaving the empire looking like a modern failed state, with "imperial" authoritarian forms of government coexisting with policies of nationalizing, while the reality on the ground was one of indomitable diversity.

War, trade, and taxation were the major macrohistorical factors that impinged on the networks of state–society relations, forcing them into new, more formal and less flexible patterns with separation and closure, and finally leading to violent nationalizing state action. How the Ottoman state responded to the challenges of war, trade, and taxation shaped the forms of centralization, as well as the discourse about and future of the empire. The first section explores the economic exigencies of war, trade, and taxation, which shaped state policies and ultimately made for financial ruin. Having allowed for a century of financial decentralization, the state was unable to rein in and to coalesce the extended networks of trade and tax farming around state needs. The second section reviews the impact of trade, reform, Balkan politicization, and Muslim refugee immigration into the heartlands of the empire. As demands for autonomy coincided with a policy of hard-core centralization, tensions mounted between different ethnic and religious groups and the state. Here, the state participated in the closure of networks across religion and ethnicity by enhancing Muslim education and separation at a time of great economic disparity between *millets*, when the Muslim populations of the empire were reeling under the stress of economic disadvantage and the refugee influx from contested regions of the empire. The last section demonstrates that the policies adopted to legitimize an unstable order were diverse, but that state policies limited the choice of legitimization increasingly toward a national order rather than an imperial one.

Toward State Centralization

We left the empire in 1808, when the notables from the provinces had marched to Istanbul to rescue the reformist forces from a coup at the center, shoring up the sultan and making their provincial voices heard and their provincial armies seen. The provincial notables not only signaled their aptitude for alliance building among themselves by becoming the main nodes of vertical and horizontal linkages in the empire, but they also positioned themselves as serious economic players, political interlocutors, and among the most progressive modernizers of the empire. If such regional activity indicates a certain amount of decentralization, did it necessarily spell the end of the empire? How do we explain the politics of centralization and reformation that ensued after 1808?

The transformation of state–society relations during the long eighteenth century (1695–1808) set the empire on a trajectory of transition from empire to multiple nation-states. It was during the eighteenth century that the changes in the nature and form of state–society relations changed enough that the imperial compact was slowly deconstructed. The empowerment of a broader social base, both politically and economically, and the resulting spread of connectivity through networks, changed the nature of imperial state control over social groups, pushing state actors toward a retightening of control and consolidation in the nineteenth century, although under a new model that was "national" rather than "imperial." The difficulty of eighteenth-century warfare continuing into the nineteenth century, especially against Russia, also pressed the Ottomans on a trajectory toward administrative and military reorganization, a route that would unravel imperial compacts and shift the empire toward the construction of new standardized forms of rule.

An alternative scenario to centralization claims that the eighteenth century had perhaps engendered sufficient indigenous modernity, with wealthy and politically powerful regional notables who could have built a federal structure, to avoid the painful and bloody change from empire to nation. I stay away from this interpretation, showing how the developments of the eighteenth century and the enmity of Russia made it necessary for the Ottoman rulers of the nineteenth century to recentralize, to renew their military forces, and to find solutions in the direction of direct and centralized taxation. Çağlar Keyder describes that at the time there was such a view that preferred federalism. It was a Tanzimat view, liberal and Ottomanist, presented and backed by the National Liberals and by Greek and Armenian merchants in Anatolia who preferred a multiethnic, federalist state. They saw such a political formation in Tanzimat terms of equality among all subjects, but with the additional benefit of federalism, that is, ethnic and territorial autonomy. Given the political climate of the period, however, Keyder is similarly doubtful of the prospective success of this approach to imperial integration. Roderic Davison makes this point differently when he argues that the Ottomans in this period did not try federalism because they understood the dangers of trying to impose such a system onto an intense mosaic of *millets*.[1] Instead, the task of centralization and national unification consumed Ottoman leadership through the nineteenth and early twentieth centuries, and they only partially succeeded; more important, centralization also led to warped understandings of the reformers' mission, with dire consequences.

From the early nineteenth century on, when various groups in the Balkans began agitating for change, the climate in the empire was somber. First among the Serbian population and then among the Greek populations of the empire, leaders began agitating for autonomy and independence. In this, they were supported by foreign powers also eager to interfere in Ottoman affairs; among them the most forceful at infiltrating the Balkans was the Russian Empire. The Ottoman Empire found itself surrounded by enemies that had managed to centralize, develop standing armies, and contest Ottoman sovereignty in many territories much more successfully than they had before, Russia being the prime example. Both the Habsburg and the Russian Empires continued their warfare against the Ottomans, but with the Russians also increasingly interfering in the affairs of the Balkan Orthodox populations, inciting them toward rebellion against the empire.

The wars with Austria and Russia were not particular to the nineteenth century, although their effect was strongly felt throughout this time period. From 1736 to 1739, Austria and Russia had inflicted some losses on the Ottomans, although they had recouped much of their territory toward the end of the conflict. For the Ottomans, the more important lesson of the war was the recognition of Russian military organization and strength, the result of administrative and military reforms starting with Peter the Great. Warfare was resumed after Catherine of Russia attacked the Ottomans on multiple fronts from 1768 to 1774, with the resulting takeover from the Ottomans of the Danubian Principalities and the Crimea. After the Treaty of Küçük Kaynarca in 1774, where the Russians asserted their claims over the Orthodox population of the empire, a third round of warfare between 1787 and 1792 ended with the Treaty of Jassy, a moment when European powers shielded the empire from further territorial losses as well as more humiliating agreements with the Russians. Experience of international warfare against increasingly better-organized adversaries would also force the Ottoman state toward the modernization implied by better armies and administrative capacities.

Reform was initiated by Selim III (1789–1807) and continued by Mahmud II, then pursued during the era of the Tanzimat (1839–1876) and finally reformulated during the reign of Abdülhamid II (1876–1909). The Young Turk

[1] Çağlar Keyder, "The Ottoman Empire," in *After Empire: Multiethnic Societies and Nation-Building, the Soviet Union and Russian, Ottoman, and Habsburg Empires*, ed. Karen Barkey and Mark von Hagen (Boulder, CO: Westview Press, 1997), 30–45; Roderic Davison, "Nationalism as an Ottoman Problem and an Ottoman Response," in *Nationalism in a Non-National State: The Dissolution of the Ottoman Empire*, ed. William W. Haddad and William Ochsenwald (Columbus: Ohio State University Press, 1977), 25–56.

Revolution was to provide another twist to reform and centralization, a result of pressure from increasing internal and international conflict. Starting with Selim, a new westernized army corps was established (the Nizam-I Cedid Army) within a larger field of reform entitled Nizam-I Cedid or the New Order (1792–1793). During the reign of Mahmud II (1808–1839), the renewed effort to continue military reforms led to the final confrontation between the state and the Janissaries, leading to their demise.[2] Mahmud's centralization effort was directed against the central and regional elements who were seen as the causes of decay and disorder: notables and military fiefholders in the provinces, and state administration at the center. He reorganized the state into units that emulated the French administrative model, with various ministries and departments, a new separation of executive and legislative branches of government, and a reformulation of the payment structure for members of the state.

When the Tanzimat was ushered in, the goals of the reformers were fairly clear; they were stated in the formal decree of Gülhane Hatt-I Hümayun in 1839. The reformers pledged to guarantee the life, honor, and property of all subjects of the sultan, as well as their equality under the law, and to establish a military system of conscription, while also reforming the antiquated tax farming system by switching to a state-controlled, direct system of taxation. The state–society reorganization that ensued was only partially successful in that, despite many attempts at standardization and rationalization, imperial forms of state–notable bargains continued and were flagrant examples of an old and rejected mode of imperial relations.[3]

There are many reasons why centralization was absolutely necessary to reformers. First, consider the international conditions within which the empire existed. The empire's fiercest adversary, Russia, was a much stronger political and military entity than the Ottomans. Russia had already started industrializing successfully during the reign of Peter the Great and had developed a standing army with the modern features of European armies.[4] In contrast to the Ottomans, the Russians had large manpower resources, and by 1750,

---

[2] There are many sources on the long nineteenth century and the reforms of the period. I have used and consulted these in the historical background materials in this chapter. Among the best known are Carter V. Findley, *Bureaucratic Reform in the Ottoman Empire: The Sublime Porte* (Princeton, NJ: Princeton University Press, 1980); Erik Zürcher, *Turkey: A Modern History* (London: I. B. Tauris, 1993); Bernard Lewis, *The Emergence of Modern Turkey*, 2d ed. (Oxford, UK: Oxford University Press, 1961); Stanford J. Shaw and Ezel Kural Shaw, *History of the Ottoman Empire and Modern Turkey*, Vol. 2: *Reform, Revolution, and Republic: The Rise of Modern Turkey 1808–1975* (Cambridge, UK: Cambridge University Press, 1977); Roderic H. Davison, *Reform in the Ottoman Empire, 1856–1876* (Princeton, NJ: Princeton University Press, 1963).

[3] Yonca Köksal, "Local Intermediaries and Ottoman State Centralization: A Comparison of the Tanzimat Reforms in the Provinces of Ankara and Edirne (1839–1878)," Ph.D. dissertation, Columbia University, New York, 2002.

[4] Peter the Great's army had grown to 200,000 in 1745, while Catherine had 500,000 in 1796, and by the Crimean War, Russia had a standing army of 800,000. See George L. Yaney, *The Systematization of Russian Government: Social Evolution in the Domestic Administration of*

Russia, with one-fifth of the revenues of the French monarchy, had the world's largest standing army.[5] It had become a formidable enemy on the battlefield, and the Ottomans saw this in the series of wars they fought against Russia, among them one from 1768 to 1774 that ended in a humiliating defeat. The Ottomans had experienced no such modernization, industrialization, or military reform as yet, and some Ottoman statesmen were sorely aware of their comparative disadvantage.

Second, the military situation of the empire ought to be considered together with its financial state, especially the state's inability toward the end of the eighteenth century to increase resources significantly. When Selim III developed a comprehensive model of military reform, establishing a fund to pay for a new military class of soldiers and developing new bases in Rumelia and Anatolia to enlist a new army, he encountered financial difficulties. The army that he formed grew from 2,000 to 120,000 in the 1830s. Income from lucrative tax farms was redirected in 1793 to endow a new treasury for the military and training needs of this army,[6] diminishing the income of the old treasury. Yet, as we know, his reign was short lived, and his efforts met with much resistance, especially from groups that were directly threatened by reform, such as the Janissaries, an institution no longer of value to the state.[7] Mahmud II was to continue with much more effect the reforms of Selim III, centralizing the state administration, reforming the military, and incorporating within the ambit of his program some of the more recalcitrant *ulema*.[8] An essential and early prerequisite of centralization would be financial recovery.

Imperial Russia, 1711–1905 (Urbana: University of Illinois Press, 1973). For reform and modernization in Russia, see Walter McKenzie Pintner, *Russian Economic Policy under Nicholas I* (Ithaca, NY: Cornell University Press, 1967); *Russian Officialdom: The Bureaucratization of Russian Society from the Seventeenth to the Twentieth Century*, ed. Walter McKenzie Pintner and Don Karl Rowney (Chapel Hill: University of North Carolina Press, 1980).

[5] Virginia Aksan, "Ottoman Military Recruitment Strategies in the Late Eighteenth Century," in *Arming the State: Military Conscription in the Middle East and Central Asia, 1775–1925*, ed. Erik J. Zürcher (London and New York: I. B. Tauris, 1999), 24.

[6] Stanford J. Shaw, *Between Old and New: The Ottoman Empire under Sultan Selim III, 1789–1807* (Cambridge, MA: Harvard University Press, 1971); idem, "The Origins of Ottoman Military Reform: The Nizam-I Cedid Army of Sultan Selim III," *Journal of Modern History* 37 (1965): 298–299; Musa Çadırcı, "Ankara Sancağında Nizam-I Cedid Ortasının Teşkili ve 'Nizam-I Cedid Askeri Kanunnamesi,'" *Belleten* 36 (1972); Sipahi Çataltepe, *19. Yüzyıl Başlarında Avrupa Dengesi ve Nizam-I Cedid Ordusu* (Istanbul: Göçebe Yayınları, 1997).

[7] It is said that at this period there were about 400,000 Janissaries who were supposed to protect the entire empire. Among these, about 60,000 were at work and in position, but only about 25,000 went to war. For the state, then, these soldiers represented wasted resources. Çadırcı, "Ankara Sancağında Nizam-I Cedid Ortasının Teşkili."

[8] Much has been written about Mahmud II as a reformer. See Shaw and Shaw, *History of the Ottoman Empire and Modern Turkey*; Halil İnalcık, "Sened-I Ittifak ve Gülhane Hatt-I Hümayunu," *Belleten* 28 (1964), 603–690; Uriel Heyd, "The Ottoman Ulema and Westernization in the Time of Selim III and Mahmud II," *Scripta Hierosolymitana* 9 (1961); Avigdor Levy, "The Ottoman Ulema and the Military Reforms," *Asian and African Studies* 7 (1971); Stanford J. Shaw, "The Nineteenth-Century Ottoman Tax Reforms and Revenue System," *International Journal of Middle Eastern Studies* 6 (1975): 421–459.

Decentralization, Decline, or Restoration under Federalism: The Role of Tax Farming

States engage in the privatization of their key functions, such as taxation, military control, or administration, either when they are in search of immediate sources of income or when the transaction costs for state officials to carry out these tasks is too great. In particular, traditional land-based empires – as far-flung territorial entities with diverse lands and peoples and less developed technology – made use of privatization. However, as even modern examples (e.g., the United States' privatization of its security forces in Iraq) clearly show, this policy may be efficient at first, but in the long run it leads to decentralization, corruption, replacement of patronage ties with the money nexus, and, most important, loss of state control of some crucial public functions.[9] As Rome demonstrated and as the Ottomans vividly experienced in the nineteenth century, the tax farming system that had been allowed to develop during one long century might have become too decentralized and was dissipated into the hands of many. Nineteenth-century dynamics required that such rich sources of taxation be reclaimed and moved from the realm of private tax farming to public tax collection. Between administrative and legal reforms and increasing military needs, the expenditures of the central government skyrocketed by 250% to 300%.[10] Such a development required better tax collection for the central treasury, especially the transformation of indirect to direct taxes as the increasingly efficient state bureaucracy took over the role of tax collection.

Countries that had successfully industrialized had also been able to shift from indirect to direct taxes and from private tax farmers to public salaried tax collectors and a stable bureaucratic apparatus. The Ottomans had effectively managed the collection of direct taxes for centuries; yet, during the eighteenth century, they had also been content to permit the development of a state-affiliated, bureaucratic, rentier class that allowed it to share the benefits of indirect tax farm–based collection of resources. The Ottomans, in the face of a severe financial crisis, tried to alleviate it through various means, among which was control over tax farming.

---

[9] Ramsay MacMullen, *Corruption and the Decline of Rome* (New Haven, CT: Yale University Press, 1988). The comparison of the United States with Rome has been made frequently in academic and journalistic circles. This comparison emphasizes that what happened in Rome – state functions being put into private hands – worked only because money became the primary determinant. The result of such privatization is decentralized control, but also less and less state control of functions that were originally public. The Roman example is being played out in America. Parts of the U.S. government are being outsourced, as we see in the military, prisons, border security, and even national intelligence operations. Rome warns us that when such privatization of functions is allowed to spread, it is harder and harder to draw them back in and reconnect them to the system for the state's benefit. See Cullen Murphey, *Are We Rome? The Fall of an Empire and the Fate of America* (New York: Houghton Mifflin, 2007).

[10] Şevket Pamuk, *The Ottoman Empire and European Capitalism, 1820–1913: Trade, Investment and Production* (Cambridge, UK: Cambridge University Press, 1987); idem, *A Monetary History of the Ottoman Empire* (Cambridge, UK: Cambridge University Press, 2000), 189.

The source of wealth and development in the provinces was the result of life-term tax farming, the quasi-privatization of local enterprise through the farming out of revenues. Between the center and the provinces, thousands of tax farmers, managers, financiers, and intermediaries spread through the empire and controlled the majority of the revenue from taxes, villages, businesses, customs duties, and many other income-producing investments. The men in the provinces had become especially adept at manipulating the system to pass their revenue streams to the next generation, while their patrons in Istanbul – who profited heavily – closed their eyes to local abuses. Even though many of these enterprises became lucrative, as I showed in Chapter 7, they were never centralized, organized as a cartel, or forced under the aegis of the state. They remained quintessentially decentralized ventures, on the verge of developing modern, capitalist, shareholding enterprises. In fact, Çizakça argues that the tax farmers were on the threshold of inventing the joint stock company as some groups had achieved many of the requirements for such institutional arrangements to emerge.[11] They never did emerge, however, because the state was not interested in providing opportunities for the tax farmers, instead wanting to eliminate them and bring in their resources.

The Ottoman state, unlike England and France, was never able to centralize the tax farms into one large, bureaucratic entity with increasingly refined modes of collection and control. As in France and England, the Ottoman state engaged in struggles with tax farmers, but always ended up in negotiated settlements with diverse groups of them, or evicted them from their tax farms. Moreover, when they tried to bypass the tax farmers and hire an entirely new staff of salaried officials (*muhassıls*) to go to the provinces to collect taxes instead of the tax farmers, they had practically no success. There were not enough officials ready to accept a salary and collect taxes, and the tax farmers were certainly not willing to relinquish their positions to become salaried officials. By 1840, the tax farming system was reestablished, and the notables had won. The response from the government was to work on reforming and increasing other taxes that could be collected directly.[12]

Besides, the life-term tax farm, the *malikane*, had been overly exploited and was not providing enough resources for the government. The average profit-to-down payment ratio of the tax farm had steadily declined, making it less profitable for the *malikane* owner, therefore curbing the interest of potential buyers. Moreover, the best available resources had been converted already, and there were not many new and lucrative *malikane*s available for exploitation. Last, the state was weary of the corruption that had set in, leaving the central authority unable to monitor the life courses of the *malikane* owners in order to

---

[11] Murat Çizakça, *A Comparative Evolution of Business Partnerships: The Islamic World and Europe, with Specific References to the Ottoman Archives* (Leiden, The Netherlands and New York: Brill, 1996).

[12] Stanford Shaw shows that many other taxes were collected more or less adequately in the early nineteenth century. See his "The Nineteenth-Century Ottoman Tax Reforms."

recapture and resell the *malikane*. Life-term tax farming was a spent force. But how does a state rein in this brittle and friable system, with so many diverse and loosely interconnected groups with an interest in the continuation of the overall practice?

If we look at this problem from an institutional point of view, it becomes clear that once the Ottomans had started on a path of tax farming and institutionalized the system, it became costly for both the state and the agents of privatization to reverse their course of action.[13] Therefore, when Ottoman state elites had adapted to the fiscal conditions of the eighteenth century by financially decentralizing and privatizing public sources of income, it became clear that they could not recentralize without great cost. The Ottomans attacked this problem from a variety of directions. They formulated alternative schemes for increasing central resources, tried to increase and enhance existing direct taxes, and attacked individual tax farmers rather than the institution itself. Each scheme essentially failed, leading to the financial collapse of the empire. With the realization that life-term tax farming did not provide enough resources and would require too much reorganization and control, and especially, after one more expensive war (with Russia from 1768 to 1774), they were forced to experiment yet again with alternatives. The Ottomans opted for an alternative financial scheme, called *esham*, a system of domestic borrowing with annual net revenues from a tax source specified in name only and divided into shares sold to the larger public for the lifetime of buyers. The annual revenue was sold for six to seven times the annual net payments; the tax farmers continued to collect the revenues. Şevket Pamuk argues that *esham* increasingly looked like life-term annuity.[14] In the tradition of maintaining multiple systems working at the same time, the state maintained *malikane*, *esham*, and a hybrid version – *malikaneli esham* – all together, undermining its own finances. It quickly became apparent that the coexistence of two cash-generating methods was problematic. Both methods were siphoning demand from the same market, and each method became a threat to the applicability and efficiency of the other.

Parallel to such efforts, government financiers also continued with the traditional method of devaluation of the silver *akçe*, especially during the reign of Mahmud II (1808–1839). One especially dramatic devaluation occurred after the abolition of the Janissaries in 1826 because they were the most threatened by such government policies and most likely to resist.[15] In the mid-nineteenth century, another solution was attempted, the printing of interest-bearing paper

---

[13] Paul Pierson, *Politics in Time: History, Institutions, and Social Analysis* (Princeton, NJ: Princeton University Press, 2004), 20. See also Thomas Ertman, *Birth of the Leviathan: Building States and Regimes in Medieval and Early Modern Europe* (Cambridge, UK: Cambridge University Press, 1997).

[14] Şevket Pamuk, "The Evolution of Financial Institutions in the Ottoman Empire, 1600–1914," *Financial History Review* 11 (2004): 18.

[15] Pamuk, *The Ottoman Empire and European Capitalism*, 193–200.

money, although this was effective only in the short term.[16] It seems that in these government financial policies, the Ottomans chose solutions that would raise money for the treasury quickly and dramatically but without lasting benefits. Again, we should extend the term "fiscalist" – used by economist Mehmet Genç to characterize the Ottoman financial mentality in the classical age – to the understanding of later centuries as well. The response to financial burdens was the immediate rethinking of taxation and monetary policy to swiftly fill the treasury, but leaving long-term needs unaddressed. This is evident in the choice of the *esham* system, a clear failure in that individuals who bought shares in the tax farms recovered their losses rather quickly and went on to make larger profits directly paid by the state. This type of arrangement was an interim rather than a planned and long-term solution.

Beyond the financial methods themselves, the government sorted out the networks of individuals entrenched in their central or provincial positions. The established tradition had been to negotiate settlements among the state, the central tax farmers, and various layers of tax farmer/notables, with a tendency to increasingly decentralize and distribute wealth rather than consolidate it. This tradition thus fit the old imperial style of a distributive, negotiated standard of state–society relations, rather than an accumulative mentality. Unshakable in this mentality, both sides – the state and the various tax farming groups – continued to accommodate and in many ways encroach on each other's resources, with neither side benefiting from the other's potential, nor with the tax farmers benefiting from their combined potential. The tax farmers often defaulted on their obligations, trying to maximize their long-term property rights, and the state tried to eliminate tax farmers, often by violent means.

There were many reasons for the difficulties inherent in the renegotiation of tax farming. Undoubtedly, the vast geography of the empire, with the extension of tax farming to many different realms of resource collection and the various levels of subcontracting, made reining in the system impossible. We also have to pay attention to the identity of the central Ottoman tax farming class. That the group of central tax farmers were members of the Ottoman state themselves, military and civilian grandees with important resources, made it unlikely that the state could impose its will on them or easily expropriate them. The rentier group of *malikane* owners was actually not doing that well financially, but nonetheless held onto positions and alliances with the provincial notables. In this way the state, by having extended tax farming contracts to its own patronage networks, and the rentier tax farmers, by having become dependent on the state, were equally constrained. The local intermediaries, the notables with multiple skills and positions, the *nouveau riche* of the provinces, also remained attached to their central rentier patrons. They gained political favors and the benefit of direct linkages to Istanbul more than financial gain because notables themselves had become the main cash-generating group in the empire. The rentier group had nowhere else to go. As a rentier class rather than as

[16] Pamuk, "The Evolution of Financial Institutions," 25.

financiers (as in France and England,) the life-term tax farmers had devolved their financial and administrative powers and delegated them to local notables, further distancing the state from its ability to negotiate directly. In this way, life-term tax farming was neither a rupture with the old forms of negotiated tax collection, nor successful in engendering a protomodern tax system. As we will see, the state attacked the people in the system more than the institution itself.

The Ottoman government, in need of cash and cognizant of European forms of public taxation, attempted to undermine the actors embedded in its ineffective, decentralized tax farming. Since 1808, it had also been clear that the notables had transformed their economic might into political power. Recentralization of resources could not be carried out without removing the notables from their positions of regional power. Mahmud II understood well this relation between economic, political centralization and the notables. He doggedly attempted to remove notables peacefully and forcefully, when necessary. Anatolian and Balkan notables who died were not replaced. Central agents were sent to take over their taxation duties. As a result, by 1820, Mahmud II had managed to bring many localities in Rumelia and the Balkans under his direct control. In the Balkans, perhaps the most difficult notable to eliminate was Ali Pasha of Janina, whose defeat in 1822 came at the price of significant military and financial resources. Combining negotiations, ruse, and force, the center also eliminated the important Anatolian notables, Çapanoğlu and Karaosmanoğlu, among the most significant players in central politics. The containment of the Arab notables was harder and took longer, although with the appointment in 1860 of Mithat Pasha as governor of Iraq, the more influential notables had been eliminated.[17]

Starting in 1820, the government tried to sever the relationship between the rentier bureaucrats at the center and the powerful notable intermediaries, hoping that by breaking these ties they would weaken tax farming. The state abolished the tax farming system in 1839, but permitted it again 2 years later. When the tax system was put under the management of salaried Ottoman officials, the surviving shareholders were summarily evicted. The state's interest, although not always successfully maintained, was that with each defeated notable, political and financial gains were to be had.

The Ottoman state did not manage successfully the transition to the centralization and nationalization of indirect sources of taxation. As we have seen, it attempted alternative financial and political means of economic rehabilitation, but the state was never able to raise the money necessary for the expenses it incurred during the wars. Especially with the establishment of European banks in the Ottoman Empire, the government began to borrow heavily from Europe. The Crimean War (1853–1856), the War of 1877–1878 against Russia, and the suppression of the Cretan Revolt in 1869 cost the Ottoman state great sums. Although the Ottoman state struggled with different economic responses to the

[17] Shaw and Shaw, *History of the Ottoman Empire*, vol. 2, 14–16.

financial crisis it had engendered in 1875, it was bankrupt, and it declared a moratorium on its foreign debt, which amounted to 200 million pounds sterling.[18] An Ottoman Public Debt Administration (PDA) was established in 1881 that put Ottoman finances under European control, especially that of France, Britain, and Germany. The financial history of the Empire until World War I went through similar crises at wartime and increased European administration to protect European investments in the empire, and to force the Ottomans to provide revenue to direct toward servicing and repaying foreign debt. Although the PDA improved Ottoman finances somewhat, the financial crisis continued through the reign of Abdülhamid II and the Young Turks, creating discontent at all layers of Ottoman society.

Returning to our original question of why the Ottomans were prone to such financial crises in the last centuries of rule, we have to compare the Ottomans' ability to end tax farming with two more successful cases of transition out of empire, England and France. At different times, but more or less through similar circumstances, the two countries forced the centralization of tax farms into one larger monopolistic entity, facilitating their eventual transition to the public domain.[19] In England, the process was initiated with the Great Farm of the customs in 1604, with this new institution incorporating many other tax revenues over time. In both cases, once the thorough centralization of tax farms into one great farm was consolidated, such a powerful and resourceful entity threatened the state, although its increasing efficiency at tax collection and centralized administration provided a model for the state to emulate. When the consolidated tax farming monopoly was transferred into public hands, in both cases the crown benefited from the tax farmers' experience in collecting indirect taxes and from the existence of an organized set of detailed management and personnel records that facilitated the bureaucratization of tax collection.

The comparative history of tax farming seems to indicate that countries that are successful at the transition from tax farming to a modern, bureaucratic form of tax collection are those where privatized tax collection was transformed into government-administered public collection. In both England and

---

[18] Manfredi Pittioni, "The Economic Decline of the Ottoman Empire," in *The Decline of Empires*, ed. Emil Brix, Klaus Koch, and Elisabeth Vyslonzil (Vienna: Verlag für Gechichte und politik, 2001), 21–44; Pamuk, "The Evolution of Financial Institutions," 26; Donald Quataert, "The Age of Reforms, 1812–1914," in *An Economic and Social History of the Ottoman Empire, 1300–1914*, ed. Halil İnalcık and Donald Quataert (Cambridge, UK: Cambridge University Press, 1994), 759–943; Roger Owen, *The Middle East in the World Economy 1800–1914* (London: Methuen, 1981); Charles Issawi, *The Economic History of the Middle East 1800–1914* (Chicago: The University of Chicago Press, 1966).

[19] John Brewer, *The Sinews of Power: War, Money and the English State, 1688–1788* (Cambridge, MA: Harvard University Press, 1988), 4–24. For excellent works on the French tax farming system, see Daniel Dessert, *Argent: Pouvoir et société au grand siècle* (Paris: Fayard, 1984); George T. Matthews, *The Royal General Farms in 18th-Century France* (New York: Columbia University Press, 1958). See also Eugene N. White, "From Privatized to Government-Administered Tax Collection: Tax Farming in Eighteenth-Century France," *Economic History Review* 57:4 (2004): 636–663.

France, tax collection, despite privatization, had remained under state control. There was ample opportunity to renegotiate state tax farming arrangements because they came up for renewal often. The Ottoman-style life-term lease made both renewal and renegotiation awkward and less frequent. The tremendous size of the empire provided the opportunity both for the spread of tax farming to faraway places on the periphery and for its establishment out of the reach of direct state or rentier supervision. The tax farmers were also not a homogeneous group in the Ottoman Empire, whereas they were from similar areas, backgrounds, and social circles in France and England. In the Ottoman Empire, central palace officials, palace women, Christians, and Jews, and, in the provinces, notables from every city, participated in the tax farming enterprise, making it extremely diverse.

The overwhelming ruling class (*askeri*) hold on the central Istanbul tax farms was also quite different from the English and French model in which tax farmers were financiers. The interests of a financier class and a rentier class are at odds. The state also allowed the proliferation, decentralization, and vast expansion of networks of *malikane mukataa*, unlike the European states that were much more concerned about containing the tax farms. As Kiser and Kane show, in France and earlier in England, indirect taxes were first centralized under the General Farm, then bureaucratized, and then slowly transferred from private to public hands.[20] The French attempt to centralize the tax farms had already started in the seventeenth century under the successful policies of Colbert, who instituted new rules for the governance of the tax farms under a unified company more inline with the centralization goals of the French state itself. In the Ottoman Empire, tax farms were never centralized; when they were too successful, they were eliminated by a state keen to reassert its central power. Therefore, it is difficult to argue that such decentralized wealth could have been usefully gathered and transferred; rather, it was confiscated through battle and opposition. Notables were eliminated, life-term tax farming was abolished, short-term tax farming continued, and reform policies had contradictory effects in that some notables lost their land and revenues, whereas others were able to consolidate their land as private property. By the time the PDA was established in 1881, the notables who remained were replaced by salaried agents collecting taxes, although not on behalf of the Ottoman state but for a foreign consortium established to manage the fiscal debt of the state.

We can then conclude that the Ottoman state did not manage successfully the transition from indirect to direct taxation, from a decentralized to a centralized administration of taxation. The highly negotiated and fragmented nature of imperial state–society relations hindered this development. Yet, we can also conclude that the Ottoman state had no other solutions available for its international and internal conundrum. It had internal revolts and international

---

[20] Edgar Kiser and Joshua Kane, "Revolution and State Structure: The Bureaucratization of Tax Administration in Early Modern England and France," *American Journal of Sociology* 107 (2001): 183–223.

enemies; it needed to finance its administration and its military, and it hoped to increase its fiscal revenues to do so; and it tried a series of adaptive reforms of its fiscal structure, but they were unsuccessful. Throughout the nineteenth century, then, the state struggled to alleviate its fiscal burden and to institute more regular and standardized forms of revenue collection, but such efforts ended up like a giant patchwork of arrangements that demonstrated a multiplicity of forms rather than standardized and regularized tax collection.

Federalism in this scenario would not have been possible because further decentralization could not have been a solution to the internal and international threats. For a state that perceived itself as incapable of collecting resources from its diverse populations, federalism was far from being an attractive option. The long eighteenth century had established a pattern of privatization of enterprise and a view that the tax farming of positions and enterprises were to be sources of profit rather than services to the state. Notables understood that it was under the aegis of an imperial system that they could benefit from the opportunities presented to them. A federal structure was beneficial to neither the state nor the notables.

Minorities at Risk: Toleration Unraveled and the Construction of "Bounded Identities"[21]

Another pillar of imperial dominance was the pragmatic and flexible management of diversity, with boundaries as *mobile markers of difference* rather than as established and rigid separations that obstructed social and economic interaction and fluidity. The Islamic script on how to deal with non-Muslim populations, as well as the highly settled and organized nature of the non-Muslim communities in the empire, had made it possible for imperial authorities to absorb such diversity, to integrate but not to change its cultural and social inheritance. Except at moments of extensive insecurity, sultans and their administrators were able to maintain a certain forbearance over subject populations, resolutely confronting the abuse of power by individual officials or perpetrators of religious and ethnic hatred. Interethnic relations, despite the potential for explosion, were maintained by a mutual interest in interethnic peace.

Yet, this particular empire, with its important heritage of religious tolerance, ended with a violent transition from empire to nation-state. The empire on the road to nonempire committed atrocities against its Greek and Armenian populations and, by 1915–1916, had enacted measures that ended in the

---

[21] I use the notion of "bounded identities" as different from "barricaded identities" from Ken Jowitt, where he argues for these kinds of identities being fueled by the fear of contamination. Bounded identities signify separation and closure of previously connected networks. See his article, "Ethnicity: Nice, Nasty, and Nihilistic," in *Ethnopolitical Warfare: Causes, Consequences, and Possible Solutions*, ed. Daniel Chirot and Martin E. P. Seligman (Washington, DC: American Psychological Association, 2001), 27–36.

large-scale destruction of a whole community, imprinting an entirely different legacy on the empire. In the nineteenth century, government-approved ethnic violence occurred against groups perceived to be in revolt or dangerous to the state, Greeks in the 1820s, Syrian and Lebanese Christians in 1860s, Bulgarians in 1876, and the Armenians of Zeytun in 1862. Yet, as Donald Bloxham argues, the last three decades of the empire were different in the level and intensity of the violence that culminated in 1915–1916 and the mass extermination of Armenians.[22] We then have to ask the following question: if empires are dominant when they manage diversity, and if the learning and application of such tolerance were so much part of the empire, what explains this particular road to cataclysm?

The question of the Armenian "genocide" remains a deep and dark challenge to historians, politicians, and scholars of diverse backgrounds. There is less and less debate about the contours of the massacres; a series of well-researched arguments explains how the Ottoman government and its henchmen could have committed such acts of terror. The case made usually presents the macrohistorical, international, and internal transformations that the empire was undergoing, its increasingly fervent nationalism, together with the perceived threat from an Armenian alliance with the Russians, to explain the structural conditions for the actions of the Young Turk leaders. However, these should not be seen as attempts to try to put into context the difficulties of the leadership of the empire, rationalizing their behavior. Rather, they should be seen as the structural conditions within which the Young Turks chose to ethnically cleanse certain regions of their Armenian populations. Here, given the way I have argued for the interaction between the macrostructural-institutional level, the meso level of networks, and individual agency, my explanation explores the transformation of the multiethnic dimension of empire at these levels. We can see the actions of the Young Turks as strategies of individuals who were trying to secure a lasting place for the empire, while operating in an environment that was inherently unstable and insecure, and where mobilizing a nationalist identity and centralization was effected within the already transformed network structure of the empire.

To be clear, macrohistorical and socioeconomic transformations reconfigured the networks of association of the empire, leading to the development of bounded entities and identities, which the leadership chose to enhance rather than broker across. That is, we have here a strategy entirely opposite from the one used in the formation of the Ottoman state, which was based on brokerage across ethnic and religious groups and centralization by incorporation and negotiation. The Ottoman post-Tanzimat administrations chose policies to enhance and mobilize corporate identities, strategizing that this was a better

[22] Donald Bloxham, *The Great Game of Genocide: Imperialism, Nationalism, and the Destruction of the Ottoman Armenians* (Oxford, UK: Oxford University Press, 2005), 15–16. See also *Der Volkermord an den Armeniern und die Shoah (The Armenian Genocide and the Shoah)*, ed. Hans-Lukas Kieser and Dominik J. Schaller (Zurich: Chronos, 2002).

choice for dealing with war and insecurity. Such elite behavior favoring the consolidation of conflictual ethnic and religious identities was becoming the preferred choice of the new national politics of many imperial formations. The Ottoman administrations of the nineteenth century espoused such policies and planned their own version of corporate politics. To describe such events is to follow the process of network manipulation and identity formation of the nineteenth century.

The emergence of ethnic and religious antagonism and state distrust of non-Muslim populations dates back to the eighteenth century, and can be seen in the changing network associations of non-Muslim and Muslim groups in the empire. The economic transformation of the eighteenth century, increasing trade with Europe, and the role of non-Muslims in European trade networks led to growing economic disparity between groups in which undue emphasis was placed on religious and ethnic rivalries. The vast spread of commercial networks and the insecurities perceived by members of different groups vis-à-vis such density and intensity of competition forced a reorganization along ethnic and religious lines, and gave rise to local moments of violence, changing the script of tolerance and the containment of violence. However, as Ken Jowitt demonstrates, corporate identities alone that are separate from one another do not represent as serious a threat as when state authorities are involved and/or are unable to deal with the conflict; such situations can end up in mass violence.[23]

Commerce with Europe changed the internal dynamics of diversity in the empire. The changes occurred in the density and shape of trade networks and in the content and meaning of these networks. Many realms, rural and urban, villages and towns, guilds and trade associations, were affected. The networks and their content affected Muslims and non-Muslims differently. The traditional narrative usually either emphasizes the commercial success of the Christian communities and the resulting development of nationalism, or the decline of Muslim communities in trade and social status. Rather, there were many different ways in which communities both benefited and endured hardship. Given the vagaries of commerce and the insecurity of the intermediate position that many non-Muslims were locked in to, they chose to revert to a community based on ethnic and religious ties, familiar local identities tying them to the national discourses available in their Western interactions. Therefore, non-Muslims who had spread throughout the empire with trade and finance and developed far-reaching networks, begun in the eighteenth century to consolidate their identities around the traditional differences maintained by empire. Muslims, in contrast, who were locked out of many trading relations because they were not Christian or did not know the European languages, became aware of their newly acquired disadvantage and united in their Muslim identities in resentment. This was a recipe for intercommunal disaster.

---

[23] Jowitt, "Ethnicity: Nice, Nasty, and Nihilistic."

The first observation we can make is that these relations of commercialization affected both Muslims and non-Muslims, but politicized their communities differently. The structural position of the non-Muslim communities was altered through the dynamics of trade and the attendant choices of different imperial and Western groups. For non-Muslim commercial communities located in Istanbul, Salonica, Izmir, Aleppo, and other trading cities, the relationship among the British, French, and Dutch merchants and the non-Muslim traders and intermediaries was not only necessary, but also prejudicial and competitive.[24] Officially, non-Muslims became associated as intermediaries with Western trade at the initiative of the Ottoman state, when the latter appointed certain non-Muslim men who were highly skilled in languages and politics as translators, *dragoman*. Western merchants who had the right to trade in the Ottoman Empire also used non-Muslim community members as links between Western merchants and local producers or landholders.

Yet, commercial linkages between different communities at different ports often complicated relations among the non-Muslim communities, the Europeans, and their consuls. The comfortable movement between communities across personal ties, conversion and marriage, and the interlocking of communities, the "convivencia" that had made the Ottomans powerful, eroded slowly by the complications of competition, greed, and European intervention. Jews and Greeks, who combined this new status of protected members of a trading community with widespread family ties abroad, were poised to expand their businesses and open trading houses at home and in the major industrial centers of Europe.[25] The unstructured and somewhat unexpected movement and settlement of Jews and Christians as a result of their increasing involvement in trade and protection from Europe even unsettled their own communities, prompting spontaneous alliances and associations. Instructive is the example of the Jews of Livorno, who were brought into the Ottoman Empire by the French, offered protection from Ottoman taxes and restrictions, and settled in port cities such as Salonica, Izmir, Istanbul, Aleppo, Alexandria, and Cairo. This led to the reorganization of trading relations, alliances, and competition both by pushing local Jews to put together local trading associations to counter

---

[24] This argument is about the relations among the companies, consuls, and individuals who engaged in commercial relations and about the nature of their relations. It does not discuss the more general question of the relations between the Ottoman Empire and its Western trading counterparts, about which there is an important literature that has been questioned in an interesting article: see Edhem Eldem, "French Trade and Commercial Policy in the Levant in the Eighteenth Century," in den Boogert and Fleet, eds., *The Ottoman Capitulations*, 26–47.

[25] Edhem Eldem, *French Trade in Istanbul in the Eighteenth Century* (Leiden, The Netherlands and Boston: E. J. Brill, 1999); Edhem Eldem, Daniel Goffman, and Bruce Masters, *The Ottoman City between East and West: Aleppo, Izmir, and Istanbul* (Cambridge, UK: Cambridge University Press, 1999); Robert Mantran, *Istanbul dans la seconde moitié du XVIIe siècle* (Paris: Adrien Maisonneuve, 1962); Ilber Ortaylı, "18. Yüzyılda Akdeniz Dünyası ve Genel Çizgileriyle Türkiye," *Toplum ve Bilim* (Spring 1977); G. R. Bosscha Erdbrink, *At the Threshold of Felicity: Ottoman–Dutch Relations during the Embassy of Cornelis Calkoen at the Sublime Porte, 1726–1744* (Amsterdam: A. L.van Gendt & Co. B.V., 1977); *Istanbul et les langues orientales*, ed. Frederic Hitzel (Paris: Harmattan, 1997).

the intruders and by promoting new commercial ties in which they relied on their coreligionists abroad, those left in Livorno, or on other members settled in Marseilles.[26]

Although Europeans were glad to have Ottoman subjects to act on their behalf in their day-to-day dealings with local officials, they were also wary of the competition from these agents, and often had their consuls issue calls for organized protection from these intermediaries.[27] European merchants were interested in developing a monopoly on trade everywhere they landed; they viewed their dependence on brokers negatively and were eager to rid themselves of those they described as entrenched, scheming speculators and creditors.[28] They also wanted to define and reorganize communities to suit their particular needs. As Greene explains in her analysis of the commercial relations in Crete between the French and the locals: "The French reports overwhelmingly concerned with commerce, present an anonymous society composed of well-defined groups: Jews, Turks and Greeks. They foreshadow the era of nationalism."[29] The blurred identities, the hybrid groups, the Levantines, the Ottomans who had Greek mothers, and the convert Jews acquired off-putting characteristics or disappeared from the larger discourse. The mixed categories were simplified and clarified. As Alexander de Groot describes, "the latter group of Ottoman subjects was generally referred to as 'Levantines,' a term which acquired a pejorative sense, denoting a hybrid race, not fully Oriental nor quite accepted socially and culturally as being Western, 'tainted with a remarkable degree of moral obliquity.'"[30] A similar simplification and hardening of categories was widespread in the Arab provinces of the empire as well.[31]

---

[26] Many of these cases are presented by Rozen in "Contest and Rivalry in Mediterranean Maritime Commerce in the First Half of the Eighteenth Century: The Jews of Salonica and the European Presence," *Revue des Etudes Juives* 147:3–4 (1988): 325–327. I have also gleaned many such cases from the Archives Nationales de France, Affaires Étrangères.

[27] The French consul to Salonica in 1779 presents one such interesting case among many in the French archives. He complains about a certain Greek *berat* holder (*barataire*), Yoanni Calamanaky, who was both the agent of the German traders in Salonica and in collusion with the *ayan* of Seres. In particular, he is accused of colluding with the *ayan* at the expense of the French and other Europeans, providing large loans to the *ayan*, who in turn either had to tax their people more or impose much higher prices on Europeans for wheat and cotton. In this particular letter, the French merchants complain about the uncharacteristic increase in cotton prices, and the consul, after some research, has found out that Calamanaky was behind such price hikes. Archives Nationales de France, Affaires Etrangeres Bi 1003 Salonique, Lettre du 8 Fevrier 1779 par M. Arazy.

[28] Felix Beaujour in his reports displays despicable forms of anti-Semitism and anti-Greek feelings when he describes these groups. See his *Tableau du Commerce de la Grèce*. As to the actions of the local forces, see Frangakis–Syrett, *The Commerce of Smyrna*, 60–65.

[29] Molly Greene, *A Shared World: Christians and Muslims in the Early Modern Mediterranean* (Princeton, NJ: Princeton University Press, 2000), 205. See also Paschalis Kitromiledes, "The Dialectic of Intolerance," *Journal of Hellenic Diaspora* 6 (1979): 5–30.

[30] Alexander H. de Groot, "Protection and Nationality: The Decline of the Dragomans," in ed. Hitzeled, *Istanbul et les langues orientales*, 235.

[31] Usama Makdisi, *The Culture of Sectarianism: Community, History and Violence in Nineteenth-Century Ottoman Lebanon* (Berkeley: University of California Press, 2000).

The non-Muslims acted in full knowledge of their dual disability. They were confronted with European merchants who undermined and despised them and Ottoman officials who did not trust them and were learning to despise them. Such insecurity brought on innovation. Over time, the non-Muslims formed multiple associations to better protect themselves. For example, to protect themselves against the Dutch, thirty Chiot merchants formed a league in 1782. They established internal rotating leadership rules and credit systems, and managed to grow in influence so that by the end of the century they were able to control the cloth trade of Izmir and the Anatolian hinterland.[32] Expanding to provide both membership and contracts to other Chiot merchants and to Ottoman non-Muslims generally, they formed important networks protecting them both from the state and from the international traders and their consuls. In such ways, the numbers of business partnerships and leagues created by non-Muslim merchant brokers increased by the late eighteenth and early nineteenth centuries.[33]

Whether they functioned as independent merchants or as local intermediaries between the European and Ottoman powers, these non-Muslims extended their networks and communication; traded goods, information, and lifestyles; and slowly helped develop the beginnings of a bourgeois culture.[34] The Greeks were by far the most successful at the organization of resources and people into leagues, clubs, and associations to further almost any economic or political goal. There were a number of reasons for this. First, the initial *millet* distribution, whereby Ottoman sultans subordinated all Orthodox Christian groups to the authority of the Greek Orthodox patriarch, structured Balkan society so that other orthodox groups learned the Greek language and Greek liturgy early on. Second, the rise to power of the Greek merchants from the Phanar district of Istanbul and their ability to use their wealth to buy political office, becoming the princes of the Romanian principalities, gave those who spoke Greek and were of the Orthodox faith a remarkable advantage. The Greek merchants and the Greek rulers of Moldavia and Wallachia extended privileges, business contracts, and patronage networks to the Greek community, expanding and widening their business dealings.[35]

---

[32] Frangakis-Syrett, *The Commerce of Smyrna*, 101–102.

[33] For example, Frangakis-Syrett provides lists of non-Muslim merchants and merchant companies involved in trade with the Dutch for 6-month periods in 1762 and 1786–1787. Just for trade with the Dutch, she provides for 22 February 1762 to 22 August 1762, 40 merchants and 12 trading partnerships, and for 22 August 1786 to 22 February 1787, 56 individuals and 25 new firms. See *Commerce of Smyrna*, 255–256.

[34] Reşat Kasaba, "Izmir," *Review* 16 (1993), special issue "Port–Cities of the Eastern Mediterranean, 1800–1914," ed. Çağlar Keyder, Y. Eyüp Özveren, and Donald Quataert, 398–402. The best examples of economic development and competition among non-Muslims and Muslims in the Arab provinces of the empire can be found in Bruce Masters, *Christians and Jews in the Ottoman Arab World: The Roots of Sectarianism* (Cambridge, UK: Cambridge University Press, 2001).

[35] *Ottoman Greeks in the Age of Nationalism*, ed. Dimitri Gondicas and Charles Issawi (Princeton, NJ: Darwin Press, 1999); Richard Clogg, *Struggle for Greek Independence* (New York:

Economic power in conjunction with political office provided Greeks with bargaining power, exemplified in the deal that Demetrios Mouroutsis struck with Selim III to start a Greek trading company, as "une grande société commerciale dite des négociants européens," with all the privileges of the European merchants.[36] Such economic and political networks that stretched from simple Greek merchants to Romanian princes to Ottoman sultans undoubtedly facilitated the activities of the revolutionary societies, such as the Philike Hetairia, that were to follow trading companies. Greeks, as a result, were among the first Christian communities of the Balkans to demand autonomy and distinct political rights.

In yet another development, relations between non-Muslim religious and ethnic communities also deteriorated. From the very beginning of western European expansion into Ottoman commercial relations, Jews and Christians struggled for commercial dominance. What seemed, therefore, a united set of non-Muslim communities was quite competitive against one another, which is surprising because they were at least originally in the same structural position, intermediaries between the Ottoman and several foreign states. Because they also had the widest and most developed interstate familial and commercial ties, Greeks and Jews were competing for economic predominance beyond Ottoman frontiers. Yet, they had also a disturbing past of animosity based on the teachings of the Christian Church, often making itself felt as blood libels during Easter. Whereas the Ottoman authorities had contained the conflict and potential for blood libel for many centuries, in the late eighteenth through early twentieth centuries, many more episodes of blood libel were recorded. The rising nationalism of the various Greek Orthodox communities where ethnic, religious, and national passions erupted did not help the Jewish populations in these areas. In the late nineteenth century, there were at least fifty blood libel accusations and violent episodes in Asia Minor.[37] At another level, ethnic relations in the Balkans became more contentious as other groups now challenged the Greek Orthodox Church that had dominated all Orthodox peoples. These groups were reorganizing their own churches in their own language and wanted to establish independent churches. Such demands for ecclesiastical

Macmillan, 1973); *Balkan Society in the Age of Greek Independence*, ed. Richard Clogg (London: Macmillan, 1981); Paschalis Kitromilides, "'Imagined Communities' and the Origins of the National Question in the Balkans," in *Enlightenment, Nationalism, Orthodoxy: Studies in the Culture and Political Thought of South-Eastern Europe*, ed. P. Kitromilides (Aldershot, UK: Variorum, 1994); Theodore H. Papadopoullos, *Studies and Documents Relating to the Greek Church and People under Turkish Domination* (Brussels: Bibliotheca Graeca Aevi Posterioris, 1952).

[36] Stoianovich, "The Conquering Balkan Orthodox Merchant," 272. See also G. G. Gervinus, *Insurrection et Régénération de la Grèce*, 2 vols., transl. J. F. Minssen and Leonidas Sgouta (Paris: A. Durand, 1863), vol. 1, 99.

[37] Yitzchak Kerem, "Relations between the Jews, the Greek-Orthodox and the Armenians in the 19th and Early 20th Centuries in the Ottoman Empire," *Acta Viennensia Ottomanica* (1999): 191–198; Moise Franco, *Essai sur l'histoire des Israelites de l'empire Ottoman: depuis les origines jusqu'à nos jours* (Paris: Librairie A. Durlacher, 1897).

independence brought about increasing ethnic awareness and tensions in many parts of the Balkans. The many alternative organizations, the ayan administration in the Balkans, and the reorganization fostered by changes in taxation systems contributed to the diminished role of the Greek Orthodox Church, which reacted by struggling against decentralization and dispersal of its ecclesiastical and administrative influence. Intercommunal violence that had been tempered and reined in by various religious and secular administrative actors could not be contained and decisively materialized in the eighteenth century.[38]

Despite the insecurity and growing intercommunal local violence, Muslim populations focused on the rapid upward mobility of non-Muslims. Eighteenth-century economic realities deeply affected the Muslim rural, mercantile, and artisan classes. On the one hand, the overall impact of the increase in economic relations with Europe was positive because it stimulated growth and development. On the other hand, when combined with changing geopolitical factors, it could become devastating to local Muslim populations. When, for example, Ottomans had to share the Black Sea trade with the Russians after the treaty of Küçük Kaynarca in 1774, the Ottoman merchants were deprived of much of their income. Still, in the Black Sea region, even though the majority of the merchant class of Trabzon had been Muslims, with Russian commerce and European intrusion, Greek merchants displaced Muslims and acquired a dominant trading position. Shifts of this sort occurred in many other centers.[39]

In the cities, artisans were affected by the increasing needs of the Ottoman state, increased taxes, provisioning, and the reduced availability of raw materials, not to mention the influx of some European goods into local markets. The guilds entered a phase through which they slowly declined, losing their monopoly over economic activities. The development of an alternative mechanism of guild maintenance, which basically ensured the stability of a guild master through a *"gedik"* certificate, transformed property relations in the guilds, making them a form of ownership subject to internal tensions. At the same time, the increasing control of Europeans affected the manufacturing markets and established non-Muslims as local agents in direct relations with Muslim guild members. Those guild members who were Christian benefited from European intervention and European demands in the Ottoman market, whereas the fortunes of Muslim guild members stagnated. Discrimination and harassment of non-Muslims ensued, and hostility was ratcheted up as the nineteenth-century

---

[38] Paschalis Kitromilides, "Imagined Communities and the Origin of the National Question in the Balkans," in *Modern Greece: Nationalism and Nationality*, ed. Martin Blinkhorn and Thanos Veremis (Athens: SAGE-ELIAMEP, 1990); *Nationalism in Eastern Europe*, ed. Peter F. Sugar and Ivo J. Lederer (Seattle and London: University of Washington Press, 1971); Papadopoullos, *Studies and Documents Relating to the Greek Church*.

[39] A. Üner Turgay, "Trade and Merchants in Nineteenth-Century Trabzon: Elements of Ethnic Conflict," in *Christians and Jews in the Ottoman Empire: The Functioning of a Plural Society*, ed. Benjamin Braude and Bernard Lewis, 2 vols. (New York and London: Holmes and Meier, 1982), 287–318.

reforms evolved.[40] In many places, Jewish and Muslim guild members who had been relegated to modest positions and could not even afford to pay their taxes revolted and attacked the wealthy Christians, who were becoming the regular targets of the mobs.[41]

Muslims' interpretation of the privileges enjoyed by non-Muslims brought them to understand their plight in religious terms. They argued that the religious differences and the preferences of the West were clear cut. With this increased awareness of religious differentiation, Muslims in turn espoused a religious discourse to explain their economic disadvantages, blaming the lack of Shar'ia law on the workings of commercial relations. For example, a well-established Syrian Muslim merchant who endured financial difficulties in the mid-eighteenth century complained to the sultan that the legal basis for the European-Ottoman Christian compact was provided not in sultanic law but in religious law, and advised the Sultan to return to the application of religious law.[42] He and many others saw in the more stringent application of Islamic law a way out of the financial conundrum of the empire. Not only had the discourse on interreligious relations changed, but it also worked to fashion a stronger Islamic identity among the disgruntled elites and masses.

In the cities, the remaining Muslim masses were either unemployed or employed at the lowest rank with the lowest salaries. The Europeans who started projects in the empire often hired cheap Muslim labor controlled by highly paid, non-Muslim Ottoman or foreign managers. The result was increased interreligious tensions, as in projects such as the Anatolian Railroad, where Muslims filled 90% of the lower positions, while Armenians and Greeks occupied half of the middle-rank, administrative positions.[43]

In the nineteenth century, especially in the Arab provinces in Aleppo in 1850 and in Damascus in 1860, more serious conflicts occurred involving the Christian inhabitants of these two cities. These episodes of violence and many smaller ones were also the result of the growing resentment of Muslims in these provinces as their economic position declined. In contrast, Christians in Syria enjoyed greater freedom, more protection due to European consulates and governments, and markedly increased opportunities for trade. In Damascus,

---

[40] Engin Deniz Akarlı, "Law in the Marketplace: Istanbul Artisans and Shopkeepers, 1730–1840," in *Dispensing Justice in Islam: Qadis and their Judgements*, ed. M. Khalid Masud, Rudolph Peters, and David S. Powers (Leiden, The Netherlands, and Boston: Brill, 2006), 245–270; Onur Yıldırım, "Ottoman Guilds as a Setting for Ethno-Religious Conflict: The Case of the Silk-Thread Spinners' Guild in Istanbul," *IRSH* 47 (2002): 407–419; Suraiya Faroqhi, "Migration into Eighteenth-Century 'Greater Istanbul' as Reflected in the Kadı Registers of Eyüp," *Turcica* 30 (1998): 163–183.

[41] Abdul-Karim Rafeq, "Craft Organizations and Religious Communities in Ottoman Syria (XVI–XIX Centuries)," in *La Shi'a nell'impero Ottomano* (Romae: Accademia Nazionale dei Lincei, 1993), 25–56.

[42] Masters, *Christians and Jews in the Ottoman Arab World*, 125.

[43] Donald Quataert, *Social Disintegration and Popular Resistance in the Ottoman Empire, 1881–1908* (New York: New York University Press, 1983); idem, *The Ottoman Empire, 1700–1922* (Cambridge, UK: Cambridge University Press, 2003).

"the splendid houses built by the rich class of Christians excited jealousy and their general prosperity tended to create in the Mussulmans feelings of envy. The persons who managed the affairs of the pashalik were Christian, they kept the public accounts and grew richer in the employment. The Christian traders were more prosperous than the Mussulmans."[44]

As these relations of competition and violence indicate, the early restlessness created by economic disparities in the eighteenth century had been severely compounded by the reforms of the mid-nineteenth century. Under the watchful eyes of the West and with Ottoman central state enthusiasm, the Tanzimat reforms (1839–1876) had inaugurated a new period of centralization and modernization. Ottoman Tanzimat leaders introduced the basics of modern Western statecraft, slowly but surely moving away from negotiated, distributive, flexible, and accomodationist forms of imperial integration and settlement toward rational settlements, uniform rules and regulations, and universal legal principles. The Ottomans enacted reforms in central administration, law and order, education, the bureaucracy, and the military to remove intermediary groups and institutions between the state and society. They had endorsed equality before the law, bringing Muslim and non-Muslim subjects to the same level, stripping each group of its particular set of privileges.

The reforms initially affected each group's ability to negotiate a place in the system, its degree of communal closure, and its internal cohesion. The Tanzimat brought regularization of state–society relations: no more individual community compacts, but rather one state–society arrangement for all. The program was defined in a document of 1839 called Hatt-i Şerif (Noble Edict of the Rose Chamber). Provincial representative assemblies were established, together with state courts that ruled independently of the *ulema*. Local administrative councils and new codes of commercial and criminal law were introduced. A conscription system based on Prussian patterns signaled the end of traditional expectations for both Muslim and non-Muslim communities. Muslims, who were expected to be the warrior class of the empire with special privileges attached to their superior status, were bound to be disappointed by the inclusion of others. Non-Muslims, who had been content in their noncombatant role, were distressed. Moreover, with the reforms that effectively instituted the rights of each individual and guaranteed their security of life, property, and honor regardless of religion, the Ottomans took a critical step away from empire. Accordingly, the empire could not claim the superiority of Islamic populations over non-Muslims. In return, the state demanded that all citizens be loyal to the sultan and to the Ottoman administration.

---

[44] Quoted in Moshe Maoz, "Religious and Ethnic Conflicts in Ottoman Syria during the Tanzimat Era," in *The Great Ottoman Turkish Civilization*, ed. Kemal Çiçek (Ankara: Yeni Türkiye Yayınları, 2000), 441; Arnon Groiss, "Minorities in a Modernizing Society: Secular vs. Religious Identities in Ottoman Syria, 1840–1914," *Princeton Papers in Near Eastern Studies* 3 (1994): 39–70; Michael Winter, "Ethnic and Religious Tensions in Ottoman Egypt," in *International Congress on the Social and Economic History of Turkey* (Istanbul: Isis Press, 1989), 309–317.

Another major reform of the Tanzimat was the formation of a modern school system with modern ideals, which, intriguingly, was not appreciated by either Muslim or non-Muslim populations. Benjamin Fortna demonstrates the degree to which the early Tanzimat reforms and the creation of schools after the 1869 Education Regulation were an attempt to transform education for all the *millet*s in the empire, but ended up promoting only Muslim schools. As a result of internal competition among groups, missionary involvement and schooling, and western involvement in separate Christian and Jewish schooling, non-Muslim schools provided a superior education.[45] The consequences of educational separation and competition were dire for interethnic relations in the empire, forcing closure in communities rather than interaction, and teaching young students separation, difference, and competition. The reform of education, which during the Tanzimat led to increased differentiation among communities and produced a sense of Muslim inferiority, pushed Sultan Abdülhamid II (1876–1909) to put enormous energy and resources into Muslim education, creating the basis of a distinct religious and national identity for the Muslim population of the empire.[46]

If major misgivings regarding ethnic and religious difference and disparity were already well rooted in the empire, competition and communal strife only got worse as Muslim refugees from the Balkans, the Caucasus, and the Crimea were settled in Anatolia. Between 5 and 7 million refugees, mostly Muslims, were settled by the Ottoman government throughout the nineteenth century, mostly in Anatolia. Kemal Karpat argues that between 1856 and 1876 at least 500,000 Crimean Tatars and 2.5 million Muslim immigrants from the Caucasus were settled in Anatolia, the Balkans, northern Syria, and Iraq. Not long after, in 1877–1878, the Caucasian population that had been settled in the Balkans was resettled in Anatolia together with a million others, mostly Muslims from the Balkans. Another 2 million took refuge in Anatolia until 1914. By the time of World War I, the immigrant population of Anatolia represented nearly 40% of the total population.[47] Such immigration, originating in the nationalist movements and independence politics of the Balkans, the Russian Wars, and the Ottoman defeats, brought in another element of Muslim discontent that not only altered the demographic balance of the empire, but also exacerbated social and economic tensions. These immigrants had arrived from lands where ethnic and nationalist identities were well formed, and although they kept these identities, in the Anatolian context they quickly espoused their

---

[45] Benjamin C. Fortna, *Imperial Classroom: Islam, the State, and Education in the Late Ottoman Empire* (Oxford, UK: Oxford University Press, 2002); Aron Rodrigue, *French Jews, Turkish Jews: The Alliance Israelite Universelle and the Politics of Jewish Schooling in Turkey, 1860–1925* (Bloomington: Indiana University Press, 1990).

[46] Ibid. Kemal Karpat's summary of the school system during the reign of Abdülhamid II provides the numbers of schools and the policies that the state was developing toward a unified Islamic identity. See *The Politicization of Islam: Reconstructing Identity, State, Faith, and Community in the Late Ottoman State* (Oxford and New York: Oxford University Press, 2001), 98–100.

[47] Karpat, *The Politicization of Islam*, 184.

Muslim identity, finding it to be a source of commonality and interaction with the local populations.

Such immigration occurred during an important pan-Islamic phase of Ottoman rule as the government of Abdülhamid II worked hard to generate Muslim unity as an essential tool for maintaining the integrity of the empire and for mobilizing its diverse population on the theme of Islam rather than around religious diversity. In fact, increasing Muslim settlement in the empire gave him the means to argue more fervently about a renewed and robust political unity, one formulated around Islam, especially Sunnî Orthodoxy. Abdülhamid made a point of reviving the caliphate, a symbol of Ottoman Islamic dominance.[48]

Whereas the commercial disparities were spreading across the empire, the tensions of religious, immigrant, and resentful Islam were located especially in eastern Anatolia, the traditional heartland of the Armenian and Kurdish populations. Although the Armenians became a clear minority in many regions, the Kurds were enveloped into an alternative process of Islamization and centralization as well as militarization. In 1891, Abdülhamid also established the Hamidiye, a Kurdish cavalry unit that quickly filled the space left by regular troops. The reorganization of eastern Anatolia was further enhanced by the settlement of tribes, sedentarized by the state to increase its control of peoples and resources. Toward the end of the nineteenth century, when tribes were settled they often engaged in struggles with the local populations, Kurdish and Armenian. The state or local authorities rarely resolved the resulting local disturbances between groups. Such conditions increased the pressures between Muslims and non-Muslims, but especially Armenians, who were most likely to be in eastern Anatolia and scattered across numerous villages.[49] At the capital, the Armenian patriarchate and the Ottoman government struggled over the settlement of Muslims and Armenians, clearly a prelude to the dispossession to come.[50] Clearly, the aim of the state was to promote homogeneity, a necessary step on the way to national state formation, although it is not clear that such a purpose had been articulated yet.

The task begun by Abdülhamid II was brought home by the Committee of Union and Progress (CUP), which brought to power a group of Young Turks committed to saving the empire and whose vision of a multinational empire was still present, although vacillating, because it defined the Armenians as the mortal enemies of such an empire. The politicization of Armenian relations with the CUP, the internationalization of the Armenian question, and the strategic decisions to eliminate the Armenians from the territories of eastern Anatolia were made in the context of intense international threats, increased

---

[48] Selim Deringil, "Legitimacy Structures in the Ottoman State: The Reign of Abdülhamid II (1876–1909)," *International Journal of Middle Eastern Studies* 23 (1991): 345–359.

[49] Martin van Bruinessen, *Agha, Shaikh and State: On the Social and Political Organization of Kurdistan* (Utrecht: The Netherlands Rijksuniversiteit, 1978); Fikret Adanır, "Armenian Deportations and Massacres in 1915," in *Ethnopolitical Warfare*, ed. Chirot and Seligman, 71–81.

[50] Bloxham, *The Great Game of Genocide*, 48.

Muslim homogeneity, and strong networks of immigrant resentment, as well as a constructed and imagined Armenian threat.[51]

Although the Ottoman Empire had been tolerant, its forbearance was built on the notion of order, which assumed the superiority of Muslims over non-Muslims. Both conditions of trade and Western intervention had played havoc with this notion of Pax Ottomanica and Islamic superiority. The late eighteenth and most of the nineteenth centuries had slowly brought wide-ranging examples of intercommunal tension among non-Muslim communities, especially Greeks and Jews, as well as increasingly among Christians and Muslims. Western support and advantages in trade, separate education, and the spread of a world system incorporating the idea of nationalism were all compounded by serious demographic instabilities.[52] Communities responded by turning in on themselves, developing their own religious and national identities, and forging closure around their communal ties. The state reaction under such conditions of increasing Christian privilege and nationalist mobilization and decreasing Muslim status and dominance, as well as the reconstitution of a more homogeneous Muslim population base across the empire, was to dispense with diversity as an asset of empire. Once diversity was recast as a weakness, another essential component of empire was stripped away. As such, economic, political, and religious transformations were occurring, and ruling groups were reconfiguring ways to maintain legitimate rule, moving toward a more uniform and national legitimacy.

Religion and Legitimacy

The emergence of the Ottomans as an imperial political formation was in large part due to their skills at brokerage across religions. As I showed in the analysis of the networks of Osman and Orhan, the first two leaders of the Ottomans, were unusual in the manner in which they promoted the coming together of different religions under the aegis of the Ottoman state and in the practical aspect of their multivocal signaling and toleration, which emerged out of organizational principles of rule. Building on such an arrangement of religious and ethnic diversity that ran parallel to an intricate composition of communities, Ottomans maintained a legitimate order focused on the harmony and peace that arose from a circle of justice.

As they acquired a deep-rooted Islamic identity, they believed in the strength and domination of a superior Orthodox Islamic empire, which organized and

[51] Ronald Grigor Suny, "The Holocaust before the Holocaust: Reflections on the Armenian Genocide," in *Der Volkermord an den Armeniern*, ed. Kieser and Schaller, 83–100; Aron Rodrigue, "The Mass Destruction of Armenians and Jews in the 20th Century in Historical Perspective, in *Der Volkermord an den Armeniern*, ed. Kieser and Schaller, 303–316; Taner Akçam, *Türk Ulusal Kimliği ve Ermeni Sorunu* (Istanbul: Iletişim, 1992).

[52] Daniel Chirot and Karen Barkey, "States in Search of Legitimacy," *International Journal of Comparative Sociology* 24:1–2 (1983).

preserved space for communities with immutable religious and ethnic differences to be located within an Islamic legitimacy. Their perception of the "other" as the ethnic, religious, and heterodox communities in the empire, as we have seen, was tempered by the order that could be established over it. That is, if the "other" could be organized and channeled for productive activity in ways that imperial rulers could control, state actors were accommodating. However, if the "other" was assembled in ways that escaped and defied organization, in loose, ramified and contentious, somewhat organized and concealed networks, estranged and detached from state networks, the center declared the "other" to be heretical and dangerous, and pursued ways to mobilize a legitimate Islamic discourse and a state-centered imperial project. In all these endeavors, the notion of a legitimate state order was harnessed and maintained in relations between state and social groups and in the pragmatic demonstration of actual benefits to the various members of the imperial community.

Even though the concept of legitimacy is dynamic and fluid and is a tool that readjusts itself to the relations between the ruled and the ruler, moments of great crisis in legitimacy can develop in which easy and smooth adaptation is impossible. The transformation of the Tanzimat reforms, the realization of European influence and coercion behind the government, and the combination of a weakened imperial position with the necessity of change constructed a legitimacy crisis for the Ottomans that was internal as much as international. From that moment on, the members of the Ottoman state paid increasing attention to the construction of a new fiction for a legitimate order, carefully crafting its content and wording.

Three different options of identity emerged and persisted throughout the three periods of Ottoman transition: the Tanzimat, Abdülhamid II, and the Young Turks. Ottomanism emerged as a discourse based on the multinational, imperial model of the empire, maintaining the integrity of empire with equality among its citizens. An Islamist or pan-Islamic discourse came into view both as the opposition to the conservative *ulema* and as the political ideology of Abdülhamid II and his vision of a consolidated Islamic empire. Finally, the pan-Turkist discourse was articulated as a counterweight to the Islamic views and promoted the more national bases of Turkishness: language and cultural traits. In this uncertain environment of international war and western interference in the internal affairs of the empire, these three ideologies became multivocal.

The Tanzimat reformers (1839–1876) had a liberal view of the position of Ottoman state–society relations, and they perceived a road out of their political dilemma that provided equal rights and opportunities for education and welfare, building on European notions of the Enlightenment and appropriating them for the consumption of an Ottoman public, which they hoped would develop such sensitivities in light of a larger Ottoman identity. In many ways, from a European perspective, reformers believed that the clear-cut administrative, political, and social changes they produced would be a panacea for all and would restore support for the state. After all, why would anyone reject legal equality for all, the rule of law, and the safeguarding of life, property, and honor for all rather than for only a small privileged group?

The Tanzimat reformers were poised to reconstruct a new legitimacy based on liberal notions of citizenship, yet they were seriously hampered internally and externally. Internally, the response to equality, educational reform, and administrative reform was mixed, and resistance arose in the least expected quarters of the empire. Furthermore, the Ottomans suffered from the same problems that other multinational states did at this time, when the idea of national self-determination had taken hold. The 1848 revolutions and the movements for national self-determination in the Habsburg lands, the autonomist and later nationalist secessionist movements in the Balkan regions of the Ottoman Empire, and the confrontation of the Russians with Muslim resistance signaled the potential disruption to come. Under such circumstances, the empires of the nineteenth century attempted to build an official nationalist ideology that would unite the different groups.[53]

It is in this context that the second attempt at building another legitimate Ottoman order and the reign of Abdülhamid II (1876–1909) has to be placed. Abdülhamid became powerful after the Russian war of 1877–1878 and after it was clear that the Tanzimat reformers had not been able sustain a significant sense of internal cohesion, especially in the face of the intensification of a sense of dismemberment. The new sultan was successful at constructing an internal legitimation based on the reformulation of Islam as the central connecting ideology of the state, and built the networks of his legitimacy through a state policy that linked and expanded the relations between Muslim subjects of the empire in unity, solidarity, and imperial continuity.

Wars and the resulting demographic conditions of the empire provided a fertile context for such an imperial ideology. After all, as we have already seen, the Ottoman Empire had gone through a significant process of ethnic separation as a result of the loss of the European provinces, the various massacres of Muslims in the Balkans, and the return of refugees from Bulgaria, Bosnia-Herzegovina, and the Caucasus. The resulting tension provided the ground on which Abdülhamid could build his policy of unity, survival, and Islamic legitimation.[54] Moving away from the traditional imperial legitimation of multiethnic diversity and toleration, Abdülhamid saw an opportunity to construct a new ideological state legitimacy based on an old component of the traditional Ottoman order, yet with a national rather than a multinational content. A new

[53] Hugh Seton-Watson, *Nations and States: An Inquiry into the Origins of Nations and the Politics of Nationalism* (Boulder, CO: Westview Press, 1977); *Nationalism and Empire: The Habsburg Empire and the Soviet Union*, ed. Richard L. Rudolph and David F. Good (New York: St. Martin's Press, 1992); Barkey and Hagen, eds., *After Empire*.

[54] Selim Deringil, *The Well-Protected Domains: Ideology and the Legitimation of Power in the Ottoman Empire, 1876–1909* (London and New York: I. B. Taurus, 1999); Albert Hourani, *A History of the Arab Peoples* (Cambridge, MA: Harvard University Press, 1991); Stephen Duguid, "The Politics of Unity: Hamidian Policy in Eastern Anatolia," *Middle Eastern Studies* 9 (1973): 139–155.

Islamic faith followed, which integrated orthodox and heterodox perspectives based on "the correction of the beliefs" of heretics and the spread of the official faith among the Muslim population of the empire.[55]

An Islamic perspective was not new. It had been part of the first effort at the redefinition of the bases of legitimacy during the Tanzimat era, although in an entirely different context. The Tanzimat leadership had been intent on creating a new Ottoman identity, based on superseding the old traditional divisions of the empire – religion, ethnicity, and regional/local divisions – and on manufacturing a new loyalty based on citizenship. Islam had provided a rationalization for the various parts of these new developments, but would also be rethought in reformist terms. That is, Abdülhamid's Islam was part of an absolutist vision of state control engaged in forming one united identity to the detriment of others.

On the positive side of the ledger, this project enhanced those determinants of a modernity that had become necessary in the transition that all three European and Eurasian empires of the region were undergoing. In the creation of a central official nationalism, the Habsburgs, Russians, and Ottomans worked with different material but toward a similar goal, a transition to a modern imperial model infused with national imagery and identity. They also similarly harnessed the powers of their new modernity: schools, the print media, and the mobilizational potential of the state. In each empire, education was the centerpiece of their rethinking of state–society relations, the creed of official nationalism and their own particular "*mission civilizatrice.*" These policies created a well-integrated Muslim educational system that spread throughout the lands, penetrating different regions and attempting to fashion them into loyal Muslim elements of the new Ottoman community. Islamization proceeded at different levels, educating the masses and reasserting core Sunnî beliefs in regions with Shi'ia convictions.

There were also negative consequences to such a quest for Islamic unity, modernity, and political nationalism. Abdülhamid II wanted to unify all the Muslims of the empire, whom he saw as unable to pursue their common interests, especially in comparison to the various ethnic, religious, and national groups of the empire. Yet, the sultan ended up creating the basis of an exclusive and "bounded" identity. Despite the fact that Abdülhamid's sense of Islam was modern and never tended in the direction of a theocracy, the modernist political plan of unifying a people under a religious ideology turned out to be disastrous for interreligious relations in the empire. Abdülhamid had spent his 31 years in power building an Islamic nation. He succeeded in raising Muslim consciousness through modern tools, yet in an antimodern and illiberal way: by raising the level of suspicion, distrust, and fear among Muslims regarding their future.

A third attempt at a state-ordered legitimacy emerged as a reaction to Abdülhamid's absolutist and Islamist policies. The Young Turks, who came

[55] Deringil, *The Well-Protected Domains*, 49.

to power through a coup d'état, were demonstrably wary of religious ideologies, much preferring secular and positivistic visions and strategies to save the state. They had started by officially embracing the state ideology of Ottomanism but were opposed to Islamism as the ideology and legitimacy building tool of Abdülhamid II. However, some had also turned toward nationalism and Turkish identity, basing their theories of the nation on European theories of race, which at the time were seen to be scientific.[56] However, the Young Turks, who were quite liberal at first, were soon confronted by enough war and upheaval that they became increasingly more authoritarian, as well as more insular and less integrated into the rest of Ottoman society. The wars they fought, the secessionist movements they confronted, the continued uprisings in Albania and Yemen, and the Italian invasion of Tripoli in 1911 exhausted their financial resources and undermined their confidence in their quest to save the empire. By the 1912–1913 Balkan Wars, the Young Turks had moved fully away from any liberal perspective on building imperial/national legitimacy.

It is possible to argue that the Young Turk leadership on the eve of World War I had been severely battered by the political and economic confrontations of a retreating empire. Their ideological formation – based on a combination of European race theories, Darwin, and Gustave Le Bon, to cite just a few in the considerable mix – drove their belligerent opposition to imperial justifications and moved in the direction of taking important steps to create a set of national institutions and classes. These included the creation of a national Turkish bourgeoisie that entailed the rejection of other groups; the compulsory use of the Turkish language; state institutions and cooperatives that furthered Turkish businesses; and, finally, the most consequential of the decisions, the mass deportations and massacres of populations.[57] To the Turkish nationalism of the Young Turks, we have to add the fact that they understood the religious Islamic strength of the core, and used Islamic symbolism and legitimation to further their national goals. Eric Jan Zürcher describes an Ottoman Muslim nationalism in his book,[58] which is essentially correct, although the new legitimating ideology of the state that the Young Turks wanted to save could be seen as an intricate mix of Ottoman, Islamic, and Turkish foundations.

An Ottoman Empire increasingly stripped of its multiethnic diversity, shored up by Islam as the integrative force of society and Turkish nationalism, as the positivist reconstruction of the Young Turks, combined to enhance the ideology of barricades. The Armenians became the victims of this new construction of a transitional legitimacy.

In the words of one of the best scholars of this Armenian tragedy, "the Genocide was rather a contingent event, initiated at the moment of imperial

[56] M. Şükrü Hanioğlu, *The Young Turks in Opposition* (New York and Oxford, UK: Oxford University Press, 1995).

[57] Çağlar Keyder, *State and Class in Turkey: A Study in Capitalist Development* (London: Verso, 1987); Zafer Toprak, *Türkiye'de Milli İktisat (1908–1918)* (Ankara: Yurt Yayınları, 1982).

[58] Zürcher, *Turkey: A Modern History.*

near-collapse," and "could be understood in the context of imperial decline, a fundamental re-conceptualization of the nature of the state along more nationalist and Pan-Turkist lines, and the radicalization of Young Turk policies in the fierce context of the First World War."[59] The Young Turks had strategized to mobilize their remaining identity fragments at the cost of the destruction of the Armenian community.

From its centuries of consolidation, the Ottoman Empire emerged as a marvel of flexible control over complexity. Its political and economic structures were decentralized just enough to maintain strong ties between the periphery and the center – society and state – with loyalties and resources focused inward and separately controlled from the center. An astonishing array of elites and ethnic and religious communities saw the advantage of their ties to the center of empire in Istanbul, absent ties between themselves. The control and integration of elites, coinciding with the tolerance and incorporation of diversity, provided for imperial legitimacy and power, connecting that center through economic and political inward pulls on a constellation of holdings. The empire prospered as a solar system, with planets circling the central sun, pulled in and held by the center's gravitational force. No other forces pulled at the periphery, nor did the orbits of the planets interact with one another, focused only on the center.

The eighteenth and nineteenth centuries saw a change of vast proportions for the Ottomans. The holdings on the periphery gained strength and grew freer of the gravity at the center, with the center unable to ensure a flow of revenue just when military needs required greater, dependable funding. The rotation of the holdings on the periphery became less connected to the center, increasingly pulled by the gravity of other centers in the international system, pulled outward by war and commercial ties. The center closed in on itself, losing its flexibility in an attempt to reform. Religious identity emerged in the center, weakening the ties of legitimation to a diverse periphery, with elites in center and periphery going their own way amid a tapestry of religious distinctiveness. Complexity was no longer maintained by flexible control. In the end, the Ottoman solar system was sufficiently weakened, and then flew apart, leaving a diminished sun.

The astronomy of empire is not a simple story of rise, decline, and failed attempts at salvage. In such a grand cosmology, the actual forces of change are obscured more than illuminated. Instead, the alterations must be understood in terms of the same set of state–society relations, the gravitation of networks that both built and changed the empire. The gravitation of legitimacy had been based on the same relations with elites and management of diversity that ended up pulling outward, in a new direction.

---

[59] Ronald Grigor Suny, "Empire and Nation: Armenians, Turks, and the End of the Ottoman Empire," *Armenian Forum* 1:2 (1998): 17–18. Also quoted in Adanır, "Armenian Deportations," 78.

The cosmic transition was evident in the weakening of the financial pull of the center, which was increasingly unable to make effective revenue demands on a highly dispersed periphery. International warfare required reform and additional resources that taxation farmed out to local notables could not meet. Granting life tenure, or additional power, to the tax farming notables reduced the central pull, with the Ottomans forced to resort to massive borrowing. Unlike in western Europe, tax farming was not consolidated into a larger entity that could then be captured by the state. It was too dispersed in a broad-reaching empire to be brought together. Long-standing indirect rule failed to centralize.

In the same period, the ethnic diversity of the empire, which had long been a source of strength, hardened into more distinct units no longer so tied to the center by flexible control and tailored needs. Complexity that had been a basis of legitimacy became a source of dispersed loyalty. Locals in the periphery built commercial ties with related groups outside the empire, establishing an alternative network from that controlled from the center. Competition fed conflict, exacerbated by international warfare and internal disputes. Muslim resentment of deteriorating conditions fed the rise of Islamism at the center, further cutting it off from the diversity of its holdings.

The more the state used ethnic favoritism to consolidate its hold on the central Muslim population, the more it appeared to spurn and was spurned by other populations. Outside states purposefully fed the growing sense of distinctiveness and alternative ties, while unintended demographic shifts also reinforced instability and the search for alternative legitimations tied to those outside forces.

Finally, the policy of flexibly managing diversity was abandoned by the center, and with it, the glue that held the empire together was lost. Religion became the basis for holding the loyalty of the center, which necessarily diminished the tolerance that had connected the periphery to the center. Islamization made religious relations rigid, where previously they had been flexible; finally, rigidity became brittleness. If empire had been built to hold diversity by respecting and using difference, when empire focused on its core cultural distinctiveness to hold that core together, the legitimacy ties and interests of the periphery to remain focused on the center was lost. Revenues did not flow sufficiently to the center to fund any forceful retention of holdings, and those holdings established ties outside while their financial and legitimation ties to the center weakened. What was left, finally, was a galaxy of nationalisms increasingly floating free from one another.

What is striking is that the same forces of control that helped create it undid the control of the empire. The dispersion of elites had been a source of strength, bolstering agents of indirect rule and taxation. However, when more resources were needed at the center for the fundamental public good of an effective military, the dispersion of power and resources could not be captured. Toleration of diversity had forged ethnicity into a basis for patronage ties to the center. Yet, outside pressures and commercial ties bolstered the ethnic sensibility of the units of the periphery, pulling them away from imperial loyalty. Religion, which had justified such flexibility and complexity, was turned to a more fundamentalist version of set uniformity, leaving non-Muslims out in the cold.

The same bases of legitimation that had tied elites and communities to the center turned to delegitimate that center. Finally, loyalty shifted outward, as manifested in a fiscal crisis of the state, and an empire was lost. Pressing questions then emerge.

The empire incorporated diversity, and to manage and control that diversity, it rested on a legitimacy that was not bound to any one unit or identity. However, with diversity and flexible responses demonstrating and reinforcing distinctive units as such, the trajectory to greater distinctiveness – and awareness of that distinctiveness – seems built in. Yet, as long as there was – or is – distinctiveness incorporated within states, potential pressures for dispersion of power remain.

These issues of direct and indirect rule are also evident in relations with elites. Like local communities so tied to the center, the elites' distinctiveness and interests were recognized by the center, and became legitimate while deals were struck. However, in unavoidably using local notables as the basis of indirect rule, the center also recognized and reinforced their distinctiveness, bolstering later claims for more independence. The seeds of empire were also the seeds of its transformation.

Is the conundrum of large-scale rule, or at least controlled coexistence, unsolvable? For the Ottomans, finally, it was, but only after centuries in which the contradictions did not preclude central power. So, the questions remain for us now, calling out from the minarets of an empire that once coordinated and enriched a wide array of difference that we have yet to see again.

Bibliography

Abdi, *1730 Patrona İhtilâli Hakkında bir Eser: Abdi Tarihi*, ed. Faik Reşit Unat. Ankara: Türk Tarih Kurumu, 1943.

Abou-el-Haj, Rifa'at Ali. *The 1703 Rebellion and the Structure of Ottoman Politics.* Istanbul: Nederlands Historisch-Archaeologisch Instituut, 1984.

———. "The Narcissism of Mustafa II." *Studia Islamica* 40 (1974): 115–131.

———. "The Ottoman Vezir and Paşa Households 1683–1703: A Preliminary Report." *Journal of the American Oriental Society* 94:4 (1972): 438–447.

———. "The Formal Closure of the Ottoman Frontier in Europe: 1699–1703." *Journal of the American Oriental Society* 89:3 (1969): 467–475.

———. "Ottoman Diplomacy at Karlowitz." *Journal of the American Oriental Society* 87:4 (1967): 498–512.

Adanır, Fikret. "Armenian Deportations and Massacres in 1915." In *Ethnopolitical Warfare: Causes, Consequences, and Possible Solutions*, ed. Daniel Chirot and Martin E. P. Seligman, 71–81. Washington, DC: American Psychological Association, 2001.

———. "The Ottoman Peasantries, c. 1360–c. 1860." In *The Peasantries of Europe from the Fourteenth to the Eighteenth Centuries*, ed. Tom Scott, 269–310. London and New York: Longman, 1998.

Agoston, Gabor. "A Flexible Empire: Authority and Its Limits on the Ottoman Frontiers." *International Journal of Turkish Studies* 9:1–2 (1993): 15–31.

———. "Muslim Cultural Enclaves in Hungary under Ottoman Rule." *Acta Orientalia Academiae Scientiarum Hung* 45:2–3 (1991): 181–204.

Akarlı, Engin. "Law in the Marketplace: Istanbul Artisans and Shopkeepers, 1730–1840," In *Dispensing Justice in Islam: Qadis and Their Judgements*, ed. M. Khalid Masud, Rudolph Peters, and David S. Powers, 245–270. Leiden, The Netherlands and Boston: Brill, 2006.

———. "Gedik: A Bundle of Rights and Obligations for Istanbul Artisans and Traders, 1750–1840." In *Law, Anthropology, and the Constitution of the Social: Making Persons and Things*, ed. A. Pottage and M. Mundy, 166–200. Cambridge, UK and New York: Cambridge University Press, 2004.

Akçam, Taner. *Türk Ulusal Kimliği ve Ermeni Sorunu*. Istanbul: İletişim, 1992.

Aksan, Virginia. "Ottoman Military Recruitment Strategies in the Late Eighteenth Century." In *Arming the State: Military Conscription in the Middle East and Central Asia, 1775–1925*, ed. Erik J. Zürcher, 21–39. London and New York: I. B. Tauris, 1999.

———. "Gedik: Implements, Masterships, Shop Usufruct and Monopoly among Istanbul Artisans, 1750–1850." *Wissenschaftskolleg Jahrbuch* (1985–1986): 223–232.

Aktepe, Münir. *Patrona İsyanı (1730)*. Istanbul: Istanbul Üniversitesi Edebiyat Fakültesi Yayınları, 1958.

Alexander, John C. "Law of the Conqueror (The Ottoman State) and Law of the Conquered (The Orthodox Church): The Case of Marriage and Divorce." *International Congress of Historical Sciences* 16 (1985): 369–371.

Alexandra-Dersca, Marie M. "Contributions a l'étude de l'apprivoisionnement en blé de Constantinople au XVIIIe siècle." *Studia et Acta Orietalia* 1 (1958): 13–37.

Altınay, Ahmet Refik. *Sokollu: Geçmiş Asırlarda Osmanlı Hayatı*. Istanbul: Tarih Vakfı Yurt Yayınları, 2001.

———. *Onbirinci Asr-ı Hicri'de Istanbul Hayatı (1592–1688)*, document no. 98, 52. Istanbul: Enderun Kitabevi, 1998.

———. *Onikinci Asr-ı Hicri'de Istanbul Hayatı (1689–1785)*. Istanbul: Enderun Kitabevi, 1988.

———. *Onuncu Asr-ı Hicri'de Istanbul Hayatı*. Istanbul: Enderun Kitabevi, 1988.

Andrews, Walter. *Poetry's Voice, Society's Song*. Seattle: University of Washington Press, 1985.

Archives Nationales de France, Affaires Etrangères, Série Sous-Série Bi, Correspondance Consulaire, vols. 1003, 1051, 1052, 1053, 1076.

Arnakis, G. G. "Futuwwa Traditions in the Ottoman Empire: Akhis, Bektashi Dervishes, and Craftsmen." *Journal of Near Eastern Studies* 7 (1953): 232.

———. "Gregory Palamas among the Turks and Documents of His Captivity as Historical Sources." *Speculum* 26 (1951): 108.

Artinian, Vartan. *The Armenian Constitutional System in the Ottoman Empire 1839–1863: A Study of its Historical Development*. Istanbul: [V. Artinian], 1988.

Aşıkpaşazade, *Tevarih-i Al-i Osman*, ed. Ali Bey. Istanbul: Matbaa-yı Âmire, 1914.

Atsız, Nihal. *Aşıkpaşaoğlu Tarihi*. Istanbul: Milli Eğitim Bakanlığı, 1970.

Aziz Efendi. *Kanun-name-i Sultani li Aziz Efendi, Aziz Efendi's Book of Sultanic Laws and Regulations: An Agenda for Reform by a Seventeenth-Century Statesman*, ed. and transl. Rhoads Murphey. Sources of Oriental Languages and Litarature no. 9. Cambridge, MA: Harvard University Press, 1985.

Babinger, Franz. *Mehmed the Conqueror and His Time*. Princeton, NJ: Princeton University Press, 1978.

Badian, Ernst. *Publicans and Sinners: Private Enterprise in the Service of the Roman Republic*. Ithaca, NY: Cornell University Press, 1972.

Baer, Marc David. "The Great Fire of 1660 and the Islamization of Christian and Jewish Space in Istanbul." *International Journal of Middle Eastern Studies* 36 (2004): 159–181.

———. "Honored by the Glory of Islam: The Ottoman State, Non-Muslims, and Conversion to Islam in Late Seventeenth Century Istanbul and Rumelia." Ph.D. dissertation, University of Chicago, Chicago, 2001.

———. "17. Yüzyılda Yahudilerin Osmanlı İmparatorluğu'ndaki Nüfuz ve Mevkilerini Yitirmeleri." *Toplum ve Bilim* 83 (Kış 1999/2000): 202–222.

Balivet, Michel. *Islam mystique et révolution armée dans les Balkans ottomans: vie du Cheikh Bedreddin le "Hallaj des Turcs" (1358/59–1416)*. Istanbul: Les Éditions Isis, 1995.

———. *Romanie Byzantine et pays de Rum Turc: Histoire d'un espace d'imbrication Greco-Turque*. Istanbul: Les Éditions Isis, 1994.

———. "Culture ouverte et échanges inter-réligieux dans les villes ottomanes du XIVe siècle." In *The Ottoman Emirate (1300–1389)*, ed. Elizabeth Zachariadou, 1–6. Rethymnon: Crete University Press, 1993.

———. "Aux origines de l'islamisation des Balkans ottomans." *Les Balkans à l'époque Ottomane, La revue du monde musulman et de la Méditerranée* 66 (1992/4): 11–20.

Barbaro, Nicolo. *Diary of the Siege of Constantinople 1453*. New York: Exposition Press, 1969.

Barbir, Karl K. *Ottoman Rule in Damascus, 1708–1758*. Princeton, NJ: Princeton University Press, 1980.

———. "From Pasha to Efendi: The Assimilation of Ottomans into Damascene Society 1516–1783." *International Journal of Turkish Studies* 1 (1980): 67–82.

Barkan, Ömer Lütfi. "Essai sur les données statistiques des registres de recensement dans l'empire Ottoman au XVe et XVIe siècle." *Journal of the Economic and Social History of the Orient* 1 (1957): 35.

———. "Osmanlı İmparatorluğu'nda bir İskan ve Kolonizasyon Metodu Olarak Sürgünler." *İktisat Fakültesi Mecmuası* 11 (1949–1950): 539–540.

———. *XV ve XVI. Asırlarda Osmanlı İmparatorluğu'nda Zirai Ekonominin Hukuki ve Mali Esasları, I, Kanunlar*. Istanbul: Burhaneddin Matbaası, 1945.

———. "Osmanlı İmparatorluğu'nda bir İskan ve Kolonizasyon Metodu olarak Vakıflar ve Temlikler I: İstila Devirlerinin Kolonizator Türk Dervişleri ve Zaviyeler." *Vakıflar Dergisi* 2 (1942): 281–365.

Barkey, Karen. "In Different Times: Scheduling and Social Control in the Ottoman Empire, 1550–1650." *Comparative Studies in Society and History* 38:3 (1996): 460–483.

———. *Bandits and Bureaucrats: The Ottoman Route to State Centralization*. Ithaca, NY: Cornell University Press, 1994.

Barkey, Karen and Mark von Hagen, eds. *After Empire: Multiethnic Societies and Nation-Building, the Soviet Union and Russian, Ottoman, and Habsburg Empires*. Boulder, CO: Westview Press, 1997.

Barkey, Karen and Ronan van Rossem, "Networks of Contention: Villages and Regional Structure in the Seventeenth Century Ottoman Empire," *American Journal of Sociology* 102:5 (March 1997): 1345–1382.

Barnai, Jacob. "The Spread of the Sabbatean Movement in the Seventeenth and Eighteenth Centuries." In *Communications in the Jewish Diaspora: The Pre-Modern World*, ed. Sophia Menashe, 313–337. Leiden, The Netherlands: E. J. Brill, 1996.

Barth, Fredrik. "Introduction." In *Ethnic Groups and Boundaries: The Social Organization of Culture Difference*, ed. F. Barth. Boston: Little Brown and Co., 1969.

Bayatlı, Osman. *Bergama'da Yakın Tarih Olayları, XVIII–XIX. Yüzyıl*. Izmir, Turkey: Teknik Kitap ve Mecmua Basımevi, 1957.

Beaujour, Felix. *Tableau du commerce de la Grèce*. 2 vols. Paris: Renouard, 1800.

Beldiceanu-Steinherr, Irene. "Loi sur la transmission du *Timar* (1536)." *Turcica* 2 (1979): 89–90.

———. "Le Regne de Selim Ier: Tournant dans la vie politique et religieuse de l'empire Ottoman." *Turcica* 6 (1975): 34–68.

Benbassa, Esther and Aron Rodrigue. *Sephardi Jewry: A History of the Judeo-Spanish Community, 14th–20th Centuries*. Berkeley: University of California Press, 2000.

Berktay, Halil. "Studying 'Relations' in Comparative Perspective." In *Chrétiens et Musulmans à la Renaissance: Actes du 37e Colloque International du CESR*, ed. Bartolomé Benassar and Robert Sauzet, 313–315. Paris: Honoré Champion Editeur, 1998.

———. "The Search for the Peasant in Western and Turkish History/Historiography." *Journal of Peasant Studies* 18 (1991): 109–184.

Bireley, Robert S. J. "Confessional Absolutism in the Habsburg Lands in the Seventeenth Century." In *State and Society in Early Modern Austria*, ed. Charles W. Ingrao, 36–53. West Lafayette, IN: Purdue University Press, 1994.

Birge, John Kingsley. *The Bektashi Order of Dervishes*. London: Luzac and Co., 1965.

Birnbaum, Pierre. *States and Collective Action: The European Experience*. Cambridge, UK: Cambridge University Press, 1988.

Bloxham, Donald. *The Great Game of Genocide: Imperialism, Nationalism, and the Destruction of the Ottoman Armenians*. Oxford, UK: Oxford University Press, 2005.

Borgatti, S. P., M. G. Everett, and L. C. Freeman. *Ucinet for Windows: Software for Social Network Analysis*. Cambridge, MA: Analytic Technologies, 2002.

Bornstein-Makovetsky, Leah. "Jewish Lay Leadership and Ottoman Authorities during the Sixteenth and Seventeenth Centuries." In *Ottoman and Turkish Jewry: Community and Leadership*, ed. Aron Rodrigue, 87–121. Bloomington: Indiana University Press, 1992.

Bosworth, C. E. "The Concept of Dhimma in Early Islam." In *Christians and Jews in the Ottoman Empire: The Functioning of a Plural Society*, ed. Benjamin Braude and B. Lewis, 37–51. 2 vols. New York: Holmes & Meier, 1982.

Bourdieu, Pierre, Loic J. D. Wacquant, and Samar Farage. "Rethinking the State: Genesis and Structure of the Bureaucratic Field." *Sociological Theory* 12 (1994): 1–18.

Brass, Paul. *The Production of Hindu–Muslim Violence in Contemporary India*. Seattle: University of Washington Press, 2003.

Braude, Benjamin. "Foundation Myths of the Millet System." In *Christians and Jews in the Ottoman Empire*, ed. Benjamin Braude and Bernard Lewis, 69–88. 2 vols. New York and London: Holmes & Meier, 1982.

Braude, Benjamin and Bernard Lewis. "Introduction." In *Christians and Jews in the Ottoman Empire: The Functioning of a Plural Society*, ed. Benjamin Braude and Bernard Lewis, 1–34. 2 vols. New York and London: Holmes & Meier, 1982.

Braudel, Fernand. *The Mediterranean and the Mediterranean World in the Age of Philip II*. 2 vols. New York: Harper & Row, 1972.

Brewer, John. *The Sinews of Power: War, Money and the English State, 1688–1788*. Cambridge, MA: Harvard University Press, 1988.

Bruinessen, Martin van. *Agha, Shaikh, and State: On the Social and Political Organization of Kurdistan*. Utrecht: The Netherlands Rijksuniversiteit, 1978.

Brunt, P. A. "The Romanization of the Local Ruling Classes in the Roman Empire." In *Assimilation et Résistance à la Culture Gréco-Romaine dans le Monde Ancien*, ed. D. M. Pippidi, 161–173. Paris: Société d'Edition "Les Belles Lettres," 1976.

Bryer, Anthony and Heath Lowry, eds. *Continuity and Change in Late Byzantine and Early Ottoman Society*. Birmingham, UK: University of Birmingham, 1986.

Burt, Ronald S. *Brokerage and Closure: An Introduction to Social Capital*. Oxford, UK: Oxford University Press, 2005.

———. "Structural Holes and Good Ideas." *American Journal of Sociology* 110 (2004): 349–399.

———. *Bandwidth and Echo: Trust, Information, and Gossip in Social Networks.* New York: Russell Sage Foundation, 2001.

Çadırcı, Musa. "Ankara Sancağında Nizam-ı Cedid Ortasının Teşkili ve 'Nizam-ı Cedid Askeri Kanunnamesi.'" *Belleten* 36 (1972):1–13.

Cahen, Claude. *Pre-Ottoman Turkey: A General Survey of the Material and Spiritual Culture and History, c. 1071–1330.* New York: Taplinger, 1968.

Cantemir, Dimitri. *History of the Growth and Decay of the Ottoman Empire.* (London, 1734).

Cassels, Lavender. *The Struggle for the Ottoman Empire 1717–1740.* London: John Murray, 1966.

Castellan, Georges. *Histoire des Balkans XIVe–XXe siècle.* Paris: Fayard, 1999.

Çataltepe, Sipahi. *19. Yüzyıl Başlarında Avrupa Dengesi ve Nizam-ı Cedid Ordusu.* Istanbul: Göçebe Yayınları, 1997.

Çavuşoğlu, Semiramis. "The Kadızadeli Movement: An Attempt of Seriat Minded Reform in the Ottoman Empire." Ph.D dissertation, Princeton University, Princeton, NJ, 1990.

Çetin, Osman. *Sicillere Göre Bursa'da İhtida Hareketleri ve Sosyal Sonuçları (1472–1909).* Ankara: Türk Tarih Kurumu Basımevi, 1994.

Cevdet, Paşa Ahmed. *Tarih-i Cevdet*, 2d ed. 12 vols. Istanbul: Matbaa-yı Osmaniye, 1884–1885.

Cezar, Yavuz. *Osmanlı Maliyesinde Bunalım ve Değişim Dönemi.* Istanbul: Alan Yayıncılık, 1986.

Chelebi, Katib. *The Balance of Truth*, transl. G. L. Lewis. London: George Allen and Unwin Ltd., 1957.

Chirot, Daniel. "Empire and Nation: Conclusion." Empire and Nation Conference, 5–7 Dec. San Diego. 2003.

———. "Modernism Without Liberalism." *Contentions* 13 (1995): 141–166.

Chirot, Daniel and Karen Barkey. "States in Search of Legitimacy." *International Journal of Comparative Sociology* 24:1–2 (1983): 30–46.

Çizakça, Murat. *A Comparative Evolution of Business Partnerships: The Islamic World and Europe with Specific Reference to the Ottoman Archives.* Leiden, The Netherlands, and New York: E. J. Brill, 1996.

Clayer, Nathalie. "Des agents du pouvoir Ottoman dans les Balkans: les Halvetis." *Les Balkans à l'époque Ottomane* 66 (1992–1994): 21–29.

Clogg, Richard. "The Greek Millet in the Ottoman Empire." In *Christians and Jews in the Ottoman Empire*, ed. Benjamin Braude and Bernard Lewis, 185. 2 vols. New York and London: Holmes & Meier, 1982.

———, ed. *Balkan Society in the Age of Greek Independence.* London: Macmillan, 1981.

———. *Struggle for Greek Independence.* New York: Macmillan, 1973.

Cohen, Amnon. "Communal Legal Entities in a Muslim Setting, Theory and Practice: The Jewish Community in Sixteenth-Century Jerusalem." *Islamic Law and Society* 3:1 (1996): 75–89.

Cohen, Mark R. "Persecution, Response, and Collective Memory: The Jews of Islam in the Classical Period." In *The Jews of Medieval Islam*, ed. Daniel Frank, 145–164. Leiden, The Netherlands: E. J. Brill, 1995.

———. *Under Crescent and Cross: The Jews in the Middle Ages.* Princeton, NJ: Princeton University Press, 1994.

Crepell, Ingrid. *Toleration and Identity: Foundations in Early Modern Thought*. New York: Routledge, 2003.

Crews, Robert. *For Prophet and Tsar: Islam and Empire in Russia and Central Asia*. Cambridge, MA: Harvard University Press, 2006.

———. "Empire and the Confessional State: Islam and Religious Politics in Nineteenth-Century Russia." *American Historical Review* 108:1 (February 2003): 50–83.

Crummey, Robert. *The Formation of Muscovy 1304–1613*. New York: Longman, 1987.

Cuno, Kenneth M. "The Origins of Private Property of Land in Egypt: A Reappraisal." *International Journal of Middle Eastern Studies* 12:3 (1980): 245–275.

Cvetkova, Bistra. "Les Celep et leur rôle dans la vie économique des Balkans à l'époque ottomane (XVe–XVIIIes)." In *Studies in the Economic History of the Middle East*, ed. M. A. Cook. London: Oxford University Press, 1970.

Darling, Linda. "Contested Territory: Ottoman Holy War in Comparative Context." *Studia Islamica* 91 (2000): 133–163.

———. *Revenue-Raising and Legitimacy: Tax Collection and Finance Administration in the Ottoman Empire 1560–1660*. Leiden, The Netherlands and New York: E. J. Brill, 1996.

David, Geza and Pal Fodor. "Introduction." In *Ottomans, Hungarians, and Habsburgs in Central Europe: The Military Confines in the Era of Ottoman Conquest*, ed. Geza David and Pal Fodor, xi–xxvii. Leiden, The Netherlands: Brill, 2000.

Davison, Roderic. "Nationalism as an Ottoman Problem and an Ottoman Response." In *Nationalism in a Non-National State: The Dissolution of the Ottoman Empire*, ed. William W. Haddad and William Ochsenwald, 25–56. Columbus: Ohio State University Press, 1977.

———. *Reform in the Ottoman Empire, 1856–1876*. Princeton, NJ: Princeton University Press, 1963.

de Groot, Alexander H. "Protection and Nationality: The Decline of the Dragomans," in *Istanbul et les Langues Orientales*, ed. Frederic Hitzel. Paris: Harmattan, 1997.

Deringil, Selim. *The Well-Protected Domains: Ideology and the Legitimation of Power in the Ottoman Empire, 1876–1909*. London and New York: I. B. Tauris, 1999.

———. "Legitimacy Structures in the Ottoman State: The Reign of Abdülhamid II (1876–1909)." *International Journal of Middle Eastern Studies* 23 (1991): 345–359.

Dessert, Daniel. *Argent: Pouvoir et société au grand siècle*. Paris: Fayard, 1984.

Dimitriades, Vasilis. "Ottoman Chalkidiki: An Area in Transition." In *Continuity and Change in Late Byzantine and Early Ottoman Society*, ed. Anthony Bryer and Heath Lowry. Washington, DC: Dumbarton Oaks Research Library and Collection, 1986.

Divitçioğlu, Sencer. *Osmanlı Beyliğinin Kuruluşu*. Istanbul: Eren Yayıncılık, 1996.

Doumani, Beshara. *Rediscovering Palestine: Merchants and Peasants in Jabal Nablus, 1700–1900*. Berkeley: University of California Press, 1995.

Doyle, Michael W. *Empires*. Ithaca, NY: Cornell University Press, 1986.

Dressler, Markus. "Inventing Orthodoxy: Competing Claims for Authority and Legitimacy in the Ottoman-Safavid Conflict." In *Legitimizing the Order: The Ottoman Rhetoric of State Power*, ed. Hakan T. Karateke and Maurus Reinkowski, 151–173. Leiden, The Netherlands and Boston: Brill, 2005.

Ducellier, Alain. "Byzantins et Turcs du XIIIe au XVIe siècle: du monde partage à l'empire reconstitué." In *Chrétiens et Musulmans à la Renaissance*, ed. Bartolomé Bennassar and Robert Sauzet, 11–49. Paris: Honoré Champion Editeur, 1998.

Duguid, Stephen. "The Politics of Unity: Hamidian Policy in Eastern Anatolia." *Middle Eastern Studies* 9 (1973): 139–155.

Dumont, Paul. "Jewish Communities in Turkey during the Last Decades of the 19th Century." In *Christians and Jews in the Ottoman Empire*, ed. Benjamin Braude and Bernard Lewis, 209–242. 2 vols. New York and London: Holmes & Meier, 1982.

Eisenstadt, S. N. "Multiple Modernities." *Daedalus* 129 (2000): 1–29.

———. *The Political Systems of Empires*. Glencoe: Free Press, 1963.

Eldem, Edhem. "French Trade and Commercial Policy in the Levant in the Eighteenth Century." In *The Ottoman Capitulations: Text and Context*, ed. Maurits H. van den Boogert and Kate Fleet. *Oriente Moderno* 22:3 (2003): 27–43.

———. *French Trade in Istanbul in the Eighteenth Century*. Leiden, The Netherlands and Boston: E. J. Brill, 1999.

———, Daniel Goffman, and Bruce Masters, *The Ottoman City between East and West: Aleppo, Izmir, and Istanbul*. Cambridge, UK: Cambridge University Press.

Eliot, Sir Charles. *Turkey in Europe*. London: Frank Cass and Co. Ltd., 1965.

Epstein, Mark. *The Ottoman Jewish Communities and Their Role in the Fifteenth and Sixteenth Centuries*. Freiburg, Germany: Klaus Schwarz Verlag, 1980.

Erdbrink, G. R. Bosscha. *At the Threshold of Felicity: Ottoman–Dutch Relations during the Embassy of Cornelis Calkoen at the Sublime Porte, 1726–1744*. Amsterdam: A. L. van Gendt and Co. B.V., 1977.

Ertman, Thomas, *Birth of the Leviathan: Building States and Regimes in Medieval and Early Modern Europe*. Cambridge, UK: Cambridge University Press, 1997.

Faroqhi, Suraiya. "Migration into Eighteenth-Century 'Greater Istanbul' as Reflected in the Kadi Registers of Eyup." *Turcica* 30 (1998): 163–183.

———. "Labor Recruitment and Control in the Ottoman Empire (Sixteenth and Seventeenth Centuries)." In *Manufacturing in the Ottoman Empire and Turkey, 1500–1950*, ed. Donald Quataert, 13–57. Albany: State University of New York Press, 1994.

———. "Crisis and Change, 1590–1699." In *An Economic and Social History of the Ottoman Empire, 1300–1914*, ed. Halil İnalcık and Donald Quataert, 538–541. Cambridge, UK: Cambridge University Press, 1994.

———. "Trade Controls, Provisioning Policies, and Donations: The Egypt–Hijaz Connection during the Second Half of the Sixteenth Century." In *Suleyman the Second and His Time*, ed. Halil İnalcık and Cemal Kafadar. Istanbul: Isis Press, 1993.

———. "Wealth and Power in the Land of Olives: Economic and Political Activities of Muridzade Haci Mehmed Agha, Notable of Edremit." In *Landholding and Commercial Agriculture in the Middle East*, ed. Çağlar Keyder and Faruk Tabak. Albany: State University of New York Press, 1991.

———. "Agricultural Crisis and the Art of Flute-Playing: The Worldly Affairs of the Mevlevi Dervishes," *Turcica* 20 (1988): 43–69.

———. "Civilian Society and Political Power in the Ottoman Empire: A Report on Research in Collective Biography (1480–1830)." *International Journal of Middle Eastern Studies* 17 (1985): 109–117.

———. "The Tekke of Haci Bektaş: Social Position and Economic Activities." *International Journal of Middle Eastern Studies* 7 (1976): 183–208.

———. "Agricultural Activities in a Bektashi Center: The Tekke of Kizil Deli 1750–1830." *Sudost-Forschungen* 35 (1976): 69–96.

Faroqhi, Suraiya and Randi Deguilhem, eds. *Crafts and Craftsmen of the Middle East: Fashioning the Individual in the Muslim Mediterranean*. London and New York: I. B. Tauris, 2005.

Fearon, James D. and David D. Laitin. "Explaining Interethnic Cooperation." *American Political Science Review* 90:4 (1996): 715–735.

Findley, Carter V. *Bureaucratic Reform in the Ottoman Empire: The Sublime Porte.* Princeton, NJ: Princeton University Press, 1980.

———"Patrimonial Household Organization and Factional Activity in the Ottoman Ruling Class." In *Türkiye'nin Sosyal ve Ekonomik Tarihi (1071–1920)*, ed. Halil İnalcık, Osman Okyar, and Ü. Nalbantoğlu, 227–235. Ankara: Meteksan, 1980.

Fine, John V. A. *The Early Medieval Balkans: A Critical Survey from the Sixth to the Late Twelfth Century.* Ann Arbor: University of Michigan Press, 1999.

———. *The Late Medieval Balkans: A Critical Survey from the Late Twelfth Century to the Ottoman Conquest.* Ann Arbor: University of Michigan Press, 1987.

Finkel, Caroline. *Osman's Dream.* New York: Basic Books, 2005.

Fleet, Kate. *European and Islamic Trade in the Early Ottoman State: The Merchants of Genoa and Turkey.* Cambridge, UK: Cambridge University Press, 1999.

Fleischer, Cornell H. *Bureaucrat and Intellectual in the Ottoman Empire: The Historian Mustafa Ali, 1546–1600.* Princeton, NJ: Princeton University Press, 1986.

Fodor, Pal. "Making a Living on the Frontiers: Volunteers in the Sixteenth Century Army." In *Ottomans, Hungarians, and Habsburgs in Central Europe: The Military Confines in the Era of Ottoman Conquest*, ed. Geza David and Pal Fodor, 229–265. Leiden, The Netherlands: Brill, 2000.

Fortna, Benjamin C. *Imperial Classroom: Islam, the State, and Education in the Late Ottoman Empire.* Oxford, UK: Oxford University Press, 2002.

Fotic, Aleksandar. "The Official Explanations for the Confiscation and Sale of Monasteries (Churches) and Their Estates at the Time of Selim II." *Turcica* 26 (1994): 33–54.

Franco, Moise. *Essai sur l'histoire des Israelites de l'empire Ottoman: depuis les origines jusqu'à nos jours.* Paris: Librairie A. Durlacher, 1897.

Frangakis-Syrett, Elena. *The Commerce of Smyrna in the Eighteenth Century.* Athens: Centre for Asia Minor Studies, 1992.

———. "Trade between the Ottoman Empire and Western Europe: The Case of Izmir in the Eighteenth Century." *New Perspectives on Turkey* (Spring 1988): 1–18.

———. "The Raya Communities of Smyrna in the 18th Century (1690–1820): Demography and Economic Activities." In *Actes du colloque international d'histoire: la ville néohellenique. Héritages Ottoman à état Grec.* vol. 1. Athens, 1985.

Frazee, Charles A. *Catholics and Sultans: The Church and the Ottoman Empire 1453–1923.* London: Cambridge University Press, 1983.

Galante, Avram. *Histoire des Juifs de Turquie.* 9 vols. Istanbul: Isis Press, 1940.

Gandev, Christo. "L'apparition des rapports capitalistes dans l'économie rurale de la Bulgarie du nord-ouest au cours du XVIIIe siècle." *Etudes Historiques* 1 (1960): 207–220.

Gara, Eleni. "In Search of Communities in Seventeenth Century Ottoman Sources: The Case of Kara Ferye District." *Turcica* 30 (1998): 135–162.

Geertz, Clifford. *Islam Observed: Religious Development in Morocco and Indonesia.* Chicago: University of Chicago Press, 1968.

Genç, Mehmet. *Osmanlı İmparatorluğu'nda Devlet ve Ekonomi.* Istanbul: Ötüken, 2000.

———. "Ottoman Industry in the Eighteenth Century: General Framework, Characteristics, and Main Trends." In *Manufacturing in the Ottoman Empire and Turkey,*

1500–1950, ed. Donald Quataert. Albany: State University of New York Press, 1994.

———. "19. Yüzyılda Osmanlı İktisadi Dünya Görüşünün Klasik Prensiplerindeki Değişmeler." *Divan* 1:6 (1991): 1–8.

———. "A Study on the Feasibility of Using Eighteenth-Century Ottoman Financial Records as an Indicator of Economic Activity." In *The Ottoman Empire and the World-Economy*, ed. Huri Islamoğlu-Inan. Cambridge, UK: Cambridge University Press, 1987.

———. "A Comparative Study of the Life Term Tax Farming Data and the Volume of Commercial and Industrial Activities in the Ottoman Empire during the Second Half of the 18th Century." In *La Révolution industrielle dans le sud-est Européen XIX siècle*. Sofia: Institut d'Etudes Balkaniques, Musée National Polytechnique, 1976.

———. "Osmanlı Maliyesinde Malikane Sistemi." In *İktisat Tarihi Semineri*, ed. Osman Okyar and Ünal Nalbantoğlu. Ankara: Hacettepe Üniversitesi Yayınları, 1975.

Gervinus, G. G. *Insurrection et Régénération de la Grèce*, transl. J. F. Minssen and Leonidas Sgouta. 2 vols. Paris: A. Durand, 1863.

Gibb, H. A. R. and Harold Bowen. *Islamic Society and the West: A Study of the Impact of Western Civilization on Moslem Culture in the Near East*. 2 vols. London: Oxford University Press, 1957.

Gibbons, H. A. *The Foundation of the Ottoman Empire: A History of the Osmanlis up to the Death of Bayezid I, 1300–1403*. London: Frank Cass and Co., 1968.

Ginzburg, Carlo. *The Cheese and the Worms: The Cosmos of a Sixteenth-Century Miller*. London: Routledge and Kegan Paul, [1976] 1980.

Goffman, Daniel. "Ottoman Millets in the Early Seventeenth Century." *New Perspectives on Turkey* 11 (1997): 135–158.

Gölpınarlı, Abdülbâki. *Melâmîlik ve Melâmîler*. Istanbul: Devlet Matbaası, 1931.

———. *Simavna Kadısıoğlu Şeyh Bedreddîn*. Istanbul: Varlık Yayınevi, 1966.

Gondicas, Dimitri and Charles Issawi, eds., *Ottoman Greeks in the Age of Nationalism*. Princeton, NJ: Darwin Press, 1999.

Goody, Jack. *The Logic of Writing and the Organization of Society*. Cambridge, UK: Cambridge University Press, 1986.

Grant, Jonathan. "Rethinking the Ottoman Decline: Military Technology Diffusion in the Ottoman Empire, Fifteenth to Eighteenth Centuries." *Journal of World History* 10 (1999): 179–201.

Greene, Molly. *A Shared World: Christians and Muslims in the Early Modern Mediterranean*. Princeton, NJ: Princeton University Press, 2000.

Greenwood, Anthony W. "Istanbul's Meat Provisioning: A Study of the Celepkeşan System." Ph.D. dissertation, University of Chicago, Chicago, 1988.

Groiss, Arnon. "Minorities in a Modernizing Society: Secular vs. Religious Identities in Ottoman Syria, 1840–1914." *Princeton Papers in Near Eastern Studies* 3 (1994): 39–70.

Güçer, Lütfi. *Osmanlı İmparatorluğunda Hububat Meselesi ve Hububattan Alınan Vergiler*. Istanbul: Sermet Matbaası, 1964.

———. "XVIII. Yüzyıl Ortalarında Istanbul'un İaşesi için Lüzumlu Hububatın Temini Meselesi." *İktisat Fakültesi Mecmuası* 11 (1949–1950): 397–416.

Güran, Tevfik. "The State Role in the Grain Supply of Istanbul: The Grain Administration, 1793–1839." *International Journal of Turkish Studies* 3 (1985): 27–41.

Habib, Irfan. *The Agrarian System of Mughal India (1556–1707)*. London: Asia, 1963.

Hacker, Joseph R. "The Sürgün System and Jewish Society in the Ottoman Empire during the Fifteenth to the Seventeenth Centuries." In *Ottoman and Turkish Jewry: Community and Leadership*, ed. Aron Rodrigue, 1–65. Bloomington: Indiana University Press, 1992.

———"Ottoman Policy toward the Jews and Jewish Attitudes toward the Ottomans during the Fifteenth Century." In *Christians and Jews in the Ottoman Empire*, ed. Benjamin Braude and Bernard Lewis, 117–126. 2 vols. New York and London: Holmes & Meier, 1982.

Halaçoğlu, Ahmet. *Teke (Antalya) Mütesellimi Hacı Mehmed Ağa ve Faaliyetleri*. Isparta: Fakülte Kitabevi, 2002.

Haldon, John. "Empires and Exploitation: The Case of Byzantium." Paper Presented at the Social Science History Institute, Stanford University, 2001.

Hanioğlu, M. Şükrü. *The Young Turks in Opposition*. New York and Oxford, UK: Oxford University Press, 1995.

Hasluck, F. W. *Christianity and Islam under the Sultans*. 2 vols. Oxford, UK: Clarendon Press, 1929.

Hattox, Ralph S. "Mehmed the Conqueror, the Patriarch of Jerusalem, and Mamluk Authority." *Studia Islamica* 90 (2000): 105–123.

Hegyi, Klara. "The Ottoman Network of Fortresses in Hungary." In *Ottomans, Hungarians, and Habsburgs in Central Europe: The Military Confines in the Era of Ottoman Conquest*, ed. Geza David and Pal Fodor, 163–193. Leiden, The Netherlands: Brill, 2000.

Hellie, Richard. *Enserfment and Military Change in Muscovy*. Chicago: University of Chicago Press, 1971.

Heyd, Uriel. "The Ottoman Ulema and Westernization in the Time of Selim III and Mahmud II." *Scripta Hierosolymitana* 9 (1961): 63–96.

———. "The Jewish Communities in Istanbul in the Seventeenth Century." *Oriens* 6 (1953): 299–314.

Hickok, Michael Robert. *The Ottoman Empire and Its Heritage: Ottoman Military Administration in Eighteenth-Century Bosnia*. Leiden, The Netherlands and New York: E. J. Brill, 1997.

Hikmet, Nazım. "The Epic of Sheik Bedreddin." In *Poems of Nazim Hikmet*. New York: Persea Books, 2002.

Hitzel, Frederic, ed. *Istanbul et les langues orientales*. Paris: Harmattan, 1997.

Hobsbawm, E. J. "How Empires End." In *After Empire: Multiethnic Societies and Nation-Building*, ed. Karen Barkey and Mark von Hagen. Boulder, CO: Westview Press, 1997.

Hoffman, George W. "Thessaloniki: The Impact of a Changing Hinterland." *East European Quarterly* 2:1 (1968): 1–27.

Hopwood, Keith. "The Byzantine–Turkish Frontier c. 1250–1300." *Acta Viennensia Ottomanica*, 153–161. Wien, Germany: Im Selbstverlag des Instituts für Orientalistik, 1999.

———. "Low-Level Diplomacy between Byzantines and Ottoman Turks: The Case of Bithynia." In *Byzantine Diplomacy*, ed. Jonathan Shepard and Simon Franklin. Aldershot, UK: Variorum, 1992.

Hourani, Albert. *A History of the Arab Peoples*. Cambridge, MA: Harvard University Press, 1991.

————. "Ottoman Reform and the Politics of Notables." In *Beginnings of Moderniza-tion in the Middle East: The Nineteenth Century*, ed. William R. Polk and Richard L. Chambers. Chicago: University of Chicago Press, 1968.

Hupchick, Dennis P. *The Bulgarians in the Seventeenth Century: Slavic Orthodox Society and Culture under Ottoman Rule.* Jefferson, NC: McFarland and Co., 1993.

————. "Orthodoxy and Bulgarian Ethnic Awareness under Ottoman Rule, 1396–1762." *Nationalities Papers* 21:2 (1993): 75–93.

Iakichitch, G. "Notes sur Pasvan-oğlu, 1758–1807, par l'adjudant commandant Meriage." *La Revue Slave* 1:1 (May 1906): 261–279; 1:2 (June 1906): 419–429; 2:1 (July–August 1906): 139–144; 2:2 (November–December 1906): 435–448; 3:1 (January–February 1907): 138–144; 3:2 (March–April 1907): 278–288.

Imber, Colin H. *The Ottoman Empire 1300–1650.* New York: Palgrave Macmillan, 2002.

————. *Ebu's-su'ud: The Islamic Legal Tradition.* Edinburgh: Edinburgh University Press, 1997.

————. "Canon and Apocrypha in Early Ottoman History." In *Studies in Ottoman History in Honour of Professor V. L. Menage*, ed. Colin Heywood and Colin Imber, 117–137. Istanbul: Isis Press, 1994.

————. "The Legend of Osman Gazi." In *The Ottoman Emirate*, ed. Elizabeth Zachari-adou. Rethymnon: Crete University Press, 1993.

————. *The Ottoman Empire: 1300–1481.* Istanbul: Isis Press, 1990.

————. "The Ottoman Dynastic Myth." *Turcica* 19 (1987): 7–27.

————. "The Persecution of the Ottoman Shi'ites according to the Muhimme Defterleri, 1565–1585." *Der Islam* 56:2 (1979): 245–273.

İnalcık, Halil. "Foundations of Ottoman–Jewish Cooperation." In *Jews, Turks, Ottomans: A Shared History, Fifteenth through the Twentieth Century*, ed. Avig-dor Levy. Syracuse, NY: Syracuse University Press, 2002.

————. "An Overview of Ottoman History." In *The Great Ottoman-Turkish Civiliza-tion* 41. vol. 1. Ankara: Yeni Türkiye, 2000.

————. "How to Read Ashik Pasha-Zade's History." In *Studies in Ottoman History in Honour of Professor V. L. Menage*, ed. Colin Heywood and Colin Imber, 139–156. Istanbul: Isis Press, 1994.

————. "The Ottoman State: Economy and Society, 1300–1600," in *An Economic and Social History of the Ottoman Empire, 1300–1914*, ed. Halil İnalcık and Donald Quataert. Cambridge, UK: Cambridge University Press, 1994.

————. "State, Sovereignty and Law During the Reign of Suleyman." In *Suleyman the Second and His Time*, ed. Halil İnalcık and Cemal Kafadar, 59–92. Istanbul: SIS Press, 1993.

————. "The Emergence of Big Farms, Çiftliks." In *Landholding and Commercial Agri-culture in the Middle East*, ed. Çağlar Keyder and Faruk Tabak. Albany: State Uni-versity of New York Press, 1991.

————. "The Status of the Greek Orthodox Patriarch under the Ottomans." *Turcica* 21–23 (1991): 407–437.

————. "Istanbul: An Islamic City." *Journal of Islamic Studies* 1 (1990): 1–23.

————. "Köy, Köylü ve İmparatorluk." In *V. Milletlerarası Türkiye Sosyal ve İktisat Tarihi Kongresi, Tebliğler.* Ankara: Türk Tarih Kurumu Basımevi, 1990.

————. "The Rise of the Turcoman Maritime Principalities in Anatolia: Byzantium and the Crusades." *Byzantinische Forschungen* 9 (1985): 179–217.

———. "Military and Fiscal Transformation in the Ottoman Empire, 1600–1700." In *Studies in Ottoman Social and Economic History*. London: Variorum Reprints, 1985.

———. "Ottoman Archival Materials on *Millets*." In *Christians and Jews in the Ottoman Empire*, ed. Benjamin Braude and Bernard Lewis, 437–449. 2 vols. New York and London: Holmes & Meier, 1982.

———. "The Question of the Emergence of the Ottoman State." *International Journal of Turkish Studies* 4 (1980): 71–79.

———. "Centralization and Decentralization in Ottoman Administration." In *Studies in Eighteenth Century Islamic History*, ed. Thomas Naff and Roger Owen. Carbondale: Southern Illinois University Press, 1977.

———. *The Ottoman Empire: The Classical Age 1300–1600*. London: Weidenfeld and Nicolson, 1973.

———. "The Policy of Mehmed II toward the Greek Population of Istanbul and the Byzantine Buildings of the City." *Dumbarton Oaks Papers* 23 & 24 (1969–1970): 231–249.

———. "Djizya." *Encyclopedia of Islam*. 2d ed, 563–565. Leiden, The Netherlands: E. J. Brill, 1965.

———. "Sened-i İttifak ve Gülhane Hatt-ı Hümayunu." *Belleten* 28 (1964): 603–690.

———. "Osmanlılarda Raiyyet Rüsumu." *Belleten* 23 (1959): 575–610.

———. "Ottoman Methods of Conquest." *Studia Islamica* 2 (1954): 103–129.

———. "Stefan Duşandan Osmanlı Imparatorluğuna: XV. Asırda Rumeli'de Hiristyan Sipahiler ve Menşeleri," *Fuad Köprülü Armağanı/Melanges Fuad Köprülü* (Istanbul: Ankara Üniversitesi Dil ve Tarih-Coğrafya Fakültesi Yayınları, 1953): 207–248.

İnalcık, Halil and Donald Quataert, eds. *An Economic and Social History of the Ottoman Empire, 1300–1914*. Cambridge, UK: Cambridge University Press, 1994.

Ingrao, Charles. *The Habsburg Monarchy 1618–1815*. Cambridge, UK: Cambridge University Press, 1994.

Issawi, Charles. *The Economic History of the Middle East 1800–1914*. Chicago: University of Chicago Press, 1966.

Itzkowitz, Norman. "Men and Ideas in the Eighteenth Century Ottoman Empire." In *Studies in Eighteenth-Century Islamic History*, ed. Thomas Naff and Roger Owen. Carbondale: Southern Illinois University Press, 1977.

———. "Eighteenth Century Ottoman Realities." *Studia Islamica* 16 (1962): 73–94.

Jennings, Ronald C. *Christians and Muslims in Ottoman Cyprus and the Mediterranean World, 1571–1640*. New York and London: New York University Press, 1993.

Jennings, Ronald, "Loans and Credit in the Early 17th Century Ottoman Judicial Records: The Sharia Court of Anatolian Kayseri." *Journal of the Economic and Social History of the Orient* 16 (1973): 168–216.

Jones, J. R. Melville. *The Siege of Constantinople 1453: Seven Contemporary Accounts*. Amsterdam: Hakkert, 1972.

Jowitt, Ken. "Ethnicity: Nice, Nasty, and Nihilistic." In *Ethnopolitical Warfare: Causes, Consequences, and Possible Solutions*, ed. Daniel Chirot and Martin E. P. Seligman, 27–36. Washington, DC: American Psychological Association, 2001.

Kafadar, Cemal. *Between Two Worlds: The Construction of the Ottoman State*. Berkeley: University of California Press, 1995.

———. "Yeniçeri–Esnaf Relations: Solidarity and Conflict." M.A. thesis, Institute of Islamic Studies, McGill University, Montreal, Quebec, Canada, 1981.

Kaldy-Nagy, Gyula. "The Holy War (Jihad) in the First Centuries of the Ottoman Empire." *Harvard Ukrainian Studies* 3–4 (1979–1980): 467–473.

Kappeler, Andreas. *The Russian Empire: A Multiethnic History*, transl. Alfred Clayton. New York: Pearson Education, 2001.

Karateke, Hakan T. "Legitimizing the Ottoman Sultanate: A Framework for Historical Analysis." In *Legitimizing the Order: The Ottoman Rhetoric of State Power*, ed. Hakan T. Karateke and Maurus Reinkowski. Leiden, The Netherlands and Boston: Brill, 2005.

Karpat, Kemal. *The Politicization of Islam: Reconstructing Identity, State, Faith, and Community in the Late Ottoman State*. Oxford, UK and New York: Oxford University Press, 2001.

———. "Millets and Nationality: The Roots of the Incongruity of Nation and State in the Post-Ottoman Era." In *Christians and Jews in the Ottoman Empire*, ed. Benjamin Braude and Bernard Lewis. 2 vols. New York and London: Holmes & Meier, 1982.

———. *An Inquiry into the Social Foundations of Nationalism in the Ottoman State: From Social Estates to Classes, from Millets to Nations*. Princeton, NJ: Center of International Studies, Princeton University, 1973.

———. "The Transformation of the Ottoman State, 1789–1908." *International Journal of Middle Eastern Studies* 3 (1972): 243–281.

———. "The Land Regime, Social Structure and Modernization in the Ottoman Empire." In *Beginnings of Modernization in the Middle East*, ed. William R. Polk and Richard L. Chambers, 69–90. Chicago: University of Chicago Press, 1968.

Kasaba, Reşat. "A Time and a Place for the Nonstate: Social Change in the Ottoman Empire during the Long Nineteenth Century." In *State Power and Social Forces: Domination and Transformation in the Third World*, ed. Joel S. Migdal, Atul Kohli, and Vivienne Shue, 207–230. Cambridge, UK: Cambridge University Press, 1994.

———. "Izmir." *Review* 16 (1993): 387–410.

———. "Migrant Labor in Western Anatolia, 1750–1850." In *Land Holding and Commercial Agriculture in the Middle East*, ed. Çağlar Keyder and Faruk Tabak. Albany: State University of New York Press, 1991.

———. *The Ottoman Empire and the World Economy: The Nineteenth Century*. Albany: State University of New York Press, 1988.

———. "Incorporation of the Ottoman Empire, 1750–1820." *Review* 10 (1987): 805–847.

Katırcıoğlu, Nurhan Fatma. "The Ottoman Ayan, 1550–1812: A Struggle for Legitimacy." M.A. thesis, University of Wisconsin–Madison, 1984.

Kerem, Yitzchak. "Relations between the Jews, the Greek-Orthodox and the Armenians in the 19th and Early 20th Centuries in the Ottoman Empire." *Acta Viennensia Ottomanica* (1999): 191–198.

Keyder, Çağlar. "The Ottoman Empire." In *After Empire: Multiethnic Societies and Nation-Building, the Soviet Union and Russian, Ottoman and Habsburg Empires*, ed. Karen Barkey and Mark von Hagen, 30–45. Boulder, CO: Westview Press, 1997.

———. "Introduction: Large-Scale Commercial Agriculture in the Ottoman Empire?" In *Landholding and Commercial Agriculture in the Middle East*, ed. Çağlar Keyder and Faruk Tabak. Albany: State University of New York Press, 1991.

———. *State and Class in Turkey: A Study in Capitalist Development*. London: Verso, 1987.

Khordarkovsky, Michael. "'Not by Word Alone': Missionary Policies and Religious Conversion in Early Modern Russia." *Comparative Studies in Society and History* 38:2 (April 1996): 267–293.

Khoury, Dina Rizk. "Administrative Practice between Religious Law (Shari'a) and State Law (Kanun) on the Eastern Frontiers of the Ottoman Empire." *Journal of Early Modern History* 5:4 (2001): 305–330.

———. *State and Provincial Society in the Ottoman Empire, Mosul, 1540–1834.* Cambridge, UK: Cambridge University Press, 1998.

Kidd, B. J. *The Churches of Eastern Christendom.* London: Faith Press, 1927.

Kieser, Hans-Lukas and Dominik J. Schaller, eds. *Der Volkermord an den Armeniern und die Shoah.* Zurich: Chronos, 2002.

Kırmızıaltın, Süphan. "Conversion in Ottoman Balkans: A Historiographical Survey." *History Compass* 5 (2007): 646–657.

Kiser, Edgar and Joshua Kane. "Revolution and State Structure: The Bureaucratization of Tax Administration in Early Modern England and France." *American Journal of Sociology* 107 (2001): 183–223.

Kissling, Hans Joachim. "The Sociological and Educational Role of the Dervish Orders in the Ottoman Empire." *American Anthropologist* 22 (1954): 23–35.

Kitromilides, Paschalis. "'Imagined Communities' and the Origins of the National Question in the Balkans." In Paschalis Kitromilides, *Enlightenment, Nationalism, Orthodoxy: Studies in the Culture and Political Thought of South-Eastern Europe.* Aldershot, UK: Variorum, 1994.

———. "Imagined Communities and the Origin of the National Question in the Balkans." In *Modern Greece: Nationalism and Nationality*, ed. Martin Blinkhorn and Thanos Veremis. Athens: SAGE-ELIAMEP, 1990.

———. "The Dialectic of Intolerance." *Journal of Hellenic Diaspora* 6 (1979): 5–30.

Kivelson, Valerie A. *Autocracy in the Provinces: The Muscovite Gentry and Political Culture in the Seventeenth Century.* Palo Alto, CA: Stanford University Press, 1996.

Koçi Bey. *Risale*, ed. Zuhuri Danışman. Istanbul: Milli Eğitim Bakanlığı Yayınları, 1972.

Köksal, Yonca. "Local Intermediaries and Ottoman State Centralization: A Comparison of the Tanzimat Reforms in the Provinces of Ankara and Edirne (1839–1878)." Ph.D. dissertation, Columbia University, New York, 2002.

Kömürciyan, Eremya Çelebi. *Istanbul Tarihi: XVII. Asırda Istanbul.* Istanbul: Eren Yayıncılık ve Kitapçılık Ltd. Şti., 1988.

Konortas, Paraskevas. "Considérations Ottomanes au sujet du statut du patriarcat orthodoxe de Constantinople 15e–16e siècles: quelques hypothèses." *Congrés international des études du sud-est Européen* 6 (1989): 213–226.

Köprülü, Fuat M. *The Origins of the Ottoman Empire*, transl. and ed. Gary Leiser. Albany: State University of New York Press, 1992.

Küçükdağ, Yusuf. "Precautions of the Ottoman State against Shah Ismail's Attempt to Convert Anadolu (Anatolia) to Shia." In *The Great Ottoman–Turkish Civilization*, ed. Kemal Çiçek, 181–193. Ankara: Yeni Türkiye, 2000.

Kunt, Metin I. "State and Sultan up to the Age of Süleymân: Frontier Principality to World Empire." In *Süleymân the Magnificent and His Age: The Ottoman Empire in the Early Modern World*, ed. Metin I. Kunt and Christine Woodhead. London and New York: Longman, 1995.

———. *The Sultan's Servants: The Transformation of the Ottoman Provincial Government 1550–1650.* New York: Columbia University Press, 1983.

Kuran, Timur, "Islam and Underdevelopment: An Old Puzzle Revisited." *Journal of Institutional and Theoretical Economics* 153 (March 1997): 41–71.

Lachmann, Richard. "Elite Self-Interest and Economic Decline in Early Modern Europe." *American Sociological Review* 68 (2003): 346–372.

Laiou, Angeliki E. "The Agrarian Economy: Thirteenth–Fifteenth Centuries." In *The Economic History of Byzantium: From the Seventh through the Fifteenth Century*, ed. Angeliki E. Laiou, 311–375. Washington, DC: Dumbarton Oaks Research Library and Collection, 2002.

Laitin, David D. *Identity in Formation: The Russian-Speaking Populations in the Near Abroad*. Ithaca, NY and London: Cornell University Press, 1998.

———. "The National Uprisings in the Soviet Union." *World Politics* 44 (1991): 139–177.

Lamont, Michele and Virag Molnar. "The Study of Boundaries in the Social Sciences." *Annual Review of Sociology* 28 (2002): 167–195.

Lampe, John R. and Marvin R. Jackson. *Balkan Economic History, 1550–1950: From Imperial Borderlands to Developing Nations*. Bloomington: Indiana University Press, 1982.

Landes, David S. *Bankers and Pashas: International Finances and Economic Imperialism in Egypt*. Cambridge, MA: Harvard University Press, 1979.

Lefort, Jacques. "Tableau de la Bithynie au XIII siècle." In *The Ottoman Emirate (1300–1389)*, ed. Elizabeth Zachariadou, 101–117. Rethymnon: Crete University Press, 1993.

Levy, Avigdor, ed., *Jews, Turks, Ottomans: A Shared History, Fifteenth through the Twentieth Century*. Syracuse, NY: Syracuse University Press, 2002.

———. *The Sephardim in the Ottoman Empire*. Princeton, NJ: Darwin Press, 1992.

———. "The Ottoman Ulema and the Military Reforms." *Asian and African Studies* 7 (1971): 13–30.

Levy, J. P. *The Economic Life of the Ancient World*. Chicago: University of Chicago Press, 1967.

Levy, Margaret. *Of Rule and Revenue*. Berkeley: University of Califonia Press, 1988.

Lewis, Bernard. *Istanbul and the Civilization of the Ottoman Empire*. Norman: University of Oklahoma Press, 1963.

———. "Ottoman Observers of Ottoman Decline." *Islamic Studies* 1 (1962): 71–87.

———. *The Emergence of Modern Turkey*. 2d ed. London: Oxford University Press, 1961.

Lieven, Dominic. *Empire: The Russian Empire and its Rivals*. New Haven, CT: Yale University Press, 2001.

Lindner, Rudi P. *Nomads and Ottomans in Medieval Anatolia*. Bloomington: Indiana University Press, 1983.

———. "Stimulus and Justification in Early Ottoman History." *Greek Orthodox Theological Review* 27 (1982): 207–224.

Lintott, Andrew. *Imperium Romanum: Politics and Administration*. London and New York: Routledge, 1993.

Locke, John. "A Letter Concerning Toleration." Indianapolis: Bobbs-Merrill Educational, 1955.

Longworth, Philip. *The Cossacks*. New York: Holt, Rinehart and Winston, 1969.

Lopasic, Alexander. "Islamization of the Balkans with Special Reference to Bosnia." *Journal of Islamic Studies* 5 (1994): 163–186.

Lowry, Heath W. *The Nature of the Early Ottoman State.* Albany: State University of New York Press, 2003.

———. *Fifteenth Century Ottoman Realities: Christian Peasant Life on the Aegean Island of Limnos.* Eren: Istanbul, 2002.

———. *Trabzon Şehrinin İslamlaşma ve Türkleşmesi, 1461–1583.* [1981]. Istanbul: Bosphorus University Press, 1998.

Luttwak, Edward N. *The Grand Strategy of the Roman Empire.* Baltimore: Johns Hopkins University Press, 1976.

Lybyer, Albert K. *The Government of the Ottoman Empire in the Time of Suleiman the Magnificent.* Cambridge, MA: Harvard Historical Studies, 1913.

Macfarlane, Charles. *Constantinople in 1828.* 2 vols. London: Saunders and Otley, 1829.

MacMullen, Ramsay. *Romanization in the Time of Augustus.* New Haven, CT: Yale University Press, 2000.

———. *Corruption and Decline of Rome.* New Haven, CT: Yale University Press, 1988.

Mahoney, James and Dietrich Rueschemeyer. *Comparative Historical Analysis in the Social Sciences.* Cambridge, UK: Cambridge University Press, 2003.

Makdisi, Ussama. *The Culture of Sectarianism: Community, History and Violence in Nineteenth-Century Ottoman Lebanon.* Berkeley: University of California Press, 2000.

Mango, Cyril, ed. *The Oxford History of Byzantium.* Oxford, UK: Oxford University Press, 2002.

Mann, Michael. *The Sources of Social Power: A History of Power from the Beginning to A.D. 1760.* Cambridge, UK: Cambridge University Press, 1986.

Mantran, Robert. *Histoire de l'empire Ottoman.* Paris: Fayard, 1989.

———. *Istanbul dans la seconde moitié du XVIIe siècle.* Paris: Adrien Maisonneuve, 1962.

Maoz, Moshe. "Religious and Ethnic Conflicts in Ottoman Syria during the Tanzimat Era." In *The Great Ottoman-Turkish Civilisation,* ed. Kemal Çiçek, 438–444. Ankara: Yeni Türkiye Yayınları, 2000.

Marcus, Abraham. *The Middle East on the Eve of Modernity: Aleppo in the Eighteenth Century.* New York: Columbia University Press, 1989.

Mardin, Şerif. "The Just and the Unjust." *Daedalus, Journal of the American Academy of Arts and Sciences* 120:3 (Summer 1991): 113–129.

———. "Religion and Secularism in Turkey." In *Ataturk: Founder of a Modern State,* ed. Ali Kazancıgil and Ergun Özbudun, 192–195. Hamden, CT: Archon Books, 1981.

———. "Power, Civil Society, and Culture in the Ottoman Empire." *Comparative Studies in Society and History* 11 (1969): 258–281.

Marx, Anthony W. *Faith in Nation.* New York: Oxford University Press, 2003.

Masters, Bruce. *Christians and Jews in the Ottoman Arab World: The Roots of Sectarianism.* Cambridge, UK: Cambridge University Press, 2001.

Matschke, Klaus-Peter. "Research Problems concerning the Transition to Tourkokratia: The Byzantinist Standpoint." In *The Ottomans and the Balkans: A Discussion of Historiography,* ed. Fikret Adanır and Suraiya Faroqhi, 79–113. Leiden, The Netherlands: Brill, 2002.

Mattern, Susan P. *Rome and the Enemy: Imperial Strategy in the Principate.* Berkeley: University of California Press, 1999.

Matthee, Rudi. "The Safavid-Ottoman Frontier: Iraq-i Arab as Seen by the Safavids." In *Ottoman Borderlands: Issues, Personalities, and Political Changes*, ed. Kemal Karpat with Robert W. Zens, 157–173. Madison: University of Wisconsin Press, 2003.

Matthews, George T. *The Royal General Farms in 18th-Century France*. New York: Columbia University Press, 1958.

Mazower, Mark. *Salonica, City of Ghosts: Christians, Muslims, and Jews 1430–1950*. New York: Alfred A. Knopf, 2005.

McGowan, Bruce. "The Age of the Ayans, 1699–1812." In *An Economic and Social History of the Ottoman Empire, 1300–1914*, ed. Halil İnalcık and Donald Quataert. London: Cambridge University Press, 1994.

———. *Economic Life in Ottoman Europe: Taxation, Trade, and the Struggle for Land, 1600–1800*. Cambridge, UK: Cambridge University Press, 1981.

McNeill, William H. *Europe's Steppe Frontier, 1500–1800*. Chicago: University of Chicago Press, 1964.

Meeker, Michael. *A Nation of Empire: The Ottoman Legacy of Turkish Modernity*. Berkeley: University of California Press, 2002.

Mélikoff, Irène. "Les origines centre-asiatiques du soufisme anatolien." *Turcica* 22 (1988): 7–18.

———. "L'Islam hétérodoxe en Anatolie: non-conformisme – syncrétisme – gnose." *Turcica* 14 (1982): 142–154.

———. "Un ordre de derviches colonisateurs: les Bektachis. leur rôle social et leurs rapports avec les premiers sultans Ottomans." In *Mémorial Ömer Lûtfi Barkan*, 149–157. Paris: Librairie d'Amérique et d'Orient Adrien Maisonneuve, 1980.

———. "Le Problème kızılbaş." *Turcica* 6 (1975): 49–67.

Mélikoff-Sayar, Irène. *Le destan d'Umur Pacha. (Düsturname-I Enveri): Texte, traduction et notes*. Paris: Presses Universitaires de France, 1954.

Ménage, V. L. "The Islamization of Anatolia." In *Conversion to Islam*, ed. Nehemia Levtzion, 65–66. New York: Holmes & Meier, 1979.

Menning, Bruce W. "The Emergence of a Military-Administrative Elite in the Don Cossack Land, 1708–1836." In *Russian Officialdom: The Bureaucratization of Russian Society from the Seventeenth to the Twentieth Century*, ed. Walter McKenzie Pintner and Don Karl Rowney, 131–135. Chapel Hill: University of North Carolina Press, 1980.

Meriwether, Margaret Lee. "Urban Notables and Rural Resources in Aleppo, 1770–1830." *International Journal of Turkish Studies* 4 (1987): 55–73.

———. "The Notable Families of Aleppo, 1770–1830: Networks and Social Structure." Ph.D. dissertation, University of Pennsylvania, Philadelphia, 1981.

Mert, Özcan. *XVIII. ve XIX. Yüzyıllarda Çapanoğulları*. Ankara: Kültür Bakanlığı Araştırma ve İnceleme Yayınları, 1980.

Meyendorff, J. "Grecs, Turcs et Juifs en Asie mineure au XIVe siècle." *Byzantinische Forshungen* 1 (1966): 211–217.

Michels, Georg Bernhard. *At War with the Church: Religious Dissent in Seventeenth-Century Russia*. Palo Alto, CA: Stanford University Press, 1999.

Miles, Gary B. "Roman and Modern Imperialism: A Reassessment." *Comparative Studies in Society and History* 32 (1990): 629–659.

Miller, A. F. *Mustapha Pacha Bairaktar*. Bucharest: Association Internationale D'Etudes du Sud-Est Europeen, 1975.

Ministère des Affaires Etrangères, Archives Diplomatiques, Mémoires et Documents, Turquie, vols. 8, 9, 13, 15.

Minkov, Anton. *Conversion to Islam in the Balkans: Kisve Bahasi Petitions and Ottoman Social Life, 1670–1730.* Leiden, The Netherlands: Brill, 2004.

Moore, R. I. *The Formation of a Persecuting Society.* Malden, MA: Blackwell, 1990.

Mordtmann, J. H. and Bernard Lewis. "Derebey." *Encyclopedia of Islam.* 2d ed. Leiden, The Netherlands: E. J. Brill, 1965.

Motyl, Alexander J. *Imperial Ends: The Decay, Collapse, and Revival of Empires.* New York: Columbia University Press, 2001.

Murphey, Cullen. *Are We Rome? The Fall of an Empire and the Fate of America.* New York: Houghton Mifflin, 2007.

Murphey, Rhoads. "External Expansion and Internal Growth of the Ottoman Empire under Mehmed II: A Brief Discussion of Some Contradictory Aspects of the Conqueror's Legacy." In *The Great Ottoman-Turkish Civilization,* ed. Kemal Çiçek, 181–193. Ankara: Yeni Türkiye, 2000.

———. "Süleyman's Eastern Policy." In *Süleyman the Second and His Time,* ed. Halil İnalcık and Cemal Kafadar, 228–248. Istanbul: Isis Press, 1993.

———. "Ottoman Census Methods in the Mid-Sixteenth Century: Three Case Histories." *Studia Islamica* 71 (1990): 115–126.

———. "Review Article: Mustafa Ali and the Politics of Cultural Despair." *International Journal of Middle East Studies* 21 (1989): 243–255.

———. "Yeni Çeri." *Encyclopedia of Islam.* 2d ed, 322–331. Leiden, The Netherlands: E. J. Brill, 1965.

Nagata, Yuzo. *Tarihte Ayanlar: Karaosmanoğulları Üzerine bir İnceleme.* Ankara: Türk Tarih Kurumu Basımevi, 1997.

———. *Studies on the Social and Economic History of the Ottoman Empire.* Izmir: Akademi Kitabevi, 1995.

———. *Materials on the Bosnian Notables.* Tokyo: Institute for the Study of Languages and Cultures of Asia and Africa, 1979.

———. *Some Documents on the Big Farms (Çiftliks) of the Notables in Western Anatolia.* Tokyo: Institute for the Study of Languages and Cultures of Asia and Africa, 1976.

Nagel, Joane. "The Political Construction of Ethnicity." In *Competitive Ethnic Relations,* ed. Susan Olzak and Joane Nagel, 93–112. Orlando, FL: Academic Press, 1986.

Nathans, Benjamin. *Beyond the Pale: The Jewish Encounter with Late Imperial Russia.* Berkeley: University of California Press, 2002.

Norris, H. T. *Islam in the Balkans: Religion and Society between Europe and the Arab World.* London: C. Hurst and Co., 1993.

Ocak, Ahmet Yaşar. "Kutb ve İsyan: Osmanlı Mehdici (Mesiyanik) Hareketlerinin İdeolojik Arkaplanı Üzerine Bazı Düşünceler." *Toplum ve Bilim* 83 (1999/2000): 48–56.

———. "Les Melamis-Bayrami (Hamzavi) et l'administration ottomane aux XVIe–XVIIe siècles." In *Melamis-Bayramis: etudes sur trois mouvements mystiques musulmans,* 99–114. Istanbul: Éditions Issis, 1998.

———. *Osmanlı Toplumunda Zındıklar ve Mülhidler (15–17. yüzyıllar).* Istanbul: Tarih Vakfı Yurt Yayınları, 1998.

———. "Les milieux soufis dans les territoires du Beylicat ottoman et le problème des Abdalan-Rum." In *The Ottoman Emirate (1300–1389),* ed. Elizabeth Zachariadou, 145–158. Rethymnon: Crete University Press, 1993.

———. "Islam in the Ottoman Empire: A Sociological Framework for a New Interpretation." In *Suleyman the Second and His Time*, ed. Halil İnalcık and Cemal Kafadar. Istanbul: Isis Press, 1993.

———. "Idéologie officielle et réaction populaire: Un aperçu général sur les mouvements et les courants socio-religieux à l'époque de Soliman le Magnifique." In *Soliman le Magnifique et son temps: Actes du Colloque de Paris, Galeries nationales du Grand Palais, 7–10 mars 1990*, ed. Gilles Veinstein, 185–194. Paris: Ecole du Louvre, 1992.

———. "XVI. Yüzyıl Osmanlı Anadolu'sunda Mesiyanik Hareketlerin Bir Tahlil Denemesi." In V. *Milletlerarası Türkiye Sosyal ve İktisat Tarihi Kongresi: Tebliğler (Fifth International Congress on the Social and Economic History of Turkey)*, 817–825. Istanbul: Türkiyat Araştırma ve Uygulama Merkezi, 1989.

———. "Quelques remarques sur le rôle des derviches Kalenderîs dans les mouvements populaires et les activités anarchiques aux XVe et XVIe siècles dans l'empire Ottoman." *Osmanlı Araştırmaları* 3 (1982): 69–80.

———. "XVII. Yüzyılda Osmanlı İmparatorluğu'nda Dinde Tasviye (Puritanizm) Teşebbüslerine bir Bakış: 'Kadızadeliler Hareketi.'" *Türk Kültürü Araştırmaları* 17–22 (1979–1983): 208–223.

Odorico, Paolo, ed. *Conseils et mémoires de Synadinos, prêtre de Serrés en Macédoine (XVIIe siècle)*. Paris: Editions de l'Association "Pierre Belon," 1996.

Olson, Mancur. *Power and Prosperity*. New York: Basic Books, 2000.

Olson, Robert W. "Jews, Janissaries, Esnaf and the Revolt of 1740 in Istanbul: Social Upheaval and Political Realignment in the Ottoman Empire." *Journal of the Economic and Social History of the Orient* 20:2 (May 1977): 185–207.

———. "The Esnaf and the Patrona Halil Rebellion of 1730: A Realignment in Ottoman Politics?" *Journal of the Economic and Social History of the Orient* 17:3 (1974): 329–344.

Ortaylı, İlber. "18. Yüzyılda Akdeniz Dünyası ve Genel Çizgileriyle Türkiye." *Toplum ve Bilim* (Kış 1977): 81–91.

Ostrogorsky, George. *History of the Byzantine State*. New Brunswick, NJ: Rutgers University Press, 1957.

Owen, Roger. *The Middle East in the World Economy 1800–1914*. London: Methuen, 1981.

Öz, Mehmet. "Ottoman Provincial Administration in Eastern and Southeastern Anatolia: The Case of Bidlis in the Sixteenth Century." In *Ottoman Borderlands: Issues, Personalities and Political Changes*, ed. Kemal Karpat and Robert W. Zens, 143–155. Madison: University of Wisconsin Press, 2003.

Özkaya, Yücel. *Osmanlı İmparatorluğu'nda Ayanlık*. Ankara: Türk Tarih Kurumu Yayınları, 1994.

———. *XVIII. Yüzyılda Osmanlı Kurumları ve Osmanlı Toplum Yaşantısı*. Ankara: Kültür ve Turizm Bakanlığı, 1985.

———. *Osmanlı Tarihinde Ayanlık*. Ankara: Ankara Üniversitesi Yayınları, 1977.

Özvar, Erol. *Osmanlı Maliyesinde Malikane Uygulaması*. Istanbul: Kitabevi Yayınları, 2003.

Padgett, John F. "Organizational Genesis, Identity and Control: The Transformation of Banking in Renaissance Florence." *Journal of Economic Literature* 41 (2003): 211–257.

Padgett, John F. and Christopher K. Ansell. "Robust Action and the Rise of the Medici, 1400–1434." *American Journal of Sociology* 98 (1993): 1259–1319.

Palmer, J. A. B. *The Origins of the Janissaries*. Manchester, UK: Manchester University Press, 1953.

Pamuk, Şevket. "The Evolution of Financial Institutions in the Ottoman Empire, 1600–1914." *Financial History Review* 11 (2004): 7–32.

———. "Institutional Change and the Longevity of the Ottoman Empire, 1500–1800." *Journal of Interdisciplinary History* 35 (2004): 225–247.

———. *A Monetary History of the Ottoman Empire*. Cambridge, UK: Cambridge University Press, 2000.

———. "Osmanlı Ekonomisinde Devlet Müdahaleciliğine Yeniden Bakış." *Toplum ve Bilim* 83 (1999/2000): 133–145.

———. "Money in the Ottoman Empire." In *An Economic and Social History of the Ottoman Empire, 1300–1914*, ed. Halil İnalcık and Donald Quataert, 947–953. Cambridge, UK: Cambridge University Press, 1994.

———. *The Ottoman Empire and European Capitalism, 1820–1913: Trade, Investment and Production*. Cambridge, UK: Cambridge University Press, 1987.

Panaite, Viorel. "The Voivodes of the Danubian Principalities: As Haracguzarlar of the Ottoman Sultans." In *Ottoman Borderlands: Issues, Personalities, and Political Changes*, ed. Kemal Karpat and Robert W. Zens, 58–78. Madison: University of Wisconsin Press, 2003.

Pantazopoulos, N. J. *Church and Law in the Balkan Peninsula during the Ottoman Rule*, no. 92. Thessaloniki: Institute for Balkan Studies, 1967.

———"Community Laws and Customs of Western Macedonia under Ottoman Rule." *Balkan Studies* 2:1 (1961): 1–22.

Panzac, Daniel. "International and Domestic Maritime Trade in the Ottoman Empire during the 18th Century." *International Journal of Middle Eastern Studies* 24 (1992): 189–206.

———. "Activité et diversité d'un grand port Ottoman: Smyrne dans la première moitié du XVIIIe siècle," and "Affreteurs Ottomans et capitaines Français à Alexandrie: la caravane maritime en Mediterranée au milieu du XVIIIe siècle," *Revue de l'occident Musulman et de la Mediterranée* 34 (1982): 23–38.

Papadakis, Aristeides. "Gennadius II and Mehmed the Conqueror." *Byzantion* 42 (1972): 93.

Papadopoullos, Theodore H. *Studies and Documents Relating to the History of the Greek Church and People under Turkish Domination*. Brussels: Bibliotheca Graeca Aevi Posterioris, 1952.

Perrot, Georges. *Souvenir d'un Voyage en Asie Mineure*. Paris: M. Levy, 1867.

Pierce, Leslie P. *The Imperial Harem: Women and Sovereignty in the Ottoman Empire*. New York: Oxford University Press, 1993.

Pierson, Paul. *Politics in Time: History, Institutions, and Social Analysis*. Princeton, NJ: Princeton University Press, 2004.

Pintner, Walter McKenzie. *Russian Economic Policy under Nicholas I*. Ithaca, NY: Cornell University Press, 1967.

Pintner, Walter McKenzie and Don Karl Rowney, eds. *Russian Officialdom: The Bureaucratization of Russian Society from the Seventeenth to the Twentieth Century*. Chapel Hill: University of North Carolina Press, 1980.

Pittioni, Manfredi. "The Economic Decline of the Ottoman Empire." In *The Decline of Empires*, ed. Emil Brix, Klaus Koch, and Elisabeth Vyslonzil, 21–44. Vienna: Verlag für Gechichte und politik, 2001.

Prunier, Gerard. *Darfur: The Ambiguous Genocide.* Ithaca, NY: Cornell University Press, 2005.

Quataert, Donald. *The Ottoman Empire, 1700–1922.* Cambridge, UK: Cambridge University Press, 2003.

———. "Ottoman History Writing at the Crossroads." In *Turkish Studies in the United States,* ed. Donald Quataert and Sabri Sayarı, 15–30. Bloomington: Indiana University Press, 2003.

———. "The Age of Reforms, 1812–1914." In *An Economic and Social History of the Ottoman Empire, 1300–1914,* ed. Halil İnalcık and Donald Quataert, 759–943. Cambridge, UK: Cambridge University Press, 1994.

———. *Social Disintegration and Popular Resistance in the Ottoman Empire, 1881–1908.* New York: New York University Press, 1983.

Raby, Julian. "East and West in Mehmed the Conqueror's Library." *Bulletin du Bibliophile* 3 (1987): 296–318.

———. "Mehmed the Conqueror's Greek Scriptorium." *Dumbarton Oaks Papers* 37 (1983): 15–34.

———. "A Sultan of Paradox: Mehmed the Conqueror as Patron of the Arts." *Oxford Art Journal* 5 (1982): 3–8.

Raeff, Marc. *Understanding Imperial Russia [Comprendre l'ancien régime russe.* Paris: Editions du Seuil, 1982], transl. Arthur Goldhammer. New York: Columbia University Press, 1984.

Rafeq, Abdul-Karim. "Craft Organizations and Religious Communities in Ottoman Syria (XVI–XIX Centuries)." In *La Shi'a nell'impero Ottomano,* 25–56. Rome: Accademia Nazionale dei Lincei, 1993.

Rauch, James E. and Alessandra Casella. "Networks and Markets." *Journal of Economic Literature* 41 (2003): 545–565.

Richards, John F. *The New Cambridge History of India I–5: The Mughal Empire* Cambridge, UK: Cambridge University Press, 1993.

Rodrigue, Aron. "The Mass Destruction of Armenians and Jews in the 20th Century in Historical Perspective." In *Der Volkermord an den Armeniern und die Shoah,* ed. Hans-Lukas Kieser and Dominik J. Schaller, 303–316. Zurich: Chronos, 2002.

———. "Difference and Tolerance in the Ottoman Empire." *Stanford Humanities Review* 5:1 (1995): 81–90.

———. *French Jews, Turkish Jews: The Alliance Israelite Universelle and the Politics of Jewish Schooling in Turkey, 1860–1925.* Bloomington: Indiana University Press, 1990.

Rozen, Minna. *A History of the Jewish Community in Istanbul: The Formative Years, 1453–1566.* Leiden, The Netherlands, and Boston: E. J. Brill, 2002.

———. "Contest and Rivalry in Mediterranean Maritime Commerce in the First Half of the Eighteenth Century: The Jews of Salonica and the European Presence." *Revue des Etudes Juives* 147:3–4 (1988): 300–320.

Rudolph, Richard L. and David F. Good, eds. *Nationalism and Empire: The Habsburg Empire and the Soviet Union.* New York: St. Martin's Press, 1992.

Runciman, Sir Steven. *The Fall of Constantinople 1453.* Cambridge, UK: Cambridge University Press, 1990.

———. *The Great Church in Captivity: A Study of Constantinople from the Eve of the Turkish Conquest to the Greek War of Independence.* Cambridge, UK: Cambridge University Press, 1968.

Sadat, Deena R. "Ayan Aga: The Transformation of the Bektashi Corps in the Eighteenth Century." *The Muslim World* 63 (1973): 206–219.

———. "Rumeli Ayanlari: The Eighteenth Century." *Journal of Modern History* 44 (1972): 346–363.

———. "Urban Notables in the Ottoman Empire: The Ayan." Ph.D. dissertation, Rutgers University, New Brunswick, NJ, 1969.

Sakaoğlu, Necdet. *Anadolu Derebeyi Ocaklarından Köse Paşa Hanedanı*. Ankara: Yurt Yayınları, 1984.

Salzmann, Ariel. *Tocqueville in the Ottoman Empire: Rival Paths to the Modern State. The Ottoman Empire and its Heritage.* Leiden, The Netherlands: E. J. Brill, 2004.

———. "The Age of Tulips: Confluence and Conflict in Early Modern Consumer Culture (1550–1730)." In *Consumption Studies and the History of the Ottoman Empire 1550–1922*, ed. Donald Quataert, 95–96. Albany: State University of New York Press, 2000.

———. "Measures of Empire: Tax Farmers and the Ottoman Ancien Regime, 1695–1807." Ph.D. dissertation, Columbia University, New York, 1995.

———. "An Ancient Regime Revisited: 'Privatization' and Political Economy in the Eighteenth-Century Ottoman Empire." *Politics and Society* 21 (1993): 393–423.

Schacht, Joseph. *An Introduction to Islamic Law*. Oxford, UK: Oxford University Press, 1964.

Scholem, Gershom. *Sabbatai Sevi and the Sabbatean Movement in His Lifetime.* Jerusalem, 1957.

Scott, James C. *Seeing Like a State: How Certain Schemes to Improve the Human Condition Have Failed.* New Haven, CT: Yale University Press, 1998.

Seton-Watson, Hugh. *Nations and States: An Inquiry into the Origins of Nations and the Politics of Nationalism.* Boulder, CO: Westview Press, 1977.

Sewell, William H., *Jr. Logics of History: Social Theory and Social Transformation.* Chicago and London: University of Chicago Press, 2005.

Shaw, Stanford J. *Mustapha Pacha Bairaktar.* Bucharest: Association Internationale d'Études du Sud-Est Européen, 1975.

———. "The Nineteenth-Century Ottoman Tax Reforms and Revenue System." *International Journal of Middle Eastern Studies* 6 (1975): 421–459.

———. *Between Old and New: The Ottoman Empire under Sultan Selim III, 1789–1807.* Cambridge, MA: Harvard University Press, 1971.

———. "The Origins of Ottoman Military Reform: The Nizam-I Cedid Army of Sultan Selim III." *Journal of Modern History* 37 (1965): 298–299.

Shaw, Stanford and Ezel Kural Shaw. *History of the Ottoman Empire and Modern Turkey.* 2 vols. Cambridge, UK: Cambridge University Press, 1977.

Shinder, Joel. "Career Line Formation in the Ottoman Bureaucracy, 1648–1750: A New Perspective." *Journal of the Economic and Social History of the Orient* 16:2–3 (1973): 217–237.

Shmuelevitz, Aryeh. *The Jews of the Ottoman Empire in the Late Fifteenth and the Sixteenth Centuries: Administrative, Economic, Legal, and Social Relations as Reflected in the Responsa.* Leiden, The Netherlands: E. J. Brill, 1984.

Silahdar Mehmed Ağa. *Nusretname*, transl. İsmet Parmaksızoğlu. 2 vols. Istanbul: Milli Eğitim Bakanlığı Yayınları, 1962–1969.

Skinner, Barbara. "Borderlands of Faith: Reconsidering the Origins of the Ukrainian Tragedy," *Slavic Review* 64 (Spring 2005): 88–116.

Skendi, Stavro. "The Millet System and Its Contribution to the Blurring of Orthodox National Identity in Albania." In *Christians and Jews in the Ottoman Empire*, ed. Benjamin Braude and Bernard Lewis, 244. 2 vols. New York and London: Holmes & Meier, 1982.

Slade, Adolphus. *Records of Travels in Turkey, Greece, &c., and of a Cruise in the Black Sea, with the Capitan Pasha, in the Years 1829, 1830, and 1831.* 2 vols. London: Saunders and Otley, 1833.

Soykan, T. Tankut. *Osmanlı İmparatorluğu'nda Gayrimüslimler: Klasik Dönem Osmanlı Hukukunda Gayrimüslimlerin Hukuki Statüsü.* Istanbul: Ütopya Kitabevi Yayınları, 1999.

Stark, David and Laszlo Bruszt. *Postsocialist Pathways: Transforming Politics and Property in East Central Europe.* New York: Cambridge University Press, 1998.

Stoianovich, Traian. *Between East and West: The Balkan and Mediterranean Worlds.* New York: Caratzas, 1992.

———. "The Conquering Balkan Orthodox Merchant." *Journal of Economic History* 20:2 (1960): 234–313.

———. "Land Tenure and Related Sectors of the Balkan Economy." *Journal of Economic History* 13 (1953): 398–411.

Sugar, Peter. *Southeastern Europe under Ottoman Rule, 1354–1804.* Seattle: University of Washington Press, 1977.

Sugar, Peter F. and Ivo J. Lederer, eds. *Nationalism in Eastern Europe.* Seattle and London: University of Washington Press, 1971.

Suny, Ronald Grigor. "The Holocaust before the Holocaust: Reflections on the Armenian Genocide." In *Der Volkermord an den Armeniern und die Shoah*, ed. Hans-Lukas Kieser and Dominik J. Schaller, 83–100. Zurich: Chronos, 2002.

———. "Empire and Nation: Armenians, Turks, and the End of the Ottoman Empire." *Armenian Forum* 1:2 (1998): 17–51.

Svoronos, N. G. *Le Commerce de Salonique au XVIIIe siècle.* Paris: Presses Universitaires de France, 1956.

Syme, Ronald. *Colonial Elites: Rome, Spain and the Americas.* London: Oxford University Press, 1970.

———. *The Roman Revolution.* London: Oxford University Press, 1960.

Tamdoğan-Abel, Işık. "Les Modalités de l'urbanité dans une ville Ottomane." Thèse de Doctorat, Ecole des Hautes Etudes en Sciences Sociales, Paris, 1998.

Thelen, Kathleen. *How Institutions Evolve: The Political Economy of Skills in Germany, Britain, the United States, and Japan.* Cambridge, UK: Cambridge University Press, 2004.

———. "How Institutions Evolve: Insights from Comparative Historical Analysis." In *Comparative Historical Analysis in the Social Sciences*, ed. James Mahoney and Dietrich Rueschemeyer, 208–240. Cambridge, UK: Cambridge University Press, 2003.

Thys-Şenocak, Lucienne. "The Yeni Valide Mosque Complex at Eminönü." *Muqarnas: An Annual of the Visual Culture of the Islamic World* 15 (1998): 58–70.

Tilly, Charles. *Durable Inequality.* Berkeley: University of California Press, 1998.

———. "How Empires End." *After Empire: Multiethnic Societies and Nation-Building*, ed. Karen Barkey and Mark von Hagen, 1–11. Boulder, CO: Westview Press, 1997.

Toprak, Zafer. *Türkiye'de Milli İktisat (1908–1918).* Ankara: Yurt Yayınları, 1982.

Turan, Osmân. "L'Islamisation dans la Turquie du Moyen Âge." *Studia Islamica* 10 (1959): 137–152.

———. "Les Souverains Seldjoukides et leurs Sujets non-Musulmans." *Studia Islamica* 1 (1953): 65–100.

Turgay, A. Üner. "Trade and Merchants in Nineteenth-Century Trabzon: Elements of Ethnic Conflict." In *Christians and Jews in the Ottoman Empire: The Functioning of a Plural Society*, ed. Benjamin Braude and Bernard Lewis, 287–318. 2 vols. New York and London: Holmes & Meier, 1982.

Tursun Beg. *The History of Mehmed the Conqueror*, transl. Halil İnalcık and Rhoads Murphey. Minneapolis and Chicago: Bibliotheca Islamica, 1978.

Tülüveli, Güçlü. "De-Mystification of the Contemporary Historiographical Paradigms: Ottoman Provincial Notables in Historical Perspective." M.A. thesis, Boğaziçi University, Istanbul, 1993.

Ülker, Necmi. "The Emergence of Izmir as a Mediterranean Commercial Center for the French and English Interests, 1698–1740." *International Journal of Turkish Studies* (Summer 1987): 1–37.

Uluçay, Çağatay. "Karaosmanoğullarına Ait Bazı Vesikalar." *Tarih Vesikaları Dergisi* (1942) II :193–207, 300–308, 434–440 & III: 13, 117–126.

Ursinus, Michael. "Millet." In *Encyclopedia of Islam*. 2d ed. Leiden, The Netherlands: E. J. Brill, 1965.

Uzunçarşılı, Ismail Hakkı. *Anadolu Beylikeri ve Akkoyunlu, Karakoyunlu Devletleri.* Ankara: Türk Tarih Kurumu Basımevi, 1988.

———. *Osmanlı Tarihi*, III. Ankara: Türk Tarih Kurumu Basımevi, 1983.

———. "Çapan Oğulları." *Belleten* 38 (1974): 215–261.

———. *Meşhur Rumeli Ayanlarından Tirsinikli Ismail, Yılık Oğlu Süleyman Ağalar ve Alemdar Mustafa Paşa.* Istanbul: Maarif Matbaası, 1942.

Vacalopoulos, Apostolos E., *Origins of the Greek Nation: The Byzantine Period, 1204–1461*, transl. Ian Moles. New Brunswick, NJ: Rutgers University Press, 1970.

Varshney, Ashutosh. *Ethnic Conflict and Civic Life: Hindus and Muslims in India.* New Haven, CT: Yale University Press, 2002.

———. "Ethnic Conflict and Civil Society." *World Politics* 53 (2001): 362–398.

Vatin, Nicolas. "L'Emploi du Grec comme langue diplomatique par les Ottomans (fin du XV͏ᵉ–debut du XVI͏ᵉ siècle)." In *Istanbul et les Langues Orientales*, ed. Frederic Hitzel, 41–47. Paris: Harmattan, 1997.

Veinstein, Gilles. "Une communauté Ottomane: Les juifs d'Avlonya (Valona) dans la deuxième moitié du XVI siècle." In *État et société dans l'empire Ottoman, XVIe–XVIIIe siècles: la terre, la guerre, les communautés*, 781–828. Aldershot, UK: Variorum, 1994.

———. "'Ayan' de la region d'Izmir et le commerce du Levant (deuxième moitié du XVIIIe siècle)." *Etudes Balkaniques* 12 (1976): 71–83.

Voltaire, François-Marie. *Toleration and Other Essays*, transl. Joseph McCabe. New York and London: Knickerbocker Press, 1912.

———. *Oeuvres complètes de Voltaire: Essai sur les moeurs et l'esprit des nations.* vol. 3. Paris: Gallimard, 1858.

von Hammer-Purgstall, Joseph. *Histoire de l'empire Ottoman*, transl. M. Dochez. 3 vols. Paris: Imprimerie de Bethune et Plon, 1844.

Vryonis, Speros, Jr. "Local Institutions in the Greek Islands and Elements of Byzantine Continuity during Ottoman Rule." *Godishnik na Sofiski a Universitet Sv. Kliment Okhridski* 83:3 (1989): 1–60.

———. *The Decline of Medieval Hellenism in Asia Minor and the Process of Islamization from the Eleventh through the Fifteenth Century.* Berkeley: University of California Press, 1971.

———. "The Byzantine Legacy and Ottoman Forms." *Dumbarton Oaks Papers* 23 (1969–1970): 251–308.

———. "Devshirme." In the *Encyclopedia of Islam*. 2d ed, 210. Leiden, The Netherlands: E. J. Brill, 1965.

———. "Isidore Glabas and the Turkish Devshirme." *Speculum* 31 (1956): 433–443.

Vucinich, Wayne S. "The Nature of Balkan Society under Ottoman Rule." *Slavic Review* 21 (1962): 608.

Wallerstein, Immanuel. *The Modern World System II: Mercantilism and the Consolidation of the European World-Economy, 1600–1750*. New York: Academic Press, 1980.

———. *The Modern World System: Capitalist Agriculture and the Origins of the European World-Economy in the Sixteenth Century*. New York: Academic Press, 1974.

Weber, Max. *Economy and Society*, ed. Guenther Roth and Claus Wittich. Berkeley: University of California Press, 1978.

———. *General Economic History*. Glencoe, IL: Free Press, 1961; reprinted 1993.

———. *The Religion of India: The Sociology of Hinduism and Buddhism*, transl. H. H. Gerth and D. Martindale. Glencoe, IL: Free Press, 1958.

Weeks, Theodore R. "Between Rome and Tsargrad: The Uniate Church in Imperial Russia." In *Of Religion and Empire: Missions, Conversion, and Tolerance in Tsarist Russia*, ed. Robert P Geraci and Michael Khordarkovsky. Ithaca, NY: Cornell University Press, 2001.

White, Eugene N. "From Privatized to Government-Administered Tax Collection: Tax Farming in Eighteenth-Century France." *Economic History Review* 57:4 (2004): 636–663.

White, Harrison. *Identity and Control: A Structural Theory of Social Action*. Princeton, NJ: Princeton University Press, 1992.

White, Harrison C., Frédéric C. Godart, and Victor P. Corona. "Mobilizing Identities: Uncertainty and Control in Strategy." *Theory, Culture, and Society* 24 (2007): 191–212.

Whittaker, C. R. *Rome and Its Frontiers: The Dynamics of Empire*. New York: Routledge, 2004.

Winter, Michael. "Ethnic and Religious Tensions in Ottoman Egypt." In *International Congress on the Social and Economic History of Turkey*, 309–317. Istanbul: Isis Press, 1989.

Wittek, Paul. *The Rise of the Ottoman Empire*. London: The Royal Asiatic Society, 1938.

Yaney, George L. *The Systematization of Russian Government: Social Evolution in the Domestic Administration of Imperial Russia, 1711–1905*. Urbana: University of Illinois Press, 1973.

Yerasimos, Stéphane. "Türkler Romalıların Mirasçısı mıdır?" *Toplumsal Tarih* 116 (2003): 68–73.

———. "La Communauté juive d'Istanbul à la fin du XVIe siècle." *Turcica* 27 (1995): 101–130.

Yücel, Yaşar. *Anadolu Beylikleri Hakkında Araştırmalar: XIII–XV Yüzyıllarda Kuzey-Batı Anadolu Tarihi*. Ankara: Türk Tarih Kurumu Basımevi, 1988.

Yıldırım, Onur. "Ottoman Guilds as a Setting for Ethno-Religious Conflict: The Case of the Silk-Thread Spinners' Guild in Istanbul." *IRSH* 47 (2002): 407–419.

Zachariadou, Elizabeth A. "In Honor of Professor İnalcık: Methods and Sources in Ottoman Studies." Presentation at Harvard University, Cambridge, MA, 29 April–2 May 2004.

———. "Co-Existence and Religion," *Archivum Ottomanicum* 15 (1997): 119–129.

———. "Histoire et legendes des premiers Ottomans." *Turcica* 27 (1995): 52–53.

———. "The Emirate of Karasi and that of the Ottomans: Two Rival States." In *The Ottoman Emirate (1300–1389)*, 225–236. Rethymnon: Crete University Press, 1993.

———. "Lauro Quirini and the Turkish Sandjaks (ca. 1430)." *Journal of Turkish Studies* 11 (1987): 240.

Zagorin, Perez. *How the Idea of Religious Toleration Came to the West*. Princeton, NJ and Oxford, UK: Princeton University Press, 2003.

Zhelyzakova, Antonina. "Islamization in the Balkans as a Historiographical Problem: The Southeast-European Perspective." In *The Ottomans and the Balkans: A Discussion of Historiography*, ed. Fikret Adanır and Suraiya Faroqhi, 223–266. Leiden, The Netherlands: Brill, 2002.

Zilfi, Madeline C. "Women and Society in the Tulip Era, 1718–1730." In *Women, the Family and Divorce Laws in Islamic History*, ed. Amira el Azhary Sonbol, 290–303. Syracuse, NY: Syracuse University Press, 1996.

———. *The Politics of Piety: The Ottoman Ulema in the Postclassical Age, 1600–1800*. Minneapolis: Bibliotheca Islamica, 1988.

———. "The Kadizadelis: Discordant Revivalism in Seventeenth-Century Istanbul." *Journal of Near Eastern Studies* 45 (1986): 251–269.

Zürcher, Erik J. *Turkey: A Modern History*. London: I. B. Tauris, 1993.

Index

Abdalan-i Rum milieu, 52
abdals. See dervishes *(babas* and *abdals),* in
    frontier society
Abdülhamid II. *See also* Committee of Union
    and Progress (CUP)
  creation of Muslim unity, 288
  education efforts of, 287
  establishment of Hamidiye, 288
  financial crisis during reign of, 275
  legitimacy building by, 291–292
  reform efforts of, 267
Abou-el-Haj, Rifa'at, 207, 210, 212, 260
accommodation policies *(istimalet),* 51, 59,
    87, 110
Achmed III, 197
Actium, Battle at (Rome), 74
actors. *See also* actors, state and social;
    governance regimes; notables *(ayan);* state
    and social actors
  attempts at undermining, 274
  banishment of, by Aziz Mehmed, 189
  central/peripheral, and Russian expansion,
    35
  challenges to state policies, 217
  communication between, 45
  and conflict resolution, 148
  contentiousness of, during Kadızadeli
    ascendancy, 183
  embedding of, 17, 24, 243, 245
  and exploitation/affirmation of boundaries,
    119
  as force for balance between state/social
    forces, 27
  frontier activities of, 29, 33, 36, 44
  legitimacy building by, 32, 44

  limited options available to, 23
  and longevity/durability of empire, 15
  mediation role of, 200
  national vs. imperial solutions sought by, 7
  peace promotion/violence prevention by,
    118
  political actors, 6, 201, 204, 206
  regional actors, 227
  and religion, 105
  social/economic ties between, 228
  state/religious, alliance between, 164, 183
  state/social, 6, 17, 21
  strategies of, 34, 118
actors, state and social
  alliances between, 68
  conflicts between, 223
  embedding of, 17, 24
  negotiation of Sened-i İttifak, 220
  resolution of differences between, 69,
    228
adaptability
  of Byzantine Empire, 19
  of Ottoman Empire, 7, 70, 85
  as sign of flexibility/pragmatism,
  of state/social forces, 69
administration. *See also* millet administrative
    system
  and Armenian incorporation, 115
  by Byzantines, for Ottomans, 81
  changes in seventeenth century, 218
  and Christian incorporation, 115
  and Jewish incorporation, 115
  by Mehmed II, 81
  Ottoman core values, 87
  responsibilities of local intermediaries, 115

323

Agency for Convert Affairs (Russian Empire), 112
Agoston, Gabor, 16, 91
Ahlati, Hüseyin, 171
Ahmed III
  abdication of, 204, 205
  appointment of Nevşehirli Damad Ibrahim Pasha, 213
  concessions made by, 213
  deposition of, 216
  replacement by Mahmûd I, 217
Ahmet Yaşar Ocak, 56
akandye (Turkish raiders), 28
Akhi brotherhoods, 43, 48, 51, 52
Akınjı. See also raiders, 50
akra (space) between Byzantine and Seljuk empires, 39
Albania, *voynuks* of, 88
Alemdar Mustafa Pasha, 218. *See also* Bayraktar Mustapha Pasha
Ali Rumi (Şeyh), 166
Amcazade Hüseyin, 209–210
Anatolia, 28
  Abdalan-I Rum milieu in, 52
  akhi (mystical corporations) in, 43
  ayan support of reforms, 222
  backing of Safavid Empire vs. Ottomans, 103
  conquests of, by Selim I, 91–103
  conversions from Christianity to Muslim, 126
  dissent in, 167
  entrance of Oghuz peoples, 30
  focus on feeding Istanbul, 97
  immigrant population of, 287–288
  infiltration by Shah Ismail, 103
  Mongol invasion of, 55
  mystic movements in, 170
  Ottoman administrative system core values, 87
  patronage networks of, 207–208
  preferences for multiethnic, federalist state, 266
  silk trade in, 40
  spread of Sufis in, 43
  trade exports of, 239
  Turkish invasion of, 28
  wartime assistance by notables, 246
Andronikos, contract with Catalans, 38
Ankara, battle of, 67
Anthony, Mark, 74
Armenians
  genocide of, 114–115, 277–278, 293–294
  incorporation/administration of, 115

millet system of, 131
movement to Istanbul, 142
relationship with Ottoman Empire, 141
religious authority centers of, 140–141
Asia Minor
  influence of Osman, 44
  invasion by Mongols, 42
askeri (ruling class), in Ottoman Empire, 70
  hold on Istanbul tax farms, 276
  vs. *reaya* (subjects), 76
assassination
  of Grand Vizier, 165
  of Menocchio, 170
  of Musa Çelebi, 172
  of Osman II, 206
  of Selim III, 220
  of Sokullu Mehmed Pasha, 165
atrocities, against Armenian/Greek populations, 277–278
Augustus (Emperor of Rome)
  comparisons with Mehmed II, 81–82
  elimination of hostile elites, 75
  imperialization of Rome, 74–75
  reshaping of military, 75
Austria. *See also* Habsburg Empire
  discussions of millet system, 153
  effects of warfare with Ottomans, 267
  Kara Mustafa's attempt to conquer Vienna, 202
  territories lost/won, 240
  warfare with Mahmud I, 204
ayan. See notables *(ayan)*; Sened-i İttifak (1808 Agreement)
Aydın *(beyliks)* emirate, 30, 45

babas. See dervishes *(babas* and *abdals)*, in frontier society
Baer, Marc, 183, 187
Bali, Hamza, 166
Balkan Wars, 293
Balkans
  agrarian transformations in, 255
  conquest by Ottomans, 11
  Enlightenment/development transmitted by, 256–257
  growing desire for independence, 267
  as hub of Ottoman fairs, 240
  infiltration by Russian Empire, 267
  integralist perspective in, 84
  katun (Balkan pastoral community), 144
  notables *(ayan)* competition for territory/influence, 219

self-government by, 87
as eighteenth-century center of new politics, 201
bandits *(celalis)*, 178–181
Barbir, Karl, 199
"barricaded social entities" concept, 118
Basra, Ottoman control of, 91
Bathory, Stephen (King), 179
battles
  at Actium, 74
  at Ankara, 67
  at Çaldıran, 176
  at Kosovo, 11–12, 30
  at Manzikert, 30, 69
  at Manzikert (Malazgirt), 30
  at Mohacs, 90
Bayraktar Mustafa Pasha, 218, 222–223. *See also* Sened-i İttifak (1808 Agreement)
  attempt at reinstatement of Selim III, 222
  cooptation of provinces by, 220
  leadership of *ayan* of Rumelia/Anatolia, 220
Bayramîs order, 161, 166, 167–168
Bedreddîn, Şeyh, 154–155, 169–175
  dissent by, 181
  early background, 171–172
  execution of rebels of, 173
  network accomplishments, 171
  promotion to army judge, 172
  as representative of Islamo-Christian synthesis, 173
  revolt of, 170
  trial/death of, 174
  use of outside contacts, 173–174
Bektaş, Hacı, 52
Bektaşî dervish community, 52, 53, 165–166
berats (documents of patriarchal authority), 134
Beyazıd I (son of Murad I), 30–31, 61, 87, 172
Beyazıd II, 70, 79
  and conversion of Jews, 126
  expansion of Janissary army, 77
  imperial formation by, 71–72
  recruitment of *akinji* raiders, 50
beys (chieftains). *See* Orhan Bey (of Ottomans); Süleyman Bey (of Karesi); Umur Bey (of Aydın)
Bithynia, Osman's networking building in, 52
Black Death, 38
Bogomilism (social-religious movement), 156
Bosnia
  confrontations with Habsburgs in, 202
  conversions from Christianity to Islam, 127
  prevalence of law and order in, 219
  voynuks of, 88

boundaries. *See also* brokerage across boundaries
  coexistence with openness, 20
  between communities, reinforcement of, 12
  and fluidity of relationships, 118–119
  fracturing of, in frontier zones, 28
  hardening of, from group competitions, 27
  influence of religion, 60–61
  institution of, in empire building, 13, 14
  internal, of Ottoman state, 63
  marking of, and Ottoman tolerance, 119–123
  as mobile markers of difference, 62, 277
  movable boundaries, 184
  among Muslims, Christians, and Jews, 56, 60
  between Muslims and non-Muslims, 122–123
  Ottoman concern for, 25
  role of, in social transactions, 119
  script model, for interactions, 119
  social boundaries, 21
bounded identities, 62
  construction of, 277–289
  Sunni/Shîa transformation to, 177
Bozcaada, reconquest of, 187
Brass, Paul, 117
Braude, Benjamin, 115
brokerage across boundaries
  with Christians, by Osman/Orhan, 56
  as foundation of Ottoman power, 53–55
  importance for state-building, 33–34, 46
brokerage across networks, 25, 28–64. *See also* frontier society; Osman
Bulgaria
  attempts at gaining control of, 170
  ethnic violence in, 278
  focus on feeding Istanbul, 97
  Murad I's defeat of Serbs in, 30
  Muslim immigration to, 127
  voynuks of, 88
Burt, Ronald, 10, 33, 34, 117
Byzantine Empire
  adaptability/flexibility of, 19
  administration for Ottoman rulers, 81
  adoption of Roman practices, 69
  architecture in Hagia Sophia, 8
  attempts at conversion of Christians/Jews, 111
  borderlands of, 36
  Byzantine-Greek entrepreneurs, 40
  Christian–Muslim trade alliances, 40
  Church of Sulu Manastır, 141
  connection with Seljuks, 33

Byzantine Empire (*cont.*)
cooperation with Turcoman warriors, 42
decline/end of, 36, 74
elites of, incorporation by Mehmed, 72
emirate raids in, 45
fights with Turcoman warriors, 38, 58
incorporation feature, 18–19
John VI Kantakouzenos vs. John V
Palaiologos, 56–57
meaning of toleration, 111
pronoia land system, 88, 89
reconquering of Constantinople, 37
religious dissent in, 156
signs of success of, 39
struggles with Seljuks, 29
tax farmers, 79
years of, 15

Çaldıran, Battle of, 176
Canboladoğlu Ali Pasha (*celali* chieftain),
179
Çandarlı family, execution of, 78–79
Candia, capture of, 187
Caniklioğlu dynasty, 246
Çapanoğlu Ahmet, 249
Çapanoğlu dynasty, 246, 254
Catalan Company (of mercenaries)
contract with Andronikos, 38
defeat of Turcoman raiders by, 58
Catherine the Great, 112, 267
Catholics/Catholicism
counter-Reformation policies, 64
deliberate violence by, 183–184
vs. Greek Orthodoxy, 42, 130
Habsburgs as protectors of, 99, 111
in Holy Roman Empire, 111
of Medieval Europe, 183–184
vs. Protestants, 159
cebecis (armorers) of Istanbul, 210
Celâl (Şeyh), 178–181
celalis (bandits), 178–181
and consent/dissent, 180–181
cooptability of, 179
dealmaking with, 179
dissent by leaders, 181
engagement by state, 179
incorporation of, 179, 181
name derivation, 180–181
perception of, vs. *kızılbaş*, 178
centralization policies of Ottoman Empire,
74–83. *See also* Mehmed II;
recentralization of resources; Tanzimat
reforms/reorganization

alternative scenario for,
askeri (ruling class) vs. *reaya* (subjects), 76
Balkans/Greece growing desire for
independence, 267
devshirme system, 76, 81
importance of for reformers, 268–269
increased expenditures caused by, 270
kul (slave–servant) system, 76
lack of success with indirect taxation
sources, 274–275
land appropriation policies, 79
Mahmud II's efforts at, 268
as measure to "save the empire," 264
preference for multiethnic, federalist state,
266
seizure of *vakıf*, conversion to *tımars*, 77
tax farm centralization failure, 271
warfare difficulties as force for, 266
*The Cheese and the Worms: The Cosmos of a
Sixteenth-Century Miller* (Ginzburg),
169–170
chiefs, neighborhood (*mahalle başı*), 143
Chirot, Daniel, 12–13
Christ, Turk recognition of, 61
Christian Orthodox Church, empowerment of,
143
Christians/Christianity
alliances with Osman, 47, 48–50, 51, 56
Byzantine Christians, 40
complaints against Jews, 187
conflicts/violence in Aleppo/Damascus,
285
conversion to, from *devshirme*, 124
conversion to Judaism, 61
conversions by, to avoid taxation, 125–126
emergence of boundaries, with Muslims, 56,
60
fertility rites shared with Muslims, 41
freedom in Syria, 285–286
guild system participation by, 145
harmony with Muslims, on frontier, 43–44
influence on Seljuk Empire, 39
Latin Christians, 80
Muslim conversions to, 62
Orthodox, incorporation/administration of,
115
participation in sultan courts, 61
population percentage, 120
privileged positions of, 88–89
raids by Umur, 56
Russian interference with, 219
struggle for commercial dominance, 283
taunting of, by Turcoman chieftains, 39–40

territorial raids by Turcomans, 36–37
trade role of, 280–281
churches. *See also* Greek Orthodox Church;
    religion/religious issues
    Bulgarian church, 137
    Byzantine Church of Sulu Manastır, 141
    Christian Orthodox Church,
    conversion to Islamic learning centers, 62,
        63, 102
    Eastern Orthodox Church (Russia), 35
    Serbian Orthodox Church, 124, 137
*çiftlik*s (plantation style estates), 252, 253,
    254
civil wars
    within Byzantium, 38
    John VI Kantakouzenos vs. John V
        Palaiologos, 56–57
    Republican Civil Wars, 72
    of Rome, 74
Çizakça, Murat, 234
cizye. *See* taxation *(cizye)*
Cleopatra, 74
commercial networks. *See also* trade
    empire integration into, 228
    Greek control of, 129
    protectionism of Ottomans, 241–242
    and spread/containment of violence, 279
    spreading of, between Ottomans and
        European port cities, 238–239
commercialization. *See also* trade
    collective response to, 255
    with Europe, 240–241
    by Karaosmanoğlu dynasty, 253
Committee of Union and Progress (CUP),
    288–289
communal forms of self-government, 144
communities. *See also* boundaries
    alternatives to religious community, 143
    "barricaded social entities" concept, 118
    conflicts/discomforts in, 116–117
    potential for/absence of violence, 117
    resistance to political manipulation, 117
comradeship *(nöker)* on the frontier, 42, 48
confiscation tool *(müsadere)*, of state, 259
conquer and rule, patterns of empires, 10
conquests
    by Beyazid, 30–31
    of Bozcaada, 187
    in central Europe, 184
    of Constantinople, 67, 73–74, 115, 132–133
    of Crete, 92–93, 230
    of Iraq, 91–92
    by Murad, 30

by Orhan, 30
by Selim I, 91–103
by Süleyman, of Gallipoli Peninsula, 58
of Syria, Jerusalem, Egypt, 91
conscription system, of Tanzimat reforms,
    286
consilia reports, 15–16
Constantinople
    aftermath of conquest, 131
    Byzantine reconquering of, 37
    claim to authority over Orthodox
        Christians, 134
    conquest of, 67, 73–74, 115, 132–133. *See
        also* millet administrative system
    deportations to, 129
    Janissary attacks on, 73
    reconstruction, into Ottoman city, 101
    sacking of, 36
conversions, 125–128
    in Anatolia, from Christianity to Muslim,
        126
    in Bosnia, from Christianity to Islam, 127
    of Christians, to Judaism, 61
    of churches, to Islamic learning centers, 62,
        102
    from *devshirme*, to Christianity, 124
    by Mehmed II, to Islamic ways, 102–103
    Muslims to Christianity, 62
    role of Sufis in Christian conversions, 125
    of *vakıf* to *tımar* system, 77
cooptation/cooptability
    of *celalis* (bandits), 179
    of elites, 87, 91, 156
    of enemies, by Ottomans, 65
    of Jews/Muslims, 156, 162
    of military notables, 199
    of provinces, by Bayraktar, 220
core provinces *(tımarlı)*, of Ottoman Empire,
    86
corporate patrimonialism, 209
Cretan Revolt (1869), 274
Crete, conquest of, 92–93, 230
Crimean War (1853–56), 274
customs zones, 98

Damad Ibrahim Pasha (grand vizier)
    appointment by Ahmed III, 213
    execution of, 216
Damad Ibrahim Pasha (grand vizier),
    execution of, 204
Darling, Linda, 31, 59
Davison, Roderic, 266–267
de Groot, Alexander H., 281

decentralization of resources. *See also*
  recentralization of resources
  devaluation of silver *akçe*, 272–273
  involvement of elites, 272
  and tax farming, 270–277
The Decline and Fall of the Roman Empire
  (Gibbons), 4
decline thesis, 22–23
deportations. *See sürgün* (deportations)
dervishes *(babas and abdals)*
  Bektaş dervish community, 52
  conflict with Ottoman state, 168
  dervish-based proselytism, 60
  in frontier society, 42–43
  opposition to Sunnî orthodox state, 167
  patronization by sultans, 169
  tarîkats (dervish orders), 186
devshirme system, 81, 123–125
  and Christian conversions, 124
  contribution to ethnic heterogeneity, 125
  earliest reference to, 123
  emergence during reign of Murad, 76
  and non-Muslims, 70, 81
  process of childrens' distribution, 123–124
dhimmi communities, 148
Diaspora, of Jews, 114, 137, 139
dissent. *See also* Bedreddîn, Şeyh
  in Anatolia, 167
  by Bedreddîn (Şeyh), 181
  in Byzantine Empire, 156
  by *celali* leaders, 181
  of dervishes, 165, 168
  in Habsburg Empire, 156
  by intellectuals/religious officials, 182
  by Jews/Orthodox, 181–190
  in Roman Empire, 156
  in Russian Empire, 156
  by Sufi groups, 162
  transformation of, in eighteenth century,
  200
divide/rule patterns of empires, 10, 12
Don Cossacks
  incorporation of, 179–180
  unpredictability of relationship with,
Doumani, Beshara, 259
Doyle, Michael, 9, 74
Dressler, Markus, 177
Dubrovnik, self-government by, 87

economic system, of Ottomans, 94–95. *See
  also* fiscalism, of Ottomans; taxation
  (cizye); trading zones
  fiscalism, provisionalism, traditionalism, 96,
  97

flexibility/openness to outside views, 96–97
  guild system, 95
  mukataa revenues/money economy, 95, 96
  privatization of revenues by notables,
  258–259
  trade capitulations to European countries,
  237
Edirne Event rebellion (1703), 206–213. *See
  also* households
  causes of, 206–207, 210
  corporate patrimonialism, 209
  demands of rebels, 211
  development of patronage networks,
  207–208, 209
  fetvas issued by *ulema*, 211–212
  growth/influence of households, 208
  resolution of, 212
  ulema concentration/reproduction of power,
  209, 210
Egypt
  conquests of, 91, 103
  economic value of, 84
  focus on feeding Istanbul, 97
  Mamluk hindrance of Ottoman expansion,
  91
  practice of tax farming, 229
  and Selim I, 93
1808 Agreement. *See also* Sened-i İttifak
  (1808 Agreement)
Eighteenth Century
  deconstruction of imperial compact, 266
  dominance of Istanbul-based *malikane*
  contracts, 233
  economic growth/beginnings of modern
  polity, 257
  Edirne Event rebellion, 206–213
  historical background, 201–204
  neglect/misunderstanding of, 197
  Patrona Halil revolt, 204, 213–217
  Sened-i İttifak, 218–224
Eisenstadt, Shmuel N., 6, 9, 257
eleutherochoria (Greek free communities), 144
elites. *See also* governance regimes; notables
  (ayan)
  cooptation/cooptability of, 87, 91, 156
  decentralization/privatization efforts of,
  272
  elimination of, by Augustus/Mehmed II, 75
  empowerment of notables in Istanbul by,
  218
  incorporation of, 70, 72, 294
  Jewish secular elites, 143
  Shiites, struggles with, 242
  status in Kazakhstan, 84

emirates. *See also* Osman; Turcomans; Umur
  Bey (of Aydın)
  Aydın *(beyliks)* emirate, 30, 45
  competition between, for resources/booty,
    30, 45
  Karesi emirate, 30
  organization of Byzantium/Seljuk frontier,
    55
empire(s)
  analytical framework, 9–15
  characteristics of, 3
  conditions for dominance, 13–14
  cultural studies of, 4
  definition (author's), 9
  divide/rule patterns of, 10, 12
  incorporation of, 18
  longevity of, 3, 6
  as macrostructural formations, 6
  as multiple networks, 11
  as multiple networks of interaction, 11
  political authority relations, 9
  segmentation/integration structure of, 10,
    17–18
  theoretical studies of, 4
Engin Akarlı, 215
England
  public to private transference of indirect
    taxes, 276
  reliance on tax farming, 230
  state control of tax collection, 275–276
esham financial scheme, 272
ethnic/religious toleration, 21–22
Europe
  attempts at creating trade monopolies,
    281
  centralization model of, 265
  commercialization of relationships with,
    240–241
  descriptions of East/West by, 198
  guild involvement/influence, 284
  linked with Asia/Africa, 7
  Ottoman borrowing from banks of, 274
  Reformation, 109
  social, political, economic actors of, 240
  trade role of non-Muslims, 279, 280
  trade/commercial networks with Ottomans,
    238–239
  violence by Catholics, 183–184
Evrenos Bey, 48–50, 51, 52, 53–55
Evrenosoğulları warrior family, 47

Fawkener, Everard, 217
Fazıl Ahmed (grand vizier), 202
Fearon, James, 118

fermâns (sultanic decrees), 120–121
fetvas (legal opinions), 187, 211–212, 216
Feyzullah Efendi (Şeyhülislam). *See also* Edirne
    Event rebellion; Mustafa II
  execution of, 203
  exploitation of tax-farming advantages, 207
fighters *(akınjı-uc beyis)*, 48
fiscalism, of Ottomans, 96, 218. *See also*
    mukataa (Ottoman fiscal unit); taxation
    (cizye)
  costliness of warfare, 230–231, 274
  devaluation of silver *akçe*, 272–273
  esham financial scheme, 272
  establishment of Public Debt
    Administration, 275, 276
  malikaneli esham financial scheme, 272
  returns from life-term tax farming, 235
  strain of warfare on, 230–231
  fifteenth/sixteenth century provisionist
    outlook, 237
Fleischer, Cornell, 125
flexibility. *See also* adaptability
  of Byzantine Empire, 19
  of empires, 3, 14
  of Ottoman Empire, 7, 70, 85
  of Russian Empire, 35
Fortna, Benjamin, 287
foundation myths, 116
France
  ancien régime, 228
  attempts at tax farm centralization, 276
  favorable trade balance of, 242
  French Revolution, 240
  public to private transference of indirect
    taxes, 276
  reliance on tax farming, 230
  state administrative model, 268
  state control of tax collection, 275–276
  war with Habsburgs, 203
  widespread trade by, 239, 240
frontier society, 28, 36–45. *See also* Anatolia;
    brokerage across networks; Osman
  Byzantine reconquering of Constantinople,
    37
  coexistence of Christians and Muslims,
    43–44
  comradeship *(nöker)* in, 42
  decline of Seljuk empire, 37
  dervishes in, 42–43
  emirate organization of, 55
  Hamid principality, 37
  hybrid culture of, 42–43
  incorporation vs. resistance in, 158
  influence of Seljuk collapse, 37

frontier society (*cont.*)
  Karamanid principality, 37
  law and order issues, 28, 44
  management of, 83–93
  Muslims vs. Muslims, 42
  myths and legends, 41
  opportunities in, 36
  Ottoman vs. Habsburg border issues, 84
  Ottoman/Russian emergence from, 29
  political layering, evolution, unpredictability
    of, 38
  raids by Greeks, 37
  relationship with sovereignty/identity
    notions, 85
  successes of Osman, 43–45
  symbiotic culture of, 41–42
  territorial raids by Turcomans, 36–37
  trading zones, 40–41

gazâ (Holy War) ideology, 31, 59
Geertz, Clifford, 17, 107
Genç, Mehmet, 273
Gengiz Khan, 30
Gennadios (Patriarch of Greek Orthodox
  Church), 133
genocide, of Armenian population, 114–115,
  277–278, 293–294
Gibbons, Edward, 4
Ginzburg, Carlo, 169–170
Glabas, Isidore, 123
Golden Horde, 29
  decline of, 35
  role in Russian Empire, 34–35
governance regimes. *See also* notables *(ayan)*
  creation of, 243
  Mahmud II's attempt at elimination of,
    242–243
  outcomes of, 243
  rise of Karaosmanoğlu dynasty, 246–248
  rise of Osman Ağa Pasvanoğlu, 248–249
  rivalries between, 251–252
  transition to modernity, 257
  Tuzcuoğlu dnasty, 250–251
Greek Orthodox Church
  administrative structure of, as state model,
    151
  attempts at forcing Jews in line with, 131
  challenges to, 283–284
  and conquests of Balkans, 133
  development of patriarchate, 136–137
  domination by, 131, 283–284
  empowerment by Ottoman state, 145
  harmony with Muslims, 55

  influence on Russians, 112
  influence on Serbian/Bulgarian churches,
    137
  interference with, by Mehmed II, 78
  Islamic authority modeled on, 112
  and Russian efforts at conversion,
  sanctioning of Gennadios as Patriarch, 133
Greeks
  as administrators for Mehmed II, 81
  battles with/conversion by Osman, 48
  as crews for raids, 37
  demands for autonomy by, 201, 219, 267
  deportation to Constantinople, 129
  and dervishes, 42–43
  ethnic violence against, 277–278
  influence of wars on trade, 239–240
  strained relationships with Jews, 117
  successful organization of resources/people,
    282
Greene, Molly, 281
guild system, of Ottomans, 95
  decline of, 284–285
  economic intervention by states, 97
  kethüdâ (guild leaders), 136, 143, 145
  Ottoman control through, 152
  participation in, by Christians and Jews,
    145
  rise of tension within, 215
  sharing of, by Muslims/non-Muslims, 148,
    215

Habsburg Empire, 7. *See also* Austria
  attempts at Transylvanian rule, 202, 203,
    230
  border issues, 84
  Catholic institutions/values of, 111
  contesting of Hungary with Ottomans, 91
  discussions of *millet* system, 153
  divisions during Protestant Reformation, 64
  economic/political/nationalist movements,
    201
  expansion by marriage alliances, 11
  Jews of, 12, 137
  meaning of toleration, 111
  monarchical basis of, 99
  nationalitatät of, 12
  openness to change/loyalty to ruling houses,
    100
  religious dissent, 156
  sense of self/legitimacy of, 99
  toleration/persecution of, on frontiers, 111
  transition to modern imperial model, 292
  war with France, 203

wars vs. Ottoman Empire, 182, 198, 202, 203
years of, 15
Hagia Sophia mosque, 102
Halvetis Sufis, 56, 184
Hamid principality, 37
Hamidiye (Kurdish cavalry unit), establishment of, 288
Hamza Bali, 161
Hatt-i Şerif (Noble Edict of the Rose Chamber), 268, 286
heterodox sects, 26, 48, 164–178
  Bedreddîn, Şeyh, 169–175
  kızılbaş (redhead) movement, 175–178
  of Sufism, in Anatolia, 164
Hikmet, Nazım, 154–155
Hocazade Mesut (Şeyhülislam), 113
Holy War *(gazâ)* ideology, 31
Hopwood, Keith, 39
Hospitalers, taking of Smyrna (Izmir), 55
Hourani, Albert, 245
households
  entry into rebel movement (Edirne Event), 210–211
  growth/influence of, 208
  Mustafa II's reliance on, 209–210
  soldiers from, vs. *devshirme* soldiers, 208
Hükümet sanjaks, 92
Hungary
  attention of Kara Mustafa, 202
  contesting of, by Habsburgs/Ottomans, 91
  costliness of frontier defense, 90
  fate of Protestants in, 12
  incorporation by Ottomans, 90
  loss of territory in, 202
  military/strategic value of, 84
  Süleyman's dealings with, 90
Hupchick, Dennis, 127
hybrid civilizations, 7–8

Ibn Abi Zimra, David, 114
Ibn Arabi, 170
Identity and Control (White), 6
iltizam. See tax farming *(iltizam)*
Imber, Colin, 32
imperial society
  state-periphery relationships, weakness of, 11
İnalcık, Halil, 32, 230, 254
incorporation. *See also* boundaries
  of Armenians, 115
  of *celalis* (bandits), 179, 181
  constrained policies of, 92

of dervishes, 165
of *devshirme* recruitment style, into slave-*kul* system, 123
of Don Cossacks, by Russia, 179–180
of eastern Anatolia, 91
of elites, 70, 72, 294
of Hungary, 90
impact of, on imperial thinking/institutional development, 85–86
integration component of, 18, 29
in Iraq, 91
of Jews, 115
of Karaosmanoğlu dynasty, 251
of non-Muslims, 120, 162
of Ottoman Empire, 19–20, 82, 84–86, 90, 174, 228, 278
preaching of, by Bayraktar Mustafa Pasha, 222–223
religious, by Russians/Habsburgs, 153
vs. resistance, in frontiers, 158
of Roman Empire, 83–84, 156
of Russian Empire, 11, 84
as source of flexibility, 14
of Sufi groups, 162, 165
Thelen's view of, 131
toleration as policy of, 110
Turkic tribal understandings of, 150
understanding of, by Byzantine rulers, 19
An Introduction to Islamic Law (Schact), 152
Iran
  hindrance of Ottoman security/expansion, 91
  seventeenth century wars with, 182, 203, 215
  spread of Oghuz peoples through, 30
  Sufi origins in, 161
  warfare with Mahmud I, 204
Iraq, 12–13, 91
  conquest of, 91–92
  representation by redhead movement, 175
  Sufi origins in, 161
Islam
  attempted codification of laws, 169
  dealing with non-Muslim communities in empire, 277
  dissent by Ultra-Orthodox, 181–190
  domination over non-Muslims, 114
  increased adoption by Ottoman Empire, 102–103
  initial encounters with Ottoman Empire, 102
  role of, 104–108
  toleration of Jews by, 110

Islam (*cont.*)
  triumph of, 102
  ulema-sponsored version of, 115
Islamization
  in Anatolia, 126
  creation of religious rigidity, 295
  as incorporation of imperial
    thinking/institutional development, 85
  of Kurds, 288
  origins/decline of, 127
  reasons for, 38, 102
  reassertion of Sunni beliefs, 292
  and Selim II, 63
  as solution to Ottoman legitimacy, 186,
    188, 190
  and *tımar* system, 88
Ismail (Shah of Iran)
  conquests of, by Selim I, 91–103
  hindrance of Ottoman expansion, 91, 103
  infiltration of Anatolia, 103
Istanbul. *See also* Edirne; life-term tax farming
    (*malikane*); tax farming (*iltizam*)
  askeri hold on tax farms, 276
  banning of Jews in, 184
  contrasting nature of, 214–215
  defiance of *cebecis* (armorers), 210
  elite's empowerment of notables (*ayan*),
    218
  establishment of dervish lodges, 169
  patronage networks, 207–208
  eighteenth-century plague epidemics, 202
  vaizans (preachers) vs. Sufi counterparts,
    185
istimalet (accommodation policies), 87
Itzkowitz, Norman, 198
Ivan III, 78, 79
Ivan IV (Ivan the Terrible), 79–80, 179–180
Izmir, trade with France, 239

Janissary corps
  alliance with *ulema*, 213, 216, 219–220, 225
  attack on Constantinople, 73
  condemnation of Achmed III, 197
  demise of, 268, 272
  dethroning of Osman II, 206
  embracement of Bektaşis, 161, 165
  expansion by Beyazıd II, 79
  inherited by Mehmed II, 76
  protection of, by Bektaş, 53
  recruitment of Christian children, 124
  running amok by, in Bosnia, 219
  support of *cebecis*, 210
Jassy Treaty, 267

Jeremie 1st (Patriarch), 136
Jerusalem, conquests of, 91, 103
Jews/Judaism. *See also* Messianic Jews;
    Sabbatai Sevi (Jewish messiah)
  accusations against, 147
  and Beyazıd II, 126
  boundaries with Christians/Muslims,
    60–61
  Christian conversion to, 61
  complaints against Christians, 187
  conversions by, to avoid taxation, 125–126
  decline of, in Ottoman Empire, 187–188
  deference towards Muslims, 120
  deportation to Constantinople, 129
  deteriorating relationship with Kadızadelis,
    182–183
  Diaspora, 114, 137, 139
  discrimination against, by
    Habsburgs/Russians, 137
  dissent by Messianic Jews, 183
  grain/wool exports of, 239
  and Greek Orthodox Church, 131
  guild system participation by, 145
  of Habsburg Empire, 12
  incorporation/administration of, 115
  Istanbul's banning of, 184
  massacre of, 183, 187
  Mehmed III's tax-exemption for, 121–122
  and Mehmed IV, 126
  millet system of, 131, 140
  organization into synagogues, 139
  participation in sultan courts, 61
  percentage of population, 120
  relationship with Ottoman Empire,
    137–140
  secular elites, 143
  Sephardic Jews, 138
  strained relationships with Greeks, 117
  struggle for commercial dominance, 283
  trade role of, 280–281
  violence against, 184, 186–187
  Western vs. Ottoman treatment of, 110
John V Palaiologos, 56–57
John VI Kantakouzenos, 56–57
John VII Kantakouzenos, 53
Jowitt, Ken, 118, 279

Kadı court, 147, 148, 149
Kadızadeli Islamic movement
  anti–non-Muslim attitude of, 187
  defining of internal/external enemies, 183
  deteriorating relationship with Jews,
    182–183

feelings of lack of respect, 185
vs. Halveti Sufis, 184
opposition to innovation *(bida)*, 185
rise of, 187
Kafadar, Cemal, 59
Kalenderîs (mystical fraternity), 165
Kamanica citadel, 184
Kamber Baba shrine, destruction of, 184
kanun (secular law), 72, 93, 105, 106,
  120–121, 134
Kara Mustafa (grand vizier), 202
Karamanid principality, 37
Karaosmanoğlu dynasty
  commercialization efforts, 253
  construction of, 246–248
  housing units/hostel endowments, 254
  incorporation policies, 251
  loans by Müridoğlu to, 250
  modernity efforts, 261
Karaosmanzade Hüseyin Pasha, 253
Karesi emirate, 30
Karlowitz Treaty, 203, 212, 249
Karpat, Kemal H., 146, 287
Kasaba, Reşat, 16
Katib Çelebi, 182
katun (Balkan pastoral community),
  144
Kazakhstan, elites of, 84
kehillah (town-wide organizations), 139
kethüdâ (guild leaders), 136, 143, 145
Keyder, Çağlar, 266
Khanate of Khazan, 112
kizilbaş (redhead) movement, 175–178
  perception of, vs. *celalis*, 178
  representation of Turcomans/Safavid rulers,
    175
  support of Safavid Shah, 175
knezina (Serbian joint family organization),
  144
Kommenian Turkophiles, 39
Kommenos, Manuel, 39
Köprülü dynasty, 208–209, 210–211
Köprülü Fazıl Ahmed Pasha, 186
Köprülü Mehmed (grand vizier), 202
Köprülü Mehmed Pasha, 186
Köse Mihal, 48–50, 51, 52, 53–55
Kosovo, Battle of, 11–12, 30
Küçük Kaynarca Treaty, 204, 267, 284
kul (slave–servant) system, 76
Kurdish tribal leaders *(sanjak beyi)*, 92. *See
  also Hükumet sanjaks*
kızıl elma (golden apple) of Roman emperors,
  73

Laitin, David, 118
Languschi, Giacomo de, 67
Latin Kingdoms, 40
legal issues
  codification of Islamic/secular laws, 169
  frontier zone law and order, 28, 44
  kadi court, 147, 148, 149
  religious law vs. secular dynastic law, 72
legitimacy, of rulership, 98–104. *See also*
  Abdülhamid II; Tanzimat
  reforms/reorganization
  acceptance/promotion of family of Osman,
    99–100 (*See also* Osman)
  of Habsburg Empire, 99
  Islamization as solution to, 186, 188, 190
  and longevity, 98–99
  of Ottoman Empire, 100
  and religion, 289–294
  role of actor, 32
  of Russian Empire, 99
  and sultans, 101–102
  Tanzimat reforms as crisis of, 290
  Weber's view on, 98
"Letter concerning Toleration" (Locke),
  109
life-term tax farming *(malikane)*, 232–235
  advantages of, 234–235
  as agent of privatization, 233
  farming out to intermediary tax farmers
    (mültezim), 234
  financing of, 233–234
  holdings of Jalilis/Umari families, 245–246
  importance for state financing, 232–233
  incentives offered by, 233
  as institution, 242
  mechanics of, 232
  monetary returns from, 235
  overexploitation, 271–272
  parceling/inheritance provisions, 259
  and reorganization of Ottoman provinces,
    257–258
  as source of wealth in provinces, 271
  stability brought by, 259–260
  state portrayal vs. tax-farmer
    representation, 258–259
Limnos, *timar* system on, 89, 91
Locke, John, 109
longevity of empires, 3, 6, 15–23
  conditions for, 13
  reasons for success of, 20–21
longue durée transformations, 15
Lowry, Heath, 32, 42, 126, 129
Luttwak, Edward, 15

Macedonia
  agrarian transformations in, 255
  fight against Christians, 57
  Serb defeats, 30
  trade exports, 239
  voynuks of, 88
mahalle başı (neighborhood chiefs), 143
mahalle (neighborhoods of religious
    communities), 144–145
Mahmud I, 204, 216, 217
Mahmud II, 3, 218
  attempt to eliminate regional governance
    regimes, 242–243
  coup d'état against Selim III, 204, 218,
    219–220
  devaluation of silver *akçe*, 272–273
  military reforms initiated by, 204, 267,
    268
  recentralization efforts of, 274
Mahmud Pasha, 80
Mahomaet II, 197
Mahomat Bey, 73
Mahoney, James, 5
malikane. See life-term tax farming *(malikane)*
malikaneli esham financial scheme, 272
Mamluks of Egypt
  conquests of, by Selim I, 91–103
  hindrance of Ottoman expansion, 91, 103
Mantran, Robert, 151–152
Manuel I, 39
Manzikert (Malazgirt), battle of, 30, 69
martolosi (auxiliaries/guards), 88
massacre of Jews, 183, 187
Masuki, Ismail, 161, 166
Mavrozomes, Manuel, 39
Mecca
  Ottoman provisioning of, 92
  and Selim I, 93
  Şeyh Bedreddîn's visit to, 171
Medicis, in Renaissance Florence, 45
Medina
  Ottoman provisioning of, 92
  and Selim I, 93
  Şeyh Bedreddîn's visit to, 171
Mehmed Efendi, 186
Mehmed II, 31, 67, 71–72, 73
  authority delegated to Grand Duke Notaras,
    133
  centralization policies, 167
  comparisons with Augustus, 81–82
  consolidation of power, 71, 72
  conversion to Islamic ways, 102–103
  creation of administrative group, 81

  elimination of hostile elites, 75
  goals accomplished by, 77
  inheritance/expansion of janissary corps, 76,
    77
  issuance of *ferman*, 150
  military reforms of, 76
  multivocal signaling of, 102
  network building by, 80
  recoordination of Ottoman factions, 75–77
  relationship between state and Orthodox
    Church, 135
  sanctioning of Gennadios, 133
  Trapezuntine palace slaves of, 78
  use of deportations, 128
Mehmed III, 121–122, 186
Mehmed IV, 186
  and conversion of Jews, 126
  deposition of, 203, 213
Melâmîs spiritual order, 166–167
Mélikoff, Irène, 175
Menocchio, assassination of, 170
Menteshe emirate, 30, 37
Messianic Jews, 155, 181–183, 190. *See also*
    Sabbatai Sevi (Jewish messiah)
Mevlânâ Celâleddin Rumi, 170
Mevlevis Sufis, 56
Mihailovic, Konstantin, 28, 34
Mihaloğulları warrior family, 47
millet administrative system, 12
  of Armenians, 131
  criticism of, 115–116
  Habsburg Empire discussions of, 153
  of Jews, 131, 140
  non-Muslim millets, 130
  of Orthodox church, 131
  as script for multireligious rule, 130
  umbrella organizations of, 145–146
Minkov, Anton, 127
mission civilisatrice theme of empires, 13
modernity
  arguments for, 259
  defined, in Ottoman context,
  indigenous, establishment of, 27, 266
  leadership by Karaosmanoğlu dynasty, 261
  notables transition to, 226–227, 256–262
  push of Ottomans towards, 258
  Weberian definition, 206
Mohacs, Battle of, 90
Mohammed, 61
Moldavia, 87, 136, 202, 282
Mongol Empire, 14, 29
  decline of, 35
  invasion of Anatolia, 55

invasion of Asia Minor, 42
  role in Russian Empire, 34–35, 36
Mosul, Ottoman control of, 91
Motyl, Alexander J., 9
Mourroutsis, Demetrios, 283
movable boundaries, 184
mukataa (Ottoman fiscal unit), 95, 96, 136
Murad I, 30, 61
Murad II, 63, 75
Murad IV, 120–121, 124
  and Halvetis/Kadızadelis
  interaction with Kadızade Mehmed Efendi,
    184
Müridoğlu, loans to Karaosmanoğlu family,
  250
Musa Çelebi, 172
müsadere (confiscation tool), of state, 259
Muscovites
  brokering/innovation by, 29, 35
  rise of, 29, 35
  tactics/policies of, 36
Muslims, 12. *See also* dervishes *(babas* and
    abdals); non-Muslims *(dhimma)*
  Abdülhamid II's attempt to create unity, 288
  alliance with Christians, vs. Jews, 187
  blurred distinction from non-Muslims,
    120–121
  colonial status of elites, 84
  complaints against Christians and Jews, 187
  conversions to Christianity, 62
  deportations to Constantinople, 129
  emergence of boundaries, with Christians,
    56, 60
  fertility rites shared with Christians, 41
  frontier harmony with Christians, 43–44
  gazâ (Holy War) ideology, 31, 59
  and guild system, 145, 148
  immigration to Bulgaria, 127
  impounding land from, 187
  and Islamization, 88
  Jewish deference towards, 120
  laying of hybrid state foundation with Greek
    Orthodox, 55
  vs. Muslims, 42, 118, 122
  nontoleration of, 160
  Osman's befriending of, 47, 48–50
  practice of tax farming, 229
  religious explanation of economic
    disadvantages, 285
  Russian perceptions of, 84
  and Selim I, 103, 104
  Seljuk's facilitation of Muslims in Anatolia,
    30

Sunnî vs. Shias, 85
tarîkats (dervish orders), 186
  ties with Byzantine Christians, 40
Mustafa II, 197, 203, 209–210. *See also*
  Edirne Event rebellion; Feyzullah Efendi
  (Şeyhülislâm)

nationalitatät of Habsburg Empire, 12
networks. *See also* boundaries; commercial
    networks; governance regimes; notables
    (ayan); Osman; patronage networks;
    political networks; social networks
  brokerage across, 25, 28–64
  embedding of actors within, 17, 24, 27, 245
  empire as, 11
  and expanded influence of leaders, 33
  of frontiers, 29
  reinforcement of ideas/prejudices, 34
  shaping of, 17
  structure of, 9, 10
  of trade/cooperation, 27
Nicholas I, 180
nishans (imperial diplomas), 135
Nizam-ı Cedid army, 220, 249, 268
Nizâm-ı-Alem (Ottoman conception of order),
    100, 162
non-Muslims *(dhimma)*, 7. *See also devshirme*
    system
  competition with Muslim merchants, 26
  and *devshirme*, 70
  incorporation policies of, 120, 162
  Islamic domination over, 114
  and millet system, 130
  vs. Muslims, 42, 118, 122
  organization by Mehmed II, 81
  protectionist associations formed by, 282
  religious/institutional boundaries from
    Muslims, 118
  state distrust of, 279
  and taxation *(cizye)*, 86, 96
  toleration/protection of, 26, 120
  trade role Europe, 279, 280
notables *(ayan). See also* Bayraktar Mustafa
    Pasha; Sened-i İttifak (1808 Agreement)
  attachments to rentier patrons, 273
  attempts at limiting power of, 251
  Caniklioğlu dynasty, 246
  Çapanoğlus dynasty, 246, 254
  competition for territory/influence, 219
  as economic/political actors, 226
  empowerment by Istanbul elites, 218
  involvement in trading, 238
  Karaosmanoğlu dynasty, 246–248

notables *(ayan) (cont.)*
  Pasvanoğlu dynasty, 248–249
  rebellion against Ottoman state, 221
  responsibilities of, 242, 245, 249
  revenue privatization by, 258–259
  rise to power, 245
  social transformation role, 226–227
  support of reforms in Anatolia, 222
  and tax farming *(iltizam)*, 246
  and trade, 252–256
  transitional modernity of, 226–227,
    256–262
  Tuzcuoğlu dynasty, 250–251
  use as military reserves, 219
  wartime assistance in Anatolia, 246
  wealth building mechanisms, 244
Notaras (Grand Duke), 133

Oghuz Khan, 99
Oghuz peoples, 30
Olson, Mancur, 34
On the Origin of the Ottoman Emperors
  (Spandugnino), 47
Orhan (son of Osman), 30
  brokerage with Christians, 56
  differences with Osman, 46–47
  involvement in Byzantium civil war,
    57
  joint raids with Umur Bey, 57
  marriages of, 53, 57, 61
  networking patterns of, 53
  promotion of religious tolerance, 289
  rivalry with Umur Bey, 55
Osman, 30
  alliance with Christians, 51
  battles with/conversions of Greeks, 48
  bridging of social gaps, 48–50, 53–55
  brokerage between Sufis and akhi
    organizations, 51
  brokerage with Christians, 56
  coming of age, 46
  concern for excess warfare, 51
  connections through marriage, 51–52
  dethroning by Janissary corps, 206
  differences with Orhan, 46–47
  establishment of power relations, 56
  as first legitimate Ottoman ruler, 99
  friendship building by, 47–50
  networks of, 33, 45–52, 58
  promotion of religious tolerance, 289
  reliance on Turcomans, for warfare, 50
  rivalry with Umur Bey, 55
  successes of, 43–45

Osmanoğulları warrior family, 47
Ottoman Empire. *See also* centralization
    policies of Ottoman Empire; economic
    system, of Ottomans; fiscalism, of
    Ottomans; guild system, of Ottomans;
    reforms in Ottoman Empire
  arrangements with Kurdish tribal leaders,
    92
  askeri status in, 70
  central meaning-based concept of, 100
  centralization policies, 74–83
  conquest of Arab land/Balkans, 11
  conquest of Gallipoli Peninsula, 58
  continents linked by, 7
  conversion of churches to Islamic learning
    centers, 62, 63, 102
  core provinces/outer provinces, 86
  encounters with Islam, in Arab provinces,
    102
  establishment of provincial rule, 83–93
  fiscal strain of warfare, 230–231
  flexibility/adaptability of, 7, 70, 85
  frontier management, 83–93
  goals of, 130
  hybrid civilization quality, 7–8
  identification with Sunni identity, 168
  incorporation policies (*See under*
    incorporation)
  initial spatial/temporal advantages, 28–29
  internal boundaries of, 58–64
  lack of class distinctions, 214–215
  meaning of toleration, 110–111
  pan-Islamic phase, 288
  policies toward diversity, 111–113
  political organization of, 8–9
  reasons for successful emergence, 34
  relationship with Armenians, 141
  relationship with Jews, 137–140
  religious foundations, 53
  religious tolerance in, 112
  struggles with Shiite elite, 176–177
  supranational ideology of, 99
  traditional historical interpretation of, 16
  transition out of empire, 257
  transition to modern imperial model, 292
  transition to modernity, 256–262
  wars vs. Habsburg Empire, 182, 198, 202,
    203
  wars with Poland, 182, 202
  wars with Russia, 203–204, 267
  wars with Safavids, 63, 85, 91, 161, 177,
    202
  years of, 15

outer provinces *(salyaneli)*, of Ottoman
Empire, 86–87

Palaiologos, Michael, 37, 39, 47
Palamas, Gregory (archbishop of Salonica),
61, 62
Pamuk, Şevket, 16, 96–97, 272
pan-Islamic phase of Ottoman Empire, 288
Parsons, Talcott, 5
Passarowitz Treaty, 203, 249
Pasvanoğlu
rebellion against Ottoman state, 221
rise to *ayan*hood, 248–249
patriarchs
financial relationship with Ottomans,
135–136
Gennadios, 133
of Greek Orthodox Church, 136–137
Jeremie 1st, 136
as Ottoman fiscal unit *(mukataa)*, 136
purchase of *berats*, 134
Serkis (of Armenia), 141
Patrona Halil revolt, 204, 213–217. *See also*
Tulip Era
coalescence into class movement, 217
conditions leading to, 215
ulema endorsement of, 216
patronage networks. *See also* Edirne Event
rebellion
and bandits, 179
and constraint of state/rentier tax farmers,
273
extension of, to Greek communities, 282
horizontal/vertical ties of association, 209
in Istanbul, Rumelia, Anatolia, 207–208
state extension of tax-farming contracts to,
273
Persia
building of empire, 14
effects of Sunnî-Shia consolidation, 177
warfare against Mahmûd, 177
Peter I (Peter the Great), 112, 180, 267, 268
Poland
massacre of Jews in, 183
Russian expansion into, 11, 78, 157
wars with, 182, 202
political networks, 204, 209, 244, 283
pomest'e system of Ivan III, 78
privatization
encouragement for, by trade/tax-farming,
227
granting of life-leases on tax farms, 231
involvement of elites, 272

of land and enterprises, 233
malikane as agents of, 233, 259
negative aspects of, U.S. example, 270
by notables, of revenues, 258
of public resources, 258
by states, of key functions, 270
pronoia land system (Byzantines), 88, 89
prophecy of Saint Augustine, 73
Protestants
of Bohemia/Hungary, 12
opposition to Habsburg rulers, 159
Protestant Reformation, 64
provincial rule, establishment of (Ottoman
Empire), 83–93
provisionalism, of Ottomans, 96, 97
Prunier, Gerard, 12–13
Public Debt Administration (PDA),
establishment of, 275, 276

Raif Mahmud Pasha, 220
reaya (subjects) vs. *askeri* (ruling class), 76
recentralization of resources, 274
reforms in Ottoman Empire. *See also*
Tanzimat reforms/reorganization
in Anatolia, 222
efforts of Selim III, 76, 219, 267, 269
endorsement of equality before the law,
286
fiscal reforms of Amcazade Hüseyin, 204
importance of centralization, 268–269
initiation by Mahmud II, 204, 267
military reforms of Mehmed II, 76
positioning against Sufis/*ulema*, 76
promulgation of tax/fiscal reforms, 231
religion/religious issues. *See also*
Catholics/Catholicism; Christianity;
churches; Greek Orthodox Church; Islam;
Jews/Judaism; Muslims; non-Muslims
(dhimma); Protestants; *sharia* (religious)
law; Sufis; *ulema* (religious leaders)
alternatives to religious communities,
143–146
of Armenians, 140–141
Bayramî order, 161, 166
boundaries between Muslims and
non-Muslims, 118
dissent in Byzantine Empire, 156
influence in boundary creation, 60–61
Kalenderî (mystical fraternity), 165
and legitimacy, 289–294
mahalle (neighborhoods of communities),
144–145
Melâmî spiritual order, 166–167

religion/religious issues (*cont.*)
    Ottoman identification with Sunnî identity,
        168
    religious law vs. secular dynastic law, 72
    Sunnî vs. Shia struggles, 85
    tolerance by Ottoman/Russian empires,
        21–22, 112
    Unity of Being (Vahdet-i Vücud) doctrine,
        166
    violence by Selim I, 113
    Weber on complexity of, 105
rentier capitalists, 270, 273. *See also* tax
        farming *(iltizam)*
    attempts at severing relationship with, 274
    as founders of tax-farming business, 258
Republican Civil Wars (Rome), 72
Rifai Sufis, 56
Rodrigue, Aron, 115
Roman Empire, 7
    Battle at Actium, 74
    citizenship as key to successes of, 70
    Civil Wars of, 74
    contributions of Augustus, 74–75
    incorporation of, 18–19, 83–84
    influence on Byzantine Empire, 19
    meaning of toleration, 111
    meaning-based concept of, 100
    military strategy/transformations, 15
    Republican Civil Wars, 72
    slavery in, 156
    weakness of, 11
    years of, 15
Romania, 201, 238, 282
Romanov Empire, 15, 180
Rozen, Minna, 120–121
Rueschemeyer, Dietrich, 5
Rum sultanate, 30
Rumelia, 103, 171, 172, 207–208, 218
Russian Empire, 7. *See also* Catherine the
        Great; Peter I (Peter the Great)
    Agency for Convert Affairs of, 112
    border wars with, 182
    conversion of non-Christians, 64
    cooptation of elites, 156
    development of standing army, 268–269
    discrimination against Jews, 137
    emergence from frontier zones, 29
    expansion into Poland, 11, 78, 157
    expansion into Ukraine, 11, 157
    flexibility/firm control by, 35
    incorporation of Don Cossacks, 179–180
    incorporation policies, 11, 84
    infiltration of Balkans, 267

    interference with Christians, 219
    Ivan III construction strategies, 78
    land appropriation policies, 79–80
    legitimacy, of rulership, 99
    meaning of toleration, 111
    origins of, 78
    policies toward diversity, 111–113
    religious dissent/tolerance/incorporation,
        112, 156
    role in Golden Horde/Mongol Empire,
        34–35
    sharing Black Sea for trade, 284
    toleration of, 111
    transition to modern imperial model, 292
    wars with Ottomans, 203–204, 267

Sabbatai Sevi (Jewish messiah)
    arrest of, 189
    rise of, 164, 183, 185, 187
    successes of, 188
    travels of, 188
Safavid Empire, 63
    Anatolia Shiite groups backing of, 103
    shared borders with Ottomans, 85
    shared frontier with Mosul and Basra, 91
    strengthening of, 102
    support of *kızılbaş* movement, 175
    wars with Ottomans, 63, 85, 91, 161, 177,
        202
Safiye Sultan, 186
Saint Augustine, prophecy of, 73
salyaneli. See outer provinces *(salyaneli)*, of
        Ottoman Empire
Salzmann, Ariel, 214, 235, 259
sanjak beyi (Kurdish tribal leaders), 92. *See
        also Hükumet sanjaks*
Sarukhan emirate, 30
Schact, Joseph, 152
script model, for interactions, 119
self-government
    by Balkans, 87
    communal forms of, 144
    by Dubrovnik, 87
    by Moldavia, 87
    by Transylvania, 87
    by Wallachia, 87
Selim I, 71–72
    adoption of Muslim ways, 103
    conquests of, 91–103
    and conversion of Bulgarians, 126
    expansion by, 93
    and Muslims, 103, 104
    religious/ethnic violence by, 113

Selim II, 64, 197
Selim III, 218. *See also* Nizam-ı Cedid army
  assassination of, 220
  assistance of Süleyman Çapanoğlu, 249
  attempted reinstatement by Bayraktar
    Mustafa Pasha, 222
  coup d'état against, 204, 218, 219–220
  initiation of reforms by, 76, 219, 267, 268,
    269
  promotion of reforms by Tirsinklioğlu, 221
  reorganization of military, 268
  rise to power, 218–219
  trade deal with Mouroutsis, 283
Seljuk empire, 25. *See also* Rum sultanate
  acceptance of Sunnî Muslims, 30
  Baba'is revolt against, 52
  decline of, 36, 37
  fragmentation of, 39
  opening of Anatolia to tolerance, 170
  preaching of Islamic–Christian synthesis,
    43
  provision of *berats* to subjugated
    populations, 133
  struggles with Byzantium, 29
  Sufis welcomed by, 161
Sened-i İttifak (1808 Agreement), 218–224
  coup d'état against Selim III, 204, 218,
    219–220
  description, 220–221
  reasons for creation of, 222
Sephardic Jews, 138
Serbia
  attempts at gaining control, 170
  cattle/pig exports of, 239
  confrontations with Habsburgs in, 202
  demands for autonomy in, 201, 219
  joint family organization *(zadruga)*, 144
  self-governing community *(knezina)*, 144
  voynuks of, 88
Serkis (Armenian Patriarch), 141
Seven Year's War, 240
Seventeenth Century
  administrative changes during, 218
  destruction of Jewish synagogues/Christian
    churches, 184
  dissent of Ultra-Orthodox/Jewish
    Messianism, 181–190
  execution/persecution of Sufis, 184
  financial burden of war during, 230–231
  fiscal system/life-term tax farming, 218
  French attempts at tax farm centralization,
    276
  household development in, 260

inception of tax farms, 245–246
Kadızadeli movement, 182–183
Messianic Jews, 181–183, 190
rebellion of Pasvanoğlu vs. Ottoman state,
  221
rise of Sabbatai Sevi, 183, 185, 187
two-fronted wars during, 182
violent conquests in central Europe, 184
wars with Iran, 182, 203, 215
Sewell, William, Jr., 199–200
Şeyhs. *See also* Bedreddîn (Şeyh)
  Ali Rumi, 166
  Celâl, 178–181
  Hocazade Mesut, 113
  relationships with *ulema*, 186
sharia (religious) law, 72, 93, 105, 106,
  120–121, 134
Shiites, 7, 30, 42, 164
  consolidation of identity, 177–178
  struggles with Ottomans, 176–177
  fifteenth/sixteenth century persecution of,
    175–176
Sivasi Efendi, 186
slavery, 63. *See also devshirme* system
  kul (slave-servant) system, 76
  in Rome, 156
  Trapezuntine slaves of Mehmed II, 78
Smyrna (Izmir)
  invasion by Hospitalers, 55
  loss of, by Umur Bey, 57
social boundaries, of empires, 21
  discomforts in communities, 116–117
  potential for/absence of violence, 117
  resistance to political manipulation, 117
social networks
  of Bedreddîn, 171
  and dissent, 159
  of Orhan, 53
  of Osman, 33, 47–48
  state attempts to minimize,
social sciences, understanding of "state," 4
Sokullu Mehmed Pasha, assassination of, 165
Soliman I, 197
states
  authority of, through supranational
    ideology, 99
  building of, encouraged by trading zones,
    40
  as central actor, 18
  European social science perspective of, 4
  Imber's viewpoint, 32
  importance of brokerage, 33–34, 46
  Inalcık/Lowry's viewpoint, 32

states (*cont.*)
  institutional integration with communities, 115–119
  massacres sponsored by, 114
  Weberian definition (of author), 32
Sufis, 7, 48, 56
  and Akhi organizations, Osman's brokerage between, 51
  Bektaşî order, 165–166
  execution/persecution of, 184
  Halvetî order, 165
  incorporation by Ottomans, 162, 165
  Ottoman nontolerance of, 26
  role in conversion of Christians to Islam, 125
  spread of, in Anatolia, 43
  spread of Sufism, 164
  welcoming by Seljuk empire, 161
Süleyman Bey (of Karasi), 71–72, 177, 254
  conquest of Gallipoli Peninsula, 58
  dealings with Hungary, 90
  involvement in Byzantium civil war, 57
sultans/sultanates
  acceptance of differences by, 119–120
  as combination of *Shari* and *kanun*, 134
  contacts with religious communities, 116 (*See also* foundation myths)
  disciplinary duties of, 182
  and legitimacy of empire, 101–102
  move away from mysticism vs. patronization of dervish mystics, 169
  pressure on, by Sunni preachers, 113
  self-stylings of, 82–83
Sunnî Muslims, 7, 30, 42, 48
  consolidation of identity, 177–178
  gradual reinforcement of, 201
  Ottoman identification with, 168
  pressure on Ottoman sultans, 113
  struggles with Shia visions of Muslim, 85
sürgün (deportations), 128–130
  of Çepni Turcomans/Tatars, 128
  to Constantinople, 129
  and Mehmed II/Jewish encounters, 138
  use of, by Mehmed II, 128
Sürmeli Ali Pasha (grand vizier), 209
Sütçü Beşir Ağa, 166
Syme, Ronald, 18
Syria
  conquests of, 91, 103
  ethnic violence in, 278
  freedom of Christians in, 285–286
  and Selim I, 93
  Sufi origins in, 161

Tanzimat reforms/reorganization, 234, 257, 268. *See also* Hatt-ı Şerif (Noble Edict of the Rose Chamber)
  attempt at building legitimacy, 290–291
  conscription system, 286
  as crisis of legitimacy, 290
  education reforms, 287
  endorsement of equality before the law, 286
  federalist preference of, 266
  as inspiration for centralization/modernization, 286
  Mahmud II creation of, 3
tarîkats (dervish orders), 186
Tatars, 29, 78, 128, 287
tax collectors (*mütesellim*), involvement in trading, 238
tax farming (*iltizam*), 218, 229–236. *See also* life-term tax farming (*malikane*); rentier capitalists
  defaults by tax farmers, 273
  definition/description, 229, 231
  failures at centralization of, 271
  importance of, 230
  inception of, 245–246
  of Istanbul, *askeri's* hold on, 276
  and notables, 246
  purpose of, 229–230, 231
  renegotiation difficulties, 273–274
  role of, 270–277
  transference to public hands, 275
  Weber's views on, 229
taxation (*cizye*), 86, 96. *See also* economic system, of Ottomans; fiscalism, of Ottomans
  avoidance of religious conversion through, 125–126
  esham financial scheme, 272
  malikaneli esham financial scheme, 272
  need for better collection methods, 270
  eighteenth century war-related, 202–203
Thelen, Kathleen, 131
Tilly, Charles, 9, 119
tımar system
  as basis for Ottoman expansion, 95, 133
  comparison with *pomest'e* system, 78
  conversion of *vakıf* to, 77
  importance of, 77
  and Islamization of Christian Balkan landed elites, 88
  on island of Limnos, 89, 91
  as reward for prowess in service, 62
  for ruling of core provinces, 86

similarities with Byzantine *pronoia* land
system, 88
tax farming parallel to, 231
Tirsinklioğlu, promotion of Selim III's reforms,
221
toleration
definition/description, 110
of diversity/dissent, 29
of Habsburgs/Russians, 111
of Jews by Islam, 110
of Ottomans, 110–111, 114, 119–123
as policy of incorporation, 110
religious toleration, 21–22
of Roman Empire, 111
toward non-Muslims, 26
unraveling of, 277–289
Toleration (Voltaire), 109
trade, 236–242. *See also* *çiftlik*s (plantation
style estates); commercial networks;
commercialization
alliance of Byzantine Christians/Muslims, 40
attempt at creating monopolies by Europe,
281
capitulations to European countries, 237
establishment of provisioning routes, 238
influence of wars on, 239–240
involvement of notables/tax collectors, 238
notables and, 252–256
rise of merchant communities, 241
role of Christians/Jews, 280–281, 283
role of non-Muslims, 279, 280
sharing Black Sea trade with Russians, 284
spread of commercial networks, 238–239
trading zones
Byzantine-Greek entrepreneurs, 40
customs zones, 98
encouragement of state-building, 40
favored status concessions, 98
of frontier society, 40–41
linking of trade/commerce zones, 97
traditionalism, of Ottomans, 96
Transylvania, 12, 203
Habsburg attempts at ruling, 202, 203, 230
loss of territory in, 202
Ottoman response to revolt, 230
self-government by, 87
Trapezuntine slaves, 78
treaties
Jassy, 267
Karlowitz, 203, 212, 249
Küçük Kaynarca, 204, 267, 284
Passarowitz, 203, 249
with Safavids (1638), 202

Tulip Era, 203, 213–214. *See also* Patrona
Halil revolt
tımarlı. *See* core provinces *(tımarlı)*, of
Ottoman Empire
Turcomans. *See also* *gazâ* thesis; *kızılbaş*
(redhead) movement
attacks on Byzantines, 38, 58
Beyazıd I's penetration into *beylik* territory,
30–31
comradeship with Christians/Muslims, 42
cooperation with Byzantines, 42
deportation of Çepni Turcomans, 128
expansion towards Aegean Sea, 37
fight with Byzantine forces, 38
frontier raids by, 39–40
land loss by, 167
leadership of, 29
participation in construction of Ottoman
Empire, 29
raids of Christian territories, 36–37
as warriors for Osman, 50
Turkey. *See* Anatolia

uc (space) between Byzantine and Seljuk
empires, 39
Ukraine
border wars with, 182
favored lord status of, 84
Russian expansion into, 11, 157
ulema (religious leaders), 79, 165
alliance with Janissary corps, 213, 216,
219–220, 225
concentration/reproduction of power, 209,
210
dissent by, 182
easy relationships with Şeyhs, 186
endorsement of Patrona Halil revolt, 216
issuance of *fetvas* at Edirne, 211–212
opposition movement participation, 201
patronage households of,
sponsored version of Islam, 115
support of *cebecis*, 210
18th century strengthening of, 200–201
Umur Bey (of Aydın), 45
establishment of power relations, 56
involvement in Byzantium civil war, 57
joint raids with Orhan, 57
naval strength of, 55
rivalry with Osman and Orhan, 55
Unity of Being (Vahdet-i Vücud) doctrine,
166
Üstüvani Mehmed Efendi (Vani Efendi), 186
Uzunçarşılı, I. H., 221

Vahdet-i Vücud (Unity of Being) doctrine, 166
vakıf (pious foundations), seizure of,
    conversion to *tımars*, 77
Varsney, Ashutosh, 117
verstehen insight, into social world, 17
violence
    by Catholics, 183–184
    of central European conquests, 184
    against Christians, in Aleppo/Damascus,
        285
    and commercial networks, 279
    destruction of Jewish synagogues/Christian
        churches, 184, 186–187
    genocide, of Armenian population,
        114–115, 277–278, 293–294
    intercommunal, absence of, 146–150
    by Ottoman officials, 113–114
    potential for/absence of, 117
    prevention of, by actors, 118
    religious/ethnic, by Selim I, 113
    state-sponsored massacres, 114
voynuks (auxiliaries/guards), 88
Vucinich, Wayne, 144

Wallachia, 87, 136, 202, 282
War of 1877–78 (against Russia), 274
War of Independence, 240
Weber, Max, 14, 17
    complexity of religion, 105
    definition of state, 32
    legitimacy of domination, 98
    modernity definition, 206
    tax farming, 229
    views on tax farming, 229
White, Harrison, 6, 44
Whittaker, C. R., 15–16
World War I, 3

Yanık citadel, 184
Young Turks
    Armenian ethnic cleansing by, 278, 293–294
    discontent created by, 275
    ideological foundations of, 293
    secular strategies for saving state, 292–293

zadruga (Serbian joint family organization),
    144

DR 531 .B37 2008
Barkey, Karen, 1958–
Empire of difference

DATE DUE
